Otto Zöckler, Charles Augustus Aiken

The Proverbs of Solomon

Theologically and homiletically expounded

Otto Zöckler, Charles Augustus Aiken

The Proverbs of Solomon
Theologically and homiletically expounded

ISBN/EAN: 9783337317751

Printed in Europe, USA, Canada, Australia, Japan

Cover: Foto ©Lupo / pixelio.de

More available books at **www.hansebooks.com**

A
COMMENTARY
ON THE
HOLY SCRIPTURES:

CRITICAL, DOCTRINAL, AND HOMILETICAL,

WITH SPECIAL REFERENCE TO MINISTERS AND STUDENTS.

BY

JOHN PETER LANGE, D.D.,

IN CONNECTION WITH A NUMBER OF EMINENT EUROPEAN DIVINES.

TRANSLATED FROM THE GERMAN, AND EDITED, WITH ADDITIONS,

BY

PHILIP SCHAFF, D.D.,

ASSISTED BY AMERICAN SCHOLARS OF VARIOUS EVANGELICAL DENOMINATIONS

VOL. X. OF THE OLD TESTAMENT: CONTAINING PROVERBS, ECCLESIASTES, AND THE SONG OF SOLOMON.

NEW YORK:
CHARLES SCRIBNER'S SONS
1898

THE
PROVERBS OF SOLOMON.

THEOLOGICALLY AND HOMILETICALLY EXPOUNDED

BY

DR. OTTO ZÖCKLER,
PROFESSOR OF THEOLOGY AT GREIFSWALD.

TRANSLATED AND EDITED BY
Rev. CHARLES A. AIKEN, D.D.,
PRESIDENT OF UNION COLLEGE, SCHENECTADY, N. Y.

NEW YORK:
CHARLES SCRIBNER'S SONS,
1898

ENTERED, according to Act of Congress, in the year 1870, by
CHARLES SCRIBNER, & CO.,
In the Clerk's Office of the District Court of the United States for the Southern District
of New York.

Trow's
Printing and Bookbinding Co.,
Printers and Bookbinders,
205-213 East 12th St.,
New York.

PREFACE BY THE GENERAL EDITOR.

The present volume corresponds to Parts XII. and XIII. of the Old Testament Division of Dr. LANGE's *Biblework*, and contains the Solomonic writings, PROVERBS, ECCLESIASTES, and the SONG OF SOLOMON. They form an important part of the Old Testament, and give us the poetry and practical philosophy of the wisest of men, with none of his follies and sins, which were overruled in his writings for the advancement of wisdom and virtue.

The English translation, with additions and improvements, was intrusted to three eminent Oriental and Biblical Scholars, too well known in America to need an introduction. They have done their work well, and have added very materially to the value as well as the size of the original.

In this volume the text of the Authorized Version is superseded by a new metrical version in accordance with the laws of Hebrew poetry. The same will be the case in the other poetical books of the O. T. To retain the prose version of King James' revisers, and to insert the corrections in brackets, would conceal to the reader the beauties of the original as a work of art. In Ecclesiastes, Prof. TAYLER LEWIS has thought best to retain the common version for the Commentary, and to give his metrical version as a separate appendix.

Some remarks will introduce the author of this part of the *Biblework*, and explain the relation which the several parts of the American edition sustain to the German.

DR. ZÖCKLER.

The author of this Commentary on the Solomonic writings belongs to the younger generation of German divines, and appears now for the first time in an English dress; none of his previous writings having been translated.

Dr. OTTO ZÖCKLER was born at Grünberg, in the Grand Duchy of Hesse, May 27, 1833. After a thorough training in classical and oriental philology, philosophy and theology, he entered the career of an academic teacher of theology, A. D., 1856, as *privatim docens*, in the University of Giessen ; he advanced to the position of professor *extraordinarius* in 1863, and in the autumn of 1866 he was called by the Prussian Government as professor *ordinarius* to the University of Greifswald, in Pomerania, where he still labors with fidelity and success. He is a very able and learned divine, a fertile author, a modest, retiring and amiable gentleman, of unblemished character, a little hard of hearing, and hence the more devoted to the cultivation of the inner life by study and contemplation, yet wide awake to all the living questions of the age. His learning covers a large ground, especially Exegesis of the O. and N. Testaments, Church History, Apologetics, Natural Sciences. His biography of St. Jerome, with which I am quite familiar, is one of the best historical monographs. He is now engaged on Daniel for LANGE's *Biblework*.

The following is a chronological list of Dr. ZÖCKLER's writings to the present date :

De vi ac notione vocabuli ἐλπίς in N. To. diss. inauguralis. Giss., 1857.

THEOLOGIA NATURALIS. *Entwurf einer systematischen Naturtheologie vom offenbarungsgläubigen Standpuncte aus.* Bd. I. Frankft. a M., 1860.

KRITISCHE GESCHICHTE DER ASKESE (*Critical History of Asceticism*); *ein Beitrag zur Geschichte christlicher Sitte und Cultur.* Frankft. 1862.

HIERONYMUS ; *sein Leben u. Wirken aus seinen Schriften dargestellt.* Gotha, 1864.

i

Die Evangelienkritik und das Lebensbild Christi nach der Schrift. 2 *Vorträge.* Darmstadt, 1864.

Commentar zu den SPRUECHEN SALOMONIS. 1866.
Commentar zum HOHENLIED U. PREDIGER. 1868. } in LANGE's *Biblework.*
Commentar zum Propheten Daniel (in course of preparation).

Die Urgeschichte der Erde u. des Menschen (The Primitive History of Earth and Man). 6 *Vorträge gehalten in Hamburg.* Gütersloh, 1868.

Prof. ZÖCKLER is also the principal editor of a valuable apologetic monthly entitled: *Der Beweis des Glaubens (The Evidence of Faith)*, Gütersloh (Westphalia), since 1865, and of the *Allgemeine Literarische Anzeiger für das evang. Deutschland (General Literary Intelligencer for Evangelical Germany)*, published at Gütersloh, since 1869.

PROVERBS.

Prof. ZÖCKLER introduces his commentary on this storehouse of practical philosophy and heavenly wisdom with the following preface:

"A theological and homiletic exposition of the Book of Proverbs has difficulties to contend with which exist in an equal degree in but few books of the Old Testament, and in none in quite the same form. Even the most searching investigation is able to gain only partially and approximately fixed points for the determination of the time when the book originated, and of the editorship of its several main divisions as it is now constructed. In almost every new group of Proverbs the linguistic and theological exposition of the individual Proverbs encounters new difficulties—and these difficulties are, in many cases, of such a sort that we must utterly despair of fully assured exegetical results. And finally, to treat the book homiletically and practically, in so far as it regards only brief passages, is rendered more difficult by the obscurity of many single sentences; and in so far as it attempts to embrace large sections, by the unquestionable lack of fixed order and methodical structure, which appears at least in the central main division of the collection (chap. x. 1—xxii. 16), as well as in the supplement added by Hezekiah's men (chaps. xxv.—xxix.).''

" To this is to be added the imperfection of previous expository works, both the scientific and the practical.'' [The author then reviews the recent commentaries of HITZIG, UMBREIT, EWALD, BERTHEAU, VAIHINGER, and ELSTER, as well as the older works of MICHAELIS, GEIER, STARKE, STÖCKER, MELANCHTHON, and concludes:]

" In view of this condition of exegetical literature, heretofore so unsatisfactory in many ways, the author has at least attempted, with the most conscientious application of his powers, and with the use of the most important works that have hitherto appeared, to effect what might be done to relieve these difficulties, which exist in all directions in considerable numbers. . . . Over many of the obscurities that exist, he hopes that he has thrown substantially the right light; with regard to others, that he has turned attention to the most promising avenues to an appropriate exposition and a useful application; and that for the whole he has proposed a meaning essentially sound, scientifically defensible, and, for that very reason, edifying.''

The work on Proverbs was first committed to the hands of the late ROBINSON P. DUNN, D. D., Professor of Rhetoric and English Literature in Brown University. He was one of the most accomplished scholars of New England, and " one of those rare men who, by a happy combination of the gifts of nature and of grace, seemed adapted to usefulness in every department of life.'' But he had scarcely collected a complete apparatus and finished the rough draft of his translation as far as the opening sentences of § 9 of the Introduction, when he was suddenly called to his rest, Aug. 28, 1867, in Newport, R. I., the place of his birth, at the age of forty-three. His last words were similar to those of Dr. NEANDER: "Good-by, I am going home.'' His pen was found in the Commentary on the Proverbs, at the page he had reached, as a sign of his last study on earth. His initials are attached to the notes he added.*

---

* An elegant memorial volume, published by his widow, pp. 237, contains a biographical sketch by Dr. SAMUEL L. CALDWELL, the Commemorative Discourse delivered, at the request of the Faculty of Brown University, by the Rev. J. L. DIMAN, Professor of History in the University, and selections from the writings of Dr. DUNN, which give evidence of his accurate scholarship, elegant taste, lovely character and elevated piety.

After the lamented death of Professor DUNN, I secured the valuable services of Dr. AIKEN, then Professor of Latin Literature in Princeton College, and since called to the Presidency of Union College, in the State of New York. A hasty glance at the translation and the grammatical and critical notes is sufficient to convince the reader how much of original research and learning, in addition to the labor of a faithful translation, has been bestowed upon this part of the American edition of LANGE. In compliance with my suggestion, the purely grammatical parts of the Commentary have been transferred as far as practicable to the textual department, in small type, which the lay reader may pass by. The same rule has been followed in Ecclesiastes, and the Song, as it had already been done in Genesis. An unusual number of grammatical references has been made to BÖTTCHER's encyclopædic *Grammar*, which, in the exhaustive fullness of its citations, amounts almost to a commentary on the Hebrew Scriptures. The same scholarly hand is seen in the large number of supplementary and illustrative notes which are scattered through the exegetical parts. The elder English commentators, like TRAPP, MUFFET, are cited not for their scientific, but for their sterling practical value. Of recent commentators, STUART and MUENSCHER, of our own country, both unknown to Dr. ZÖCKLER, have justly been laid under contribution. Considerable additions have also been made to the homiletical department from our rich and varied literature.

ECCLESIASTES.

After the translating and editing of ZÖCKLER's Koheleth had been undertaken by Prof. TAYLER LEWIS, who had so admirably edited the greater part of Genesis, it was found that the state of his health, and the heavy additions which he felt it necessary to make, rendered assistance indispensable. By my advice, therefore, there was procured the valuable aid of his colleague, Prof. WELLS, of Union College. To him that important part, the translation, is due. For the added introductions, dissertations, annotations, the Metrical Version, and the editing generally, Prof. LEWIS is responsible. It is trusted that these will afford no little aid to a better comprehension of this strange and wonderfully impressive portion of Holy Scripture. We have here the ripe fruits of long continued biblical studies from one of our most venerable scholars, who is a man of genius as well as learning. The Metrical Version in Iambic measure, with an introduction thereto, is a new feature, to which we direct the special attention of the lovers of Hebrew poetry.

As a help to the reader, it is thought best to give, as was done in the volume containing Genesis, an index to the principal additions of Prof. LEWIS. Some of these are of considerable extent and unusual interest, and they may all be divided into two classes, according as they are contained in the body of the pages, or in marginal notes.

I. EXTENDED DISSERTATIONS ON LEADING IDEAS.

1. Appendix to ZÖCKLER's Introduction, defending the Solomonic origin of the book against the objections drawn from the style, and the alleged later Hebrew.......... pp. 28–35
2. Excursus on the Olamic or Æonian Words in Scripture—Eternities, or *World-times* in the plural. Ch. i. 3.. 44–51
3. The Inquisition of the Ages. Ch. iii. 11-15. Cyclical Ideas in Koheleth................... 72–76
4. Alleged Historical Allusions in Koheleth. Ch. iv. 14, 15.. 84–87
5. Koheleth's Idea of the Dead. Ch. ix. 15.. 129–131
6. The Alleged Epicureanism of Koheleth. His Mournful Irony. Ch. ix. 7-10; xi. 9, 10. 131–136
7. The Unknown Way of the Spirit. Life. The Divine Secret in Nature. Ch. xi. 5... 147–151
8. Koheleth's Description of Old Age intended for the Sensualist........ 152–154
9. Beth Olam, or "the Eternal House." xii. 5.. 158–160
10. Introduction to Metrical Version, maintaining the Poetical Character of the Book.... 171–181
11. Metrical Version, divided into 40 Meditations.. 183–199

II. THE PRINCIPAL MARGINAL NOTES.

1. The metaphor of the Horses of the Sun. i. 5.. 38
2. The Reining of the Flesh; the Word כשר. Ch. ii. 3... 54–55
3. שדה ושדות, ii. 8, falsely rendered "*musical instruments*"................................... 56–57

4.	The word *chance*..	54
5.	Exclamatory style of Koheleth..	54
6.	"There is nothing better for a man," *etc.* (controverted). ii. 24.......	56
7.	"The world in their heart." iii. 11..	67–68
8.	*Here, there—Diesseits, Jenseits,* or the coming retribution. iii. 17.....	69–70
9.	"Who knoweth the spirit of man that goeth upward?" iii. 21...............	71–72
10.	The Melancholy of Epicureanism, as contrasted with the style of the Sacred Poetry.....	80–81
11.	Vain Predictings, Superstitions, *etc*..	91
12.	The King, and the Field..	92
13.	Spirituality of the Hebrew Accents, "The *Good* that is *Fair*"......................	94–95
14.	The Naming—Adam. vi. 10..	101
15.	The "Light of thy countenance"..	101
16.	The oppression of the wise man...	106
17.	"Wisdom giveth life." vii. 12...	107
18.	Over-righteousness, Over-wisdom..	108
19.	Soliloquizing style of Koheleth...	113–114
20.	"The wicked buried"—the "going to and from the Holy Place." viii. 10.............	119
21.	"The days of thy vain life." Pathetic Repetition. ix. 9...................	126
22.	False logical and ethical divisions of many commentators...................	137
23.	"Dead flies." x...	138
24.	"Knows not how to go to the city;" interpretation of x. 14, 15................	141–142
25.	Speech of the prattling fool. False view of Hitzig.........................	142
26.	"The sight of the eyes," and "the way of the heart." xi. 9..................	152
27.	"Keepers of the house"—"the Grinders"—"the Light darkened"—"Clouds after rain."	154
28.	"Those who look out of the windows." "The doors shut in the streets."........	155
29.	The Mill, and the constant grinding of an ancient household; with illustration from the Odyssey.............	155–156
30.	The Almond Tree..	157
31.	Images of the Silver cord, the Golden bowl, the Fountain, *etc*.........................	160
32.	Creationism. xii. 27...	164
33.	The "making many books"..	168

To these may be added many minor marginal notes, together with the notes on particular words, the ancient versions, and various readings, as they are attached to each division of the text. Special attention is here paid to words alleged to belong to the later Hebrew.

THE SONG OF SOLOMON.

The Commentary on the Song of songs [שִׁיר הַשִּׁירִים, Sept.: Ἄσμα ᾀσμάτων, Vulg.: *Canticum canticorum*], as this most beautiful of poems of pure and holy love is called, was prepared by the Rev. Dr. GREEN, Professor in the Theological Seminary at Princeton.

The difficulty of the book is such as to allow considerable latitude of individual opinion, but it is all important to have a proper view of its spirit and aim. The German author justly rejects both the profane *rationalistic* exposition which can see no more in the Song than a sensual erotic poem, and the opposite *allegorical* interpretation which regards the persons and objects described as mere figures or names for spiritual persons and objects, leaving a large margin for random guess-work and unbridled extravagance.* Most nearly agreeing with his friend, Prof. DELITZSCH,

---

* The allegorical interpretation, it must be admitted, has the authority of many of the greatest divines, both Jewish and Christian, Catholic and Evangelical, and is also sanctioned by the headings of our English Bible. It will probably always retain the ascendancy in the pulpit, and in books for popular devotion. Many of the most eloquent sermons (as ST. BERNARD'S *Sermones in cant. cant.*, and KRUMMACHER'S *Salomo und Sulamith*), and of the sweetest hymns (by GERHARDT, DESSLER, DAENE, ZINZENDORF, WESLEY, and GUSTAV HAHN'S, *Das Hohe Lied in Liedern*, Halle, 1853) are based upon this view. If we distinguish carefully between *exposition* and *application*, we may allow a considerable latitude for homiletic and ascetic purposes. One of the very best legitimate practical applications of the passage ii. 15, I have seen, is in a little book of Mrs. H. Beecher Stowe, where the "little foxes that spoil the vines" (ii. 15), are applied, in a series of entertaining homilies, to little faults that disturb domestic happiness. But in an exegetical point of view most of the allegorical interpretations turn out to be arbitrary *impositions* rather than *expositions*. Just as I write, a new attempt in this line comes to my eyes in the *British and Foreign Evangelical Quarterly Review* for Oct. 1869, pp. 773–796. The writer of this article discovers in the Song

he adopts the *typical* or *typico-Messianic* view, which is not so old and generally received among orthodox divines as the allegorical, but which has the sanction of such eminent names as LIGHTFOOT, BOSSUET, LOWTH, and is more natural and in harmony with the typical and prophetical character of the whole ancient theocracy, as foreshadowing the substance of Christianity, and preparing the way for its introduction.

The Canticles are probably a nuptial song or lyric drama (melo-drama) from Solomon's best period, and present the ideal Hebrew view of marriage as established by God Himself in Paradise on the basis of the strongest and tenderest passion He has implanted in man; and this ideal is realized in the highest and holiest sense in the relation of Christ to His Church (Comp. Eph. v. 32).

The American editor, while recording his approval of ZÖCKLER's method and standpoint in general, especially his typical view (see pp. 19-25), has expressed his dissent from certain parts of his scheme. He inclines to regard the Canticles as a series of unconnected scenes rather than a well-arranged, continuous drama, with a regularly unfolded plot, as is done by ZÖCKLER and DELITZSCH, also, with various modifications, by LOWTH, EWALD, UMBREIT, BÖTTCHER, HITZIG, RENAN. He is moreover of the opinion that the Song should be more favorably interpreted by itself than from the history and later character of Solomon as given in the first book of Kings. In this last point I entirely agree. Any reference to Solomon's polygamy, unless it be in the way of rebuke, would mar the beauty and purity of the poem, and make it unworthy of its place in the canon.

The next most considerable addition is to the bibliography at the close of the Introduction (pp. 43-47), where a pretty full account is given of English and American Commentators on the Song. The critical and grammatical notes have been very materially enriched both from the editor's own researches and from the early English translations, and from English commentators.

I must add that Dr. GREEN had inserted a considerable number of Arabic and Persian words, but erased nearly all of them in the proof sheets, because, after the type had been procured at considerable trouble, it was found almost impossible to obtain accuracy in characters unknown to the compositors, and because they rather disfigured the pages.

I now commit this new volume to the churches of the English tongue, with the wish that it may be as cordially welcomed, and prove as useful, as the other parts of this Commentary.

PHILIP SCHAFF.

5, *Bible House*, NEW YORK, Nov. 19, 1869.

---

a progressive drama beginning at the gates of Eden and running through the light and shade of the history of Judaism and Christianity till the glory of the millennium. He distinguishes in it the following parts:

1. The Church before the advent, waiting and longing for the coming of Christ. 2d. The theocracy under Solomon, which in the temple and its worship, afford the fullest and clearest typical revelation of Christ which that dispensation admitted of. 3d. The gradual decadence that followed, in both type and prophecy, which went on till at last it deepened into the darkness of the captivity. 4th. The sudden opening of the gospel day in the advent of the Saviour, and the preaching of the apostles—the voice of the turtle, and the flowers that now begin to cover the earth. 5th. A second night, during which Christ is again absent; this lasts longer than the first, and during it a deeper sleep oppresses the church. On awakening, she is seen seeking her beloved, wounded and bleeding, from the sword of persecution. 6th. The bursting out of the day of the Reformation—the morning of the millennium—and then the church is beheld "terrible as an army with banners," clothed with truth, and shining with a light which makes her the admiration of the nations,—"fair as the moon, clear as the sun."

A few specimens of interpretation on this scheme, will suffice. The kisses of the Bridegroom are the promises of Christ's coming; the "Virgins" who love the spouse (ch. i. 3), like the Virgins in the Apocalypse, represent those who had not defiled themselves with the idolatrous rites of pagan or papal worship; the "wilderness" from which the bridegroom comes on the day of his espousals (iii. 6), is Jewish formalism, Gentile scepticism, and pagan idolatry; and the clouds of smoke, which attended the royal progress, are the symbols of mysterious providences.

THE
PROVERBS OF SOLOMON.

INTRODUCTION.

§ 1. THE ETHICAL AND RELIGIOUS RANK AND SIGNIFICANCE OF THE PROVERBS OF SOLOMON.

The collection of Proverbs which bears the name of Solomon is the chief storehouse of moral instruction and of practical wisdom for the chosen people of God under the old dispensation. It forms, therefore, the principal documentary source of the Ethics of the Old Testament, just as in the successive steps of a gradual revelation, it is the peculiar office of the Pentateuch to exhibit the fundamental truths of its Theology, the Psalter those of its Anthropology, and the Prophetical Books those of its Christology and Soteriology. Some of the more general principles and postulates of Ethics, especially much of what belongs to the province of the so-called doctrine of the Highest Good, and, as might be expected, the whole doctrine of the Moral Law, are indeed found in the Books of Moses. Single topics connected with the doctrine of virtue and obligation are occasionally more fully discussed in the Psalms and the Prophets. But the special doctrine of virtue and duty, which must ever hold the chief place in the system of Ethics, finds nowhere else in the Old Testament so thorough, so individualizing, and so lively a presentation as in the Proverbs; and even the more general principles of Ethics, as well as the fundamental maxims of rectitude and law are, if not directly referred to in them, at least incidentally assumed.*

Resting on the basis of the widest and most diverse experience, and adopting the form of the most thoughtful, pithy and suggestive apothegms, they apply to the life of man in all positions, relations and conditions, the moral precepts contained in the law. In other words, what the law reveals as a universal rule for the national life of the covenant people in a religious and a political aspect, the Proverbs apply to the relations and obligations of the private life of each individual of that people. The principle of consecration through fellowship with Jehovah, the God of the Covenant, which was revealed through Moses, and established in general in his legislation, is individualized and developed in detail by Solomon with reference to the special domestic and social relations of his countrymen.

NOTE.—It has been often observed that the Proverbs of Solomon are the chief source of the Old Testament Ethics. ORIGEN, in the Preface to his exposition of the Song of Solomon, expressed the opinion that in the Proverbs Solomon had aimed to discuss the ἠθική, in Ecclesiastes the φυσική, and in the Canticles the λογική or θεωρική (the science of the contemplation of Divine things), and JEROME adopted from him this view (Preface to the Comm. on Eccles., Ep. 30 to Paula).†

---
* [This threefold division of Ethics, originating with SCHLEIERMACHER, and closely adhered to by ROTHE, is generally adopted in Germany. "*Güterlehre*" is the doctrine of the Good as an object of desire or a thing to be attained. "*Tugendlehre*" is the doctrine of the sentiments and inclination towards virtue. "*Pflichtenlehre*" is the doctrine of the right as the foundation of law. The first and the last are objective; the second is subjective.—R. P. D.]

† In his 107 Ep. to Læta in reference to the education of her daughter Paula, JEROME says: "*Discat primo Psalterium, his se canticis sanctam vocet, et in Proverbiis Salomonis erudiatur ad vitam.*" Compare the title παιδαγωγική σοφία which GREGORY of Nazianzus was wont to give to the Book of Proverbs.

LUTHER, in his Preface to the Books of Solomon, written in 1524 (Erlangen ed., Vol. LXIII., p. 35), says of the Proverbs: "It may be rightly called a book of good works; for he (Solomon) there teaches the nature of a godly and useful life,—so that every man aiming at godliness should make it his daily Handbook or Book of Devotion, and often read in it and compare with it his life." STARKE (Introd. to the Proverbs, Synops., Pt. IV., p. 1591) thus describes its contents: "It is for the most part a school of Christian Morals; upon the basis of faith it founds the wisest counsels in reference to the believer's duties towards God, towards his neighbor, and towards himself. . . . . By means of a great variety of sententious maxims this book teaches man how to escape from sin, to please God, and to secure true blessedness." The elder MICHAELIS (CHRISTIAN BENEDICT) gives a like estimate of the ethical value of the Proverbs. He passes from an exposition of the Psalms to one of the Proverbs with these words: "From the oratory of David we now proceed to the school of Solomon, to find in the son of the greatest of theologians the first of philosophers." On account of the ethical wisdom of the Proverbs of Solomon, the Würtemberg Theosophists, BENGEL and OETINGER, preferred them to most of the other books of the Old Testament. They made them the theme of their devout meditations, and earnestly sought to penetrate their deeper meaning. (See for BENGEL: OSK. WAECHTER'S "*Joh. Alb. Bengel: Life, Character*, &c., p. 166). OETINGER, when, as a youthful master of arts, he resided at Halle, thought of lecturing on "*Philosophiam sacram et applicatam*, drawn from the Scriptures, especially the Proverbs of Solomon." This plan he did not, however, carry out. At a later period, when he was a pastor first at Hirsau and then at Walddorf, he diligently studied the Proverbs as the chief repository and source of what he called "*Sensus communis*." He used them for purposes of religious instruction; he wrote them on separate slips of paper, put them in a box, and made his scholars draw them out as lots. He also published a little book of a catechetical nature, with the title "How shall the head of a family exemplify at home the Proverbs of Solomon?" and a larger work called "Common Sense in the Proverbs and Ecclesiastes," Stuttgard, 1753. "The Proverbs," he once observed, " exhibit Jesus with unusual clearness, and he who cannot perceive this knows not Paul's meaning when he says, 1 Cor. xiv. 20, 'In understanding be men'" (see EHMANN's "*Life and Letters of Oetinger;*" also the essay in VILMAR's *Past.-theol. Bll.*, 1865, I., pp. 265 sq, on "Theosophy: Oetinger and the Lutheran Church."— Still earlier the Rostock theologian, SAMUEL BOHL, had attempted in his *Ethica Sacra* (1640) a systematic exhibition of the ethics of Solomon, in the form of a continuous commentary on the first nine and the last two chapters of Proverbs. Most of the modern interpreters have in like manner justly appreciated the superior ethical value of this book. According to KAHNIS (*Luth. Dogmatik*, I., 282) its peculiar excellence lies in the skill with which its author "has presented the maxims of a practical wisdom which aims in all the human relations of the Kingdom of God to govern the lives of men in harmony with the intentions of its founder." ELSTER (*Deutsche Zeitschr. für Christl. Wissenschaft*, 1859, and in his Commentary on the Proverbs) ascribes the importance of this book of Solomon to the fact that "it consists of a didactic religious discussion of practical experience," in the form of proverbial wisdom, which is not mere human prudence, but "a new emanation from the Divine essence itself, a new communication of eternal wisdom, which alone is true wisdom." It is a proverbial wisdom which, "like the Law and the Prophets, has its own peculiar and most important province," and has upon the varied and symmetrical development of the individual man an influence which should be deeply felt and fully recognized. BRUCH (*Weisheitslehre der Hebräer*, pp. 102 sq.), OEHLER (*Die Grundzüge der alttestamentl. Weisht*, pp. 5 sq.), DELITZSCH (Article *Sprüche Salomo's* in HERZOG's *Real-Encyclopädie*), express themselves in similar terms with reference to the high ethical and religious rank of this book. Even HITZIG, while denying its inspiration, and perceiving in it nothing but human wisdom, recognizes in it "a religious consecration and an irresistible attraction of the heart towards morality," which distinguish this monument of Hebrew proverbial wisdom above all similar productions, whether of Arabian literature or of the Semitic mind in general ("*Die Sprüche Salomo's übersetzt und ausgelegt*," p. xii.).

[COLERIDGE says: "The Book of Proverbs is the best statesman's manual which was ever written. An adherent to the political economy and spirit of that collection of apothegms and essays would do more to eradicate from a people the causes of extravagance, debasement and ruin, than all the contributions to political economy of SAY, SMITH, MALTHUS and CHALMERS together."—Prof. M. STUART says (Preface to his Comm. on Proverbs, p. 9): "All the heathen moralists and proverbialists joined together cannot furnish us with one such book as that of the Proverbs." In his Introd., p. 64, he says: "After all the light which Christianity has shed upon us, we could not part with this book without a severe loss." "The book contains a striking exhibition of practical wisdom, so striking that it can never be antiquated."—J. MUENSCHER, in his Introd. to his Comm. on Proverbs, says, p. xliv.: "The moral precepts of Solomon rest on the foundation of religion and true piety, and in this respect differ heaven-wide from the systems of the ancient heathen moralists."—R. P. D.]

[Dr. GRAY observes, The Proverbs of the inspired son of David "are so justly founded on principles of human nature, and so adapted to the permanent interests of man, that they agree with the manners of every age, and may be assumed as rules for the direction of our conduct in every condition and rank of life, however varied in its complexion or diversified by circumstances; they embrace not only the concerns of private morality, but the great objects of political importance." —Dr. JORTIN says: "They have not that air of smartness and vivacity and wit which modern writers have usually affected in their maxims and sentences; but they have what is better, truth and solid good sense." "Though the composition be of the disjointed kind, yet there is a general design running through the whole, which the author keeps always in view; that is, to instruct the people, and particularly young people, at their entrance into public and active life,— to give them an early love and an earnest desire of real wisdom, and to lay down such clear rules for their behaviour as shall carry them through the world with peace and credit." (See D'OYLY and MANT, Introd. to Proverbs).

BRIDGES (Exposition of the Proverbs, Am. Ed., Pref., pp. iii., vii., ix., etc.) says: "This wonderful book is indeed a mine of Divine wisdom. The views of God are holy and reverential. The observation of human nature is minute and accurate." "Doubtless its pervading character is not either *explicit* statement of doctrinal truth or lively exercises of Christian experience. Hence the superficial reader passes over to some (in his view) richer portion of the Scriptural field." "While other parts of Scripture show us the glory of our high calling, this may instruct in all minuteness of detail how to 'walk worthy of it.' Elsewhere we learn our completeness in Christ (Col. ii. 10); and most justly we glory in our high exaltation as "joint heirs with Christ," etc. (Rom. viii. 17; Eph. ii. 6). We look into this book, and, as by the aid of the microscope, we see the minuteness of our Christian obligations; that there is not a temper, a look, a word, a movement, the most important action of the day, the smallest relative duty, in which we do not either deface or adorn the image of our Lord, and the profession of His name."

WORDSWORTH (Introd. to Proverbs, pp. ix., x.) says: "The Book of Proverbs is an inspired book adapted to the circumstances of the times of Solomon." "The Holy Spirit, in inspiring Solomon to write the Book of Proverbs, supplied an antidote to the poison of those influences (temptations attending the splendor and prosperity of the times), and has given to the world a moral and spiritual manual, which has its special uses for those who dwell in populous towns and cities, and who are busily engaged in worldly traffic, and are exposed to such temptations as are rife in an age and country like our own, distinguished by commercial enterprise and mechanical skill, and by the production of great works of human industry, in Art, Literature and Science, and also by religious activity, especially of that kind which aims to give to Religion external dignity and beauty, such as reached its highest pitch in the Temple of Solomon." Again, "The Proverbs of Solomon come from above, and they also look upward. They teach that all True Wisdom is the gift of God, and is grounded on the fear of the Lord. They dwell with the strongest emphasis on the necessity of careful vigilance over the heart which is manifest only to God; and on the right government of the tongue, whose sins are rarely punished by human laws; and on the duty of acting, in all the daily business and social intercourse of life, with an eye steadily fixed on the throne of God, and with habitual reference to the only unerring standard of human practice, His Will and Word. In this respect the Book of Proverbs prepared the way for the preaching of the Gospel; and we recognize in it an anticipation of the Apostolic precept concerning all domestic and social relations, 'Whatsoever ye do, do it heartily, as unto the Lord.'"

Dean STANLEY (*History of the Jewish Church*, II., 269, Am. Ed.), looking at the other side of the shield, says, This book "has even something of a worldly, prudential look, unlike the rest of the Bible. But this is the very reason why its recognition as a Sacred Book is so useful. It is the philosophy of practical life. It is the sign to us that the Bible does not despise common sense and discretion. It impresses upon us in the most forcible manner the value of intelligence and prudence, and of a good education. The whole strength of the Hebrew language, and of the sacred authority of the book, is thrown upon these homely truths. It deals too in that refined, discriminating, careful view of the finer shades of human character, so often overlooked by theologians, but so necessary to any true estimate of human life."

Dr. GUTHRIE (*Sunday Magazine*, Oct., 1868, p. 15) calls attention in his forcible way to other qualities of the book, and bears a valuable testimony to its experimental worth in a wide sphere. "It fulfils in a unique and pre-eminent degree the requirements of effective oratory, not only every chapter, but every verse, and almost every clause of every verse expressing something which both 'strikes and sticks.'" "The day was in Scotland when all her children were initiated into the art of reading through the Book of Proverbs. . . . I have no doubt whatever—neither had the late Principal LEE, as appears by the evidence he gave before a committee of parliament—that the high character which Scotsmen earned in bygone years was mainly due to their early acquaintance with the Proverbs, the practical sagacity and wisdom of Solomon. . . . The book has unfortunately disappeared from our schools; and with its disappearance my countrymen are more and more losing their national virtues—in self-denial and self-reliance, in foresight and economy, in reverence of parents and abhorrence of public charity, some of the best characteristics of old manners and old times."—A.]

A.—GENERAL INTRODUCTION TO THE PHILOSOPHICAL LITERATURE ASCRIBED TO SOLOMON.

§ 2. THE PHILOSOPHY OF THE OLD TESTAMENT IN GENERAL, IN ITS RELATION TO THE PHILOSOPHY OF OTHER NATIONS.

The peculiar form in which the ethical doctrines and precepts of the Proverbs are presented is that of the Hhokmah, or Proverbial Philosophy of the Hebrews. It is a species of moral and philosophical instruction in practical wisdom, which though distinguished by its thoroughly religious character from the secular philosophy of all other races, stands in the same relation to the spiritual development of the covenant people as that occupied by this philosophy in reference to the general culture of men who are without the Scriptures. For, whatever answer be given to the somewhat perplexing question, whether the Hebrews can be properly said to have had a philosophy, it is certainly true, that the essential feature of philosophy, the striving after objective wisdom, or after a true conception of the absolute fitness of the world to accomplish its ends, in both a theoretical and a practical aspect, is most completely presented in the Hhokmah of the old dispensation; and that in fact it is only the peculiar form in which this striving develops itself in the Old Testament literature, which distinguishes this Hhokmah from the philosophy of Greek and Roman antiquity. The wisdom of the people of God under the Old Testament is the art of so shaping life in harmony with the divine will, and in obedience to its peculiar laws learned by experience and reflection, as to make one an upright subject of the kingdom of God, in other words, so as to secure at once the divine favor and earthly blessedness. [When NOYES (*A new Translation of the Proverbs, etc.*, Introd. to Proverbs, p. xiv.) says: "It is true that the religion and morality of the Book of Proverbs will not bear a favorable comparison with those of Jesus Christ. Its morality is much less disinterested, being for the most part founded in prudence rather than in love. Its motives generally are of a much less elevated kind than those which Christianity presents . . . . Prudential motives, founded on a strict earthly retribution, are the principal encouragements to a life of virtue which he presents," etc., we recognize the truth which he exhibits, but notwithstanding his supplementary and balancing statements prefer ISAAC TAYLOR's mode of exhibiting the truth. Speaking immediately of the 23d Psalm he says (*Spirit of Hebrew Poetry*, Am. 12mo. ed., p. 38): "The bright

§ 2. THE PHILOSOPHY OF THE OLD TESTAMENT.

idea of *earthly well-being* pervades the Old Testament Scriptures; and this worldly sunshine is their distinction as compared with the New Testament; but then there are many cognate ideas which properly come into their places around the terrestrial idea.... A feeling is here indicated which was of that age, and which was approvable then, although it has been superseded since by sentiments of a higher order, and which draw their reason from the substitution of future for present good."—A.] In so far as God is alike the beginning and the end of this pursuit of wisdom, or in so far as it both necessarily springs from the fear of God,—Prov. i. 7; ix. 10; comp. Job xxviii. 28; Ps. cxi. 10; Ecclesiast. i. 16,—and leads to a purifying fellowship with Him, Prov. viii. 35; iii. 16, *etc.*, it has an essentially religious and practical character. Its sphere of reflection and of action must therefore be also more limited than that of the old classical or of the modern philosophy, both of which delight in profound theoretical inquiries in reference to created existence, and investigations of not only the end but also the origin of both nature and man. Those questions concerning the origin of the world and the origin of evil which play so conspicuous a part in the philosophy of ancient and of modern times, are only incidentally discussed in the Hebrew literature of wisdom, whether in the works ascribed to Solomon, the book of Job, or the kindred Psalms; and then only in their relation to the motives and tendencies to practical morality. The divine wisdom which establishes the relation of God to the world, and is at once the chief source and fundamental law of both the subjective and the objective wisdom of men, (Prov. viii. 21; ix. 12; Job xxviii. 24 sq.; Ecclesiast. xxiv.) is always represented rather as the medium of the foreknowledge and the providence of God, than as a creative power, or even as the ideal pattern of the world (the κόσμος νοητός of PLATO). In fine, the essential character of the Hebrew philosophy is far more practical than speculative; it is as little inclined to pursue or to prompt genuine speculation as it is to identify itself with secular philosophy in general, and with unaided human reason to investigate the final causes of things. It is essentially a divine philosophy planting its feet upon the basis of the divine revelation, and staying itself upon the eternal principles of the divine law; and it is this determinate and positive character of its method of conceiving and teaching, that chiefly distinguishes it from the philosophy of other nations and of other times. Moreover, the habitual, and not as was the case with many ancient philosophers, the occasional, adoption of the poetical form of the Gnome or didactic apothegm for conveying its instructions, must be regarded as a marked and important feature of this whole body of Old Testament literature, and as a decided indication of its method and of its tendencies.

NOTE 1.—The Strasburg theologian, J. F. BRUCH, in his "*Weisheitslehre der Hebräer; ein Beitrag zur Geschichte der Philosophie,*" Strasburg 1851, thoroughly discusses the question whether or not the doctrine of the Hhokmah in the Old Testament is to be considered philosophy in the strict sense, and decides it in the affirmative. This was the prevailing opinion in former times among the theologians of all the churches. Jesuits, *e. g.* MENOCHIUS in his learned work, "*De Republica Hebræorum,*" Book VII., Chap. 1; many of the Reformers of the 17th and 18th centuries, especially the followers of DESCARTES and COCCEIUS; and Lutherans like the aforementioned BOHLIUS in his "*Ethica Sacra,*" or the eminent BUDDÆUS in his "*Introductio ad Historiam philosophiæ Hebræorum,*" 2d ed., Leipsic. 1720, all spoke without hesitation of the Hebrew philosophy, of the philosophy of Solomon, David, Moses, Joseph, and Abraham. Indeed they often ventured to trace the philosophy of the patriarchs as far back as to Adam. Even at the beginning of the present century BLESSIG, in his Introduction to J. G. DAULER s "*Denk- und Sittensprüchen Salomo's*" (Strasburg, 1810), unqualifiedly characterized the proverbial poetry of the Hebrews as philosophical; DE WETTE, in his Hebrew Archæology, spoke of " the speculative and practical philosophy of the Hebrews;" and STAEUDLIN wrote a dissertation on " The Philosophy, the Origin and Design of the Book of Job." (See his "*Beiträge zur Philosophie und Geschichte der Religion und Sittenlehre,*" II., 133 sq.; compare the same author's "*Geist der Sittenlehre Jesu,*" I., 74 sq.). Theologians of the most diverse schools agreed in assuming in general the existence among the early Hebrews of a style of wisdom which might claim the undisputed title of a philosophy.

The opposite view is represented not only by many later philosophers especially those of the critical school of KANT, but also by such theologians as limit the notion "philosophy" to the scholarly scientific speculative inquiries peculiar to modern times, and must therefore consider not only the Hebrews, but all the Semitic races, and indeed the Orientals in general, as totally destitute of a philosophical habit of mind. Such was the opinion of BRUCKER before the time of KANT, when he asserted in his Critical History of Philosophy (Leipsic, 1767, I., 64), "*non confundendam esse Hebræorum sapientiam cum philosophia proprii nominis atque significationis.*" KRUG (*Philosophisch-Encyclopädisches Lexicon*, II., 328) thinks that anything like philosophy or philosophical wisdom is not to be looked for among the ancient Hebrews." REINHOLD (*Lehrbuch der Geschichte der Philosophie*, p. 15) denies in general the existence of any proper old Oriental philosophy side by side with the Greek. RITTER (*Geschichte der Philosophie*, I., 48) bluntly says, "Of the only Asiatic nations whose literature is known to us, we may venture to assert, without fear of much contradiction, that in the early times they had no philosophy. Among these are the Hebrews," *etc.*

Of the more recent theologians R. F. GRAU ("*Semiten und Indogermanen in ihrer Beziehung zu Religion und Wissenschaft*," p. 28 sq.) has warmly and zealously supported the proposition that "the Semitic mind in general has no capacity for either philosophy or science," and LUTHARDT (in the "*Leipziger Vorträge über die Kirche, nach Ursprung, Geschichte und Gegenwart*, pp. 18 sq. [pp. 19 sq. of the translation published by Messrs. T. & T. Clark, Edinburgh, 1867]) adopts his opinion at least in reference to the Hebrews.

All these scholars manifestly have too limited and partial a conception of philosophy. They with one consent understand by it an exercise of the human intellect controlled by the rigid laws of logic and carried on in a scientific method such as was never seen among the early Hebrews, or indeed among any of the older Eastern nations. But philosophy means far more than this. It is in itself, as its etymology, φιλοσοφία, *i. e. studium sapientiæ* [love of wisdom], indicates, and as the whole practice and method of the oldest Greek philosophers down to the time of ARISTOTLE demonstrates, nothing but a love for wisdom; an earnest endeavor to find a theoretical and a practical solution of the problems of our earthly life; that intellectual effort which strives to re-establish the proper relation between the absolute omniscience of God, and the relative knowledge possessed by the reason of man. A philosophy and philosophical science in this wider sense must be claimed for the people of God under the Old Testament. We cannot, however, quite agree with BRUCH (*ut supra*, p. 20 sq.) when, having defined philosophy in its *objective* aspect as "the science of the Absolute, or the science of the supreme necessary causes of all that is or that must be," and in its subjective aspect, "as the unaided inquiry after the absolute, or rational thinking in so far as renouncing all external authority it investigates the supreme necessary causes of all that is or that must be," he ascribes both to the Hebrews. For, in the first place, that which among them corresponds to the philosophy of other nations is not properly science, but rather a knowledge and comprehension, an intellectual effort and reflective process in general; and in the next place, it is not so much the "supreme necessary causes" as the chief practical ends of our earthly life and being which occupied the mind of the Hebrew thinker. It is then only philosophy in its subjective character, as above defined, which can in the main be ascribed to the Hebrews, and even this in a form quite unlike that in which it presents itself to BRUCH, one which secures the full recognition of its predominant practical and theological character. A philosophy consisting in such an essentially practical or ethical tendency of the mind, which by an examination of the highest moral and religious ends of all human and superhuman existence, seeks to determine the normal relation between God and the world, and thus to point out the way to truth and blessedness, may without hesitation be ascribed to the people of the Old Covenant. It is indeed a philosophy, which though its shape and dress are religious and poetical rather than didactic and scientific, contains within itself all the elements which are essential to strictly scientific development, or to an entrance into the sphere of dogmatic and moral and theological speculation.

In this properly limited sense has EWALD, among others, (*Geschichte des Volkes Israel*, III., 82) recognized the existence of an old Hebrew Philosophy. "Philosophy," says he, "may exist even where the rigid laws of thought (logic) are not observed, or where no attempt is made to reduce all truths and conceptions to a symmetrical whole (a system). This, it may be admitted, is its final aim,—though this aim like every other human aspiration is so often thoroughly erroneous and misleading ;—it is not, however, its beginning nor its constant living impulse. Its beginning and very life is rather the intense and unquenchable desire for investigation, and for the investigation of all objects, both higher and lower, remote and near, human and divine. Where the problems of existence allow thoughtful men no rest, where they provoke among the mightiest intellects of any people, or of several nations at once, an unwearied rivalry in the attempt to solve them, Philosophy is in the bloom and vigor of youth. In that earlier time the noblest of the Semitic races had plainly reached that stage when the Greeks were far from having approached it; and Israel, whose higher religion furnished besides a special impulse to reflection on the relations of things, now entered with them upon this nobler field of honor in the most generous rivalry."

Similar views are expressed by UMBREIT in his ingenious and instructive, though somewhat prolix observations "on the wisdom of the East" (*Commentar über die Sprüche Salomo's, Einleitung,* pp. iii. sq.); by DELITZSCH (Article "*Sprüche Salomo's,*" in HERZOG's *Real-Encycl.,* XIV., pp. 712 sq.), as well as by the editor of this Biblework in his General Introduction to the Old Testament (Genesis p. 19, [Am. Ed.]). OEHLER in his work "*Die Grundzüge der alttestam. Weisheit,*" pp. 5 sq., as well as his follower KAHNIS (*Lutherische Dogmatik,* I., 304), essentially agrees with the above statements. The latter says excellently, among other things, "To find in the life of nature and of man, in the revelations of the kingdom of God, in the whole world, the divine 'wherefore,' the divine fitness to accomplish the proposed end, was the great aim of the wisdom of Solomon. Here unquestionably existed a tendency to science, to philosophy. But the national life of Israel rested on too divine a foundation to permit great freedom of inquiry, and the kingdom of God had too many practical aims to favor a purely theoretical exploration of the objects of existence. Springing from the practical this wisdom sought to further the practical," *etc.*

NOTE 2.—In harmony with his above-quoted definition of the philosophy of the Hebrews, as an inquiry into the highest necessary causes of all that is or that shall be, BRUCH (pp. 69 sq.) introduces the cosmogony of the first two chapters of Genesis into his representation of the philosophy of the Old Testament. He thus regards the substance of these chapters as a portion of a philosophical system, and indeed in its essential features as the earliest instance of philosophical reflection among the Hebrew race. (HERDER, as is well known, held similar views. In his "*Ideen zur Philosophie der Geschichte der Menschheit*" he termed the Mosaic cosmogony "an ancient philosophy of the history of man"). This view of BRUCH's is connected with his assumption of the purely human and moreover half-mythical character of the Mosaic narrative. It is therefore to be decidedly rejected, together with his opinion that the Old Testament "wisdom" is the product of unaided human speculation, and that no divine or specifically supernatural factor is to be recognized in the Old Testament revelation in general.

NOTE 3.—The word חָכְמָה primarily denotes (in accordance with the fundamental meaning of the root חכם, حكم in Arabic, where it means to fasten, to hold fast, and then to separate, to decide) the fixing of an object for cognition, and secondarily, simply knowledge, insight. It is therefore in Prov. i. 2 used as precisely synonymous with דַּעַת, and elsewhere, as in Isa. xi. 2 sq., as at least parallel with בִּינָה. The חָכָם is then in the first instance the wise, the learned man in general (comp. Jer. viii. 9), whether he be a judge (1 Kings iii. 28 : comp. the corresponding Arabic word which always signifies a judge), or an artificer (Ex. xxviii. 3; xxxi. 6; Jer. x. 9), or finally a cunning, subtle man who can use his craft for his own or for others' advantage (Job v. 13, comp. 2 Sam. xiii. 3; xx. 16). In the religious realm חָכְמָה naturally denotes insight into that upright dealing which pleases God and conforms to the divine law, a knowledge of the right way which is to be followed before God, and of the wrong one which is to be shunned. In short it is that practical uprightness, founded on religious enlightenment, in which the true happiness of man consists, and which is therefore frequently represented by הוּשִׁיָּה (*i. e.* well being and wisdom in one), *e. g.* Prov. ii. 7; iii. 21; viii. 14; xviii. 1; Job xi. 6; xii. 16; xxvi. 3. Compare in general HITZIG, *Die Sprüche Salomo's, Einleitung,* p. lii.

sq. The latter, however, gives a somewhat different and less correct etymology of the word. He defines חָכָם as one who possesses the spiritual power of control and determination, and חָכְמָה as the power of moral self-subjugation. He thus gives to the notion of government a prominence which is by no means justified by the Arabic حكم.

NOTE 4.—The מָשָׁל or Hebrew gnome, as the distinctive artistic form adopted by the Old Testament philosophy and proverbial poetry, will be particularly discussed in a later section. We may, however, here observe that of all the titles borrowed from kindred secular literature, and applied to the Proverbs of Solomon on account of their peculiar form, none appears more just and appropriate than that adopted by BRUCH, who terms them (p. 104) an Anthology of Hebrew Gnomes. In the explanation and justification of this title he, however, as he does elsewhere, disparages the theopneustic character of this Book of Scripture.

§ 3. THE AGE OF SOLOMON, OR THE GOLDEN AGE OF THE HEBREW LITERATURE OF WISDOM.

As among other nations philosophy is not wont to assume its proper form till a long time after the religious and civil foundations of national culture are securely laid, so in Israel no season of undisturbed reflection and of philosophical inquiry and instruction could be enjoyed, before the protracted storms and conflicts of the period of the Judges had fixed the religion of the law in the depths of the popular consciousness, or before the reigns of Saul and David, the earliest kings, had firmly established the theocratic national life. The power of external enemies must first in some way be broken and overthrown, and the prosperity of the citizen and the political and social influence of the nation upon the life of the surrounding nations must be to a certain degree secured; but this could not be effected before the brilliant and glorious though warlike reign of David. Furthermore, as an element of the internal culture of the nation, the spirit of the law must have begun to receive a new invigoration and a fresh inculcation, which it derived from the schools of the prophets which sprung up after the time of Samuel. Hand in hand with the directly religious activity of this prophetic company the national poetry must make its earliest start, and create for that philosophy a proper literary and æsthetic form.

These conditions were not all of them fully realized until the time of Solomon, when the people were blessed with a long period of peace, rich in earthly possessions and enjoyments of all sorts; they then began a lively and widely extended intercourse with foreign nations, and with an extending view reaching even to Tarshish and Ophir, their thought and their activity received the most various impulses in a direction which was no longer narrow and strictly national, but more or less universal and as broad as humanity itself.* There was therefore associated with the priests, the prophets, the warriors, the judges, a new class of notables, that of the Hhakamim (חֲכָמִים, 1 Kings iv. 30, 31; Jer. xviii. 18; Prov. i. 6; xiii. 20; xxii. 17), the wise, or the teachers of wisdom, who began to bear their part in the whole work of training the nation. A pretty large number of such wise men, of considerable importance, must have appeared under Solomon, and have been associated with him as the most famous of all. For the books of the Kings mention besides him some of his contemporaries, viz.: "Ethan, the Ezrahite, and Heman, Chalcol and Darda, the sons of Mahol," as representatives of the wisdom of that time (1 Kings iv. 31; comp. 1 Chron. ii. 6), and compare the wisdom of these Hebrew Hhakamim with that of all the children of the East country, and all the wisdom of Egypt" (1 Kings iv. 30). Whether they did or did not form a well de-

---

* ("That stately and melancholy figure (Solomon's)—in some respects the grandest and the saddest in the sacred volume—is, in detail, little more than a mighty shadow. But, on the other hand, of his age, of his court, of his works we know more than of any other." (STANLEY, *Jewish Church*, II., 184). And the accomplished author goes on to indicate the multiplying points of contact with the outer and the later world, and with secular history; and adds (p. 186): "To have had many such characters in the Biblical History would have brought it down too nearly to the ordinary level. But to have one such is necessary, to show that the interest which we inevitably feel in such events and such men has a place in the designs of Providence, and in the lessons of Revelation." See also pp. 252 sq.—Prof. B. B. EDWARDS (*Writings, etc.*, II., 402), speaking of the fitness of the age to develop this species of poetry, says: "It was the period of peace, extended commerce, art, reflection, when the poet could gather up the experiences of the past, and embody them in pithy sayings, sharp apothegms, instructive allegories, or spread them out in a kind of philosophical disquisition." - A.]

fined, exclusive class of popular teachers gathered about some leader or master, whether there were thus special schools for the wise, or the schools of the prophets were also chief places of culture for the disciples of the Hhokmah, these Hhakamim of the age of Solomon and of subsequent ages must be considered a very important factor in the limited mental development of the people, and as a factor possessing, like the prophetic and the priestly order, an independent importance (comp. Jer. xviii. 18; Ez. vii. 26). They had doubtless offered a vigorous resistance to those frivolous impulses of the לֵצִים, the freethinkers and insolent scoffers, that had manifested themselves since the times of Saul and of David. Their positive agency was exerted in the propagation and dissemination of that deeper religious knowledge and practical wisdom of life, beside which all worldly prudence, fine culture and enlightenment must appear as foolishness (comp. נְבָלוֹת נְבָלָה נָבָל, etc.; Prov. xiii. 20; xvii. 21; Ps. xiv. 1; Is. xxxii. 6). The first decided manifestation of this new intellectual tendency, together with the literature produced by it under Solomon's peaceful reign, marks this bright summit of the entire theocratic development in the Old Testament as the golden age and the really classic epoch of this especially important branch of the intellectual culture in the life of the covenant people.

Note 1.—The independent significance of the חָכְמָה as a special tendency of the mind, exerting with the נְבוּאָה, or the gift of prophecy, an important influence has been recently estimated with special correctness by Ewald. In his dissertation "on the popular and intellectual freedom of Israel in the time of the great prophets down to the destruction of Jerusalem" (*Bibl. Jahrbücher*, I, 96 sq.), he says, among other things, "It is not easy to conceive correctly how high a development was reached in the pursuit of wisdom (Philosophy) in the first centuries after David—and it is not usual to consider how mighty was the influence which it exerted on the entire development of the national life of Israel. The more closely those centuries are reviewed, the greater must be the astonishment at the vast power so early exerted on all sides by wisdom as the peculiar concern of many men among the people. It first openly manifested itself in especial circles of the nation, whilst in the peculiarly propitious age after Solomon eager and inquisitive pupils gathered about individual teachers until ever-improving schools were thus formed. But its influence gradually pervaded all the other pursuits of the people, and acted upon the most diverse branches of authorship." The existence of especial schools of the wise, like those of the Prophets, thus asserted, cannot be satisfactorily proved. Delitzsch's remark in favor of this assumption (*ut supra*, p. 717), that the usual form of address in the Proverbs, בְּנִי, my son, which is not that of a father to a son, but of a teacher to a scholar, implies that there were then בְּנֵי חָכְמָה, *i. e.*, pupils of the wise, just as there were "sons of the prophets," and that there must also have been "schools of wisdom." is and must remain a mere hypothesis. It is moreover an hypothesis, which from the acknowledged wide application of the conception בֵּן, son, in Hebrew, and its almost absolute lack of all support in the Proverbs as well as in the other books of the Old Testament, must always be regarded as a rather unsafe one. Comp. Bruch, pp. 57 sq., who is at all events so far correct that he observes: "The Hebrew wise men were not philosophers by profession; they constituted no class distinct from others, but might belong to different classes." For there is the less reason for supposing from the above cited passage (Jer. xviii. 18) that there was a special class of Hhakamim, beside that of the priests and the prophets, from the fact that in the parallel passage, Ez. vii. 26, the notion of "the wise" is represented by that of "the ancient," זְקֵנִים.

Note 2.—The antithesis between לֵץ and חָכָם which runs through the entire body of Old Testament literature pertaining to wisdom has been discussed in an eminently instructive manner by Delitzsch, *ut supra*, pp. 713 sq. He shows very strikingly how "in the age of Solomon, which was peculiarly exposed to the danger of sensuality and worldliness, to religious indifference and freethinking latitudinarianism," the number of לֵצִים necessarily increased, and their skepticism and mockery must have assumed a more decided and aggravated form. "For those men who despised what is holy, and in doing so laid claim to wisdom (Prov. xiv. 6), who, when permitted to speak, indulged in contention and bitterness (xxii. 10), who carefully shunned the company of the Hhakamim, because they fancied themselves superior to their reproofs (xv. 12), the age of Solomon," he says, "first invented the title לֵץ [scorner]. For in the Psalms of the time of David their common designation is נָבָל (which occurs in Prov. xvii. 21 only in the general sense of low fellow, Germ. *Bube* [Eng. 'Booby.' It occurs also in Prov. xvii. 7, and xxx. 22, and the corresponding verb in xxx. 32—R. P. D.], while the word לֵץ is found in no other than the 1st Psalm, which has a later origin. One of the proverbs of Solomon (xxi. 24, comp. xxiv. 8) gives a definition of the new term: "Proud and haughty scorner (לֵץ) is his name who dealeth in proud wrath." The conscious self-sufficiency of his ungodly thoughts and deeds distinguishes him from the פֶּתִי, the simple, who has been only misled, and may therefore be reclaimed (Prov. xix. 25; xxi. 11). His disowning the Holy, in opposition to a better knowledge and better opportunities, distinguishes him from the כְּסִיל ["foolish," *i. e.*, gross or stupid], the אֱוִיל ["foolish," *i. e.*, lax or remiss], and the חֲסַר־לֵב [the man "void of understanding," lit., lacking heart, *i. e.*, sense], all of whom despise truth and instruction through want of understanding, narrowness and forgetfulness of God, rather than from essential perverseness."

NOTE 3.—Of the four wise contemporaries of Solomon mentioned in 1 Kings v. 11 (iv. 31 according to the older division of chapters [the one followed in our English Bible]) Heman and Ethan appear in Ps. lxxxviii. 1 and lxxxix. 1 as "Ezrahites," *i. e.*, descendants of Ezrah or Zerah, the son of Judah (Num. xxvi. 13, 20). Chalcol and Darda (in the parallel passage, 1 Chron. ii. 6, Dara) are designated as בְּנֵי מָחוֹל, *i. e.*, either "sons of Machal," a man otherwise unknown, or if מָחוֹל be taken as an appellative, "sons of verse," *i. e.*, singers, leaders of the chorus (comp. Eccl. xii. 4). LUTHER's translation, "poets," and his reference of the title to all the four, are unsupported by the original. Comp. KEIL, *Commentar zu den Büchern der Könige*, pp. 42 sq.

§ 4. SOLOMON AND THE POETRY OF WISDOM WHICH MAY BE CALLED SOLOMON'S IN THE STRICTEST SENSE.

As the chief representative and promoter of the Jewish literature of wisdom, we have Solomon himself ["not only the AUGUSTUS of his age, but its ARISTOTLE" (STANLEY)]. The Old Testament exalts the wisdom of this monarch, as a direct gift of Divine grace * (1 Kings iii. 5-12; iv. 29), high above that of all other wise men, whether of his own or of other nations,—especially above that of the teachers of wisdom already named, Heman, Ethan, Chalcol and Darda (1 Kings iv. 30, 31). This is described as consisting, in the first place, in the highest virtues of the ruler and the judge, or, as it is expressed in 1 Kings iii. 9, in "an understanding heart to judge thy people, that I may discern between good and bad;" and in the second place, in an unusually wide and varied knowledge as the basis of his teaching, which related to all the possible relations of created existence. [Comp. STANLEY's *Jewish Church*, II., pp. 254 sq.]

It is this vast erudition which is referred to in the expression "largeness of heart † (רֹחַב לֵב) even as the sand that is on the sea shore," which, with the words "wisdom and understanding exceeding much," is used in 1 Kings iv. 29 to describe his extraordinary endowments. With the same intent it is said of him, ver. 33, that "he spake of trees, from the cedar tree that is in Lebanon even unto the hyssop that springeth out of the wall; he spake also of beasts, and of fowl and of creeping things and of fishes." Among these discourses of his upon all possible manifestations of life in nature are doubtless meant wise sayings in reference to their deeper sense, and the Divine majesty and wisdom reflected in them, physico-theological observations and descriptions, therefore, such, for example, as still present themselves to us in the concluding chapters of the Book of Job (chaps. xxxviii.—xli.), and in several of the sublimest Psalms (viii.; ix.; civ., *etc.*); or shorter aphorisms, parabolic reflec-

---

* ["He showed his wisdom by asking for wisdom. He became wise because he had set his heart upon it. This was to him the special aspect through which the Divine Spirit was to be approached, and grasped, and made to bear on the wants of men; not the highest, not the choice of David, not the choice of Isaiah; but still the choice of Solomon. 'He awoke, and behold, it was a dream.' But the fulfilment of it belonged to actual life." DEAN STANLEY, *History of the Jewish Church*, II., 196.—A.]

† LUTHER's translation, "*getrostes Herz*" [a comforted, then a courageous or confident heart], must be rejected as contrary to the sense of the original. Comp. KEIL *in loc.*, who correctly explains "largeness of heart" as "comprehensive understanding," "intellectual capacity to grasp the widest realms of knowledge."

tions and pointed sentences, such as are quite numerous in the Proverbs and in Ecclesiastes (e. g., Prov. vi 6–8; xx. 1 sq.; xxvi. 1 sq.; xxvii. 3 sq.; xxx. 15 sq.; comp. Eccles. i. 5 sq.; vii. 1 sq.; x. 1 sq.; xii. 1 sq.). It is the manifold materials and themes of both the lyrical and the didactic poetry of Solomon (or, according to 1 Kings iv. 32, his " Proverbs " and " Songs "), which in that noteworthy passage are mentioned as proofs of the unusual extent of his knowledge, this theoretical foundation of his wisdom, or are pointed out by the prominence given to a few noted examples from the vegetable and the animal world. JOSEPHUS indeed rightly understood the passage as a whole, when he found that it ascribed to Solomon a comprehensive knowledge and a profound philosophical view of natural objects (*Antt.*, VIII., 2, 5 : οὐδεμίαν τούτων φύσιν ἠγνόησεν οὐδὲ παρῆλθεν ἀνεξέταστον ἀλλ' ἐν πάσαις ἐφιλοσόφησεν [he was not ignorant of the nature of any of these things, nor did he pass them by unexamined, but he philosophized concerning them all]. A similar correct estimate of the nature and extent of the philosophical knowledge of this great monarch is found in IRENÆUS (*Adv. haer.*, IV., 27, 1), who, on the authority of the same passage says of Solomon, "*eam quæ est in conditione* (i. e., κτίσει) *sapientiam Dei exponebat physiologice.*" He thus in like manner ascribes to him not perhaps a purely descriptive or historical knowledge of natural objects, but a knowledge of nature serving as a basis for fine religious and philosophical observations and ethical instructions in wisdom.

Many of the fruits of this learned pursuit of wisdom must have had a literary character. According to 1 Kings iv. 32 " he spake three thousand proverbs, and his songs were a thousand and five." Not only then had he inherited from his father David, in undiminished fertility, the power of composing songs, the gift of both sacred and secular lyrical verse, but he also originated and established a new species of Hebrew poetic art, that of gnomic didactic poetry, of which before his time there had existed but mere germs, imperfect attempts completely eclipsed by his achievements. Proportionably few specimens of either class of his poetical productions have come down to us. Instead of one thousand and five songs we have in the Canon but two Psalms, which bear his name, the 72d and the 127th. The exclusion of so large a number of his lyrics from the collection of the religious verse of his nation may have been occasioned either by their lack of a directly religious character, or by their too individual bearing. In reference to another monument of the lyrical poetry associated with the name of Solomon, the Canticles, it is still an undecided and controverted question whether Solomon was the proper and immediate author of it, or rather some contemporary poet who chose him as its subject (see § 5).

The remains of his gnomic didactic poetry, as they are presented in the Proverbs, are much more numerous. Even this collection, however, contains not more, perhaps, than one quarter of those 3,000 sayings which Solomon uttered ; inasmuch as several parts of the book are by their titles expressly ascribed to other authors, and of the remaining 746 verses hardly the whole can be directly ascribed to him (see § 12). It will always be uncertain whether those 3,000 proverbs of which it is expressly said that he "spake" them, were all actually recorded by him or one of his contemporaries, or whether many of them, as matters of merely oral tradition, were not gradually lost.

That in general he spoke more than he wrote, so that the greater part of the utterances of his wisdom consisted in pithy maxims and acute sayings, like the riddles of the modern Orientals, may be pretty safely inferred from the statement, that "there came of all people to hear the wisdom of Solomon, from all kings of the earth, which had heard of his wisdom " (1 Kings iv. 34). The same inference may be drawn partly from the Scripture narrative, and partly from the old Jewish tradition preserved by JOSEPHUS in reference to the Queen of Sheba's visit to his court (1 Kings x. 1 sq.), as well as from the account of his contest with King Hiram, and with the Tyrian Abdemon, in the proposing of ingenious riddles. (JOSEPHUS, *Antt.* VIII., 5, 3).

NOTE 1.—Besides songs (שִׁירִים), gnomes or maxims (מְשָׁלִים), and riddles (חִידוֹת), HITZIG, *ut supra*, p. xvi., ascribes fables to Solomon. " The discourse concerning beasts, trees, fowl, *etc.*, ascribed to him (in 1 Kings iv. 33)," he thinks, "cannot be properly referred to the substance of his maxims, but is most naturally understood of his invention of fables." This is a rather arbitrary conceit of HITZIG's, which he unsuccessfully tries to sustain by the hypothesis which he throws in, that "perhaps in the אֵזוֹב, 1 Kings iv. 33 (hyssop), the name of Æsop lies concealed" (Αἴσωπος=ἔσσωπος??). Notwithstanding the contrary assertion of HERDER, in his well-known work, "The Spirit of Hebrew Poetry" (II., p. 13), the Old Testament offers no example of a proper fable. The story of the bramble invited by the trees to be their king (Judg. ix. 8-15) is in its whole plan and tendency much more of a parable than a fable.

NOTE 2.—According to Oriental traditions in reference to Solomon and the Queen of Sheba, her name was Balkis or Belkis; she became Solomon's concubine, or his actual wife (the first is asserted by the Himyaritic Arabs, the latter by the Æthiopians); she bore him a son, Menilehek, with the surname *Ibn-el-hagim*, son of the wise; she first brought to Palestine the root of the genuine balsam, afterwards cultivated at Jericho and near Engedi (comp. 1 Kings x. 10, and in addition JOSEPHUS, Antt. VIII. 6, 6), *etc.* Legends of this sort, invented especially by the Rabbis to heighten the kingly glory and wisdom of Solomon, and found some of them in JOSEPHUS (*ut supra*), others in the Talmud (*e. g. Jalkub Melachim*, p. 195), others in the Koran (Sura 27), others in later Arabic, Æthiopic and Persian documents, abound in the compreher ave Turkish work *Suleiman name, i. e.* the Book of Solomon, which, according to VON HAMMER, consists of 70 folio volumes. Comp. VON HAMMER "*Rosenöl*, or Oriental Legends and Traditions from Arabic, Persian and Turkish sources," Vol. I., pp. 147-257. See also H. LUDOLF, *Hist. Æthiop.*, II, c. 3, 4: POCOCKE, *Specimen hist. Arab.*, p. 60; CAUSSIN DE PERCEVAL, *Essai sur l'histoire des Arabes*, I., pp. 76 sq.; and P. CASSEL, *Elagabal*, in the Elberfeld "*Vortrage f. d. gebildete Publikum*," 1864, p. 182.

NOTE 3.—[The question of Solomon's moral qualification to be the author of some of the books contained in the canon of the Scriptures has sometimes perplexed honest disciples, and been made a specious argument in the mouths of cavillers. The point is well put and the answer well given by ARNOT, *Laws from Heaven for Life on Earth*, pp. 11-13. "The choice of Solomon as one of the writers of the Bible at first sight startles, but on deeper study instructs. We would have expected a man of more exemplary life—a man of uniform holiness. It is certain that, in the main, the vessels which the Spirit used were sanctified vessels: 'Holy men of old spake as they were moved by the Holy Ghost.' .... But the diversity in all its extent is like all the other ways of God; and He knows how to make either extreme fall into its place in the concert of His praise. He who made Saul an apostle did not disdain to use Solomon as a prophet. .... If all the writers of the Bible had been perfect in holiness,—if no stain of sin could be traced on their character, no error noted in their life, it is certain that the Bible would not have served all the purposes which it now serves among men. It would have been Godlike indeed in matter and mould, but it would not have reached down to the low estate of man—it would not have penetrated to the sores of a human heart. .... Practical lessons on some subjects come better through the heart and lips of the weary, repentant king than through a man who had tasted fewer pleasures, and led a more even life. .... Here is a marvel ; *not a line of Solomon's writings tends to palliate Solomon's sins.* .... The glaring imperfections of the man's life have been used as a dark ground to set off the lustre of that pure righteousness which the Spirit has spoken by his lips."—A.]

§ 5. THE SONG OF SOLOMON IN ITS RELATION TO THE LITERATURE OF WISDOM ASSOCIATED WITH SOLOMON.*

The opinion that the Song of Solomon is not only a production of the age of Solomon, but most probably the work of Solomon himself, is favored both by its numerous allusions to the personal and historical relations of this king (*e. g.* iii. 2; iv. 4; vi. 8; vii. 5; viii. 11), and by its general æsthetic character, its lively conception of nature. Thus it manifests a decided preference for comparisons with natural objects of all sorts, especially with such as are distinguished

---

* [While there must be conceded to be weight in the objections urged by ISAAC TAYLOR (chap. iii. of his "*Spirit of Hebrew Poetry*") to the recognition of a proper *drama* in the Scriptures, we cannot agree with him that it is only with "a very forced meaning" that such books as Job and Solomon's Song can be called dramatic. There is, on the other hand, need to guard against the fondness of some for assimilating the Scriptures in their descriptive terms to secular literature; is there not in the other direction such an error as hyper-fastidiousness?—A.]

either by their beauty or their variety ; it refers not only to numerous important places of both Northern and Southern Palestine, but also to regions, cities and persons beyond the limits of Palestine (e. g. Kedar, Damascus, Pharaoh, etc.). Had it been composed merely with reference to Solomon, it would not have been ascribed to this monarch either in the title of the Masoretic text, or by the unanimous tradition of Jewish antiquity. It is manifestly a product of that extremely rich and fruitful poetical activity of Solomon, described in 1 Kings iv. 32, 33. In virtue of its erotic contents it belongs essentially to that division of his poetry which is there indicated by the mention of the songs which were a thousand and five, and thus to the lyrical class, whose characteristic features must be recognized in it, though with UMBREIT, EWALD, DELITZSCH and others, we regard it as a dramatic composition. For even though this pre-eminently probable view of its artistic form be adopted,—a view which alone offers a thorough and generally satisfactory refutation of the recently somewhat popular theory, which divides the entire composition into a simple cycle of "love songs,"—the essentially lyrical and erotic character of its separate parts is ever unmistakable ; so that the name of a drama in the narrower and stricter sense of the word is not on the whole applicable to it, but rather only that of a "lyrical drama" (BÖTTCHER), a garland of erotic songs joined in dramatic unity (DELITZSCH). But notwithstanding this its lyric and dramatic, or perhaps even melo-dramatic form, and notwithstanding its somewhat wide deviation from the Maschal form of the Proverbs, there exists between its fundamental idea and that of the strictly didactic or aphoristic poetry of Solomon a significant inner connection. The Song of Solomon must undoubtedly be classed with the Hhokmah poetry in its wider sense, because its fundamental idea when rightly viewed, must be admitted to belong to the circle of those ethical ideas which form the chief and the favorite subjects of Solomon's doctrine of wisdom. This fundamental idea consists in the exaltation of conjugal love and faithfulness as the most excellent and sure foundation of earthly prosperity, as a moral force in life triumphing over all the misery and mischief of this earth and even death itself. This fundamental idea is prominent in passages like chap. vii. 7, 8, and viii. 6–8, which are closely related to expressions like those found in Prov. v. 18, 19 ; xviii. 22 ; xix. 14 ; xxxi. 10 sq. This must be admitted to be the chief topic in the poem and the central point in its descriptions, whether we assume, with EWALD and others, that the design is to celebrate the changeless constancy and innocence of the Shulamite, that was proof against all the flatteries and artful temptations of the luxurious Solomon, or with DELITZSCH, that the work belongs to an earlier period in the life of that king, before he had sunk into the foul depths of polygamy and idolatry, and that consequently it refers to his chaste relations to a single wife. It is evident that the latter view is more harmonious with the opinion which, on both internal and external grounds, asserts the authorship of Solomon, than is that of EWALD, or than the interpretation most nearly related to it adopted by HUG, BOTTCHER and the author of this general commentary ; it also favors equally, if not still better, the recognition of a secondary or a mystical reference of the poem to the Messiah. For as a representation of the rapturous joy and bliss arising from the conjugal relation between Solomon, the prince of peace, and his beloved Shulamite, the poem admits of innumerable typical and prophetic applications to Christ and His Church. And these applications render superfluous all other expositions of its Christological contents, such as have resorted to various allegorizing expedients, from the earliest periods of the Church down to the time of H. A. HAHN and HENGSTENBERG [with whom must be reckoned as in general sympathy a considerable number of British and American expositors, among the most conspicuous and emphatic of whom is Bishop WORDSWORTH]. The mystery of the Song of Solomon is that of the marriage relation, and therefore the poem not only admits of that somewhat general Messianic sense which belongs to every poetical celebration of bridal love and conjugal faithfulness within the range of the Scriptures (comp. Eph. v. 32), but also appears as a Messianic prophecy of a specific typical significance, as a prediction in which the marriage of a theocratic king of Israel is described as an especially suggestive analogue and type of the relation of Christ to the Church of the New Testament. In this aspect it closely resembles the 45th Psalm, which likewise celebrates an Old Testament royal marriage as a type of the New Testament covenant relation between Christ and His Church ; this Psalm, however, probably refers to a later prince than Solomon, and both by this its origin, in a period after Solomon, and by the unmistakable decrease, in its delineations, of the favorite ideas and characteristic imagery of Solomon's poetry, it shows that it must have sprung from another sphere of spiritual culture and production than that of the classic Hhokmah literature of the earlier age.

[All comment on this view of Solomon's Song, together with all comparative and supplementary presentation of views that have been held in Great Britain and America, is deferred to the Introduction and Exegetical notes connected with our author's companion Commentary on the Book, which is contained in the present series and will be found translated in the present volume].

NOTE.—In these hints with reference to the relation in which the Song of Solomon stands to the literature of wisdom which bears his name, we have mainly followed DELITZSCH. In his "*Untersuchung und Auslegung des Hohenliedes,*" 1851, p. 171, he does not hesitate to designate it as "a production of the Hhokmah,"—a species of literature cultivated and employed by Solomon with conspicuous skill. This he does in virtue of the broadly human and ethical character of the idea of conjugal love and union which forms its chief theme. "For," he adds, arguing pertinently in support of his view, "the Hhokmah of the age of Solomon is devoted to the exposition of those creative ordinances of the Cosmos, which have a broader range than the national limits of Israel, and of the universal axioms of religion and morality. The poetry of the Hhokmah is therefore didactic; and both proverbial poetry and drama were developed by it."

DELITZSCH's view of the Song of Solomon and of its ethical and theological value, is in general more interesting and in all respects more satisfactory than any other modern one; it is also preferable to that of the respected founder of this general Commentary, who, on p. 36 [Am. Ed.] of the General Introduction to the Old Testament, expresses the view "that the poem doubtless sprung from the theoretic indignation provoked by the anticipated allowance of religious freedom by Solomon, his polygamy implicating him with heathenism." The fundamental idea is therefore held to be that "the Virgin of Israel, or the theocracy, refuses to be numbered with the heathen wives, or religions, as the favorite of Solomon, but turns to her true betrothed, the still remote Messiah."

We cannot adopt this view, chiefly because the arguments for the genuineness of the poem or the authorship of Solomon, seem to us to outweigh all that lie against it. As little, and indeed still less, can we approve the two conceptions most nearly related to this of LANGE. That of HUG ("*Das Hohelied in einer noch unversuchten Deutung,*" 1813) refers the poem to the time of Hezekiah, and considers it as a symbolical expression of the desire of the ten tribes of Israel for reunion with the kingdom of Judah represented by the king of peace, Hezekiah—Solomon. That advocated by BÖTTCHER (*Die ältesten Buhnendichtungen*, 1850) regards it as a lyrical drama, produced and represented in the kingdom of Israel about the year 950 B. C., some time after Solomon's death, and aimed at the royal house and the manners of the harem, so hostile to the life of the family. A more extended critical discussion of these views would here be out of place. An examination of the various modifications of the Messianic allegorical interpretation, as well as of the purely historical or profane erotic view (THEODORE of Mopsuesta, CASTELLIO, J. D. MICHAELIS, HERDER, EICHHORN, HITZIG, *etc.*), must be left for the Introduction to this book of Scripture.

§ 6. THE BOOK OF JOB, CONSIDERED AS A PRODUCT OF THE POETRY OF WISDOM, KNOWN IN THE BROADER SENSE AS SOLOMON'S.

The Book of Job must also be without doubt classed with the productions of the poetical Hhokmah literature, and indeed, as a whole, with even more justice than the Song of Solomon. For although its composition cannot be confidently referred to the time of Solomon, since verbal and other considerations seem to indicate a later period for its origin, its inner relationship to the chief characteristic productions of that literature, to the Proverbs on the one hand and to Ecclesiastes on the other, is so much the less doubtful. Its ethical and religious tendency, developed in the representation of the conflict and the victory of a godly man in sore trial, and in the justification of the divine dealing in the face of the apparent injustice of such sufferings as his, and the peculiar method in which it develops this fundamental thought, by means of conversations and discourses which are made up now of gnomes or moral maxims strung together like pearls, and again of lively and symbolical pictures from nature and from human life,—both alike prove the close connection of this didactic poem with the proverbial poetry of Solomon, as we have above (§§ 3, 4) characterized it. Moreover, the manner in which the poet in chap. xxviii. rises to the idea of the absolute wisdom of God, and represents a participation in it as dependent on a godly and upright course, is very closely related to that which appears in passages like Prov. viii. 22; ix. 12; Eccl. xii. 13; Prov. i. 7; iii. 16, *etc.* The fundamental principle and the didactic tendency of the book seem in all essential features to have sprung from the same style of seeking after wisdom and of religious and philosophical inquiry as the Proverbs and Ecclesiastes; and if, in consequence of a certain tinge of skepticism peculiar to its theological views and reflections, in which the decidedly skeptical attitude of the Preacher to a certain extent betrays itself, it forms a sort of connecting link between these two books, so on the other hand it is by virtue of its poetical form most nearly related to the Song of Solomon. For like this it appears in the poetical garb of a drama, of a drama, however, which, in so far as it bears an impress of an *epico*-dramatic rather than of a *lyrico*-dramatic (melodramatic) kind, deviates from the pure central and typical form of this species of poetry in a different direction from that taken by the Song of Solomon. It is on this account, therefore, to be likened to such intellectual creations as DANTE's *Divine Comedy* (or even as the philosophical dialogues of Plato, so far as these may be considered as artistic poetical productions in the wider sense), rather than to the erotic lyrical dramas or idylls of other nations.*

At all events the interlocutory dramatic style of the poem prompts one to fix the time of its composition as near as possible to that of the Song of Solomon, and to regard it as having originated, if not under Solomon, at least in the age immediately following him. This period is indicated on the one hand by the sublime character of its descriptions of nature, reminding one strongly of the universally extended horizon of the epoch of Solomon (compare especially chaps. xxxviii.-xli. with 1 Kings iv. 30), and on the other by the traces appearing in passages like ix. 24; xii. 17 sq.; xv. 18 sq., of a decline already begun in the glory of the kingdom, and of heavy national calamities. That the whole book must in any case have appeared long before the Babylonish captivity, is evident from such a familiarity with its contents as a whole, and with individual descriptions in it, as is exhibited by the prophets Ezekiel (xx. 14, 20) and Jeremiah (xx. 14 sq., comp. Job iii. 3 sq.). This origin before the exile is to be claimed also for the discourses of Elihu in chaps. xxxii.-xxxvii. the more confidently, in proportion as they unmistakably form an essential and indispensable link of connection between the conversation of Job with his three friends, and the manifestation of Jehovah which brings the final solution of the whole problem.

[Among English authors who agree in this classification of the Book of Job few are more emphatic in their assertions or more felicitous in their illustration than Dean STANLEY (*Jewish Church*, II., 270-1): "Nothing but the wide contact of that age with the Gentile world could, humanly speaking, have admitted either a subject or a scene so remote from Jewish thought and customs, as that of Job." "The allusions to the horse, the peacock, the crocodile and the hippopotamus, are such as in Palestine could hardly have been made till after the formation of Solomon's collections. The knowledge of Egypt and Arabia is what could only have been acquired after the diffusion of Solomon's commerce. The questions discussed are the same as those which agitate the mind of Solomon, but descending deeper and deeper into the difficulties of the world," *etc.*—On the other side, apart from formal commentaries, one will hardly find a clearer and more vigorous presentation of the reasons, both in the style and substance of the Book of Job, for assigning it an earlier date, "an age as early at least as that of the Israelitish settlement in Palestine," than is given in chap. 8 of ISAAC TAYLOR's *Spirit of Hebrew Poetry*.—A.]

NOTE.—If the Book of Job belongs to the epoch of Solomon, there is the more reason for re-

---

* Compare the excellent essay of G. BAUR, "*Das Buch Hiob und Dante's göttliche Komödie, eine Parallele,*" in the *Studien und Kritiken*, 1856, III.

garding this period as one of unequalled richness in the manifold variety of its poetical ideas, its species and forms of poetic art. For besides the religious lyric and the proverbial poetry, both of the chief forms of the Old Testament drama, the religious-erotic and the religious-didactic or philosophical, must have attained their maturity during this period; and there is the more truth in what EWALD—who, moreover, refers the Book of Job to the period just before the exile—remarks in characterizing this epoch: "Thus at this time poetry expands, seeking new paths in every possible direction, though she could only enter them. This is the period of the full formation and broadest development of Hebrew poetry, when it reveals all its latent capacities, and gathers up all its scattered forces; and it is just this that is here new and peculiar" (*Die poetischen Bücher des alten Bundes*, I., p. 19). Compare HAEVERNICK, *Einleit. in das A. T.*, *herausg. von* KEIL, Bd. III., p. 12: "Thus Solomon excels his father in fruitfulness of poetic inspiration, and this fruitfulness testifies to the great wealth of this period in poetical productions. As the splendor and richness of Solomon's peaceful reign is a fruit of David's strifes and victories, so the poetry of his time is but the rich unfolding of the fruit planted and nourished by David. It proves itself to be such by its peculiar character of peaceful objectiveness, while the poetry of David is the thorough expression of deeply stirred subjective emotion. The blessedness of the peace, which, after long and bitter conflicts, the theocracy enjoyed under Solomon, reflects itself as clearly in the 72d and 127th Psalms as in the Song of Solomon, and gives to the latter, notwithstanding its thoroughly emotional contents, a repose and objectiveness of attitude which has long since overcome all struggle and conflict. With this is also connected the broader horizon which poetry gains under Solomon, as well as the complete development and rounding out of its form which likewise marks this period," etc. Many of the characteristics here mentioned belong as well to the book of Job; this is not, however, the case with all of them. The passages above quoted [on the preceding page], for example, refer rather to a disturbed and troublous period, than to the peaceful repose and glory of Solomon's reign. On this account we do not venture to adopt without hesitation the view that the book originated in this period, as held by LUTHER, DOEDERLEIN, STAEUDLIN, HAEVERNICK, KEIL, SCHLOTTMANN, HAHN, VAIHINGER, and others. We regard as more probable the assumption of a somewhat later composition (adopted by the general Editor; see *Introd.*, etc., p. 35). We do not, however, for that reason, with EWALD, HIRZEL, HEILIGSTEDT, BLEEK, and others, assign its origin to the seventh century before Christ; or, with CLERICUS, GESENIUS, UMBREIT, VATKE, BUNSEN, and others, refer it to the exile or the period that immediately followed it.

§ 7. THE LITERATURE OF WISDOM AFTER SOLOMON; *a*) ECCLESIASTES.

To the productions of the Hhokmah that undoubtedly belong after Solomon is to be referred Koheleth or the Preacher (קֹהֶלֶת, Ἐκκλησιαστής). This is a didactic poem, which not only by its extended monologue in the Maschal form, but also by its express designation of the speaker as "the son of David," and "King in Jerusalem," seems to betray an origin direct from Solomon. The entire weight of all those considerations, whether of an internal or a verbal character, which claim attention, compel the assumption of an origin not only after Solomon, but even after the exile. For the numerous Chaldaisms in its diction, the references to the oppressive rule of unworthy kings of a non-Israelitish race, *e. g.*, iv. 13-16; v. 8; viii. 1 sq.; x. 4 sq., as well as many allusions to circumstances and events after the exile, such as vi. 2, 3; viii. 10; ix. 13 sq.; xii. 12—all together compel us to recognize the book as a literary monument of the later Persian period. Complaints of the vanity of all earthly things, in the form of disconnected monologues, not, however, exactly separate aphoristic sentences like those of the Proverbs, but rather as somewhat extended reflections, are here put into the mouth of the wise King Solomon. The rhetorical dress by means of which this is accomplished appears the more suitable, since a king who had not only acquired an unusually extended knowledge of earthly things, but also had surrendered himself to the inordinate enjoyment of them, should be regarded as a pre-eminently appropriate preacher concerning their nothingness and transitoriness. The complaints which the book contains on this topic sometimes rise to doubts in reference to the moral government of the world; *e. g.*, iii. 10 sq.; iv. 1 sq.; vi. 8 sq.; vii. 15 sq.; ix. 2 sq., or where this is not the case, at least

§ 7. THE LITERATURE OF WISDOM AFTER SOLOMON.

leave apparently unreconciled the contradiction between the Divine perfection and the vanity of the world. Its philosophy of life has therefore with a certain degree of justice been explained as a sceptical one. It has indeed even received the name of a "Song of Songs of Scepticism."[*] The entire absence of the Divine covenant name, Jehovah, and the occurrence of frequent exhortations to the cheerful enjoyment of life, instead of possible admonitions to obedient subjection to the law (ii. 24-26; iii. 12 sq; iii. 22; v. 17-19; viii. 15; ix. 7-10, xi. 7 sq.; xii. 7 sq.), might besides seem to justify the suspicion of an attitude religiously indifferent and morally lax, which is not seldom charged upon the author. He was, however, far removed from proper Epicureanism, or indeed from atheistic impulses. He in fact never contents himself with uniting the traditional faith and his sceptical view of the world in a merely external "Concordat between the fear of God and the cheerful enjoyment of the present." (KAHNIS, ut supra, p. 309). But in a time inclined to the abandonment of faith in God's holy and just government of the world, he clings to such a faith with a touching constancy, and defends the fact of the wise rule of the Eternal and Omnipotent God against all the frivolous scoffs of fools (ii. 26; iii. 20 sq.; v. 1; v. 17-19; viii. 14; ix. 1-3; compare ii. 13; iv. 5; x. 2 sq.; x. 13, 14). And in an age when his people had little or nothing to hope for in the way of external national prosperity and increase, when moral dullness, apathy and despondency might thus easily master the individual members of this people, he is never weary of pointing out the righteous retributions of the future as a motive to the fear of God, the chief and all-comprehending virtue of the wise (iii. 14-17; v. 6; vi. 6, 10; viii. 12 sq.; xi. 9; xii. 13, 14), and of commending unwavering constancy in individual callings as the best prudence and the surest defence against the sufferings and the temptations of our earthly life (compare ii. 10; iii. 22; v. 17, 18; viii. 15, etc.). It is especially the high estimate which he puts upon this faithful endeavor to fulfil one's earthly duty, this "cheerfulness in labor," which reveals the close relationship between his practical view of life and that of the Proverbs of Solomon, and reveals his place within the circle of those Hhakamim whose spiritual thought and action in the earlier age has left its worthiest monument in that collection of Proverbs, and in the Book of Job.

NOTE 1.—The assumption that Solomon was the immediate author of the Book of Ecclesiastes, which once exclusively prevailed, and is still at this time defended by L. VAN ESSEN (*Der Prediger Salomo's*, Schaffh., 1856), M. A. HAHN, *Commentar, etc*., 1860), and E. BOHL (*Dissertatio de Aramaismis libri Koheleth*, Erlangen, 1860), is refuted not only by the arguments above given, which favor its origin in the period of the Persian sway, but still more especially by many passages in which the use of the name of King Solomon is manifestly but a free and poetical one, e. g., i. 12; i. 16; ii. 6; and particularly xii. 9-14, in which the author speaks of his own person in distinction from the Preacher. Compare BLEEK, *Einleitung*, p. 645; KEIL, *Einleitung* p. 435.

NOTE 2.—The charges which have of late been often brought against the Book of Ecclesiastes, viz., that it teaches merely a "religion of the present," that its moral and religious tendency is simply negative, that it inclines to fatalistic scepticism and to the lax morality of Epicureanism (LOWTH, DOEDERLEIN, DE WETTE, KNOBEL, in part also HITZIG and BRUCH, according to whom "the scepticism of this book rises even to bitter anguish and utter despair of finding any aim or order in human life" [*ut supra*, pp. 68, 238 sq., 383 sq.]), are met by the passages above cited, in which patient devotion to one's personal earthly calling, together with a cheerful mind and thankful enjoyment of God's temporal gifts, is recommended. These passages are of special importance, since they significantly exhibit the peculiar practical tendency of the book. It is the New Testament virtues, ὑπομονή, χαίρειν τῇ ἐλπίδι, ἐργάζεσθαι μετὰ ἡσυχίας (Rom. xii. 12; 2 Thes. iii. 12, *etc.*), in their peculiar Old Testament form, and in accordance with that view of the world inculcated in the more advanced Hhokmah doctrine, which are here substantially exhibited and commended to the tempted saints of the theocracy after the exile.

Compare LUTHER's Preface to the writings of Solomon—" The other book is named Koheleth, which we call the Preacher; and it is a book of consolation. When a man would live obediently

---

[*] So HEINRICH HEINE designates it in his "*Vermischte Schriften*," 1854, I. In like manner DELITZSCH, *Commentar zum Buch Hiob* (In KEIL und DELITZSCH's *Bibl. Comm. zum A. T.*), p. 5.

according to the teaching of the first book (*i. e.*, the Proverbs), and perform the duties of his calling or of his office, the devil, the world, and his own flesh oppose, so that he is wearied of his condition. . . . . Now as Solomon in the first book teaches obedience, as against foolish desire and curiosity, so in this book he teaches patience and constancy in opposition to discontent and temptation, and a peaceful and joyful waiting for the final hour." Comp. the *Preface to the Latin Commentary* (*Opp. exeget. ed. Schmid et Irmischer*, T. XXI., p. 5): *Hunc librum Ecclesiasten rectius nos vocaremus Politica vel Œconomica Salomonis, qui viro in politia versanti consulat in casibus tristibus et animum erudiat ac roboret ad patientiam, etc.* ["This book, Ecclesiastes, we should more correctly call the Politics or Economics of Solomon; for he is giving counsel in adversity to a man engaged in public life, and is training and strengthening his spirit to patience," etc.] For similar passages see ELSTER, *Commentar über den Prediger Sal.*, 1855, Introd., pp. 14 sq. Besides this expositor (see especially pp. 27 sq.), EWALD (*Einl. zu Koheleth*, pp. 177 sq.), HAEVERNICK (*Einl.* III., 449 sq.), VAIHINGER (*Ueber den Plan Koheleth's, Stud. und Krit.*, 1848, pp. 442 sq.), and HENGSTENBERG (*Der Prediger Salom. ausgelegt*, 1859), have, among recent writers, with cogent arguments, defended the ethical character and contents of the book against such attacks. Compare also the profound essay of VILMAR, "*Ueber Kohcleth*," in the *Pastoraltheol. Bll.*, 1863, 1, 241 sq.

§ 8. CONTINUATION. *b*) THE PSALMS OF WISDOM.

Proverbial poetry most clearly combined with lyrical appears not only in the writings of Solomon, but also in those of many poets of the later age. Certain intermediate forms of composition therefore occur which may be classed with one as well as with the other species of poetry. Such are those Psalms, which, though they do not directly teach wisdom, yet sing the praise of the fear of God as the source of all wisdom, and exhibit a didactic tendency, both by the Maschal form which they adopt, and by proclaiming the praise of the law of the Lord and their exhortations to its faithful observance. They may be briefly designated as Hhokmah-Psalms, and may be regarded as gnomes expanded into lyrics, or as the combination of several wise adages into a lyrical didactic whole. The shortest of the two Psalms ascribed to Solomon, the 127th, appears to be in a measure a gnome thus expanded into a lyrical form. Of the later Psalms those belong to the same category, which consist of praises of a life led in the fear of God and the faithful observance of the law,—Ps. i., cxi., cxii., cxxv. and cxxviii. Of these the second is especially worthy of notice, in that it closes with the same commendation of the fear of God as the beginning of wisdom (ver. 10), which is found at the beginning of Solomon's Book of Proverbs (Prov. i. 7, comp. ix. 10, etc.), and at the end of Ecclesiastes and of the 28th chapter of the Book of Job. The 119th Psalm is also a Psalm of wisdom on a magnificent scale, an alphabetical arrangement [lost of course in our versions] of inspired praises of the Divine word, and of the blessings which result from obeying it,—which LUTHER has well styled "the Christian A. B C. of praise, love, power, and use of the word of God." Here belongs also the 49th Psalm, which describes the transitoriness of the happiness of the ungodly, and contrasts with it the hope of the righteous resting on God. For this purpose it adopts a form which is expressly termed "speaking of wisdom" (ver. 3 [E. V.]), a "parable," a "dark saying" (ver. 4 [E. V.]). The 78th Psalm, which belongs to Asaph, asserts its didactic character by the use of similar expressions. Yet its contents, which are descriptive of the history of redemption rather than gnomically instructive or contemplative, show that it ought not to be classed with the proper psalms of wisdom, even though its tendency, like that of several other of the Psalms of Asaph, might in general be called didactic. Those Psalms of David also, which contain didactic matter, differ almost throughout both in their contents and their form from the Hhokmah poetry of the age of Solomon and of that immediately succeeding, and only incidentally coincide with a few of the above named psalms of wisdom; *e. g.*, Ps. xv. 2 sq., with Pss. i., cxi., cxii.; Ps. xiv. 8 sq., with Ps. cxix.

The title מַשְׂכִּיל borne by some of David's psalms, *e. g.*, Pss xxxii., lii, as well as by Asaph's, the 78th, affords no ground for regarding these songs as productions of the Hhokmah poetry, or in general as merely didactic poems; for מַשְׂכִּיל is to be rendered neither as "Instruction" nor as "Didactic poem," but most probably with DELITZSCH as "Meditation," or even with HITZIG and others, as "Form, Image, Invention." The Psalter then contains in general no Hhokmah poems of the period before Solomon, since the above named psalms of this class, all belong more probably to a later age, and indeed for the most part to the period after the exile; they are consequently contemporary with Ecclesiastes rather, perhaps, than with the Book of Job, or with the original materials of the Book of Proverbs.

§ 9. CONCLUSION.—*c*) THE APOCRYPHAL LITERATURE OF WISDOM (SIRACH, BARUCH, THE BOOK OF WISDOM, *etc.*).

In the Apocryphal writings of Jesus, son of Sirach (Σοφία τοῦ Σειράχ, Ecclesiasticus), and of the anonymous author of the book of Baruch, and of the "Wisdom of Solomon," the Hebrew literature of wisdom celebrates its second spring-time upon Alexandrian Hellenistic soil. No one of these works can have originated earlier than the second century before the Christian Era, at least in the linguistic form and structure in which they now exist. For the Ptolemy under whom the younger son of Sirach* clothed in its present Greek garb the Hebrew work of his grandfather of the same name (a Jew of Palestine), can be no other than Ptolemy Physcon, or Ptolemy Euergetes II. (B. C. 170–117). The Book of Wisdom, according to internal evidence, belongs rather to the more advanced than to the earlier period of Alexandrianism; it must probably have been produced, therefore, not until near the age of Philo, rather than have been composed by a contemporary of Aristobulus, or, as some claim, by Aristobulus himself. The book Baruch, finally, which has as little to do with the old Baruch of the school of the prophets, as the "Letters of Jeremiah" which it contains have to do with the old prophetic teacher, is very certainly quite a late post-canonical production. No one of these works—and this is quite as true of the book Tobias, and the "Prayer of Manasseh," which exhibit at least some points of contact with the later Jewish literature of wisdom—reaches back even as far as the time of Ecclesiastes, the latest production of the canonical or classical Hhokmah poetry. In their literary artistic character, and their religious didactic substance, the three works named above are distinguished one from another in this, that the collection of gnomes by Jesus, son of Sirach, in regard to contents as well as form, appears to be mainly an imitation of the Proverbs, without, however, attaining the classical excellence of its model; that, furthermore, the "Wisdom of Solomon," less rich in genuine theological and ethical substance, in its didactic form (as a monologue) and its free poetical appropriation of the person of Solomon, approaches Ecclesiastes quite as much as it differs from it in the, not sceptical but, Platonic speculative stamp of its argument; and that finally Baruch, which attempts to array the fundamental ideas of the doctrine of wisdom in the form of the old prophetic admonitions, commands, and letters, reaches nothing better than a dull, spiritless reproduction of these prophetic forms, of as little theological as philosophical value.

NOTE.—The collection of proverbs by the son of Sirach, in spite of the occasional originality and beauty of its contents, still falls far below the poetic perfection and the theological ripeness of the model furnished by Solomon. It therefore cannot be regarded as a composition bearing the stamp of inspiration and worthy of a place in the Canon. These points are conceded even by several of the most recent defenders of the Apocrypha against the criticisms of the English Reformed School; *e. g.*, HENGSTENBERG (*Evang. Kirchen-Zeitung*, 1853, Nos. 54 sq.; 1854, Nos. 29 sq.) and BLEEK (*Studien und Kritiken*, 1853, II.). BRUCH also, in particular, has commented very justly on the literary value of Ecclesiasticus as compared with the Proverbs. He says in his "*Weisheitslehre der Hebräer*," p. 273: "The true Hebrew gnome did indeed stand before this sage as a lofty ideal. This was the goal toward which he pressed, but which he was not able to reach. Only now and then does he attain in his proverbs the condensed brevity, the suggestive fullness of meaning, and the telling rhythm of proposition and antithesis, which

---

* [A genealogy based on the assumed correctness of the first prologue to the Book of Ecclesiasticus has been constructed as follows: 1. Sirach. 2. Jesus, son (father) of Sirach (*author of the book*). 3. Sirach. 4. Jesus, son of Sirach (*translator of the book*). See B. F. WESTCOTT's articles, "Jesus, the son of Sirach," and "Ecclesiasticus," in SMITH's *Dictionary of the Bible.*—A.]

distinguish the Proverbs of Solomon. In many cases it is only with difficulty that he succeeds in comprehending a thought, in its rounded fullness of meaning, within the narrow limits of a single proposition. Still less frequently does he bring corresponding members into a true antithetic relation. He usually carries out his thoughts through a series of complementary proverbs, which not seldom run out at last into dull prose. The true poetic spirit is altogether wanting to the son of Sirach. He frequently expresses himself, it is true, in imagery, but then he heaps figure upon figure improperly, and in his similes falls into the inflated and fantastic. The quiet attitude of reflection would better befit the whole individuality of this Jewish sage," etc.

Furthermore, that Sirach, notwithstanding his comparative lack of originality and independent creative power, was still no mere imitator of Solomon's Proverbs, but that besides this he made use of other collections of ancient and esteemed maxims, appears from some hints in his own book (e. g., xxiv. 28; xxxiii. 16). It appears also from the fragments of ancient Hebrew proverbs which still occur here and there in the Talmudic literature of the Jews, which fragments point to the existence of similar collections of gnomes by the side of and before that of the son of Sirach. Comp. BRUCH, p. 274; DELITZSCH, "*Zur Geschichte der Hebräischen Poesie,*" pp. 201 sq.; BERTHEAU, "*Exeget. Handbuch zu den Spr. Sal.,*" Introd., pp. xlii. sq.

In regard to the literary and theological character of the Book of Wisdom, in its relations to the canonical literature of wisdom in the Old Testament, comp. BRUCH (the work above cited), pp. 322 sq., and GRIMM, in the "*Kurzgef. exeget. Handbuch zu den Apocryphen,*" Vol. 6, Introduction ; and likewise KUEBEL (Pastor in Wurtemberg), "*Die ethischen Grundanschauungen der Weisheit Salomos: ein Beitrag zur Apocryphenfrage,*" *Studien und Kritiken*, 1865, IV., pp. 690 sq.

In regard to the book Baruch, see O. F. FRITZSCHE, in the "*Kurzgef. exeg. Handb. zu den Apocr.*," I., 167 sq., and BRUCH, in the work already cited, pp. 319 sq. [Dean STANLEY (*Jewish Church*, II., 272) says of the Book of Wisdom: "It is one link more in the chain by which the influence of Solomon communicated itself to succeeding ages. As the undoubted 'Wisdom,' or Proverbs of Solomon, formed the first expression of the contact of Jewish religion with the philosophy of Egypt and Arabia, so the apocryphal 'Wisdom of Solomon' is the first expression of the contact of Jewish religion with the Gentile philosophy of Greece. Still the apologue and the warning to kings keeps up the old strain; still the old 'wisdom' makes her voice to be heard; and out of the worldly prudence of Solomon springs, for the first time, in distinct terms, 'the hope full of immortality'" (Wisdom i. 1; vi. 1, 9; iii. 1–4; v. 1–5, *etc.*)—A.]

§ 10. SYSTEM OF THE LITERATURE OF WISDOM IN THE OLD TESTAMENT, AND THE RELATIVE PLACE OF THE PROVERBS OF SOLOMON.

So far as the entire literature of wisdom in the Old Testament can be treated as an organic whole, and this whole be viewed as the didactic part of the religious literature of the Old Testament, as distinguished from its other main divisions, we recognize first a classical and a post-classical period [post-heroic, compared by the author to the age of the Epigoni in Greek legend. —A.] as the most strongly marked phases in the course of its development. And within each of these two periods there grows up side by side with gnomic poetry, or the Hhokmah literature in the narrower sense, a similar literature of broader range. In the classical period, or within the bounds of the canonical literature of the Old Testament, the Hhokmah poetry in the strictest sense is represented by the Proverbs of Solomon, with their maxims of wisdom aiming to secure a conception and treatment of nature and of the life of man that shall be conformed to the will of God. Side by side with its profound, concise, vigorous, marrowy sentences we find the glowing delineations and soaring lyrical effusions of Solomon's Song, this glorification of the mystery of love, as it is contemplated from wisdom's point of view. The traditional triple chord in the harmony,—the trilogy in the drama,—of the writings ascribed to Solomon, is completed by the broader reflections to which the Preacher (Ecclesiastes) gives utterance concerning the nothingness of all that is earthly, and the duty of a cheerful but also grateful and devout enjoyment of life. Outside this trilogy, which contains at least one work not immediately from Solomon, we find some other products of the Hhokmah literature in the wider sense. There are the didactic Psalms of later date than Solomon, which most resemble the Maschal poetry of the Book of Proverbs, since they are mainly nothing more than gnomes, developed in poetic form. And there is the Book of Job, the dramatic form of whose dialogue is analogous to that of Solomon's Song, while it reveals a certain internal likeness to Ecclesiastes in its devotion to the problems of the day, although at the same time it gives expression to many sceptical thoughts.

Of the productions of the post-classical age, or the literature of wisdom contained in the Jewish Apocrypha, the collection of proverbs by the son of Sirach [Ecclesiasticus], represents the Hhokmah poetry in the narrower sense; for it is a direct imitation of the Proverbs, and in part a later gleaning from the same field. Of the writings which are to be classed here only in the broader sense, the Book of Wisdom stands parallel to Ecclesiastes, and Baruch to the Song of Solomon: still further, if one will, in Tobit a counterpart may be found for Job, and in the Prayer of Manasseh for many of the didactic Psalms.

The Proverbs of Solomon appear therefore, as the central spring and storehouse of the gnomic wisdom of the Old Testament; or, as the true and main trunk of the tree of Hhokmah poetry, widely branching and laden with fruit. And it is mainly on account of this radical impulse, and because of this main trunk, consisting so largely of elements really furnished by Solomon, that the whole development deserves to be called in a general and comprehensive way an intellectual production of the wisest of all kings in Israel.

NOTE 1.—Exhibited in a tabular form the above representation of the literature of wisdom in the Old Testament would stand somewhat as follows,—according to its genetic development and its organic relations:

I. Classical or Hebrew canonical period of the Hhokmah.
  1. Hhokmah poetry in the strictest sense, or in the primitive form of the Maschal (the true gnomic poetry of Solomon):
    The Proverbs.
  2. Hhokmah poetry in the broader sense; or in various transformations and modifications of the primitive type:
    A. The Maschal form transformed to dramatic dialogue:
      a) **Solomon's Song.**—a didactic drama, with strongly marked lyrical and erotic character.
      b) **Job,**—a didactic drama, with a preponderance of the epic character.
    B. The Maschal form expanded in monologue:
      a) **Ecclesiastes,**—a collection of reflective philosophical monologues, constructed from the point of view of the Hhokmah.
      b) The **didactic Psalms,**—specimens of the lyrical development of some fundamental ideas and principles of the Hhokmah.

II. Post-classical period, or Hhokmah literature of the Jewish Apocrypha.
  1. True Hhokmah poetry, with a direct imitation of the old Maschal form:
    Ecclesiasticus.
  2. Hhokmah compositions in the broader sense:
    A. With evident leaning toward the elder literature of the prophetic, or epic and dramatic style:
      a) **Baruch.**
      b) **Tobit.**
    B. With leanings toward elder didactic and lyrical compositions, reflective and philosophical:
      a) The **Wisdom of Solomon.**
      b) The **Prayer of Manasseh.**

NOTE 2.—The grouping of Proverbs, Solomon's Song and Ecclesiastes as a trilogy of compositions by Solomon cannot be critically and chronologically justified. Nevertheless it finds its partial truth and justification in the fact that precisely these three works constitute the normal types of the entire literature of wisdom, in respect both to substance and form (see the Table in note 1). If they be contemplated ideally from this point of view, we cannot refuse to recognize a degree of truth in the old parallel drawn by ORIGEN and JEROME between this trilogy, and the philosophical triad,—*Ethics, Logic, Physics*. Attention has been already called to this in the note to ¿ 1. Compare also page 67 of the General Introduction to the Old Testament section of this Commentary, where the author has given a classification of the writings of Solomon, or, as he puts it, "of the general didactic system of Solomon," which likewise includes the above trilogy.

An analysis of the literature of wisdom in the Old Testament which differs in several points from our own, while it also brings out clearly many correct points of view, is proposed by BRUCH, pp. 67 sq. 1. Period before the Exile: *a*) Monuments of the practical philosophy of this period: Proverbs; *b*) Theoretical philosophy: Job; *c*) compositions of partly practical, partly theoretical nature: the older didactic Psalms. II. Period after the exile: *a*) Practical philosophy; Ecclesiasticus; *b*) Theoretical: Solomon's Song; *c*) partly practical, partly theoretical; the later didactic Psalms, and also the Book of Wisdom, which at the same time forms the transition to the Alexandrian philosophy.

By others the apocryphal literature is ordinarily excluded from the classification, and, on the other hand, all the lyrical poetry of the Psalter brought in, so that the result is a classification of all the poetical literature of the Old Testament Canon. See, *e. g.*, HAEVERNICK and KEIL's *Einleitung*, Vol. III., page 81, where the two great departments of lyrical poetry שִׁיר, and gnomic poetry מָשָׁל are distinguished, and to the first are assigned Psalms, Solomon's Song, and Lamentations,—to the latter, Proverbs, the discourses of Job, and the reflections of Ecclesiastes. FREDERIC SCHLEGEL (*Lectures on the History of Literature*, 4th Lecture), and following him, DELITZSCH (in HERZOG's "*Real-Encyclopädie*," XIV., 716), propose two main classes of Old Testament writings: 1, historico-prophetic, or books of the history of redemption,—and 2, poetical, or books of aspiration.

The latter class, according to them, includes Job, the Psalter, and the writings of Solomon, and these correspond to the triple chord of faith, hope and love. For Job is designed to maintain faith under trials: the Psalms breathe forth and exhibit hope in the conflict of earth's longings; the writings of Solomon reveal to us the mystery of Divine love, and Proverbs in particular makes us acquainted with that wisdom which grows out of and is eternal love.

With reference to the position to be assigned to Proverbs within the circle of the poetical literature of the Old Testament, these classifications are very instructive. And this is especially true of that last mentioned, which is as evidently correct in its exhibition of the relation of Proverbs to Job and the Psalms, as it is defective with respect to the third of Solomon's writings, Ecclesiastes (which surely has very little to do with "the mystery of Divine love").

In one passage, J. A. BENGEL (in his "*Beiträge zur Schrifterklärung*," edited by Osc. WAECHTER, Leipsic, 1866, p. 27) expresses himself singularly in regard to the significance of the grouping, that has been so long traditional, of Proverbs, Job and Solomon's Song in a trilogy. "The reason why Proverbs, Job and the Canticles stand together in the best Hebrew codices is this,—man standing under paternal discipline needs the Proverbs; when he has passed out from this into the fellowship of suffering he needs Job: after he has been perfected he enters into the *unio mystica* (mystical union) and comprehends Canticles."

B.—SPECIAL INTRODUCTION TO THE PROVERBS OF SOLOMON

¿ 11. NAMES OF THE COLLECTION.

The superscription of the book which has been handed down in the Masoretic text, and which rests upon several passages of the book itself (see especially i. 17; x. 1; xxv. 1) is מִשְׁלֵי שְׁלֹמֹה is more correctly rendered, not "Proverbs" (*Sprüchwörter*), but Sayings of Solomon (*Sprüche*).*

---

* [To speak of the *Proverbs* of Solomon, or any other one man, is, in the strict use of terms, a self-contradiction. A *proverbium*, a *Sprüchwort*, a proverb, is strictly an old and popular saying. Archbishop TRENCH (see Lecture I. in his valuable little work " On the lessons in Proverbs ") speaks of "popularity—acceptance and adoption on the part of the people," as "the most essential of all " the qualities of a proverb. A little later he adds, " Herein, in great part, the force

This corresponds with the Παροιμίαι of the LXX, and the *Parabolæ*, not *Proverbia*, of the Vulgate. For the word מָשָׁל does indeed sometimes describe proverbs in the true sense, or general, practical maxims, growing out of the spirit of a people and expressed in popular form (*e. g.*, 1 Sam. x. 12; Ezek. xvi. 44; xviii. 2). But in itself it signifies only resemblance, likeness (*simile, comparatio,* παραβολή, παροιμία); it is therefore used, according to the peculiarity of Oriental poetry, to designate symbolical or parabolic apothegms, or poetic and philosophical maxims in the widest sense. [The verb מָשַׁל is found with two quite distinct significations—to *command*, and to *compare*. GESENIUS (*Thesaurus*, s. v.), after proposing two different ways of deriving these from one primary radical meaning, suggests that possibly there are two independent radicals. FUERST regards them as wholly distinct, the primary meaning of the one being "to be strong," of the other "to combine, connect, entwine." Some old commentators erroneously derive the noun from the first of these two verbal roots; *e. g.*, TRAPP (Comm. on Prov., i. 1): "Master sentences; maxims, axioms, speeches of special precellency and predominancy."—A.] Accordingly prophetical predictions (*e. g.*, those of Balaam, Num. xxiii. 7, 18; xxiv. 3; comp. Is. xiv. 4; Mich. ii. 4; Hab. ii. 6), as well as didactic Psalms (*e. g.*, Ps. xlix. 5; lxxviii. 2) or sententious discourses of wise men (*e. g.*, Job xxvii. 1; xxix. 1) are designated as מְשָׁלִים. In the special and predominant sense מָשָׁל is however the designation of a maxim or gnome from within the sphere of the Hhokmah; it is therefore the sentiment or the moral axiom of a Hhakam (see above, §§ 2, 3). For it was just these men, the Hhakamim of the Old Testament economy, that exhibited their main strength in giving utterance to pertinent comparisons, and significant truths of general practical value, and who were accustomed to impart their instructions chiefly in the form of maxims (Prov. i. 7; xxv. 1). An old synonym of the title "Book of Proverbs" or "Proverbs of Solomon" is therefore "Book of Wisdom" סֵפֶר חָכְמָה. [Comp. FUERST'S *Kanon des alten Testaments, etc.*, 1868, pp. 73 sq.—A.]. The book probably received this title now and then in the old Hebrew times. At any rate it is so called several times in the Talmud (*e. g.*, Tosephoth to Baba Bathra, f. 14, *b*), and among the earliest Fathers of the Greek Church, like CLEMENT, HEGESIPPUS, IRENÆUS, *etc.*, it received the name ἡ πανάρετος σοφία [wisdom including all virtues]. Comp. EUSEBIUS, *Chh. Hist*, IV., 22, 26, according to whom MELITO of Sardis also gave the book a similar title, Σολομῶντος παροιμίαι ἡ καὶ Σοφία [similitudes of Solomon, which is also wisdom]. Compare further the titles σοφὴ βίβλος and παιδαγωγικὴ σοφία ["the wise book" and "instructive wisdom"] which DIONYSIUS of Alexandria and GREGORY of Nazianzum employ. We may therefore even now give to our collection of Proverbs the title of "Book of Wisdom," as well as the more common designation of "Proverbs." And this is all the more allowable, because this collection is far better entitled to be called a "Book of Wisdom" than the Alexandrian apocryphal work which has assumed the name; it is also far more worthy than Ecclesiastes and Ecclesiasticus, to which old Jewish and Christian works not unfrequently apply the title in question (חָכְמָה, Σοφία).

NOTE 1. HAEVERNICK (III. 386) and KEIL (*Introd.*, § 117, p. 396) are in error when they dispute the opinion put forth by BERTHEAU, that the designation of the Proverbs as סֵפֶר חָכְמָה originated among the early Jews. The words of MELITO quoted by EUSEBIUS (passage above cited) are a conclusive proof of the correctness of this view, as they belong to a passage whose express object is to give the designations of the books of the Bible that were current *among the Jews*. Comp. DELITZSCH (work above quoted, p. 712).

NOTE 2. As synonymous with מָשָׁל there occur in the Proverbs of Solomon and elsewhere in the Old Testament the words חִידָה (Prov. i. 6; Ps. xlix. 5; lxxviii. 2; Hab. ii. 6) and מְלִיצָה (Prov.

---

of a proverb lies, namely, that it has already received the stamp of popular allowance." He calls attention to the Spanish name of the proverb, "*refran*, which is a *referendo*, from the oftenness of its repetition." The probable etymology of παροιμία, as "a trite, wayside saying," points the same way.—Dean STANLEY (*Jewish Church*, II., 267), illustrating the same view, says of the Proverbs of Solomon: "They are individual, not national. It is because they represent not many men's wisdom, but one man's superennient wit, that they produced so deep an impression. They were gifts to the people, not the produce of the people," etc. The adage, *adagium*, is of doubtful etymology; probably from "*ad agendum aptu*." The παραβολή, from παρα-βάλλω, to cast or put beside, is in form a comparison, in purpose an illustration. An instructive and entertaining discussion of this subject, enriched with the amplest illustration, may be found in the *London Quarterly Review*, July, 1863.—A.]

i. 6; Hab. ii. 6). The first expression, which properly signifies "enigma" (comp. Judg. xiv. 14; 1 Kings x. 1, etc.), [Etym., knotted, involved, intricate, GESEN., FUERST, etc.], stands for any dark, involved, profound utterance whatsoever; as in Matth. xiii. 35 the חִידוֹת כִּי קֶדֶם is rendered by κεκρυμμένα ἀπὸ καταβολῆς (instead of the προβλήματα ἀπ᾽ ἀρχῆς of the LXX). Compare AUGUSTINE, who uniformly explains *œnigma* by *obscura allegoria*: comp. also LUTHER'S "*in einem dunklen Worte*" [through an obscure word] for the phrase ἐν αἰνίγματι ["darkly," Eng. vers.,—"by means of a mirror in riddles," DE WETTE,—"still darkly as in riddles," VAN ESS, ALLIOLI]. If therefore an ethical axiom, a gnome or parable be designated as this חִידָה this is always done with reference to the deeper meaning hidden in it under a figurative veil (comp. in addition to the passages above cited Ezek. xvii. 2). Examples of these enigmatical proverbs ["dark sayings"] in our collection are to be found especially in the "words of Agur," in chap. xxx. Comp. the remarks on xxx. 15, 16.

The meaning of מְלִיצָה is disputed. According to GESENIUS, BERTHEAU, and HITZIG it is equivalent to "interpretation," "discourse requiring interpretation," (comp. the σκοτεινὸς λόγος of the LXX, Prov. i. 6). According to DELITZSCH, HAEVERNICK and KEIL it is "brilliant or pleasing discourse," *oratio splendida, luminibus ornata*." [FUERST adheres to the derivation first preferred by GESENIUS (following SCHULTENS) according to which לוּץ (obs. in Kal), Arab. لاص signifies "to be involved, entangled," and used of discourse, "to be obscure, and ambiguous,"—and מְלִיצָה "figurative, involved discourse." GESENIUS afterward developed the meaning of the noun from the radical idea of "stammering."—A.]. A sure decision can hardly be reached; the analogy of כְּלִיץ, however, Job xxxiii. 23, Gen. xlii. 23, Isa. xliii. 27, etc., seems to speak for the first interpretation, to which the second may be appended, as appropriate at least for Hab. ii. 6. The radical word is then לוּץ, *torquere*, to twist,—and מְלִיצָה is properly *oratio contorta sive difficilis* [involved or difficult discourse], just as חִידָה (from חוּד *deflectere* [to turn aside]) is properly *oratio obliqua sive per ambages* [oblique or ambiguous discourse].

NOTE 3. With reference to the true conception of the "Proverbs" of Solomon as compared with the proverbs (properly so called) of the Hebrews, and of various other nations, see especially BRUCH, p. 103. "The maxims which are here collected (in the Proverbs) are a product not of the popular spirit of the Hebrews, but of Hebrew wisdom. They have not sprung up unsought, but rather betray deliberate reflection. * * * * They do not lie separate and isolated, like the proverbs of a people, but rest upon certain fundamental conceptions, and together make up a whole. They bear the impress of the Hebrew spirit, but only so far forth as the wise men from whom they come themselves rendered homage to this spirit; in many other respects they rise, as their authors did, essentially above the spirit of the Hebrew nation. They contain rules for conduct in the most diverse conditions of life; but having a bond of connection in general truths, they reach far beyond the sphere of mere experience. Now and then they take a speculative flight, and give utterance to profound conceptions and doctrines of philosophy. * * * * All are clothed in the garb of poetry; every where the law of parallelism prevails in them. That elevation of language which is characteristic of Hebrew poetry is apparent in most of them, while the true *proverbs* of the people are for the most part expressed in prosaic forms, and often in very common language.

It is therefore altogether erroneous to compare this Book of Proverbs with the collections of Arabic proverbs; it might be more fitly compared with the gnomic poetry of the Greeks. It is strictly an *Anthology of Hebrew gnomes*." Comp. § 2, note 4.

The comparison of the Hebrew Maschal-poetry with the sententious and proverbial poetry of the Arabs, although so peremptorily denied by BRUCH, is not without its justification. See UMBREIT's *Commentary*, Introduction, p. lv., where the two Arabic collections of proverbs, by the grammarian AL MEIDANI († 1141). are named as affording at least some parallels to the Proverbs of Solomon. Reference is made beside to H. A. SCHULTENS' *Anthologia sententiarum Arabicarum* (Leyden, 1772), and to the collections of ERPENIUS, GOLIUS, KALLIUS, etc. (in

Schnurrer's *Bibliotheca Arabica*, pp. 210-221) as furnishing such parallels in rich abundance. The latest and best edition of these collections of Arabic proverbs is that of Freytag, *Arabum proverbia sententiarque proverbiales*, Bonn, 1838-43, which not only contains entire the collection of Meidani numbering above 9,000 proverbs, but also gives information concerning the 29 collections of gnomes existing in Arabic literature before Meidani. Comp. also Haevernick and Keil, III., 381 sq., and Bleek's Introduction, p. 632, where among other things an interesting observation of Al Meidani is given, with reference to the great value of the proverbial wisdom; "acquaintance with proverbs does not merely adorn with their beauties all circles of society, and grace the inhabitants whether of cities or of the desert; it imparts brilliancy to the contents of books, and by the allusions which are hidden in them sweetens the words of the preacher and teacher. And why should it not? since even the word of God, the Koran, is interwoven with them,—the discourses of the Prophet contain them,—the most eminent scholars, who have trodden the path of a mysterious wisdom have won this knowledge as their friend?" "Proverbs are to the soul what a mirror is to the eyes." Manifestly it is not common popular proverbs to which this enthusiastic praise refers, but maxims from the schools of the sages, and of a poetic, philosophic character, similar to those of the Old Testament, though mainly of far inferior worth. (This is pertinent also as a reply to Delitzsch, p. 694, who following Ewald, declares the comparison of the Hebrew with the Arabic collections of proverbs altogether inadmissible).

§ 12. ORIGIN AND COMPOSITION OF THE COLLECTION.

The collection of the Proverbs of Solomon in its present form opens with a long superscription, which, in the style of oriental titles, praises the whole book for its important and practically useful contents. This is followed by three main divisions of the book, of unequal length and distinguished by separate titles, to which are appended two supplements. The *first* main division (chap. i.—ix.) subdivided into three sections (chaps. i.—iii., iv.—vii., viii.—ix.) contains an exhibition of wisdom as the highest good to be attained. To the attainment and preservation of this in the face of the dangers that threaten the possession of it,—sensuality, impurity, adultery, etc.,—youth in particular are admonished: and this is done in the form of instructions or admonitions, somewhat prolonged, and having an inward connection of parts, addressed by a father to his son,—and not in brief, aphoristically separated maxims.

The *second* main division (chap. x.—xxiv.) again comprises three sections, not symmetrical but of quite unequal length; *a*) chaps. x. 1—xxii. 16, with the superscription מִשְׁלֵי שְׁלֹמֹה, a collection of separate, loosely connected, and for the most part very short maxims, which in part depict wisdom and the fear of God, and in part folly and sin, according to their chief manifestations and results; and this they do without rigid adherence to a fixed train of ideas, with so loose a coherence of the individual sentences that either no connection of thought appears, or one merely external, brought about by certain characteristic words or terms of expression.

b) chap. xxii. 17—xxiv. 22: a Maschal introduced by a special injunction to hearken to the words of the wise (chap. xxii. 17—19), quite well connected in its parts, and evidently forming one whole; this contains various prescriptions of equity and worldly prudence.

c) chap. xxiv. 23—34; a short appendix, which by its superscription גַּם אֵלֶּה לַחֲכָמִים ["these also are the words of the wise"], is described as the work of various wise men, no longer definitely known; it consists of some maxims which, although nearly all having the form of commands or prohibitions, have no internal mutual connection.

Then follows the *third* main division (chap. xxv.—xxix.) having the superscription, "These also are proverbs of Solomon, which the men of Hezekiah, the King of Judah, collected:"—a collection of single, loosely grouped proverbs, among which are found an unusually large number of pointed comparisons and antitheses.

The two supplements of the collection are, 1) chap. xxx. "The words of Agur the son of Jakeh," a compilation of maxims distinguished by their peculiarly artificial garb, and the partial obscurity of their meaning; 2) chap. xxxi. bearing the superscription "Words of Lemuel the king of Massa, which his mother taught him."* Under this title (in regard to which we shall soon have

---

* [For the various explanations of the verse see Comm. on xxxi. 1].

more to say) the chapter contains *a*) a series of maxims for kings, and *b*) the praise of a virtuous matron, which is clothed in the form of an alphabetic song (vers. 10-31).

That the collection as a whole is not the immediate work of Solomon, or in other words, that the introductory words of the first superscription (chap. i. 1) " Proverbs of Solomon, son of David, king of Israel," so far as they relate to the whole, design to claim the authorship for Solomon only in the most general sense, appears from the most hasty glance at our abstract of the contents. For apart from the fact that at the opening of the second main division there is a repetition of the title " Proverbs of Solomon,"—the last divisions, from xxii. 17 onward, are introduced by quite different superscriptions, two of which refer vaguely to " wise men" as the authors of the respective sections, and two to definite persons (although these are otherwise unknown), while the one which contains again the expression " Proverbs of Solomon" designates as the " collectors" of these " Proverbs of Solomon" the " men" of a king of Judah who did not live until 300 years after Solomon. [FUERST's inference from these diverse superscriptions and appellations is thus stated (*Canon des alten Testaments*, p. 74); " that it is not the originating of all the proverbs with Solomon that was emphasized, though he be regarded as their main source, but only the aim and effect of the proverbs to promote wisdom."—Dean STANLEY, (*ubi supra*, p. 268) says " as in the case of the word 'wisdom,' the connection of 'Proverbs' with Solomon can be traced by the immense multiplication of the word after his time."—A]. And not only these diverse superscriptions, but various peculiarities of language, style, *etc.*, such as present themselves to the attentive observer in each section in a characteristic way, bear witness to the gradual growth of the collection under the hands of several authors of a later day than Solomon's, each complementing the rest. We might put the whole work of compilation to the account of the " men of Hezekiah," (chap. xxv. 1), and so assume that the maxims of Solomon, before scattered, and transmitted in part orally, in part by less complete written records, were collected, and, with the addition of sundry supplements brought into their present form by certain wise men from the court of the devout king Hezekiah (B. C. 727—697). The verb הֶעְתִּיקוּ which in the passage cited above is used to describe the agency of these men, would well accord with this assumption ; for it signifies, not " appended" (LUTHER), but " brought together, arranged in order," in as much as הֶעְתִּיק properly means " to remove from its place, to set or place somewhere;" and in the passage before us it is rendered correctly by the ἐξεγράψαντο of the LXX, and the *transtulerunt* of the Vulgate. But the relations of the matter are not quite so simple that the whole compilation and revision can be referred to these wise men of Hezekiah. For from the quite numerous repetitions of whole proverbs, or at least parts of proverbs from earlier sections, such as occur in the division chaps. xxv.—xxix. (compare *e. g.*, xxv. 24 with xxi. 9,— xxvi. 22 with xviii. 8,—xxvii. 12 with xxii. 3,—xxvii. 21 with xvii. 3,—xxix. 22 with xv. 18, *etc.*) it seems altogether probable that the preceding sections existed as an independent whole, before the attachment of chaps. xxv. sq. This is confirmed by the fact that certain characteristics noticeable in the structure of clause and verse, and many peculiarities of phraseology and idiom likewise indicate that between the sections preceding chap. xxv. and the last seven chapters a wide difference exists, and one that points to the greater antiquity of the first and largest division. Hezekiah's wise men appear therefore substantially as supplementing, or more exactly as continuing and imitating a larger collection of Solomon's proverbs already in existence before their day : and the existence of this they must not only have known but studiously regarded, for the great majority of the maxims and axioms there found they did not take into their new collection, but sought to present that which was mainly new and independent; in consequence however of the similarity of the sources from which they drew to those of the earlier collection, they could not but reproduce much in a similar form, and some things in a form exactly corresponding with the earlier. [The Jewish tradition as given by FUERST (*ubi supra*, p. 75) ascribes the collection of the proverbs of the first three sections, chaps. i.—ix., x.—xxii. 16, and xxii. 17—xxiv. to the men of Hezekiah. And it finds this view confirmed by the very fact that the next section begins (xxv. 1) with the words "*These also*, are proverbs," *etc.* But the subsequent collection (chap. xxv. sq. is " continued" by them, the proverbs being searched out elsewhere and transferred to this place; " proverbs not hitherto publicly employed for the education of the people they brought into a collection, to be in like manner used as a collection of Solomon's proverbs." The "men of Hezekiah" he regards moreover as not all contemporaries and agents of the good king, but as organized into a "college," continued for literary, religious, and judicial purposes 280 years, seven full generations. This is Jewish tradition.—A.].

That the older collection is not however to be itself regarded as all of one casting, but likewise as a product of the activity of one or several editors collecting and combining from still earlier sources, appears from several facts. Within this section, as well as the later, instances occur of the repetition of single proverbs in an identical or analogous form (comp. *e. g.* xiv. 12 with xvi. 25,—xvi. 2 with xxi. 2,—x. 2 with xi. 4,—xiii. 14 with xvi. 27,—xix. 12 with xx. 2, *etc.*). We have, besides, this fact, which is still more significant, that here again a diversity appears, marked by decided peculiarities of form as well as substance, between the two large subdivisions, chaps. i.—ix., and chaps. x. 1—xxii. 16. In the second of these sections we find mainly verses symmetrically constructed,—so-called "antithetic couplets,"—and each verse presents an idea quite complete and intelligible. It is the simplest and, as it were, the ideal type of the Maschal that here predominates; and since the simplest is wont to be as a general rule the most primitive, this fact suggests the conjecture that we are dealing here simply with genuine, original proverbs of Solomon. In other words, *Chapters x.—xxii. 16 comprise the proper germ of the gnomic poetry of the Old Testament, which is in the strictest sense to be referred to Solomon and his age.* In the two supplements to this central main division, chap. xxii. 17—xxiv. 22, and chap. xxiv. 23—34 we observe in respect to form quite another character in the individual proverbs, although in their ethical tenor and substance they correspond with the preceding. They lose something of the telling, pointed brevity, the inward richness of meaning, the condensed power, that characterize the earlier proverbs; and instead of "the rapid alternation of clause and counter-clause" before every where perceptible, there is apparent here less uniformity of structure, and an effort to expand the brief axiom to the longer discourse, admonitory, didactic, or illustrative of some moral truth. Still more entirely is the simple and beautiful form of the Maschal, compact, pithy and symmetrical, disregarded and cast aside in chaps. i.—ix. These present nothing but longer admonitory discourses, moral pictures full of warning, and ethico-religious contemplations of broader compass, in all of which the simple, short proverb is only exceptional, and "proverbial poetry evidently took the form of admonition and preaching, but for this very reason became much more flexible, flowing and comprehensible." The technical language of the Hhokmah appears here in various ways expanded and refined,—especially in the application of such full allegorical delineations as are contained in chap. ix. (in the description of Wisdom's house with its seven pillars, and her feast,—and also in that of the conduct of the אֵשֶׁת כְּסִילוּת the personification of Folly). The nearly equal length, moreover, of the three sections into which this entire admonitory address to youth is divided, (see the earlier part of the §), the quite regular and frequent recurrence of the בְּנִי, "my son," which shows this to be its chief application, (i. 8; ii. 1; iii. 1, 11, 21; iv. 10, 20; v. 1, *etc.*), the adherence to certain leading thoughts through all the change and variety in expression and delineation,—all this points us to a single author, who different as he was from the author of the collection following (x. 1—xxii. 16), designed to furnish an appropriate introduction to this collection of older proverbs, and to commend it to the Israel of his own time, especially to its younger generation.

That the mutual relations of the various parts of the Book of Proverbs are to be judged substantially in this way, most of the recent commentators are agreed. [This general view both of the structure and authorship of our book is taken by most of our English and American scholars, with some divergencies of course, in the details. Thus, STUART, NOYES, MUENSCHER, W. ALDIS WRIGHT, *etc.* STUART sums up his view of the authorship thus (Comm. p. 63): "Solomon selected many, composed others, and put together those which he judged to be true, most striking, and most worthy to be preserved. . . . . It matters not how much of the book of Proverbs Solomon actually composed; we only need his sanction to what it now contains." Portions of the book moreover do not even purport to be Solomon's.—A.]. We may make an exception, perhaps, of H. A. HAHN, HAEVERNICK, and KEIL, who, in spite of all internal and external differences between the several sections, which they are forced to acknowledge,—in spite of the various introductory superscriptions,—still feel constrained to maintain Solomon's immediate authorship of the whole, with the sole exception of the two supplements in chaps. xxx., xxxi. (see especially HAEVERNICK and KEIL's *Introduction*, III., 392 sq.). [This is WORDSWORTH's position. It is moreover characteristic of him to look on the proverbs as having "also a typical character and inner spiritual significance, concerning heavenly doctrines of supernatural truth." He finds support for this view in the fact that the collection is in its introduction said expressly to comprise enigmas and dark sayings.—A.]. Inasmuch as this conclusion is made necessary neither by reasons, internal or external, [in the book itself], nor by any general theological interest in maintaining the inspired character of Scriptures, we must, unquestionably, adopt one of those views which represent the present collection as growing up gradually in the time between Solomon and Hezekiah, or even within a period ending somewhat later, and which discriminate between an original nucleus that is from Solomon, and the accretions of various ages, which are due to later collectors and editors.

The more important of these theories are (1) that of EWALD (*Poet. Bücher des Alten Test.*, IV. 2 sq.). According to this, chap. x. 1—xxii. 16 forms the earliest collection, originating perhaps two hundred years after Solomon, yet inspired throughout by Solomon's spirit; to this were appended, first, in Hezekiah's time chap. xxv.—xxix., which also contain much that is the genuine work of Solomon,—then, in the following century, the Introduction, chap. i.—ix.,—then the supplements to the central main division, chap. xxii. 17—xxiv. 34,—and lastly the supplements chaps. xxx., xxxi; and all these last are to be regarded as the independent composition of unknown sages of the later period before the exile, without any elements whatever that are Solomon's.

We have (2) the view of BERTHEAU (*Commentary*, *Introd.*, pp. xxiii. sq.). According to this it is as impossible to demonstrate with certainty an origin earlier than the days of Hezekiah for the second collection (chap. x. 1—xxii. 16) as for the first (chap. i.—ix.), the third (chap. xxii. 17—xxiv. 34), or the fourth (chap. xxv.—xxix.); we must therefore in general maintain the merely negative conclusion, that the book of Proverbs in its present form originated after the time of Solomon, and that it flowed from sources oral and written that are perhaps very numerous. We have (3) the view of HITZIG ("*Das Königreich Mus a*" in ZELLER's *Theol. Jahrb.* 1844, pp. 269 sq., and *Commentary*, Introd. pp. xvii. sq.). This represents the present order of the parts as substantially that of their composition. It accordingly conceives of the first collection (chaps. i. —ix.) as originating pretty soon after Solomon, in the 9th century B. C.; it then appends to this, shortly before the times of Hezekiah, or in the first half of the 8th century, the second (chap. x. 1—xxii. 16) together with the latter part of the fourth (chap. xxviii. 17—xxix. 27); to this it attaches "in the last quarter of the 8th century" the anthology in chaps. xxv.—xxvii., and about a hundred years later (at the beginning of the period following the exile) the intruded section, chap. xxii. 17—xxiv. 34, and the fragment, chap. xxviii. 1—16; finally, at a still later day it adds the supplements in chaps. xxx , xxxi.

We have (4) the view of DELITZSCH (in HERZOG's *Encycl.*, as above quoted, especially pp. 707 sq.), with which that developed by BLEEK (*Introd.*, pp. 634 sq.) agrees in the main point,—*i. e.*, apart from some subordinate details in which it approaches more nearly the theory of EWALD. According to this the first and largest section of the Book of Proverbs (chap. i. 1—xxiv. 22) comes from an age earlier than Hezekiah, the second and smaller commencing with xxiv. 23, from Hezekiah's times. The compiler of the first half lived possibly under Jehoshaphat, within a century of Solomon. As material for the middle and main division of this work,—the germ. the main trunk, consisting of the genuine proverbial wisdom of Solomon as contained in chap. x. 1—xxii 16,—he availed himself above all of the rich treasures of the 3,000 proverbs of Solomon, which were undoubtedly all fully preserved to his day, and from which he may be assumed to have taken at least all that were of religious and ethical value. Still he appears to have gathered up much that is not from Solomon, and therefore to have united in one collection the noblest and richest fruits of the proverbial poetry of the wise king. with the most valuable of the " side shoots which the Maschal poetry put forth, whether from the mouth of the people or the poets of that day." To this collection he prefixed the long Introduction in chaps. i.—ix.; a monument of his high poetic inspiration, not in the strict form of the Maschal, but that of long poetic admonitions,—in which he dedicated the whole work to the instruction of youth. At the same

§ 12. ORIGIN AND COMPOSITION OF THE COLLECTION.

time he added an appendix, chap. xxii. 17—xxiv. 22, consisting of proverbs from various wise men, and commencing with an apostrophe to youth (chap. xxii. 17—21) the tone of which reminds one of the longer Introduction.

While according to this view the first and larger section purports to be essentially a book for youth, the second and shorter division, whose nucleus is formed by the proverbs of Solomon compiled by the men of Hezekiah, is evidently a book for the people, a treasury of proverbial wisdom for kings and subjects,—as is indicated by the first, introductory proverb: "It is the glory of God to conceal a thing, and the honor of kings to search out a matter." After the analogy of the first collection, to these proverbs gathered by Hezekiah (or this treasury of "Solomon's wisdom in Hezekiah's days," in STIER's apt phrase), a sort of introduction was prefixed, chap. xxiv. 23-34, and a supplement was added, consisting of the proverbial discourses of Agur and Lemuel, and the poem in praise of a virtuous matron, in chap. xxx., xxxi. Thus, like the older collection of the proverbs of Solomon, this made by Hezekiah has " proverbs of wise men on the right and on the left;" "the king of proverbial poetry stands here also in the midst of a worthy retinue." As to the time of the origin of the second collection, we are indeed not to assume the reign of Hezekiah itself, but the next subsequent period. The personality of the collector of this second main division stands far more in the background than that of the author of the first, larger collection, who in its introductory chapters has given rich proofs of his own poetical endowments and his wisdom. From which of the two the general superscription of the whole, chap. i. 1–6, has come, must remain a question; yet it is from internal evidence more probable that it was the last collector who prefixed this to the book.

We have presented with especial fullness this hypothesis of DELITZSCH in regard to the origin of the Book of Proverbs, because it is in itself the most attractive of all, and offers the most satisfactory explanation of the various phenomena that arrest the attention of the observant reader, as he considers the superscriptions and the internal peculiarities of the several parts. It is less forced and artificial than the theory of HITZIG, which shows itself arbitrary and hypercritical, especially in breaking up the section, chap. xxv.—xxix.; and it does not rest content with the mere negative results of criticism, like the analysis of BERTHEAU, which is also chargeable with excess of critical sharpness. In comparison with EWALD's hypothesis it has the advantage, that it rests upon a more correct conception of the order of the development of gnomic poetry among the ancient Hebrews. For it rejects as a one-sided and arbitrary dictum, EWALD's axiom, that the antithetic verse of two members which predominates in chap. x. 1—xxii. 16, is the oldest form of the Maschal, and that all proverbs and gnomic discourses otherwise constructed, by their departure from the typical form betray their origin as decidedly later than the days of Solomon. It accordingly allows that sections in which there is a preponderance of gnomic discourses and gnomic songs,—such as chap. i.—ix. and xxii. 17—xxiv. 22, may come, if not from Solomon himself, at least from the age immediately after Solomon. It likewise recognizes in the collection that dates from Hezekiah's day proverbial poetry which is mainly the genuine work of Solomon, or at least stands very near his day, and whose artistic character by no means (as EWALD thinks) contains traces of a decay in purity and beauty of form that is already quite far advanced.

Only in this particular are we unable altogether to agree with DELITZSCH, that he would find in chap. x.—xxii. together with a selection from the 3,000 proverbs of Solomon, much that is his only in a secondary sense. We believe rather that it is just this main division which contains nothing but fruits of Solomon's gnomic wisdom in the narrowest and strictest sense, and that repetitions of individual proverbs within the section, which are partly identical and partly approximative, in which especially DELITZSCH thinks he finds support for the view that we are now combating, are to be otherwise explained. They are, like the repetitions of discourses of Christ in the Gospels, to be partly charged to diversity in the sources or channels of the later oral or written tradition, and in part recognized as real tautologies or repetitions which the wise king now and then allowed himself. We should, on the other hand, be disposed rather to conjecture, that in the supplements, chap. xxii. 17—xxiv. 34, which are expressly described as "words of wise men," and perhaps also in Hezekiah's collection, chap. xxv.—xxix., there is no inconsiderable number of utterances of wise men of Solomon's time, such as Heman, Ethan, Chalkol, *etc.*; and this simply for the reason, that the superscriptions דִּבְרֵי חֲכָמִים (xxii. 17) [words of wise men], and גַּם אֵלֶּה לַחֲכָמִים (xxiv. 23) [these also are from wise men], together with the peculiarity of diction which points to a high antiquity, make such a conjecture reasonable. The short section beginning with the superscription last cited, chap. xxiv. 23–34, we should be most inclined, in concurrence with the majority of expositors, to regard as a second appendix to the first main collection, because the assumption of DELITZSCH that it is a sort of Introit to the second main division, of the same age as the section, chap. xxv.—xxix., strikes us in no other way than as too bold and destitute of all adequate foundation.

It remains only to speak briefly of the superscriptions to the two supplements in chapters xxx., xxxi. The "Agur, son of Jakeh" (?) to whom the contents of chapter xxx. are accredited, is a wise man otherwise altogether unknown, whose era we are as unable to determine with certainty as his residence, whose very name is almost as difficult and uncertain in its interpretation as are the words next succeeding in chapter xxx. 1. הַמַּשָּׂא נְאֻם הַגֶּבֶר לְאִיתִיאֵל לְאִיתִיאֵל וְאֻכָל. Perhaps instead of the common translation of these words: "the prophetic address of the man to Ithiel, to Ithiel and Ucal" ["even the prophecy; the man spake unto Ithiel, even unto Ithiel and Ucal," E. V.], the interpretation of HITZIG, adopted also by BERTHEAU, HAHN and DELITZSCH, should be followed. According to this, the words בֶּן יָקֶה [" son of Jakeh "] by a change of punctuation are to be connected closely with the word הַמַּשָּׂא; thus for the beginning of the whole superscription we reach this meaning: "Words of Agur, the son of her whose dominion is Massa" (בֶּן יָקְהָה מַשָּׂא), i. e., son of the queen of Massa. This queen of Massa we should then have to regard as the same person who in the superscription to the next supplement (chap. xxxi.) is designated as the " mother of King Lemuel." For in this passage also מַשָּׂא must be regarded as the name of a country, and the מֶלֶךְ מַשָּׂא [King of Massa] as perhaps an Israelitish Arab, or, as DELITZSCH suggests, an Ishmaelitish prince, whose kingdom, to judge from the mention of it in Gen. xxv. 14; 1 Chron. i. 30, must have lain in Northern Arabia, and whose brother would have been the Agur in question. [FUERST (ubi supra, pp. 76–7) regards מַשָּׂא as a common noun, singular in form, but collective in import, having the meaning common in the prophets, "a prophetic or inspired utterance." The symbolical meaning found here by Jewish tradition may be reserved for the exegetical notes on this chapter.—A.] Further arguments in support of this interpretation (first presented by HITZIG in the Articles in ZELLER's *Theol. Jahrb.*, 1844, cited above, and adopted, although with various modifications, by the other interpreters whom we have named), and in reply to all conflicting interpretations, will be brought forward in the special exegesis of the passages involved. We shall there have occasion to discuss the further question, whether the whole substance of chap. xxx. is to be referred to Agur, and all in chap. xxxi. to Lemuel, or whether at least the Alphabetic poem in praise of a virtuous matron must not be regarded (as is done by nearly all the recent commentators) as the work of another author.

§ 13. THE RELATION OF THE MASORETIC TEXT OF THE COLLECTION TO THE ALEXANDRIAN.

In the LXX there occur many, and in some instances very remarkable deviations from the common Hebrew text of the Proverbs. These consist in glosses to many obscure passages (*i. e.*, either in readings that are actually correct and primitive, as, *e. g.*, xi. 24; xii. 6; xv. 28; xviii. 1; xix. 28; xxi. 6, 28, *etc.*, or in wild emendations, as in xii. 12; xviii. 19; xix. 25; xxiv. 10, *etc.*), in completing imperfect sentences (as, *e. g.*, xi. 16; xvi. 17; xix. 7), in independent additions or interpolations (*e. g.*, after i. 18; iii. 15; iv. 27; vi. 8, 11; viii. 21; ix. 6, 10, 12; xii. 13; xiii. 13, 15, *etc.*), in double versions of one and the same proverb (*e. g.*, xii. 12; xiv. 22; xv. 6; xvi. 26; xvii. 20; xviii. 8; xxii. 8, 9; xxix. 7, 25; xxxi. 27, in the omission of whole verses (*e. g.*, i. 16; xvi. 1, 3; xxi. 5; xxiii. 23, *etc.*), and finally in the transposition of entire passages of greater length. Accordingly, of the proverbs of Agur, the first half (chap. xxx. 1–14) is inserted after chap. xxiv. 22, and the second, chap. xxx. 15–33, together with the words of King Lemuel, after xxiv. 34; the two supplements, therefore with the exception of the praise of the excellent matron (chap. xxxi. 10 sq.) appear associated with the "words of wise men" which stand between the elder and the later collection of proverbs.

These deviations are so considerable that they compel the assumption that there were quite early two different recensions of the Book of Proverbs, one belonging to Palestine, the other to Egypt, the former of which lies at the basis of the Masoretic text, the latter, of the Alexandrian version. The Egyptian text appears in general to abound more in corruptions and arbitrary alterations of the original; sometimes, however, it preserves the original most correctly, and seems to have drawn from primitive sources containing the genuine proverbial wisdom of Solomon. Especially is it true that not a few of the additions which it exhibits on a comparison with the Hebrew text, breathe a spirit, bold and lofty, as well as thoughtful and poetic (see, *e. g.*, iv. 27; ix. 12; xii. 13; xix. 7, *etc.*); these appear, therefore, as fruits grown on the stock of the noble poetry of wisdom among the ancient Hebrews,—in part even as pearls from the rich treasures of Solomon's 3,000 proverbs (1 Kings iv. 32).

NOTE 1.—The critical gain for the emendation of the text and for the interpretation of the Book of Proverbs that is yielded by the parallels of the LXX may be found most carefully tested and noted—though not without many instances of hypercritical exaggeration and arbitrary dealing—in FR. BÖTTCHER'S "*Neue exegetisch-kritische Aehrenlese zum A. T.*," III., pp. 1–39; in P. DE LAGARDE'S "*Anmerkungen zur griechischen Uebersetzung der Proverbien*" (Leipz., 1863); in M. HEIDENHEIM'S Article, "*Zur Textkritik der Proverbien*" (*Deutsche Vierteljahrsschr. für englisch-theol. Forschung*, u. s. w., VIII., Gotha, 1865, pp. 395 sq.); as well as in the Commentaries of BERTHEAU (see especially Introd., pp. xlv. sq.) and HITZIG (Introd., pp. xix. sq.; xxiii. sq.). The last mentioned writer has also thoroughly discussed the variations of the Syriac version (Peschito), the Vulgate and the Targum (pp. xxvii. sq.); of these, however, in general, only the first named are of any considerable critical value, and that usually only in the cases where they agree with those of the LXX.

Compare furthermore the earlier works of J. G. JAEGER, *Observationes in Provv. Salom. versionem Alexandrinam*, Lips., 1786; SCHLEUSSNER, *Opuscula critica ad versiones Graecas V. T. pertinentia*, Lips., 1812, pp. 260 sq.; and also DATHE, *De ratione consensus versionis Chaldaicae et Syriacae proverbiorum Salomonis* (in *Dathii Opusc.* ed. ROSENMUELLER, pp. 106 sq.).

NOTE 2.—UMBREIT in his Commentary has taken special notice of several other ancient Greek versions beside the LXX, especially the *Versio Veneta*, which is for the most part strictly literal. Another text which is likewise quite literal, which PROCOPIUS used in his Ἑρμήνεια εἰς τὰς παροιμίας, and which ANGELO MAI has edited in Tom. IX. of his *Class. Auctor.*, may be found noticed in HEIDENHEIM (as above).

§ 14. THE POETICAL FORM OF PROVERBS.

The simplest form of the Maschal, or the technical form of poetry among the Hebrews, is a verse consisting of two short symmetrically constructed clauses,—the so-called distich (*Zweizeiler,*)as DELITZSCH calls it, following EWALD's peculiarly thorough investigations on the subject before us. The mutual relation of the two members or lines of this kind of verse shapes itself very variously, in accordance with the general laws for the structure of Hebrew poetry. There are *synonymous* distichs, in which the second line repeats the meaning of the first in a form but slightly changed, for the sake of giving as clear and exhaustive a presentation as possible of the thought involved (*e. g.*, xi. 7, 25; xii. 28; xiv. 19; xv. 3, 10, 12, *etc.*). There are *antithetic* distichs, in which the second illustrates by its opposite the truth presented in the first (*e. g.*, x. 1 sq.; xi. 1 sq; xii. 1 sq.; xv. 1 sq.). There are *synthetic* distichs, the two halves of which express truths of different yet kindred import (*e. g.*, x. 18, 24, *etc.*). There are *integral* (*eingedankige*) distichs, in which the proposition commenced in the first half is brought to completion only by the second, the thought which is to be presented extending through the two lines (as in xi. 31; xiv. 7, 10; xvi. 4, 10; xxii. 28). There are finally *parabolic* distichs, *i. e.*, maxims which in some form or other exhibit comparisons between a moral idea and an object in nature or common life: and this is effected sometimes by כְּ [as] in the first clause and כֵּן [so] in the second, that is, in the form natural to comparisons,—sometimes, and more usually, in such a way that the proposed object and its counterpart are set loosely side by side, with a suggestive, emblematic brevity, with or without the copulative ו (xi. 22; xvii. 3; xxv. 25; xxvi. 23; xxvii. 21, *etc.*). In the central main division of the collection, chap. x.—xxii. 16, all the proverbs are these short distichs, and, as has been already said, the larger part of them (especially in the first six chapters of the section) *antithetic* distichs, distinguished by the "but" (Hebr. ¹) at the beginning of the second line (compare § 12, p. 27, and below, § 15). In the supplements to the oldest collection (xxii. 17—xxiv. 34) as well as in the gleanings of Hezekiah's men, there are found however not a few instances of the extension of the simple typical distich to a verse of several lines, or of the multiplication of the couplet to four-, six- or eight-lined verses.*

In the case of these longer proverbs, which comprise several verses, we find repeated, if not every one, yet the greater part of the diverse relations of the first to the second half of the proverb, which we had observed in the distichs. There are, it is true, no antithetic stanzas of four lines,—but there are *synonymous* verses (e. g., xxiii. 15 sq.; xxiv. 3 sq; xxiv. 28 sq.),—*synthetic* (xxx. 5 sq.),—stanzas with a *single idea* (xxii. 22 sq., 26 sq.; xxx. 17 sq.),—and *parabolic* verses (xxvi. 18 sq.; xxv. 4 sq.). Specimens of the six-lined stanzas (which are constructed mainly with a single thought, or in the synthetic form) are to be found, *e. g*., in xxiii. 1-3, 12-14, 19-21, 26-28; xxiv. 11-12; xxx. 29-31. Verses 22-25 of chapter xxiii. compose a stanza of eight lines, synthetic in its structure. Side by side with this normal multiplication of the couplet to form stanzas of four, six or eight lines, there are abnormal or one-sided growths, resulting in triplets, with the first division of two lines and the second of one (*e. g.*, xxii. 29; xxiv. 3; xxvii. 22; xxviii. 10, *etc.*),—or in stanzas of five lines (xxiii. 4 sq.; xxv. 6 sq.; xxx. 32 sq.), or in stanzas of seven lines, of which at least one example appears in chap. xxiii. 6-8.

If the proverb extends itself beyond the compass of seven or eight lines, it becomes the Maschal (or *gnomic*) poem, without a fixed internal order for the strophes. Such a poem (or song) is, for example, the introductory paragraph [of one main division], chap. xxii. 17-21; and again, the meditation on the drunkard, xxiii. 29-35; that on the lazy husbandman, xxiv. 30-34; the admonition to diligence in husbandry, xxvii. 23-27; the prayer for the happy medium between poverty and riches, xxx. 7-9; the prince's mirror, xxxi. 2-9, and the alphabetically constructed song in praise of the matron, xxxi. 10-31.

The introductory main division, chap. i. 7—ix. 18, consists wholly of these proverbial poems, and of 15 of them (see in § 16 the more exact enumeration of these 15 subdivisions, which may again be classed in three larger groups). Inasmuch as the rhetorical presentation throws the poetical in these cases usually quite into the background, these Maschal poems may almost be called with greater propriety Maschal discourses. Yet within these there is no lack of poetical episodes, lofty and artistic in their structure, among which we would name especially the allegory of the banquet of Wisdom and Folly (chap. ix. 1 sq.), and also the numerical proverb in eight lines concerning "the six things which the Lord hates and the seven that are an abomination to Him" (in chap. vi. 16-19). Of these numerical proverbs, or מִדּוֹת, as they are called in the poetry of the later Judaism, chap. xxx., as is well known, contains several (vers. 7 sq., 15 sq., 18 sq., 21 sq., 24 sq.). In the Son of Sirach's collection of proverbs likewise we find several examples of the same kind (*e. g.*, Ecclesiasticus xxiii. 16; xxv. 7; xxvi. 5, 28). Further observations on the origin and import of this peculiar poetic form may be found in notes on chap. vi. 16. Now and then the Book of Proverbs contains forms analogous to the *Priamel* [*praeambulum*, a peculiar type of epigram, found in German poetry of the 14th and 15th centuries—A.]; see, *e. g.*, xx. 10; xxv. 3; xxvi. 12; xxx. 11-14; yet this form is hardly found except in the most imperfect state.

The last of the technical forms of the poetry of the Book of Proverbs is that of the Maschal-series, *i. e.*, a sequence of several proverbs relating to the same objects, *e. g.*, the series of proverbs concerning the fool, chap. xxvi. 1-12,—the sluggard, xxvi. 13-16,—the brawler, xxvi. 20-22,—the

---

* [In English Biblical literature, Bishop Lowth's discussion and classification has been the basis generally assumed. We know no clearer and more concise exhibition of this system and the various modifications that have been proposed than that given by W. Aldis Wright in Smith's *Dictionary of the Bible* (Article *Poetry, Hebrew*). Lowth who is closely followed by Stuart, Edwards and others, regards a triple classification as sufficient: *synonymous, antithetic* and *synthetic* parallelisms. An infelicity in the term *synonymous*, in view of the extent and variety of its applications, was recognized by Lowth himself, but more strongly urged by Bishop Jebb, who proposed the term *cognate*. This appears to be a real improvement in terms. Moenscher (Introd., pp. xlv. sq.) proposes two additional classes, the *gradational* and the *introverted*, the first of which is well covered by the term *cognate*, while the second, which had been proposed by Jebb, seems open to Wright's exception, that it is "an unnecessary refinement." This objection does not seem to lie against the new terms proposed in Zöckler's nomenclature.—A.]

spiteful, xxvi. 23–27. This form belongs, however, as DELITZSCH correctly observes, "rather to the technical form of the collection than to the technical form of the poetry of proverbs." That the former [the arrangement] is far more imperfect and bears witness to far greater indifference than the latter,—in other words, that the logical construction, the systematic arrangement of individual proverbs according to subjects, especially within the central main division, is far from satisfactory, and baffles almost completely all endeavors to discover a definite scheme,—this must be admitted as an indisputable fact, just in proportion as we give fit expression on the other hand to our admiration at the wealth of forms, expressive, beautiful and vigorous, which the collection exhibits in its details.

NOTE.—With reference to the connection of the several proverbs one with another, and also with respect to the progress of thought apparent in the collection as a whole, we can by no means concur in the opinion of J. A. BENGEL,—at least in regard to the main divisions, x. 1 sq.; xxii. 17 sq.; xxv. 1 sq. The collection of proverbial discourses, i. 7—ix. 18, being intentionally arranged according to a plan, is of course excluded from such a judgment. BENGEL says: "I have often been in such an attitude of soul, that those chapters in the Book of Proverbs in which I had before looked for no connection whatever, presented themselves to me as if the proverbs belonged in the most beautiful order one with another" (OSK. WAECHTER, *Joh. Albrecht Bengel*, p. 166). We must pass the same judgment upon many other expositors of the elder days, who wearied them. selves much to find a deeper connection between the several proverbs (see, *e. g.*, S. BOHLIUS, *Ethica Sacra*, I., 297 sq., "*de dispositione et cohærentia textus;*" and STÖCKER in the Introduction to his "*Sermons on the Proverbs of Solomon*"). In regard to this matter as old a commentator as MART. GEIER judged quite correctly :* "*Ordo-frustra quæritur ubi nullus fuit observatus. Quamquam enim sub initium forte libri certa serie Rex noster sua proposuerit,—attamen ubi ad ipsas proprie dictas parabolas aut gnomas devenitur, promiscue, prout quidque se offerebat, consignata videmus pleraque, ita ut modo de avaritia, modo de mendaciis, modo de simplicitate, modo de timore Dei vel alia materia sermonem institui videamus*," etc. As in the case of the great majority of the songs of the Psalter, in which the arrangement is merely and altogether external, determined often by single expressions, or by circumstances wholly accidental, there is found among the germinal elements of the Book of Proverbs little or no systematic order. The whole is simply a combination of numerous small elements in a collection, which was to produce its effect more by the total impression than by the mutual relation of its various groups or divisions. To use HERDER's language (*Spirit of Hebrew Poetry*, II., 13), it is "a beautiful piece of tapestry of lofty didactic poetry, which spreads out with great brilliancy its richly embroidered flowers," which, however, is constructed according to no other rules of art than those perfectly simple and elementary ones to which the pearl jewelry and bright tapestries of Oriental proverbial wisdom in general owe their origin. Comp. furthermore the general preliminary remarks prefixed to the exegetical comments on chap. x.

§ 15. THE DOGMATIC AND ETHICAL SUBSTANCE OF THE PROVERBS, EXHIBITED IN A CAREFUL SURVEY OF THE CONTENTS OF THE BOOK.

Inasmuch as our book, considered as an integral part of the entire system of the Scriptures of the Old Testament, stands before us as the central and main source of Solomon's doctrine of wisdom (in the wider sense),—and so bears as it were written on its brow its Divine designation to be the chief storehouse of ethical wisdom and knowledge within the sphere of Old Testament revelation (see above, § 1, and § 10, latter part) we must anticipate finding in it great treasures of ethical teachings, prescriptions, rules and maxims for the practical life of men in their moral relations. In fact, the ethical contents of the collection far outweigh the doctrinal. And deeply significant as may be its contributions to the development of individual subjects in dogmatic theology, such as are found in various passages (*e. g.*, iii. 19 and viii. 22 sq. in their bearing upon the doctrine of

---

* It is in vain to seek for order where none has been observed. For while perhaps near the beginning of the book our king arranged his material with a definite plan,—yet when we come to the parables or gnomes properly so called we find the greater part recorded at random, as one after another suggested itself, so that we see the discourse turning now upon avarice, then upon falsehoods, again upon simplicity, and once more upon the fear of God, or some other subject," etc.—TR.

the creation;—viii. 22—ix. 12 as related to the doctrine of the eternal Word of God, and the doctrine of the Hypostasis or of the Trinity in general;—xv. 11; xvi. 9; xix. 21; xx. 27, *etc.*, as connected with Biblical Anthropology; or xi. 7; xiv. 32; xv. 24 in connection with the Old Testament doctrine of Immortality and the hope of a Resurrection, *etc.*); still, as a general rule, practical and ethical subjects are treated not only more thoroughly but with a far more direct interest. The book deserves much more the name of a school of morals, or of a Codex of Ethical Precepts for old and young, for princes and people, than that of Archives of Dogmatic Theology, or a prolific Repository of dogmatic propositions and proof-texts.

The dogmatic propositions do not, however, by any means stand in the midst of the greater wealth of ethical teachings and precepts, isolated and interspersed without system. They form rather every where the organic basis. They give expression to the absolute and primary premises for all the moral instruction, knowledge and conduct of men. They appear therefore inseparably combined with those propositions that are properly of an ethical or admonitory nature. It is pre-eminently the central idea of the DIVINE WISDOM as the mediator in all the activity of God in the world and in humanity, that shines out bright as the sun upon this background of religious truth which is every where perceptible in the book, and that more or less directly illuminates every moral utterance. As this eternal Divine wisdom is the original source in all God's revelation of Himself in natural and human life,—as it is especially the mediating and executive agency in the Divine revelation of the way of life in the law of the Old Covenant, and must therefore be the highest source of knowledge and the standard for all the religious and moral life of man,—so likewise does it appear as the highest good, and as the prescribed goal toward which men are to press. And the subjective wisdom of man is nothing but the finite likeness of the wisdom of God, which is not only objective, but absolute and infinite; nothing but the full unfolding and normal development of the noblest theoretical and practical powers of the moral nature of man. It can be attained only by the devotion of man to its Divine original; it is therefore essentially dependent upon the fear of God and willing subjection to the salutary discipline (מוּסָר, i. 2, 8; iv. 1, *etc.*) of the Divine word. He who does not seek it in this way does not attain it, but remains a fool, an opposer of God and of Divine truth, who in the same ratio as he fails to raise his own moral nature by normal development to a living likeness to God, fails also to share in any true prosperity in the present life, to say nothing of the blessed rewards of the future. He who because of the fear of God strives after true wisdom, on the contrary unfolds his whole inner and outer life to such a symmetry of all his powers and activities as not only secures him the praise of a wise man in the esteem of God and men, but also establishes his true and complete happiness for time and eternity.

A presentation of these fundamental ideas in the ethics of Solomon, well connected, systematically arranged and exhibited, cannot possibly be expected consistently with the note appended to the preceding section in reference to the composition of the Book of Proverbs. If we therefore now endeavor to give a table of contents as complete as possible, following the arrangement of the Masoretic text and the ordinary division of chapters, we shall be quite as unable to avoid a frequent transition to heterogeneous subjects, as on the other hand a return in many instances to something already presented; we must in many cases dispense with even aiming at a strict logical order of ideas. We follow in the main the "Summary of the Contents of the Proverbs of Solomon," given by STARKE at the end of his preface, pp. 1593 sq. Only with respect to the first nine chapters do we adopt the somewhat different summary and division which DELITZSCH has given (pp. 697 sq.) of the "fifteen proverbial discourses" of the first main division.

GENERAL SUPERSCRIPTION OF THE COLLECTION.

Chap. I. 1—6.

Announcement of the author of the collection (ver. 1) of its object (vers. 2, 3), and of its great value (vers. 4-6).

I. Introductory Division.

Chap. I. 7—IX. 18.

True wisdom as the basis and end of all moral effort, impressed by admonition and commendation upon the hearts of youth.

Motto: *"The fear of the Lord is the beginning of all knowledge;"* i. 7.

1. Group of admonitory discourses; i. 8—iii. 35.
    1. Admonition of the teacher of wisdom to his son to avoid the way of vice; I. 8-19.
    2. Warning delineation of the perverse and ruinous conduct of the fool, put into the mouth of Wisdom (personified); I. 20-33.
    3. Exhibition of the blessed consequences of obedience and of striving after wisdom; II. 1-22.
    4. Continuation of the exhibition of the salutary results of this devout and pious life; III. 1-18.
    5. Description of the powerful protection which God, the wise Creator of the world, grants to those that fear Him; III. 19-26.
    6. Admonition to charity and justice; III. 27-35.

2. Group of admonitory discourses; IV. 1—VII. 27.
    7. Report of the teacher of wisdom concerning the good counsels in favor of piety, and the warnings against vice, which were addressed to him in his youth by his father; IV. 1-27.
    8. Warning against intercourse with lewd women, and against the ruinous consequences of licentiousness; V. 1-23.
    9. Warning against inconsiderate suretyship; VI. 1-5.
    10. Rebuke of the sluggard: VI. 6-11.
    11. Warning against malice and wanton violence; VI. 12-19.
    12. Admonition to chastity, with a warning delineation of the fearful consequences of adultery; VI. 20-35.
    13. New admonition to chastity, with a reference to the repulsive example of a youth led astray by a harlot; VII. 1-27.

3. Group of admonitory discourses; VIII. 1—IX. 18.
    14. A second public discourse of Wisdom (personified) chap. VIII., having reference
        a) to the richness of her gifts (vers. 1-21);
        b) to the origin of her nature in God (vers. 21-31); and
        c) to the blessing that flows from the possession of her (vers. 32-36).
    15. Allegorical exhibition of the call of men to the possession and enjoyment of true wisdom, under the figure of an invitation to two banquets (chap. IX.),
        a) that of Wisdom; vers. 1-12.
        b) that of Folly; vers. 13-18.

II. Original nucleus of the collection,—genuine proverbs of Solomon; X. 1—XXII. 16.

Ethical maxims, precepts, and admonitions, with respect to the most diverse relations of human life.

1. Exhibition of the difference between the pious and the ungodly, and their respective lots in life; chap. X.—XV.*

    a) Comparison between the pious and the ungodly with reference to their life and conduct in general; X. 1-32.
    b) Comparison between the good results of piety, and the disadvantages and penalties of ungodliness (chap. XI.—XV.), and particularly
        a) with reference to just and unjust, benevolent and malevolent conduct toward one's neighbor; chap. XI.;
        β) with reference to domestic, civil and public avocations; chap. XII;
        γ) with reference to the use of temporal good, and of the word of God as the highest good: chap. XIII.;
        δ) with reference to the relation between the wise and the foolish, the rich and the poor, masters and servants: chap. XIV.;
        ε) with reference to various other relations and callings in life, especially within the sphere of religion: chap. XV.;

2. Exhortations to a life in the fear of God, and in obedience; (chap. XVI. 1—XXII. 16); and in particular

    a) to confidence in God as the wise regulator and ruler of the world; chap. XVI.;
    β) to contentment and a peaceable disposition; chap. XVII.;
    γ) to affability, fidelity, and the other virtues of social life; ch. XVIII.;
    δ) to humility, meekness and gentleness; chap. XIX.;
    ε) to the avoidance of drunkenness, indolence, quarrelsomeness, *etc.*; chap. XX.;
    ζ) to justice, patience, and dutiful submission to God's gracious control; chap. XXI.;
    η) to the obtaining and preserving of a good name; chap. XXII. 1-16.

III. **Additions made before Hezekiah's day to the genuine proverbs of Solomon which form the nucleus of the collection;** chap. XXII. 17—XXIV. 34.

1st Addition: Various injunctions of justice and prudence in life; XXII. 17—XXIV. 22.
    a) Introductory admonition to lay to heart the words of the wise; XXII. 17-21;
    b) Admonition to justice toward others, especially the poor; XXII. 22-29;
    c) Warning against avarice, intemperance, licentiousness and other such vices: chap. XXIII.;
    d) Warning against companionship with the wicked and foolish; chap. XXIV. 1-22.

2d Addition: chap. XXIV. 23-34.
    a) Various admonitions to right conduct toward one's neighbor; vers. 23-29.
    b) Warning against indolence and its evil consequences: vers. 30-34.

IV. **Gleanings by the men of Hezekiah;** chap. XXV.—XXIX.

True wisdom proclaimed as the highest good to Kings and their subjects.
    Superscription; XXV. 1.

1. Admonition to the fear of God and to righteousness, addressed to Kings and subjects; chap. XXV.

---

* The justification for comprehending the contents of these chapters under the above heading is to be found in this,—that the so called antithetic Maschal form is decidedly predominant in them. Comp. above § 14, p. 32, and also the general prefatory remarks which introduce the exegetical comments on chap. x.

2. Various warnings: *viz.*

   a) Against disgraceful conduct (especially folly, indolence, and malice) chap. XXVI.

   b) Against vain self-praise and arrogance; chap. XXVII. (with an exhortation to prudence and frugality in husbandry; vers. 23-27).

   c) Against unscrupulous, unlawful dealing, especially of the rich with the poor; chap. XXVIII.

   d) Against stubbornness and insubordination; chap. XXIX.

V. The Supplements: chaps. XXX., XXXI.

1st Supplement: the words of Agur; chap. XXX.

   a) Introduction: Of the word of God as the source of all wisdom; vers. 1-6.

   b) Various pithy numerical apothegms, having reference to the golden mean between rich and poor, to profligacy, insatiable greed, pride, arrogance, *etc.;* vers. 7-33.

2d Supplement: The words of Lemuel, together with the poem in praise of the matron; chap. XXXI.

   a) Lemuel's philosophy for kings; vers. 1-9.

   b) Alphabetic poem in praise of the virtuous, wise, and industrious woman; vers. 10-31.

NOTE. The more thorough presentation of the didactic substance of the proverbs is reserved for the exposition that is to follow, and especially for the rubric "Doctrinal and Practical." As the best connected discussion of this subject (biblical and theological) we should be able without hesitation to commend that of BRUCH (*Weisheitslehre der Hebraer*, pp. 110 sq.), if it were not characterized by the fault which pervades BRUCH's treatise, so meritorious in other respects,—that in the interest of critical and humanitarian views it misrepresents the stand-point and the tendency of the Hhokmah-doctrine. That is to say, it insists that there is in this attitude of mind a relation of indifference or even of hostility toward the theocratic cultus and the ceremonial law, like the relation of the philosophers and free-thinkers of Christendom to the orthodox creed. No less clearly does he insist upon the general limitation to the present life of every assumption of a moral retribution; and in his view there is an entire absence of the hope of immortality from the view of the world taken in our book. For the refutation of these misconceptions of BRUCH (which are undeniably in conflict with such passages as, on the one side, xiv. 9; xxviii. 4 sq.; xxix. 18, 24; xxx. 17; and on the other xii. 28; xiv. 32; xv. 24; xxiii. 18, *etc.*), OEHLER's able treatise may be referred to: "*Grundzüge der alttestamentl. Weisheit*" (Tüb. 1854, 4); although this deals more especially with the doctrinal teachings of the Book of Job, than with Proverbs. See likewise EWALD (as above quoted, pp. 8 sq.; ELSTER, § 1, pp. 1-6; DELITZSCH, pp. 714-716, and even HITZIG, pp. xii. sq.)

§ 16. THEOLOGICAL AND HOMILETICAL LITERATURE ON THE BOOK OF PROVERBS.

Beside the general commentaries (of which we shall have especial occasion to make use of STARKE's *Synopsis*, the *Berleburg Bible*, J. LANGE's *Licht und Recht*, WOHLFARTH and FISCHER's *Prediger-Bibel*, the *Calwer Handbuch*, and VON GERLACH's Commentary) we must mention the following as the most important exegetical helps to the study of the Proverbs. MELANCHTHON: *Explicatio Proverbiorum*, 1525 (*Opp.*, T. XIV.); SEBAST. MUNSTER, *Prov. Salom. juxta hebr. verit. translata et annotationibus illustrata* (without date); J. MERCERUS, *Comm. in Salomonis Proverbia, Eccl. et Cantic.*, 1573; MALDONATUS, *Comm. in præcipuos libros V. Testamenti*, 1643; F. Q. SALAZAR. *In Prov. Sal. Commentarius*, 1636-7; MART. GEIER, *Prov. Salomonis cum cura enucleata*, 1653, 1725; THOM. CARTWRIGHT, *Commentarii succincti et dilucidi in Prov. Sal.*, 1663; CHR. BEN. MICHAELIS, *Annotationes in Prov.* (in J. H. MICHAELIS, "*Uberiores annotationes in Hagiogr. V. Test. libros*," 1720, Vol. 1); A. SCHULTENS, *Prov. Salom. vers. integram ad Hebr. fontem expressit atque comm. adjecit*, 1748; (*In compend. redegit obss. critt. aurit* G. J. L. VOGEL, Hal., 1768-9); J. D. MICHAELIS, *Die Sprüche Sal. und der Prediger übs. mit Anmerkungen, für Ungelehrte,* 1778; J. CHR. DÖDERLEIN, *Die Sprüche Salomonis mit Anmerkungen,* 1778, 3d edn. 1786; W. C. ZIEGLER, *Neue Uebers. der Denksprüche Salomonis,* 1791; H. MUNTINGHE, *Uebers. der Spr., a. d. Holländ. von* SCHOLL, 1800-2; CHR. G. HENSLER, *Erläuterungen des 1 Buches Samuels und der Salom. Denksprüche,* 1796; J. FR. SCHELLING, *Salomonis quæ supersunt omnia lat. vertit notasque adjecit,* 1806; J. G. DAHLER, *Denk- und Sittensprüche Salomos, nebst den Abweichungen der Alex. Vers. ins Deutsche übers. mit Vorrede von* BLESSIG, 1810; C. P. W. GRAMBERG, *Das Buch der Sprüche Sal., neu übersetzt, systemat. geordnet, mit erkl. Anm. u. Parall.,* 1828; F. W. C. UMBREIT, *Philol.-Krit. und Philos. Comm. uber die Sprüche Sal., nebst einer neuen Uebers. Einl. in die morgenl. Weisheit überhaupt u. in d. Salomonische insbes.,* 1826; H. EWALD, *die poetischen Bücher des A. Bundes,* Th. IV., 1837; F. MAURER, *Comm. gram. crit. in Prov., in usum academiarum adornatus,* 1841; C. BRIDGES, An exposition of the Book of Proverbs, 2 Vols., Lond., 1847 [1 Vol., New York, 1847]; E. BERTHEAU, *Die Sprüche Sal.* in the "*Kurzgef. exeg. Handb. z. A. T.,*" 1847; VAIHINGER, *Die Spr. Sal.,* 1857; F. HITZIG, *Die Spr. Sal. übers. u. ausgelegt,* 1858; E. ELSTER, *Comm. über d. Salomonischen Sprüche,* 1858. [ADOLF KAMPHAUSEN, in BUNSEN'S *Bibelwerk,* 1865].

[Besides the standard general Commentaries of HENRY, PATRICK, ADAM CLARKE, GILL, ORTON, SCOTT, TRAPP and others, a considerable number of special commentaries on Proverbs have been written by English and American scholars. Among these are BEDE, *Expositio allegorica in Salom. Proverbia;* M. COPE, Exposition upon Proverbs, translated by M. OUTRED, London, 1580; P. A. MUFFET, a Commentary on the Proverbs of Solomon, 2d ed. London, 1598; republished in NICHOL's Series of Commentaries, Edinburgh, 1868; T. WILCOCKS, a short yet sound Commentary on the Proverbs of Solomon (in his works); JOHN DOD, a plain and familiar exposition of Proverbs (chap. ix. to xvii.), 1608-9; JERMIN, Paraphrastical Meditations by way of Commentary on the whole Book of Proverbs, London, 1638; F. TAYLOR (Exposition with practical reflections on chaps. i.—ix.), London, 1655-7; Sir EDWARD LEIGH, in his "Annotations on the Five Poetical Books of the Old Testament," London, 1657; H. HAMMOND, Paraphrase and Annotations, *etc.;* RICHARD GREY, The Book of Proverbs divided according to metre, *etc.,* London, 1738; D. DURELL, in his "Critical Remarks on Job, Proverbs, *etc.,*" Oxford, 1772; T. HUNT, Observations on several passages, *etc.,* Oxford, 1775; B. HODGSON, The Proverbs of Solomon translated from the Hebrew, Oxford, 1788; G. HOLDEN, An Attempt towards an Improved Translation, *etc.,* Liverpool, 1819; G. LAWSON, Exposition of the Book of Proverbs, Edinb., 1821; R. J. CASE, Comm. on the Proverbs of Solomon, London, 1822; FRENCH and SKINNER, a new translation, *etc.,* Camb., 1831; W. NEWMAN, The Proverbs of Solomon, an improved version, London, 1839; B. E. NICHOLLS, The Proverbs of Solomon explained and illustrated, London, 1842; G. R. NOYES, in his "New Translation of the Proverbs, Ecclesiastes and the Canticles," *etc.,* Boston, 1846; M. STUART, Commentary on the Book of Proverbs, Andover, 1852; J. MUENSCHER, The Book of Proverbs in an amended Version, *etc.,* Gambier, 1866; CHR. WORDSWORTH, Vol. IV., Part III. of his Commentary on the Bible, London, 1868.]

Jewish Rabbinic Expositions; ANT. GIGGEJUS, *In Proverbia Salomonis commentarii trium Rabbinorum; Sal. Isacidis, Abr. Aben Ezræ, Levi ben Ghersom, quos A. Gigg. interpret. est, castig., illustr.,* Mediolan, 1620. Of the more recent Rabbinical commentaries, that in Hebrew by LÖWENSTEIN, Frkft. a. M., 1838, is of special importance, and also that by L. DUKES, in COHEN's Commentary (Paris, 1847; *Proverbes*), where the earlier expositions of learned Jews upon our book, 38 in all, from SAADIA to LÖWENSTEIN, are enumerated and estimated.

Literature in Monographs. 1. Critical and exegetical: J. F. HOFFMANN and J. TH. SPRENGER, *Observationes ad quædam loca Proverbb. Sal.,* Tubing. 1776; * J. J. REISKE, *Conjecturæ in Jobum et Provv. Salom.,* Lips. 1779; A. S. ARNOLDI, *Zur Exegetik und Kritik des A. Tests,* 1. *Beitrag; Anmerkungen über einzelne Stellen d. Spr. Sal.,* 1781; J. J. BELLERMANN, *Ænigmata hebraica,* Prov. xxx. 11 sq., 15 sq., *explicata,* spec. 1-3, Erford. 1798-9; H. F.

---

* In UMBREIT (p. lxvi.) and in KEIL (p. 395) CHR. FR. SCHNURRER is incorrectly named as the author of this little treatise. It was rather a dissertation defended by the scholars above named under SCHNURRER'S rectorate.

MUEHLAU, *De proverbiorum quæ dicuntur Aguri et Lemuelis* (Prov. xxx. 1—xxxi. 9) *origine atque indole*, Leips., 1869.—Compare moreover the works already named in § 13, note 1, among which especial prominence should be given to FR. BÖTTCHER's "*Neue exegetisch-kritische Aehrenlese z. A. Test.* (Abth. III., herausg. von. F. MUEHLAU, Lips. 1865), as likewise to the treatises which are there mentioned by P. DE LAGARDE and M. HEIDENHEIM (the former judging somewhat too unfavorably of the LXX, the latter in some cases contesting the exaggerations of the former, and in other instances reducing them to their proper measure); for these are important aids to the criticism and exegesis of single passages.

2. Practical and Homiletical: SAM. BOHLIUS, *Ethica sacra*, Rost. 1640 (compare note to § 1); J. STÖCKER (Pastor at Eisleben, died in 1649) Sermons on the Proverbs of Solomon; OETINGER, *Die Wahrheit des sensus communis in den Sprüchen und dem Prediger Salomonis*, Stuttg., 1753; STAUDENMAIER, *Die Lehre von der Idee* (1840), pp. 37 sq. (valuable observations on Prov. viii. 22 sq.); C. I. NITZSCH, on the essential Trinity of God, *Theod. Stud. u. Krit.*, 1841, II., 295 (on the same passage; see especially pp. 310 sq.); R. STIER, *Der Weise ein König*, Solomon's Proverbs according to the compilation of the men of Hezekiah (chap. xxv.—xxix.), expounded for the School and the Life of all times, Barmen, 1849 (the same work also elaborated for the laity, under the title "Solomon's wisdom in Hezekiah's days"); same author: "The Politics of Wisdom in the words of Agur and Lemuel," Prov. xxx. and xxxi. Timely scriptural exposition for every man, with an appendix for scholars, Barmen, 1850. [In English no other recent work of this sort can be compared with ARNOT's "Laws from Heaven for Life on Earth," 2d edn. Lond., 1866. Bishop HALL's "Characters of Virtues and Vices," London, 1609, is designed to be an epitome of the Ethics of Solomon. R. WARDLAW: Lectures on the Book of Proverbs (a posthumous publication), 3 Vols., London, 1861].

THE

PROVERBS OF SOLOMON.

General Superscription to the Collection.

Announcement of the Author of the Collection, of its Object, and of its great value.

Chap. I. 1-6.

1 Proverbs of Solomon, the son of David,
   the King of Israel:
2 to become acquainted with wisdom and knowledge,
   to comprehend intelligent discourse,
3 to attain discipline of understanding,
   righteousness, justice and integrity,
4 to impart to the simple prudence,
   to the young man knowledge and discretion;—
5 let the wise man hear and add to his learning,
   and the man of understanding gain in control,
6 that he may understand proverb and enigma,
   words of wise men and their dark sayings.

Introductory Section.

True wisdom as the basis and end of all moral effort, impressed by admonition and commendation upon the hearts of youth.

Chap. I. 7—IX. 18.

7 The fear of Jehovah is the beginning of knowledge;
   wisdom and discipline fools despise.

First group of Admonitory or Gnomic Discourses.

Chap. I. 8—III. 35.

I. The teacher of wisdom admonishes his son to avoid the way of vice.

Chap. I. 8-19.

8 Hearken, my son, to thy father's instruction,
   and refuse not the teaching of thy mother;
9 for they are a graceful crown to thy head,
   and jewels about thy neck.—
10 My son, if sinners entice thee,
   consent thou not!

11 If they say, "Come with us, and we will lie in wait for blood,
   will plot against the innocent without cause;
12 we will swallow them, like the pit, living,
   and the upright, like those that descend into the grave;
13 we will find all precious treasure,
   will fill our houses with spoil!
14 Thou shalt cast in thy lot among us;
   one purse will we all have!"
15 My son! go not in the way with them,
   keep back thy foot from their path!
16 For their feet run to evil,
   and haste to shed blood;
17 for in vain is the net spread
   before the eyes of all (kinds of) birds:
18 and these watch for their own blood,
   they lie in wait for their own lives.
19 Such are the paths of every one that grasps after unjust gain;
   from its own master it taketh the life.

Chap. I. 20-33.

2. Warning delineation of the perverse and ruinous conduct of the fool, put into the mouth of wisdom (personified).

20 Wisdom crieth aloud in the streets,
   on the highways she maketh her voice heard:
21 in the places of greatest tumult she calleth,
   at the entrances to the gates of the city she giveth forth her words:
22 " How long, ye simple, will ye love simplicity,
   and scorners delight in scorning,
   and fools hate knowledge!
23 Turn ye at my reproof!
   Behold I will pour out upon you my spirit,
   my words will I make known to you!
24 Because I have called and ye refused,
   I stretched out my hand, and no man regarded it,
25 and ye have rejected all my counsel,
   and to my reproof ye have not yielded;
26 therefore will I also laugh at your calamity,
   will mock when your terror cometh;
27 when like a storm your terror cometh,
   and your destruction sweepeth on like a whirlwind,
   when distress and anguish cometh upon you.
28 Then will they call upon me, and I not answer,
   they will seek me diligently and not find me.
29 Because they have hated sound wisdom
   and have not desired the fear of Jehovah,
30 have not yielded to my counsel
   and have despised all my reproof,
31 therefore shall they eat of the fruit of their way
   and be surfeited with their own counsels.
32 For the perverseness of the simple shall slay them,
   and the security of fools destroy them:
33 he, however, who hearkeneth to me shall dwell secure,
   and have rest without dread of evil!"

GRAMMATICAL AND CRITICAL.

Ver. 2. [We have in vers. 2, 3, 4, 6 final clauses, introduced by ל, and indicating the object with which these wise sayings are recorded. That purpose is disciplinary, first with reference to "the young man," and then to him who is already "wise." This discipline is contemplated not from the point of view of him who imparts, but that of those who receive it. These considerations determine our choice of words in translating several of the terms employed. Thus in ver. 2 we render לָדַעַת not "to know," as this suggests the finished result rather than the process, which is "to become acquainted with, to acquire;" so ZÖCKLER, *zu erkennen*; DE WETTE, *kennen zu lernen*; NOYES, "*from which men may learn;*" a little less definitely, E. V., "to know;" incorrectly HOLDEN, "respecting the knowledge." These wise sayings are to guide to and result in knowledge; but the verbs, except in ver. 4, represent not the teaching, imparting, communicating, but the discerning and seizing. In respect to the two shades of meaning to be given to חֹכְבָּד see the exeg. notes.

GESEN. and FUERST agree in the etymology (יסר); FUERST, however, carries back the radical meaning one step farther; G., "to chastise, correct, instruct;" F., "to bind or restrain, chastise," etc. It should, therefore, be borne in mind that more than the imparting of information is intended by the word, it is *discipline*, sometimes merely intellectual but more frequently moral.—אִמְרֵי בִינָה, lit., "words of discernment," "words of understanding" (so E. V., NOYES, MUENSCHER); STUART, "words of the intelligent;" DE WETTE like ZÖCKLER, "*verständige Reden;*" VAN ESS and ALLIOLI, with whom HOLDEN seems to agree, "*die Worte (Regeln) der Klugheit,*" "the words (rules) of prudence."—A.].

Ver. 3. מוּסַר הַשְׂכֵּל.—our author's conception (see exeg. notes) corresponds with that of FUERST also, who makes the genitive not merely objective, as DE WETTE, etc., seem to do ("discipline of understanding," "*die Zucht der Vernunft*"), but makes it final, contemplating the end: FUERST, "*Z. zur Besonnenheit,*" ZÖCKLER, "*einsichtsvolle Zucht;*" discipline full of discernment, insight, understanding, *i. e.*, in its results. The rendering of most of our English expositors is ambiguous or suggests other ideas: E V. and MUENSCHER, "*instruction of wisdom;*" HOLDEN, "*instruction in wisdom ;*" NOYES, "*the instruction of prudence ;*" STUART, "*of discreetness.*"—מֵישָׁרִים, plural of that which is "ideally extended" and pleasurable; BÖTTCHER, *Ausf. Lehrb.*, § 699.—A.].

Ver. 5. [E. V., followed by HOLDEN and MUENSCHER, "a wise man will hear ;" NOYES, "may hear ;" STUART, more forcibly, "let the wise man listen," like our author, "*es höre,*" and BÖTTCHER (§ 950, d., "*Fiens debitum*") "*es soll hören.*" DE WETTE makes this a final clause, like those of the three preceding verses, "*dass der Weise höre ;*" but see exeg. notes.—וְיוֹסֵף is given by BÖTTCHER (§ 964, 2) as an illustration of the "consultive" use of the Jussive ; STUART makes it an ordinary Imperf., and renders "and he will add ;" but his explanations are not pertinent; the ו need not be "conversive," it is simply copulative, and יוֹסֵף which he assumes as the normal Imperf., is already a Jussive.—A.].—לֶקַח, properly that which is "taken, received, transmitted" (comp. the verb לקח, "to attain," above in ver. 3) is like the Aram. קַבָּלָה (from קבל, to take), and like the Latin *traditio* [in its passive sense]. The parallel term תַּחְבֻּלוֹת (from חֵבֶל, to lead, according to the analogy of the Arabic, and cognate with חֶבֶל, cable, and חֹבֵל, steersman) is by the LXX correctly rendered by κυβέρνησις.

Ver. 6. LUTHER's translation of the 1st clause, "that he may understand proverbs and their interpretation," cannot possibly be right; for מְלִיצָה, if it was designed to convey any other idea than one parallel to מָשָׁל could not on any principle dispense with the suffix of the 3d person (הֵן־), its, comp. Vulgate: "*animadvertet parabolam et interpretatimem.*" [This is also the rendering of the E. V., which is followed by HOLDEN, while NOYES, STUART, MUENSCHER and WORDSWORTH, DE WETTE and VAN ESS agree with the view taken by our author.—A.].

Ver. 7. אֱוִילִים, derived from אוּל, *crassus fuit;* to be gross or dull of understanding ;—GESEN., however, derives it from the radical idea "to be perverse, turned away," and FUERST "to be slack, weak, lax or lazy." [WORDSWORTH adopts the latter explanation.—A.].

Ver. 8. [The different renderings given to the verb of the 2d clause while agreeing in their substantial import, "forsake," "neglect," "reject," do not reproduce with equal clearness the radical idea, which is that of "spreading," then of "scattering."—A].

Ver. 10. תֵּבֹא, *scriptio defectiva*, for תָּבוֹא, as some 50 MSS. cited by KENNICOTT and DE ROSSI in fact read, while some others prefer a different pointing אַל־תָּבֹא [thou shalt not go], which is however an unwarranted emendation. The LXX had the correct conception: μὴ βουληθῇς, and the Vulgate: *ne acquiescas.*—[Comp. GREEN's *Heb. Gram.*, § 111, 2, b, and § 177, 3. BÖTTCHER discusses the form several times in different connections. §§ 325, *d*, and n. 2,—429, B, and 1164, 2, b,—and after enumerating the six forms which the MSS. supply, תָּבוֹא, תָּבֹא, תֵּאבֶה, תַּאְבָּא, תֹּבֶה, and תּוֹבָא decides that the original form, whose obscurity suggested all these modifications, was תֵּבֹא = תֹּאבֶה. In signification he classes it with the "dehortative" Jussives.—A.].

Ver. 11. [E. V., NOYES, WORDSWORTH, LUTHER, VAN ESS agree with one another in connecting the adverb with the verb, while DE WETTE, HOLDEN, STUART, MUENSCHER regard it as modifying the adjective, "him whose innocence is of no avail to protect him."—A.].

Ver. 12. [E. V., STUART and MUENSCHER, like our author connect חַיִּים with the object of the main verb; UMBREIT and HITZIG (see exeg. notes) are followed by DE WETTE, HOLDEN, NOYES in connecting it with the comparative clause.—יוֹרְדֵי בוֹר, for construction see *e. g.*, GREEN, § 271, 2 and 254, 9, b.—A.].

Ver. 16. [יְרוּצוּ, masc. verb with feminine subject; BÖTT., § 936, II.; *C. a;* GREEN, § 275, 1. c.—A.].

Ver. 20. The Wisdom who is here speaking is in this verse called חָכְמוֹת, which is not a plural but "a new abstract derivative from חָכְמָה, formed with the ending וֹת" (EWALD, § 165, c); a form which is also found *e. g.*, in תַּחֲמוֹת, Ps. lxxviii. 15. The name recurs in the same form in ix. 1; xxiv. 7. [BÖTTCHER, however, regards this as an example of the *pluralis extens.*, to denote emphatically "true wisdom," §§ 679, d, 689, C, b, 700, c and b, 42 and 4. There is no difficulty in connecting a verb fem. sing. with a subject which although plural in form is singular in idea.—A.].—תָּרֹנָּה, crieth aloud, from רָנַן, comp. Lam. ii. 19; 3d sing. fem. as also in viii. 3 (EWALD, 191, c). [Comp. GREEN, § 97, 1, a, and BÖTT., § 929, d, who with his usual minuteness endeavors to trace the development of this idiom.—A.].

Ver. 21. ZÖCKLER, *an den lärmvollsten Orten;* DE WETTE, *an der Ecke lärmender Strassen;* FUERST, *der bewegten Strassen;* HOLDEN, like the Eng. Ver., *in the chief place of concourse.*

Ver. 22. [For the vocalization of הָאֱהַב see GREEN, §§ 60, 3, c., 111, 2, e. For the use of the perfect חָכְדוּ see BÖTT., § 948, 2. He illustrates by such classical perfects as ἔγνωκα, οἶδα, μέμαα, memini, novi, and renders this form by *concupiverint*.—A.].

Ver. 23. [יָעֲנֶה, an Instance of the intentional Imperf., in what DÖTTCHER calls its "voluntative" signification,— § 965, 1.—A.].

Ver. 27. [כְּשׁוֹאָה, K'ri כְּשׁוֹאָה, the former derived from שָׁאוּ or שָׁאָה, the latter from שׁוּא, of which verbs the latter is obsolete except in derivatives, while the former occurs in one passage in Is. in the Niphal. The signification seems to be one, and the forms variations growing out of the weakness of the 2d and 3d radicals. Comp. BÖTT., §§ 474, a, and 811, 2.—A.].

Instead of the Infin. בְּבוֹא, we have in the 2d member, since בְּ is not repeated, the Imperf. יֶאֱתֶה (EWALD, 337, b) [STUART, § 129, 3, n. 2].—A.

Ver. 28. יְקָרָאֻנְנִי, יְשַׁחֲרֻנְנִי, יִמְצָאֻנְנִי. These are among the few instances in which the full plural ending וּן is found before suffixes. GREEN, § 105, c., BÖTT., § 1047, f.—A.].

Ver. 29. For the use of "תַּחַת כִּי," "therefore because," compare Deut. xxxiv. 7, and also the equivalent combination תַּחַת אֲשֶׁר in 2 Kings xxii. 7; 2 Chron. xxi. 12.

EXEGETICAL.

1. Vers. 1–6. The superscription to the collection, which is quite long, as is common with the titles of Oriental books, is not designed to be a "table of contents" (UMBREIT), nor to give merely the aim of the book (so most commentators, especially EWALD, BERTHEAU, ELSTER, etc.). But beside the author of the book (ver. 1), it is intended to give first its design (vers. 2, 3), and then, in addition, its worth and use (vers. 4–6), and so to commend the work in advance as salutary and excellent (STARKE, DELITZSCH). Accordingly it praises the book as a source of wholesome and instructive wisdom: 1) for the simple-minded and immature (ver. 4); 2) for those who are already wise and intelligent, but who are to gain still more insight and understanding from its maxims and enigmas (vers. 5, 6).—**Proverbs of Solomon,** *etc*.—In regard to the primary meaning of מָשָׁל, and in regard to the special signification which prevails here in the superscription, "Proverbs of Solomon" (maxims, aphorisms, not proverbs [in the current and popular sense]), see Introd., § 11.—**To become acquainted with wisdom and knowledge.**—In respect to חָכְמָה and its synonyms (בִּינָה and דַּעַת) consult again the Introd., § 2, note 3. מוּסָר properly "chastisement," signifies education, moral training, good culture and habits, the practical side, as it were, of wisdom (LXX: παιδεία; Vulg.: *disciplina*). In ver. 2 the expression stands as synonymous with "wisdom" (חָכְמָה), as in iv. 13; xxiii. 23, and frequently elsewhere; in ver. 3, on the contrary, it designates an element preparatory to true wisdom and insight,—one serving as their foundation, and a preliminary condition to them. For the "discipline of understanding" (מוּסַר הַשְׂכֵּל, ver. 3) is not, as might be conceived, "discipline under which the understanding is placed," but "discipline, training to reason, to a reasonable, intelligent condition" (as HITZIG rightly conceives it); compare the "discipline of wisdom" (מוּסַר חָכְמָה), xv. 33, and for "understanding" (הַשְׂכֵּל), insight, discernment, a rational condition, see particularly xxi. 16. UMBREIT and EWALD regard הַשְׂכֵּל as equivalent to thoughtfulness ("a discipline to thoughtfulness," *Zuchtigung zur Besonnenheit*"); by this rendering, however, the full meaning of the conception is not exhausted.—**Righteousness, justice and integrity.** The three Hebrew terms צֶדֶק, מִשְׁפָּט and מֵישָׁרִים are related to each other as "righteousness, justice, and integrity, or uprightness" (*Gerechtigkeit, Recht und Geradheit*). The first of the three expressions describes what is fitting according to the will and ordinance of God the supreme Judge (comp. Deut. xxxiii. 19); the second, what is usage and custom among men (Is. xlii. 1; 1 Sam. xxvii. 11): the third, what is right and reasonable, and in accordance with a walking in the way of truth, and so denotes a straight-forward, honorable and upright demeanor.

Ver. 4. **To impart to the simple prudence.**—The telic infinitive (לָתֵת) is co-ordinate with the two that precede in vers. 2 and 3, and has the same subject. Therefore the same construction is to be employed here also (to become acquainted with—to attain—to impart); and we are not, by the introduction of a final clause, to make the contents of this 4th verse subordinate to the preceding, as the LXX do (ἵνα δῷ κ. τ. λ.), and likewise the Vulg. (*ut detur, etc.*), and LUTHER ("that the simple may become shrewd, and young men reasonable and considerate"). The "simple" (פְּתָאיִם), properly, the "open," those who are readily accessible to all external impressions, and therefore inexperienced and simple, νήπιοι, ἄκακοι (as the LXX appropriately render the word in this passage; comp. Rom. xvi. 18). With respect to the relation of this idea to that of the "fool" (כְּסִיל נָבָל) compare what will be said below on i. 32, and also Introd., § 3, note 2.—**Prudence** (עָרְמָה), derived from עָרַם) signifies properly nakedness, smoothness (comp. the adj. עָרוּם ["subtle," E. V.], naked, *i. e.*, slippery, crafty; used of the serpent, Gen. iii. 1); therefore metaphorically "the capacity for escaping from the wiles of others" (UMBREIT), "the prudence which guards itself against injury" (xxii. 3; 1 Sam. xxiii. 22).—**To the young man knowledge and discretion.**—Discretion, thoughtfulness (מְזִמָּה, LXX, ἔννοια), denotes here in connection with "knowledge" (דַּעַת) the characteristic of thoughtful, well considered action, resting upon a thorough knowledge of things,—therefore, circumspection, caution.

Ver. 5. Not the simple and immature only, but also the wise and intelligent, are to derive instruction from Solomon's proverbs. This idea is not, as might be supposed, thrust in the form of a parenthesis into the series of final clauses beginning with ver. 2, and reaching its conclusion in ver. 6, so that the verb (יִשְׁמַע) is to be conceived of as rendering the clause conditional, and is to be translated "if he hears" (UMBREIT, ELSTER); it begins a new independent proposition, whose imperfect tenses are to be regarded as voluntative, and upon which the new infinitive clause with ל in ver. 6 is dependent (EWALD, BERTHEAU, and commentators generally).—Let the wise man hearken and add to his learning.—As to the expression "add to his learning" (יוֹסֶף לֶקַח) comp. ix. 9; xvi. 12. The peculiar term rendered "learning" (see critical notes above) is a designation of knowledge, doctrine, instructive teaching in general; comp. vers. 22 and 29. The word rendered "control," or mastery, is an abstract derivative, strengthened by the ending ת (EWALD, Gramm., § 179 a., note 3), and expresses here in an appropriate and telling figure the idea of "skill and facility in the management of life." Comp. xi. 14; xii. 5; Job xxxvii. 12, etc. Its relation to "learning" (לֶקַח) is quite like that of "discipline" to "wisdom" in ver. 2; it supplies the practical correlative to the other idea which is predominantly theoretical.

Ver. 6. To understand proverb and enigma, etc.—["The climax of the definition of wisdom"—STANLEY]. The infinitive (לְהָבִין) supplies the announcement of the end required by ver. 5: to this end is the wise man to gain in knowledge and self-command or self-discipline, that he may understand the proverbs and profound sayings of the wise, i. e., may know how to deal appropriately with them. It is not the mere understanding of the wisdom of proverbs by itself that is here indicated as the end of the wise man's "increase in knowledge and mastery," but practice and expertness in using this wisdom; it is the callere sententias sapientum which imparts a competence to communicate further instruction to the youth who need discipline. If the telic infinitive (לְהָבִין) be taken in this frequent sense, for which may be compared among other passages Prov. viii. 9; xvii. 10, 24; Dan. i. 27, we do not need with BERTHEAU to give the expression a participial force (by virtue of the fact that he understands,—understanding proverbs, etc.).—nor to maintain with HITZIG and others that ver. 6 is not grammatically connected with ver. 5, on the ground that it is not conceivable that the "learning to understand the words of wise men" should be made an object of the endeavor of such as are wise already. It is an intensified acquaintance with wisdom that is here called for, a knowledge in the sense of the passage, "to him that hath shall be given, and he shall have abundance," Matth. xiii. 12; comp.

John i. 16; Rom. i. 17; 2 Cor. iii. 18. For the verbal explanation of "enigma" and "dark saying" (חִידָה and מְלִיצָה) see Introd., § 11, note 2. Certain as it is that both expressions here are only designed to embody in a concrete form the idea of obscure discourse that requires interpretation (the parallelism with "proverbs" and "words of wise men" (דִּבְרֵי חֲכָמִים and מָשָׁל) shows this beyond dispute), we have no warrant for finding in this verse a special allusion to the obscure, enigmatical contents of chap. xxx., and so for insisting upon its very late origin, as HITZIG does (see in reply EWALD). Nevertheless, it follows from the comprehensiveness of the plural expression "words of wise men" (comp. xxii. 17 and Eccles. ix. 17; xii. 11) that no one could have prefixed to his work an introduction like that before us, who was not conscious that he had collected with proverbs of Solomon many others that were not directly from him (comp. § 12 of the Introd.).

2. Ver. 7 is not to be regarded as a part of the superscription, as EWALD, BERTHEAU, ELSTER, KEIL, etc., treat it, but is the general proposition introducing the series of didactic discourses that follows:—a motto, as it were, for the first or introductory main division of the book, as UMBREIT happily expresses it; comp. HITZIG in loc. The proverb has also passed into the Arabic, and here also frequently stands at the commencement of collections of proverbs, whether because it is ascribed to Mohammed, as is sometimes done in such cases, or because it is cited as coming from Solomon. Compare VON DIEZ, Denkwürdigkeiten, II., 459; MEIDANI, ed. Freytag, III., 29, 610; ERPENIUS, Sent. qued. Arab., p. 45. In the Old Testament [and Apocrypha], moreover, the same maxim occurs several times, especially in Prov. ix. 10; Ecclesiast. i. 16, 25; Ps. cxi. 10. From the passage last cited the LXX repeat in our verse the words appended to the first clause: Ἀρχὴ σοφίας φόβος κυρίου, σύνεσις δὲ ἀγαθὴ πᾶσιν τοῖς ποιοῦσιν αὐτήν ["and a good understanding have all they that do it"].—Beginning.—(רֵאשִׁית) is here equivalent to תְּחִלָּה found in the parallel passage, ix. 10; it is therefore correctly rendered in Ecclesinst. and the LXX by ἀρχή in the sense of "beginning"); compare chap. iv. 7, "the beginning of wisdom:" not, as the words themselves would allow, "that which is highest in wisdom," "the noblest or best wisdom." [The latter is given as a marginal reading in the E. V., and is retained and defended by HOLDEN; so also by TRAPP and others.—A.].—Fools.—The word designates properly the hardened, the stupid,—those fools who know nothing of God (Jer. iv. 22), and therefore refuse and contemptuously repel His salutary discipline (comp. above, note to ver. 2).

3. Vers. 8–19. These verses show in an example so shaped as to convey an earnest warning, how we are to guard ourselves against the opposite of the fear of God, against depravity, which is, at the same time, the extremest folly. They contain, therefore, a warning against turning aside to the way of vice, given as the first illustration of the truth expressed in ver. 7.—Vers. 8, 9 —My son.—The salutation of the

teacher of wisdom, who is here represented as "father" in order to illustrate to his pupil the inner reality and nature of their mutual relation (comp. 1 Cor. iv. 15; Philem. 10). The "mother" who is mentioned in connection with this "father" is only a natural expansion of the idea of the figure, suggested by the law of poetic parallelism,—and not a designation of wisdom personified, who does not appear before ver. 20. [WORDSWORTH and many of the older English expositors regard this as a specific address by Solomon to Rehoboam; this interpretation, however, lacks the support of Oriental usage, and too much restricts the scope of the Book of Proverbs. The large majority, however, of English and American commentators (e. g., TRAPP, HOLDEN, BRIDGES, WORDSWORTH, MUENSCHER) find here a more specific commendation of filial docility and obedience. STUART more nearly agrees with our author in making the "father" and "mother" figurative rather than literal terms—A.].

—**Law** (תּוֹרָה), here *doctrina*, instructive precepts in general; as in several other instances in our book it is used of the instruction given by parents to their children, e. g., iii. 1; iv. 2; vii. 2; xxviii. 7, 9.—**For they are a graceful crown to thy head.**—"Wreath of grace" (לִוְיַת חֵן) graceful crown, as in iv. 9. The comparison of the teachings of wisdom with pearls which one hangs as a necklace about the neck, a figure which is a great favorite every where in the East, recurs again in iii. 3; vi. 21; Ecclesiast. vi. 30.

Ver. 10. Transition to an intelligible admonitory example; hence the repetition of the familiar salutation "My son," which occurs once more in ver. 15, at the beginning of the apodosis. **Sinners** (חַטָּאִים).—Sinners by profession, habitual sinners, as in Ps. i. 1; here those in particular whose business is murder (comp. Gen. iv. 7, 8), robbers who are murderers.—Ver. 11. **We will lie in wait for blood,** *etc.*—The two verbs (אָרַב and צָפַן) both signify to lie in wait for, to lay snares artfully (as the huntsman for the game, with noose and net). The adverb (חִנָּם) is probably more correctly construed with the verb (lie in wait without cause, *i. e.*, without having any reason for revenge and enmity), than with the adjective,—although this latter combination is also grammatically admissible. But with the conception "him that is innocent in vain," *i. e.*, the man to whom his innocence shall be of no avail against us, the parallel passages (Ps. xxxv. 19; lxix. 4; Lam. iii. 52) correspond less perfectly than with that to which we have given the preference; comp. HITZIG *in loc.*—Ver. 12.—**Will swallow them, like the pit, living.**—The "living" (חַיִּים) can refer only to the suffix pronoun (in נִבְלָעֵם). The connection with "like the pit" (כִּשְׁאוֹל), to which UMBREIT and HITZIG give the preference, gives the peculiarly hard sense "as the pit (swallows) that which lives." Comp. rather Ps. lv. 15: "they must go down living into the pit;" and also Ps. cxxiv. 3; Prov. xxx. 16, and the account of the destruction of Korah's company, Numb. xvi. 30,

33.—**The upright** (תְּמִימִים) is accusative, object of the verb (בָּלַע), and therefore stands evidently as synonymous with נָקִי (innocent, comp. Ps. xix. 13); it is accordingly to be interpreted as referring to moral integrity or uprightness, and not of bodily soundness (as EWALD, BERTHEAU, and others claim).—**Those that descend into the grave** (יוֹרְדֵי בוֹר)—that sink into the sepulchre, *i. e.*, the dead; comp. Ps. xxviii. 1; lxxxviii. 4; cxliii. 7.

Vers. 13, 14. Reasons for the treacherous proposal of the murderers.—**Thou shalt cast in thy lot among us**—*i. e.*, thou shalt, as one having equal right with us, cast lots for the spoil, comp. Ps. xxii. 18; Nehem. x. 35.—Vers. 15 sq. The warning,— given as an apodosis to the condition supposed in ver. 11. As to the figurative expressions in ver. 15, comp. Ps. i. 1; Jer. xiv. 10; Prov. iv. 26; for ver. 16 compare Is. lix. 7, and the passage suggested by it, Rom. iii. 15. Without adequate grounds, HITZIG conjectures that ver. 16 is spurious, because, he says, it agrees almost literally with Isaiah (as cited), and, on the other hand, is wanting in the Cod. Vatic. of the LXX. Literal quotations from earlier Biblical writers are in Isaiah above all others nothing uncommon; and with quite as little reason will the omission of a verse from the greatly corrupted LXX text of our book furnish ground, without other evidence, for suspecting its genuineness (see Introd., § 13).—Ver. 17. "The winged" (properly "lords of the wing;" בַּעַל כָּנָף, as in Eccles. x. 20) is hardly a figurative designation of those plotted against by the robbers, and threatened by treacherous schemes, so that the meaning would be "in vain do they lie in wait for their victims; these become aware of their danger, and so their prize escapes the assailants" (so DÖDERLEIN, ZIEGLER, BERTHEAU, ELSTER, *etc.*). For 1) the causal conj. "for" (כִּי) authorizes us to look for a direct reason for the warning contained in ver. 15; 2) the allusion to the possible failure of the plans of the wicked men would not be a moral motive, but a mere prudential consideration, such as would harmonize very poorly with the general drift of the passage before us; and 3) the expression "before the eyes" (בְּעֵינֵי) stands evidently in significant contrast with "in vain" (חִנָּם); it is designed to set the fact that the net is clearly in sight over against the fact that the birds nevertheless fly into it,—and so to exhibit their course as wholly irrational.—Therefore we should interpret with UMBREIT, EWALD, HITZIG, *etc.*, like thoughtless birds that with open eyes fly into the net, so sinners while plotting destruction for others plunge themselves in ruin. Only with this explanation, with which we may compare Job xviii. 8, will the import of ver. 18 agree: there "and these, these also" (וְהֵם) puts the sinners in an emphatic way side by side (not in contrast) with the birds, and the suffixes designate the *own* blood, the *own* souls of the sinners. Between the two verses there is therefore the relation of an imperfectly developed comparison suggested by the "also" (וְ) as in xxv. 25; xxvii.

21; comp. Introd., § 14. [The view of English expositors is divided, like that of the German scholars cited by our author. Bishop HALL, TRAPP, HENRY and NOYES, e. g. agree with him in finding here a comparison, while D'OYLY and MANT, HOLDEN, BRIDGES, WORDSWORTH, STUART, MUENSCHER find a contrast. The argument based on the particles כִּי and ‍ן it must be admitted has very little force; for כִּי (see EWALD, § 321, b.) may be used positively or negatively in intense asseveration, "yea, surely," or "nay;" while ‍ן, it is well known, has a very generous variety of uses, among which is the antithetic, in which case it may be rendered "but" or "and yet" (EWALD, § 330, a.).—A.].—**They lie in wait for their own lives.** The LXX, which at the end of this verse adds the peculiar but hardly genuine clause, ἡ δὲ καταστροφὴ ἀνδρῶν παρανόμων κακή ("and the destruction of transgressors is evil, or great") seems, instead of "they lie in wait for their own lives" (יִצְפְּנוּ לְנַפְשֹׁתָם), to have read "they heap up evil" (יִצְבְּרוּ רָע לִי); for it renders the second number by "θησαυρίζουσιν ἑαυτοῖς κακά" (they treasure up evils for themselves). Comp. HEIDENHEIM in the article cited in the Introd., § 13. note 1.—Ver. 19. Retrospect and conclusion; comp. Job viii. 13; xviii. 21.—Spoil (בֶּצַע) gain unlawfully acquired, as in xxviii. 16. The combination בֹּצֵעַ בָּצַע is found also in xv. 27. The subject of the verb "takes" (יָקַח) is בָּצַע; "the life of its owner it, unjust gain, takes away." LUTHER, following the LXX, Vulgate, and most of the ancient expositors, renders "that one (i. e., of the rapacious) takes life from another." But the idea "ownership, owner" (בְּעָלִים) has no reference to the relation between partners in violence and those like themselves, but to that existing between an object possessed and its possessor.

4. Vers. 20–33. After this warning against the desperate counsels of the wicked there follows in this second admonitory discourse a warning against the irrational and perverse conduct of fools. In the former case it was contempt of the fear of God, in the latter it is contempt of wisdom against which the warning is directed. Both passages, therefore, refer back distinctly to the motto that introduces them in ver. 7. The admonition against folly, which is now to be considered, is put appropriately into the mouth of wisdom personified,—as is also, later in the book, the discourse on the nature and the origin of wisdom (chap. viii. 1 sq).—On the street and in public places wisdom makes herself heard; not in secret, for she need not be ashamed of her teaching, and because she is a true friend of the people seeking the welfare of all, and therefore follows the young and simple, the foolish and ungodly, everywhere where they resort; comp. Christ's command to His disciples, Matt. x. 27; Luke xiv. 21. As in these passages of the New Testament, so in that before us, human teachers (the wise men, or the prophets, according to Ecclesiast. xxiv. 33; Wisdom vii. 27) are to be regarded as the intermediate instrumentality in the public preaching of wisdom.—Ver. 21. **In the places of greatest tumult she calleth,** etc. "The tumultuous" (הֹמִיּוֹת), comp. Isaiah xxii. 2; 1 Kings i. 41, can signify here nothing but the public streets full of tumult, the thoroughfares. The "beginning" (רֹאשׁ) of these highways or thoroughfares is, as it were, their corner; the whole expression points to boisterous public places. The LXX seem to have read חוֹמוֹת "walls," since it translates ἐπ' ἄκρων τειχέων [on high walls]. Before the second clause the same version has the addition "ἐπὶ δὲ πύλαις δυναστῶν παρεδρεύει" [and at the gates of the mighty she sits], an expansion of the figure in which there is no special pertinence. **In the city** (בָּעִיר) is probably to be regarded as a closer limitation of "at the entrances of the gates" (פִּתְחֵי שְׁעָרִים), i. e., on the inner, the city side of the entrances at the gates: it is not then to be regarded as an antithesis, as UMBREIT, BERTHEAU, HITZIG, etc., claim, [nor is it to be detached and connected with the next clause, as STUART claims].—Ver. 22. **How long, ye simple, will ye love simplicity?** The discourse of Wisdom begins in the same way as Ps. iv. 2. In regard to the distinction between "simple" (פֶּתִי) and "scorner" (לֵץ), comp. Introd. § 3, note 2; and above, the remarks on ver. 4.—The perfect tense in the second clause (חָמְדוּ), which standing between the imperfects of the 1st and 3d clauses is somewhat unusual, is to be conceived of as inchoative (like the verb "despise" בָּזוּ in ver. 7), and therefore properly signifies "become fond of," and not "be fond of." [See, however, the critical note on this verse].—Ver. 23. **Turn ye at my reproof.**—i. e., from your evil and perverse way. **I will pour out upon you my spirit.** The spirit of wisdom is to flow forth copiously, like a never-failing spring; comp. xviii. 4; and with reference to the verb "pour out" (הַבִּיעַ) which "unites in itself the figures of abundant fullness and refreshing invigoration" (UMBREIT, ELSTER) comp. xv. 2; Ps. lxxviii. 2; cxix. 171.—Ver. 24, in connection with 25, is an antecedent clause introduced by "because" (יַעַן), to which vers. 26, 27 correspond as conclusion. The perfects and imperfects with ן consec. in the protasis describe a past only in relation to the verbs of the apodosis, and may therefore well be rendered by the present, as LUTHER has done: "Because I call and ye refuse," etc. To **stretch forth the hand,** in order to beckon to one, is a sign of calling for attention,—as in Isa. lxv. 2. The verb in ver. 25, f. c. (פָּרַע) is doubtless not "undervalue, despise" as HITZIG explains, following the analogy of the Arabic), but "cast off, reject," as in iv. 15, (UMBREIT, EWALD, ELSTER and commentators generally; comp. LUTHER's "let go, fahren lassen"). [As between the two the English Version is equivocal, "set at naught"].—Ver. 26. "Laugh" and "mock" (שָׂחַק and לָעַג) here as in Ps. ii. 4.— Ver. 27 depicts the style and manner in which calamity comes upon fools, "and accumulates

expression to work upon the fancy" (HITZIG). Instead of the K'thibh כשואה according to the K'ri we should read כְּשׁוֹאָה, and this should be interpreted in the sense of "tempest" (comp. iii. 25; Zeph. i. 15). Thus most commentators correctly judge, while HITZIG defends for the expression the signification "cataract," which however is appropriate in none of the passages adduced, and also fails in Job xxx. 14 (comp. DELITZSCH on this passage).—In regard to the alliteration צָרָה וְצוּקָה **distress and anguish,** comp. Isa. xxx. 6; Zeph. i. 15.—Ver. 28. **They shall seek me diligently.** שָׁחַר, a denominative verb from שַׁחַר, "the morning dawn," signifies to seek something while it is yet early, in the obscurity of the morning twilight, and so illustrates eager, diligent seeking. [Of the recent commentators in English, NOYES only retains and emphasizes the rendering of the E. V., "they shall seek me *early*." The rest do not find the idea of *time* in the verb, except by suggestion.—A.]. Comp., with respect to the general idea of the verse, Prov. viii. 17; Hos. v. 15. [Observe also the force of the transition from the 2d person of the preceding verse, to the 3d person in this and the verses following.—A.].— Ver. 29. The "because" (תַּחַת כִּי) is not dependent on ver. 28, but introduces the four-fold antecedent clause (vers. 29, 30), which ver. 31 follows as its conclusion. With ver. 31 comp. Is. iii. 10; Ps. lxxxviii. 3; cxxiii. 4, where the figure of satiety with a thing expresses likewise the idea of experiencing the evil consequences of a mode of action. מוֹעֵצוֹת, evil devices, as also Ps. v. 10.—Vers. 32, 33. Confirmatory and concluding propositions, connected by "for" (כִּי).— מְשׁוּבָה; turning away from wisdom and its salutary discipline, therefore resistance, rebelliousness. Comp. Jer. viii. 5, Hos. xi. 5, where it signifies turning away or departure from God. "Security" (שַׁלְוָה) idle, easy rest, the carnal security of the obdurate; comp. Jerem. xxii. 21. A beautiful contrast to this false case is presented in the true peace of the wise and devout, as ver. 33 describes it.

DOCTRINAL AND ETHICAL.

As long ago as the time of MELANCHTHON it was recognized as a significant fact, that wisdom claims as her hearers and pupils not only the simple, the young and the untaught, but those also who are already advanced in the knowledge of truth, the wise and experienced. He remarks on ver. 5: "To his proposition he adds an admonition what the hearer ought to be. A wise hearer will profit, as saith the Lord: To him that hath shall be given. And again, He shall give the Holy Spirit to those that seek, not to those that despise, not to those that oppose with barbarous and savage fierceness. These despisers of God, the Epicureans and the like, he here says do not profit, but others, in whom are the beginnings of the fear of God, and who seek to be controlled by God, as it is said: Ask and ye shall receive."* Susceptibility therefore both must manifest,—those who are beginners under the instruction of wisdom, and those who are more advanced; otherwise there is no progress for them. It is indeed divine wisdom in regard to the acquisition of which these assertions are made; and in the possession of this wisdom, and in the communication of it as a teacher, no man here below ever attains perfection, so as to need no further teaching. It is precisely as it is within the department of the New Testament with the duty of faith, and of growth in believing knowledge, which duty in no stage of the Christian life in this world ever loses its validity and its binding power. Comp. Luke xvii. 5; Eph. iv. 15, 16; Col. i. 11: ii. 19; 2 Thess. i. 3; 2 Pet. iii. 18.

2. **The thoroughly religious character of wisdom** as our book designs to inculcate it, appears not only in the jewel which sparkles foremost in its necklace of proverbs (ver. 7: "The fear of Jehovah is the beginning of wisdom, *etc.*"), but also in the fact that in the introductory admonition, in ver. 10, it is **Sinners** (so designated without preamble or qualification), the חַטָּאִים (LUTHER, "the base knaves," *die bösen Buben*), whose seductive conduct is put in contrast with the normal deportment of the disciple of wisdom. Observe further that in the very superscription, vers. 2 and 3, the ideas of discipline, righteousness, justice and uprightness are appended to that of wisdom as synonymous with it. The wise man is therefore *eo ipso*, also the just, the pious, the upright, the man who walks the way of truth. Inasmuch, however, as the ideas of righteousness, justice and uprightness (מֵישָׁרִים, מִשְׁפָּט, צֶדֶק), here, as every where else ... the Old Testament, express the idea of correspondence with the revealed moral law, *the* law, the law of Moses, therefore the wise man is the man who acts and walks in accordance with law, the true observer of the law, who "walks in all the commandments and ordinances of the Lord blameless" (Luke i. 6; comp. Deut. v. 33; xi. 22; Ps. cxix. 1). True wisdom, knowledge, and spiritual culture, are to be found within the sphere of Old Testament revelation only where the law of the Lord is truly observed. Mere morality in the sense of the modern humanitarian free-thinking and polite culture could not at all show itself there; moral rectitude must also always be at the same time legal rectitude. Nay it stands enacted also under the New Testament that "whosoever shall break one of these least commandments, and shall teach men so, shall be called the least in the kingdom of heaven" (Matth. v. 19); that "the weightier matters of the law, judgment, mercy and faith," together with its less significant demands, must be fulfilled (Matth. xxiii. 23); that he only can be called a possessor of "the wisdom that is from above," and "a perfect man," who "offends not in word" (James iii. 2, 17). The fear of the Lord, which according to ver. 7 is the beginning of wisdom, while again in ver. 29 it is

---

* *Propositioni addit admonitionem, qualem oportet auditorem esse. Sapiens auditor proficiet, sicut Dominus inquit: Habenti dabitur. Item: Dabit spiritum sanctum petentibus, non contemnentibus, non repugnantibus barbarica et cyclopica ferocia. Hos contemptores Dei, ut Epicureos et similes, ait hic non proficere, sed alios, in quibus sunt initia timoris Dei, et qui petunt se regi a Deo, sicut dicitur Petite et accipietis.*

presented as the synonyme of the same idea (comp. ii. 5; ix. 10, etc.) consists, once for all, in a complete devotion to God, an unconditional subjection of one's own individuality to the beneficent will of God as revealed in the law (comp. Deut. vi. 2, 13; x. 20; xiii. 4; Ps. cxix. 63, etc.). How then can he be regarded as fearing God, who should keep only a part of the divine commands, or who should undertake to fulfil them only according to their moral principle, and did not seek also to make the embodying letter of their formal requirements the standard of his life—in the Old Testament with literal strictness, in the New Testament in spirit and in truth?

From these observations it will appear what right BRUCH has to maintain (in the work before cited, p. 128), that in the collection of the Proverbs of Solomon, and in general in the gnomic writers of Israel, the idea of wisdom is *substituted* for that of righteousness which is common in other parts of the Old Testament. Righteousness and wisdom according to this view would be essentially exclusive the one of the other; since the former conception "had usually attached itself to a ceremonial righteousness through works," and had appeared "to make too little reference to the theoretical conditions of all higher moral culture." In the Introduction, (§ 15, note) we have already commented on the one-sidedness and the misconception involved in this view, according to which the doctrine of wisdom (the Hhokmah-system) was Antinomian and rationalistic in the sense of the purely negative Protestantism of modern times. Further arguments in its refutation we shall have occasion to adduce in the exposition of the several passages there cited (see particularly xiv. 9; xxviii. 4 sq.; xxix. 18, 24, etc.) See also the doctrinal observations on iii. 9.

3. That the reckless transgressor destroys himself by his ungodly course, that he runs with open eyes into the net of destruction spread out before him, and, as it were, lies in wait for his own life to strangle it,—this truth clearly presented in vers. 17, 18 is a characteristic and favorite tenet in the teaching of wisdom in the Old Testament. Comp. particularly chap. viii. 36, where wisdom exclaims "Whoso sinneth against me, wrongeth his own soul; all they that hate me love death." So also xv 32; xxvi. 27; Eccles. x. 8; Ps. vii. 15; Ecclesiast. xxvii. 29 (the figure of the pit which the wicked digs, to fall into it at last himself). But in the Prophets also essentially the same thought recurs; thus when Jehovah (in Ezek. xviii. 31; xxxiii. 11) exclaims "Why will ye die, ye of the house of Israel?" Of passages from the New Testament we may cite here Rom. ii. 5; 1 Tim. vi. 9, 10; Gal. vi. 8; James v. 3–5, etc. Both propositions are alike true, that true wisdom, being one with the fear of God and righteousness, is "a tree of life to all that lay hold upon her" (Prov. iii. 18; xi. 30; xv. 4; comp. iv. 13, 22; xix. 23, etc.),—and that on the other hand a walking in folly and in forgetfulness of God is a slow self-murder, a destruction of one's own life and happiness. See the two concluding propositions of our chapter (vers. 32, 33) and the admirable poetic development of this contrast in the Ps. i. 4. The explanation given above (on ver. 20) of the fact that wisdom is exhibited as preaching upon the streets, *i. e.*, in reference to her benevolent and philanthropic character, which impels her to follow sinners, and to make the great masses of the needy among the people the object of her instructive and converting activity, seems to us to correspond better with the spirit of the doctrine of wisdom in the Old Testament, than either that of UMBREIT, according to which "it is only in busy life that the rich stream of experience springs forth, from which wisdom is drawn," or that of EWALD, which recognizes, in the free public appearance of wisdom an effective contrast to the light-shunning deeds, and the secret consultations of the sinners who have just been described, (which explanation, besides, would apply only to this passage, and not to its parallels in viii. 2, 3, and ix. 3). The tendency of the Old Testament Hhokmah was essentially popular, looking to the increased prosperity of the nation, to the promotion of philanthropic ends in the noblest sense of the word. Love, true philanthropy is everywhere the keynote to its doctrines and admonitions. "Forgiving, patient love (x. 12), love that does good even to enemies (xxv. 11 sq.), which does not rejoice over an enemy's calamity (xxiv. 17 sq.), which does not recompense like with like (xxiv. 28 sq.), but commits all to God (xx. 22), love in its manifold varieties, as conjugal love, parental love, the love of a friend, is here recommended with the clearness of the New Testament and the most expressive cordiality." (DELITZSCH, as above cited, p. 716). Why then should not that yearning and saving love for sinners which ventures into the whirl and tumult of great crowds to bear testimony to divine truth, and to reclaim lost souls,—why should not this also constitute a chief characteristic in this spiritual state modelled so much like the standard of the New Testament? It appears—in how many passages!—as the type of, nay, as one with the spirit of Him who also "spake freely and openly before the world, in the synagogue and in the temple whither the Jews always resorted" (John xviii. 20); who, when He said something in secret to His disciples, did it only to the end that they should afterward "preach it upon the housetops" (Matth. x. 27); who allowed himself to be taunted as "a man gluttonous, and a wine-bibber, a friend of publicans and sinners," because He had come to seek and to save the lost (Matth. xi. 19; Luke xix. 10). It is at least significant that the Lord, just in that passage in which he is treating of the publicity of His working, and of the impression which His condescending intercourse with publicans, sinners and the mass of the people had made upon the Jews, designates Himself distinctly (together with His herald and forerunner, John the Baptist) as the personal Wisdom; Matth. xi. 19; Luke vii. 35. It is as though He had by this expression intended to call up in fresh remembrance Solomon's representation of wisdom preaching in the streets, and to refer to His own identity with the spirit of the Old Testament revelation that spoke through this wisdom (the "spirit of Christ," 1 Pet. i. 11). Comp. MART. GEIER and STARKE on this passage. These authors appropriately remind us of the universality of the New Testament's proclamation of salvation, and its call penetrating everywhere (Rom. x. 18; Col. i. 6, 28); they are in error, however, in suspecting in the supposed plural חָכְמוֹת (ver. 18) an intimation of the numberless ways in which wisdom is proclaimed in the world. The true conception of this seeming plural may be found above in the Exegetical and Critical Notes on this passage.

HOMILETICAL AND PRACTICAL.

Homily upon the entire *first chapter*. Solomon's discourse upon wisdom as the highest good. 1) Its design, for young and old, learned and unlearned (vers. 1–6). 2) Its substance: commendation of the fear of God as the beginning and essence of all wisdom (ver. 7). 3) Its aim: *a)* warning against betrayal into profligacy as being the opposite of the fear of God (vers. 8–19); *b)* warning against the foolish conduct of the world as being the opposite of wisdom (vers. 20–33).—The wisdom of the Old Testament as a type of true Christian feeling and action: *a)* with respect to God as the supreme author and chief end of all moral effort (vers. 1–9); *b)* with respect to the world, as the seducing power, that draws away from communion with God (vers. 10–19); *c)* with respect to the way and manner in which Divine wisdom itself reveals itself as an earnest and yet loving preacher of righteousness (vers. 20–33).—Fear of God the one thing that is needful in all conditions of life: *a)* in youth as well as in age (vers. 4 sq.); *b)* in circumstances of temptation (vers. 10 sq.); *c)* in the tumult and unrest of public life (vers. 20 sq.); *d)* in prosperity and adversity (vers. 27 sq.).

STÖCKER:—Threefold attributes of the lover of wisdom: 1) in relation to God: the fear of God (1-7); 2) in relation to one's neighbors,—and specifically, *a)* to one's parents: obedience (8, 9); *b)* to others: the avoidance of evil company (10-19); 3) in relation to one's self: diligent use of the opportunity to become acquainted with wisdom.

Separate passages.—Vers. 1-6. See above, Doctrinal and Ethical principles. 1.—

STARKE:—The aim of the book, and that which should be learned from it, are pointed out in these verses in various almost equivalent words. The aim is, however, substantially twofold: 1) that the evil in man be put away; 2) that good be learned and practised.—WOHLFARTH:—the necessity of the culture of our mind and heart. Not the cultivated, but the undisciplined, oppose the law! God "will have all men come to the knowledge of the truth," 1 Tim. ii. 4.—[Ver. 4. CARTWRIGHT (quoted by BRIDGES): —"Over the gates of Plato's school it was written—Μηδείς ἀγεωμέτρητος εἰσίτω—Let no one who is not a geometrician enter. But very different is the inscription over these doors of Solomon— Let the ignorant, simple, foolish, young, enter!"]

Vers. 7-9. The blessedness of the fear of God, and the unblessed condition of forgetfulness of God,—illustrated in the relation 1) of children to their parents; 2) of subjects to authorities; 3) of Christians to Christ, the Lord of the Church. —The proposition "The fear of the Lord is the beginning of wisdom" must constitute the foundation of all the culture of the children of God, as the experience of the truth that "to love Christ is better than all knowledge" is to constitute its capstone and completion.—Vers. 8, 9, in general a peculiarly appropriate text for a sermon on education.—LUTHER (a marginal comment on ver. 7): "He who would truly learn must first be a man fearing God. He, however, who despises God asks for no wisdom, suffers no chastisement nor discipline."—MELANCHTHON (on ver. 7):—The fear of God, which is one with true reverence for God, includes: 1) right knowledge of God; 2) a genuine standing in fear before God; 3) faith, or the believing consecration to God, which distinguishes this fear from all servile dread, and fleeing from God; 4) the worship of God which aids to a true reconciliation with Him, a well ordered and assured control of the whole life. Therefore the fear of God is not merely beginning—it is quite the sum of all wisdom, the right manager of all our counsels in prosperity and adversity.—MELANCHTHON (again) on vers. 8, 9:—He only reveals genuine fear of God who hearkens to the divinely instituted ministry (*ministerium docendi*) in the Church; and to this ministry parents also belong, so far forth as they are to "bring up their children in the nurture and admonition of the Lord," Eph. vi. 4. "Forsake not the law of thy mother," *i. e.*, hearken always to the word of God as it has been communicated to the Church, and through the Church to all the children of God in the writings of the Prophets and Apostles. As a reward God here promises to those who practise this obedience to His word a wreath upon the head and a beautiful necklace about the neck. The wreath betokens dominion, distinction, successful results in all that one undertakes for himself and others, so that he becomes an instrument of blessing and a vessel of mercy for the people of God, according to the type of the devout kings, David, Jehoshaphat, Hezekiah, *etc.*, and not a vessel of wrath after the likeness of a Saul, Absalom, *etc.* The necklace signifies the gift of discourse, or of the command of wholesome doctrine, through the power of the word.—STARKE (on ver. 7):—True wisdom is no such thing as the heathen sages taught, built upon reason and the human powers, inflated, earthly, and useless with respect to salvation: but it is "the wisdom that is from above, which is first pure, then peaceable, gentle and easy to be entreated, full of mercy and good fruits, without partiality and without hypocrisy" (James iii. 17). The fear of God is, however, of two kinds, the servile and the childlike; and only the latter is here meant, 1 John iv. 18.—On Vers. 8, 9. From the fear of God as belonging to the first table of the law, Solomon passes on to the second table, and begins with obedience to parents: in this connection however it is assumed that parents also fulfil their duty, with regard to the correct instruction of their children; Eph. vi. 4.—ZELTNER:—Many simple ones, who, however, fear God from the heart, have made such progress in the knowledge of the Holy Scriptures, that they have outstripped many of the learned. True wisdom is easy to be learned, if only there be true fear of God in the heart, Ecclesiast. i. 22 sq.—LANGE:—(*Salom. Licht und Recht*). The fear of God is a desire flowing from the knowledge of the essence of all essences—of the will and the gracious acts of God,—a sincere desire heartily to love Him as the highest good, in deepest humility to honor Him, in child-like confidence to hope the best from Him, and to serve Him with denial of self, willingly and steadfastly; and all this in conformity to His revealed will. Comp. above, MELANCHTHON, and also S. BOHLIUS, *Ethica Sacra*: "To fear God is nothing but to follow God, or to imitate none but God."*

[Ver. 7. ARNOT:—"What God is inspires awe; what God has done for His people commands affection. See here the centrifugal and centripetal forces of the moral world, holding the creature reverently distant from the Creator, yet compassing the child about with everlasting love, to keep him near a Father in heaven." —Ver. 8. "This verse of the Proverbs flows from the same well spring that had already given forth the fifth commandment."]

Vers. 10-19 *Calwer Handbuch*: The first rule for youth, "Follow father and mother," is immediately followed by the second, "Follow not base fellows."—STARKE:—As a good education of children lays the first foundation for their true well being, so temptation lays the first foundation for their destruction.—The world, in order the better to lead others astray, is wont to adorn its vices with the finest colors. There be most of all on thy guard; where the world is most friendly it is most dangerous. It is a poisoned sweetmeat.—If thou art God's child, engrafted in Christ the living vine by holy baptism, thou hast received from Him new powers to hate evil and conquer all temptations.—On vers. 16-19:—The ungodly have in their wickedness their calamity also,—and must (by its law) prepare this for one another.—LUTHER (marginal comment on ver. 17): "This is a proverb, and means "It fares with them as is said, 'In vain is the net,' *etc.*; *i. e.*, their undertaking will fail, they will themselves perish."

[Ver. 10. ARNOT:—This verse, in brief compass and transparent terms, reveals the foe and the fight. With a kindness and wisdom altogether paternal, it warns the youth of the *Danger* that assails him, and suggests the method of *Defence*.]

Ver. 20 sq. GEIER (on ver. 20, 21):—"All this declares the fervor and diligence of heavenly wisdom in alluring and drawing all to itself: just as a herald with full lungs and clear voice endeavors to summon all to him."—LANGE:—Eternal wisdom sends forth a call of goodness and grace to the pious, and a call to holiness and righteousness addressed to the ungodly. O that all would read and use aright this record written out thus in capitals!—*Calwer Handb*.:—Wisdom's walk through the streets. The Lord and His Spirit follows us every where with monition and reminder. Here wisdom is portrayed especially as warning against the evil consequences of disobedience, and as pointing to the blessings of obedience.—WOHLFARTH: The words of grief over the unthankfulness and blindness of men which Solomon here puts into the mouth of wisdom,— we hear them, alas! even to-day. Truth has become .... the common property of all men: in thousands upon thousands of churches and schools, from the mouth of innumerable teachers, in millions of written works, it speaks, instructs, warns, pleads, adjures, so that we with wider meaning than Solomon can say, it is preached in highways and byways. If, on the one hand, we must greatly rejoice over this, how should we not in the same measure mourn that so many despise and scorn this call of wisdom! Is it not fearful to observe how parents innumerable keep their children from schools—how many despise the preaching of the gospel, *etc.*? Let us therefore learn how slow man is to good, how inclined to evil, how careless he is just in connection with his richest privileges, *etc.*

Vers. 22 sq. STARKE:—Wisdom divides men here into three classes: 1) The simple or foolish; 2) mockers; 3) the abandoned. Through her call, "Turn you at my reproof," *etc.*, she aims to transform these into prudent, thoughtful, devout men. —No one can receive the Holy Spirit of Christ and be enlightened with Divine wisdom, and not turn to the sacrifice of Christ (John xiv. 15 sq.—xvi. 7 sq.), renounce evil, and begin a new life (Ps. xxxiv. 15).—LANGE:—If man does not follow the counsel of eternal wisdom, but walks according to the impulse of his own will, he comes at last to the judgment of obduracy.—W. STEIN (Fast day sermon on i. 23-33):—How does eternal, heavenly wisdom aim to awaken us to penitence? 1) She uncovers our sins; 2) she proclaims heavy judgments; 3) she offers us shelter and points out the way of eternal salvation.—[Ver. 23. FLAVEL:—This great conjunction of the word and Spirit makes that blessed season of salvation the time of love and of life.—J. HOWE:—When it is said, "Turn," *etc.*, could any essay to turn be without some influence of the Spirit? But that complied with tends to pouring forth a copious effusion not to be withstood.—ARNOT:— The command is given not to make the promise unnecessary, but to send us to it for help. The promise is given not to supersede the command, but to encourage us in the effort to obey.—When we turn at His reproof, He will pour out His Spirit; when He pours out His Spirit, we will turn at His reproof; blessed circle for saints to reason in.—Ver. 24-28. ARNOT:—When mercy was sovereign, mercy used judgment for carrying out mercy's ends; when mercy's reign is over and judgment's reign begins, then judgment will sovereignly take mercy past, and wield it to give weight to the vengeance stroke.—Ver. 32. SOUTH:—Prosperity ever dangerous to virtue: 1) because every foolish or vicious person is either ignorant or regardless of the proper ends and rules for which God designs the prosperity of those to whom He sends it; 2) because prosperity, as the nature of man now stands, has a peculiar force and fitness to abate men's virtues and heighten their corruptions; 3) because it directly indisposes them to the proper means of amendment and recovery.—BAXTER:—Because they are fools they turn God's mercies to their own destruction; and because they prosper, they are confirmed in their folly.]

---

* "*Timere Deum nihil aliud est quam sequi Deum sive neminem imitari præter Deum.*"

3. Exhibition of the blessed consequences of obedience and of striving after wisdom.

Chap. II. 1–22.

1 My son, if thou receivest my words
 and keepest my commandments by thee,
2 so that thou inclinest thine ear to wisdom,
 and turnest thine heart to understanding;
3 yea, if thou callest after knowledge,
 to understanding liftest up thy voice;
4 if thou seekest her as silver,
 and searchest for her as for hidden treasure;
5 then shalt thou understand the fear of Jehovah,
 and find knowledge of God;—
6 for Jehovah giveth wisdom,
 from his mouth (cometh) knowledge and understanding:
7 and so he layeth up for the righteous sound wisdom,
 a shield (is he) for them that walk uprightly,
8 to protect the paths of justice,
 and guard the way of his saints;—
9 then shalt thou understand righteousness and justice
 and uprightness,—every good way.
10 If wisdom entereth into thine heart,
 and knowledge is pleasant to thy soul,
11 then will discretion watch over thee,
 understanding will keep thee,
12 to deliver thee from an evil way,
 from the man that uttereth frowardness,
13 (from those) who forsake straight paths,
 to walk in ways of darkness;
14 who rejoice to do evil,
 who delight in deceitful wickedness;
15 whose paths are crooked,
 and they froward in their ways;—
16 to deliver thee from the strange woman,
 from the stranger who maketh her words smooth,
17 who hath forsaken the companion of her youth
 and forgotten the covenant of her God.
18 For her house sinketh down to death
 and to the dead (lead) her paths;
19 her visitors all return not again,
 and lay not hold upon paths of life.
20 (This is) that thou mayest walk in a good way
 and keep the paths of the righteous!
21 For the upright shall inhabit the land,
 and the just shall remain in it:
22 but the wicked are cut off from the land,
 and the faithless are driven out of it.

GRAMMATICAL AND CRITICAL.

[Ver. 1 sq. De Wette and Noyes conceive of the first two verses as not conditional, but as containing the expression of a direct and independent wish: *Oh that thou wouldest receive*, etc. The LXX, *Vulg.*, Luther, etc., make the first verse conditional, but find the apodosis in ver. 2. Muenscher finds in ver. 2 an independent condition, and not a mere sequence to the preceding; so Holden, with a slightly different combination of the parts of ver. 2: *If by inclining thine ear . . . thou wilt incline thine heart*, etc. M., H., Stuart and others find the apodosis of the series of conditional clauses in ver. 5, agreeing in this with the E. V. These diverse views do not essentially modify the general import of the passage. ZÖCKLER it will be observed finds the apodosis in vers. 5 and 9, vers. 6-8 being parenthetical.—A.].

Ver. 7. For the construction with the stat. constr. compare Isa. xxxiii. 15. [Compare GREEN, §§ 254, 9, b and 274, 2.]

Ver. 8. The infinitive לִנְצֹר is followed by the Imperf. יִשְׁמֹר as above in ver. 2. [For explanations of the nature and use of this infinitive construction see EWALD, § 237, c. The literal rendering would be "for the guarding, protection, keeping," etc." Whose keeping the paths, etc.? HOLDEN understands it of the righteous: "who walk uprightly by keeping the paths, etc." Most commentators understand it of God, who is "a shield for the protection, i. e., to protect, etc." ZÖCKLER in translation conforms the following Kal pret. to this infin., while most others reverse the process.—A.]

Ver. 10. [The כִּי with which the verse commences is differently understood, as conditional or temporal, or as causal. Thus E. V., N., M., "when wisdom, etc.;" S., K., VAN ESS, "for wisdom, etc.;" DE W., Z., "if wisdom, etc." Between the first and last there is no essential difference, and this view of the author is probably entitled to the preference.—A.].

The feminine דַּעַת, "knowledge" (which is used here, as in i. 7, as synonymous with חָכְמָה "wisdom") has connected with it the masculine verbal form יִנְעָם, because this expression "it is lovely" is treated as impersonal, or neuter, and חָיָה is connected with it as an accusative of object [acc. synecd., "there is pleasure to thy soul in respect to knowledge"]. Comp. the similar connection of דַּעַת with the masculine verbal form נָקֵל in chap. xiv. 6;—also Gen. xlix. 15, 2 Sam. xi. 25.

Ver. 11. [For the verbal form הַנַּרְכָּה, with נ unassimilated, "for the sake of emphasis or euphony," see BÖTT., § 1100, 3.—A.].

Ver. 12. רַע is a substantive subordinate to the stat. constr. דֶּרֶךְ as in viii. 13, or as in תַּהְפֻּכוֹת רָע ver. 14, in אַנְשֵׁי־רָע, chap. xxviii. 5, etc.

Ver. 18. שָׁחָה־בֵּיתָהּ. בַּיִת which is everywhere else masculine is here exceptionally treated as feminine; for שָׁחָה is certainly to be regarded as 3d sing. fem. from שׁוּחַ, and not with UMBREIT and ELSTER as a 3d sing. masc., for only שׁוּחַ and not שָׁחָה (to stoop, to bow) has the signification here required, viz., that of sinking (Lat. sidere). The LXX read שָׁתָה from שִׁית, and therefore translate: ἔθετο γὰρ παρὰ τῷ θανάτῳ τὸν οἶκον αὐτῆς [she set her house near to death] in which construction however שָׁתָה sidere, is incorrectly taken as transitive. [Both BÖTTCHER and FUERST recognize the possibility of deriving this form as a 3d sing. fem., either from שׁוּחַ or from שָׁחַח, which have a similar lutrans. meaning. To שִׁית neither RÜDIGER (GESEN. Thes.) nor ROBINSON's Gesenius, nor FUERST gives any other than a transitive meaning.—A.]. Perhaps BÖTTCHER (De Inferis, §§ 201, 292; Neue Aehrenl., p. 1) has hit upon the true explanation, when he in like manner makes the wanton woman the subject, but treats בֵּיתָהּ not as object but as supplementary to the verb, and therefore translates "for she sinks to death with her house, and to the dead with her paths. [Rüb. (Thesaur. p. 1377, 3) expresses his agreement with B., but states his view differently: "de ipsa muliere cogitavit scriptor initio he-mistichii prioris, tum vero in fine ad complendam sententiam loco mulieris subjectum fecit בֵּיתָהּ." FUERST also pronounces it unnecessary to think of any other subject than בֵּיתָהּ.—A.]. Compare however HITZIG's comment on this passage, who remarks in defence of the common reading that בַּיִת is here exceptionally treated as feminine, because not so much the house itself is intended as "the conduct and transactions in it" (comp. vii. 27; Isa. v. 14).

Ver. 22. With יִקָּרֵתוּ, the expression which is employed also in Ps. xxxvii. 9, to convey the idea of destruction, there corresponds in the 2d clause יִסְּחוּ, which as derived from נסח (Deut. xxviii 63; Ps. lii. 5; Prov. xv. 25) would require to be taken as Imperf. Kal and accordingly to be translated actively: "they drive them out," i. e., they are driven out (so e. g., UMBREIT, ELSTER, and so essentially BERTHEAU also). But inasmuch as the parallelism requires a passive verb as predicate for בּוֹגְדִים (i. e., the faithless, those who have proved recreant to the theocratic covenant with Jehovah, comp. xi. 3, 6; xiii. 2; xxii. 12) which is employed unmistakably as synonymous with רְשָׁעִים,—and inasmuch as no verb נָסַח exists as a basis for the assumed Niphal form יִסְּחוּ, we must probably read with HITZIG יֻסְּחוּ, as an Imperf. Hophal from נָסַח and compare יֻקַּח as an Imperf. Hophal of לָקַח (used with the Pual of the same verb).

EXEGETICAL.

1. Vers. 1-9. This first smaller division of the chapter forms a connected proposition, whose hypothetical protasis includes vers. 1-4, while within the double apodosis (vers. 5 and 9) the confirmatory parenthesis, vers. 6-8 is introduced. The assertion of EWALD and BERTHEAU [with whom KAMPHAUSEN and STUART agree] that the entire chap. forms only one grand proposition, rests on the false assumption that the "if" כִּי in ver. 10 is to be regarded as a causal particle, and should be translated by "for,"—to which idea the relation of ver. 10 both to ver. 9 and to ver. 11 is opposed. Comp. UMBREIT and HITZIG on this passage. [On the other hand, the LXX, Vulg., LUTHER, etc., complete the first proposition, protasis and apodosis, within the first two verses; the Vulgate e. g. renders "si susceperis . . . inclina cor tuum, etc.," and LUTHER "willst du meine Rede annehmen . . . So lass dein Ohr u. s. w." The E. V. ends the proposition with ver. 5 as the apodosis.—A.].—**If thou receivest my words.** To the idea of "receiving" that of "keeping" stands related as the more emphatic, just as "commandments" (מִצְוֹת) is a stronger expression than "words" (אֲמָרִים). In the three following verses also we find this same increased emphasis or intensifying of the expression in the second clause as compared with the first,—especially in ver. 4, the substance of which as a whole presents itself before us as a superlative, or final culmination of the gradation which exists in the whole series of antecedent clauses, in so far as this verse sets forth the most diligent and intent seeking after wisdom.—Ver. 3. **Yea, if thou callest after knowledge,** i. e., if thou not only inclinest thine ear to her when she calls thee, but also on thine own part callest after her, summonest her to teach thee, goest to

meet her with eager questioning. This relation of climax to the preceding is indicated by the אם כי, imo, yea, rather; comp. Hos. ix. 12; Is. xxviii. 28; Job xxxix. 14 [comp. EWALD, § 343, b]. The Targum translates the passage "If thou callest understanding thy mother," and must therefore have read כי אם But the Masoretic pointing is to be preferred for lexical reasons (instead of אם, according to the analogy of Job xvi. 14 we should have expected אמי, "my mother"), and because of the parallelism between vers. 1 and 3. Still "knowledge" (בינה), as well as "understanding," which is named as its counterpart in the parallel clause, appears evidently as personified.—Ver. 4. **If thou seekest her,** etc.—"The figure of diligent seeking is taken from the tireless exertion employed in mining, which has before been described in the Book of Job, chap. xxviii., with most artistic vivacity in its widest extent. The מטמנים are surely the treasures of metal concealed in the earth (comp. Jerem. xli. 8; Jos. vii. 21)," UMBREIT. [For illustrations of the peculiar significance of this comparison to the mind of Orientals, see THOMSON's *Land and Book*, 1., 197.—A.].

Ver. 5. **Then wilt thou understand the fear of Jehovah.**—"Understand" is here equivalent to taking something to one's self as a spiritual possession, like the "finding" in the second clause, or like δέχεσθαι ["receiveth"] in 1 Cor. ii. 14. The "fear of Jehovah" (comp. i. 7) is here clearly presented as the highest good and most valuable possession of man (comp. Is. xxxiii. 6), evidently because of its imperishable nature (Ps. xix. 9), and its power to deliver in trouble (Prov. xiv. 26; Ps. cxv. 11; Ecclesiast. i. 11 sq.; ii. 7 sq.).—**And find knowledge of God.**—Knowledge of God is here put not merely as a parallel idea to the "fear of Jehovah" (as in chap. ix. 10; Is. xi. 2), but it expresses a fruit and result of the fear of Jehovah, as the substance of the following causal proposition in vers. 6-8 indicates. Comp. the dogmatical and ethical comments. [Is the substitution of *Elohim* for *Jehovah* (in clause 6) a mere rhetorical or poetical variation? WORDSWORTH calls attention to the fact that this is one of five instances in the Book of Proverbs in which God is designated as *Elohim*, the appellation Jehovah occurring nearly ninety times. The almost singular exception seems then to be intentional, and the meaning will be, the knowledge of "*Elohim*—as distinguished from the knowledge of man which is of little worth." In explaining the all but universal use of *Jehovah* as the name of God in our book, while in Eccles. it never occurs, WORDSWORTH says, "when Solomon wrote the Book of Proverbs he was in a state of favor and grace with Jehovah, the Lord God of Israel; he was obedient to the law of Jehovah; and the special design of the Book of Proverbs is to enforce obedience to that law," etc. (see Introd. to Eccles., p. 78)—A.].

Vers. 6-8. The Divine origin of wisdom must make it the main object of human search and effort, and all the more since its possession ensures to the pious at the same time protection and safety.—**And so he layeth up for the righteous sound wisdom.**—So we must translate in accordance with the K'thibb וְצָפַן which is confirmed by the LXX and *Pesch.* as the oldest reading. The K'ri יִצְפֹּן, without the copulative, would connect the proposition of ver. 7 with ver. 6 as essentially synonymous with it, to which construction the meaning is however opposed. [The majority of commentators prefer the K'ri, making this verse a continuation and not a consequence of the preceding. KAMPHAUSEN agrees with our author in what seems to us the more forcible construction, which has the advantage also of resting on the written text; comp. BÖTTCHER, § 929, b.—A.]. צָפַן to protect, to preserve, after the manner of a treasure or jewel, over which one watches that it may not be stolen; comp. above, ver 1, and also vii. 1; x. 14. —In regard to תּוּשִׁיָה [rendered "sound wisdom" by the E. V. here and in iii. 21; viii. 14; xviii. 1] properly prosperity and wisdom united, see Introd., § 2, note 3. The word is probably related to יֵשׁ, and denotes first the essential or actual (so e. g., Job v. 12), and then furthermore help, deliverance (Job vi. 13), or wisdom, reflection, as the foundation of all safety; so here and iii. 21; viii. 14; xviii. 1; Job xi. 6 sq.; Is. xxviii. 29. Comp. UMBREIT and HIRZEL on Job v. 12. HITZIG (on iii. 21) derives the word from the root שָׁוָה, which he says is transposed into וְשָׁה (??), and therefore defends as the primary signification of the expression "an even, smooth path," or subjectively "evenness," i. e., of thought, and so "considerateness;" he compares with this כִּישׁוֹר which signifies "plain" as well as "righteousness."—**A shield for them that walk blamelessly.**—The substantive מָגֵן (shield) is most correctly regarded as an appositive to the subject, "Jehovah:" for also in Ps. xxxiii. 20; lxxxiv. 11; lxxxix. 18, Jehovah is in like manner called a shield to His saints. In opposition to the accusative interpretation of מָגֵן [which is adopted by STUART among others], as object of the verb צָפַן (he secureth, or ensureth) we adduce, on the one hand, the meaning of this verb, and on the other the fact that we should expect rather הָיָה כְּמָגֵן (as an appositive to תּוּשִׁיָה). The old translations, as the LXX and Vulgate, furthermore read the word as a participle (מְגֵן or מָגֵן); they translate it by a verb (LXX: ὑπερασπιεῖ τὴν πορείαν αὐτῶν).—הֹלְכֵי תֹם, literally the "walkers of innocence," are the same as "those that walk uprightly," Prov. x. 9 (the הוֹלְכִים בַּתֹּם) or Ps. lxxxiv. 11 (the הוֹלְכִים בְּתָמִים).—**To protect the paths of justice,** etc.—The 8th verse gives more specifically the way in which God manifests Himself to the pious as a shield, and the ensurer of their safety. "Paths of justice" are here, by the substitution of the abstract for the concrete expression, paths of the just, and therefore essentially synonymous with the "way of the pious" in the second clause. Comp. chap. xvii. 23.—Ver.

9 carries out the import of the parallel ver 5 as the particle אָז repeated from the preceding verse shows.—**Every good path**—This expression (כָּל־מַעְגַּל־טוֹב) includes the three conceptions given above, justice, righteousness and integrity, and thus sums up the whole enumeration. Therefore, it is attached without a copula; comp. Ps. viii. ver. 9 b.

2. Vers. 10-19 form a period which in structure is quite like vers. 1-9; only that the hypothetical protasis is here considerably shorter than in the preceding period, where the conditions of attaining wisdom are more fully given, and with an emphatic climax of the thought. This is connected with the fact that in the former period the Divine origin of wisdom, here, on the contrary, its practical utility for the moral life and conduct of man forms the chief object of delineation. There wisdom is presented predominantly as the foundation and condition of religious and moral rectitude in general,—here specially as a power for the consecration of feeling and conduct, or as a means of preservation against destructive lusts and passions.—**If wisdom entereth into thine heart.**—This "coming into the heart" must be the beginning of all attaining to wisdom; then, however, she who has, as it were, been received as a guest into the heart must become really lovely and dear to the soul. There is, therefore, a climax of the thought, as above in vers 1-4 The *heart* is here, as always, named as the centre and organic basis of the entire life of the soul, as the seat of desire, and the starting point for all personal self-determination. The *soul*, on the contrary, appears as the aggregate and sum total of all the impulses and efforts of the inner man. The former designates the living centre, the latter the totality of the personal life of man. Comp. BECK, *Bibl. Seelenlehre*, p. 65; DELITZSCH, *Bibl. Psychol.*, pp. 248 sq.; VON RUDLOFF, *Lehre vom Menschen*, pp. 59 sq. What the last mentioned author, pp. 64 sq, remarks in criticism upon DELITZSCH'S too intellectual conception of the idea of the heart as the "birthplace of the thoughts,"—that every where in the Scriptures it appears to belong more to the life of desire and feeling, than to the intellectual activity of the soul,—this view finds foundation and support especially in the passage now before us, as well as in most of the passages which mention heart and soul together (*e. g.*, Prov. xxiv. 12; Ps. xiii. 2; Jerem. iv. 19; Deut. vi. 5; Matth. xxii. 37; Acts iv. 32). Comp. also HITZIG on this passage.—**And knowledge is pleasant to thy soul**—[For a peculiarity of grammatical structure in the original, see critical notes.]—Ver. 11. **Then will reflection watch over thee.** שָׁמַר עַל, as in vi 22. שָׁמַר (construed, however, with a mere accusative of the object) and נָצַר have already been found connected in ver. 8 above, and occur again in chap. iv. 6. מְזִמָּה here reflection, considerateness (LXX: βουλή καλή). properly "wisdom, so far forth as its direction is outward, and it presents itself in relation to the uncertain, testing it, and to danger, averting it" (HITZIG).

Ver. 12. **To deliver thee from an evil way**—properly "from the way of evil."—**From the man that uttereth perverseness.**—תַּהְפֻּכוֹת perverseness, a strong abstract form [found almost exclusively in Proverbs—FUERST] which expresses the exact opposite of מֵישָׁרִים ("uprightness," ch. 1. 3; ii. 9),—it is therefore deceitfulness, subtlety, maliciousness. Comp the expressions, "mouth of perverseness," chap. viii. 13; x. 32; "tongue of perverseness," x. 31; "man of perverseness," xvi. 28; also passages like vi. 14; xvi. 30; xxiii. 33.—Vers. 13-15 Closer description of the wayward or perversely speaking man, in which, because of the generic comprehensiveness of the conception אִישׁ, the plural takes the place of the singular.—**Who forsake straight paths**—The participle הָעוֹזְבִים expresses, strictly interpreted, a preterite idea, "those who have forsaken;" for according to ver. 15 the evil doers who are described are already to be found in crooked ways.—**In dark ways.**—Comp. Rom. xiii. 12; Eph. v. 11; 1 Thess. v. 5; also Job xxiv. 16; Is. xxix. 15.—**Deceitful wickedness**—literally "perverseness of evil" (comp. remarks on ver. 12) a mode of combining two nouns which serves to strengthen the main idea.—**Whose paths are crooked**—literally, "who in respect to their ways are crooked;" for the prefixed אָרְחֹתֵיהֶם is to be construed as an accusative of relation belonging to the following עִקְּשִׁים; comp. xix. 1; xxviii. 6. In the second clause in the place of this adverbial accusative, there is substituted the more circumstantial but clearer construction with בְּ "perverse *in* their ways."

Vers. 16-19. The representation passes into a warning against being betrayed by vile women, just as in v. 3; vi. 24; vii. 5 sq.—**From the strange woman, from the wanton woman.**—As "strange woman" (אִשָּׁה זָרָה) or a "wanton woman" (נָכְרִיָּה, properly "unknown," and so equivalent to "strange or foreign woman") the betrayer into unchastity is here designated, so far forth as she is the wife of another (comp. vi. 26), who, however, has forsaken her husband (ver. 17), and therein has transgressed also God's commandment, has broken the covenant with her God (ver. 17, l. c.)—The person in question is accordingly at all events conceived of as an Israelitess; and this is opposed to the opinion of those who, under the designation "the strange, or the foreign woman" (especially in connection with the last expression which appears as the designation of the adulteress in chap. v. 20; vi. 24; vii. 5; xxiii. 27), think first of those not belonging to the house of Israel, because the public prostitutes in Israel were formerly, for the most part, of foreign birth (so especially J. F. FRISCH: *Commentatio de muliere peregrina apud Ebræos minus honeste habita*. Leips., 1744, and among recent commentators, *e. g.*, UMBREIT). This view is in conflict with the context of the passage before us quite as decidedly as is the idea of the LXX, which interprets the foreign and wanton woman as the personification of temptation in contrast with wisdom (i. 20 sq.), but to carry out this view is obliged to introduce all manner of arbitrary relations,—*e. g.*, referring that of the "companion of youth" in ver. 17 to the instruction in Divine truth (διδασκαλία νεότητος), which was a guide in youth. It is decisive against this allegorical conception of the strange woman, which has been a favorite with some Christian expositors also, such as MELANCHTHON, JOACH. LANGE, CHR. B. MICHAELIS, that the wicked and perverse men in vers. 12-15 cannot possibly be interpreted figuratively, but certainly only as individual concrete representatives of moral evil. [This word נָכְרִיָּה is "especially applied to those 'strange women' whom Solomon himself loved in his old age, and who turned away his heart from the Lord his God, and beguiled him to favor and encourage the worship of their false gods (see 1 Kings xi. 1-8; comp. Neh. xiii. 26, 27). Here is a solemn lesson. Solomon warns his son against that very sin of which he himself was afterwards guilty. Thus by God's goodness Solomon's words in this Divinely inspired book were an antidote to the poison of his own vicious example." WORDSWORTH].—**Who maketh her words smooth**—*i. e.*, who knows how to speak flattering and tempting words; comp. vii. 21; Ps. v. 9; Rom. iii. 13.—Ver. 17. **The companion of her youth.**—The same expression occurs also in Jerem. iii. 4; comp. Ps. lv. 13, where אַלּוּף in like manner means companion, confidant. The forsaking of this "companion of youth," *i. e.*, the first lawful husband, is, at the same time, a "forgetting of the covenant of her God," *i. e.*, a forgetting, a wilful disregard of that which she has solemnly vowed to God. Marriage appears here not merely as a covenant entered into in the presence of God, but in a certain sense one formed with God. Quite similar is the representation in Mal ii. 14, where the adulterous Israelite is censured for the faithless abandonment of his אֵשֶׁת נְעוּרִים (wife of youth) because God was witness with her at the formation of the marriage covenant. That the marriages of the Israelites "were not consummated without sacred rites connected with the public religion, although the Pentateuch makes no mention of them," is accordingly a very natural assumption,—one which, *e. g.*, EWALD, BERTHEAU, HITZIG, REINKE, V. GERLACH, *etc.*, have made on the ground of the two passages here under consideration, especially the passage in Malachi. Yet compare besides A. KÖHLER on the latter passage (*Nachexil. Prophh.*, IV. 102 sq.), who finds there a witness of Jehovah, not at the consummation, but at the violation of marriage.— Vers. 18, 19. **For her house sinks down to death,** *etc.*—A reason for the strong expression in ver. 16, "to deliver thee from the strange woman."—**And to the dead her paths.**—The רְפָאִים (*i. e.*, properly the weak, languid, powerless [GESEN., *Thes.: quieti, silentes*,—FUERST, "the dark, the shadowy"]; comp. the εἴδωλα καμόντων of HOMER, and the *umbræ* of VIRGIL) are the dwellers in the kingdom of the dead (comp. ix.; xxi. 16; Ps. lxxxviii. 10; Is. xiv. 9; xxvi. 14, 18, 19), and stand here, like the Latin *inferi*, for the world of the dead, or Sheol itself.—**Her visi-** tors all return not again,—because from Sheol there is no return to the land of the living; see Job vii. 9, 10,—and comp. Prov. v. 5, 6.— **Paths of life,** as in Ps. xvi. 11; Prov. v. 6.

3. Vers. 20-22. While the לְמַעַן [in order that] is strictly dependent on ver. 11, and co-ordinate with the לְ of the two final clauses in vers. 12 sq. and 16 sq., still we are to recognize in the announcement of a purpose which it introduces, a conclusion of the entire admonitory discourse which this chapter contains,—an epilogue, as it were ("all this I say to thee in order that," *etc.*), which again may be resolved into a positive and a negative proposition (vers. 20, 21 and ver. 22).

UMBREIT's translation of לְמַעַן by "therefore" is ungrammatical, nor can it be justified by reference to passages like Ps. xxx. 12; li. 4; Hos. viii. 4.—**The upright shall inhabit the land.**—In the description of the highest earthly prosperity as a "dwelling in the land" (*i. e.*, in the native land, not upon the earth in general, which would give a meaning altogether vague and indefinite), we find expressed the love of an Israelite for his fatherland, in its peculiar strength and its sacred religious intensity. "The Israelite was, beyond the power of natural feeling, which makes home dear to every one, more closely bound to the ancestral soil by the whole form of the theocracy; torn from it he was in the inmost roots of life itself strained and broken. Especially from some Psalms belonging to the period of the exile this patriotic feeling is breathed out in the fullest glow and intensity. The same form of expression has also passed over into the New Testament, comp. Matth. v. 5, and also, with regard to the idea as a whole, Ps. xxxvii. 9, 11, 29; Prov. x. 30" (ELSTER).—**But the wicked shall be rooted out from the land.**—See critical notes above.

DOCTRINAL AND ETHICAL.

He only who seeks after wisdom, *i. e.*, who turns his practical efforts wholly toward it, and walks in its ways, finds true wisdom. For wisdom in the objective sense, is a gift of God, an effluence from Him, the only wise (Rom. xvi. 27). It can therefore come into possession of him alone who seeks appropriately to make his own the true subjective wisdom, which is aspiration after God and divine things; who in thought and experience seeks to enter into communion with God; who devotes himself entirely to God, subjects himself fully to His discipline and guidance, in order that God in turn may be able to give Himself wholly to him, and to open to him the blessed fulness of His nature.—This main thought of our chapter, which comes out with especial clearness in vers. 5, 6, is essentially only another side, and somewhat profounder conception, of the motto which, in i. 7, is prefixed to the entire collection, viz., that the fear of Jehovah is the beginning of wisdom,—or again, of the significant utterance in chap. xxviii. 5: "They that seek God understand all things." Within the limits of the New Testament we may compare above all else, what the Lord, in John vii. 17, presents as the condition of a full comprehension of Himself and of the divine truth revealed in Him: "If any man will do His will he shall know whether this doctrine be of God;" likewise: "Ask and it shall be given you; seek and ye shall find," etc. (Matt. vii. 7); and also: "Awake thou that sleepest, and arise from the dead, and Christ shall give thee light" (Eph. v. 14). Comp. further the passage from the Book of Wisdom (chap. vi. 12, 13), which MELANCHTHON, with perfect propriety, cites in this connection: "Wisdom is willingly found of them that seek her, yea, she cometh to meet and maketh herself known to those that desire her;" and also David's language: "In thy light do we see light" (Ps. xxxvi. 9), the well-known favorite motto of AUGUSTINE, which in like manner, as it was employed by the profound metaphysician MALEBRANCHE, ought to be used by all Christian philosophers as their daily watchword and symbol.

In the second section of this admonition (vers. 10-19) this true wisdom, to be conferred by God, to be found only with God, is more completely exhibited, on the side of its salutary influence upon the moral life of humanity, especially as a preserver against sin and vice and their ruinous consequences. After this in conclusion the epilogue (vers. 20-22) contrasts the blessed results of wise and righteous conduct and the punishment of ungodliness in strongly antithetic terms, which remind us of the close of the first Psalm and of the Sermon on the Mount (Matt. vii. 24-27; comp. Ps. i. 6). Comp. the exegetical comments on these two sections.

HOMILETIC.

Homily on the entire chapter: The main stages in the order of grace, contemplated from the point of view of the wisdom of the Old Testament: 1) The call (vers. 1-4); 2) Enlightenment (vers. 5, 6); 3) Conversion (vers. 7-10); 4) Preservation or sanctification (vers. 11-20); 5) Perfection (vers. 21, 22).—STARKE:—The order of proceeding for the attainment of true wisdom and its appropriate use: 1) the order for the attainment of wisdom consists in this,—that we a) ask for it, (1-3), b) search for it with care and diligence (4). 2) The wisdom thus attained is the only true wisdom, as appears a) from its own characteristics (5), b) from the person of its giver (6), c) from the conduct of the men who possess it (7, 8). 3) This only true wisdom is profitable, a) for the attainment of righteousness in faith and life (9-11), b) for deliverance from evil (12-19), c) for the steadfast maintenance of an upright life (20-22).—Simpler and better STÖCKER:—*Studiosi sapientiæ* 1) *officium* (1-8); 2) *præmium* (9-22). [The student of wisdom 1) in his duty, 2) in his reward].—*Calwer Handb.:* The way to wisdom consists 1) in listening to its call (1, 2); 2) in searching for it prayerfully (3-6); 3) in deference to that portion of wisdom which one has already attained, by earnestness in a holy walk (7-9); 4) in the experience of the power of wisdom, which lies in this, that it preserves from ways of evil, especially of impurity (10-22).

Vers. 1-9. MELANCHTHON:—"He admonishes how we may make progress (in wisdom): for he combines two causes: 1) God's aid; 2) our own zeal." (No. 2 ought here necessarily to have been put first—an improvement which was made by STÖCKER in his reproduction of this analysis of MELANCHTHON).—STÖCKER:—The rounds upon which one must, with divine help, climb up to the attainment of wisdom are seven: 1) eager hearing; 2) firm retention; 3) attentive meditation; 4) unquestioned progress; 5) due humiliation; 6) devoted invoking of God's help; 7) tireless self-examination.—[CHALMERS (on vers. 1-9):—The righteousness of our conduct contributes to the enlightenment of our creed. The wholesome reaction of the moral on the intellectual is clearly intimated here, inasmuch as it is to the righteous that God imparteth wisdom].—STARKE (on vers. 1-4):—As the children of the world turn their eyes upon silver and treasures, run and race after them, make themselves much disquiet to attain them, though after all they are but shadows and vanity; so ought the children of God to use much more diligence to attain heavenly wisdom, which endures forever, and makes the man who possesses it really prosperous.—[Vers. 1-6, BRIDGES:—Earthly wisdom is gained by study; heavenly wisdom by prayer. Study may form a Biblical scholar; prayer puts the heart under a heavenly pupilage, and therefore forms the wise and spiritual Christian. But prayer must not stand in the stead of diligence. Let it rather give life and energy to it.—ARNOT (vers. 2):—The ear inclined to divine wisdom will draw the heart: the heart drawn will incline the ear. Behold one of the circles in which God, for His own glory, makes His unnumbered worlds go round.—(Ver. 4). Fervent prayer must be tested by persevering pains.—TRAPP (ver. 2):—Surely as waters meet and rest in low valleys, so do God's graces in lowly hearts.—(Ver. 3). A dull suitor begs a denial].—STARKE (On vers. 5-9):—Righteousness of faith and righteousness of life are closely connected. As soon as the first exists (vers. 5-8) the other must also show itself in an earnest and pure walk before God and man, Luke i. 74, 75; Phil. i. 11.—LANGE (on ver. 6):—One may indeed by natural knowledge very readily learn that God is a very benevolent being; but how He becomes to a sinner the God of love, this can be learned only from the mouth of God in the Holy Scriptures.—[TRAPP (ver. 9):—"Thou shalt understand righteousness," not as *cognoscitiva*, standing in speculation, but as *directiva vitæ*, a rule of life.]

Vers. 10-22.—[Ver. 11. BRIDGES:—Before wisdom was the object of our search. Now, having found it, it is our pleasure. Until it is so it can have no practical influence.—ARNOT:—It is pleasure that can compete with pleasure; it is "joy and peace in believing" that can overcome the pleasure of sin.]—STÖCKER (on vers. 10-12):—Wisdom helps such as love her in all good, and preserves them against all evil; she directs them to the good and turns them from the evil way.—(On vers. 12-19):—Wisdom delivers from the three snares of the devil, viz., 1) from a godless life; 2) from false doctrine; 3) from impurity and licentiousness.—STARKE (on vers. 12 sq.):—Daily experience teaches us that we are by nature in a condition from which we need deliverance. But how few are there of those who are willing to be delivered, Matt. xxiii. 37!—(On vers. 20-22):—Not merely some steps in the right way, but continuing to the end brings blessedness, Matt. xxiv. 13!—Granted that for a time it goes ill with the godly in this world, God's word must nevertheless be made good, if not here, surely in eternity, Ps. cxxvi. 5.—[BRIDGES:—The spell of lust palsies the grasp by which its victim might have *taken hold of the paths of life* for his deliverance.]—HASIUS (on vers. 21, 22):—People who mean rightly neither with God nor men are with their posterity rooted out of the world. He who observes will even now see plain proofs of this, Ps. lxxiii. 19; xxxiv. 16.—VON GERLACH (on ver. 21:)—The meaning of the promise, so common in the law, of "the pious dwelling in the land" depends especially on the fact that Canaan was type and pledge of the eternal inheritance of the saints in light.

---

4. Continuation of the exhibition of the salutary results of a devout and pious life.

CHAP. III. 1-18.

1   My son, forget not my doctrine,
    and let thy heart keep my commandments;
2   for length of days and years of life
    and welfare will they bring to thee.
3   Let not love and truth forsake thee;
    bind them about thy neck,
    write them upon the tablet of thy heart;
4   so wilt thou find favor and good reputation
    in the eyes of God and of men.
5   Trust in Jehovah with all thy heart,
    and rely not on thine own understanding.
6   In all thy ways acknowledge him,
    and he will make smooth thy paths.
7   Be not wise in thine own eyes;
    fear Jehovah and depart from evil.
8   Healing will then come to thy body
    and refreshing to thy bones.
9   Honor Jehovah with thy wealth,
    and with the best of all thine income;
10 so will thy barns be filled with plenty
    and with new wine will thy vats overflow.
11 Jehovah's correction, my son, despise not,
    neither loathe thou his chastening;
12 for whom Jehovah loveth, him he chasteneth
    and holdeth him dear, as a father his son.
13 Blessed is the man that hath found wisdom,
    and he that attaineth understanding;
14 for better is its accumulation than the accumulation of silver,
    and her gain (is better) than the finest gold.
15 More precious is she than pearls,
    and all thy jewels do not equal her.
16 Long life is in her right hand,
    in her left hand riches and honor.
17 Her ways are ways of pleasantness,
    and all her paths (are paths) of peace.
18 A tree of life is she to those that lay hold upon her,
    and he who holdeth her fast is blessed.

5 Description of the powerful protection which God, the wise Creator of the world, ensures to the pious.

Chap. III. 19–26.

19 Jehovah hath with wisdom founded the earth,
   the heavens (hath he) established by understanding;
20 by his knowledge were the floods divided,
   and the clouds dropped down dew.
21 My son, never suffer to depart from thine eyes,
   maintain (rather) thoughtfulness and circumspection;
22 so will they be life to thy soul
   and grace to thy neck.
23 Then wilt thou go thy way in safety
   and thy foot will not stumble.
24 When thou liest down thou wilt not be afraid,
   and when thou liest down thy sleep is sweet.
25 Thou needst not fear from sudden alarm,
   nor from the destruction of the wicked when it cometh.
26 For Jehovah will be thy confidence
   and keep thy foot from the snare.

6. Admonition to benevolence and justice.

Chap. III. 27–35.

27 Refuse not good to him to whom it is due,
   when thine hands have power to do it.
28 Say not to thy neighbor: "Go and come again;"
   or "to-morrow I will give it"—while yet thou hast it.
29 Devise not evil against thy neighbor
   while he dwelleth securely by thee.
30 Contend with no man without cause,
   when he did thee no evil.
31 Imitate not the man of violence
   and choose none of his ways.
32 For an abhorrence to Jehovah is the deceiver,
   but with the upright he maintaineth true friendship.
33 Jehovah's curse dwelleth in the house of the wicked
   but the home of the just he blesseth.
34 If he scorneth the scorners,
   to the lowly he giveth grace.
35 Honor shall the wise inherit,
   but shame sweepeth fools away.

GRAMMATICAL AND CRITICAL.

Ver. 6.—[The idea of the verb יְיַשֵּׁר is not that of guidance [E. V.: "shall direct thy paths"], but that of making straight (Stuart), or, perhaps, better still, making smooth (Fuerst, De W., Kamph.).—A.]

Vers. 7, 8.—[אַל־תְּהִי. the "dehortative" use of the Jussive, Bött., § 964, 8; while in ver. 8 we have an example of the "desponsive" use—*it shall be*.—לְשָׁרְךָ. For the doubling of the ר by Dagesh see Bött., § 392 c. He explains it as "mimetic for greater vigor." Some texts carry this even into the succeeding ךְ, § 885, A. Fuerst (Lex., sub verbo) pronounces it unnecessary to change the vocalization as proposed by some commentators and preferred by Zöckler, and agrees with Umbreit in his view of the meaning.—A.]

Ver. 12.—In the ordinary rendering, "even as a father the son in whom he delighteth," or "whom he holds dear" [which is the rendering, e. g., of the E. V., De Wette, Stuart, Noyes, Muensch.], יִרְצֶה is construed as in a relative clause. But then we should expect rather the perfect רָצָה; and there should have been in the first clause a comparative proposition of like construction with the one before us. The LXX, from which Heb. xii. 5 is literally quoted in rendering which Holden adopts and defends, appears to have read כְּאָב instead of וּכְאָב, for it translates the second clause by μαστιγοῖ δὲ πάντα υἱὸν ὃν παραδέχεται [scourgeth every son whom he receiveth]. This old variation, however, appears to owe its origin to the endeavor to secure a better parallelism. [Kampn. adopts a slightly different rendering, which makes the latter part of the clause relative, but makes the relative the subject and not the object of the verb, thus obviating the objection in regard to tense; *and* (dealeth) *as a father* (who) *wisheth well to his son*. The אֶת for אֶת at the beginning of the verse is explained by Bött., § 362, 3, as the result of assimilation to the subsequent אֶת.—A.]

Ver. 18.—In the Hebrew וְתִמְכֶיהָ מְאֻשָּׁר the plural הַתֹּמְכִים is employed distributively, or, as it were, of undefined individuals, for which reason its predicate stands in the singular; comp. Gen. xlvii. 3; Num. xxiv. 9; Gesen., *Lehrgeb.*, p. 713; Ewald, § 309, a [Bött., § 702, 8]

Ver. 26.—The בְ in בְכִסְלֶךָ is the so-called בְ *essentiæ*, which serves for the emphatic and strengthened introduction of the predicate, as, *e. g.*, in בְּעֹזְרִי, Ex. xviii. 4 (Gesen., *Lehrgeb.*, 839, Ewald, *Lehrb*, 217 f.).

Ver. 27.—"When thy hands have power to do it;" literally "when thy hands are for God." With this phrase compare יֶשׁ לְאֵל יָד, Gen. xxxi. 29, Micah ii. 1; or אֵין לְאֵל יָד, Deut. xxviii. 32; Neh. v. 5. [The weight, both of lexicographical and exegetical authority, is, and, we think, plainly should be, against this view of the author. See, *e. g.*, Gesen. and Fuerst; אֵל has assigned to it distinctly the signification "strength," the abstract quality corresponding to the concrete, "the strong," *i. e.*, God. It belongs to the power—it is in the power]. Inasmuch as in these idioms the singular יָד always occurs, the K'ri reads in our passage also יָדְ, and the LXX for the same reason had translated ἡ χείρ σου (the translation being a free one; Frankel, *Vorstudien zur Septuaginta*, p. 239]. Yet there is no grammatical reason whatever for the change.

Ver. 28.—[לְרֵעֶיךָ, K'thibh, another distributive plural, where the K'ri has a singular; see Bött., §§ 702, d—866, c.—A.]

Ver. 30.—[Holden translates the last clause "surely he will return thee evil," because the ordinary rendering "gives to the word גָּמַל the sense of doing or performing, which it seems never to bear, but always that of *returning, requiting, recompensing*." The primary import, however, seems to be to *collect*, to *complete*, which fact, together with the tense, justifies the almost entire unanimity which sustains the ordinary rendering.—A.]

EXEGETICAL.

1. The close connection between this group of admonitions and chap. ii. appears at once externally in the resuming of the address "My son" (ii. 1), which recurs three times in chap iii , vers. 1, 11, 21,—without, however, for that reason, introducing in each instance a new paragraph; for in ver. 11 at least the series of admonitions beginning in ver. 1 continues in its former tone without interruption (comp. especially ver. 9),—and again the new commencement in ver. 21 does not equal in importance that in ver. 19 sq., or that in ver. 27 sq.—Hitzig maintains that vers. 22-26 are spurious, inasmuch as the promise of reward which it contains, after the earlier briefer suggestions of virtue's reward in vers. 4, 6, 8, 10, seems tedious and disturbing; inasmuch as their style of expression appears tame, prosaic, and even, in some degree, clumsy; inasmuch as there may be detected in them traces of a strange and later idiom (*e. g.*, the חַיִּים וְחֵן [life and grace] in ver. 22; the שׁוֹאָה [destruction] in ver. 25, the מִלֶּכֶד [from the snare] in ver. 26); and finally—the thing which appears in fact to have given the chief impulse to his suspicion—inasmuch as from the omission of these five verses there would result another instance of the decimal grouping of verses before we come again to the address to the "children" of wisdom in chap. iv. 1, just as before the בְּנִי [my son] in vers. 11 and 21 was repeated in each case after ten verses. But since no kind of external testimony can be adduced in support of this assumption of an interpolation, while, on the other hand, a version as old as the LXX contains the verses entire, the suspicion appears to rest on grounds wholly subjective, and to be supported by reasonings that are only specious. This is especially true of the fact that there are in each instance ten verses between the first addresses, "my son,"—which loses all its significance when we observe that in chap. i. the same address recurs at much shorter intervals,—that between the "my son" in chap. ii. 1 and the first in the third chapter there are no less than 22 verses,—and that finally the paragraphs or "strophes" formed by the repetition of this address in the two following chapters (iv. 10 sq.; iv. 20 sq.; v. 1 sq.) are by no means of equal length, and can be brought into uniformity only by critical violence (the rejection of chap. iv. 16, 17 and 27).—If we therefore cannot justify Hitzig's endeavor to produce by the exclusion of several verses a symmetrical external structure for our chapter, *i e.*, a division of it into three equal strophes, we are also obliged to differ with him when he conceives of the contents as mainly admonitory, in contrast with the more descriptive character of chap. ii. For here as there we find admonitions, direct or indirect, to the securing and retaining of wisdom (vers. 1, 3, 5, 7, 9, 11, 21, 27 sq.) alternating with delineations of the blessedness which becomes the portion of its possessors (vers. 4, 6 b, 8, 10, 22 sq., 32 sq.), or with praises of wisdom itself (vers. 13 sq., 19 sq.). Especially are the commencement and conclusion of the chapter in close correspondence with those of chap. ii., and accordingly justify our conception of the general import of the proverbial discourses which it contains, as being a sort of continuation of the longer discourse which constitutes the preceding chapter. Only in two points do we find essentially new material introduced into the representation, which is now mainly admonitory and again chiefly descriptive,—*viz.*, in vers. 19 sq., where the protecting and preserving power of wisdom is illustrated by a reference to God's creative wisdom as the original source and model of all human wisdom,—and in vers. 27 sq., where in the place of the previous admonitions of a more general nature there appears a special admonition to love of one's neighbor, as the sum and crown of all virtues. Therefore (with Delitzsch, comp. above, Introd., § 15) at each of these points we begin a new section.

2. *Continued representation of the salutary consequences of a wise and devout life.* Vers. 1-18.

Vers. 1, 2. **Forget not my teaching.**—The substance of this teaching (תּוֹרָה, as in i. 8), or the enumeration of the individual commands (מִצְוֹת) of which it consists, begins with ver. 3.—**Length of days**, properly "extension of days" (אֹרֶךְ יָמִים) as in Ps. xxi. 4), is a description of earthly prosperity as it is promised to wisdom for a reward. Comp. Ex. xx. 12; 1 Kings iii. 14. For that this long life is a happy one, a "living in the promised land" (Deut. iv. 40; v. 30; vi. 2; xi. 9; xxii. 7; xxx. 16), an "abiding in the house of the Lord" and under His blessing (Ps. xv. 1; xxiii. 6; xxvii. 3),—this is plainly assumed. Comp. the parallel expression שָׁלוֹם [peace] in the second member, which here, as below in ver. 17, describes the safety which belongs only to the pious, the religious peace of mind of which the ungodly know nothing (Is. xlviii. 22; lvii. 21).—Vers. 3, 4. The first of the commandments announced in ver. 1, with the corresponding promise of reward.—**Love and truth.**—These ideas חֶסֶד וֶאֱמֶת which are very often associated, in our Book, e. g., in xiv. 22; xvi. 6; xx. 28,—are, when predicated of man, the designation of those attributes in which the normal perfection of his moral conduct towards his neighbor expresses itself. חֶסֶד, which, as a Divine attribute, is equivalent to mercy or grace, designates "the disposition of loving sympathy with others, which rests upon the feeling of brotherhood, the feeling that all men are of like nature, creatures of the same God." This feeling, which is the prime factor in our moral life by which society is constituted, has for its natural basis the destitution and defencelessness of isolated man; from which springs the deeper necessity not only to augment power by mutual outward help, but also by the interchange of thoughts and emotions to effect a richer development of spiritual life, and to discern what in one's own feeling is purely individual, and what is common and eternal" (ELSTER). אֱמֶת then designates inward truthfulness, the *pectus rectum*, the very essence of a true man opposed to all hypocrisy and dissimulation, the endeavor to mould every form into the closest possible correspondence with the nature of the thing, on which depends all the reliableness and security of life's relations" (ELSTER, comp. UMBREIT). The proofs of a life regulated by "love" and "truth," and so of conduct toward one's neighbor, as loving as it is true, a genuine ἀληθεύειν ἐν ἀγάπῃ [truth in love, Eph. iv. 15] are suggested in the following admonitory discourse in vers. 27 sq.—**Bind them about thy neck**—not as talismans and amulets, as UMBREIT suggests, but simply as costly ornaments, which one wears upon the neck (comp. i. 9; also vii. 3); or again as treasures which one will secure against loss, and therefore (if valued like a signet ring, Gen. xxxviii. 18; Jer. xxii. 24) wears attached to a chain about the neck. The latter explanation, to which HITZIG gives the preference, seems to be favored especially by chap. vi. 21, and also by the analogy of the parallel expression "write upon the tablet of the heart," *i. e.,* thoroughly impress upon one's self and appropriate the virtues in question (love and truth—not perchance the "commandments" mentioned in ver. 1, of which C. B. MICHAELIS and others here think without any good reason); comp. Jer. xxxi. 33; 2 Cor. iii. 3 [" To bind God's law about the neck is not only to *do* it, not to *rejoice* in doing it; to put it on, and to exult in it as the fairest ornament." WORDSW.].—**So wilt thou find favor and good reputation**—literally, "and so find," *etc.* (וּמְצָא); the Imper. with ו *consec.* stands for an Imperf. (EWALD, *Lehrb.*, 235); for "by the command the certainty that obedience will follow is promoted." HITZIG. Comp. iv. 4; xx. 13; Gen. xlii. 8; Isa. viii. 9; xlv. 22. [BÖTT. calls this the "desponsive" imperative; see § 957, 6—A.].—"Find favor or grace" (מְצָא חֵן) as in Jer. xxxi. 2; 1 Sam. ii. 26; Luke ii. 52; only that in these passages, instead of "in the eyes of God" (*i. e.,* according to God's judgment, comp. Gen. x. 9; 2 Chron. xxx. 22) the simpler phrase "with God" (אֱלֹהִים, παρά) is combined with the formula under discussion.—**Good reputation.**—Thus we translate, as HITZIG does, the expression שֵׂכֶל טוֹב, which below in chap. xiii. 15, as in Ps. cxi. 10, conveys the idea of good understanding or sagacity [so the E. V., BERTHEAU, KAMPH., render it in this passage also]; but here, as in 2 Chron. xxx. 20, denotes the judgment awarded to any one, the favorable view or opinion held concerning any one. [FUERST, VAN ESS, *etc.,* prefer this rendering, while GESEN., DE W., STUART, NOYES, MUENSCHER translate "good success."—A.]. With this interpretation the "finding favor" will have reference more to God, the "finding good opinion or favorable judgment" predominantly to men. [KAMPH., however, insists that the idea is indivisible—universal favor.]

Vers. 5, 6. **Trust in Jehovah with all thine heart,** *etc.:* the fundamental principle of all religion, consisting in an entire self-committment to the grace and truth of God, with the abandonment of every attempt to attain blessedness by one's own strength or wisdom; comp. Ps. xxxvii. 3 sq.; cxviii. 8, 9; Jer. ix. 22.—**Regard him**, דָּעֵהוּ, strictly "take notice of him," *i. e.,* recognize Him as the unconditional controller over all thy willing and doing. Comp. the opposite: 1 Sam. ii. 12, and in general for this pregnant use of the verb יָדַע Ps. i. 6; xxxvii. 18; Am. iii. 2, *etc.*—Vers. 7, 8. **Fear Jehovah and depart from evil** (comp. xiv. 16; xvi. 6; Job i. 1; xxviii. 28); an absolute contrast to the first clause of the verse; for he who fears God distrusts his own wisdom, when this perchance presents evil and wayward action as something agreeable and desirable (Gen. iii. 5).—**Healing will then be** (come) **to thy body.** Thus probably is the phrase רִפְאוּת תְּהִי to be explained, with BERTHEAU and HITZIG,—for to express the idea "healing is this to thy body," (UMBREIT, EWALD, ELSTER, and most of the elder commentators) רְפָאוּת הִיא would rather have been required.—Instead of לְשָׁרֶּךָ thy navel (which, according to UMBREIT, here, unlike Ezek. xvi. 4; Song of Sol. vii. 3, is intended to be a designation of the whole body by a part of special physiological importance) it will probably be correct to read לְשָׁרֶךָ as a contraction of לִבְשָׂרֶךָ, or לִשְׁאֵרֶךָ as in chap. iv. 22. For translations as early as the LXX and Peshito express simply the idea "to thy body," to which furthermore the parallel "to thy bones" corresponds better (comp. xiv. 30; Micah iii. 2) than to the very far-fetched expression "to thy navel."—**Refreshing to thy bones.** שִׁקּוּי strictly irrigation, watering, then refreshing, invigoration; here in contrast with the "languishing of the bones" (Ps. xxii. 3, 4), i. e., their drying up under a fever heat or an inward anguish of soul, e. g., the pangs of a troubled conscience. Comp. Job xxi. 24; Is. lviii. 11.

Vers. 9, 10. **Honor Jehovah with thy riches.** The מִן in מֵהוֹנֶךָ and the following phrase מֵרֵאשִׁית כָּל־תְּבוּאָתֶךָ is certainly not to be construed as partitive, as though God was to be honored with a part only of one's wealth and of the first fruits of one's increase (so e. g., BERTHEAU), but the preposition מִן here expresses the idea of a coming forth out of something, as in Ps. xxviii. 7; 2 Kings vi. 27. In opposition to the comparative idea which EWALD endeavors to bring out from the מִן ("more than thy wealth") see HITZIG on this passage. With regard to the idea itself compare passages like Ex. xxiii. 19; Deut. xviii. 4 sq.; xxviii. 8 sq.; Mal. iii. 10-12. That the offering in sacrifice the first fruits of the field and of the other revenues of one's possessions or labors was not only enjoined by their law upon the people of God under the Old Testament, but that it was also practiced by other ancient nations as a usage connected with religious worship, appears from passages in classical authors, c. g., DIOD. SICUL. l.. 14; PLUT. de Iside, p. 377; PLINY'S Hist. Nat., 18, 2. Comp. in general SPENCER, De legibus Hebræorum ritualibus, p. 713, sq ("de primitiarum origine"). [Be not content with lip-service, but obey God's law by making the prescribed oblation and by bringing also free-will offerings to Him."—WORDSW. Our author's notes, in their distinct recognition of the first fruits as required for and by Jehovah, are to be preferred to his version, which has the more general but less Jewish idea that "the best" should be given.—A.]—**With new wine will thy vats overflow.** יִפְרְצוּ, literally: they will extend themselves, separate, swell up. Comp. the use of the same verb פָּרַץ with reference to rapidly increasing flocks; Gen. xxx. 20; Job i. 10.—Similar strong metaphors for the description of a rich abundance and the blessing of the harvest may be found, e. g., Joel iv. 18; Amos ix. 13; Lev. xxvi. 5.

Vers. 11,12. **Jehovah's correction despise thou not.** To the "despising" (מָאַס) here as in the quite similar passage Job v. 17 [from which WORDSW. thinks our passage to be derived]), the "loathing" or "abhorring" (קוּץ) is evidently the climax. [In the E. V. generally this distinction between the two verbs is very fairly made; the prevailing rendering of the former being "despise, disdain, reject, refuse,"

while that of the latter is "loathe, abhor." In the present instance the rendering might easily be taken as an anti-climax—A.].—**And holds him dear as a father his son.** For the general idea that God's corrections are essentially nothing but revelations of His educating love and fatherly faithfulness, comp. in the Old Testament especially Deut. viii. 5; Ps. cxviii. 18; Lam. iii. 33 sq.

Vers. 13-18. Enthusiastic praise of true wisdom, which is one with the fear of God.—**Blessed is the man that hath found wisdom.** The perfect מָצָא, **who hath found,** expresses the idea of permanent possession; the parallel imperfect יָפִיק (from פּוּק, procedere; therefore, to bring forth, to bring to view, to bring to pass, comp. viii. 35; xii. 2; xviii. 22) denotes a continually renewed and repeated attaining. The ἐκβάλλειν ("bring forth") used of the scribe "instructed unto the kingdom of heaven," Matt. xiii. 52, cannot be compared directly with our expression, since הֵפִיק clearly contains an idea synonymous and not one contrasted with מָצָא.—**Better is her accumulation than the accumulation of silver.** סַחְרָהּ does not, like the corresponding term פִּרְיָהּ in the parallel passage, viii. 19, denote what wisdom brings by way of gain, but the very act of gaining and acquiring (ἐμπορεύεσθαι, LXX). So with תְּבוּאָתָהּ, that which comes with and in herself, the gain which exists in herself. [The "merchandise" of the E. V. is unfortunately obscure and misleading].—**Than the finest gold.** חָרוּץ signifies, according to most of the old interpreters, the finest and purest gold (Vulg.: aurum primum). The etymology leads, in the unmistakable identity of the root חרץ with that of the Greek χρυσός, at first only to the idea of clear or bright shining, gleaming or glittering (coruscare). Gold is therefore, on the ground of its brilliancy, named in the climax as a more precious possession than silver, to which in ver. 15 the "**pearls**" (instead of the K'thibb פְּנִיִּים we shall be constrained to give an unqualified preference to the K'ri פְּנִינִים, comp. viii. 11; xx. 15: xxxi. 10, etc.) supply the culmination in the series, and the generalizing term "all thy jewels" includes the three specified items with all similar articles of value. Comp. viii. 11; Job xxviii. 18, where our verse recurs almost literally. In the latter passage (Job xxviii. 15-19) besides silver, gold and pearls, various other gems, e. g., onyx, sapphire, coral, amber, topaz, etc., are mentioned as falling far below the value of wisdom. In the LXX there appear both in ver. 15 and in 16 amplifying additions, in respect to which HITZIG, while not regarding as original the double clause interpolated in ver. 15 between the two members: οὐκ ἀντιτάσσεται αὐτῇ οὐδὲν πονηρόν. Εὔγνωστός ἐστιν πᾶσιν τοῖς ἐγγίζουσιν αὐτῇ [no evil thing competes with her. She is well known to all those that approach her], yet considers it as resting upon an interpolation that had already made its way into the Hebrew text. The supplement added to ver. 16: ἐκ τοῦ στόματος αὐτῆς ἐκπορεύεται δικαιοσύνη, νόμον δὲ καὶ ἔλεον ἐπὶ γλώσσης φορεῖ [from her mouth proceedeth righteousness, law and mercy doth she bear upon her tongue] HEIDENHEIM regards as the gloss of an Alexandrian Jew, who designed with it to oppose certain Pharisaic interpretations (?).—**Long life is in her right hand,** *etc.* Wisdom here appears personified, endowed with a human body and members,— and in ver. 16 at first in a general way, in ver. 17 so that she is represented as walking, in ver. 18 so that she appears standing like a tree, that dispenses shade and precious fruits. בִּימִינָהּ and

בִּשְׂמֹאולָה in ver. 16 are at any rate not to be translated "*at* her right hand," and "*at* her left hand" (so LUTHER and many old interpreters, conforming to Ps. xvi. 8; xlv. 9; cx. 5), but "*in* her right and left hand," in accordance with Ps. xvi. 11; Is. xliv. 20, where the preposition בְּ expresses the same idea.—"**Long life,**" literally, "**length of days,**" as above, in ver. 2, from which passage the LXX has here repeated also the phrase "καὶ ἔτη ζωῆς."—**Riches and honor,** as in viii. 18; xxii. 4. "The blessings which wisdom offers are appropriately distributed between the hands, according to their essential difference. The right hand is regarded as the nearer; and that one live is the foundation for his becoming rich and honored, as health is a condition preliminary to the enjoyment of prosperity. Compare accordingly the arrangement in 1 Kings iii. 11-14" (HITZIG). [An over-fanciful elaboration of the simple idea of the passage.—A.].—**All her paths are** (paths of)

peace. שָׁלוֹם can be regarded as a genitive, in which case the construction is the same as in Ps. xlv. 6 (according to the interpretation which is probably correct), Ps. xxx. 7; Lev. vi. 3, *etc.;* comp. GESENIUS, *Gramm.* § 121, 6; NAEGELSBACH, § 64, g.;—or as a nominative, "her paths are peace," *i. e.*, peaceable, peaceful, instead of strife and alarm offering pure peace and joy (so nearly all recent commentators, with the exception of UMBREIT and ELSTER, who seem with good reason to prefer the former view). **A tree of life** wisdom is called in ver. 18, as in chap. xi. 30 the "fruit of the righteous" is described by the same figurative expression, in xiii. 12 the fulfilment of an ardent desire, and finally, xv. 4, "temperateness of the tongue." The expression doubtless contains an allusion to the tree of life mentioned by Moses in Gen. ii. 9; iii. 22, although there the definite article stands before חַיִּים, because it was intended to designate the particular tree bearing this name in Paradise. The עֵץ הַחַיִּים of Genesis and the עֵץ חַיִּים of Proverbs are therefore related to each other as the familiar ὁ υἱὸς τοῦ ἀνθρώπου of the Gospels to the υἱὸς ἀνθρώπου without the article in John v. 27. ELSTER, without reason, attempts to deny altogether the reference to Gen. ii. 9, and to make the expression parallel with other figurative representations, like "fountain of life," *etc.* In his observation that the figure of the tree in this passage is based upon the previous personification of wisdom, and that Sol. Song, vii. 9 is therefore to be compared, HITZIG is certainly right (comp. also passages like Is. lxi. 3; Jer. xvii. 8; Ps. i. 3; xcii. 12). We must, however, regard as less pertinent the other proposition of the same commentator, according to which the tree of life in our passage corresponds not only with the tree of the same name in Paradise, but at the same time also with the tree of knowledge (Gen. iii. 3), and so exhibits the identity of the two trees of Paradise. For as a thoroughly practical demeanor, consisting in the fear of God and obedience (see i. 7) the true wisdom of the Book of Proverbs unquestionably presents as complete a contrast to all assuming and "devilish" wisdom from beneath (James iii. 15) as the tree of life in Paradise to that of knowledge.—**And he who holds her fast is blessed.** See critical notes. See also below, notes on chap. xv. 22.

3. *Description of the wisdom of God that created the world, as the mighty protector of him that fears God:* vers. 19-26.—**Jehovah hath with wisdom founded the earth,** *etc.* A connection undoubtedly exists between this allusion to the divine archetype of all human wisdom and what has been before said, so far forth as the paradisiacal tree of life of primitive time seems to have called to the mind of the author the creation of the world, and therefore afforded him occasion for the brief delineation of the creative wisdom of God that lies before us, of which the passage, chap. viii. 22 sq., is only a fuller development (comp. also Job xxviii. 12 sq.; Ecclesiast. xxiv. 2 sq.). Yet if the connection were really as close as it is commonly regarded (*e. g.*, by BERTHEAU, who finds in vers. 19, 20 the conclusion of the series of thoughts beginning in ver. 11; by ELSTER, who discerns here "in a certain sense a metaphysical confirmation of the foregoing:" and in general also by HITZIG, *etc.*), the demonstrative conjunction כִּי (for) would unquestionably stand at the beginning of the 19th verse: this, however, is wanting both in the original text and in the older versions, and was first introduced by LUTHER. Therefore as the words stand, with an emphatic prefixing of the subject "Jehovah" (as at the commencement of many Psalms, *e. g.*, Ps. xxvii.; xcvii.; xcix., *etc.*), they are evidently designed not so much to serve as a continuation of representations already begun, as for the introduction of ideas essentially new,—and these new thoughts are the promises contained in vers. 21-26, of the divine protection and blessing, of which the wise man, *i. e.*, he who acts and walks in accordance with this divine wisdom, will infallibly have the full enjoyment. Furthermore, comp., with reference to the idea of the conformity of the practical, ethical wisdom of man with the absolute creative wisdom of God, the "Doctrinal and Ethical" notes. — **With wisdom.** בְּחָכְמָה, literally "through" wisdom, *i. e.*, not merely with the manifestation of wisdom as an attribute of His, but by means of the personal, essential wisdom, as an independent, creative power indwelling in Him from eternity, comp. viii. 22 sq. In the same hypostatic sense, therefore, are also the interchangeable ideas of "understanding" תְּבוּנָה ver. 19 l. c., and "knowledge" דַּעַת in ver. 20, to be understood. [With this view of the author BERTHEAU agrees, so TRAPP and some others of the old English expositors: SCOTT, HOLDEN

suggest it as possible; while STUART, MUENSCHER and others, judging more correctly, we think, find here none of those personal attributes which are so conspicuous in chap. viii. and there so clearly shape the interpretation —A.]. On ver. 19 comp. in addition Jer. x. 12, and on ver. 20, Gen. i. 6 sq.; ii. 6.—**Did the seas divide.** The perf. נִבְקָעוּ, "they have divided," refers to the primary creative act of the division once for all of the masses of water above and beneath the firmament, Gen. i. 6 sq., while the imperf., יִרְעֲפוּ, relates to the constantly repeated and still continued emptying of the clouds in rain, as a consequence of that sundering of the waters which belongs to the history of creation. [The E. V. loses this distinction and refers both to the present, "are"].

Vers. 21, 22. **My son, never suffer to depart from thine eyes,** *etc.* אַל יָלֻזוּ (for which, perhaps, in conformity with iv. 21 we ought to read יִלֹזוּ) signifies literally, "there must not escape, slip aside" (from לוּז) *deflexit, a via declinavit*). As subjects for the plural verb we usually find supplied from the preceding, especially from ver. 1 sq., the idea "my doctrines, my commands," [as in the E. V. and the commentaries of STUART, MUENSCHER and others]. But this is plainly quite too far-fetched. It is simpler, with UMBREIT, HITZIG, *etc.*, to conceive of the following hemistich, "thoughtfulness and circumspection," as at the same time subjects of the verb in the first, and to explain their omission in the former clause to which they should properly have been attached, on the ground of the peculiar vivacity of the representation. This liveliness of expression can in some measure be preserved in our version by a "rather" after the verb of the second clause.—**Maintain thoughtfulness and circumspection.** The more uncommon תֻּשִׁיָּה (comp. above ii. 7) stands here instead of חָכְמָה (wisdom) ver. 19, and also the less frequent מְזִמָּה instead of בִּינָה which occurs there, in order to suggest the difference between the absolute wisdom and insight of God and the corresponding attributes of man. The LXX instead of the present order appear to have found the reverse, as they translate βουλὴν καὶ ἔννοιαν. Comp. HEIDENHEIM (as above cited).—**So will they be life to thy soul,** *etc.* In reply to HITZIG's disparagement of the genuineness of vers. 22-26, see remarks above, at the commencement of the exegesis. With respect to the thought of ver. 22 f. c., comp. above vers. 2, 16, 18; also iv. 22; viii. 35, *etc.* For last clause comp. i. 9; iii. 3.

Ver. 23. **Then wilt thou go thy way in safety.** לָבֶטַח, in security, free from care, full of trust and good confidence, as below in ver. 29. ["Thou shalt ever go under a double guard, the 'peace of God' within thee (Phil. iv. 7) and the 'power of God' without thee, (1 Pet. i. 5)."—TRAPP.—For illustrations drawn from travellers' experience near Jerusalem, see THOMSON's *Land and Book*, 1., 109.—A].

The simple בֶּטַח is used in the same way in chap. x. 9. For ver. 23 l. c. compare Ps. xci. 12, for the whole verse Prov. iv. 12.—Ver. 24. **When thou liest down.** The imperf. תִּשְׁכַּב in the first member probably designs to express the idea of "laying one's self down to rest," while the following perf. וְשָׁכַבְתָּ would designate the effect and consequence of this act, the reclining and sleeping. Thus most interpreters have correctly judged. HITZIG amends according to the LXX: אִם תֵּשֵׁב, if thou sittest, which is plainly needlessly arbitrary. For the thought comp. furthermore chap. vi. 22; Deut. xxviii. 66.—Ver. 25. **Thou needest not fear from sudden alarm.** אַל־תִּירָא literally **fear thou not.** Since however the אַל in ver. 23 still has its effect, the expression is not to be taken merely as an admonition, but at the same time as a description of the future condition (EWALD, *Lehrbuch* 310, a). [BÖTT. § 964, a, classes it with the "permissive negatives"].—**Nor from the destruction of the wicked.** שֹׁאַת רְשָׁעִים the old commentators unanimously regard as active; the onset of the wicked, the storm which they raise against the pious (*procella quam impii excitant*, CHR. B. MICHAELIS). So recently HITZIG, while nearly all other modern interpreters since DÖDERLEIN prefer the passive conception; the storm or destruction that will sweep away the wicked. A positive decision is probably not possible. Yet the parallel in Ps. xxxv. 8, seems to favor the latter view [which is adopted also by STUART and MUENSCHER]. With reference to the subject compare further, for clause *a*, Ps. xci. 5; Prov. i. 27; xxiv. 22; and for *b*, Job v. 21.—Ver. 26. **For Jehovah will be thy confidence:** literally, will be in thy confidence. כֶּסֶל is here unquestionably trust, confidence, as in Job viii. 14; xxxi. 24; Ps. lxxviii. 7. The signification "loins, side," which the Vulgate has given to the expression ("*Dominus erit in latere tuo*") and, in imitation of this, *e. g.*, ZIEGLER, MUENTINGHE, *etc.*, agrees indeed with passages like Job xv. 27; Lev. iii. 4, 10; xv. 4, *etc.*, but not with the one before us.—**And keep thy foot from the snare.** The substantive לֶכֶד, snare—for which more usually יָקוּשׁ or פַּח —occurs only here, is not, however, for that reason necessarily to be regarded, as HITZIG would have it, as a sign of a later phraseology.

4. *Admonition to benevolence and justice:* Vers. 27-35. A connection of this exhortation with some more specific point in the foregoing (with ver. 21 or ver. 20, *e. g.*, as HITZIG suggests, assuming vers. 22-26 to be spurious) need not be attempted, since the whole of this brief section definitely enough distinguishes itself from the longer series of proverbial discourses, as an independent and peculiar whole.—**Refuse not good to him that deserves it**: literally, "hold not good back from its master," *i. e.*, from him to whom it belongs ["either by the law of equity or of charity," TRAPP,—"whether upon their deserving or upon their need," BR. HALL.], him who is at the same time deserving and needy

(LXX: εὖ ποιεῖν ἐνδεῆ).—Ver. 28. **And yet thou hast it**: literally, and it is yet with thee on hand, there is yet a store [there is with thee]. The LXX adds to this admonition to ready giving and to quick relief (according to the principle: *bis dat qui cito dat*, "he gives twice who gives quickly"), the words appropriate in themselves, "οὐ γὰρ οἶδας τί τέξεται ἡ ἐπιοῦσα" (for thou knowest not what the morrow shall bring forth), which, however, occur in their original place in chap. xxvii. 1.—Ver. 29. **Devise not evil**. The verb חָרַשׁ here as in vi. 14, 18; xii. 20; xiv. 22, expresses the idea of contriving, and that as a development of the idea of "forging" (Ez. xxi. 36) and not that of "ploughing" (as EWALD, following some older interpreters, maintains).—Ver. 30. **Without cause**, Heb. חִנָּם, LXX, μάτην, comp. δωρεάν in John xv. 25. What is meant by this "contending without cause" is made more apparent in the 2d member. In regard to the ethical significance of this precept comp. "Doctrinal and Ethical" notes, No. 3.—Ver. 31. **Emulate not the man of violence**. For this signification of אַל־תְּקַנֵּא, which is found as early as the Vulgate (*ne æmuleris hominem injustum*), the strongest support is the parallel thought in the 2d member; while unquestionably in passages like Ps. xxxvii. 1; lxxiii. 3; Prov. xxiv. 1, the expression קָנָא בְ denotes rather a "falling into a passion" about some one, a "being envious." Yet comp. Prov. xxiii. 17, where the meaning plainly resembles that before us. [The difference among these expositors, we think, is more seeming than real. Thus STUART renders, "Be not envious toward," etc., and explains "do not anxiously covet the booty which men of violence acquire;" MUENSCHER renders, "Envy thou not the man," etc., and explains, "Do not be offended by the success and prosperity," etc., "so as to imitate," etc.— A.]—**And choose none of his ways**. For תִּבְחַר the LXX (μηδὲ ζηλώσῃς) must have read תֶּחַר, a reading which HITZIG is disposed to accept as the original. But how easily could this change be introduced, following as a standard Ps. xxxvii. 1, or Prov. xxiv. 19, where no doubt תֶּחַר stands as the only appropriate reading!

Vers. 32-35 supply a ground in the first instance for the counsels contained in vers. 27-31, but further in general for those of the whole chapter: thus ver. 35 in particular, by its contrasting the comprehensive terms "fool" and "wise," reveals a far reaching breadth and compass in its reference, like the similar expressions at the close of the 1st and 2d chapters.—**An abhorrence to Jehovah is the deceiver**.—נָלוֹז, properly the "perverse," he who is deceitfully crooked and secret (comp. ii. 15), and so is in direct contrast with the "upright" or straightforward. [תּוֹעֵבָה] which in the E.V. is always translated by "abomination," or some cognate term, is often used in other sacred books of idolatry. In the twenty or more passages in the Book of Proverbs in which the word is found it has this signification in no single instance. "It would seem," says WORDSWORTH, *in loc.*, "as if, when Solomon wrote the

Proverbs, he regarded *idolatry* as a thing *impossible*. He therefore left out idolatry as the Greek Legislator omitted parricide from his code—as a thing too monstrous to be contemplated. And yet Solomon himself afterwards fell into idolatry," etc.—A.].—**With the upright he maintains true friendship**.—Literally, "with the upright is his secret compact" (סוֹד), his intimacy, his confidential intimacy. Comp. Job xxix. 4; Ps. xxv. 14.—**Jehovah's curse dwells in the house of the wicked**.—Comp. the אָלָה, the cursing which, according to Zech. v. 4, will take possession of the house of the wicked, and destroy it (in accordance with Deut. xxviii. 17 sq.); and for the term מְאֵרָה, Mal. ii. 2 (and KÖHLER on both passages).

Ver. 34. **If he scorneth the scorners**.—To this hypothetical protasis the apodosis is not found in ver. 35, as BERTHEAU [and STUART] hold, but immediately after, in the second clause of ver. 34. As in Job viii. 20; Lam. iii. 32, there is an *argumentum a contrario*. Comp. our mode of constructing propositions, with "while on the one hand—so on the other." For the sentiment of the 1st member, comp. Ps. xviii. 26; for that of the whole verse the passages in the N. T. which cite freely from the LXX, 1 Pet. v. 5; James iv. 6, and also above, i. 26 sq.—Ver. 35. **Shame sweeps fools away**.—קָלוֹן מֵרִים literally "shame lifts up," *i. e.*, in order to sweep away and destroy them: Comp. Ez. xxi. 31; Is. lvii. 14, and the corresponding use of נָשָׂא, *tollere=auferre*: Is. xli. 16; Job xxvii. 21. The expression קָלוֹן, *ignominia*, properly *levitas* (lightness), at once reminds us directly of the familiar figure of chaff whirled away by the wind (Ps. i. 4 ; Is. xvii. 3 ; xxix. 5, *etc.*). Therefore we need not take מֵרִים as the predicate of כְּסִילִים (fools) and translate it by *suscipiunt* in the sense of "gather up," "carry away," as HITZIG does, following the LXX, Targ., VATABL., and ROSENMUELLER [so NOYES, MUENSCHER, WORDSW., while DE WETTE, STUART, *etc.*, agree with our author—A.]; although the distributive use of the participle in the singular instead of the plural, would have a sufficient parallel in the passage already explained, chap. iii. 18 *b*.

DOCTRINAL AND ETHICAL.

1. "*Wisdom is life and gives life.*" This proposition, which finds its most pregnant utterance in ver. 18, and is formulated as a sort of Epitome of the whole chapter, is especially in the first admonitory discourse (vers. 1-18) expressed in manifold ways and exhibited in its bearing upon the most diverse relations, those of the present life first. Above all it is *long life*, to which walking in true wisdom aids (ver. iii. 16), and this for this reason,—because such a course is the indispensable condition of physical as well as spiritual health,—or because, as ver. 8 expresses it, "the wise findeth health for his body and refreshing for his frame." He who is truly wise aims infallibly at the needful temperance, and a prudent self-restraint in his physical and mental

regimen, and thereby promotes health, his inward and outward well-being in the highest possible degree. He contributes by his obedient subjection to the Divine grace, to the emancipation of his noblest spiritual powers and capacities,—secures these as well as the functions of his bodily organization against morbid excitement or torpidity, and so develops generally his entire personal life, body, mind and spirit, to its normal harmony, and the most vigorous manifestation possible of its diverse and cardinal activities. He who has in this way become inwardly free through the fear of God and real wisdom in life, attains necessarily also to the confirmation of this his godlike freedom and vital power in connection with the phenomena of the outward natural life, as surely as the laws of the economy of nature are the same as those of the ethical sphere in the kingdom of God. He who is inwardly free becomes also naturally free. To him who has attained true mastery over himself there is soon restored dominion over the outward creation,—that heritage of the true children of God from Paradise,—at least in its essentials. And so outward prosperity is added in his experience to inward peace; God "smooths his paths" (ver. 6); fills his garners and cellars with abundance (ver. 10), makes him great through riches and honor (ver. 16), and guides him during this whole life in ways of delight, peace, and prosperity (ver. 17; comp. vers. 2 and 18). A thing, however, that rises far above all these external blessings, above gold, silver and all the treasures of the earth (see vers. 14 and 15), is the grace and favor which the wise man finds not only with men, but much more with God (ver. 4). This *favor of God and of men,*—*i. e.*, not of all indiscriminately, but first and pre-eminently of the wise and devout, such as agree with God's judgment, is evidently in the view of the poet the highest and most precious of the multiform blessings of wisdom which he enumerates. What, however, is this "favor with God and men," the inseparable attendant and consequence of genuine wisdom (1 Sam. ii. 26; Luke ii. 52), what is this but the being a true child of God, the belonging to the fellowship of God and His people, the co-citizenship in the kingdom of truth and of blessedness?—We stand here manifestly at the point at which the eudæmonism of the author, in itself comparatively external and inclining to that which is partial and sensuous, joins hands with the true doctrine of Christianity,—where, therefore, the Old Testament doctrine of retributions predominantly earthly begins to be transformed into the supersensual or spiritual realistic doctrine of the New Testament (Matth. v. 10–12; xix. 28–30). For if to be a child of God and to stand in relations of grace appears as the chief value and most precious reward of wisdom, the goal of prosperity at which the lovers of this wisdom aim is far more a heavenly than an earthly one; and fellowship with God, obedient, loving dependence on Him, is then not merely the end, but at the same time the principle and motive for all the thought, effort and action of the wise. As a way to the attainment of this end no other whatsoever can come under consideration but that opened and pointed out by God himself—that is, the way of faith in the revelation of His grace. Believing self-devotion to the salvation which God bestows, which in the Old Testament is still essentially placed in the future, but in Christ as the Mediator of the New Testament, has become real and present, is there as well as here the condition of the attainment of wisdom, of progressive growth and strength in its possession, and finally of the enjoyment of the blessed reward. That our poet also walks in this path, that he is a representative of the "*fides Veteris Testamenti*," that he belongs to that host of witnesses, exemplars of faith under the Old Testament, which is brought before us in Hebrews xi.; this is incontrovertibly established by the way in which he speaks of the conditions of attaining to the blessed reward of wisdom, or of the practical demeanor of the wise man in its details. There we hear nothing of outward works of the law, of meritorious services, of the fulfilling of God's will with one's own strength or reason; but "trust in the Lord with all thine heart" is enjoined in emphatic contrast with "leaning upon one's own prudence" (ver. 5); the being "wise in one's own eyes" is put in significant contrast with the fear of God and the avoiding of all evil (ver. 7); yes, willing submission to God's salutary correction, humble and grateful subjection even to the strict disciplinary regulations which His fatherly love finds it good to employ; this constitutes the substance of the dispositions and modes of action which are here prescribed (vers. 11, 12; comp. Heb. xii. 5 sq.). With good reason did MELANCHTHON direct attention to the genuinely evangelical, and even profoundly Christian character of this admonition to the patient endurance of sufferings as wholesome disciplinary ordinances of God. He remarks on vers. 11, 12: "Here the whole doctrine of the cross is to be brought into view, and the distinction considered between Philosophy and the Gospel. Philosophy and human reason judge otherwise of the causes of death and of human calamities than does the voice of the Gospel. . . . . Christian and philosophic patience must also be distinguished." And further, on ver. 13 sq.: "These praises of wisdom are rightly understood of revealed wisdom, *i. e.*, of the word of God manifested in the Church, of the Decalogue and the Gospel. Nor yet is it strange that antiquity applied these praises to the person who is the Son of God, who is the revealer of the word resounding in the Church, and is efficient by this word, and in it shows forth what God is, and what is His will." How far, furthermore, the point of view of our teacher of wisdom is removed from all possible Antinomian disparagements of positive moral requirements, how clearly, on the other hand, the wisdom that he teaches appears to be regulated by both factors of Divine revelation, law and gospel, shows itself from the emphatic prominence given to "love and truth" (חֶסֶד וֶאֱמֶת ver. 3; comp. the previous analysis of these two ideas on p. 61) as the chief manifestations of a spirit that fears God, and of a scrupulously dutiful course in intercourse with one's neighbor. Love is, therefore, according to him, also, the fulfilling of the law (Rom. xiii. 10; Gal. v. 14), and indeed to such a degree that, according to his conception, the compliance with special prescriptions of the positive external ceremonial law, e. g., the ordinances which relate to the bringing of the offerings of first fruits (see above on ver. 9), must be to it an easy thing. With the proposition of BRUCH, that our author found himself in a sort of free-thinking opposition to the positive prescriptions of the Mosaic ceremonial law (comp. Introd., § 15, note), this admonition to a conscientious devotion of the first fruits to Jehovah, plainly cannot be reconciled.

2. As wisdom alone ensures true joy in life and abiding prosperity, it also shows itself man's most reliable protection (vers. 19-26), his defender and guardian in all the inward temptations as well as the outward dangers of this earthly life. And this essentially for this reason, because it consists in trusting devotion to the eternal and absolute wisdom of God, which most richly and gloriously manifests its exhaustless power, and its compassionate love and faithfulness, as formerly in the creation of the world, now also in its preservation and government. For he who loves wisdom is also loved by her; and he who by walking in faith, love, and the fear of God, confesses himself here below a friend of the Divine word,—in his behalf does the eternal Word make confession above before the throne of the Heavenly Father.—For further remarks upon the relation to the Logos or the Son of God, of the Divine wisdom, which is here in vers. 19-20, for the first time, hypostatically presented in its quality as the power that created the world, see below on chap. viii. 22 sq. (Doctrinal and Ethical comments). [As will be seen from the Exegetical notes on ver. 19, the best modern exegesis is not unanimous in applying this passage, like chap. viii., to the hypostatic wisdom. Our author's remarks, therefore, however just in themselves, may be regarded as here out of place, so far forth as they involve the personality of wisdom—A.]

3. The conditions for the attainment of true wisdom and its blessing, which are again emphasized in the concluding verses (27-35), are comprehended in the single requirement of love to one's neighbor as the fulfilling of the Divine law. As special manifestations of this love of our neighbor, we have made prominent, charitableness and constant readiness to give (27, 28), sincerity and an unfeigned frankness of disposition (29), peaceableness and placability (30), gentleness and abstinence from all violence (31), straightforward, honorable and upright deportment in one's general transactions (32, 33), humility and the avoidance of all arrogant, frivolous and scornful demeanor (34).—These admonitions do not rise to the full moral elevation of the New Testament's requisitions of love. Thus there is noticeably wanting here the demand of love to enemies, although not in chap. xxv. 21, and instead of this there is, it is true, no hatred of one's enemy recommended (as in the casuistic ethics of the later Pharisaic Judaism, according to Matth. v. 43), but yet a restriction of all dispute and controversy to one's relations with an actual offender; see ver. 30. The specification of duties to one's neighbor that is here presented is therefore related to one truly Christian, very much as the moral precepts which, according to Luke iii. 10-14, John the Baptist gave to the multitude that followed him, if compared with that fulfilment of the law presented by Jesus in the Sermon on the Mount as the standard for the conduct of the children of God under the New Testament (Matth. v. 20-48). Let us observe also the fact, which is certainly not accidental, that all the moral precepts in our passage are given in the form of negative imperatives or warnings, while, e. g., in the Sermon on the Mount, in the concluding and admonitory chapters of Paul's Epistles, and in general in most of the counsels of the New Testament, the positively admonitory and preceptive tone has a decided preponderance over the prohibitory.

HOMILETIC AND PRACTICAL.

Homily on the entire chapter, starting with the central thought in ver. 18: True wisdom as a tree of life,—considered 1) in the precious fruits which it bestows upon us (1-18);—2) in the solid ground in which it is rooted (19-26);—3) in the cultivation which we must bestow upon it by a loving and faithful integrity (27-35).—Comp. M. GEIER's analysis of the chapter, which, treating the four introductory verses as an exordium for the whole, finds prescribed in it three main classes of duties: 1) to God (5-26);—2) to our neighbor (27-30);—3) to ourselves (31-35).—So STARKE: Solomon's exhortation to the manifestation of that piety which flows from true wisdom, viz.: 1) of piety in itself (1-12);—2) of wisdom as its celestial source (13-26);—3) of love to our neighbors as its chief earthly fruit and result (27-35).

Vers. 1-12. MELANCHTHON (on vers. 5-12, after treating the first four verses as an Introduction): Three precepts of divine wisdom; 1) Trust in God and fear of God (5-8);—2) the support of the ministry of the word by offerings and gifts (9, 10);—3) patience under crosses and sufferings (11, 12, comp. above, p. 65).—GEIER (on 5-18): Six cardinal duties to God: 1) confidence,—2) reverence,—3) humility,—4) honor, —5) patience,—6) zeal for wisdom.—STARKE: An exhortation to true piety; and 1) a preliminary encouragement to attention (1-4);—2) the direct admonition to the manifestation of true piety, a) in confidence in God (5),—b) in a living knowledge of God (6),—c) in the fear of the Lord with a renouncing of one's own wisdom (7, 8),—d) in the right payment of all gifts that are due (9, 10),—e) in the patient bearing of the cross (11, 12).—*Calwer Handb.:* The multiform blessings of a multiform wisdom; vers. 1, 2: long life, prosperity and peace;—3, 4: favor with God and men;—5, 6: a right guidance;—7, 8: even physical well-being;—9, 10: full garners and presses;—11, 12: grace from God also in trials and sufferings.

On vers. 1-4. EGARD: See to it that on the tablet of thine heart nothing be found but the word of God and Jesus Christ. According to what is written on the tablet of thine heart, (2 Cor. iii. 3) will endless pain or eternal joy await thee, Matth. x. 32, 33.—On vers. 5-8. HASIUS: It is a characteristic of true wisdom that one regards himself as simple; men who are wise in their own eyes are far removed from true wisdom.—ZELTNER: Where true fear of God exists, there is also true humility of soul, and renunciation of self. Ecclesiast. i. 17, 18, etc.—[Ver. 5. TRAPP: They trust not God at all that do it not alone.—ARNOT: Trust is natural to the creature, though trust in the Lord be against the grain to the guilty. God complains as much of a divided allegiance as of none. In cleaving to Christ the effort to reserve a little spoils all. The command to "trust" is encouraging as well as reproving. The genuine spirit of adoption may be best observed in little things.—R. M. M'CHEYNE: Every enlightened believer trusts in a divine power enlightening the understanding; he therefore follows the dictates of the understanding more religiously than any other man.—Vers. 8. ARNOT: He who makes holiness happy in heaven, makes holiness healthful on earth.]—On vers. 9, 10. STARKE: We should above all things seek the kingdom of God, and share our means with those who labor in the word, and the extension of God's kingdom; but not hold our goods for gain in order so to avoid God's service. It is unbelief if one accounts that lost which he voluntarily devotes to churches and schools, and to the maintenance of the ministry of the word. Matth. x. 42; 2 Cor. ix. 6; Gal. vi. 6, etc.— ZELTNER: Thankfulness opens the fountain of the divine blessing, unthankfulness closes it.— STÖCKER: Liberality toward the clerical office, considered 1) in and by itself,—2) according to the manner of its exercise,—3) in its reward.— [W. BATES: Charity is a productive grace, that enriches the giver more than the receiver. The Lord signs Himself our debtor for what is laid out for Him, and He will pay it with interest].— On vers. 11, 12. EGARD: God's strokes are better than Satan's kiss and love; God smites for life, Satan caresses for death.—J. LANGE: The kingdom of God in this world is a kingdom of the cross; but all suffering tends evermore to the testing and confirmation of faith. 1 Pet. i. 6, 7. —Berleb. Bible: God's chastenings and corrections are no signs of anger, but of love; they are the pains which our healing and cure demand. Those who lie under the cross are often more acceptable to God, than those who taste and experience His dainties. He finds pleasure in our crosses and sufferings for this reason, because these are His remembrance and renewal of the sufferings of His Son. His honor is also involved in such a perpetuation of the cross in His members (Eph. iii. 13; Col. i. 24, etc.) and it is this that causes Him this peculiar joy!

[Vers. 11, 12. ARNOT: Let your heart flow down under trouble, for this is human; let it rise up also to God, for this is divine.—TRAPP: He that escapes affliction may well suspect his adoption. God's house of correction is His school of instruction.]

Vers. 13-18. EGARD: Silver, gold and pearls, serve and adorn the body only, wisdom, however, serves and adorns mainly the soul. As much as the soul is nobler than the body, so much is wisdom also nobler than all treasures. Beware lest thou with the children of this world look with delight upon the forbidden tree, and with them eat death from it. Beware lest thou choose folly instead of wisdom!—STÖCKER: Whosoever desires to regain what our first parents squandered and lost by the fall, namely, eternal life—let him hold fast upon heavenly wisdom—i. e., God's revealed word. This is a tree of life to all those who in true faith lay hold upon it.—Berleb. Bible: Solomon here testifies that wisdom even in Paradise nourished and supported men, and that the same is for this reason also in the restoration (the restitution of all things by Christ, Acts iii. 21) ordained for their spiritual maintenance. In this originates that most blessed condition of the new man, who gradually becomes again like and equal to the man of Paradise.—WOHLFARTH: The tree of life of which we are to eat day by day is faith, love, hope. Faith is its trunk, hope its flowers, love its fruit.

[Vers. 16, 17. ARNOT:—If the law were according to a simple calculation in arithmetic, "the holiest liver, the longest liver," and conversely, "the more wicked the life the earlier its close;" if this, unmixed, unmodified, were the law, the moral government of God would be greatly impeded, if not altogether subverted. He will have men to choose goodness for His sake and its own; therefore a slight veil is cast over its present profitableness.—SOUTH (ver. 17): The excellency of the pleasure found in wisdom's ways appears 1) in that it is the pleasure of the mind;—2) that it never satiates nor wearies;—3) that it is in nobody's power, but only in his that has it.]

Vers. 19-26. STÖCKER:—Inasmuch as wisdom is so grand a thing that all was made and is still preserved by it, we are thence to infer that we also can be by it preserved for blessedness. We should hold dear the heavenly wisdom revealed to us in the word, and earnestly crave it, should learn to keep our eye upon God Himself, should entreat Him for all that we need, depend upon His omnipotence and faithful care, despond under no adversities, etc., etc.—[BRIDGES: (Ver. 23) Habitual eyeing of the word keeps the feet in a slippery path].—STARKE: He who orders his ways to please the Lord, can in turn depend upon His gracious oversight and protection.—Our unrest and fear spring mainly from an evil conscience; divine wisdom however keeps the conscience from heavy sins, and stays the heart on God.—VON GERLACH: The wisdom which God imparts to the man who hearkens for His voice is no other than that by which He founded the earth; the holy order, which forms, keeps, supports, holds together, develops into life, advances all. As now all that God has made is very good, each thing according to the law of the divine order that dwells in it, so in and for man all becomes good that conforms to this order.—WOHLFARTH (on ver. 21-26): The holy rest of the pious. Little as the heart's innocence, this fairest fruit of wisdom, can preserve and wholly free us from the sufferings which God suspends over us for our refining, so surely however does it turn away the worst and saddest consequences of sin, and ensures even amidst the storms of this life a rest that nothing can disturb.—[Ver. 26. ARNOT: It is the peace of God in the heart that has power to keep the feet out of evil in the path of life.]— Ver. 27-35. STÖCKER: The virtues of beneficence and patience are here developed after the method of the second table of the ten commandments; it is therefore taught how the believing Christian is in his relations to his neighbor to exercise himself in true charity, steadfast patience and forbearance.—CRAMER (in STARKE): When God richly bestows upon us spiritual treasures, ought it to be a great matter, if we to honor Him give alms from our temporal goods?—(On ver. 32 sq.); If an ungodly man rises in prosperity, look not upon his prosperity, but upon his end; that can easily deter you from imitating him.—WOHLFARTH (on vers. 27, 28): Thankfulness toward God requires beneficence toward one's brethren.—VON GERLACH: Divine wisdom teaches the true communism,—makes all things common.

According to true love earthly goods belong to "their lord" (ver. 27) i. e, to him who needs them.—[Ver. 27. ARNOT: The poor have not a right which they can plead and enforce at a human tribunal. The acknowledgment of such a right would tend to anarchy. The poor are placed in the power of the rich, and the rich are under law to God.—Ver. 33. ARNOT: In addition to the weight of divine authority upon the conscience, all the force of nature's instincts is applied to drive it home.—Ver. 34. TRAPP: Humility is both a grace and a vessel to receive grace.]

Second Group of Admonitory or Gnomic Discourses.

CHAP. IV. 1—VII. 27.

7. Report of the teacher of wisdom concerning the good counsels in favor of piety, and the warnings against vice, which were given him in his youth by his father.

CHAP. IV. 1–27.

1 Hearken, ye children, to a father's instruction,
and attend to know understanding:
2 for I give you good doctrine;
forsake not my law.
3 For I was also a son to my father;
a tender and only (son) for my mother;
4 and he taught me and said to me:
"Let thine heart hold fast my words;
keep my commandments and thou shalt live!
5 Get wisdom, get understanding;
forget not, turn not from the words of my mouth!
6 Forsake her not and she shall preserve thee;
love her and she shall keep thee.
7 The highest thing is wisdom; get wisdom,
and with all that thou hast gotten get understanding!
8 Esteem her and she will exalt thee,
will bring thee honor if thou dost embrace her.
9 She will put upon thine head a graceful garland,
a glorious crown will she bestow upon thee.
10 Hearken, my son, and receive my sayings;
and the years of thy life shall be many.
11 In the way of wisdom have I taught thee,
I have guided thee in right paths.
12 When thou goest thy step shall not be straitened,
and when thou runnest thou shalt not stumble.
13 Hold fast upon instruction; let not go;
keep her, for she is thy life.
14 Into the path of the wicked enter thou not,
and walk not in the way of the evil.
15 Avoid it, enter not upon it;
turn from it, and pass away.
16 For they sleep not unless they sin;
their sleep is taken away unless they have caused (others) to fall;

17 for they eat the bread of wickedness,
   and the wine of violence do they drink.
18 But the path of the just is like the light of dawn,
   that groweth in brightness till the perfect day.
19 The way of the wicked is as darkness,
   they know not at what they stumble.
20 My son, attend to my words,
   incline thine ear to my sayings.
21 Let them not depart from thine eyes:
   keep them in the midst of thine heart.
22 For they are life to those who find them,
   and to their whole body health.
23 Above all that is to be guarded keep thy heart,
   for out of it flow the currents of life.
24 Put away from thee perverseness of mouth,
   and waywardness of lips put far from thee.
25 Thine eyes should look straight forward,
   and thine eyelids look straight before thee.
26 Make straight the path of thy foot
   and let all thy ways be established.
27 Turn not to the right or to the left,
   remove thy foot from evil!"

GRAMMATICAL AND CRITICAL.

Ver. 2. [נָתַתִּי, an "affirmative" perfect (Bött. § 947, f.), anticipating a sure result, and so confirming confidence; not merely have I already given, *etc.*; it will always be found true. See like instances in ver. 11.—A.].

Ver. 10. [A masculine verb agreeing with a fem. subject, the more readily because the verb precedes. The same thing recurs in ver. 25; in v. 2; vii. 11; x. 21, 32; xv. 7; xvi. 3; xviii. 6.—A.]

Ver. 13. The fem. suffix in נִצְּרֶהָ refers strictly to חָכְמָה (מוּסָר being masculine), which idea, on account of its close relationship, could be easily substituted for מוּסָר (comp. i. 3; xv. 33), and all the more readily because this idea was constantly before the poet's mind as the main subject of his discourse. Like anomalies in the gender of suffixes may be found, *e. g.* in Isa. liii. 10, Judg. xxi 21. [To emphasize the injunction the form of the verb is expanded from the simple נָצְרָה by doubling the middle radical by Dagesh forte *dirimens*, and by attaching the suffix in its fullest form. See Bött. § 500, 12; §§ 1042, b, 1043, 6.—A.].

Ver. 14. [Fuerst takes הָאַשֵּׁר in its more common causative and therefore transitive sense, supplying as its object לִבְּךָ; he reaches, however, the same result. The third declarative use of the Piel we have not found given here by any modern commentator.—A.].

Ver. 16. [For the form given in the K'thibh וּכְשִׁילוּ, see Green, § 88, Bött. § 367, A.—A.].

Ver. 20. [The paragogic imperative usually and naturally takes its place at the beginning of the clause; הַקְשִׁיבָה here, and in ver. 1 follows its object as well as the vocative בְּנִי. Bött. § 960, *e.*—A.].

Ver. 21. יָלִינוּ fut. Hiphil from לוּן with a doubling of the first radical, as in יְלִינוּ from לוּן. [Verb עוּ treated like a verb עִי.—Green, § 160, 1; Bött., § 1147, B. 3.—A.].

Ver. 25. [Holden makes לְנֹכַח an object and not an adverbial modifier—"behold that which is right." This can hardly be reconciled with the strict meaning of נֹכַח. For the peculiar יַיְשִׁרוּ, in which the first radical retains fully its consonant character, resisting quiescence, see Stuart, § 69, 2; Green, § 150, 1; Bött., § 458, *a.* § 408, 12.—A.]

EXEGETICAL.

1. The address to the sons, *i. e.*, the pupils or hearers of the teacher of wisdom, in the plural number, appearing for the first time in ver. 1, and then recurring twice afterward, in v. 7 and vii. 24 (as well as in one later instance, in the discourse of the personified Wisdom, chap. viii. 32) announces the beginning of a new and larger series of proverbial discourses. This extends to the end of chap. vii., and is characterized by a preponderance of warning, and also by the clear and minute delineation of the by-paths of folly and vice which are to be avoided, that now takes the place of the tone, hitherto predominant, of positive appeals to strive after wisdom and the fear of God. A starting point for these admonitory discourses is furnished by the communication made in the preceding chapter, concerning the good instructions which the author as a child had had urged upon his notice by his father. The negative or admonitory import of these teachings of the father is now more fully developed in the discourses, some longer, some shorter, of the next three chapters. And among these special prominence is given to sins against chastity, which had not, it is true, been expressly named by the father, but still must now come under consideration as involving dangers especially seductive and ruinous for the son, as he grew up from boyhood to youth. To these there-

fore the poet reverts no less than three times in the course of the admonitions which he attaches to his account of the precepts of his father as given in chap. iv. (viz., v. 3 sq.; vi. 24 sq.; vii. 5 sq). And in each instance the transition is made in a peculiarly natural way, and with a far more complete delineation of the repulsive details than had been earlier given on a similar occasion (chap. iii. 16-19). Of the older expositors *e. g.*, EGARD, J. LANGE, STARKE, and of the more recent ELSTER are in favor of extending the father's admonition from ver. 4 to the end of this chapter. In favor of these limits may be adduced especially the fact that vers. 26, 27 form a peculiarly appropriate conclusion for the father's discourse,—far more so not only than ver. 9 (with which JEROME, BEDE, LAVATER, the *Würtemberg Bible*, and most commentators of modern times, *e. g.*, EWALD, BERTHEAU, HITZIG, [MUENSCHER, KAMPH.] would close the discourse) but also than ver. 20, (to which point *e. g.*, UMBREIT would extend it). Against those who would regard chap. v. 1-6 as also belonging to the father's address (HANSEN, DELITZSCH) we have the substance of these verses, which, at least from ver. 3 onward, seem no longer appropriate to an admonition addressed to a boy still "tender" (see iv. 3); we have besides the still more weighty fact that chap. v. forms an indivisible whole, from which the first six verses can plainly not be separated, on account of the reference to them contained in ver. 8. It is furthermore by no means necessary that the address "ye sons" (v. 7) should stand at the very commencement of the discourse where the poet resumes it. In reply to HITZIG who, for the sake of restoring a symmetrical relation of numbers, in the present chapter once more pronounces certain verses spurious (vers. 16, 17 and 27), see the special remarks on these verses.

2. Ver. 1-3. **Hearken, ye children.** It seems quite certain that this address, occurring only here and in chap. v. 7 and chap. vii. 24, is occasioned by the fact, that the author designed to represent himself in and after ver. 4 as himself a son and the object of his father's counsels and warnings. The aim was to present the example of the one son plainly before the many sons; for this is the relation in which the teacher of wisdom conceives of his hearers or readers. For this reason again he does not say, "*my sons*," but "*ye sons, ye children*," here as well as in chap. v. 7.—**To a father's correction**, *i. e.*, to the instruction of a man who is your spiritual father; not to the instruction of your several fathers. For, just as in chap. i. 8, the author does not intend in the first line to exhort to obedience to parents, but simply to obedience in general.—**To learn understanding.** The לָדַעַת בִּינָה here corresponds with לָדַעַת חָכְמָה in the superscription, chap. i. 2, and is therefore to be similarly understood. HITZIG's idea "to know *with the understanding*" is evidently needlessly artificial.—Ver. 2. **For good doctrine,** etc. לֶקַח, something received, handed over (see on i. 5); the author here describes his doctrine in this way because he himself received the substance of it from his father.

The LXX here translate the word outright by δῶρον (Vulg. *donum*).—Ver. 3. **For I also was a son to my father**, *i. e.*, "I also once stood in the relation to my (actual) father, in which you stand to me, your paternal instructor," (BERTHEAU). [MUENSCH. less forcibly makes בִּי temporal: *when* I was, *etc.*]—**A tender and only** (son) **to my mother**, strictly, **before** my mother, in her sight; comp. Gen. xvii. 18. The mention of the mother is probably occasioned here, as in i. 8, by the poetic parallelism; for in what follows it does not occur again.—**Tender,** רַךְ, not equivalent, as sometimes, to "susceptible of impressions, tractable," as the LXX conceive in translating it by ἐπήκοος; but the expression, in connection with יָחִיד, "an only one" (comp. Gen. xxii. 2), indicates that the child has been to his parents an object of tender care; comp. Gen. xxxiii. 13, where Jacob speaks of the tenderness of his children. Furthermore the LXX, doubtless in remembrance of the fact that Solomon, according to 1 Chron. iii. 5, was not the only son of his mother, renders יָחִיד by ἀγαπώμενος (beloved). That several ancient manuscripts and versions have substituted for אַפִּי, לִפְנֵי אַפִּי, the *sons* of my mother, doubtless rests upon the same consideration. The earlier exegesis in general thought far too definitely of Solomon as the only speaking subject in the whole collection of proverbs, and therefore imagined itself obliged in every allusion to a "father" or a "mother" of the poet, to think specifically of David and Bathsheba. This is also the explanation of the fact that the LXX in the verse following exchanged the singular, "he taught me and said," for a plural (οἳ ἔλεγον καὶ ἐδίδασκόν με), and accordingly represented all that follows as instruction proceeding from both parents.

3. Vers. 4-9. **Let thine heart hold fast my words.** The father's instruction begins quite in the same style as all the other admonitions in this first main division of the Book of Proverbs. At the end of ver. 4 the Syrian Version adds the words "and my law as the apple of thine eye," which is, however, plainly a supplementary gloss from chap. vii. 2, in which passage also the expression occurs, "keep my commandments and thou shalt live." BERTHEAU regards the addition as original here also, in order thus to do away with the peculiarity of three members in ver. 4 (which is surrounded by nothing but distichs), and to make of the three clauses four. But the triple structure owes its origin simply to the fact that the first member, as an introductory formula for the following discourse, must necessarily be made to stand outside the series of clauses which are otherwise always arranged in pairs.—Ver 5. **Get wisdom, get understanding,** literally, "*buy* wisdom, *buy* understanding." The doubling of the verb makes the demand more vehement; as UMBREIT explains it, an "imitation of the exclamation of a merchant who is offering his wares."—**Forget not, turn not from the words of my mouth.** The zeugma appears only in the translation, not in the original, since the verb

שָׁכַח elsewhere, *e. g.*, Ps. cii. 5, is found construed with לְ. In the idea of forgetting there is naturally involved a turning aside or away from the object.—Ver. 7. **The highest thing is wisdom.** This is the interpretation to be here given, with Hitzig (following Mercer, De Dieu and some older expositors), to the expression רֵאשִׁית חָכְמָה. It is usually rendered "The beginning of wisdom," [*e.g.* by the LXX, Vulg., Luther] and the following clauses, "get wisdom, *etc.*" are taken as the designation of that in which the beginning of wisdom consists, *viz.*, in the "resolution to get wisdom" (Umbreit), or in the instant observance of the admonition which relates to this (comp. Elster on this passage [and also Kamph.]). But as the beginning of wisdom the fear of God is every where else designated (see Obs. on i. 7); and for the absolute use of רֵאשִׁית in the sense of *præstantissimum, summum* (the highest, most excellent thing) we may compare on the one hand Job xxix. 25, and on the other Gen. i. 1.—**And with all that thou hast gotten get understanding.** The beautiful verbal correspondence in the Hebrew phrase is well indicated in the above rendering [in which the ambiguity of the E. V. is avoided; *with* is not to be taken in the sense of *in connection with*, but *with the expenditure of*, or *at the price of*,—German *um* or *für*]. For the thought comp. iii. 14 sq.—Ver. 8. **Esteem her.** The verb סִלְסֵל which occurs only here,—the Pilel of סלל,—might possibly, as an intensive formed from this verb, which as is well known signifies "to heap up, to build a way by mounds and embankments," express the idea of enclosing with a wall, of a firm surrounding and enclosure. So the LXX understood it, translating by περιχαράκωσον αὐτήν; so also the Chald., Syr., Vulg., and several modern interpreters, *e. g.*, Bertheau,—all of whom find expressed in the word the idea of a loving clasp and embrace. It is however probably simpler and more in accordance with the sense of רוֹמֵם in the parallel clause to take the word, as Aben Ezra, Luther, and most modern interpreters do, in the sense of "to exalt, esteem;" [So H., M., N., St. agreeing with the E. V.]. With this conception also the second clause best agrees, for in this there is added to the exhortation to prize and honor wisdom, the other admonition to love her.—**If thou dost embrace her.** Wisdom here appears personified as a loved one or wife, whom one lovingly draws to him, and embraces; comp. v. 20; Eccl. iii. 5.— Ver. 9. **She will put upon thy head a graceful wreath.** Comp. i. 9.—**Will she bestow upon thee.** The rare verb מִגֵּן which again in Hos. xi. 8 stands parallel with נָתַן, according to this passage and Gen. xiv. 20 undoubtedly signifies to offer, to give, to present some one with something (construed with two accusatives). The old translations took it sometimes in the sense of protecting (LXX: ὑπερασπίσῃ σου; Vulg.; *protegat te*; so the Syriac), as though it were a denominative from מָגֵן shield. With this, however, the "glorious crown" does not correspond, which is evidently introduced as an ornament, and not as a protection and defence.

4. Vers. 10-19. The father instructs his son concerning the way of wisdom (vers. 11, 18) in which he should walk, in contrast with the ruinous path of impiety (vers. 14, 19).—**So shall the years of thy life be many.** Comp. chap. iii. 2. [Wordsworth says "This word חַיִּים is plural in the original, as in iii. 2, as if Solomon would comprehend the future life with the present, and add Eternity to Time." He forgets that the abstract idea of life is never expressed by the singular of this noun except as its *stat. constr.* חַי is used in formulas of adjuration, *e. g.*, Gen. xlv. 15, 16; 1 Sam. i. 26, *etc.* See Lexicons generally, and Bött. § 697, 2. § 689, B. a. A.]—Ver. 11. **In the way of wisdom,** *i. e.*, not "in the way *to* wisdom," but in the way in which Wisdom walks, here also again as it were personified,—a way which is lovely and peaceful (according to iii. 17), a way with "right paths" (lit., "paths of straightness," comp. ii. 9, 12) as the 2d member and the following verse describe it (comp. Job xviii. 7).—[Ver. 12. The peculiar significance of such promises to an inhabitant of Palestine, see illustrated, *e. g.*, in Hackett's *Illustrations of Scripture*, p. 20.—A.].—Ver. 13. **Hold fast upon instruction; let not go; keep her; she is thy life,** as the bestower of long life; iii. 2, 16, 18; see below, ver. 23.—Ver. 14. **And walk not.** *etc.* אֲשֶׁר properly, to go straight on, here used of the bold, arrogant walk of the presumptuous; comp. ix. 6; xxiii. 19. To translate אַל־תְּאַשֵּׁר by "do not pronounce happy" (comp. iii. 18) as the LXX, Vulg., and Syr. propose, contradicts the parallelism with "enter not" in the first member.—Ver. 15. **Avoid it.** On פָּרַע to abhor, reject, comp. i. 25.—**Turn from it and pass away.**—*i. e.*, even if thou hast entered upon it (יָעַל) still turn aside from it and choose another way, which carries thee by the ruinous end of that one.—Ver. 16, 17. **For they cannot sleep unless they sin,** *etc.* Hitzig thinks that in this reference to the energy of the wicked in sinning there can be found no appropriate ground for the warning in ver. 15; he therefore declares vers. 16, 17 a spurious interpolation, and at the same time inverts the order of the two following verses, *i. e.*, makes the 19th the 18th; he then connects the כִּי, "for," the only genuine fragment remaining of ver. 16, immediately with the דֶּרֶךְ רְשָׁעִים *etc.*, of ver. 18 (19); "For . . . the way of the wicked is as midnight, *etc.*" Since however no ancient MSS. or translation exhibits anything that favors this emendation, and since a certain irregular movement, an abandonment of that order of ideas which would seem simpler and more obvious, corresponds in general with the style of our author (comp. i. 10 sq.; iii. 3 sq.; viii. 4 sq.), we may fairly disregard so violent a treatment. Besides, the substance of vers. 16, 17, so far forth as they depict the way of the wicked as a restless, cruel and abominable course of procedure, is plainly quite pertinent as the foundation of a warning against this way. And

that subsequently the concluding description of this way as a way of darkness (ver. 19) is not introduced until after the contrasted representation of the way of the pious (ver. 18), is an arrangement favorable to the general rhetorical effect of the whole, like several which we have already found, especially in chap. iii. 34, 35, and also at the end of chapters i. and ii.— **Unless they have caused** (others) **to fall**, *i. e.*, unless they have betrayed into sin; the object—*viz.*, others, in general—does not need to be here distinctly expressed. For the Hiphil יַכְשִׁילוּ, which should be the reading here according to the K'ri, in the ethical sense of "causing to stumble" in the way of truth and uprightness, comp. especially Mal. ii. 8, where the "causing to fall" is brought into even closer connection than in our passage with the idea of "turning from the way." [The K'thibh would require the translation "they have stumbled," *i. e.*, (figuratively) sinned].—**For they eat bread of wickedness, and wine of violence do they drink.** Against the translation of SCHULTENS, MUENTINGHE, UMBREIT, ELSTER, [KAMPHAUSEN]: "for wickedness do they eat as bread, and violence do they drink as wine" (comp. Job xv. 16; xxxiv. 7), may be adduced the position of the words, which should rather stand somewhat in this way—for they have eaten wickedness as bread for themselves—if designed to convey the meaning of a mere comparison. The expressions "bread of wickedness, wine of violent deeds," plainly conveying a stronger meaning, remind us of the "bread of affliction," Deut. xvi. 3; of the "bread of sorrows," Psalm cxxvii. 2, and likewise of the "wine of the condemned" (יֵין אֲנוּשִׁים) Am. ii. 8.

Ver. 18, 19. **Like the light of dawn that groweth in brightness till the perfect day,** literally, "that grows and brightens (familiar Hebrew idiom, as in Judges iv. 24; Esth. ix. 4; comp. EWALD, *Lehrb.* 280 b.) even to the establishing of the day." נָכוֹן (*const. state* of the part. Niphal of כּוּן) lit., the established, the (apparently) stationary position of the sun at noon (comp. the Greek τὸ σταθερὸν τῆς μεσημβρίας, which however the LXX do not here employ). For נֹגַהּ, used of the brightness of the rising sun, comp. Isa. lx. 3; lxii. 1. The comparison of the path, *i. e.*, the moral course, of the just with the light of the rising sun, bright and ever brightening, is most appropriate. If the whole path is light, a bright, clear knowledge of salvation, illumination by the heavenly light of divine revelation (comp. vi. 23; xxviii. 5; Isa. ii. 5, *etc.*) there can naturally be no idea of stumbling and falling suggested (comp. John xi. 9, 10); rather will he who walks in this way attain more and more to perfect clearness in the inward state of his heart and conscience, and therewith also in increasing measure to outward prosperity.— **The way of the wicked is as darkness,** the exact opposite to that of the righteous. אֲפֵלָה strictly "thick darkness," midnight gloom. The degree of this darkness and its evil consequences for him who walks in it, the 2d clause clearly depicts; comp. John xi. 9, 10, and for the general subject, the previous delineation of the sudden destruction of the ungodly, i. 27 sq.; also ii. 18, 22; iii. 35.

5. Ver. 20-27. The father's admonition closes with an urgent warning to the son against forgetting this counsel, with a special reference to the ruinous consequences which such a forgetting will ensure.—**Let them not depart from thine eyes.** The meaning is "depart, escape," just as in iii. 21. BERTHEAU's interpretation is needlessly artificial,—"let them not withdraw them" (3 Plur. without a definite subject), *i. e.*, let them not be withdrawn.—Ver. 22. **For they are life to those who find them**: comp. iii. 2, 16; iv. 13: and especially for the use of "find" in the sense of to attain or to be blessed with anything, see iii. 13; viii. 35.—**And to their whole body health.** Comp. iii. 8, where רִפְאוּת is found instead of the כַּרְפֵּא of our passage.—Ver. 23. **Above all that is to be guarded keep thy heart** מִכָּל־מִשְׁמָר literally, "more than every object of watching," for this is beyond all question the sense of מִשְׁמָר, and not, as ABEN EZRA and JARCHI take it, "a thing against which one must guard," which would not correspond with the radical meaning of שָׁמַר. The heart as the chief object of moral watchfulness, is plainly nothing but the conscience, the pure moral consciousness of man, the ἀγαθὴ συνείδησις, 1 Tim. i. 5, 19; 1 Pet. iii. 16. So HITZIG, with unquestionable correctness, referring to Ps. li. 10; Job xxvii 6; 1 Sam. xxv. 31.—**For out of it (flow) currents of life.** Lit., "issues of life" (BERTHEAU) *i. e.*, of life in the physico-organic as well as in the ethical sense; of life so far forth as it manifests itself in the normal course and movement of the functions of the bodily organism, just as also in the full development of the spiritual powers and their working upon external nature. Comp. remarks on ii. 8 sq. HITZIG also, who translates תּוֹצְאוֹת חַיִּים not quite appropriately by "paths of life," admits the fact that the expression rests upon the recognition of the heart as the seat and fountain of the blood, and therefore also as the central home of the entire life of the physical being (in accordance with Lev. xvii. 11; Deut. xii. 23; and in opposition to BERTHEAU, who denies this reference). So also UMBREIT, except that he, with a view somewhat partial and obscure, conceives of the heart as the "seat of the sensibilities," and the life that flows from it as the "general sensation of being." ["All vital principles are lodged there, and only such as are good and holy will give you pleasure. The exercises of religion will be pleasant when they are natural, and flow easily out of their own fountain." JOHN HOWE, *Delighting in God.*—A.].— Ver. 24. **Put away from thee perverseness of mouth,** *etc.* "Following the first clause of ver. 23 the 24th and 25th verses warn against an arbitrary perverting of the moral judgment, into which evil passions so easily betray, and admonish not to give a misdirection to thought (the *aries animi*) within the department of morality" (HITZIG).—**Let thine eyes look straight forward,** *etc.* A prohibition not of an indolent "gazing about" (BERTHEAU), but of the false

and evil look of the self-seeking, who does not intend honorable dealing with his neighbor, but seeks in all his course and dealing to outwit, to deceive and overpower him; comp. vi. 13; x. 10; xvi. 30; Ecclesiast. xxvii. 25; Matth. vi. 23.—Ver. 26. **Make straight the path of thy foot.** Plainly something that is possible only in connection with eyes that look straight forward and correctly; this is therefore the necessary practical consequence of the course commended in the preceding verse. He only who is from the heart honorable and upright is able also in the individual forms of his moral action to avoid every false step.—**Let all thy ways be established.** יִכֹּנוּ does not mean "let them be sure" (BERTH.), but "let them be definite, fixed," which can be the case only with a course rightly regulated, straightforward, and sure; comp. Ps. cxix. 133; Heb. xii. 13. The latter passage plainly contains an allusion to our verse, the first member of which according to the LXX reads: Ὀρθὰς τροχιὰς ποίει σοῖς ποσίν.—Ver. 27. **Turn not to the right or to the left, keep thy foot far from evil.** This fuller explanation of that fixedness and certainty of the way which is demanded in ver. 26 completes the further's admonition in a way altogether appropriate, and is therefore neither to be declared, with HITZIG, a spurious addition, nor is it, in agreement with BERTHEAU, to be deprived of its position and meaning as a concluding appeal, by receiving into the text as genuine the two verses which appear after it in the LXX (and Vulgate): Ὁδοὺς γὰρ τὰς ἐκ δεξιῶν οἶδεν ὁ θεός, διεστραμμέναι δέ εἰσιν αἱ ἐξ ἀριστερῶν. Αὐτὸς δὲ ὀρθὰς ποιήσει τὰς τροχιάς σου, τὰς δὲ πορείας σου ἐν εἰρήνῃ προάξει. These two verses, whose substance appears to be a mere repetition from vers. 26, and 27, seem to owe their origin to the design to secure here again, as in the preceding section (vers. 10-19) a full decade of verses. In opposition to this view, arbitrary and theoretical, that the structure of the paragraphs or strophes in the chapters before us is uniformly equal, *i. e.*, always consisting of ten verses—a view to which even BERTHEAU attaches much importance—see, above, the Exeget. Notes on chap. 3, No. 1.

DOCTRINAL AND ETHICAL.

The counsel given by the pious and wise father to his son begins with the appeal to him to hold fast his words (ver. 4), and ends with an earnest warning against a course made insecure and dangerous by disregard of these words (vers. 20-27). *Obedience to the word of revealed truth as transmitted within the community of the children of God, and bequeathed by parents to their sons,*—this is the general statement of the import of the demands of this chapter as a whole, so far forth as it may be reduced to a single brief expression. It is essentially, as MELANCTHON says, "*adhortationes ad studium obedientiæ et ad diligentiam regendi disciplinam,*" that are contained in this passage. The whole is a chapter on *the right* (Christian) *training of children*, an exhibition of the nature of that chief manifestation of the Hhokmah [practical wisdom], which in the general superscription of the book (i. 3; comp. i. 7) was designated as מוּסָר or *discipline.** To this chief end, the holding his son to discipline, to obedience, and the cherishing of his wholesome words and teachings, all the other prominent ideas which find expression in the father's discourse are made subservient; the exhibition of wisdom as the one costly jewel, whose acquisition is above every other, and if necessary, at the cost of all other possessions, to be sought and secured (vers. 5-9; comp. Matth. xiii. 44-46); the emphatic admonition to be subject to "discipline," and not to let it go, even because it is *the life* of the true and obedient child of God (ver. 13); the clear delineation of the two paths; the way of darkness in which the ungodly walk, and the way of light in which the pious and wise are found (vers. 14-19); the counsel to guard with all diligence not merely the word of truth received into the heart (vers. 20-22; comp. the ἔμφυτος λόγος, Jas. i. 18), but also the heart itself, as the seat of the conscience, and the source of all life and prosperity (ver. 23); and finally the commendation of a life of honor and integrity, without turning to the right hand or to the left, as the salutary result of that inward disposition which is both pure and sure (vers. 24-27). That a pure heart, *i. e.*, one purified by the grace of God, and with this a firm heart, *i. e.*, one firmly rooted in truth as its ground, is the source and common fountain for the successful development of all the main activities and functions of human life, those belonging to the sphere of sense, as well as to the psychical and spiritual realms, and that this must more and more manifest itself as such a centre of the personality, sending forth light and life:—this thought, expressed in ver. 23 in a way peculiarly vigorous and suggestive, unquestionably presents the most profound, comprehensive and controlling truth, that the father, in the course of his counsels and warnings, gives to his son, standing before the portal of the school of life, to be borne with him on his way (comp. the advice of Tobias to his son: Tob. iv. 6).—Yet we must also mark as one of the most noteworthy of the fundamental ideas of this discourse, the designation, contained in ver. 7, of wisdom as the "chief thing," which is to be sought above all things else, and to be prized above all possessions and treasures. Yet this passage probably requires a different conception and application from that which is usually found,—so far forth as the thought which has already been expressed, *e. g.*, above, in chap. ii. 3 sq., "that one must practise wisdom to become wise" (comp. MELANCTHON on this passage; STARKE, and of recent writers, especially ELSTER), probably does not correspond with the true import of רֵאשִׁית חָכְמָה; the expression being designed rather to serve for the designation of wisdom as the highest end of all human counsel and action.

---

* In this particular, BOMAUS certainly took the correct view, that in his otherwise remarkable classification of the contents of the first nine chapters according to the seven *principia ethices divinæ deductiva* (Daath, Binah, Sechel, Tuschijah, Musar, Meimmah, Ormah), he assigns to the 4th chapter the Musar (or the *colligata informatio*, as he explains the term). See *Ethica Sacra*, Disp. VI., p. 65 sq.

HOMILETIC AND PRACTICAL.

Homily on the entire chapter: The two paths in which youth can walk,—that of obedience and that of vice (or the way of wisdom and that of folly; the way of light and that of darkness; comp. the minute picture of the two ways in the *Ep. Barnabæ,* § 18-20).—Educational Sermon: The fundamental principles of a truly Christian education of children, exhibited according to the standard of the counsels of a sage of the Old Testament to his son. 1st principle: True wisdom (which is equivalent to the fear of God) the highest end of all regulations adopted in the educational action of parents (vers. 4-9); 2d principle: As means to this end, an earnest insisting both upon the reward of walking in the light, and upon the punishment for walking in darkness (vers. 10-19); 3d principle: Results to be anticipated simply from this, that God's word be received and cherished in a susceptible and good heart (vers. 20-27).— Comp. STÖCKER: Warning against evil companionship: 1) the simple command that one must avoid evil company (vers. 1-19); 2) the way in which this can be done (vers. 20-27).—STARKE: How David admonishes Solomon: 1) to the reception of wisdom (4-13); 2) to the avoidance of impiety (14-19); 3) to the practice of piety (20-27).

Vers. 4-9. STARKE:—Should the case arise, that one must lose either true wisdom or all temporal good, forego rather the latter; for wisdom is better than gold (chap. xvi. 16; Matth. xix. 29). Honor, accomplishments, graces, esteem, each man desires for himself. If thou wouldst attain this wish of thine, then seek wisdom; she gloriously rewards her admirers.—[Ver. 4. BRIDGES:—This heart-keeping is the path of life. GOULBURN:—Endeavor to make your heart a little sanctuary, in which you may continually realize the presence of God, and from which unhallowed thoughts and even vain thoughts must carefully be excluded.]—*Berleb. Bible:*—The two conditions of the Christian life: 1) its commencement, the seeking and finding of wisdom (ver. 7, according to the common interpretation); 2) its continuance, dependent upon preserving wisdom, and thereby being preserved, advanced, and brought to honor by it (vers. 8, 9).—[Ver. 7. TRAPP: Make religion thy business: other things do by the by].—Vers. 10-19. HASIUS: To set one's foot in the way of good is ofttimes not so difficult as to go vigorously forward in it. The power of temptation is great; the tinder of vice is naturally in us; even a little spark can kindle it.—ZELTNER: Impossible as it is that a stone fall into the water and remain dry, so impossible is it that a lover of evil company be not betrayed, Ecclesiast. xiii. 7; 1 Cor. xv. 33.—[Ver. 19. ARNOT: The sun is an emblem not of the justified, but of the justifier. Christ alone is the source of light: Christians are only its reflectors. The just are those whom the Sun of righteousness shines upon; when they come beneath His healing beams, their darkness flies away. They who once were darkness are light now, but it is "in the Lord."]—STARKE: The pious can avoid the snares of destruction through the light of the Holy Spirit; but the ungodly stumble in darkness and fall into the pits of death. As one from darkness walks on in darkness, so from light into light (ver. 18; comp. Prov. xii. 28; Ps. lxxxiv. 7; Job v. 12-14).—*Berleb. Bible:* The soul in its conversion to God must 1) hear His word; 2) receive the influence of this word, and by it be directed to the way of truth; 3) be guided by God in this way; 4) under God's guidance and protection learn so to run in this way that it shall nowhere stumble nor fall.—[Ver. 19. EMMONS: Sinners are in such darkness that they are insensible to the objects that are leading them to ruin: thus they stumble *a*) at the great deceiver; *b*) at one another; *c*) at Divine Providence; *d*) at their common employments; *e*) at the nature and tendency of their religious performances; *f*) at the preaching they hear; *g*) at the blindness of their own hearts.]

Vers. 20-27. J. LANGE:—The inner spiritual life begins with the heart. As is the heart so are all its issues; for "from the heart proceed evil thoughts," *etc.*, Matth. xv. 19; xii. 35.—*Berleb. Bible:* The heart must keep the doctrine, and the doctrine the heart. Both are so intimately connected that neither can be without the other. . . . Nature herself in the natural heart shows with what care we must keep the spiritual (ethical) heart. In this we can never be too precise, too sharp, or too careful. If we guard our house, much more must the heart be guarded; the watches must there be doubled, *etc.*—In this all the duties of a door-keeper combine, reminding us who goes in and out, what sort of thoughts enter into the heart, what sort of desires go out, *etc.* Self-denial is the best means to such a keeping of the heart. It must stand as porter before the heart's door; and the cross and the patience of Christ is the best door of the heart, well preserved with bolts and bars against all intrusion or violence.—SAURIN (sermon on ver. 26):—On the needful attention which each should give to his ways.—*Calwer Handb.:*—Threefold counsel in regard to the way and means of continuing in the right path: 1) give good heed to thy heart; 2) put away a perverse mouth (ver. 24); 3) let thine eyes look straightforward (vers. 25-27).—VON GERLACH:—The first and most immediate thing proceeding from the heart is words, then deeds. Let the former be above all things truthful and sincere; the latter circumspect, well considered, and then executed with certainty and confidence (vers. 26, 27). Comp. Rom. xiv. 23; and SENECA's well known maxim: *Quod dubitas, ne feceris.*—[ARNOT: We cry to God in the words of David, Create in me a clean heart, and He answers back by the mouth of David's son, Keep thy heart. Keep it with the keeping of heaven above, and of the earth beneath,—God's keeping bespoken in prayer, and man's keeping applied in watchful effort.—Ver. 27. TRAPP: Keep the king's highway: keep within God's precincts, and ye keep under His protection.—BRIDGES: Though to keep the heart be God's work, it is man's agency. Our efforts are His instrumentality.]

8. Warning against intercourse with wanton women, and against the ruinous consequences of licentiousness.

Chap. V. 1–23.

1 My son, give heed to my wisdom,
   to my prudence incline thine ear,
2 so that thou maintain discretion,
   and thy lips preserve knowledge.
3 For the lips of the strange woman distil honey,
   and smoother than oil is her mouth:
4 but at last she is bitter as wormwood,
   sharp as a two-edged sword.
5 Her feet go down to death,
   her steps lay hold upon the lower world;
6 the path of life she never treadeth,
   her steps stray, she knoweth not whither.
7 And now, ye children, hearken to me,
   and depart not from the words of my mouth!
8 Turn away thy path from her,
   and draw not near to the door of her house!
9 that thou mayest not give to others thine honor,
   and thy years to a cruel one;
10 that strangers may not sate themselves with thy strength,
   and (the fruit of) thy labor (abide) in a stranger's house,
11 and thou must groan at last
   when thy body and thy flesh are consumed,
12 and say, "Why then did I hate correction
   and my heart despised reproof?
13 and I did not hearken to the voice of my teachers,
   did not incline mine ear to those that instructed me?
14 Well nigh had I fallen into utter destruction
   in the midst of the assembly and the congregation!"
15 Drink waters from thine own cistern,
   and flowing streams from thine own well spring!
16 Shall thy streams flow abroad
   as water brooks in the streets?
17 Let them be thine alone,
   and none belong to strangers with thee.
18 Let thy fountain be blessed,
   and rejoice in the wife of thy youth,
19 the lovely hind, the graceful gazelle;
   let her bosom charm thee always;
   in her love delight thyself evermore.
20 Why, my son, wouldst thou be fascinated with a stranger,
   and embrace the bosom of a wanton woman?
21 For before the eyes of Jehovah are the ways of man,
   and all his paths He marketh out.
22 His own sins overtake him, the evil doer,
   and by the cords of his sin is he held fast.
23 He will die for lack of correction,
   and in the greatness of his folly will he perish.

CHAP. V. 1-23.

GRAMMATICAL AND CRITICAL.

Ver. 1.—[The shortened Imperative is even more than the paragogic entitled to the first place in its clause; here הַט follows its object, BÖTT., § 960, c. ex. (comp. critical note on Iv. 20).—A.]

Ver. 2.—[לִשְׁמֹר. The construction in the Hebrew is the same as in chap. ii. 8; the Infinitive with לְ is followed by the finite verb. [יִנְצֹרוּ, a masc. verbal form with a fem. subject,—comp. note on iv. 10. For emphasis or euphony the assimilation of the נ is sometimes dispensed with. BÖTT., § 1100, 3.—A.]

Ver. 14.—[וָיְהִי, a Perf. with the signification of a pluperf. subj.; a very little and I *should have fallen*. Comp. BÖTT., § 947, d.—A.]

Ver. 18 [BÖTT., § 964, 6, makes יְהִי an example of the *desponsive* use of the Jussive, and therefore makes it more than the expression of a wish (see Exeg. notes); it becomes an anticipation or promise.—A.]

Ver. 22.—[יִלְכְּדֻנוֹ, a unique example of the attachment of ו, a more common suffix of the Perf., to the lengthened form of the third plur. masc. of the Imperf. See BÖTT., §§ 881, λ,—1042, 5,—1047, ex., correcting EWALD, § 250 b, who makes the נ epenthetic. See also GREEN, § 105, c.—A.]

EXEGETICAL.

1. In opposition to the opinion of those who refer vers. 1-6 to the discourse of the father in ch. iv. 4 sq., consult above, p. 71. J. A. BENGEL appears even to have regarded the entire fifth chapter as a continuation of that discourse, for he remarks on ver. 1, "Inasmuch as David's careful directions to Solomon bear upon unchastity, it seems likely that David and Bathsheba were concerned lest Solomon might also pursue a course like that in which the parents sinned together" (see *Beiträge zu J. A. BENGEL'S Schrifterklärung, mitgetheilt von Dr. OSK. WAECHTER*, Leips., 1865," p. 26). But the son addressed in the preceding chapter was conceived of as a "tender child;" the one now addressed is a young man already married, see vers. 15-19. For, as in the similar admonitions of the 6th and 7th chapters, it is not simple illicit intercourse, but such an intercourse within marriage relations, adulterous intercourse with lewd women, that constitutes the object of the admonitory representations of the teacher of wisdom.—Furthermore, as BERTHEAU rightly observes, the passage before us, in its substance and its form, variously reminds us of chap. ii., especially in respect to its form, by its long propositions extended through several verses (3 sq., 8 sq., 15 sq.). As the three main divisions of the discourse are of not quite equal length, we may with HITZIG distinguish the introductory paragraph, vers. 1-6; the central and chief didactic section, vers. 7-20; which again falls into two divisions, vers. 7-14 and 15-20; and the epilogue, vers. 21-23.

2. Vers. 1-6. **My son, give heed to my wisdom**, *etc*.—Quite similar are the demands which introduce the two subsequent warnings against unchastity.—Chap. vi. 20 and vii. 1.—**So that thou maintain discretion**—literally reflection, מְזִמּוֹת, which elsewhere is usually employed in a bad sense, of base deceitful proposals, but here denotes the wise prudential consideration, the circumspect demeanor of the wise; comp. the singular in ch. i. 4.—**And thy lips preserve knowledge**.—The *lips*—not precisely the heart, chap. iii. 1—are to preserve knowledge so far forth as it is of moment to retain literally the instructions of wisdom and often to repeat them.—Ver. 3. **For the lips of the strange woman distil honey**.—The "stranger" is the harlot, as in chap. iii. 16. Her lips "drop honey" (נֹפֶת, comp. Ps. xix. 11) because of the sweetness not of her kisses but of her words. Comp. the quite similar representation, Song Sol. iv. 11, and as a sample of the wanton woman's words that are sweet as honey, Prov. vii. 14 sq. —**Smoother than oil is her mouth**.—The palate (חֵךְ) as an instrument of discourse occurs also chap. viii. 7; Job vi. 30; xxxi. 30. The "smoothness" of discourse as a symbol of the flattering and seductive, chap. ii. 16; vi. 24.— Ver. 4. **But at last she is bitter**—literally "her last is bitter" (comp. xxiii. 32), *i. e.*, that which finally reveals itself as her true nature, and as the ruinous consequence of intercourse with her.—**As wormwood** (לַעֲנָה, for which the LXX inaccurately gives χολή, gall), a well known emblem of bitterness, as in Deut. xxix. 18; Jer. ix. 15; Am. v. 7; vi. 12. It is "a plant toward two feet high, belonging to the Genus *Artemisia* (Spec. *Artemisia absinthium*), which produces a very firm stalk with many branches, grayish leaves, and small, almost round, pendent blossoms. It has a bitter and saline taste, and seems to have been regarded in the East as also a poison, of which the frequent combination with רֹאשׁ gives an intimation" (UMBREIT; comp. CELSIUS, *Hierobot*. I. 480; OKEN, *Naturgesch*. III. 763 sq.).—**As a two-edged sword**—literally as a sword of mouths, a sword with more than one mouth (חֶרֶב פִּיּוֹת, comp. Ps. cxlix. 6; Judg. iii. 16). [The multiplicative plural is sometimes used thus even of objects that occur in pairs; comp. BÖTT., § 702, 3—A.] "The fact that the surface of the sword is also smooth is in this antithesis to the second clause of ver. 3 properly disregarded," HITZIG.—Vers. 5 and 6 explain and confirm more fully the statement of ver. 4.—**Upon the lower world her steps lay hold**—*i. e.*, they hasten straight and surely to the kingdom of the dead, the place of those dying unblessed. [The author cannot be understood as meaning that שְׁאוֹל is *always* and *only* the place of those dying *unblessed*. The passage cited, chap. i. 12, is inconsistent with this,—so is the first passage in the O. T. where the word occurs, Gen. xxxvii. 35,—so is the last passage, Hab. ii. 5,—so are many intervening passages, especially such as Ps. xvi. 10; Eccles. ix. 10. If the word here has this intensive meaning, it must

appear from the connection. See, therefore, חַיִּים in ver. 6, which plainly has a moral import. Comp. FUERST's *Handw.*—A.] Comp. ii. 18; vii. 27,— and on שְׁאוֹל, Hades, the lower world, i. 12.— **The path of life she never treadeth.**—The verb פָּלַס, here just as in iv. 26, means to measure off (not to "consider," as BERTHEAU maintains), to travel over. The particle פֶּן, *ne forte*, stands here, as in Job xxxii. 13, "independent of any preceding proposition, and in accordance with its etymology signifies substantially 'God forbid that,' *etc.*, or 'there is no danger that,'" *etc.*, HITZIG; it is therefore equivalent to "surely not, nevermore." ABEN EZRA, COCCEIUS, C. B. MICHAELIS and others regard תְּפַלֵּס as second pers. masc.; "*viam vitæ ne forte expendas, vagantur orbitæ ejus*" ["lest perchance thou shouldst ponder the way of life, her paths wander;" which is very nearly the language of the E. V.]. But the second clause shows that the wanton woman must be the subject of the verb. BERTHEAU's translation is however also too hard and forced, according to which the first clause is dependent upon the second, but it is to be regarded as a negative final clause prefixed; "that she may not ponder (!) the path of life, her paths have become devious," *etc.* [This is the view adopted by HOLDEN, STUART, WORDSWORTH, and DE WETTE; KAMPH. has the same conception of the relation of the clauses, but prefers the verb *einschlagen*, adopt or enter—A.] The LXX, Vulg. and other ancient versions already contain the more correct interpretation, regarding פֶּן as here essentially equivalent to לֹא; only that the emphatic intensifying of the negation should not be overlooked.— [FUERST (*Handw.*) is also decidedly of this opinion; he renders "*dass ja nicht*"=*so that by no means*; he explains the idiom as representing a necessary consequence as an object contemplated. —A.]—**Her steps stray, she knoweth not whither.**—נָעוּ is here doubtless not intended as an inceptive ("they fall to staggering"), nor in general does it design to express a "staggering of the tracks or paths," a figure in itself inappropriate. It probably signifies rather a roving, an uncertain departure from the way (*vagi gressus*, Vulg.); and the לֹא תֵדָע which is connected with it is not to be explained by "she marks it not, without her perceiving it, unawares " (as it is usually taken, after the analogy of Job ix. 5; Ps. xxxv. 8) [so by NOYES, STUART, MUENSCH.; while the E. V. follows the old error of making the verb a second person.—A], but by "she knows not whither," as an accusative of direction subordinated to the foregoing idea (HITZIG, DE WETTE).

2. Vers. 7-14. **And now, ye children, hearken to me.**—וְעַתָּה draws an inference from what precedes, and introduces the following admonition; comp vii. 24. The "words of my mouth" are the specific words contained in ver. 8 sq.—Ver. 9. **That thou mayest not give thine honor to others**—*i. e.*, as an adulterer, who is apprehended and exposed to public disgrace.—**And thy years to a cruel one**—*i. e.*, to the injured husband, who will punish the paramour of his faithless wife with merciless severity, perchance sell him as a slave, or even take his life. [This explanation is grammatically better than that (of HOLDEN, *e. g.*) which makes the "cruel one" the adulteress, and more direct than that (of STUART and others) which makes him the purchaser of the punished adulterer.— A.]. Comp. vi. 34, and below, ver. 14.—Ver. 10. **That strangers may not sate themselves with thy strength.**—כֹּחַ might, strength, is here undoubtedly equivalent to property, possessions, as the parallel עֲצָבֶיךָ, thy toils, *i. e.*, what thou hast laboriously acquired, the fruit of thy bitter sweat (Vulg. *laboris tui*), plainly indicates. The idea is here plainly this, that the foolish paramour will be plundered through the avaricious demands of the adulterous woman (comp. vi. 26), and that thus his possessions will gradually pass over into other hands (Ecclesiast. ix. 6). A different explanation is given by EWALD, BERTHEAU, ELSTER (in general also by UMBREIT); that the proper penalty for adultery was according to Lev. xx. 10; Deut. xxii. 22 sq.: John viii. 5, stoning; in case, however, the injured husband had been somewhat appeased, the death penalty was on the ground of a private agreement changed into that of a personal ownership, the entrance into the disgracefully humiliating condition of servitude, and that allusion is here made to this last contingency. But while the superficial meaning of vers. 9 and 10 could be reconciled with this assumption, yet there is nothing whatsoever known of any such custom, of transmuting the death prescribed in the law for the adulterer by a compromise into his sale as a slave; and as the entire assumption is besides complicated with considerable subjective difficulties (see HITZIG on this passage), the above explanation is to be preferred as the simpler and more obvious.—Ver. 11. **And thou must needs groan at last**—literally "at thine end," *i. e.*, when thou hast done, when all is over with thee. נָהַם used of the loud groaning of the poor and distressed also in Ez. xxiv. 23: comp. Prov. xix. 12; xx. 2: xxviii. 15, where the same word describes the roaring of the lion. The LXX (καὶ μεταμεληθήσῃ) appear to have read וְנִחַמְתָּ, a gloss containing a true explanation, but needlessly weakening the genuine sense of the word. —**When thy body and flesh are consumed.**—בְּשָׂרְךָ וּשְׁאֵרֶךָ, *i. e.*, plainly *thy whole body*; the two synonymes, **the first of which describes the** flesh with the frame, and the second the flesh in the strictest sense, without the bones, are designed to emphasize the idea of the body in its totality, and that with the intention of marking "the utter destruction of the libertine" (UMBREIT).—Ver. 12. **Why did I then hate correction?**—Literally, How did I then hate correction? *i. e.*, in what an inexcusable way? How could I then so hate correction?—Ver. 14. **A little more, and I had fallen into utter destruction**—*i. e.*, how narrowly did I escape a fall into the extremest ruin, literally, "into entireness of misery, into completeness of destruction!" As the second clause shows, the allusion is to the danger of condemnation before

the assembled congregation, and of execution by stoning; see above on ver. 10.—**Assembly and congregation**—Hebrew קָהָל and עֵדָה—stand in the relation of the convened council of the elders acting as judges (Deut. xxxiii. 4, 5), and the concourse of the people executing the condemning sentence (Numb. xv. 35; comp. Ps. vii. 7). For קָהָל is in general always a convened assembly, *convocatio;* עֵדָה on the contrary is a multitude of the people gathering without any special call, *coetus sive multitudo.*

4. Vers. 15-20. To the detailed warning set forth in vers. 8-14 there is now added a corresponding positive antithesis, a not less appropriate admonition to conjugal fidelity and purity.— **Drink waters out of thine own cistern**, etc., *i. e.*, seek the satisfaction of love's desire simply and alone with thine own wife. "The wife is appropriately compared with a fountain not merely inasmuch as offspring are born of her, but also since she satisfies the desire of the man. In connection with this we must call to mind, in order to feel the full power of the figure, how in antiquity and especially in the East the possession of a spring was regarded a great and even sacred thing. Thus the mother Sarah is compared to a well spring, Is. li. 1, and Judah, the patriarch, is spoken of as 'waters,' Is. xlviii. 1; as also Israel, Num. xxiv. 7; Ps. lxviii. 26" (UMBREIT). Compare also Song Sol. iv. 12.— **And flowing streams from thine own well spring**—With בּוֹר, *i. e.*, properly "cistern," an artificially prepared reservoir, there is associated in the second clause בְּאֵר, fountain, *i. e.*, a natural spring of water conducted to a particular fountain or well spring. Only such a natural fountainhead (comp. Gen. xxvi. 15-20) can pour forth נֹזְלִים, *i. e.*, purling waters, living, fresh, cool water for drinking (Song Sol. iv. 15; Jer. xviii. 14).—Ver. 16. **Shall thy streams flow abroad as water brooks in the streets?**— To supply פֶּן (GESENIUS, UMBREIT) or אַל (EWALD, BERTHEAU, ELSTER [STUART], *etc.*) is needless, if the verse be conceived of as interrogative, which, like Prov. vi. 30; Ps. lvi. 7 sq., is indicated as such only by the interrogative tone. So with unquestionable correctness HITZIG. A purely affirmative conception of the sentence, according to which it is viewed as representing the blessing of children born of this lawful conjugal love under the figure of a stream overflowing and widely extending (SCHULTENS, DÖDERLEIN, VON HOFMANN, *Schriftbew.*, II., 2, 375 [HOLDEN, NOYES, MUENSCHER, WORDSW.], *etc.*) would seriously break the connection with ver. 17. As to the subject, *i. e.*, the description of a wife who has proved false to her husband and runs after other men, comp. especially chap. vii. 12.—Ver. 18. **Let thy fountain be blessed.** —יְהִי "attaches itself formally to the jussive יְהִי of the preceding verse" (HITZIG), and so adds to the wish that conjugal fidelity may prevail between the married pair, the further wish that prosperity and blessing may attend their union. בָּרוּךְ doubtless used of substantial bless-

ings, *i. e.*, of the prosperity and joy which the husband is to prepare for his wife, as an instrument in the favoring hand of God. This, which is HITZIG's view, the connection with the second clause recommends above that of UMBREIT, which explains בָּרוּךְ as here meaning "extolled," and also above that of BERTHEAU, which contemplates "children as the blessing of marriage." — **And rejoice with the wife of thy youth.**— Comp. Deut. xxiv. 5; Eccles. ix. 9. "Wife of thy youth," *i. e.*, wife to whom thou hast given the fair bloom of thy youth (UMBREIT). Compare the expression "companion of youth" in ii. 17. In a needlessly artificial way EWALD and BERTHEAU have regarded the entire eighteenth verse as a final clause depending on the second member of ver. 17: "that thy fountain may be blessed, and thou mayest have joy," etc. HITZIG rightly observes that to give this meaning we should have expected וִיהִי instead of יְהִי, and likewise וְשָׂכַחְתָּ instead of שְׂמַח, and that in general ver. 18 does not clearly appear to be a final clause. [STUART makes the second clause final, depending on the first, which is also unnecessarily involved.] —Ver. 19. **The lovely hind, the graceful gazelle.**—Fitly chosen images to illustrate the graceful, lively, fascinating nature of a young wife; comp. the name "gazelle" (צְבִי, Ταβιθά and its equivalent Δορκάς as a woman's proper name; Acts ix. 36; also Song Sol. ii. 9, 17; viii. 14. UMBREIT refers to numerous parallels from Arabic and Persian poets, which show the popularity of this figure in Oriental literature. ["These pretty animals are amiable, affectionate and loving by universal testimony—and no sweeter comparison can be found." THOMSON, *The Land and the Book*, I., 252—A.]—**Let her bosom charm thee always.**—Instead of דַּדֶּיהָ, her breasts, the *Versio Veneta* reads דֹּדֶיהָ her love (αἱ ταύτης φιλίαι), which reading HITZIG prefers ("*ihre Minne*"). A needless alteration and weakening of the meaning, in accordance with Song Sol. i. 2; Prov. vii. 18, as rendered by the LXX. Comp. rather the remarks below on ver. 20.—**In her love delight thyself evermore.** שָׁגָה elsewhere used of the staggering gait of the intoxicated (chap. xx. 1; Isa. xxviii. 7), here by a bold trope used of the ecstatic joy of a lover. That the same word is employed in the next verse for the description of the foolish delirium of the libertine hastening after the harlot, and again in ver. 23 of the exhausted prostration of the morally and physically ruined transgressor,—and is therefore used in each instance with a somewhat modified meaning, indicates plainly a definite purpose. The threefold use of שָׁגָה is intended to constitute a climax, to illustrate the sad consequences of sins of unchastity.—Ver. 20. Emphatic sequel to the foregoing, concisely and vigorously summing up the admonitory and warning contents of vers. 8-19. **And embrace the bosom of a wanton woman.** This expression (תְּחַבֶּק חֵק) testifies to the correctness of the reading דַּדֶּיהָ in ver. 19.

5. Vers. 21-23. Epilogue for the monitory presentation of the truth that no one is in condition

to conceal his adultery, be it ever so secretly practiced,—that on the contrary God sees this with every other transgression, and punishes it with the merited destruction of the sinner.—**For before Jehovah's eyes are the ways of man, and all his paths He marketh.**—(פָּלַס here also not to "ponder," but to "mark out," see note on ver. 6.) An important proof text not merely for God's omniscience, but also for His special providence and "*concursus*" [coöperation in human conduct]. Comp. Job xxxiv. 21; xxiv. 23; xxxi. 4, *etc.*—Ver. 22. **His sins overtake him, the evil doer.** The double designation of the object, by the suffix in יִלְכְּדֻנוֹ and then by the expression "the evil doer," added for emphasis, gives a peculiar force. Comp. xiv. 13; Ezek. xvi. 3; Jer. ix. 25.—**By the cords of his sin.** Comp. Isa. v. 18, and in general, for the sentiment of the whole verse, chap. i. 31, 32; xi. 5; xviii. 7; xxix. 6; Ps. vii. 15; xl. 12; John viii. 34; 2 Pet. ii. 19.—Ver. 23. **For lack of correction.** This is undoubtedly the explanation of בְּאֵין מוּסָר, and not "without correction" (UMBREIT). The בְּ is not circumstantial, but causal (instrumental), as in the 2d member.—As to the meaning of שָׁנָה see above, remarks on ver. 19.

DOCTRINAL, ETHICAL, AND HOMILETIC.

That our chapter holds up in opposition to all unregulated gratification of the sexual impulses, the blessing of conjugal fidelity and chastity, requires no detailed proof. It is a chapter on a *pious marriage relation*, appropriately attached to the preceding, on the right training of children; for pious and strict discipline of children is impossible, where the sacred bonds of marriage are disregarded, violated and trampled under foot. In conformity with the thoroughly practical nature of the doctrine of wisdom (the Hhokmah), the author, as vers. 15-20 show, completely overthrows all the demands and suggestions of a sensual desire that has broken over all the sacred bounds prescribed by God, and so, as it were, has become wild and insane, by exhibiting the satisfaction of the sexual impulse *in marriage* as justified and in conformity with the divine rule. An important hint for a practical estimate of the contents of this chapter, from which evidently there may be drawn not merely material and arguments for a thorough treatment of the Christian doctrine with respect to the sixth commandment in general, but specially for the exhibition of the true evangelical idea of marriage, in contrast with the extravagant asceticism of Romish theology, and also of many sects both of ancient and modern times (Montanists, Eustathians, Cathari, Gichtelites, *etc.*). In this connection 1 Cor. vii. must also, naturally, be brought into the account, especially the 6th verse of this chapter, which exhibits the fundamental idea of vers. 15-20 of our section, reduced to the briefest and most concise form that is possible; with the addition of the needful corrective, and the explanation that is appropriate in connection with the "always" and "evermore" of ver. 19, which might possibly be misunderstood.

As a *homily*, therefore, *on the entire chapter*: On the right keeping of the 6th commandment, a) through the avoidance of all unchastity; b) through the maintenance of a faithful (vers. 15-20) and devout (vers. 21-23) demeanor in the sacred marriage relation.—MELANCHTHON: The sum of the matter is: Love truly thine own wife, and be content with her alone, as this law of marriage was at once ordained in Paradise (Gen. ii.): "they shall be one flesh," *i. e.*, one male and one female united inseparably. For then also, even if human nature had remained incorrupt, God would have wished men to comprehend purity, and to maintain the exercise of obedience by observing this order, *viz.*, by avoiding all wandering desires. Comp. AUGUSTINE: Marriage before the fall was ordained for duty, after the fall for a remedy.

Vers. 1-4. EGARD:—A harlot is the devil's decoy, and becomes to many a tree of death unto death. The fleshly and the spiritual harlot most fill hell (chap. vii. 27). The devil comes first with sweetness and friendliness, to betray man, afterward however with bitterness, to destroy the soul.—[Ver. 3. TRAPP: There is no such pleasure as to have overcome an offered pleasure; neither is there any greater conquest than that that is gotten over a man's corruptions.]—STARKE: Beware of the spiritual antichristian harlot, who tempts the whole world to idolatry, and to forsaking the true God (1 John v. 21).—There are in general many allegorical interpretations in the old writers, in which the strange, lascivious woman is either partially or outright assumed (as, *e. g.*, more recently in the *Berleb. Bible*) to be the designation of "the false church," of antichrist, or worldly wisdom, *etc.* [See also WORDSW. *in loc.*, and also on ver. 19, together with his citations from BEDE, *etc.* —A.]. For Evangelical preaching, naturally, only a treatment that is partially allegorical, can be regarded admissible, and in the end expedient; such a treatment as consists in a generalization of the specific prohibition of unchastity into a warning against spiritual licentiousness or idolatry in general.

Ver. 15-23. STARKE: An admonition to hold to one's own wife only; 1) the admonition (15-17); 2) the motives: a) the blessing on such conjugal fidelity (18, 19); b) the dishonor (20, 21) and c) the ruinous result of conjugal unfaithfulness (22, 23).—[Ver. 15. ARNOT: God condescends to bring His own institute forward in rivalry with the deceitful pleasures of sin. All the accessories of the family are the Father's gift, and He expects us to observe and value them.—H. SMITH (quoted by BRIDGES): First choose thy love; then love thy choice.]—EGARD: A married life full of true love, joy and peace, is a paradise on earth; on the other hand, a marriage full of hate, unfaithfulness and strife is a real hell.—VON GERLACH: The loveliness and enjoyment of a happy domestic relation as the earthly motive, the holy ordinance of matrimony watched over by God with omniscient strictness, as the higher motive to chastity.—*Calwer Handbuch:* Be true to thine own wife; therein is happiness! Sin against her, and thou becomest through thine own fault wretched!—[Ver. 21. TRAPP: A man that is about any evil should stand in awe of himself; how much more of God!—ARNOT: Secrecy is the study and hope of the wicked. A sinner's chief labor is to hide his sin; and his labor is all lost. Sin becomes the instrument of punishing sinners—retribution in the system of nature, set in motion by the act of sin].

9. Warning against inconsiderate suretyship.

CHAP. VI. 1–5.

1 My son, if thou hast become surety for thy neighbor,
  hast given thine hand to a stranger;
2 if thou art entangled through the words of thy mouth,
  art snared by the words of thy mouth:
3 then do this, my son, and free thyself,
  since thou hast come into the hand of thy neighbor:
  go, bestir thyself, and importune thy neighbor!
4 Give no sleep to thine eyes,
  nor slumber to thine eyelids;
5 free thyself, like a roe, from his hand,
  and like a bird from the hand of the fowler.

10. Rebuke of the sluggard.

CHAP. VI. 6–11.

6 Go to the ant thou sluggard;
  consider her ways and be wise!
7 which hath no governor,
  director, or ruler;
8 (yet) she prepareth in summer her food,
  she gathereth in harvest her store!
9 How long wilt thou lie, O sluggard?
  when wilt thou rise from thy sleep?
10 "A little sleep, a little slumber,
   a little folding of the hands to rest;"—
11 then cometh thy poverty like a robber,
   and thy want as an armed man!

11. Warning against deceit and violent dealing.

CHAP. VI. 12-19.

12 A worthless creature is the deceiver,
   he that walketh in perverseness of speech;
13 he who winketh with his eye, who speaketh with his foot,
   who hinteth with his finger.
14 Perverseness is in his heart,
   he deviseth evil at all times;
   he stirreth up strifes.
15 Therefore suddenly shall his destruction come,
   in a moment shall he be destroyed, and there is no remedy.
16 These six things Jehovah hateth,
   and seven are an abhorrence of his soul;
17 haughty eyes, a lying tongue,
   and hands that shed innocent blood;

18 a heart that deviseth evil plots,
   feet that make haste to run to evil;
19 one that uttereth lies as a false witness,
   and one that stirreth up strifes between brethren.

12. Admonition to chastity with a warning delineation of the fearful consequences of adultery.

CHAP. VI. 20–35.

20   Keep, O my son, thy father's commandment,
     and reject not the law of thy mother:
21 bind them to thy heart evermore,
   fasten it about thy neck.
22 When thou walkest let it guide thee,
   when thou liest down let it guard thee,
   and at thy waking let it talk with thee.
23 For a lamp is the commandment, and the law a light,
   and the reproofs of corrections are a way of life;
24 to keep thee from the vile woman,
   from the flattering tongue of the strange woman.—
25 Long not for her beauty in thy heart,
   and let her not catch thee with her eyelids!
26 For for the sake of a harlot one cometh to a loaf of bread,
   and a man's wife lieth in wait for the precious life.
27 May one take fire in his bosom,
   and his clothes not be burned?
28 Or may one walk upon coals,
   and his feet not be scorched?
29 So he who goeth to his neighbor's wife;
   no one that toucheth her shall be unpunished.
30 Men do not overlook the thief, when he stealeth
   to satisfy his craving when he is hungry;
31 if he be found he must restore seven fold,
   the whole wealth of his house must he give.
32 He who committeth adultery is beside himself;
   he that destroyeth himself doeth such things.
33 Stripes and disgrace doth he find,
   and his reproach will not pass away.
34 For jealousy is man's fierce anger,
   and he spareth not in the day of vengeance.
35 He regardeth not any ransom,
   and is not willing if thou increase thy gift.

GRAMMATICAL AND CRITICAL.

Vers. 1, 3. The form רֵעֶיךָ, which is found in some texts, is not a plural, but the ־ "indicates in pause the pronunciation with ־ as in Gen. xvi. 5; Ps. ix. 15," HITZIG. Many MSS., moreover, exhibit here the regular form רֵעֲךָ [BÖTTCHER, § 888, n. 2, utterly rejects the possibility that רֵעֶיךָ can be a singular form, and also that the plural form is admissible here. HOLDEN's rendering "thy friends," is incorrectly based upon the plural reading.—A.]

Ver. 5. [Note the appropriate change of tense. The future הָכִין, "fiens solitum," BÖTT. § 943, b, and the perf. אָנְרָה, "Perfectum effectivum," §§ 940, 4; 950, 4; the continually recurring "preparation," the assured "gathering."—A.]

Ver. 12. הָלַךְ stands here with the simple accusative without בְּ, as in Mic. ii. 11; Is. xxxiii. 15; Ps. xv. 2.

Ver. 13. [קֹרֵץ used here alone with בְּ, usually with a direct object.] מֹלֵל; the verb is in use only in Piel. For the occurrence of participial forms in Piel thus resembling Kal, see FUERST (sub. v. כָּלַל), and BÖTT. § 994, 4.—A.].

Ver. 14. For the explanation of the K'ri כִּדְיָנִים (instead of the K'thibh כִּדְיָנִים) see HITZIG on this passage, who is probably right in referring to Gen. xxxvii. 36 as the source and occasion of this substitution.

Ver. 16. [The fem. הֵנָּה used of that which is distinctly neuter. See BÖTT. § 862, 4.—A.].

Ver. 19. The יָפִיחַ can be regarded as a relative Imperf., with which the participle מְשַׁלֵּחַ interchanges, or it may be regarded as an irregular participial form, lengthened from יָפֵחַ Ps. xxvii. 12, and formed like יָצִיא, נָטִיל etc.

(So HITZIG explains the form) [FUERST regards it an Imperf., but BÖTT., very decidedly as a Hiph. participal, here and in xii. 17; xiv. 25; xix. 5, 9; Ps. xii. 6; xxvii. 12. See § 994, 9.—A.].

Ver. 21. קָשְׁרֵם, a masc. suffix referring to fem. nouns. BÖTT. § 877, 3, declares it characteristic of "secular prose, popular poetry, and the majority of the later Hebrew writers" thus to disregard exactness in the use of the suffix pronouns. Chap. xx. 12 is the only similar example adduced from Proverbs. Comp. GREEN, § 104, g.—A.].

Ver. 32. מַשְׁחִית, a future participle. The suffix in עֹשָׂהּ refers to the נֹאֵף which is readily supplied from the נֹאֵף אִשָּׁה of the first member. [Interpretations divide as to the subject and predicate clause of the sentence. MUENSCHER, NOYES, HOLDEN agree with the E. V. in making destruction the predicted fate of the adulterer; STUART, KAMPH., and DE W. agree with our author in making adultery the natural and certain course of the self-destroyer.—A.].

EXEGETICAL AND CRITICAL.

1. The sixth chapter consists of four independent admonitory discourses of unequal length, of quite different contents, and a merely external and circumstantial connection (through points of contact, as between "sleep and slumber" in ver. 4 and the same expressions in ver. 10; through the triple warning against impoverishment; vers. 11, 15 and 26, etc.). This is as apparent as is the fact that it is only in the last of these four sections that the subject of adultery, that was treated in the fifth chapter, is resumed. It is nevertheless arbitrary and lacks all clear proof, when HITZIG declares the three preceding sections to be the addition of an interpolator different from the author of chaps. i.-ix., who is supposed to have taken them from some old book of proverbs, and to have enlarged the third by adding vers. 16-19. For, it is argued, this numerical group of proverbs, of eight members, clearly shows itself to be the personal production of the interpolator, who was led by the sixfold division of the categories in vers. 12-14 to the composition of this group of the six things that the Lord hates. As though this parallel sixfold or rather sevenfold arrangement in vers. 12-19 could not be the work of the composer of the entire group of proverbial discourses that lies before us, just as in the series of similar numerical proverbs contained in chap. xxx. (comp. Introd. § 14)! And still further, as if there had not been already in what has gone before at least one isolated warning against unchastity and adultery, as a demonstration of the fact, that in this connection also the advisory and admonitory discourses that relate to this matter (chap. v. 1 sq.; vi. 20 sq.; vii. 1 sq.), must not necessarily form a whole continuing without interruption, but might very naturally be interspersed with other shorter passages of differing contents, like those forming the first half of chap. vi.—Apart from this, HITZIG is undoubtedly correct in judging, that attention should be called to the close connection of vers. 16-19 with vers. 12-15, and that the first mentioned group should be regarded as a mere continuation and fuller expansion of the import of the last mentioned. A special argument for this is the literal repetition of the expression, "stir up strifes," from ver. 14 in ver. 19. The view recently prevalent (see e. g., UMBREIT, BERTHEAU, ELSTER on this passage), according to which vers. 16-19 form a separate group of verses as really independent as the rest (1-5, 6, 11, etc.) is to be estimated by what has been already said. The correct division has been before presented by DELITZSCH (HERZOG's Real. Encycl. XIV., 698), and also by EWALD (on this passage).

2. Vers. 1-5. Warning against suretyship.—**My son, if thou hast become surety for thy neighbor.**—The frequent warnings which our book contains against giving security for others (comp. in addition xi. 15; xvii. 18; xx. 16; xxii. 26), are to be explained doubtless by the severe treatment, which, in accordance with the old Hebrew jurisprudence, was awarded to sureties; for their goods might be distrained or they even sold as slaves, just as in the case of insolvent debtors (2 Kings iv. 1: Matth. xviii. 25; comp. Ecclesiast. viii. 13; xxix. 18-25, and also the warning maxim of the Greek philosopher THALES: "ἐγγύα, πάρα δ' ἄτα" [give surety, and ruin is near], and the modern popular proverb "Bürgen soll man würgen" [the alliteration cannot be translated; an approach can be made to it in "worry a surety"].—In the passage before us the warning is not so much against suretyship in general, as merely against the imprudent assumption of such obligations, leaving out of account the moral unreliableness of the man involved; and the counsel is to the quickest possible release from every obligation of this kind that may have been hastily assumed.—**Hast given thine hand to a stranger.**—The stranger (זָר) is not the creditor, but the debtor, who in the first clause had been designated as "neighbor." For according to Job xvii. 3 the surety gave his hand to the debtor as a sign that he became bound for him. Therefore the translation of EWALD and ELSTER, "for a stranger," is unnecessary as it is incorrect.—Ver. 2. **If thou art entangled through the words of thy mouth.**—This second half of the protasis, which, according to Hebrew idiom, is still dependent on the "if" of ver. 1, refers to the involved and embarrassed condition of the surety some time after his inconsiderate giving of bonds.—Ver. 3. **Then do this, my son,** etc.—The apodosis, with its emphatic warning (which extends through ver. 5), is fitly introduced by the intensive particle אֵפוֹא, now, now therefore. Comp. Job xvii. 15; Gen. xxvii. 32; xliii. 11.—**Since thou hast come into the hand of thy neighbor.** HITZIG, interpreting the כִּי, as in ii. 10, as equivalent to אִם, translates "if thou hast come," etc. But the introduction of a reason is here more pertinent, since the case of an unfortunate issue to the suretyship had already been assumed in ver. 2.—**Stamp with the foot.**—This meaning of הִתְרַפֵּס, which is attested also by Ps. lxviii. 30, is urgently commended by the following, "importune thy neighbor" (רְהַב רֵעֶיךָ). [In our version of this phrase in its connection we have substituted FUERST's interpretation which is also HOLDEN's. The verb is found only here and in Ps. lxviii. 30. GESENIUS and many others, start-

ing with the radical idea, "to trample," which they find in רפס and assume in רפם, translate the Hithp. in both passages, "suffer thyself to be trampled," i. e., "prostrate thyself." [So the E. V., DE W., M., N. and ST.]. HUPFELD (see Comm. on Ps. lxviii. 31) and others adopt the indirect reflexive as the true meaning,— "prostrate before thyself, i. e., subdue." FUERST, distinguishing the two verbs, interprets רפס as meaning, in accordance with many Arabic analogies, "to move, stir, hasten," and the Hithp. as meaning "*sich beeilen, sich sputen*," i. e., in the Imperative, make haste, bestir thyself. Although this rendering has not in its favor the weight of authorities, the internal evidence appears to us to be decidedly for it.—A.] The meaning is that one should in every way force the heedless debtor—for it is he, and not possibly the creditor, that is here again intended by the "neighbor"—to the fulfilment of his obligations, before it is too late, i. e., before the matter comes to the distraint of goods or other judicial processes on the part of the creditor.—Ver. 5. **Free thyself as a roe from his hand, and like a bird,** *etc*.—Gazelle and bird—in the original a paronomasia: צְבִי and צִפּוֹר—are appropriate emblems of a captive seeking its freedom with anxious haste and exertion. The way is already prepared for these figures by the expressions employed in ver. 2. Instead of, כַּף "out of the hand," all the old versions, except the Vulg. and Venet., had the reading מִפַּח, "out of the snare." But this is an attempt at rhetorical improvement (perhaps according to the analogy of Ps. xci. 3), "in which it was overlooked, that the hand was introduced the first as well as the second time with a reference to the giving of the hand on becoming security" (ver. 1). Comp. UMBREIT and HITZIG on this passage.

3. Vers. 6-11. **Go to the ant, thou sluggard.**—The ant, ever working of its own impulse quietly and unweariedly, is proverbial as an emblem of industry, both among Orientals and in the West; comp. MEIDANI'S *Arabic Proverbs*, III., 468; SAADI'S Persian fable of the ant and the nightingale; ARISTOTLE'S *Historia Anim.*, 9, 26; VIRGIL'S *Georg.*, I., 186 sq.; HORACE, *Serm.*, I., 1, 33; also the German word "*ämsig*" (Old High Germ. *emazic*), which is derived from "*Ameise*" (WEIGAND, *deutsches Wörterb.*, I., 35). [See THOMSON'S *Land and Book*, I., 519, 520, for illustrations both of the diligence of the ant and the utter laziness of Oriental laborers, "which have no governor, director, or ruler."—A.]—Ver. 7. **Which hath no governor, director or ruler.**—The three expressions קָצִין and שֹׁטֵר and מֹשֵׁל are relatively like the Arabic official titles, "Kadi," "Wali," and "Emir." The שֹׁטֵר in particular is the manager, the overseer, who, *e. g.*, in connection with public works urges on to labor (Ex. v. 6, 14 sq.).—Furthermore, compare chap xxx. 27, where also the first clause of ver. 8 recurs, in almost literal agreement with our passage.

Vers. 9-11 add to the positive admonition to industry an emphatic warning against the evil consequences of its opposite. — **How long wilt thou lie, O sluggard?**—Literally: till when wilt thou, *etc*. The עַד־מָתַי of the first clause and כְּתַי of the second stand in the same order as in Nehem. ii. 6. The meaning of the two parallel questions is substantially "Wilt thou continue lying forever?—Wilt thou never rise?" The double question is, as it were, a logical protasis to the apodosis which follows in ver. 11 after the interposing of the sluggard's answer (ver. 10): "then cometh (Heb. בָּא) like a robber," *etc*. Comp. BERTHEAU on this passage.—**A little sleep,** *etc*.—Ironical imitation of the language of the lazy man; literally repeated in chap. xxiv. 33.—**A little folding of the hands**—i. e., a little folding of the arms, a well-known attitude of one who is settling himself down to sleep (comp. Eccl. iv. 5), and who in that act does just the opposite of that for which the hands and arms are naturally designed, that is, for vigorous work.—**Then cometh thy poverty like a robber.**—כְּהַלֵּךְ strictly *grassator*, a frequenter of the roads, a highwayman, a footpad (LXX: κακὸς ὁδοιπορος). The parallel passage, xxiv. 34, has the Hithp. participle כְּמִתְהַלֵּךְ without בְּ, which gives the far weaker sense: "then cometh *quietly* thy poverty." —**As an armed man**—lit., as one armed with a shield (אִישׁ מָגֵן); for even the assailing robber, since he must necessarily be prepared for resistance, must carry with weapons of offence the means of defence.

4. Vers. 12-19. **Against the deceitful and violent.**—Concerning the relation of the two divisions of this group of verses, the first of which (vers. 12-15) depicts the seven modes of deceitful action, while the second (vers. 16-19) expressly designates them a seven hated by God, repeating also their enumeration,—see above, § 1 of these exegetical comments.—**A worthless man is the deceiver.**—In support of this construction of אִישׁ אָוֶן as the subject and of the prefixed אָדָם בְּלִיָּעַל as the predicate [a construction preferred also by NOYES, KAMPH, *etc*.] we have, besides the arrangement, especially the substitution of אָדָם בְּ for אִישׁ בְּ, which was rather to have been expected according to the analogy of 2 Sam. xvi. 7, *etc*. If the second expression were only "an intensive appositive to the first" (BERTHEAU; see also LUTHER [WORDSW., M., ST., II., in agreement with the E. V.]: "a heedless man, a mischievous person"), then we should have looked for אִישׁ in both instances. With אָוֶן אִישׁ, "man of deceit, of falsity, of inward untruth and vileness," comp. furthermore אָוֶן כְּתֵי, Job xxii. 15; and also, below, ver. 18.—**He that walketh in perverseness of speech.**—Comp. iv. 24; xxviii. 18.—Ver. 13. The three participles of this verse are best understood, with HITZIG, as prefixed appositives to the subject contained in בְּלִבּוֹ, ver. 14, which is indeed the same as that of the 12th verse.—**Who winketh with his eyes.**—Comp. x. 10; Ps. xxxv. 19.—**Who speaketh with his feet**—*i. e.*, gives signs in mysterious ways (LXX: σημαίνει), now with one foot, then with the other.—**Who hinteth with**

his fingers.—מוֹרֶה Hiph. part. from ירה, here used in its most primitive meaning. The evil intent involved in the three forms of the language of signs as here enumerated is of course implied.—Ver. 14. He deviseth evil at all times.—Comp. iii. 29.—He stirreth up strife.—Literally "he lets loose contentions" (Hitzig), or "he throws out matters of dispute" (Bertheau); comp. ver. 19 and chap. xvi. 28.—Ver. 15. Therefore suddenly shall his destruction come.—Comp. i. 17; iii. 25; xxiv. 22.—Quickly will he be destroyed, etc.—Comp. xxix. 1; Is. i. 28; xxx. 14; Jer. xix. 11.—Without remedy.—Comp. iv. 22.

Ver. 16. These six things Jehovah hateth, and seven, etc.—Of the origin of this peculiar proverbial form, using symbolical numbers, a form for which Arabic and Persian gnomic literature supply numerous illustrations (comp. UMBREIT on this passage), ELSTER probably gives the simplest and most correct explanation, deriving it "purely from the exigencies of parallelism." "The form of parallelism could not, on account of harmony, be sacrificed in any verse. But how should a parallel be found for a number? Since it was not any definite number that was the important thing, relief was found by taking one of the next adjacent numbers as the parallel to that which was chiefly in mind." In a similar way HITZIG on Amos i. 3 (where the numbers put into this relation are three and four); "To the number three the number four is appended to characterize the first as one optionally taken, to convey the idea that *there are not understood to be precisely three and no more, but possibly more*." At any rate, those expositors are in the wrong, who, as *e. g.*, recently BERTHEAU and VON GERLACH, find the design of this mode of numeration in the fact that the last of the enumerated elements, the seventh vice therefore in the case before us, is to be brought out with especial emphasis. [STANLEY (*Hist. Jewish Church*, II. p. 258), adduces this as a probable example of the "enigmas" or "riddles," which were one of the most characteristic embodiments of the wisdom of the wise king.—ARNOT: There is one parallel well worthy of notice between the seven cursed things here, and the seven blessed things in the fifth chapter of Matthew. The first and last of the seven are identical in the two lists. "The Lord hates a proud look" is precisely equivalent to "blessed are the poor in spirit;" and "he that soweth discord among brethren" is the exact converse of the "peacemaker."—A.].—Ver. 17. Haughty eyes: literally, high or lofty eyes; comp. xxx. 13; Ps. xviii. 27; cxxxi. 1; Job xxi. 22; xl. 11; also the Latin expression *grande supercilium*.—Hands that shed innocent blood. Comp. i. 11 sq., and Isa. lix. 7, with which passage ver. 18 also corresponds in the form of expression, without for that reason being necessarily derived from it, as HITZIG holds. For in case of such derivation the order of words ought to correspond more exactly with the alleged original, as in Rom. iii. 15-17.—Ver. 19. One that uttereth lies as a false witness, literally, one that breathes lies. The same characterization of the false witness is found also in chap. xiv. 5, 25; xix. 5, 9. As respects the arrangement in which the seven manifestations of treach-

erous dealing are enumerated in these verses, it does not perfectly correspond with the order observed in ver. 12-14. There the series is mouth, eyes, feet, fingers, heart, devising evil counsels, stirring up strifes: here it is eyes, tongue, hands, heart, feet, speaking lies, instigating strife. With reference to the organs which are named as the instruments in the first five forms of treacherous wickedness, in the second enumeration an order is adopted involving a regular descent (ver. 16-19, eyes, tongue, hands, etc.); the base disposition to stir up strife, or to let loose controversy (see rem. on ver. 14) in both cases ends the series.

5. Vers. 20-24. *Admonition to chastity*, preparing the way for a subsequent warning against adultery.—Keep, O my son, thy father's commandment, etc. This general introduction to the new warning against adultery corresponds with the similar preparatory admonitions in chap. v. 1, 2 and vii. 1-5, and serves, like these, to announce the great importance of the succeeding warnings. With respect to ver. 20 in particular comp. i. 8.—Ver. 21. Bind them to thy heart evermore, etc. So chap. iii. 3 and vii. 3. On account of the plural which occurs in the verse, with which the singular is interchanged in ver. 22, HITZIG conjectures the insertion of this verse by a late interpolator, and that in accordance with the standard furnished by chap. iii. 3, in which place the passage is held to be original. This is arbitrary, for no single ancient manuscript or version confirms the suspicion. Just as well might ver. 22 be declared interpolated, inasmuch as only in this is the singular form found, while immediately after, in ver. 23, the double designation "commandment" and "doctrine" returns.—Ver. 22. When thou walkest let it guide thee. The contrast between walking and sleeping or lying is like that in iii. 23, 24.—When thou wakest let it talk with thee. The accusative suffix in תְּשִׂיחֶךָ is here employed as in Ps. v. 4 ; xlii. 4 ; Zech. vii. 5, etc., for the designation of the person to whom the intercourse indicated in the action of the verb relates. With regard to שִׂיחַ to take, to converse, comp. also Ps. lxix. 13; with reference to the sentence as a whole comp. Ps. cxxxix. 18.—Ver. 23. For the reproofs of correction are a way of life, *i. e.*, they lead to life, comp. ii. 19; iii. 2, 16. "Reproofs of discipline" (תּוֹכְחוֹת מוּסָר) corrective reproofs, reproofs whose aim is correction.—Ver. 24. From the vile woman, strictly the woman of evil, of vileness. רָע (for which the LXX here read רֵעַ) is therefore a substantive, as in the phrase "the way of evil" in chap. ii. 12.—From the flattering tongue of the strange woman; literally, from the smoothness of the tongue of the strange woman. For instead of לָשׁוֹן, from which reading of the Masoretic text the meaning would result "from the smoothness of a strange tongue," we must doubtless point לְשׁוֹן (*construct state*), since the subject of remark here is the strange, wanton woman (just as in ii. 16; v. 20), while the thought of a foreign language (γλῶσσα

ἀλλοτρία, LXX) is altogether remote from the context. In opposition to the translation of EWALD, BERTHEAU and ELSTER, "from the smooth-tongued, the strange woman," comp. HITZIG on this passage.

6. Ver. 25-35. Warning against adultery itself.—**With her eyelids**, with which she throws amorous and captivating glances at her lover, comp. Ecclesiast. xxvi. 9. The eyelids (or, more literally, eyelashes) are here compared with the cords of a net, as in Eccles. xii. 3, with the lattice of a window, or as in the erotic songs of the Arabs and Persians, with darts, with lances, daggers or swords.—Ver. 26. **For, for the sake of a harlot one cometh to a loaf of bread**, *i. e.*, to the last bit, the last morsel of bread, as a sign and emblem of utter poverty (thus SCHULTENS, C. B. MICHAELIS, UMBREIT, ELSTER); or again, the meaning may be to the begging a loaf of bread, to beggary (thus ABEN EZRA, VATABLUS, ROSENMUELLER, ELSTER, HITZIG). In opposition to the translation defended by most of the ancient expositors, and recently by ZIEGLER, EWALD, BERTHEAU, *etc.*, "For as the hire of a harlot one gives hardly a bit of bread," or as others prefer "merely a bit of bread," may be adduced 1) the context, see the 2d clause; 2) the lexical fact that עַד can neither mean "hardly" nor "merely;" 3) the fact, historical and archæological, established by Gen. xxxviii. 17, *etc.*, that the harlot's reward in ancient Palestine doubtless amounted to more than a mere loaf of bread, *e. g.* a kid, as in the case cited from Genesis, or a price considerably higher, as seems to follow from Prov. xxix. 3; Ecclesiast. ix. 6; Luke xv. 30.—**Lieth in wait for the precious life**. Very appropriately is נֶפֶשׁ, "life," the predicate יְקָרָה "costly" connected with it; for its value rises above all mere property; comp. Ps. xlix. 8.—Ver. 27-29. The meaning is this: impossible as it is that the clothing on one's breast, or that one's feet should remain unharmed by scorching if fire be brought near them, so inconceivable is it that the adulterer should follow his unlawful intercourse without evil consequences and just retribution. The two questions in vers. 27, 28 imply a strong negation, like the interrogative clauses in Amos iii. 4-6. Ver. 29 is connected with the two negative antecedent clauses as a correlative consequent, and is therefore introduced by כֵּן, so.—Vers. 30, 31. A new figure to illustrate the punishment, surely impending and severe, which threatens the adulterer.—**Men do not overlook the thief**, *etc.*; literally "they do not contemn it in the thief." The imperf. יָבוּזוּ expresses the idea of custom, that which occurs in accordance with experience. [Interpreters are divided between the two ideas of "scorn" and "disregard" as proper renderings of the verb. STUART, MUENSCH., WORDS. adopt the former; men do not despise the thief, though he must be punished; they do despise the adulterer. WORDS. calls attention to a disposition in modern society to reverse this judgment. NOYES, HOLDEN, like DE W., FUERST and our author, adopt the other view.—A.].—**To satisfy his craving when he is hungry**. This circumstance, which exhibits the guilt of the thief in a milder light, serves evidently to display the punishment that befalls the adulterer with whom he is here compared, as one more richly deserved. For the more presumptuous his crime, the less excused, or, as it were, demanded by his necessities, the more just is the punishment that comes upon him! If HITZIG had taken due notice of this meaning of ver. 30, which is transparent enough, he would have seen in advance how unnecessary and excessively artificial is the attempt to explain the verse as interrogative. [KAMPH. adopts his view but does not strengthen it].—**He must restore sevenfold**. According to the prescriptions of the law in Ex. xxi. 37; xxii. 1 sq., it should strictly be only four or fivefold (comp. the publican Zaccheus, Luke xix. 8). But in common life these prescriptions were probably not ordinarily observed: the injured party allowing his silence, his declining a judicial prosecution of the matter, to be purchased at a higher rate than was exactly allowed. Furthermore, that "sevenfold" is here used loosely, only as a round number (comp. Gen. iv. 15), and is not designed, as might be thought, to mark the highest conceivable ransom, appears from the 2d member, which suggests the probability of losing "the whole wealth of his house."—Ver. 32 stands in the same relation to the two preceding as ver. 29 to 27 and 28; it expresses the conclusion that is to be drawn from the meaning, which is clothed in the form of an analogy or parable, with reference to the well-deserved recompense of the adulterer. It is therefore hasty and arbitrary in HITZIG to reject this as a spurious gloss, and to find in ver. 33 the direct continuation of the thief's punishment, which has been depicted in ver. 31.—**He that destroyeth himself doeth such things**. Literally, "whoso will destroy his life, he does it."—Ver. 33. **Stripes and disgrace**. The נֶגַע, *plaga*, may here very well stand in its literal sense, and so designate the blows with which the adulterer detected in the act will be visited by the husband of the unfaithful wife, and will be driven from the house (UMBREIT, HITZIG).—Ver. 34. **For jealousy is man's fierce anger**, *i. e.*, the jealousy (קִנְאָה as in chap. xxvii. 4) of the injured husband is a fire blazing fiercely, burning and raging with all the might of a man; comp. "the hurling of a man" [or as others "a mighty prostration"] Is. xxii. 17. The 2d half of the verse explains this somewhat brief expression, "man's wrath," which, moreover, appears to be chosen not without collateral reference to the more rapidly evaporating wrath of women.—Ver. 35. **He regardeth not any ransom**, literally, "he does not lift up the face of any ransom," *i. e.*, does not receive it as adequate to allay his wrath—as one lifts up the face of a suppliant when his request is granted or favorably received.—**And is not willing**, *i. e.*, to forego his strict right of revenge.

DOCTRINAL AND ETHICAL.

1. The warning against improvident suretyship in the unqualified form, and the urgent and almost passionate tone in which it is presented

in vers. 1-5, rests upon the consideration that "all men are liars" (Ps. cxvi. 11; Rom. iii. 4), that therefore no one can be trusted (comp. Jer. xvii. 5; "Cursed be the man that trusteth in man"), that every neighbor is at the same time in a certain sense a "stranger" to us (see above on ver. 1), in a word, that one must be prepared for manifestations of unfaithfulness, or unreliableness, on the part of any one whatever, though he stood ever so near us. Hence the duty, for the sake of preserving one's own independence and sparing one's own strength for his personal work (bodily as well as mental), of extricating one's self at any cost and as speedily as possible from every relation of suretyship, from the continuance of which injurious consequences might result to our own freedom and welfare. With the admonitions of our Lord in the Sermon on the Mount, to be ready at all times for the lending and giving away of one's property, even in cases where one cannot hope for the recovery of what has been given out (Luke vi. 30, 34, 36; comp. 1 Cor. vi. 7) this demand is not in conflict. For Christ also plainly demands no such readiness to suffer loss on account of our neighbor, as would deprive us of personal liberty, and rob us of all means for further beneficence; and yet this sort of evil result from suretyship is what the author of our passage has in his eye.

2. Also in the subsequent warning against slothfulness (vers. 6-11) the reference to the danger of impoverishment appears to be the main motive, brought forward with especial emphasis. This is above all things else the precise thing to be learned from the example of the ant, that it is important to gather diligently "in summer," that one may not suffer in winter,—that the "harvest time," when all is within reach in abundance, is the time for earnest and unceasing toils, that one may be able calmly to meet the later seasons of want which offer to the most willing and vigorous industry no opportunity for acquiring. Comp. the example of Joseph in Egypt (Gen. xli. sq.), and apply all this to the spiritual department of labors in Christ's service, e. g., those of the pastor, the missionary, etc.

3. The six or seven vices, twice enumerated in different order and form of expression, against which the paragraph vers. 12-19 warns (comp. the exegetical notes on ver. 19), are at the same time all of them manifestations of hatred against one's neighbor, or sins against the second table of the Decalogue; yet it is not so much a general unkindness as rather an unkindness consisting and displaying itself in falseness and malice that is emphasized as their common element. And only on account of the peculiarly mischievous and ruinous character of just these sins of hatred to one's neighbor, is he who is subject to them represented as an object of peculiarly intense abhorrence on the part of a holy God, and as threatened with the strongest manifestations of His anger in penalties (vers. 15, 16).

4. As a fundamental proposition for the successful avoidance of all converse with impure wantons, and of the dangers thence resulting, there is introduced in the 1st clause of ver. 25 a warning even against the very first beginnings of all unlawful sexual intercourse, against impure longings, or unchaste desires and thoughts of the heart. Comp. the last commandment of the Decalogue (Ex. xx. 17), as well as Christ's intensifying and spiritualizing of the Mosaic prohibition of adultery; Matth. v. 28.—The admonition also, which is prefixed as introductory, to keep continually before the eyes and in the heart the teachings of Divine wisdom (comp. Tob. iv. 6), serves as an emphatic utterance of this "*Obsta principiis!*" or the exhibition of the necessity that the very first germs and roots of the sin of unchastity must be rooted out.

HOMILETIC AND PRACTICAL.

In the endeavor to comprehend in one homiletic whole the four main divisions of the chapter, one would first of all need to have clearly in view the suggestions given in vers. 2, 11, 15 and 26 sq., with reference to the danger of sinking into poverty and destitution, and to employ these in fixing his central idea. In some such way as this then: Even in the present life want and evil of every sort are wont to be the attendants *a*) of the lighter offences 1) of inconsiderateness (vers. 1-5) and 2) of slothfulness (vers. 6-11); *b*) of the grosser transgressions and vices, such as result 1) from pride and malignity (vers. 12-19), and 2) from lust of the eyes and sensuality (vers. 20-35).—Comp. STÖCKER: Against unfaithfulness in life and conversation, as it displays itself 1) in suretyship; 2) in fulfilling the duties of one's calling; 3) in daily converse with human society; 4) in married life.

Ver. 1-5. STARKE: A teacher of the divine word becomes in a certain sense a surety to God for the souls of his hearers (Ezek. iii. 18); therefore must he watch over them day and night, that none be lost through fault of his (Acts xx. 28).— J. LANGE: In Christ our friend we have a faithful surety who can and will free us from all our debt.—WOHLFARTH: From credulity to put at risk one's property, to which one's children have the first claim, and which one should employ only for the general good, and thereby to give an impulse to the follies and sins of others, is quite as ruinous as it is morally blameworthy.

Ver. 6-11. MELANCHTHON: Diligence is the virtue by which we are disposed steadfastly and firmly for God's sake, and the common welfare, to perform the labors belonging to our calling, with the aid of God, who has promised aid to those that seek it. The extremes of this virtue are indolence and a busy officiousness (πολυπραγμοσύνη). The indolent omits too much; the officious, either from excess of ardor, undertakes many things that are not necessary, or undertakes by-works (πάρεργα) and interferes with others' vocations." *etc.*—EGARD: God will not support these without work, but by work; that is His holy ordinance (Gen. iii. 19). Do thy part, and God will do His. . . . To know how rightly to employ time and opportunity is great wisdom. Gather in summer that thou mayest have in winter; gather in youth that thou mayest have in old age!—*Berleb. Bible:* Where the ways of Christianity are not directed in accordance with the perfect law of liberty (James i. 25) and according to the impulse of the Spirit of God, but according to any human constitution, there men go more foolishly to work than the ants in their labor.—[TRAPP: They are utterly out that think to have the pleasure of idleness, and the plenty of painfulness].

Vers. 12-19. EGARD: A proud heart has never done anything specially for God's honor and a neighbor's good; through humble hearts God does great things.—STARKE: The evil heart cannot long be hidden; it soon shows itself in evil gestures, words and deeds.—(On ver. 18): The heart underlies the seven vices which are an abomination to God, and in the midst, because it is the fountain from which evil flows in all directions (Matth. xii. 34, 35; xv. 19). The Lord therefore hates not only the actual outbreakings of sins, but also the devices of the ungodly with which they encompass day and night.—(On ver. 16 sq.): Eyes, hands, tongue, heart, feet, are in themselves good and well-pleasing to God; but when they turn from the path of virtue and incline to vice, then they are evil and cannot please God.—WOHLFARTH: Before the Lord proud eyes, false tongues, guilty hands, *etc.*, cannot stand. His hand lays hold upon all such transgressors according to the holy law according to which every kind of evil finds its penalty.—[Ver. 16, 17. W. BATES: Pride is in the front of those sins which God hates, and are an abomination to Him. Pride, like an infectious disease, taints the sound parts, corrupts the actions of every virtue, and deprives them of their true grace and glory.—J. EDWARDS: It is vain for any to pretend that they are humble, and as little children before God, when they are haughty, impudent, and assuming in their behavior amongst men.]

Vers. 20-35. STÖCKER (on ver. 25): Solomon here warns chiefly against the things by which one may be enticed into adultery, namely 1) against evil desire and lust in the heart; 2) against wanton, over-curious eyes.—STARKE (on ver. 25): Since evil lusts spring up in the heart, Solomon would have us at the very beginning stop up the fountains, *i. e.*, suppress the very first instigations of corrupt flesh and blood (James i. 14, 15). For it is always more difficult to extinguish sparks already existing than to guard against the heart's receiving any.—VON GERLACH (on vers. 34, 35): The fearful rage of the jealous husband grows out of the deep feeling that the wife is one with her husband, a part of him, whose worth cannot be counterbalanced by any possession however great, outside of him.—Comp. J. LANGE: Just as little as the adulterer taken in his adultery is left unpunished by the injured husband, so little, yea even less will the spiritual adulterer remain unpunished of the Lord (1 Cor. iii. 17).

---

13. New admonition to chastity, with a reference to the warning example of a youth led astray by a harlot.

CHAP. VII. 1-27.

1   My son, keep my words,
    and treasure up my commandments with thee.
2   Keep my commandments and thou shalt live—
    and my instruction as the apple of thine eye.
3   Bind them to thy fingers,
    write them on the tablet of thine heart.
4   Say to wisdom "Thou art my sister!"
    and call understanding " acquaintance,"
5   that they may keep thee from the strange woman,
    from the stranger that flattereth with her words.—
6   For through the window of my house,
    through my lattice I looked out,
7   and I saw among the inexperienced ones,
    discerned among the youths, a young man void of understanding.
8   He passed along the street near her corner,
    and sauntered along the way to her house,
9   in the twilight, in the evening of the day,
    in the midst of the night and darkness.
10 And lo, a woman cometh to meet him,
    in the attire of a harlot, and subtle in heart.
11 Boisterous was she, and ungovernable;
    her feet would not tarry in her house;
12 now in the street, now in the market places,
    and at every corner did she watch.

13 And she laid hold upon him, and kissed him,
   put on a bold face and said to him,
14 "Thankofferings were (binding) upon me,
   to-day have I redeemed my vows;
15 therefore came I out to meet thee,
   to seek thy face, and I have found thee.
16 Tapestries have I spread upon my couch,
   variegated coverlets of Egyptian linen;
17 I have sprinkled my couch
   with myrrh, aloes and cinnamon.
18 Come, let us sate ourselves with love till morning,
   and enjoy ourselves in love!
19 For the man is not at home,
   he has gone a long journey;
20 the purse he has taken with him;
   not till the day of the full moon will he return."
21 She beguiled him with the multitude of her enticements,
   by the allurements of her lips she led him astray.
22 He followed her at once,
   as an ox goeth to the slaughter,
   and as fetters (serve) for the correction of fools—
23 till an arrow pierceth his liver:—
   as a bird hasteneth to the snare,
   and knoweth not that his life is at stake.—
24 And now, ye children, hearken to me,
   and observe the words of my mouth!
25 Let not thine heart incline to her ways,
   and stray not into her paths.
26 For many slain hath she caused to fall
   and all her slain are many.
27 Ways of hell (is) her house
   going down to the chambers of death.

GRAMMATICAL AND CRITICAL.

Ver. 7. [אֲבִינָה, the ו consec. omitted, as is sometimes the case, the form resembling a simple Intentional. GESEN. *Lehrgeb.* p. 874., BÖTT. §§ 930, 6; 973, 5. STUART (comm. in loc.) seems to be in error in regarding this a real voluntative, and rendering "that I might see among the simple, and observe, *etc.*"—A.].

Vers. 8. [For the form הֵמָּה instead of the full form כָּתְּהָ (with the ordinary form of fem. nouns with suff.), see BÖTT. § 724, b. Comp. however Exegetical notes in regard to the proper reading.—A.].

Ver. 11. [יָשְׁבוּ, used of repeated recurrence in the past—*Fiens multiplex præteriti* according to the terminology of BÖTT. § 949, f.—A.].

Ver. 13. In the verb הֶחֱזִיקָה (lit., she made hard, *corroboravit*) the doubling of the 2d radical is omitted, as in הֶחֱלָה, Jud. xx. 40. [Given by BÖTT. § 500, 5, as an example of the simplifying of that which is usually doubled, to express the idea of the permanent, gradual or gentle. See also § 1123, 3. Comp. GREEN, § 141, 1; STUART, § 63, 11.—A.].

Ver. 15. [STUART'S rendering of the last clause as final, "that I might find, *etc.*," is unnecessary; it is rather a simple consecutive.—A.].

Ver. 18. [נִתְעַלְּסָה, the *cohortative* use of the Intentional. BÖTT. § 963, 2.—A.].

EXEGETICAL.

1. From the preceding warnings against unchastity and adultery (chap. ii. 16–19; chap v.; chap. vi. 20–35) the one now before us is distinguished by the fact, that the poet, after a preliminary general introduction (vers. 1–5; comp. chap. vi. 20–24), for the sake of delineating more clearly the repulsiveness and various consequences of intercourse with wanton women, depicts in narrative form the example of a single adulterous woman, who by her lascivious arts betrays a foolish youth into adultery. This is therefore a didactic narrative, with a purpose of earnest warning, here presented as a conclusion to the second larger group of admonitory discourses. It is not possibly an allegory, for nothing whatsoever in the text points to such a conception of the adulteress, by virtue of which she might be regarded as introduced as a personification of the abstract idea of folly (in contrast with that of wisdom personified). Not till we come to chap. ix. 13 sq. do we find such a presentation of folly under the image of a wanton, adulterous woman.—In contrast with the expositors of the ancient church, most of whom gave allegorical interpretations, the correct view is

found as early as M. GEIER, VATABLUS, MERCERUS, EGARD, HANSEN, MICHAELIS, STARKE, and also in nearly all the moderns except VON GERLACH. The view of several of those named, especially that of STARKE, that the whole narration is to be regarded a true history, an actual experience of the poet, lacks sufficient support in the style and form of the delineation. The history may just as well be imaginary as the contents of many narrations of Christ,—*e. g.*, that of the good Samaritan, of the prodigal son, *etc.*

2. Vers. 1–5: Introduction in a general form, in which ver. 1 reminds us of chap. i. 8; ii. 1; vi. 20; so ver. 2 of iv. 4; ver. 3 of iii. 3; vi. 21; ver. 5 of ii. 16; vi. 24.—Ver. 2. **And my teaching as the apple of thine eye**, lit. "as the little man in thine eye." The same figurative description is found in Arabic and Persian (see UMBREIT on this passage). Comp. also the Greek κόρη, κοράσιον (=בַּת־עַיִן [the daughter of the eye] Lam. ii. 18) and the Latin *pupa, pupilla*. The apple of the eye is also in Deut. xxxii. 10; Ps. xvii. 8; Zech. ii. 12, the emblem of a precious possession guarded with peculiarly watchful care.—Ver. 3. **Bind them to thy fingers**, not precisely as an amulet, as UMBREIT thinks, but as an ornament, a costly decoration, like a ring; comp. Song Sol. viii. 6, and the observations on iii. 3.—Without adequate reason HITZIG regards the verse as spurious, on account of its partial correspondence with Deut. vi. 8; xi. 18. As though the figures here employed, especially that in the first clause, did not occur very frequently within the sphere of the Old Testament, and that in every instance with a form somehow slightly modified! Comp. *e. g.*, Ex. xiii. 9, 16; Jer. xxii. 24; Hag. ii. 23.—Ver. 4. "**Thou art my sister!**" Comp. Job xvii. 14; xxx. 29; Wisd. viii. 2. The parallel "acquaintance" in the 2d clause corresponds with the Hebrew expression מֹדָע, which denotes knowledge, acquaintance, and then (abstract for the concrete, as occurs, *e. g.*, also in the use of the French *connaisance* [and the English "acquaintance"]) one well known, a friend, *familiaris*. The same expression is found also in Ruth ii. 1 as the K'ri. Comp. P. CASSEL on this passage, who however both for that passage and the one before us gives the preference to the K'thibh מְיֻדָּע (comp. Ps. lv. 14; lxxxviii. 9) as the more primitive reading.

3. Vers. 6–9. *The foolish young man.*—**Through my lattice I looked out.** Comp. the quite similar representation in the song of Deborah, Judges v. 28. אֶשְׁנָב denotes as it does there a latticed aperture, an arrangement for the circulation of fresh air (HITZIG).—Ver. 7. **And I saw among the inexperienced**; literally, among the νηπίοις, the simple; comp. remarks on i. 4, where the same expression פְּתָאיִם is used, synonymous with נַעַר, boy, as here with בָּנִים. It is not necessary, with ARNOLDI, BERTHEAU and HITZIG, to explain the expression in exact accordance with the Arabic by *juvenes* [young men].—Ver. 8. **Near a corner.**—The Masoretic punctuation פִּנָּהּ with mappik in the ה (comp. כֹּרָה, Job xi. 9) represents the corner as hers, *i. e.*, the corner of the adulteress, the corner of her house,—and many recent expositors, *e. g.*, UMBREIT and HITZIG, translate and explain accordingly. But inasmuch as according to ver. 12 (which HITZIG, without any reason, pronounces spurious), the adulteress is accustomed to watch "at every corner," therefore at street corners in general, it is not quite needful to refer the corner here mentioned to her dwelling. All the ancient versions moreover have read only the simple פִּנָּה (LXX: παρὰ γωνίαν; Vulg.: *juxta angulum, etc.*). —**And sauntered along the way to her house.**—Psychologically it is pertinent to depict the young man predisposed to sin as strolling before the house of the adulteress, and this as the beginning of his imprudence, so far forth as he thus plunges himself into temptation. The verb צָעַד is fairly chosen, as it always expresses a certain care and intention in his going. We say substantially "he measures his steps, he paces before her door" (UMBREIT).—Ver. 9. **In the twilight, in the evening of the day.**— The accumulation of the expressions is explained by the fact that it was fitting to characterize the action and conduct of the young man as belonging to the works of darkness, the deeds of night. Comp. Luke xxii. 53; Rom. xiii. 12; 1 Thess. v. 4–7, *etc.* There is furthermore no contradiction between the notation of time in the first clause and that in the second; for נֶשֶׁף strictly signifies not the first evening twilight, but the later period of evening darkness, from 9 o'clock to 12 (see Job vii. 4; xxiv. 15), and so the time immediately bordering upon the true black night or midnight. —**In the blackness of night**—literally, "in the pupil of the night," comp. xx. 20, K'ri. The *tertium comparationis* is to be found, doubtless in both, the blackness and the middle, and not in the first alone, as UMBREIT holds. Comp. besides the phrase "heart of the night" in the poetic language of the Persians (see UMBREIT on this passage).

4. Vers. 10–20. *The adulteress.*—**In the attire of a harlot.**—שִׁית זוֹנָה, dress of a harlot (comp. with respect to שִׁית, dress, apparel, Ps. lxxiii. 16), stands here with no connecting word in apposition to "woman;" a woman a harlot's dress, as though the woman herself were nothing more than such a dress. Thus, and with good reason, BERTHEAU explains [and WORDS.], while HITZIG altogether artificially explains שִׁית by שָׁוָה (from שָׁוָה) as equivalent to דְּמוּת, likeness, and accordingly translates "with the outward appearance of a harlot;" in the same way also the LXX: εἶδος ἔχουσα πορνικόν.—**Subtle in heart.**—נְצֻרַת לֵב is strictly "one who is guarded in heart," *i. e.*, one whose heart is guarded and inaccessible, who locks up her plans and counsels deep in her breast, comp. Is. lxv. 4. Thus Chr. B. MICHAELIS (citing the French *retenu*), UMBREIT, BERTHEAU, ELSTER, *etc.*, and from earlier times at least the *Vers. Veneta*: πεφυλαγμένη τὴν καρδίαν. [With these WORDSW. is in substantial agreement; "her heart is like a walled fortress," *etc.*]. The other ancient versions expressed the idea "one carrying away the heart of the young man," as though they had read נֹצֶרֶת (so also recently

AARNOLDI). EWALD explains "of hardened heart, bold and confident;" HITZIG, in accordance with the Arabic and comparing the *saucia* in VIRGIL's *Æneid*, IV. 1: "an arrow in her heart. wounded by love's dart," and therefore ardent and wanton—both of these being plainly altogether artificial and adventurous. [FUERST, treating the adjective as fem. constr. from צֹרֶר, renders "watching (for hearts of young men")].— **Boisterous was she and ungovernable.**—With the first epithet (literally, shouting) comp. chap. ix. 13; with the second, Hos. iv. 16, where the same word is used of a wild heifer that will not submit its neck to the yoke.—Ver. 12. **Now in the street**, etc.—That we have only here a custom, a habit of the wanton woman described, while in the preceding verse we have delineated her condition in a single instance, is an entirely arbitrary assumption of HITZIG's, which is altogether opposed by the use of the Imperfect in both cases (שָׁכְנוּ, ver. 11, and הָאָרַב, ver. 12). Therefore the argument that the verse is spurious, resting as it does mainly on this alleged difference in the substance and scope of the verse, is to be rejected (comp. above, remarks on ver. 8).—Ver. 13. **Put on a bold face.**—Comp. chap. xxi. 29; Eccles. viii. 1.—Ver. 14. **Thank-offerings were binding upon me**—that is, in consequence of a vow, as the second clause shows. She has therefore on the day that is hardly gone ("to-day"—the day is here represented as continuing into the night) slain a victim in sacrifice that had been vowed to the Lord for some reason or other, and has prepared for a meal the flesh of this animal, which in accordance with the law, Lev. vii. 16, must be eaten on the second day, at the latest. To this meal, which, to judge from the description of the luxurious furnishing of the chamber, in vers. 16 sq., is no simple affair, she now invites the young man.—Ver. 16. **Variegated coverlets of Egyptian linen.**—חֲבֻבוֹת which the older translators nearly all interpret as "variegated coverlets," the larger number derive from the Arabic خطب to be many colored (therefore *tapetes versicolores s. picti*, as it is found as early as the Vulgate); BERTHEAU, on the contrary, derives from חטב = חצב to cut, to make stripes or strips (therefore *striped* material); HITZIG finally derives from the Arab. عطب cotton, appealing to PLINY, *H. N*., XIX., 1, 2, according to whom cotton fabrics in great quantity were manufactured from native material. The first of these explanations, as the simplest and best attested, deserves the preference.—אֵטוּן is equivalent to the Ægypt. *Athiouniau*, linen, and is found in Greek also in the form ὀθόνη or ὀθόνιον. [The rendering of the E. V. "with carved works, with fine linen of Egypt" conforms too closely to the primary meaning of the verb חָטַב "to carve." It cannot refer to any carved frame work of the bed, but rather to the embroidered figures which resemble carving—A.].—Ver. 17. **I have sprinkled my couch**, etc.—HITZIG, who translates the verb by "I have perfumed," has in mind a mere perfuming of the bed or of its apparel by means of the swinging of a censer filled with myrrh, aloes and cinnamon. But while נוף does properly signify to raise, to swing, yet the signification "sprinkle" is easily enough derived from this: and although the spices in question were not sprinkled precisely in the form of water holding them in solution, they still produced a satisfactory result if strewed upon the coverlets of the couch in little bits, fragments of the bark, fibres or scales. In no other way than this is it to be supposed that the same fragrant materials (with *cassia*) were employed, according to Ps. xlv. 8, in perfuming the king's robes of state; comp. also Song Sol. iii. 6; iv. 14.—Ver. 18. **Let us sate ourselves with love**, etc.—Comp. v. 19, and also the phrase שִׁכְרוּ דוֹדִים, Song Sol. v. 1.— **Enjoy ourselves in love.**—Instead of the meaning "enjoy" or "delight one's self," well attested by Job xx. 18; xxxix. 13, the old interpreters give to the verb in this instance the stronger meaning "to embrace passionately, to cohabit" (LXX: ἐγκυλισθῶμεν ἔρωτι; AQUILA and THEODOTION: συμπεριπλέκωμεν; so also HITZIG: "let us join in love's indulgence!"). But it is plainly unnecessary to substitute an obscene import, artificially and with a possible appeal to the Arabic, for the simpler meaning, which is abundantly attested by the *usus loquendi* of the Old Testament.—Ver. 19. **The man is not at home.**—Let it be observed with how cold and strange a tone the faithless wife speaks of her husband.—**He has gone a long journey.**— Lit., "upon a journey from afar;" the idea "from afar" is loosely appended to that of "journey" in order to represent not so much the way itself as rather the person traversing it as far removed.—Ver. 20. **The purse he hath taken with him**—and therefore proposes extensive transactions at a distance from home, and will continue journeying a considerable time.— **On the day of the full moon he will return.** —In the Hebrew the כֶּסֶא (for which in Ps. lxxxi. 4 we have the form כֶּסֶה) forms an alliteration with the כְּפוֹ in the first member, which is probably not undesigned; "the verse flows so smoothly along (comp. ii. 13) and one imagines that he hears the sweetly musical voice of the betrayer" (HITZIG). Furthermore the "day of the full moon" is not a designation of the full moon of the feast of tabernacles which was celebrated with peculiar festivities (UMBREIT, ELSTER), but the expression plainly relates to the next succeeding full moon. Since now, according to ver. 9, the time to which the narrative relates must be about new moon, the cunning woman means to hint that her husband will not return for about a fortnight. See HITZIG on this passage.

5. Vers. 21-23. *The result of her enticing arts.* Ver. 21. **With the multitude of her enticements.**—לֶקַח, learning (i. 5; ix. 9) is here ironically employed of the skilful and bewildering rhetoric which the adulteress has known how to employ.—With the expression "smoothness of lips" comp. "smoothness of tongue," chap. vi.

24.—Ver. 22. **At once**, Hebrew פִּתְאֹם, implies that he had at first hesitated, until this fear of his to take the decisive step was overcome by evil appetite, and he now with passionate promptness formed the vile purpose and executed it at once, to cut off all further reflection. Here is evidently a stroke in the picture of the profoundest psychological truth.—**As an ox goeth to the slaughter.**—Therefore following another, and with a brutish unconsciousness. Comp. the corresponding figure, which, however, is used with a purpose of commendation, in Is. liii. 7. **And as fetters** (serve) **for the correction of the fool.**—With the fetters (עֶכֶס comp. Is. iii. 18) we have here compared, of course, the adulteress who suddenly and by a single effort prevails upon the thoughtless youth,—and not, possibly, the young man himself (as UMBREIT supposes, who finds the significance of the comparison in this, that the foolish and ensnared youth is represented first as a dumb beast, and then as a simply material physical thing, as a mere dead instrument. As the obstinate fool (אֱוִיל) who treads a forbidden path, is suddenly caught and held fast by the trap lying in it, so has the deceitful power of the adulteress caught the foolish young man. Thus, and with probable correctness, ELSTER, and long ago many of the older expositors, like SOL. GLASS, *Philol. Sacra*, p. 738, and M. GEIER on this passage (only that they unnecessarily explain by an *hypallage*: "as fetters for the correction of a fool," in other words, "as the fool (comes) to the correction of fetters"). Somewhat differently BERTHEAU, and before him LUTHER, STARKE, *etc.* [and recently STUART]; "He comes as if to fetters, which are decreed for the correction of the fool;" but to supply before עֶכֶס אֶל from the preceding has the order and parallelism against it. [FUERST regards the noun as an instrumental accus., and translates "and as in fetters, *i. e.*, slowly, the fool is led to correction,"—but regards the evidence as all indicating a defective text. NOYES and MUENSCHER treat the noun as instrumental, but vary the construction of the other words: "as one in fetters to the chastisement of the fool." WORDSW. suggests two or three renderings, of which that of NOYES is one, but indicates no preference. ZÖCKLER'S rendering is brought, we think, with the least violence, into correspondence with the other two comparisons, where the idea is plainly that of a certain fate, notwithstanding unconsciousness of it. So fetters await the fool, though he may not be aware of it—A.] Many older interpreters, either failing to understand the figure, or judging it inconsistent with the context, have sought relief in more violent ways. The LXX, *Peschito* and Targums explain the עֶכֶס or some word substituted for this, as referring to a dog (LXX: ὥσπερ κύων ἐπὶ δεσμοῖς), which is here made a parallel to the ox and then the bird in the following verse; so also more recent commentators, like MICHAELIS, KÖHLER, *etc.* The Vulgate probably read כֶּבֶשׂ instead of עֶכֶס, since it translates "as a wanton and stupid lamb." Others, as of the older class the LXX, *Peschito*, Targums, Arabic vers., *etc.* altered the אֱוִיל to אַיָּל stag, and connected it with ver. 23; so also more recently SCHELLING and ROSENMUELLER, *e. g.*; "and like a deer rushing into fetters." HITZIG finally treats the passage with the greatest violence, since he transfers ver. 23, third clause, to the place of the 2d clause in ver. 22; in this line, by altering עֶכֶס to בַּעַס he changes the meaning to "for the fool is angry at correction;" he finally transposes the first and third clauses of ver. 23, so that the two verses have this general import:

Ver. 22. "He followeth her at once,
as an ox that goeth to the slaughter,
and as a bird hasteneth to the snare.

Ver. 23. For the fool is angry at correction,
and seeth not that it is for his life,
until an arrow pierceth his liver."

This might indeed have been originally the meaning of the passage; but inasmuch as neither manuscripts nor old versions give any evidence of any other arrangement as having ever existed, the whole emendation retains only the value of a bold hypothesis.—Ver. 23. **Till an arrow pierceth his liver.**—Since this clause plainly refers to the young man, and neither exclusively to the ox nor the fool, the two examples of a self-destroying folly which in the second and third clauses of ver. 23 are compared with him, its position is parenthetical (UMBREIT, ELSTER, BERTHEAU, *etc.*); for in the following clause still another example is added to the two mentioned before,—that of the bird hastening to the snare. The "liver" stands here as the representative of the vitals in general (comp. Lam. ii 11) as in some instances the heart or again the reins (Ps. xvi. 27; lxxiii. 21; Prov. xxiii. 16, *etc.*). According to DELITZSCH, *Bibl. Psychol.*, pp. 275 sq., the liver is here made prominent as the seat of sensual desire. Since the ancient Greeks, Arabians and Persians in fact connected this idea with the organ under consideration, and since modern Oriental nations also predicate of the liver what we say of the heart as the seat of the feelings and sensibilities (*e. g.*, the Malays in Java, see *Ausland*, 1863, p. 278), this view may be received as probably correct. By no means is the designation of the liver in the passage before us to be regarded as a purely arbitrary poetical license or as a mere accident.—**And knoweth not that his life is at stake.** Literally, "that it is for his soul;" the expression בְּנַפְשׁוֹ signifies "at the price of his life," comp. Numb. xvii. 3.

6. Vers. 24-27. *Concluding exhortation* introduced by "and now," like the corresponding final epilogue, chap. viii. 32; comp. also v. 7.—Ver. 25. **And stray not**, אַל תֵּתַע, [a dehortative] from תָּעָה, to go roaming about, comp. שָׁגָה chap. v. 20.

Ver. 26. **And all her slain are many.** עֲצֻמִים, meaning "strong" (BERTHEAU), is nevertheless on account of the parallelism with רַבִּים in the first member to be taken in the sense of "numerous, many," comp. Ps. xxxv. 18; Joel i. 5. [HOLD., NOYES, MUENSCH., DE W., K., agree with our author; STUART and WORDS., like the E. V., keep closer to the original idea of strength;

"many strong men" have been her victims.—A.] With the expression in the first member comp. Judges ix. 40.

Ver. 27. **Ways of hell—her house.** "Her house" is the subject, having here a plural predicate connected with it, as chap. xvi. 25; Jer. xxiv. 2.—**Chambers of death.** Comp. "depths of death" or "of hell," chap. ix. 18: and with reference to the general sentiment of the verse, chap. ii. 18; v. 5.

DOCTRINAL, ETHICAL, HOMILETIC AND PRACTICAL.

From the earlier and copious warnings against adultery the one now before us is distinguished by the fact, that while chap. v. contrasted the blessing of conjugal fidelity and chaste marital love with unregulated sexual indulgence, and chap. vi. 20-35 particularly urged a contending against the inner roots and germs of the sin of unchastity,—our passage dwells with special fullness upon the temptations from without to the transgression of the sixth commandment. It also sets forth the folly and the ruinous consequences of yielding to such temptations, by presenting an instructive living example. What elements in this vivid moral picture stand forth as ethical and psychological truths to be taken especially to heart, has been already indicated by us in the detailed interpretation. Aside from the fact that it is nocturnal rambling, that delivers the thoughtless, heedless and idling youth into the hands of temptation (ver. 9), and aside from the other significant feature, that after a first brief and feeble opposition he throws himself suddenly and with the full energy of passion into his self-sought ruin (ver. 22; comp. James i. 15), we have to notice here chiefly the important part played by the luxurious and savory feast of the adulteress as a coöperating factor in the allurement of the self-indulgent youth (see ver. 14 sq.). It is surely not a feature purely incidental, without deeper significance or design, that this meal is referred to as preceding the central and chief sin; for, that the tickling of the palate with stimulating meats and drinks prepares the way for lust and serves powerfully to excite sexual desire, is an old and universal observation, comp. Ex. xxxii. 6 (1 Cor. x. 17). "The people sat down to eat and to drink, and rose up to play:" as also similar passages from classical authors, e. g. EURIPIDES, Alcestis, 788; PLAUTUS, Miles gloriosus, III., 1, 83; ARRIAN, Anab. Alex., II., 5, 4; and the well-known Roman proverb from TERENCE (Eunuch., IV., 5, 6; comp. APPUL., Metam., II., 11), "Sine Cerere et Libero friget Venus" [without Ceres (food) and Bacchus (wine) Venus (love) is cold]: and finally TERTUL-LIAN, de jejun. adv. Psychicos, c. 1: "Lust without gluttony would indeed be deemed a monstrosity, the two being so united and conjoined that, if they could by any means be parted, the sexual parts would first refuse to be attached to the belly. Consider the body; the region is one, and the order of the vices conforms to the arrangement of the members; first the belly, and all other sensuality is built immediately upon gluttony; through indulgence in eating sensual desire ensues," etc.

In the homiletic treatment we are naturally not to dwell too long upon these details, lest the entire impression produced by the picture of the young man ensnared by the adulteress be unduly weakened. An analysis of the chapter into several texts for sermons is inadmissible on account of the closely compacted unity of the action. At the most, the five introductory verses may be separated as a special text (comp. STARKE); yet even these would better be connected closely with the whole, and all the more since they conform very nearly in expression and contents to similar introductory paragraphs of a somewhat general nature, of which there have already been several (see exeget. notes, No. 2).

The homily that should comprehend the entire chapter might therefore present some such theme as this: *How the dangers from temptation to unchastity are to be escaped.* Answer: 1) By avoiding idleness as the beginning of all vice (ver. 6, sq.); 2) By shunning all works of darkness (ver. 9); 3) By subduing the sensual nature, and eradicating even the minor degrees of evil appetite (ver. 14 sq.); 4) By the serious reflection, that yielding to the voice of temptation is the certain beginning of an utter fall from the grace of God, and of eternal ruin (vers. 21, 27).—Comp. STARKE: Sin is like a highway robber, that at first joins our company in an altogether friendly way, and seeks to mislead us from the right path, that it may afterwards slay us (Rom. vii. 11).—Imaginary pleasure and freedom in the service of sin are like gilded chains with which Satan binds men. Though the tempter is deeply guilty, he who suffers himself to be tempted is not for that reason excused. Let every one therefore flee from sin as from a serpent (Ecclesiast. xxi. 2).—Comp. M. GEIER: Be not moved by the flattering enticements of the harlot, the world, false teachers (that betray into spiritual adultery and abandonment of God), or of Satan himself. Close thine ears against all this, i. e. refuse in genuine Christian simplicity and faithful love to the Lord to hearken to any solicitation to disobedience. Follow not Eve's example, but Joseph's, Gen. xxxix. 8, etc.—[TRAPP: (ver. 9) Foolish men think to hide themselves from God by hiding God from themselves.—(Ver. 22). Fair words make fools fain].

Third Group of Admonitory or Proverbial Discourses.

Chap. VIII. 1—IX. 18.

14. A second public discourse of wisdom personified.

Chap. VIII. 1–36.

a) The richness of her gifts.

(Vers. 1–21.)

1 Doth not wisdom cry aloud,
 and understanding lift up her voice?
2 Upon the top of the high places, by the way,
 in the midst of the way she placeth herself.
3 By the side of the gates, at the exit from the city,
 at the entrance to its doors she calleth aloud:
4 "To you, ye men, I call,
 and my voice is to the sons of men!
5 Learn wisdom, O ye simple ones,
 and ye fools, be of an understanding heart!
6 Hear, for I speak plain things,
 and the utterances of my lips are right things;
7 for my mouth meditateth truth,
 and wickedness is an abomination to my lips.
8 All the words of my mouth are right,
 there is nothing crooked or false in them;
9 they are all right to the man of understanding,
 and plain to them that have attained knowledge.
10 Receive my instruction and not silver,
 and knowledge rather than choice gold!
11 For wisdom is better than pearls,
 and no precious things equal her.
12 I, wisdom, dwell with prudence,
 and find out knowledge of sagacious counsels.
13 The fear of Jehovah is to hate evil,
 pride, arrogance and an evil way,
 and a deceitful mouth do I hate.
14 Counsel is mine, and reflection;
 I am understanding; I have strength.
15 By me kings reign
 and rulers govern justly.
16 By me princes rule
 and nobles, all the judges of the earth.
17 I love them that love me,
 and they that seek me find me.
18 Riches and honour are with me,
 increasing riches and righteousness.
19 Better is my fruit than the purest, finest gold,
 and my revenue than choice silver.
20 In the way of righteousness do I walk,
 in the midst of the paths of justice,
21 to ensure abundance to those that love me,
 and to fill their treasuries.

b) The origin of her nature in God.

(Vers. 22–31.)

22 Jehovah created me as beginning of his way,
  before his works of old.
23 From everlasting was I set up,
  from the beginning, before the foundation of the earth.
24 When there were as yet no floods was I brought forth,
  when there were no fountains abounding with water.
25 Before the mountains were settled,
  before the hills was I brought forth;
26 while as yet he had not made land and plains
  and the first clods of the earth.
27 When he prepared the heavens I was there,
  when he stretched out the firmament over the deep;
28 when he established the clouds above,
  when the fountains of the deep raged loudly;
29 when he set to the sea its bounds,
  that the waters should not pass its border;
  when he settled the foundation pillars of the earth;
30 then was I at his side as director of the work,
  and was delighted day by day,
  rejoicing before him continually,
31 rejoicing in his earth,
  and my delight did I find in the sons of men.

c) The blessing that flows from the possession of her.

(Vers. 32–36.)

32 And now, ye children, hearken unto me:
  Blessed are they that keep my ways!
33 Hear instruction, and be wise,
  and be not rebellious.
34 Blessed is the man that heareth me,
  watching daily at my gates,
  waiting at the posts of my doors!
35 For whosoever findeth me findeth life
  and obtaineth favor from Jehovah;
36 and whosoever sinneth against me wrongeth his own soul:
  all they that hate me love death."

GRAMMATICAL AND CRITICAL.

Ver. 2. בֵּין־בֵּית, *in the midst*, is an Aramaic idiom, occurring also in Ezekiel xli. 9.—A.

Ver. 3. As to the form תרלה comp. i. 20. [Bött. 929, δ.—A.]

Ver. 5. Instead of לב הָבִינוּ [understand ye in heart, "be ye of an understanding heart," E. V.], we should probably read with the LXX [ἐνθεσθε καρδίαν], Vulg., Arnoldi and Hitzig הָבִינוּ לֵב, direct your heart, *i. e.*, exert your understanding, *applicate animum*. Comp. לֵב נָכוֹן, Ps. lvii. 8; and also 1 Sam. vii. 3; Job xi. 13; and to illustrate the use of לֵב in the sense of the understanding, the reason, comp. several other passages in the Proverbs, especially xv. 32; xvii. 16; xix. 8.

Ver. 6. נְגִידִים. [An illustration of the principle that "single adjectives describing what is pre-eminent or striking appear in the more elevated style, raised as it were to personality, and are therefore put in the masc. plural;" see Böttcher, § 707, 2.—A.]

Ver. 13. שְׂנֹאת, [an infinitive of a verb לא having the feminine termination of the verbs לה; see Bött., § 1083, 13.—A.].

אֹהֵב [regularly אָאֱהַב.—after the rejection of one of the weak consonants, the vowel is "assimilated" from the initial vowel of the neighbouring form אֱהַב; for examples of the normal modification, אֹהֵב, with and without suffixes, see Mal. i. 2; Hos. xi. 1; xiv. 5; Ps. cxix. 167.—Bött., § 425, h.—A.]

כִּנְאֲצֻנִי, [an example of the retention of the fuller form of the plural ending with weakened vowel and toneless suffix; see Bött., § 1047, *f*.—A.]

Ver. 24. כִּינוֹת. With this fem. plural form there occurs in an isolated instance, Ps. civ. 10 [together with four others of construct and suffix forms], the masculine כִּינִים ; for which reason the masc. of the adjective נִכְבֵּד is the less striking (BERTHEAU).
Ver. 25. [Perfect tense with טֶרֶם in the sense of a Pluperfect. BÖTT., § 947, c.—A.]
Ver. 26. [וְלֹא יַעַבְרוּ. Imperfect with וְלֹא in sense of an Imperf. Subj., "so that," etc. BÖTT., § 940, § 2.—A.]
Ver. 29. בְּחֻקּוֹ stands either for בְּחֻקּוֹ, or as HITZIG perhaps more correctly assumes for the Poet form בְּחוֹקְקוֹ. [BÖTTCHER prefers the first of these explanations, citing this as an example of usage varying in certain words, and suggesting as a reason for the adoption of the fuller form in this case, correspondence with בְּשׂוּמוֹ in the first clause. See §§ 766, η, and 1147.—A.]

EXEGETICAL.

1. Preliminary Remark. From the preceding larger group of admonitory discourses (chap. iv.–vii.), that now before us, comprising only chap. viii. and ix., is distinguished chiefly by the fact that it returns to the representation, which has already been made in chapters i.–iii. of Wisdom as a person. And this is so done that the two features of the representation which there appeared separately; the exhibition of Wisdom as a public preacher (i. 20-33), and as a divine agent in the creation of the world (iii. 19–26), are now combined in one whole. Here Wisdom appearing as a preacher herself testifies to the aid which she rendered God at the creation (viii. 22 sq.). Besides this point of contact with the first main group, we may also direct attention to the mention of the fear of God as a disposition in the most intimate alliance, and even identical with wisdom (viii. 13); this also is common to the division before us and the first; for only in chapters i.–iii. (see i. 7; i. 29; ii. 5; iii. 7) was any express utterance given to this form of the Hhokmah doctrine. The middle group (chap. iv.–vii.) nowhere contains the expression "the fear of Jehovah." There are however continually coming to view many connections between the second and third groups; especially the plural address "ye children," repeated in the discourse of the personal Wisdom (viii. 32) from chap. iv. 1; v. 7; vii. 24 (see above, p. 95). Observe also the representation of Folly personified, as a counterpart to Wisdom (chap. ix. 13-18), appearing as an adulteress of mien and bearing quite like the adulterous woman of chap. vii. who is as it were exhibited here, "developed into a more comprehensive character" (comp. HITZIG, p. 69).—Furthermore this last section of the first main division of the Book of Proverbs consists of only two discourses of unequal length, chapters viii. and ix. each of which, however, in turn includes several subdivisions clearly distinguishable,—chap. viii., comprising the three that have been given above, and chap. ix. the two parallel delineations of the personal Wisdom (vers. 1-12) and Folly personified (vers. 13-18).—The unequal length of the two discourses HITZIG seeks to a certain extent to remove by striking out from chap. viii. a large number of verses, sixteen, and from chap. ix. a smaller number, six, as spurious additions by a later hand. His grounds of distrust are, however, here again of a purely subjective kind, and do not present for a single one of the passages in question any reliable evidence of their spurious character, as we shall hereafter have occasion to show in detail.

2. Vers. 1-3. Doth not wisdom cry aloud? This form of interrogation (with הֲלֹא) which expects as its answer an assenting and emphatic "Yes, truly!" points to the fact clearly brought to view in all that has preceded, that wisdom bears an unceasing witness in her own behalf in the life of men.
Ver. 2. **Upon the top of the high places by the way,** in order that those who pass along by the way may observe her. **In the midst of the way.** This Aramaic idiom gives no occasion for pronouncing the passage spurious (contrary to the view of HITZIG, who furthermore takes exception to the allusion to "high places" in the 1st clause, and therefore summarily pronounces the entire 2d verse interpolated). UMBREIT translates "at the house where roads cross," and interprets, not indeed of an inn located at cross-roads (as DÖDERLEIN does), but still of a house situated at the junction of several streets. But these "ways" are roads, solitary paths, not streets in the city, and the delineation proceeds in such an order as to exhibit Wisdom first, in ver. 2, as a preacher in the open country, in grove and field, on mountains and plains, and then in ver. 3 to describe her public harangues in the cities, and in the tumult of the multitudes. The condition therefore is unlike both to that presented in i. 20, 21, and to that in ix. 13, where in both cases the interior of a city alone furnishes the scene for Wisdom's activity as a preacher.
Ver. 3. **At the exit from the city,** literally "towards the mouth of the city," i. e., standing at the gate and facing the streets which centre there.—**At the entrance to its doors,** (comp. i. 21), i. e., standing on the farther (outer) side of the gateway.
3. Vers. 4–11. This more general introduction to Wisdom's discourse, with the addition of ver. 12, HITZIG declares spurious, partly on account of the alleged tautological nature of vers. 6-9, giving no genuine progress to the thought,—partly because ver. 10 is almost identical with viii. 19, and ver. 11 with iii. 15,—and lastly, partly because of the peculiar form אִישִׁים in ver. 4, which is said to betray a later date. Yet this very form is found also in Isa. liii. 3, and Ps. cxli. 4, for both of which passages the later origin (in the exile, or even after the exile) is in like manner yet to be established. And as respects the alleged tautologies and repetitions, similar ones occur throughout the entire Book of Proverbs (comp. Introd. § 12). The codices and old versions, however, know nothing whatever of the absence from the text of even a single one of these verses.
Ver. 5. **Learn wisdom, O ye simple ones.** Comp. i. 4.—**Ye fools, show understanding,** see critical note, above.

Ver. 6. **I speak plain things.** The word here translated "plain" might, it is true, designate "noble, princely things," (comp. the αεμνά of the LXX, the "*res magnæ*" of the Vulg., etc.); [So WORDSW., HOLDEN, N. and M.], the parallelism however renders more natural the signification "plain, evident" (*clara, manifesta*); [So STUART]; comp. a similar term in ver. 9. This only appropriate sense we find already given in the Chaldee and Syriac versions.

Ver. 7. **For my mouth meditateth truth,** literally, "my palate," comp. Song Sol. v. 16; Job xxxi. 30. The function of speech does not appear to be here immediately associated with the palate, but, as the antithesis in the 2d clause shows, rather the inward moulding of the word as yet unspoken, by the silent working of the spirit,—the reflective consideration which precedes speech.

Ver. 8. **Right,** literally, "in righteousness." For this use of the preposition employed to introduce the predicate, and forming as it were the transition to the ב *essentiæ*, compare passages like Prov. xxiv. 5; Ps. xxix. 4, and EWALD, § 217 f.

Ver. 9. **Right to the man of understanding . . . plain to them that have attained knowledge.** *Straight* and *plain* stand contrasted with the *crooked* and *false* of the preceding verse. [TRAPP: "Plain in things necessary to salvation; for as all duties so all truths do not concern all men. God doth not expect or require that every man should be a doctor in the chair; but those points that direct to duty here and salvation hereafter, are clear, express and obvious to them that desire to understand them."] The "man of understanding" is he who is so wise as not to despise the words of wisdom, who rather duly takes them to heart. "They that have attained knowledge," literally "the finders of knowledge," are those who have made progress in the sphere of ethical knowledge, the "knowing," the mature and experienced. UMBREIT incorrectly interprets "to them that wish to find knowledge;" the participle is here to be taken in a preteritive sense; comp. Gen. xix. 11; Neh. x. 29. [Other examples may be found cited by BÖTCHER. § 997, 2, 11.]

Ver. 10. **Receive my instruction and not silver,** *i. e.,* when you have the choice prefer my instruction to silver. There is therefore here a comparison like that in the 2d clause, only somewhat otherwise expressed.—**Rather than choice gold.** HITZIG, following the LXX and Chald., "than tried gold." But נִבְחָר means "selected, chosen," and we have no trace elsewhere of the use of the partic. נָבֹן, which is indeed similar in form and easily substituted, for the designation of *tried* gold (χρυσίον δεδοκιμασμένον). Comp. besides ver. 19, and in the foregoing, iii. 14; with ver. 11 comp. iii. 15.

4. Vers. 12-21. **I, Wisdom, dwell with prudence.** That Wisdom who is speaking here emphatically calls herself by name is doubtless to be explained by the fact that only just before, in ver. 11, she had spoken of herself in the 3d person. Very unwarrantably HITZIG infers from this circumstance the spuriousness of this verse also.—The "dwelling" of wisdom "with pru-dence" expresses a confidential or friendly relation,—the same idea which is elsewhere indicated by the Hiphil of the closely related verb סכן; comp. Ps. cxxxix. 3; Job xxii. 21. Inasmuch as the verb stands here with the simple accusative of the noun, without the prepositions ordinarily signifying "with" (for this construction comp. *e. g.,* Ps. v. 5) many translated "I inhabit prudence" and so conceive of prudence either as the sheltering roof (as *e. g.,* UMBREIT explains), or as a property subject to the disposal of prudence (thus BERTHEAU); but both are alike harsh and inapposite. The correct view is found in EWALD, HITZIG, ELSTER, the last of whom illustrates the relation of wisdom to prudence by the remark, "prudence (עָרְמָה) denotes here right knowledge in special cases, in contrast with the more comprehensive idea of intelligence in general; the practical realization of the higher principle of knowledge found in wisdom (חָכְמָה)."—**And find out knowledge of sagacious counsels.** "To find out knowledge" here stands for "to know" (comp. Job xxxii. 13); the expression as a whole would therefore find its equivalent in the simpler "and know sagacious counsels" (יָדַע מְזִמּוֹת). Comp. furthermore the notes on i. 4.

Ver. 13. **The fear of Jehovah is to hate evil.** Only thus far is the 1st member of this ver. to be carried; the following expressions, "pride," "arrogance," and "an evil way" (literally, "way of evil") are, in spite of the present accentuation, to be regarded as prefixed objects to the verb "I hate," so that the meaning of the entire verse is substantially this; "Inasmuch as the fear of God, this beginning of all wisdom (see i. 7; ix. 10) comprises within itself as a distinguishing characteristic the hatred of evil, I, wisdom, accordingly hate everything proud, wicked and crafty." (Comp. HITZIG on this passage). The general proposition forming the first member of the ver., which naturally gives us no exhaustive definition of the fear of God, but only a description of it by one of its chief characteristics (comp. Heb. xi. 1), is therefore, as it were, the major premise, from which the conclusion is drawn that forms the 2d and 3d members. The minor premise, however, which might have had some such form as the first clause of chap. ix. 10, is omitted; the reasoning, as it here stands, taking the form of a *lemma.* In opposition to the diverse methods of punctuating and interpreting, such as are found in UMBREIT, BERTHEAU, and most of the earlier commentators, comp. HITZIG and ELSTER on this passage.—For the expression "mouth of deceit" or "crafty mouth" comp. ii. 12; x. 31.

Ver. 14 HITZIG pronounces an addition growing out of the similar passage Job xii. 13, as he also explains the two following verses as "founded upon the reading of Isa. xxxii. 1," and condemns them. But the accordance with these other passages is far too remote and partial to permit us to think of a derivation from them. In the case of ver. 14 and Job xii. 13 we might more readily think of the converse relation of dependence, in case one must at all maintain any such relation as existing, which seems hardly necessary. For as respects the expressions "wisdom," "coun-eel," "understanding," and "strength," which are brought into combination in these verses, they are found, with the exception of the second, combined elsewhere, especially in Isa. xi. 2, where they are adduced quite as they are here, as attributes of the true ruler. The instances of *paronomasia*, however, in vers. 15 and 16, ("kings are kings," and "rulers rulers"), were of themselves so natural, and suggested themselves so obviously, that neither for the author of our verses was there need of any reading of Isa. xxxii. 1, nor for Isaiah of any recollection of Prov. viii. 15, 16, to give occasion for the employment of this trope.—[WORDSW.: Sound wisdom, the very essence of things, whence they derive their soundness and strength].—**I am understanding, I have** (lit. "mine is") **strength.** This change in the pronouns is certainly not undesigned: "understanding" is to be exhibited as one with wisdom, "strength" however (*i. e.*, true efficiency or energy), as a possession, or more precisely a result of wisdom, just as previously in the first clause "counsel" and "reflection" (comp. with respect to them ii. 17) are named as constant products, possessions, or attributes of wisdom.

Ver. 16. **And nobles, all Judges upon earth.** These two subjects, attached without any copula to the "princes" of the 1st clause, are plainly intended to signify that all possible diverse classes of princes or rulers derive their power from the celestial wisdom of God (comp. the similar enumerations in Eph. i. 21; Col. i. 16, *etc.*). The idea that this proposition can hold only of *just* rulers, owes its origin doubtless to the old reading "judges of righteousness" (צֶדֶק) instead of "judges of the earth" (אָרֶץ), (found in Syr., Chald., Vulg, R. NORZI, and still preferred by BERTHEAU). See objections to this and arguments in support of the Masoretic text in HITZIG.

Ver. 17. **I love them that love me.** This conforms to the pointed text (אֹהֲבַי). The written text (אֲהֻבֶיהָ), "them that love her (Wisdom)" is not in keeping with the context, seems to have been occasioned by a wandering of the transcriber's eye to the form of the verb following [which although a peculiar form of the 1st person—see critical note above—might, unpointed, be mistaken for a form of the 3d person], and has therefore with abundant reason been rejected by all the old versions, several MSS., and by most of the recent interpreters (UMBREIT, EWALD, ELSTER, and HITZIG).—With the 2d clause of ver. 17, comp. i. 28.

Ver 18. Comp. iii. 16.—**Increasing riches.** This is probably the meaning which, with HITZIG, we should adopt (growing means, "*wachsend Vermögen*"); for the common rendering, "old" or "durable" riches, seems less appropriate, since the old is by no means necessarily the sound and permanent. Comp. rather, with reference to the idea of a steadily growing or accumulating wealth, Ps. lxii. 10.—**And righteousness.** What this here signifies is more fully explained in the first clause of ver. 20.

Ver. 19. **Better is my fruit,** comp. the representation of wisdom as the tree of life in chap. iii. 18, and to illustrate the "purest, finest gold" (in Hebrew properly two synonymous expressions for the idea of "fine gold," comp. Ps. xix. 11; xxi. 4; Song Sol. v. 11) compare iii. 14.

Ver. 21. **To ensure abundance to those that love me.** The word here translated "abundance" (יֵשׁ) must here necessarily be a substantive, of similar import with a derived form (תֻּשִׁיָּה) occurring in ii. 7, and substantially equivalent to the ὕπαρξις of the LXX and the οὐσία of the Venetian version. For the verb "to ensure" plainly requires an object, and the position of this noun at the end of the clause shows that this is precisely the object governed by the verb. Moreover, if HITZIG's conception of the expression as an impersonal verb in the sense of *praesto est*, it is at my command, ("I have it") were correct, we ought rather to have a pronominal object (יֵשׁ לִי, "there is to me"). The verse as a whole, therefore, forms a conclusion to the preceding, setting forth the object of Wisdom's walking in paths of righteousness as described in ver. 20; in other words, what result follows from such a course to her friends and attendants. Comp. BERTHEAU on this passage. After ver. 21 the LXX has the words, "If I declare to you the things that occur day by day, I will remember to enumerate the things that are from eternity" [ἐὰν ἀναγγείλω ὑμῖν τὰ καθ' ἡμέραν γινόμενα, μνημονεύσω τὰ ἐξ αἰῶνος ἀριθμῆσαι]. This addition is evidently designed to prepare the way for the subsequent description of the antemundane origin and working of Wisdom; it appears, however, as ill adapted to this as to any possible place either at the beginning of the chapter, such as JAEGER proposes to assign it (*Observatt.*, p. 63), or again before ver. 10, where HITZIG would be disposed to transfer it.

5. Vers. 22-26. In this delineation of the divine origin of the personal Wisdom, the first half directs attention first to her existence before time, or her creation as the first of all created things.—**Jehovah created me as the beginning of his course.** Thus versions as old as the LXX (ἔκτισε), Chald., Syriac, with most of the modern commentators;—while the exegesis of the ancient church from the time of the Arian controversy judged itself compelled to render the verb in the sense of *possedit me* (Vulg.), or ἐκτήσατο (thus the Vers. Venet. and even AQUILA): and this turn of expression was given, that the idea of a creation of eternal Wisdom, or what was equivalent, of the personal Word of God, might be excluded. But against the rendering, "Jehovah possessed me," may be adduced, 1) the fact that the verb (קָנָה) does not signify simply "to possess," but "to attain to the possession," "to acquire," which latter signification would find here a poor application; 2) the fact that the adjunct of the verb (רֵאשִׁית דַּרְכּוֹ) agrees better with the idea of creating than that of possessing; 3) that the double mention of Wisdom's "being born," in vers. 24, 25, and not less the expression in ver. 23, "I was set up" ("or wrought out"), corresponds better with the idea of a creation than with that of possessing or having; and 4) that the parallel passages, Ecclesiast. i. 4, 9; xxiv. 8, which are evidently

formed on the model of that before us, also employ the verb κτίζειν (create), and not some such as ἔχειν or κέκτησθαι (have or possess). Even though accordingly the personal Wisdom is represented as one *created* at the beginning of the divine activity, not *begotten*, as a κτίσμα, οὐ γέννημα, still we may by no means draw from this the conclusion of the correctness of the well-known Arian dogma that the Son of God is the first creation of God. For the delineations of the whole passage before us are of a poetical nature, and are not adapted to a direct application in forming dogmatic conceptions; and the personal Wisdom of our didactic poem is by no means simply identical with the Logos, or the Son of God. Comp. the Doctrinal notes.— "The beginning of His way" is a second accusative depending on the verb; "as beginning or first fruit of His way," *i. e.* His activity, His creative efficiency, His self-revelation. Instead of the singular, "His way," we ought perhaps, with the LXX, the Vulgate, and many recent expositors, especially Hitzig, to read in the plural "His ways" (דְּרָכָיו); the parallel expression "before His works" seems to speak decidedly for this reading.—**Before his works.** The word here translated "works" (מִפְעָלִים) occurs only here; yet comp. the corresponding feminine form in Ps. xlvi. 9 (מִפְעָלוֹת). The word translated "before" (קֶדֶם) Hitzig regards as also a substantive, synonymous with "beginning" (רֵאשִׁית), and therefore translates "as foremost of His works." Yet the conception of it as a preposition is favored by the usage of the O. T. elsewhere.—**Of old** (מֵאָז), long ago, literally, "from long ago," comp. Ps. xciii. 2.

Ver. 23. **From eternity.** It seems necessary, with the expositors of the early church and many of recent times, such as Umbreit, Bertheau, Elster, *etc.*, to regard this difficult verb which follows as a Niphal from נָסַךְ, and therefore to translate it "I was anointed," *i. e.* consecrated to a priestly royalty; comp. the *ordinata sum* of the Vulgate. But the verb is not elsewhere used in this conjugation; and the parallelism with ver. 22, as well as with those following, calls for a verb having some such meaning as "establish, create, call into being." It seems therefore needful to read with the LXX, "I was established" (נוֹכַרְתִּי=ἐθεμελίωσέν με"), or, which would be better advised, so to interpret the form in the text as to give the idea of a being created, or something equivalent. To this end we may either translate, with the *Versio Veneta*, comparing Ecclesiastic. i. 9 (ἐξέχεεν αὐτήν), κέχυμαι, "I was poured forth," or which is on the whole to be preferred, with Hitzig we may vary the punctuation (נִסַּכֹּתִי), so that the expression shall stand as Perfect Niphal, of the verb נָסַךְ, and have the signification "I was woven or wrought;" with this may be compared Ps. cxxxix. 15; Isa. xxxviii. 12.—**From the beginning, from the foundation of the earth** "From the beginning," as in Isa. xlviii. 16. "The foundation of the earth," an expression like that occurring in Isa. xxiii. 7 (קַדְמַת אֶרֶץ), denoting the earliest primæval period, the time of the beginning, the origin of the earth. How this establishment or production of Wisdom "from the foundation of the earth" is to be understood, namely, in the sense of an existence of Wisdom even prior to the earth (comp. Ps. xc. 2), appears from the three following verses.

Ver. 24. **When there were as yet no floods.** Hitzig regards the mention of the waters before the mountains as inappropriate, and therefore conjectures that the verse is spurious. As though in Ps civ. 6 and Job xxxviii. 8 the seas were not mentioned immediately before the earth as a whole, and also before the mountains!—**Fountains abounding with water.** The meaning is, doubtless, the springs from which the floods or the deep broke forth; comp. Gen. vii. 11, and below, ver. 28.

Ver. 25. **Before the mountains were as yet settled,** with their "roots" (Job xxviii. 9) in the pliant earth; comp. Job xxxviii. 6, where mention is made of the settling even of the pillars of the earth (in the infinite space of the heavens). With the second clause comp. Ps. xc. 2.—**Land and plains.** The LXX had in their day correctly rendered חוּצוֹת by ἀοικήτους [uninhabitable places]; these are "unoccupied commons or plains," regions lying outside the occasionally occupied land (comp. Job v. 10).—**The first clods of the earth.** Thus, with Hitzig, are we to understand this expression, and not "the sum or mass of the clods of the earth" (Cocceius, Schultens, Bertheau, Elster, *etc.*); and still less "the first men" (Jarchi), or even "man as born of the earth" (Umbreit); these last interpretations are plainly too far-fetched.

6. Vers. 27-31. From the antemundane existence of Wisdom the poet now passes over to the description of her active coöperation in the creation of the world. The same progress from the pre-existence to the world-creating activity of the divine Logos is found in several passages of the N. T., especially in John i. 1-3, Col. i. 15-16. —**When he stretched out the firmament over the deep,** *i. e.* when He fixed the vault of heaven, the arch of heaven (comp. Gen. i. 8; Job xxii. 14), over the waters of the earth, as a barrier between the upper and lower waters (Gen. i. 6; Job xxvi. 10). Over the deep, in the Hebrew literally "upon the surface of the deep," comp. Gen. i. 2.

Ver. 28. **When he fixed the clouds above.** Literally, "when He made firm, made strong" (בְּאַמְּצוֹ); *i. e.* the clouds are, as in Job xxvi. 8; xxxviii. 37, conceived of as bags, which only in case they are suitably secured and do not burst, prevent the mighty outpouring of the upper waters upon the earth.—**When the fountains of the deep** (see ver. 24 above) **raged violently.** This is the interpretation to be given, with Umbreit, Winer, Hitzig, *etc.*; for the verb here unquestionably has the intransitive meaning, *invalescere, vehementer agitari* (comp. in Isa. xliii. 16 the "mighty waters"). The transitive signification, "when He made firm, *i. e.* restrained, bound up" (LXX; most of the other versions, and recent interpreters like ELSTEN) is inadmissible from the absence of the suffix with the infinitive.

Ver. 29. **When he set to the sea its bounds.** "Bound" here in its local sense, limit, barrier, as in Jer. v. 22; substantially the same as "its border" (גְּבוּל) in the 2d member. For this expression (פֶּה הַיָּם) mouth or shore of the sea, instead of the phrase, elsewhere usual, "lip of the sea" (שְׂפַת הַיָּם), as in Gen. xli. 3; comp. Isa. xix. 7; and for the description of the separation between the sea and the land in general, see Gen. i. 9, 10; Ps. xciv. 9.—**When he settled the foundation pillars of the earth**; end of the description of the earth's creation, comp. Job xxxviii. 6.

Ver. 30. **Then was I at his side as directress of the work.** This noun, derived from a verb (אָמַן) signifying to be firm, true, reliable (and also kindred to יָמִין, dexter, "the right hand," yet not to be regarded as HOFFMANN takes it, Schriftbew., 1. 95, as an infinitive absolute used adverbially, but necessarily as a substantive), denotes like the parallel form found in Song Sol. vii. 2, "artifex, artist, master of the work." [So WORDSW., HOLD., MUENSCH., NOYES: STUART translates "confidant."—A.] Comp. the description, undoubtedly based on the passage before us, found in Wisdom vii. 21: ἡ τῶν πάντων τεχνῖτις σοφία ("wisdom which is the worker of all things"); comp. the epithet ἁρμόζουσα (adapting) in the LXX, and the cuncta componens of the Vulgate, in our passage. In opposition to the rendering of אָמוֹן by "foster-child, alumnus, nutricius" (AQUILA, SCHULTENS, ROSENMUELLER, ELSTER) may be urged first, that then in accordance with Lam. iv. 5 we ought to point אָמוּן, [which pointing BÖTTCHER favors, see § 660, 6 and n. 1], and then, that this form could hardly have stood in the text as a substantive without some adjunct defining it more closely. The verb should be rendered, not "then became I" (BERTHEAU), but "then was I." For the existence of wisdom before the world's creation and at the time of the world's creation formed the principal subject of the preceding description, and not, e. g., her passing from previous rest to more active relations.—**And was delighted day by day.** Literally, "I was delight day by day." This abstract noun plainly stands in the predicate quite as appropriately as the parallel term in the 3d clause (the participle מְשַׂחֶקֶת) and aims like this expression to indicate that wisdom enjoyed and delighted in her creative activity. For the idiomatic use of this abstract noun comp. e. g., Ps. cix. 4 ("but I am prayer"); also notes on vii. 10 above.—The verse following then declares that this her delight and exultation relates particularly to the manifold creatures of the earth, chiefly to man. The creative agency and control of the wisdom of God in the origin of the earth and its inhabitants, is therefore here represented as attended and sustained by the heartiest satisfaction in the natures that are created, especially in man, the personal image of God; and this is quite in harmony with the "God saw that it was good" of the six days of creation (Gen. i. 10, 12, 18, 31); comp. also Wisdom vii. 22, 27, 29 sq. A reference of these expressions in ver. 31 to any period subsequent to the creation (UMBREIT: "In his earth do I now delight and am the joy of the children of men," comp. MERCERUS and many of the elder interpreters, and also LUTHER), is suggested by nothing in the context, and is rather decidedly at variance with the connection. Not before ver. 32 does the author with "and now" return from the past to the present. When HITZIG feels constrained to strike out as spurious the second clause of ver. 30 ("and I was in joy of heart day by day"), and also the 1st clause of ver. 31 ("sporting in His earth"), this results from the fact that he has wholly missed the progressive character of the description, which gradually descends from God and His seat in the heavens to earth, and more specifically to the human race: just as, in his representation which shows throughout a peculiarly external and mechanical conception of the nature of wisdom, he maintains, "The 1st clause of ver. 31 comes into contradiction with the first of ver. 30: for if wisdom is near Jehovah she cannot appropriately be at the same time disporting herself on the earth!" A mere hasty glance at the later representations of the nature and activity of the hypostatic Wisdom, like Wisd. vii. 8; Ecclesiast. xxiv., etc., might have convinced HITZIG of the superficial and untenable nature of such a view. Yet this is in truth nothing more than the necessary fruit of his entire rationalistic view of God and the world.

7. Vers. 32-36. *Concluding admonition and promise*, based on ver. 22-31 as well as ver. 1-21. —Ver. 33. **Hear instruction**, etc. HITZIG would have this whole verse stricken out "because it has no rhythm," and because it comes in only as a disturbing element between the benedictions in ver. 32, 2d clause, and ver. 34. But the lack of rhythm that is asserted rests on the conception of the subjective taste: and the position between two benedictions produces no distraction whatever; all the more since to the first and shorter of these two sentences beginning with "Blessed," a corresponding admonition had been prefixed, ver. 32, 1st clause.—**And be not rebellious.** Thus with UMBREIT, ELSTER, etc., must we understand the prohibition without a grammatical object (וְאַל תִּפְרָעוּ). To supply from the 1st clause the idea "instruction" is unnecessary, especially since the intransitive "and be wise" had been interposed as the immediate antithesis to the verb "refuse, or rebel." For the etymology and signification of this verb (פָּרַע) see, furthermore, notes on i. 25.

Ver. 34. **That hearkeneth to me, watching**, etc. The expression, "so that he watch" (לִשְׁקֹד) like the following phrase "so that he keep," expresses not so much the design as the result of hearkening to wisdom; these expressions give, as it were, the manner of this hearkening, and thus correspond with the ablative of the gerund in Latin, or with the pres. participle (LXX: ἀγρυπνῶν—τηρῶν).—**For whosoever findeth me, findeth life.** This is in accordance with the K'ri. The K'thibh is somewhat more artificial, "for the finders of me are finders of life," *i. e.*, those who find me, they find life. One may choose between the two readings which in import do not differ. [RUETSCHI proposes (*Stud. u. Krit.*, Jan. 1868, p. 134) to solve the difficulty in another way, retaining the consonants of the K'thibh, but modifying the punctuation, so that the two forms will be singular and apparently identical (מָצְאִי), the second being a form artificially constructed with ־ֹ as a "union vowel," (EWALD, § 211, *b*, 1), so as to secure the juxtaposition of two forms apparently the same.—A.].—**And obtain favor from Jehovah.** Literally "and draws forth," *i. e.*, gains for himself, harvests, bears away.

Ver. 36. **And whosoever sinneth against me.** Literally "who misseth me" in contrast with "who findeth me" in ver. 35. Comp. Job v. 24; Judges xx. 16.—**All they that hate me love death.** Comp. iv. 13, 22; vii. 27, and also Ezek. xviii. 31.

DOCTRINAL AND ETHICAL.

1. For a correct understanding of the section before us two things in general are to be observed: 1) that the entire discourse is poetical, and that therefore the personification of Wisdom which forms its chief subject is also to be regarded as essentially, and in the first instance, the product of a bold poetical sweep of thought, and of a vivid oriental imagery; 2) that, however, because of the solemn earnestness and profoundly religious character of the discourse, its figurative element cannot possibly be viewed as the mere play of fancy; or an empty ringing of phrases, but must rather every where stand in more or less exact harmony with the supersensuous truth that is to be set forth. Wisdom, which here appears personified, as the principle of the world's creation, as well as of its preservation and government, having sprung from God himself, and being absolutely supernatural, is no unsubstantial phantom, no unreal fiction of the fancy, no poetic creation without an underlying higher reality. It is rather a result of the profoundest religious and ethical inquiry, an object of the purest and most genuine knowledge of divine things, nay a product of divine revelation—only that this revelation has here passed through the medium of a poetic conception and representation, and for that very reason appears in its formal relations partially reflected, broken, or inaccurately exhibited. It is really the free poetic form, ideal in its portraiture, to which must be charged whatever in the statements before us is partially inadequate, inconsistent, and not directly applicable in the formation of dogmatic ideas. The substance, which is easily separable from this form, bears the impress of the most genuine divinely revealed truth, and forms one of the most important and strongest of the foundation pillars of Old Testament theology, on which the theology and Christology of the New Testament is reared, the doctrine of the Trinity in the ancient church, and indeed the whole glorious structure of Christian dogmatics.—Comp. STAUDENMAIER, *Die Lehre von der Idee*, pp. 31 sq., and particularly NITZSCH, *Ueber die wesentl. Drei-einigkeit Gottes* (Letter to Lucke, in the *Stud. und Krit.*, 1841, ii.; especially pp. 310 sq.).

2. In the picture of wisdom drawn in our chapter the two conceptions of the divine wisdom, and the wisdom of the creature, or of the celestial type of the Hhokmah and its earthly and human counterpart, are plainly so combined that they more or less flow into each other, and without a clear discrimination of their difference interchange, (as in the shorter description of the protection and blessing going forth from God's creative wisdom for those who honor it,—chap. iii. 19-26). That wisdom is at the outset introduced as teaching and preaching (vers. 1 sq.), shows at once that she is regarded essentially as a self-conscious personal being, as a reflection therefore of the absolute personality, or the Godhead. And even within the first section (vers. 4-21), which refers in the first instance only to her manifestations in the moral and religious life of man, several features suggest the supernatural in her nature and relations. Thus especially the predicates "counsel, understanding, strength," (in ver. 14) with which she is endowed as the Messiah is in Isa. xi. 2. So also the allusion to the fact that she imparts to and preserves for the kings, rulers, princes, and judges of the earth, all their power (vers. 15, 16); and finally, with no less plainness, the declaration that she "loves them that love her," and accordingly shows herself to be the dispenser of all benefits and blessings to her faithful ones (ver. 16-21). Of a purely earthly and creature principle all this could not be asserted. It is plainly not an abstract conception of moral philosophy, or any definition pertaining to the moral and intellectual conduct of men, that is thus described, but something higher, a nature fundamentally identical with the divine providence, the activity of God in preserving and ruling the world,—a personal principle belonging to God's revelation of Himself, which is not essentially different from the Logos of the New Testament or the Son of God.

This conception of the idea of a superhuman wisdom, which determines and controls with absolute power and knowledge the destinies of our race, conducts, however, immediately to the proper and hypostatic representation of Wisdom as an emanation from God's eternal nature, as the partaker and mediator in His absolutely creative activity. From the description of Wisdom as the mediating principle in divine Providence (vers. 14-21), the poet passes to the exhibition of her mediating participation in the creation of the world, and in this connection he reveals in the same act the deepest sources and beginnings of her nature (vers. 22-31). Wisdom is, it is true, also a creation of God, but one coming into being before all other creatures, a "first born" (πρωτόκτιστον) a "beginning of the creation of God" (ἀρχὴ τῆς κτίσεως τοῦ θεοῦ), comp. Rev. iii. 14. And for that very reason she took part in His work of creation; she was not merely witness, but helper in the revelation of His power in the primitive creation that called His heavens and earth into being. She manifested herself as the regulative and formative principle, who in those mighty acts of creation "rejoiced before Him," *i. e.*, developed before Him in free, happy action, as it were in joyous sport and play, her infinitely rich life, and thus produced an infinite number and variety of creature forms. This creative activity of wisdom found however its end and its completion in the creation of men in whom she has her delight in an altogether pre-eminent degree (ver. 31) for they are called to be her conscious recipients, and under her enlightening influence to grow up into a walk in holy fellowship with God. Precisely for this reason the possession of wisdom, *i. e.*, in the first instance that comparative, creative wisdom which is identical with the fear of God and righteousness, is the sum of all that can be recommended to man as the means to the attainment of the highest temporal and eternal welfare. For this relative wisdom is in fact nothing but the reflection and emanation of that which is absolute. It is the absolute divine wisdom as this has found its individual reflection in the life of individual man,—the eternal wisdom of God entering into the subjective conditions of man, and so becoming creatural. When the concluding verses of the chapter (vers. 32–36) emphatically advise the obtaining of this wisdom which has thus become mundane and human, and point to the blessed consequences of its possession, they seize again upon that which was the starting-point in the whole admonition, and show how the secondary wisdom is derived from the primitive and conducts again to it, how the same holy life-power infinite in its perfection, which was active in the first creation of the world and of man, must also be efficient in their moral recreation and their perfecting after God's likeness. Comp. STAUDENMAIER, as cited above, p. 38: "The eminence of man consists not merely in the fact that wisdom comes in him to self-consciousness, but also in the fact that by the Creator there has been conferred upon him in the gift of freedom the power to become as it were the second creator of his own life according to the innate divine idea. This idea appears therefore now a practical one: the impulse to become practical existed already in its living energy, or was this very energy; and with this it is at the same time clear that man with his freedom has pre-eminently a practical religious and moral problem set before him. Since however by this very freedom he also has it in his power not to follow his destination, and even to resist it, Wisdom appeals to him to hear her voice, and does this as she speaks to him both from within and from without,—from within by ideas (through the voice of reason and conscience), from without, through divine revelation in which absolute wisdom dwells."

3. This representation of wisdom as a personal principle mediating between God and man, existing in God as the prototype, in man in the antitype, plainly stands in the closest relationship to the doctrine of the Logos in the New Testament.*

The connection, it is true, with a right exegesis of the main points involved (see notes on vers. 22, 23, and 30, above), does not reach so far that wisdom is described outright as a child of God, begotten in eternity and "anointed," *i. e.*, solemnly consecrated and sealed,—and so is attended by those characteristic predicates with which Christ describes His absolutely unique metaphysical relation as Son to God (John x. 36; v. 26; xvii. 5; comp. i. 1, 18). And yet when she also is declared to have been created as beginning of the ways of God, there are surely not wanting emphatic intimations that her character is absolutely above that of creatures in both respects, that which concerns her coming into being before all creatures, and also her intimate fellowship of essence and of life with God. While furthermore the primæval consecration to be a ruler over all things, to the ranks of a priestly regal mediatorship between God and His creation is not to be found among the points expressly emphasized in the description of Wisdom, yet the way in which she is described in vers. 14–16, as possessor and dispenser of all sovereign power and wisdom, reminds us distinctly enough of the omnipotence in heaven and earth that is given to the Son, and of His being endowed with the undivided fulness of the Divine Messiah-Spirit,—which Isaiah in his day pronounces a spirit of all wisdom and understanding, all counsel, all strength, knowledge, and holy fear (Isa. xi. 2; comp. John iii 34; Matth. xxviii. 18). And although, finally, the name "son" or "child" is not given to her, and the "exultation" in the presence of God at the time of His creative activity, cannot fitly be conceived of as the intimation of a relation in any way like that existing between a sportive favorite child and his father, still the appellation "directress of the work" characterizes this being distinctly enough as a personal emanation from the very nature of God. And a mediatorial participation not only in the creative, but also in the redemptive and sanctifying activity of God is suggested, if only in gentle intimation, by what is said of her "delight in the sons of men." To these points of correspondence which are presented in the chief individual features of the picture in Prov. viii. 22 sq., there may be added several unmistakable allusions to our chapter found in the New Testament. Among these the essential identity of the creative wisdom of God that is here described, with the Logos or the pre-existent Christ stands out most distinctly. When our Lord in Matth. xi. 19 (Luke vii. 35) and probably also in Luke xi. 49 (comp. VAN OOSTERZEE on this passage) designates himself as the "Wisdom of God," and at the same time speaks of "children of this wisdom," meaning by this the men who are subject to her revealing and enlightening influence, especially the Jews, as having been Divinely influenced by law and prophecy, He can have chosen this mode of designating Himself only with His eye upon the Biblical delineations that were familiar to His hearers; and to these, beside Ecclesiasticus xxiv. and Wisdom vii.–ix., *etc.*, the passage be-

---

* Comp. NITZSCH as cited above: "Do you see here no trace of a divine process a germ of an ontological self-distinction in God? For this Wisdom is indeed a first God's communication localized in the world, particularly in man, and still more especially in Israel. Yet it will be understood as no mere creature like others, no angel, no dependent power or effect; it claims to be known and honored in its divinity. Without exhausting the idea of divinity it claims to be God of God—"Jehovah created me"—a creation which according to the connection gives no natural, creaturely being but has a significance plainly transcending these bounds, *etc.*"—

The truth of this representation holds also as against that which VON HOFMANN (*Schriftbew*, 1. pp. 95 sq.) has brought forward in support of the opposite view, *i. e.*, that which denies the hypostatic nature of wisdom in our passage.

fore us would pre-eminently belong. When John ascribes to the Divine Logos both alike, the acting as medium of the activity of God in the creation of the world, and the accomplishment of His enlightening and saving efficiency on the world,—when he in doing this distinctly characterizes the Logos not as a mere attribute or impersonal reason of God, but as a hypostasis self-conscious and freely coming forth from the absolute ground of the Divine essence, as a Divine personality seeking incarnation (John i. 1-18), the harmony of this description of his with Solomon's praise of the Divine Wisdom cannot have continued to be merely unconscious. And this is all the less possible, from the consideration that this wisdom had already before his time and in manifold instances been designated by the name Λόγος, e. g., Ecclesiast. i. 4 (comp. xxiv. 3), Wisdom, ix. 1. When Paul in numerous passages asserts the same of his pre-existent Christ (especially 1 Cor. viii. 6; Col. i. 15 sq.; Phil. ii. 5 sq.), among the passages from the Old Testament lying at the foundation of his views in this matter, Prov. viii. 22 sq., cannot have been wanting. And furthermore his designation of the Son as the "Wisdom of God" (1 Cor. i. 24, 30; comp. Rom. xiii. 27; Col. ii. 3) cannot have developed itself on any other basis. The same holds finally also of the author of the Epistle to the Hebrews (see Heb. i. 2 sq.), as well as of the writer of the Apocalypse, who, by his emphatic use of the name of the Logos (Rev. xix. 13), shows himself plainly enough to be no other than the Evangelist John. His peculiar designation of Christ, already adduced above, as "the beginning of the creation of God" (chap. iii. 14) may perhaps be viewed outright as a literal allusion to verse 22 of our chapter.*

If this were the case, the idea of a "beginning of the creation of God" would by no means for that reason require to be interpreted in the Arian sense. For in an author who elsewhere adopts the doctrine of the Logos the representation of Christ as the first creature of God would palpably be a monstrosity. John can in this expression intend to designate the Lord only as the active principle in the creation (comp. DUESTERDIECK on this passage). In just this active sense shall we be obliged to interpret the expression which possibly suggested John's language,—the "beginning of the ways of Jehovah" in our chapter, i. e, as relating to the activity of the eternal Wisdom of God which commenced His manifestation of Himself in creation, its mediating coöperation in God's world-creating act (see remarks on this passage above).

4. The only noteworthy difference between the idea of the Logos in the New Testament, and the hypostatic Wisdom of our passage consists, therefore, in the decidedly *created* character ascribed to the latter by the expression "Jehovah created me" in ver. 22, and the parallel expression in ver. 23. Our teacher of wisdom in the Old Testament, near as he may have come to the idea, was therefore unable to rise to an altogether clear discernment of the relation existing between God and His eternal Word, who in all His likeness of nature is yet personally distinct, and while appearing as the "first-born of every creature," still on the other hand appears also as the only begotten Son of the living God, or as eternal personal emanation from the Divine essence. The hypostatic Hhokmah of our author (and also the Σοφία of the Apocrypha, which differs from it in no essential characteristic) appears accordingly as an imperfect introduction and preparation for the idea of the Logos in the New Testament, the conception not having yet reached a full symmetrical development. So also the "Spirit of God" in the prophetic literature of the O. T. shows itself to be the prototype, the germinal basis for the πνεῦμα ἅγιον of the N. T., this distinctly personal third Divine agent in salvation, with the Father and the Son.*

In any event, however, this conception stands much nearer to the idea of the Logos or the Son in the New Testament, and contributed more directly to its development, than that personification of the creative "word of Jehovah" which appears here and there in Psalmists and prophets (e. g., Ps. xxxiii. 6; cxlvii. 15; Is. lv. 11, etc.). For this last expression has, after all, no other value than poetic figures in general, hastily thrown out. The Hhokmah of our passage, however, is, notwithstanding the poetic character of its drapery, a conception developed with the greatest care, a fruit of profound and consecrated speculation, a bright ray of Divine revelation, which, among the Messianic prophecies of the O. T. that relate to the Divine side of the Redeemer's nature, holds one of the most conspicuous places. Comp. NITZSCH, as above cited, pp. 319, 320.

[5. The error in our English exegetical and theological literature with respect to our passage has been, we think, the attempt to force upon it more of distinctness and precision in the revelation of the mysteries of the Divine nature than is disclosed by a fair exegesis. Sometimes it is the doctrine of the Logos that is made to stand out with all the clearness of the New Testament announcement; sometimes it is "the eternal generation of the Son" that Solomon is made, as the Spirit's mouthpiece, to reveal. OWEN's elaborate arguments (Comm. on the Epistle to the Hebrews, Exercitation xxvii.), and HOLDEN's extended and learned comments (Comm. in loc.), appear to us very plainly to err in this excess. If it be not unworthy of the Holy Spirit to employ a bold and graphic personification, many things in this chapter may be said of and by the personified Wisdom, which these and other similar authors regard as triumphantly proving that we have here the pre-existent Christ, the Son of God. How weak would that personification be which did not ascribe to the imagined person *hate, love, power,* etc. (see HOLDEN)! Why cannot a personified attribute, if the personification be at all successful, be represented as being born, as being by or near the Deity, as rejoicing in His sight, *etc.* (see HOLDEN again)? And yet we need not

---

* We here presuppose the spurious character of the ἐκκλησίας (which, besides, was early expunged by the correctors of the text) standing in the place of κτίσεως in the Cod. S'n If this remarkable reading were genuine, the meaning of the expression would certainly be altogether different. But the assumption can hardly be avoided that there is here no attempted emendation in the interest of the Antimonarchians or Anti-arians.

* Comp. also subsequent notes on ch. xxx. 3 sq.

go so far as OWEN and say, "A personal transaction before the creation of the world, between the Father and the Son, acting materially by their One Spirit, concerning the state and condition of mankind, with respect to Divine love and favor, is that which we inquire after, and which is here fully expressed." WORDSWORTH not agreeing with GESENIUS, etc., in regard to the primary meaning of the much debated קָנָה* admitting that it originally signifies *acquire*, nevertheless agrees with GESEN., HUPFELD (?), NOYES, STUART and others in here rendering it "created," because he wants an "eternal generation" as the product of his exegesis,—a product far enough from the thoughts of most of those who agree with him in his rendering. We can, to say the least, go no farther than our author has done in discovering here the foreshadowings of the doctrine of the Logos. We are inclined to prefer the still more guarded statements, e. g., of Dr. J. PYE SMITH (*Scripture Testimony to the Messiah*, I., 352), that this beautiful picture "cannot be satisfactorily proved to be a designed description of the Saviour's person;" or that of Dr. JOHN HARRIS (Sermon on Prov. viii. 30-36). "At all events, while, on the one hand, none can *demonstrate* that Christ is here directly intended,—on the other, none can *prove* that He is not contemplated; and perhaps both will admit that under certain conditions language such as that in our text may be justifiably applied to Him. One of these conditions is, that the language be not employed *argumentatively*, or in *proof* of any thing relating to Christ, but only for the purpose of illustration; and another is that when so employed, it be only adduced to illustrate such views of the Son of God as are already established by such other parts of Scripture as are admitted by the parties addressed."—A.]

HOMILETIC AND PRACTICAL.

Homily on the entire chapter. See the translation above, and comp. STÖCKER: The heavenly Wisdom which is the word of God is urgently commended to us: 1) by the good opportunity which we have to study it (vers. 1-5); 2) by the rich blessing that it brings us (vers. 6-21); 3) by the eminence and majesty of the teacher who teaches it, and who is no other than Christ, the eternal Son of God (vers. 22-36).—STARKE: The true Wisdom's invitation of all men to the Kingdom of God: 1) the invitation itself (vers. 1-10); 2) the inducements to give heed to it, namely: *a*) the inestimable value of wisdom (vers. 11, 12); *b*) the blessings of those who accept her invitation to the Kingdom of God (vers. 13-36).— *Culwer Handbuch*: Wisdom commends herself: 1) in general (vers. 1-5); 2) by her truthfulness (vers. 6-9); 3) by the prudence, understanding, honor and power that she imparts to her followers (vers. 10-21); 4) by her eternal existence, her participation in the creation, her delight in the sons of men (vers. 22-36).—WOHLFARTU: Wisdom the truest and best friend of men, her doors (ver. 34) standing open day by day to every one that needs and desires her.

*[For a very full and candid discussion of this with other related points, see an article by Prof. E. P. BARROWS, *Biblioth. Sacra*, April, 1858; also, LIDDON's *Bamp. Lectures*, pp. 60, 61. —A.]

Vers. 1-11. EGARD:—The Eternal Son of God gathers, plants, builds His Church by a voice, *i. e.*, His word. All true teachers of the word are crying voices through which Christ calls.— Out of Christ's school is no true wisdom; they who deem themselves wise and shrewd are unfitted to learn of Him.—So long as Christ's wisdom is still speaking outside of thee it avails thee nothing; but when thou allowest it to dwell in thee it is thy light and thy life.—Thou shouldst have one heart and one mouth with Christ; if false and perverse things are found in thy mouth thou art still far from Christ.—Silver and gold is mere vanity and nothingness; what can it help in the day of wrath and judgment? Let God's word be thy highest and best treasure— *Berleb. Bible:* Wisdom (who speaks to us not only through the word written and preached, but also inwardly, as God's voice in our hearts) is so far from keeping silence, that although we stop our ears, we yet hear her correction within at the entrances and doors of the heart; and although we will not understand her, we must nevertheless feel her. And this is a testimony how desirous God is of our blessedness.

Vers. 12-21. MELANCHTHON (on vers. 14 sq.): Those counsels are just which agree with the word of God; and these counsels will at length have joyful issues, with the aid of the Son of God, who wills to aid those that continue in the word which He has given, and who call upon Him.—LUTHER (marginal comment on vers. 15, 16): "Princes should act, speak, work, honorably and praiseworthily, that men may glory in and follow their example; and not as the tyrants, the foul, the cyclops," etc.—HASIUS: When true wisdom is taken into counsel in every thing, then in all ranks that will occur which each one's purpose demands according to a perfect ideal. Kings, princes, nobles, counsellors will act in conformity with the aim of their calling (2 Chron. xix. 6, 7).—Things would stand much better in the world if men exercised their spirit more after holiness, and strove with greater zeal for wisdom, Matth. vi. 33. — *Berleburg Bible:* No one can rightfully take to himself the name of a Christian ruler, but he who subjects himself in spirit and truth, in humble obedience to the control of the Almighty, lays himself at His feet and allows himself to be wholly ruled by Him. Others exercise a rude, violent and tyrannical control, and an assumed authority over the person of men.—VON GERLACH: The wisdom who here announces herself is the very wisdom of God, and is therefore also, as all good can be from God alone, the soul of all good laws and ordinances (vers. 14-17), and must, as every thing earthly is ruled, disposed and rightly distributed among men by God, necessarily reward her disciples with welfare, honor and riches (vers. 18-21). [Ver. 12. CHARNOCK: All arts among men are the rays of Divine wisdom shining upon them. Whatsoever wisdom there is in the world, it is but a shadow of the wisdom of God.— Ver. 13. ARNOT: To fear retribution is not to hate sin; in most cases it is to love it with the whole heart. It is when sin is forgiven that a sinner can hate it. Then he is on God's side. Instead of hating God for his holiness, the forgiven man instinctively loathes the evil of his own heart.—JONA. EDWARDS: "The affection of hatred as having sin for its object is spoken of in Scripture as no inconsiderable part of true religion. It is spoken of as that by which true religion may be known and distinguished."—Ver. 15. Bp. SANDERSON: On the efficient cause and consequent obligation of human law.—HOOKER: "By me kings reign," etc. Not as if men did behold that book and accordingly frame their laws; but because it worketh in them, because it discovereth and (as it were) readeth itself to the world by them, when the laws which they make are righteous.—Ver. 18. ARNOT: The riches which the King of saints imparts along with the patent of nobility to support its dignity withal, are linked to righteousness and last forever. Handfuls are gotten on the ground, but a soulful *is* not to be had except in Christ.]

Vers. 22-31. GEIER:—From this delineation there follows: 1) the personal difference of the Son from the Father; 2) the essential likeness of the Son to the Father, as partaker of the Divine activity in creation; 3) the unutterable love of the Father to the Son (ver. 30?); 4) the deep and grateful love which we in turn owe to this Divinely loved director and mediator in creation and redemption.—ZELTNER: All the works of God's omnipotence and wisdom thou shouldst contemplate with holy joy and wonder, praise the Creator for them, and with them strengthen thyself in faith in His paternal providence.—As an essential and indescribable fellowship exists between the Father and the Son, so does there exist between God and the believer a gracious spiritual union, on which the Christian must be most intent.—STARKE: All things have had their beginning except the Son of God regarded in His Divine nature. He is with the Father and the Holy Ghost true God from everlasting to everlasting. All that this Eternal Wisdom does in the kingdom of nature, as well as in that of grace, she does with gladness and delight: yea, there is in this work so lovely and wise an alternation and manifoldness, that we must in reason wonder at it (comp. Eph. iii. 10, "the manifold wisdom of God"). — VON GERLACH: — That "play" of wisdom in which the Lord takes pleasure, and her joyousness on the earth, in which she finds her joy among men, points to the childlike gladness of the love that ruled in creation, and to the confidential relation into which the children of wisdom on earth (Matth. xi. 19) enter, to her the very wisdom of God; comp. Prov. x. 23. In this passage there is a most clearly prophetic gleam of the light of the New Testament; God's eternal wisdom comes forth from Him that He may delight Himself in her activity; His own eternal nature the Father for his own blessedness contemplates in the Son. And it is in a love most intimately blended with wisdom that the Father created the world, to His own blessedness and that of His creatures.

Vers. 32-36. GEIER: The true fruits of obedience should follow the hearing of the word. To these belong: 1) walking the prescribed way; 2) willing reception of the Divine correction; 3) the extirpation of all inner opposition; 4) zealous and persistent seeking after salvation; 5) thankful enjoyment of the true wisdom when found.— VON GERLACH (on vers. 34 sq.): Wisdom here appears as a sovereign, separate and secluded in the style of Oriental monarchs, so that only those know any thing of her who diligently keep watch at her doors. Wisdom, who is universal in her call and invitation (vers. 1-3), yet in the course of communication, in order to test the fidelity of her admirers, veils herself at times in a mysterious darkness, and reveals herself only to those who never intermit their search (Matth. vii. 7) —[JOHN HOWE: There ought to be an expectation raised in us that the vital savor diffused in and by the word may reach us; and many are ruined for not expecting it, not waiting at the posts of wisdom's door.—TRAPP: Hear, *etc.* This way wisdom enters into the soul. Hear, therefore, for else there is no hope; hear, howsoever.—FLAVEL: It is good to lie in the path of the Spirit.]

15. Allegorical exhibition of the call of men to the possession and enjoyment of true wisdom, under the figure of an invitation to two banquets.

CHAP. IX. 1-18.

a) The banquet of wisdom: Vers. 1-12.

1 Wisdom hath builded her house,
 she hath hewn out her seven pillars.
2 hath slaughtered her beasts, spiced her wine,
 hath also spread her table;
3 hath sent out her maidens; she inviteth
 on the highest points (summits of the high places) of the city:
4 "Whosoever is simple, let him come hither!"—
 Whoso lacketh understanding, to him she saith:

5 "Come, eat of my bread
   and drink of the wine I have mixed!
6 Forsake the simple, and live,
   and walk in the way of understanding.
7 He who correcteth a scorner draweth upon himself insult,
   and he who rebuketh the wicked, it is his dishonor.
8 Reprove not the scorner lest he hate thee;
   admonish the wise and he will love thee.
9 Give to the wise and he becometh yet wiser,
   instruct the upright and he learneth yet more.
10 The beginning of wisdom is the fear of Jehovah,
   and knowledge of the Holy (one) is understanding.
11 For by me will thy days become many,
   and the years of thy life will increase.
12 Art thou wise, thou art wise for thyself,
   and if thou scornest thou alone shalt bear it."

b) The banquet of Folly: Vers. 13-18.

13 A simple woman (and) clamorous,
   is Folly, and knoweth nothing whatsoever.
14 She sitteth at the door of her house
   enthroned in the high places of the city,
15 to invite the wayfarers
   who go straight on their ways:
16 "Whosoever is simple let him come hither!"—
   whoso lacketh understanding to him she saith:
17 "Stolen waters are sweet,
   and bread taken in secret is pleasant,"
18 and he knoweth not that the dead are there,
   in the depths of hell (the lower world) her guests.

GRAMMATICAL AND CRITICAL.

Ver. 3. [BÖTTCHER cites בְּרֹמֵי as illustrating a peculiar Hebrew idiom by which the emphatic plural of generic designations of persons, places and things is used for the singular with an indefinite article, which the Hebrew lacked, and only in its later periods began to supplement by the numeral. He would therefore translate "on one of the high places of the city." See *Ausführl. Lehrb.*, § 702, d.].

Vers. 4. [סָר, an example of the "consultive" use of the Jussive form (see D ਜ. § 964, 2), which under the influence of the succeeding word retains the *u* vowel (§ 956, g.—§ 1132, 3), the ordinary Jussive being יָסֹר. אָמְרָה Perf. consec. employed, as it sometimes is in the lively discourse of oratory and poetry, without the connective ן, B. § 974].

Ver. 9. [וְהֶחְכַּם, וְיוֹסֶף, examples of Jussive with ן consec., in the "*consecutive-affirmative*" sense, as giving an assured result. BÖTT. § 964, α.].

Ver. 13. [מָה is regarded by BÖTTCHER also as an indefinite, *quidquid* or *quidquam*, (§ 699, c), as it is by GESENIUS and FUERST. GESEN. however finds a different shade of meaning in the verb, and translates "and careth for nothing"].

Ver. 16. [וְאָמְרָה, an example of the Perf. consec. in the sense of the "*Fiens solidum*," the "future" with the idea of customary action. BÖTT. § 981, B. β.].

EXEGETICAL.

1. Vers. 1-3. **Wisdom hath builded her house.** The figure of the building of a house which is readily suggested by the appellation "director of the work" in chap. viii. 30, appropriately provides for a transition from the description of the agency of eternal Wisdom in the creation of the world, to that here symbolized as an invitation to a banquet,—her activity among men, summoning and morally instructing them. Comp. chap. xiv. 1.—The designation of Wisdom (חָכְמוֹת) is the same as in i. 20.—**Hath hewn out her seven pillars.** This hewing out of pillars suggests the splendor of the completed building. The sevenfold number represents this as a sacred work; for seven stands here, as it so frequently does in the Old and New Testaments, as a sacred number (comp. my article "*Siebenzahl*" in HERZOG's *Theol. Real-Encycl.*, XIV. 353 sq.). The house of the celestial Wisdom is by this peculiar and emblematic description represented, as it were, in advance, as a temple, and the banquet offered in it as a sacred sacrificial meal. Special significance in the seven pillars, *e. g.*, in connection with the seven attributes of the higher wisdom enumerated in James iii. 17; or the seven gifts of the Holy Spirit referred to in Rev. i. 4, 12 sq.; iii. 1; iv. 5; v. 6, *etc.* (VI-

CHAP. IX. 1-18.

TRINGA, C. B. MICHAELIS, J. LANGE, VON GERLACH, etc.), or the seven *principia deductiva Ethices divinæ* (according to S. BOHLIUS, comp. remarks above, p. 74, note), or finally, the first seven chapters of the Book of Wisdom now before us,—all this is indicated by nothing whatever in the context, and is therefore wholly arbitrary. The suffix in עֲפֻרֶיהָ, since בַּיִת is usually masc., seems to refer to Wisdom as the subject of the proposition,—*her*, not *its* seven pillars.

Ver. 2. **Hath slaughtered her beasts.** Notwithstanding the sacred character of the banquet, טִבְחָה is still not to be necessarily translated "her victims," but signifies "that which is slaughtered," slain animals in general. There is probably no reference to vii. 14.—The "mixing of the wine" seems not to refer to a mere mixing of wine with water, but to the preparation of a strong spiced wine with myrrh, *etc.*; comp. Isa. v. 22; Prov. xxiii. 30, *etc.*

Ver. 3. **She inviteth on the highest points of the city**, *i. e.*, so that her servants must ascend the highest elevations of the city (not specifically the roofs of palaces), from which their calls of invitation to the banquet are most widely heard. HITZIG singularly translates "on the bare elevations of the city," because גַפֵּי in Exod. xxi. 3, 4, and according to the Arabic, means naked, unclothed (?).—Furthermore the maidens sent forth, the servants of Wisdom, correspond to the servants by whom the Lord in the Gospel (Luke xiv. 16 sq.; Matth. xxii. 1 sq.) has the guests invited to his banquet.

2. Vers. 4-12. "**Whosoever is simple let him come hither!**" *etc.* On account of the similarity of this verse to ver. 16, which contains the words of Folly's invitation, and on account of the summons to eat *bread* (ver. 5) which does not agree with the mention of the slain beasts in ver. 2, HITZIG pronounces vers. 4 and 5 spurious. But it is very significant and pertinent that Wisdom's invitation appears clothed in the same words as that of Folly (comp. the analogous verbal repetitions in Christ's parables and didactic narratives, *e. g.*, Matth. xxv. 20, 22; Luke v. 6, 9; xvi. 6, 7, *etc.*); and to "eat bread" stands here as in iv. 7, and indeed frequently (*e. g.*, Gen. iii. 19; Lev. xxvi. 5; Deut. xxix. 6; Judges xix. 5; 1 Sam. ii. 36, *etc.*), by synecdoche for "the partaking of food, the taking a meal" in general. [The allegorical view of this passage as held, *e. g.*, by WORDSW., and in his Commentary supported by ample use of the Church Fathers, may be illustrated by the supposed reference of ver. 5 to "the Body of Christ, the Living Bread, and the mystery of His blood, by which we are refreshed at His Holy Table." A.].—**The destitute of understanding, to him she saith.** Before the חֲסַר־לֵב there is to be supplied from the 1st member the pronoun כִּי,—literally, therefore "who is destitute of understanding, to him she saith." The discourse accordingly here (and in the 2d member of ver. 15) falls back from the style of recital to that of description.

Ver. 6. **Forsake the simple.** It will be easiest to take this phrase in its literal sense.

For the verses following give this very counsel, not to keep company longer with the simple, with fools and scorners, because these are still incorrigible. The old versions and most modern commentators [as *e. g.*, ST., N., M] regard the noun as abstract (equivalent to the sing. פֶּתִי in i. 22, or the abstract derivative פְּתַיּוּת in ver. 13), and therefore translate "Forsake simplicity, let your simplicity go." [As TRAPP, in his pithy way expresses it: "No coming to this feast in the tattered rags of the old Adam: you must relinquish your former evil courses and companies"]. But such a signification of this plural is attested by no example whatsoever. Just as unadvisable is it to construe the verb absolutely, by which HITZIG reaches the translation, "Cease, ye simple," *etc.*; for in Jer. xviii. 14, the verb is construed not absolutely, but rather with כִּן; and the connection with what follows at least decidedly favors our explanation, which is supported by UMBREIT also among others of the later expositors.

Ver. 7. **He who correcteth the scorner draweth upon himself insult.** Usually the connection with ver. 4-6 is so conceived as if Wisdom were here (in ver. 7-10) explaining her conduct in inviting especially the simple; she is supposed to turn to these alone, for the reason that if she wished to invite the scornful and wicked also she would only expose herself to indignities, and yet would effect nothing. But against this view of the course of thought may be urged decidedly, the warning and admonitory tone of vers. 8, 9, and the didactic nature of ver. 10, which make it easy to find expressed in ver. 7 also the spirit of dissuasion, and so to regard vers. 7-10 as an argument in support of the demand embodied in the 1st clause of ver. 6, to avoid further intercourse with the simple, scorners, villains, *etc.* A comparison with i. 22 shows that under the "simple" may be included very readily mockers, the violent, *etc.*, as belonging to the same category; so does also the name "simplicity" (פְּתַיּוּת) which is below, in ver. 13, directly given to the personification of Folly. "Abandon intercourse with such persons" is therefore Wisdom's admonition, "for you gain from it nothing but insult, hate and contempt; forsake the camp of the simple (פְּתָאִים) and come over into that of the wise (חֲכָמִים), whose watchword is the fear of God and knowledge of the Holy; so will you find abundance of happiness and blessing."—HITZIG, whose conception of the 1st clause of ver. 6 makes the recognition of this as the true connection of thought from the first impossible, summarily rejects ver. 7-10 as a later interpolation. But if in fact the "if thou scornest" in the 2d clause of ver. 12 suggested this interpolation, the verses introduced would both in form and substance have been essentially different. And in the form in which the passage has come down in the manuscripts HITZIG's hypothesis of an interpolation here again finds no kind of support.—**And he who rebuketh a wicked man to him it is a shame.** The word כִּלְמוֹ (his fault or shame) cannot be dependent on the verb (לקה) of the first clause which is associated with לוֹ [he taketh to himself his shame], but must be regarded as a predicate: "this is to him shame, such action is his disgrace." Comp. Eccl. v. 16; Ps. cxv. 7.

Ver. 9. **Give to the wise and he becometh wiser.** Comp. chap. i. 5, which passage although expressing an idea like that before us, must not for that reason be regarded as derived from this (in opposition to Hitzig). [Lord Bacon (*Adv. of Learning*, Book II.) says, "Here is distinguished the wisdom brought into habit, and that which is but verbal and swimming only in conceit; for the one upon the occasion presented is quickened and redoubled, the other is amazed and confused"]. With ver. 10 comp. i. 7; ii. 5. Corresponding with the "Knowledge of God" in the latter passage we have here "knowledge of the holy," *i. e.* not "knowledge of the holy" [in plural] (LXX, Vulgate, and most Catholic expositors), but "of the Holy" [in singular, "*des Heiligen*"], *i. e.* of God. Comp. further for this *plur. majest.* chap. xxx. 3 and Hos. xii. 1. [See still further examples of the use of participial plurals in the same way in Isa. liv. 5; Ps. cxxi. 5; Eccl. xii. 1, *etc.*, EWALD, *Lehrb.*, § 178, *b*, BÖTT., § 701, GREEN, § 202.— With regard to the interpretation compare Dr. J. PYE SMITH (*Script. Test. to the Messiah*, I., 311): "According to the usual construction of Hebrew poetry, the plural epithet "the Holy" must be understood in apposition with JEHOVAH in the former half of the distich." So H., ST. M., and N.—A.]

Vers. 11, 12 are not to be regarded as taking up the discourse after the alleged digression in vers. 7–10, and attaching themselves to the words of invitation in vers. 4–6 to justify them (BERTHEAU, HITZIG), but give the reason for the general affirmation in ver. 10, which had been added as a peculiarly strong motive to the acceptance of Wisdom's invitation. The address in the singular has therefore nothing remarkable in it; it simply follows vers. 8, 9.—**By me will thy days become many,** *etc.* Comp. similar promises of long life, chap. iii. 2; iv. 10. [For the use of this 3d pers. plural יוֹסִפוּ see the grammars generally, *e. g.* GES., § 134, 3; GREEN, § 243, 2, *b*, but more fully BÖTT., § 935, 6].—**Art thou wise, thou art wise to thyself.** The same thought is found somewhat more fully developed in Job xxii. 2, 3; xxxv. 6–9; comp. also Rom. xi. 35; Rev. xxii. 11, 12.—**If thou scornest thou alone shalt bear it.** Comp. Numb. ix. 13; Jer. vii. 19; Job xxxiv. 31, and also the Latin *dictum* of PETRONIUS, "*Sibi quisque peccat.*" The LXX offer in ver. 12, 1st clause, the fuller reading "thou shalt be wise for thyself and for thy neighbor" (καὶ τῷ πλησίον) which is surely the result of interpolation, like the addition which they append to ver. 10 (τὸ γὰρ γνῶναι νόμον διανοίας ἐστὶν ἀγαθῆς). The longer additions also of three verses each, which they with the Syriac and Arabic translators exhibit after ver. 12 and ver. 18, hardly rest upon a genuine original text that was before them, although they may readily be rendered back into Hebrew (see HITZIG's attempts at this, pp. 86 and 88), and therefore very probably date from pre-Alexandrian times.

Vers. 13–18. **A simple woman, clamorous, [violently excited] is Folly.** The abstract כְּסִילוּת, simplicity, foolishness (see above remarks on ver. 7) is here plainly the subject, and designates the personified Folly, the exact opposite of Wisdom in ver. 1. With this subject is associated and prefixed as the main predicate, the appellation "woman of folly," *i. e.*, simple woman; the הוֹמִיָּה "clamorous, boisterous" is in turn an attribute of this predicate, and describes the passionately excited, wanton desire of the foolish woman represented as an adulteress, just as in vii. 11, with which delineation that before us has a general and doubtless intentional correspondence.—**And knoweth nothing whatever.** In this way in accordance with Job xiii. 13, this phrase of the Masoretic text (וּבַל־יָדְעָה מָּה) must unquestionably be interpreted. *Utter ignorance* (comp. John xi. 49, "ye know nothing at all") would accordingly be what is here asserted of Folly. But perhaps HITZIG is right, according to the LXX (ἣ οὐκ ἐπίσταται αἰσχύνην, "who knoweth not shame") in reading כְּלִמָּה instead of מָה (the disappearance of the two consonants might easily have been occasioned by the false reading כָּל־מָה), and therefore in translating "and knoweth no shame," which agrees admirably with the "boisterous" of the 1st clause.

Ver. 14. **She sitteth at the door of her house,** like harlots who watch for passers by; comp. Jer. iii. 2; Gen. xxxviii. 14, and the conduct of the adulteress described in chap. vii. 10 sq.—**Seated in the high places of the city.** The place thus described is not the same as that in the 1st clause, but some other, farther removed from the door of the house. The harlot is therefore quite like the one in chap. vii. 10 sq., represented as running irregularly this way and that and often changing her place. In this, however, the representation accords with that in ver. 3; as Wisdom so also Folly sends forth her call of invitation from elevated places of the city (comp. also chap. viii. 2). A real throne as her seat, which she has erected under the open air, and which, in contrast to the "bald, uncovered heights" (?) mentioned in ver. 3, is supposed to be covered with tapestry (HITZIG), is certainly not intended; but the "throne" is here metaphorical; a "lofty throne of the city" (UMBREIT) is a figurative and probably an ironical representation of a specially high place on which the wanton harlot has stationed herself, and therefore is as it were enthroned.

Ver. 15. **Who go straight on their ways,** and therefore quiet, unwary travellers who take no thought of circuits or by-paths. The expression is doubtless to be taken literally, and yet not without a secondary moral significance.

Ver. 17. **Stolen waters are sweet,** *etc.* Plainly words of Folly, and not of the author (EWALD, BERTHEAU), or even of one who has been assailed and ensnared by Folly's allurements (ELSTER): for the suggestion of the attraction and charm of forbidden pleasures appears most appropriately in the mouth of the beguiler. Comp. UMBREIT on this passage. Instead of wine (ver. 5) water is here mentioned as the ingredient of the feast, probably with reference to the waters mentioned in chap. v. 15. —**Bread of secrecy,** *i. e.* not simply bread secretly enjoyed, but also unjustly gained; an image of the forbidden enjoyment on which the adulterer seizes (comp. chap. xxx. 20).

Ver. 18. **And he knoweth not,** *i. e.* the foolish victim who heeds her call and enters her house (comp. viii. 22).—**That the dead** (shades) **are there,** *i. e.* children of death, who are surely moving on toward the horrors of the lower world, and therefore even now, while the body still lives, are tenants of the lower world (רְפָאִים, comp. ii. 18), or "dead" (thus quite correctly according to the sense, LUTHER [the English version, *etc*.]: comp. Matt. viii. 22; Eph. ii. 1, *etc*.) —**In the depths of hell her guests;** literally, "in the depths (not as UMBREIT and EWALD would read 'in the valleys') of Sheol her invited ones." Therefore although in the house of Folly and to be found at her banquet those ensnared by her are in truth already in hell. For that house as a throat of hell reaches down to it (comp. ii. 18; vii. 27), is as it were only a station on the way of these sinners, which leads surely and irresistibly down to hell. Thus, and doubtless correctly, HITZIG, in opposition to others who make this language only anticipative. As to the three verses which the LXX supply after ver. 18 see above on ver. 12.

DOCTRINAL AND ETHICAL, HOMILETIC AND PRACTICAL.

The prototypical relation of the contents of this chapter to our Lord's parables founded on banquets (Mt. xxii. 1-14; Lu. xiv. 16-24) is evident, and therefore its special importance to the doctrine of the call to salvation. What peculiarly characterizes the representation before us is, however, the twofold banquet to which invitation is given, and the correspondent resemblances and differences in the two feasts with their accompaniments. In both instances, at Wisdom's feast as well as that of Folly, it is the "simple," *i. e.* the great mass of the unrenewed, the children of this world, those indeed needing but not yet partaking the divine salvation, to whom the call goes forth. It also goes in both cases (Ver. 4 and 16) with the same words of invitation, and under quite similar conditions,—that is, in such a way that those to be invited are laid hold upon in the street, and at once taken into the house (comp. Matt. xxii. 9; Luke xiv. 21). With these analogies which are found mainly at the beginning of the acts compared, how great are the differences, how fearful the contrasts! In the former case it is a splendid palace with its columns, a holy temple of God, in which the feast occurs; in the latter a common house, a harlot's abode, built over an entrance to the abyss of hell! In the first the entertainer, represented as the princely occupant of a palace, remains quietly at home, while her servants take charge of the invitations; in the last the common woman goes out herself on the streets and high places of the city, that sitting in the attire of a harlot (comp. vii. 10), with the open heavens as a canopy above her, she may craftily and shamelessly attract as many as may be affected and ensnared by the contagion of her wanton lust! In the former instance it is simple words of God that make up the inviting testimony, words that in part with a literal exactness agree with the gracious calls of mercy and love with which the Son of Man once called sinners to repentance (comp., for example, ver. 5 with John vi. 35, vers. 7, 8 with Matt. vii. 6; ver. 9 with Matt. xiii. 12; vers. 6, 11, 12 with Matt. xi. 28-30); in the latter it is a Satanic voice of temptation that is heard, setting forth with the boldest effrontery as a commendable principle to which we should conform our lives, the well-known "we ever strive for the forbidden, and desire the denied" (*nitimur in vetitum semper cupimusque negata*)! comp. ver. 17 with Matt. iv. 3, 9; Rom. i. 32, *etc.*

In the *homiletic treatment of the passage as a whole* it will be appropriate to set in the clearest light this parallelism of the banquets that are compared, with their special resemblances and contrasts; in some such way as this then: The friends of the kingdom of heaven and the friends of this world; or, The call of Christ to His Church, and the enticement of Satan to the service of sin; or, The feast of death, *etc.* Comp. STÖCKER: Christ's wisdom and humanity (φιλανθρωπία); Antichrist's folly and destructiveness.— STARKE:— A lesson on the founding of the church of the Messiah, and the collection of its members: 1) The founding of the Church by the work of redemption (vers. 1, 2). 2) The invitation to the enjoyment of the blessings of Christ's salvation in the Church; and in particular: *a*) How Christ invites to the enjoyment of these blessings of His salvation (vers. 3-6); *b*) How this invitation is foolishly despised by many men, and the allurements of sin preferred to it. —WOHLFARTH :—The cross-roads; while wisdom calls us to the way of virtue and offers herself as our guide on it, at the same time the pleasure of this world calls and offers everything imaginable to draw to itself earth's pilgrims of all races, ages and conditions.

Single passages. On vers. 1-6. STÖCKER:— (Sermon on Christmas eve); Christ's friendliness and condescension, as it appears 1) from the founding of His Church and its maintenance by "seven pillars," *i. e.* by the apostles endowed with the manifold gifts of the Holy Ghost (ver. 1); 2) from His costly work of redemption in His own sacrificial death (ver. 2); by the institution of the means of grace in His Word and Sacrament (vers. 2-3); 4) from the gracious invitation to partake of all this (vers. 4 sq.).

On vers. 7, 8. CRAMER:—In the office of the Christian ministry the function of discipline must also be especially maintained. It does not, however, produce uniform fruits; some reform, some are and continue scorners.—[Ver. 7. FLAVEL:—What we fear might turn to our benefit. The reproof given is duty discharged; and the retort in return is a fresh call to repentance for sin past, and a caution against sin to come.—Vers. 7-9. ARNOT:— Reproof—how to give it and how to take it. There should be jealousy for the Lord's honor, and compassion for men's souls like a well-spring ever in the heart; and then the outgoing effort should be with all the wisdom of the serpent and the harmlessness of the dove. For rightly receiving reproof the rule is, be more concerned to get the benefit of the reproof than to wreak vengeance on the reprover.]

On ver. 7-12. *Calwer Handbuch;* Reflections on the reception which Wisdom's invitation finds among men; mockers answer it with derision; wise, *i. e.* God-fearing men, and such as continue in sanctification grow not only in wisdom, but also in outward prosperity: the gain is in every case ours, as the loss is the scorner's.—On vers. 11, 12. HASIUS:—Wisdom and virtue lose nothing by being reviled and defamed; he, however, inevitably loses who makes sport of them.—[T. ADAMS:—Wisdom is the mother of abstinence, and abstinence the nurse of health; whereas voluptuousness and intemperance (as the French proverb hath it) dig their own grave with their teeth.]

On vers. 13-18. STARKE:—If the temptation of Satan and his agents is so strong so much the more needful is it to try the spirits whether they be of God, and to beseech God that He will guide us in the right way. Alas! to many men in consequence of their corrupted taste in spiritual things there is more relish in the bread of vice and in draughts from the impure sloughs of the world, than in what is offered to them on the table of Jesus' grace.—*Berleburg Bible:*—The more faithfully one serves the world, the more he allows himself to be led by corrupt reason and gives ear to the fascinating voice of temptation, the more enamored he is of the deceitful harlot, so much the deeper will he sink into the lowest depths of hell . . . . Who would prefer hell to heaven! who would go after death that may attain life!—[Ver. 17. TRAPP:—Many eat that on earth that they digest in hell.—ARNOT:—When you have tasted and seen that the Lord is gracious, the foolish woman beckons you toward her stolen waters, and praises their sweets in vain: the new appetite drives out the old].

II. ORIGINAL NUCLEUS OF THE COLLECTION—GENUINE PROVERBS OF SOLOMON.

Ethical maxims, precepts and admonitions with respect to the most diverse relations of human life.

(Proverbs mainly in the form of antithetic distichs.)

CHAP. X. 1—XXII. 16.

1. *Exhibition of the difference between the pious and the ungodly, and their respective lots in life.*

Chap. X-XV.

a) Comparison between the pious and the ungodly with respect to their life and conduct in general. Chap. X.

1   Proverbs of Solomon.
  A wise son maketh glad his father,
  but a foolish son is the grief of his mother.
2 Treasures of wickedness do not profit,
  but righteousness delivereth from death.
3 Jehovah will not suffer the righteous to famish [E. V.: the soul of the righteous],
  but the craving of the wicked He disappointeth.
4 He becometh poor that worketh with an idle hand,
  but the hand of the diligent maketh rich.
5 He that gathereth in summer is a wise son,
  but he that sleepeth in harvest is a bad son.
6 Blessings are upon the head of the just,
  but the mouth of the wicked hideth violence.
7 The memory of the just is blessed,
  but the name of the wicked shall rot.
8 Whoso is wise in heart will receive precepts,
  but he who is of foolish lips shall fall.
9 He that walketh uprightly walketh securely,
  but he that perverteth his way shall be made known.

10 He that winketh with the eye causeth trouble,
   and he that is of foolish lips is overthrown.
11 A fountain of life is the mouth of the righteous,
   but the mouth of the wicked hideth violence.
12 Hate stirreth up strife,
   but love covereth all transgressions.
13 On the lips of the man of understanding wisdom is found,
   but a rod (is) for the back of the fool.
14 Wise men store up knowledge,
   but the mouth of the fool is a near (speedy) destruction.
15 The rich man's wealth is his strong city,
   the destruction of the poor is their poverty.
16 The labour of the righteous (tendeth) to life,
   the gain of the wicked to sin.
17 A way to life is he who heedeth correction,
   he who resisteth reproof leadeth astray.
18 He that hideth hatred (hath) lying lips,
   and he who spreadeth slander is a fool.
19 In much talking transgression is not wanting,
   but he that governeth his lips doeth wisely.
20 Choice silver is the tongue of the righteous,
   the heart of the wicked is of little worth.
21 The lips of the righteous feed many,
   but fools die for want of knowledge.
22 Jehovah's blessing,—it maketh rich,
   and labour addeth nothing thereto.
23 It is as sport to a fool to do mischief,
   but to the man of understanding wisdom.
24 What the wicked feareth cometh upon him,
   but the desire of the righteous is granted them.
25 When a storm sweepeth by the wicked is no more,
   but the righteous is an everlasting foundation.
26 As vinegar to the teeth and smoke to the eyes,
   so is the sluggard to them that send him.
27 The fear of Jehovah multiplieth days,
   but the years of the wicked are shortened.
28 The expectation of the righteous is gladness,
   but the hope of the wicked shall perish.
29 Jehovah's way is a bulwark to the righteous,
   but destruction to evil doers.
30 The righteous shall never be moved,
   but the wicked shall not abide in the land.
31 The mouth of the righteous bringeth forth wisdom,
   but the perverse tongue shall be rooted out.
32 The lips of the righteous know what is acceptable,
   but the mouth of the wicked perverseness.

GRAMMATICAL AND CRITICAL.

Ver. 1.—[חָפֵץ; cited by BÖTT (§§ 943, c, e; 950 e) as an illustration of the employment of the Imperf. to express what must be from the very nature of the case,—*Fiens debitum*,—"most gladdeo."—A.]

Ver 2.—[יוֹעִילוּ: as above, with the meaning "cannot profit:" § 950, c, ß.—A.]

Ver. 3.—[יַרְעִיב; an example of the *Fiens solitum*, what is *wont* to be; § 950, b.]—The LXX, arbitrarily assimilating the language of the first and second clauses, read in the second חַיַּת רְשָׁעִים, for they translate "the life of the ungodly," ζωὴν δὲ ἀσεβῶν ἀνατρέψει. [הַוַּת has been quite variously rendered. The E. V. translates "substance," the object of the desire of the wicked. LUTHER, following the *insidias* of the Vulg., renders by "*Schinderei*—*exactions or oppression*." HOLDEN translates "iniquity." N., ST., and M. agree with our author in retaining the simple meaning "craving, or greedy desire." So GESEN., FUERST, etc.—A.]

Ver 5.—[כָּבִישׁ is taken by GESEN., FUERST, STUART as intransitive, in the sense of "acting basely." N. M., H. agree

with the E. V. In deriving it from a different radical idea in the verb, and making it a causative Hiphil. The difference in the final import is not very great, yet the former conception of the word appears to have the best warrant.—A.]
Ver. 8.—[חֲקַ֣ר, *Fiens licitum*, "is disposed to receive," *etc*. Bött, § 950, c.—A.]
Ver. 21.—חֲסַר־ is here *stat. constr.* not of the adj. חָסֵר, as *e. g.* above in ver. 13, but of the noun חֶסֶר, as the old translators correctly judged. BERTHEAU is therefore wrong in rendering "through one void of understanding." FUERST takes our author's view; so Bött. (§ 794), who would interpret ver. 10 in the same way, "the back of folly."—A.]

EXEGETICAL.

1. *General preliminary remark.* The main division of the collection of proverbs that begins with chap. x., by the scattered isolation and the mosaic-like grouping of its individual elements contrasts quite strongly with the longer and well compacted proverbial discourses of the first nine chapters. And yet one would go too far in assuming an entirely planless and unregulated accumulation of the proverbs contained in chaps. x.–xxii., and failing to recognize at least an attempt of the collector to secure a methodical grouping of the rich store of maxims that he has to communicate. HITZIG's assumption, it is true, seems altogether artificial, and tenable only as the result of violent critical dealing,—*viz.*, that chaps. x.–xxi. may be resolved into four sections of equal length, of about 90 verses each; 1) chaps. x.–xii. (xiii. 1 making a commencement parallel to x. 1); chap. xiii.–xv. 32 (in which division xiii. 23 is to be stricken out to make 91 verses, as in the preceding section); chap. xv. 33–xix. 3 (where by omitting xvi. 25 and inserting two verses from the LXX after xvi. 17 the number of 89 verses must be reached that shall correspond with the section following); and chap. xix. 4–xxi. 31. He also assumes that within these four principal subdivisions groups of verses symmetrically constructed of six, seven and eight verses respectively, succeed one another. But although such a construction according to definite relations of numbers is not demonstrable, or at least is demonstrable only in single instances (*e. g.*, chap. xv. 33–xvi. 15; see remarks on this passage), still the existence of larger or smaller groups of proverbs of similar import cannot be denied; and many of these groups relating to one and the same subject are very probably attached one to another according to a definite plan or construction of ideas. And yet these in most cases stand in a loose co-ordination, and withal quite frequently appear accompanied or interspersed by single verses that are altogether isolated. In the chapter before us groups of this sort, governed by a certain unity of idea, may be found in vers. 2–7, 8–10, 11–14, 15–21, 22–25, 27–30. Vers. 1, 26, 31, 32 stand isolated. HITZIG's attempt to construct from x. 1–xi. 3 exactly five groups of seven proverbs each appears untenable after an unprejudiced examination of the real relations of the matter.— With reference to the contents of the six groups of verses, together with the individual verses accompanying them, and also with respect to central thoughts that may possibly be drawn from these elements, see the "Doctrinal and Ethical" notes.

2. Vers. 1. **A wise son maketh glad his father**, *etc*.—This thought, which is quite general, is plainly designed to serve as an introduction to the entire collection of proverbs that succeeds; comp. i. 8. As in that instance, and as in xv. 20; xvii. 25; xxiii. 24 there is found here an attempt, by means of an antithetic parallelism, at *Metalepsis* or the distribution of the propositions between father and mother in detail. [Ingenious expositions of the diverse effects of different kinds of conduct upon the father and the mother, like that of Lord BACON in the "*Advancement of Learning*," and more elaborately in the "*De Augmentis Scientiarum*," overlook the nature of the Hebrew parallelism—A.] "Grief, anxiety," derived from תּוּגָה (*moestus esse, dolere*), LXX : λύπη; comp. xiv. 13; xvii. 21; Ps. cxix. 28.

3. Vers. 2–7. Six verses or three pairs of verses relating to the earthly lot of the just and the unjust, the diligent and the sluggish.—**Treasures of wickedness profit not.**—Because they cannot avert the sudden and unhappy death that awaits the wicked; comp. vers. 25–27. With the second clause compare chap. xi. 4–19.

Ver. 3. **Jehovah will not suffer the righteous to famish.**—Literally, "the spirit of the righteous;" for this is the sense which in agreement with most interpreters we must find here, and not "the desire, the craving of the righteous," as ELSTER thinks, appealing for confirmation to vi. 30; xxiii. 2. For this strong expression is inappropriate before we come to the antithesis in the second member, and here the idea is plainly enough expressed by the word הַוָּה, "longing" (comp. אָוָה, Deut. xii. 15; 1 Sam. xxiii. 30). Compare xi. 6.

Ver. 4. **He becometh poor that worketh with an idle hand.**—כַּף־רְמִיָּה, not a "deceitful, crafty hand," but an "idle, sluggish hand," *manus remissa* (Vulg.); comp. xii. 24, 27; xix. 15; Jer. xlviii. 10.—רָאשׁ, for which the LXX and Vulg. must have read רָאשׁ the substantive (πενία, *egestas*), is the third Sing. Perf. Kal [or the participle] with the *scriptio plena* (like קָאם in Hos. x. 14), and with the signification "he is impoverished," *inops fit*; comp. Ps. xxxiv. 10. With the phrase יָד עָשָׂה, to stir the hand, to work with the hand, comp. Jer. xlviii. 10.—**But the hand of the diligent**—literally, " of the sharpened," comp. xii. 24.

Ver. 5. **He that gathereth in summer is a wise man**—lit., "is a son that doeth wisely," and so in the second member, "a son that doeth badly." These same predicates stand contrasted also in chap. xiv. 35, in that case to define more closely the term "servant," but here as attributes of the "son," which designation is chosen in this instance rather than "man," probably because "the heavy labors of the field which are here spoken of devolve especially upon the younger men, and also because idleness is particularly ruinous to youth" (ELSTER).—For the general sentiment comp. also chap. vi. 8, 9.

Ver. 6. **Benedictions (come) upon the head**

of the just, but the mouth of the wicked hideth violence.—In this strictly literal rendering of the verse there is no sharp antithesis between the first and second clauses, for which reason many, following the LXX and Vulg., reverse the relation of subject and object in the second clause, and either translate with DÖDERLEIN, DATHE, etc., "wickedness closeth the mouth of the vicious," or, inasmuch as the noun חָכָב cannot possibly be used in this sense of "wickedness, evil disposition," explain with UMBREIT among others, "the mouth of the profligate crime covereth." [E. V.: "violence covereth the mouth of the wicked."] (This is substantially the explanation of HITZIG also, except that he points פֶּה instead of פִּי, and takes the noun חָכָב contrary to usage in the sense of "pain, ruin;" "the mouth of the wicked is covered with sorrow.") [WORDS. gives a doubtful support to this view.] But why in just this passage and the second hemistich of ver. 11 which corresponds literally with it, it should be particularly the *mouth* and not the *face* of the wicked that is named as the object to be covered with crime, is not readily seen; and to read "face" (פָּנָי) instead of "mouth" (פִּי) in accordance with Ps. xliv. 16; Jer. li. 51, would evidently not answer on account of the double occurrence of the expression. Therefore, with BERTHEAU, ELSTER, etc. [N., ST., and M. in a qualified way], we should hold fast the above explanation as the simplest and most obvious, and accordingly reckon our verse among the exceptions, which, moreover, are not very rare, to that antithetic mode of constructing propositions which altogether predominates in the division of the book now before us. [RUEETSCHI, in the *Stud. und Krit.*, 1868, I., 135, not only agrees with our author in his construction of the verse, but endeavors more fully to justify the parallelism by the following explanation. "While the righteous, who is himself for others a fountain of life and blessing (ver. 11), nothing but love and fidelity, is himself also to expect blessing (ver. 7), the wicked has in himself only destruction; he hides it, covers it, it is true (comp. כָּסָה, ver. 18), with his mouth, yet has it in him (Ps. v. 9); and this very fact, that he covers in himself ruin for others, turns the blessing away from him."]

Ver. 7. The name of the wicked rotteth, strictly "will rot or moulder." *i. e.*, the memory of the wicked not only disappears quickly and surely, but also so as to excite sensations of abhorrence and disgust in other men (like ill smelling mould).

4. Vers. 8-10. Three proverbs bearing upon the contrast between wise men and fools.—He who is of foolish lips is overthrown.—With the wisely *disposed* (in the first clause) there is significantly contrasted the foolish *speaker*, the froward *talker*, and that, too, with the designation suggested by the organ of his foolish discourse, "the fool in lips." The verb (יִלָּבֵט), for the most part misunderstood by the older translators, can express only the meaning of being brought to a downfall, being overthrown, *præcipitari*, and accordingly sets forth the consequence of that refusal to receive commandments which characterizes the fool in contrast with the wise man.

To secure a stronger antithesis to the verb of the first clause HITZIG reads יְלַבֵּט, or יְלַבֵּט, "casts them away," *i. e.* the commandments. But it is precisely the correspondence with the 2d clause of ver. 10. where HITZIG must admit the passive meaning of the verb, that makes it certain that this is here also the intended meaning; for such verbal repetitions of whole or of half verses are among the fancies of the author of this division of our book; see above, remarks on ver. 6. [The wise "speaks little, but hears much: receives commands; therefore it goes well with him" (ver. 9, 1st clause; chap. iii. 1 sq.); but he "who is of foolish lips," who by his words shows himself a fool, is ever talking and not receiving instruction, is ruined; literally, is overthrown. It is in general a peculiar charm of many proverbs that the parallelism is not perfectly close, but it remains the function of the reader to seek out the intermediate thoughts, and to make the deductions." RUEETSCHI, as cited above].

Ver. 9. Is made manifest, lit., "is made known," *i. e.* as a sinner deserving punishment, an allusion to the judicial strictness of God, the All-seeing, [so WORDSW.], (the verb, therefore, not used as in chap. xii. 16). HITZIG strangely renders "made wiser," as though the Niphal were here passive of the Hiphil. [RUEETSCHI again (as cited above, p. 136) agrees with ZÖCKLER, and thus develops the antithesis: "he adopts crooked ways in order, as he thinks, to be able to practice iniquity more secure and unobserved; but he is ever known and exposed, he must himself always fear recognition, and this gives to his walk 'insecurity'"].

Ver. 10. He that winketh with the eye. Comp. vi. 13, where as here the "winking with the eye" immediately follows the mention of crooked and perverse action. Instead of the 2d clause, which is identical with the 2d clause of ver. 8, and which here yields no antithetic parallelism to the 1st clause, KENNICOTT, DATHE, BERTHEAU, ELSTER prefer the very different reading of the LXX: ὁ δὲ ἐλέγχων μετὰ παρρησίας εἰρηνοποιεῖ (but he that rebuketh boldly maketh peace). This however appears rather to be an attempted emendation, the result of well-meaning reflection than the restoration of an original Hebrew text. We must here again assume a momentary departure of the poet from his ordinary strictly antithetical construction of his sentences. In connection with this, however, we are not to give to the verb יְלַבֵּט conjecturally the meaning of "stumbling" or of "groping blindly" (HITZIG), but that which is found also in ver. 8, "having a fall," "self-destruction" (UMBREIT). [Here again RUEETSCHI comes to the defence of the poet's antithesis, with the explanation "he that winketh, the false, causes sorrow, produces vexation to himself, and he who in his folly openly utters evil falls." The results differ according to the nature of his wickedness; "vexation when he has done wrong secretly, overthrow, destruction, when he has done it openly" (as above cited, p. 136)].

5. Vers. 11-14. Two pairs of sentences concerning the contrast between good and evil, wisdom and folly, associated by the mention which

is common to the first and last proverb, of the *mouth* of those in whom the contrast appears (as the preceding group was characterized by the mention of the *lips* in vers. 8 and 10).—**A fountain of life is the mouth of the righteous**, on account of the hearty, edifying, loving character of its utterances. For this figure compare xiii. 14; xviii. 4. For the 2d clause see remarks above on ver. 6.

Ver. 12. **Hate stirreth up strife**, lit., "disputes," "litigations;" comp. vi. 14.—**All transgressions love covereth over**, by ignoring them, by palliating words, by considerate and conciliatory demeanor; comp. xvii. 9; James v. 20; 1 Pet. iv. 8; 1 Cor. xiii. 4.—[TRAPP: Love hath a large mantle].

Ver. 13. **A rod for the fool's back**, *i. e.* merited punishment overtakes him, the man void of understanding whose lips lack wisdom (comp. xxvi. 3; xix. 29). The imperfect and suggestive form of the antithesis is like that in vers. 6 and 8.

Ver. 14. **Wise men reserve knowledge**, lit., "conceal knowledge," *i. e.* husband the knowledge and understanding which they possess for the right time and place, do not squander it in unseasonable talk and babbling (comp. ver. 8). [So W., N., ST., and M.]. In the parallel passage xiii. 23 the synonymous verb to "cover" (פָּכָה) corresponds with the one here used. Comp. also Mal. ii. 7.—**Is a near destruction**, *i. e.* is ever inclined to break forth with its foolish suggestions, and thereby to bring upon itself and upon others alarm and even destruction. Comp. the sentiment of chap. xiii. 8, which although indeed somewhat differently constructed is still in general similar. ["Near" is an adjective, and the rendering should be more distinct than the ambiguous and misleading translation of the E. V. The mouth of the wicked is not simply passively near to being destroyed; it is a quickly destroying agency.—A.]

6. Vers. 15–21. Seven proverbs mostly relating to earthly good, its worth, and the means of its attainment,—connected with the two preceding groups (although only loosely and externally) by the "destruction" of ver. 15, and the allusion to the lips in vers. 18 and 19. With the 1st clause of ver. 15 comp. xviii. 11; Ecclesiast. xl. 26; and Eccles. vii. 12.—**The destruction of the poor is their poverty**, *i. e.*, on account of their destitution there is every instant threatening them an utter destruction or the sundering of all their relations; they therefore come to nothing, they are continually exposed to the danger of a complete ruin in all their circumstances, while to the rich man his means secure a sure basis and a strong protection in all the vicissitudes of life. Naturally the author is here thinking of wealth well earned by practical wisdom: and this is at the same time a means in the further efforts of wisdom; and again, of a deserved poverty which while the consequence of foolish conduct, always causes one to sink deeper in folly and moral need. Comp. the ver. following. HITZIG here following Jer. xlviii. 39 takes this destruction (כְּחִתָּה) subjectively, as equivalent to "consternation, terror," [NOYES], which view, however, is opposed by the use of the expression in the preceding verse and in ver. 29.

Ver. 16. **The labor of the righteous**, his acquisitions, his earnings, comp. 2 John 8.—**Tendeth to life**, comp. xi. 19 and also xvi. 8. The contrast to this, "tendeth to sin," includes the idea not fully expressed, "and accordingly to all misfortune and ruin as the result of sin." HITZIG, "to expiation," *i. e.* to making good the losses which his sins bring upon him as just penalties (with a reference to Zech. xiv. 19; Jer. xvii. 3); SCHULTENS, ARNOLDI, UMBREIT, etc., "to downfall, to misfortune." Both expositions fail to conform to the usual signification of חַטָּאת.

Ver. 17. **A way to life is he who heedeth correction**. "A way to life," (a well-known expression like "a way, or path of life" in chap. v. 6, and therefore not to be changed by a new punctuation into אֹרַח לְחַיִּים, "a traveller to life," as ZIEGLER and EWALD propose): so the wise observer of good instruction is here named because he also guides others to life, in contrast with the מַתְעֶה, him who misleads, the despiser of wholesome discipline and correction, who not only fails of the right way himself, but shows himself an evil guide to others also (Matt. xv. 14). [The rendering of the E. V., "is in the way," although followed by H., N., M., W., is not full and exhaustive enough. Such a man is not merely "in the way to life;" he is a guide, by a bolder figure he is a way to other men.—A.] The intransitive conception of this participle (LXX, Vulg., LUTHER, and also UMBREIT, EWALD, *etc.*), may if necessary be reached by modifying the punctuation מַתְעֶה (Hithp., HITZIG); but the "going astray" even then does not correspond remarkably with the "way to life," so far as this expression is correctly understood. ["This sentence is an example how sometimes that which is simplest and most obvious can be persistently missed: these words so simple and true have been refined upon because the real idea was not taken. The meaning is simply this: example is efficacious;" *etc.* RUEETSCHI, as above, p. 137].

Ver. 18. **He that hideth hatred** (hath) **lying lips**, strictly, "is lips of falsehood," *i. e.* is a man of deceitful lips. [Here again the E. V. sacrifices much of the original. "Lying lips" is not here instrumental; it is the predicate. So H., N., S., M., W.—A.] Comp for this immediate personification of the sinning organ, chap. xii. 19, 22, where in the first instance the "lying tongue" and then the "lying lips" appear personified. For the sentiment comp. xxvi. 24. Peculiarly hard and arbitrary is HITZIG's exposition; that instead of שֶׁקֶר (falsehood) we should read קֶשֶׁר (union), and that the expression thus resulting, "close, compressed lips" (?) is to be taken as the description of the deceitfully and maliciously compressed mouth of the man who is full of hate! EWALD is also arbitrary (although following the LXX); that instead of שֶׁקֶר we should read צֶדֶק (righteousness); "the lips of the righteous hide hatred," *i. e.* cover their enmity with love (?).—**He who spreadeth slander is a fool**. The meaning of this 2d clause does not stand in the relation of an antithesis to the preceding, but that of a climax, adding a worse case to one not so bad. If one conceals his hatred within himself he becomes a malignant flatterer; but if he gives expression to it in slander, abuse and base detraction, then as a genuine fool he brings upon himself the greatest injury. [RUEETSCHI objects to this, 1) that the analogy of xii. 19, 22 does not justify our taking the expression "lying lips" in the 1st clause as the predicate, and 2) that the emphatic pronoun "he" (הוּא) in the 2d clause is still less intelligible on this view of the structure of the verse; he regards this rather as one of the instances, of no very rare occurrence, in which the two clauses make but one proposition, and renders, "whoso conceals hatred with lying lips and at the same time utters slander—*he* is a fool," adding the explanation "one of the most odious of vices is where one conceals hatred under fine speech, and yet slanders behind the back; such a man is in sight of God and men despised and spurned"].

Ver. 19. **Transgression is not wanting.** In this way is the verb to be rendered, with UMBREIT, HITZIG and most others: and not with BERTHEAU, transgression "does not vanish" (as though we had here something to do with a removal or obliteration of actual guilt); only with the former rendering does the antithesis in the 2d member correspond, where it is plain that taciturnity and discretion in speech are recommended; comp. xiii. 3; xvii. 27, 28. [NOYES'S translation, "offence," has the fault, rare with him, of obscurity or ambiguity]. With the expression "to govern the lips" compare the Latin *compescere linguam* and the parallels from Arabic and Persian poets which UMBREIT adduces in illustration of our passage.

Ver. 20. **Choice silver**, as in chap. viii. 19 (comp. 10) is here used to indicate a very great value.—**Is of no worth**, literally, "is as nothing, is as a trifle,"—a popular and proverbial circumlocution for the idea of utter nothingness or worthlessness.—Ver. 21. **Feed many**, *i. e.* nourish and refresh many with the wholesome doctrines of godliness (comp. Eccles. xii. 11; Ezek. xxxiv. 2 sq; Acts xx. 28).—**But fools die for want of knowledge**, *i. e.* persistent fools (אֱוִילִים) are not only incompetent to become to others teachers of truth and guides to life; they are in themselves children of death for their lack of understanding.

7. Vers. 22–25. Four proverbs relating to the conduct of the righteous and the ungodly and their respective lots. The lot of the righteous, which consists in God's blessing which makes rich without any effort, forms the starting point of the description in ver. 22.—**And labor addeth nothing beside it**, *i. e.* as supplementary and exterior to it, that divine blessing which is all in all, which enriches the friends of God even in sleep (comp. Ps. cxxvii. 2 [and in connection with this HUPFELD'S comments: "Naturally this is not to be taken literally, as though perchance labor in itself were cast aside, and the Oriental indolence commended; nor again is the privilege given to the pious of being released from ordinary human toils, and of folding their hands in reliance on their powerful Friend; the aim is only, after the emphatic and one-sided manner of the proverb to make prominent the other side of the case, overlooked by restless toilers, what God does in the matter, so as to warn against the delusion that man can conquer by his toil alone," *etc.*]). This view is correctly taken by JARCHI, LEVI BEN GERSON, EWALD, HITZIG, *etc.*, while others (LXX, Vulg., UMBREIT, BERTHEAU, ELSTER, [the E. V., H., N., ST., M.]) translate "and addeth no sorrow thereto." But then instead of עֶצֶב we should rather have had עָלֶיהָ (comp. Jer. xlv. 3).

Ver. 23. **As sport to a fool is the practice of iniquity**, literally, "like a laugh is it to the fool to execute evil counsel." This "like sport" is then to be supplied also before the 2d member; "but to the man of understanding wisdom is as an enjoyment." [M. agrees with our author whose view is both more forcible and more accordant with the Hebrew idiom than that expressed in the E. V. and retained by N. and S.: "a man of understanding has wisdom." More than this is meant: wisdom is his delight.—A.] The verb to practice (עֲשׂוֹת) is probably not to be supplied here before "wisdom" (חָכְמָה); it is self-evident (in opposition to HITZIG'S view) that wisdom is considered here as something practiced and not merely possessed. With the phrase "man of understanding," the discerning man, comp. xi. 12.

Ver. 24. **What the wicked feareth**, lit., "the dread of the wicked," comp. Isa. lxvi 4; Job iii. 25; Prov. xi. 27.—**The desire of the righteous is granted them.**—The verb (יִתֵּן) can be regarded either as impersonal [like the German "*es gibt*," there is: comp. xiii. 10 and Job xxxvii. 10], or directly changed to the passive (יֻתַּן) as the Vulg., the Targums, and among recent interpreters EWALD and HITZIG. *e. g.*, do. To supply as the subject "Jehovah" (ABEN EZRA, UMBREIT, ELSTER, STUART, *etc.*) has its parallels indeed in xiii. 21, 22, but is here less natural than there.

Ver. 25. **When a storm sweepeth by the wicked is he no more.** Thus correctly EWALD, BERTHEAU, HITZIG, [HOLDEN, STUART, MUENSCHER]. Against the conception of the first phrase (כַּעֲבוֹר) as a comparison, "as a storm sweepeth by, so," *etc.* (UMBREIT, ELSTER, [E. V., NOYES], *etc.*) we may urge the conjunction וְ before אֵין as well as the idea of an "everlasting foundation" in the 2d member. With the latter expression comp. ver. 30, and also Ps. cxv. 1. With the first clause comp. Job i. 19; Isa. xxviii. 18, 19; Prov. i. 27.

8. Ver. 26. An isolated proverb relating to the uselessness and repulsiveness of the sluggish. Comp. xxii. 13, and also vi. 6 sq.; xii. 27; xix. 24.—**As vinegar to the teeth.** So the majority correctly render, while the LXX, Pesch., Arab., *etc.*, falsely translate the noun (חֹמֶץ, comp. Num. vi. 3; Ps. lxix. 22) by "sour grapes" (ὄμφαξ).—**To them that send him.** Perhaps this phrase as referring to the idea which must be supplied, the authority, the master (אֲדוֹנִים), comp. xxv. 13, might be translated by "his sender, his employer." Comp. HITZIG on this passage.

9. Vers. 27–30. Four proverbs bearing upon the prosperity of the pious and the ruin of the ungodly. With ver. 27 comp. iii. 1; ix. 11; xiv. 27.—Ver. 28. **The expectation of the righteous is gladness,** *i. e.* as its object comes into possession of him who indulges it. With the 2d clause comp. xi. 7; Job viii. 13; Ps. cxii. 10.

Ver. 29. **Jehovah's way is a bulwark to the innocent.** The meaning doubtless is, Jehovah's way in the administration of the world, His providence, His righteous and gracious rule, proves itself to the pious a strong protection and defence (comp. the "strong city" of ver. 15, also Ps. xxxi. 21; xxxvii. 39; xliii. 2, *etc.*) [Wordsw.: wherever he *goes* he is in a *castle*]. Only with this objective conception of "Jehovah's way" does the antithesis in the 2d clause agree (comp. vers. 14, 15), and not with the subjective, which makes it religion, a devout life. Many, however, (Arnoldi, Ziegler, Umbreit, Elster, [Noyes], *etc.*) unite דֶּרֶךְ in one conception with תֹּם and translate "A fortress is Jehovah to the innocent" (upright in his way); comp. Prov. xiii. 6; Job iv. 6. One must make his choice between the two interpretations, as both are grammatically admissible and yield essentially the same meaning.—Ver. 30. With the first clause comp. xii. 3; with the second, ii. 21; Ps. xxxvii. 29.

10. Vers. 31, 32. Two proverbs standing isolated, treating of the mouth of the righteous and that of the ungodly and their respective utterances or fruits. **The mouth of the righteous putteth forth wisdom,** as the sap of a fruitful tree develops beautiful flowers and fruits; comp. the "fruit of the lips," Isa. lvii. 19 and the corresponding expression καρπὸς χειλέων in Heb. xiii. 16.—In the 2d clause this figure is abandoned, so far as respects the expression "the perverse tongue;" but the "is destroyed" reminds distinctly enough of the hewing down and dying out of unfruitful trees; comp. Matth. iii. 10. vii. 19.—Ver. 32. **Know what is acceptable,** *i. e.,* are familiar with it, know how to say much of it. The noun רָצוֹן is here objective in its meaning, used of that which produces delight (with God and men) the lovely, the charming (comp. Luke iv. 22).—Hitzig on account of the ἀποστάζει of the LXX (they distil, they send forth) reads יַבִּיעַ instead of יֵדְעוּן from which we do certainly gain a better parallelism of meaning with the 1st clause of the preceding verse. And yet it seems at least suspicious to go so far in this endeavor to secure a parallelism in the contents of the two verses, as actually to transpose, as Hitzig does, the order of their second clauses, and so combine them in the following order: 31, 1st—32, 2d—32, 1st—31, 2d. [Rueetschi, in his criticism upon this tampering with forms and arrangement, says: "It is all needless—nay, it destroys a beautiful, life-like thought, and substitutes for it a dry commonplace." Ver. 31 says: "The mouth of the righteous shooteth forth wisdom, but the perverse tongue is rooted out;" if the mouth of the righteous may be compared to a good tree or field, that must yield good fruit, the deceitful tongue is a bad tree, that can bear only rotten fruit, and for that very reason is cut down, rooted out, destroyed. Ver. 32 adds "The lips of the righteous know," *etc.* "The righteous finds always, as if instinctively, what is acceptable—is, as it were, inspired with it, so that his lips, as it were, naturally find it, while, on the other hand, the wicked knows and understands only what is distorted or perverse, and his mouth therefore speaks only this" (as cited above, p. 138)].

DOCTRINAL AND ETHICAL.

The contrast between the righteous and the wicked, or between the wise and foolish, forms evidently the main theme of our chapter. This contrast, after being suggested in a general and prefatory way in ver 1, is developed with special reference, 1) to the attainment or non-attainment on both parts of earthly possessions, especially riches and a good name (vers. 2–7); 2) to their differing dispositions as expressed by mouth and lips, the organs of speech, with diverse influence on their prosperity in life (vers. 8–14); 3) to the effect, tending on the one side to blessing, on the other to destruction, which the labor of the two classes (whether with the hands or with the lips) has upon themselves and upon others (vers. 15–24 and ver. 26); 4) the different issues of the lives of both (vers. 25, 27–32). With the individual groups of proverbs, as we had occasion to combine them above in the exegetical notes, these main divisions in the treatment of the subject correspond only in part; for the formation of the groups was determined as we saw in manifold ways, and by quite external circumstances and relations.

A peculiarly rich return, in an ethical view, is yielded by those maxims which refer to the earthly revenues and possessions of the pious and the foolish (2–7, 15, 16, 22, 27 sq.). They all serve to illustrate the great truth, "On God's blessing every thing depends," while they no less interpret that other saying (2 Thess. iii. 10; comp. vers. 4, 5 of our chapter), "If any man will not work, neither shall he eat." Eminently important and comparatively original (*i. e.*, never before brought to an emphatic utterance) are also the proverbs relating to the worth of a circumspect reserve in speech (vers. 8, 10, 13, 14, 18, 19, comp. James iii. 3–12); those relating to the ease with which the evil man brings forth his evil and the good his good—plainly because an evil heart underlies the works of the one, a loving spirit the other's whole mode of action (ver. 23; comp. vers. 11, 12, 18, 20, and passages of the New Testament like Matth xii. 33–35; 1 John iii. 7 sq.; v. 3); and lastly those relating to the spiritual blessings for others also that spring forth from the mouth of the pious as the wholesome fruit of his wisdom (vers. 11, 21, 31; comp. Matth. vii. 16 sq.; John xv. 4 sq.; Gal. v. 22; Phil. i. 11; James iii. 18).

HOMILETIC AND PRACTICAL.

Homily on the entire chapter. The pious and the ungodly compared in respect, 1) to their earthly good; 2) to their worth in the eyes of men; 3) to their outward demeanor in intercourse with others; 4) to their disposition of heart as this appears in their mien, their words, their acts; 5) to their diverse fruit, that which they produce in their moral influence on others; 6) to their different fates, as awarded to them at last in the retribution of eternity.—Comp. STÖCKER: True righteousness: 1) its basis (ver. 1); 2) its manifestation and maintenance in life (vers. 2-5); 3) its utility (vers. 6, 7); 4) the manner of its preservation and increase (ver. 8 sq.).*

STARKE:—The great difference between the pious and the ungodly: 1) in respect to temporal blessings (vers. 1-7); 2) in respect to conduct (vers. 8-26); 3) in respect to their prosperity and the issue of their deeds (vers. 27-32).— *Calwer Handbuch:* Of righteousness through wisdom and of unrighteousness through folly and mockery. 1) Warning against the vices which quench delight in righteousness (1-14); 2) admonition to the careful government of the tongue as that on which above all things else the life and the true fruits of righteousness depend (15-21); 3) allusion to riches, long life, the joyful attainment of one's hopes, confidence in God, security, good counsel, *etc.*, as impelling to righteousness, as well as to the opposite of all these as the evil result of sin (22-32).

Vers. 1-7 (Text adapted to a sermon on Education). EGARD: Wilt thou have joy and not sorrow in thy children, then train them in the nurture and admonition of the Lord (Eph. vi. 4).—STÖCKER: Are there to be people that walk justly, *i. e.*, honorably and sincerely before God, then must they be trained to it from childhood. The education of children is the foundation that must be laid for righteousness.—Ver. 3 sq. STARKE: Although all depends chiefly on God's blessing, yet not for that reason is man discharged from labor. Labor is the ordinance in which God will reveal His blessing (Ps. cxxviii. 2).—VON GERLACH: The Lord maketh rich, but by the industry which the righteous by His grace exercise.—[Bp. BUTLER: Riches were first bestowed upon the world as they are still continued in it, by the blessing of God upon the industry of men, in the use of their understanding and strength.]—Vers. 6, 7. OSIANDER (in STARKE): A good name among men is also reasonably to be reckoned among the excellent gifts of God, Ps. cxii. 6; Eccles. vii. 1.— GEIER: To the righteous not only does God grant good in this life and the future; all good men also wish them all good and intercede for it day by day, without their knowing or suspecting it, that it may descend on them from God. Many righteous men unknown, or even hated during their life, are first truly known after their death and distinguished by honors of every kind, as the Apostles, Prophets, Martyrs, *etc.* The offensiveness of the ungodly, on the contrary, where even so much as the mention of their name is involved, is perpetual.—Funeral discourse on ver. 7. ZIEGLER (in ZIMMERMANN's *Sonntagsfeier*, 1858, pp. 760 sq.): The memory of the just is blessed 1) because of his winning friendship; 2) because of his unfeigned piety; 3) because of his steadfast patience; 4) because of his noble, public-spirited activity.—[Ver. 7. J. FOSTER: The just show in the most evident and pleasing manner the gracious connexion which God has constantly maintained with a sinful world; they are verifying examples of the excellence of genuine religion; they diminish to our view the repulsiveness and horror of death; their memory is combined with the whole progress of the cause of God on earth,—with its living agency through every stage.—TRAPP: Be good and do good, so shall thy name be heir to thy life.]

Vers. 8-14. GEIER (on ver. 8): Long as one lives he has to learn and to grow in knowledge, but above all also in the art of governing the tongue. A fool is in nothing sooner and better recognized than in his conversation.—[Ver. 9. BARROW: Upright simplicity is the deepest wisdom, and perverse craft the merest shallowness; he who is most true and just to others is most faithful and friendly to himself, and whoever doth abuse his neighbor is his own greatest cheat and foe.—BRIDGES: "Show me an easier path" is nature's cry. "Show me," cries the child of God, "a *sure* path." Such is the upright walk, under the shield of the Lord's protection and providence; under the shadow of His promises, in the assurance of His present favor, and in its peaceful end.]—J. LANGE (on ver. 10): In his very bearing and gestures the Christian must so carry himself that there can be read in them true love, due reverence and sincerity.—He who has too many compliments for every body is seldom sincere; trust not such a one, *etc.*—[Ver. 11. ARNOT: The Lord looks down and men look up expecting to see a fringe of living green around the lip of a Christian's life course.]—ZELTNER (on ver. 12): Love is the noblest spice in all things, the first fruit of faith, the most useful thing in all conditions, yea, a truly Divine virtue, for God Himself is love.—Take love out of the world, and thou wilt find nothing but contention. Of the utility of true love one can never preach enough. [T. ADAMS: "Love covereth all sins," saith Solomon: covers them partly from the eyes of God, in praying for the offenders; partly from the eyes of the world in throwing a cloak over our brother's nakedness; especially from its own eyes, by winking at many wrongs offered it.]— CRAMER (on vers. 13, 14): It is no shame to know nothing, but it is indeed to wish to know nothing. Learn in thy youth, and thou hast benefit therefrom thy life long.—HASIUS (on ver. 13): He who makes his tongue a rod to scourge others with, must often in turn give his back to correction.—VON GERLACH: The fool must like the beast be corrected with the stick, since he is capable of no rational teaching.—[BRADFORD: He that trembleth not in hearing shall be broken to pieces in feeling.]

Vers. 15-26. GEIER (on vers. 15, 16): Riches are a means that may be employed for good, but

---

* STÖCKER brings the contents of chaps. x.—xxiv. in general under five titles, corresponding to the five chief virtues: Justice, Modesty, Wisdom, Temperance, Patience. To Justice he assigns the contents of chapters x and xi.; to Moderation chaps. xii. and xiii.; to Wisdom chaps. xiv—xvi.; to Temperance chaps. xvii.—xxii.; to Patience chap. xxiv. He himself admits the arbitrariness of this division, and yet thinks there is no undue violence done thereby to the proverbs in question; for there is "On these proverbs of Solomon (in chaps. x.—xxiv.) in general a certain quality such as we may have seen in a beautiful green meadow, on which all manner of beautiful, lovely, glorious flowers of many sorts and colors are to be fallen in with or found, which stand wonderfully mixed and confused, and are only afterwards to be brought and placed in a certain order by some maiden who gathers them for a wreath." (*Sermons, etc.*, p. 166.)

as, alas, generally happens, may be misused in the service of vanity and evil. Poverty is in itself a sad thing (Prov. xxx. 8), and brings besides serious dangers to the soul; for an humble heart, however, that, child-like, submits to God's correction and guidance, it may also become a security against many kinds of sins.—[Vers. 15, 16. TRAPP: Surely this should humble us, that riches—that should be our rises to raise us up to God, or glasses to see the love of God in—our corrupt nature uses them as clouds, as clogs, etc., yea, sets them up in God's place.—Lord BACON: This is excellently expressed, that riches are as a stronghold in imagination, and not always in fact; for certainly great riches have sold more men than they have bought out.—BRIDGES: Our labor is God's work—wrought in dependence on Him—not for life, but to life.—Ver. 18. BARROW: Since our faculty of speech was given us as in the first place to praise and glorify our Maker, so in the next to benefit and help our neighbor, it is an unnatural, perverting and irrational abuse thereof to employ it to the damage, disgrace, vexation or wrong in any kind of our brother.—ARNOT: Strangle the evil thoughts as they are coming to the birth, that the spirits which troubled you within may not go forth embodied to trouble also the world.—They who abide in Christ will experience a sweet necessity of doing good to men; they who really try to do good to men will be compelled to abide in Christ.]—STARKE (on ver. 18). Open hatred and secret slander are both alike works of Satan against which a true Christian should be on his guard — (On vers. 19-21): The more one gives free course to his tongue, the more does he defile his conscience, comes too near God and his neighbor. But how usefully can a consecrated tongue be employed in the instruction, consolation and counsel of one's neighbor! Therefore let the Holy Spirit of God rule thy heart and thy tongue, Eph. iii. 29. (On ver. 23): It is devilish to sin and then boast of sin. The wanton laughter of the wicked is followed at last, and often soon enough, by weeping and wailing, Luke vii. 25.—(On ver. 24): With all the good cheer of sinners there is yet sometimes found in them a strange unrest. Their own conscience chastises them and causes dismay.—(On ver. 26): Indolence is injurious to every one, whether in a spiritual or a secular calling. Not by ease, but by diligence and fidelity does one honorably fulfil his office; 1 Cor. iv. 2.—[BUNYAN: All the hopes of the wicked shall not bring him to heaven; all the fears of the righteous shall not bring him to hell.—ARNOT:—Fear and hope were common to the righteous and the wicked in time: at the border of eternity the one will be relieved from all his fear, the other will be deprived of all his hope. —(On ver. 26): The minor morals are not neglected in the Scriptures. He who is a Christian in little things is not a little Christian. He is the greatest Christian and the most useful. The baptism of these little outlying things shows that he is full of grace, for these are grace's overflowings.]—Berleb. Bibel (on vers. 19-21): As silence is in many ways needful, as Christ Himself hath taught us by His own example, so on the other hand we should offend God and rob Him of His honor if we would keep silence when He will have us speak. The lips of the righteous often serve God as an instrument by which He speaketh and instructeth him that needeth.

Vers. 27-32. ZELTNER: There is no grosser self-deception than when one in persistent impenitence and impiety yet imagines that he is at last to live in heaven.—GEIER: If thy hope of eternal blessedness is not to fail thee, it must be based on the righteousness of Christ appropriated by faith, for this alone avails with God.—(On vers. 30): Let us love and long for that which is really eternal and unchangeable; for only then can we say "I shall not be moved," Ps. x. 6; xxx. 6.—STARKE (on vers. 31, 32): When God's honor and the edification and improvement of one's neighbor is not the chief end of our speaking; it is a sign that eternal wisdom has not yet wholly sanctified our hearts, comp. ver. 13, 14.—WOHLFARTH (on vers. 23-32): The sinner's fear and the hope of the righteous (comp. 1 John iv. 18; iii. 3).

---

b) *Comparison between the good results of piety and the disadvantages and penalties of ungodliness.*

CHAPS. XI.—XV.

a) With reference to just and unjust, benevolent and malevolent *conduct towards one's neighbor.*

CHAP. XI.

1   A false balance is an abomination to Jehovah,
    but a true weight is his delight.
2 Pride cometh, then cometh shame,
    but with the humble is wisdom.
3 The integrity of the upright guideth them,
    but the perverseness of the ungodly shall destroy them.

4 Riches profit not in the day of wrath,
  but righteousness delivereth from death.
5 The righteousness of the upright maketh smooth his way,
  but by his wickedness doth the wicked fall.
6 The integrity of the upright delivereth them,
  but by their transgressions shall the wicked be taken.
7 With the death of the wicked (his) hope cometh to nought,
  and the unjust expectation hath perished.
8 The righteous is delivered from trouble,
  and the wicked cometh in his stead.
9 The hypocrite with his mouth destroyeth his neighbor,
  but by the knowledge of the righteous shall they (he) be delivered.
10 In the prosperity of the upright the city rejoiceth,
  but at the destruction of the wicked (there is) shouting.
11 By the blessing of the upright is the city exalted,
  but by the mouth of the wicked it is destroyed.
12 He that speaketh contemptuously of his neighbor lacketh wisdom,
  but a man of understanding is silent.
13 He who goeth about as a slanderer revealeth secrets,
  he who is of a faithful spirit concealeth the matter.
14 Where there is no direction the people fall,
  but in a multitude of counsellors is safety.
15 He shall fare ill that is security for a stranger,
  but whoso hateth suretyship liveth in quiet.
16 A pleasing woman retaineth honor,
  and strong men retain riches.
17 A benevolent man doeth good to himself,
  and the cruel troubleth his own flesh.
18 The wicked gaineth a deceptive result,
  but he that soweth righteousness a sure reward.
19 He that holdeth fast integrity (cometh) to life,
  but he that pursueth evil to his death.
20 An abomination to Jehovah are the perverse in heart,
  but they that walk uprightly His delight.
21 Assuredly (hand to hand) the wicked goeth not unpunished,
  but the seed of the righteous is delivered.
22 A jewel of gold in a swine's snout,
  (and) a fair woman that hath lost discretion.
23 The desire of the righteous is good only,
  the expectation of the wicked is (God's) wrath.
24 There is that scattereth and it increaseth still,
  and (there is) that stinteth only to poverty
25 A liberal soul shall be well fed,
  and he that watereth others is also watered.
26 Whoso withholdeth corn the people curse him,
  but blessings (come) upon the head of him that selleth it.
27 He that striveth after good seeketh favor,
  but he that searcheth for evil, it shall find him.
28 He that trusteth in his riches shall fall,
  but as a green leaf shall the righteous flourish.
29 He that troubleth his own house shall inherit wind,
  and the fool shall be servant to the wise in heart.
30 The fruit of the righteous is a tree of life,
  and the wise man winneth souls.
31 Lo, the righteous shall be recompensed on earth,
  much more the ungodly and the sinner.

GRAMMATICAL AND CRITICAL.

Ver. 2.—נָא is given by Böttcher, § 950, 1, as an example of the *Perfectum relativum*, the precise time being a matter of indifference. The Imperf. that follows is then a contingent tense describing a normal consequence, § 950 B.]

Ver. 3.—שָׁדָם, to be read יְשָׁדֵם with the K'ri. [Böttcher, in explaining forms like this, of which he adduces a considerable number, § 929, β, refers to but rejects the old explanation which makes the ן an older form of the 3d personal prefix (from the pronoun הֵן), and regards it as representing in the view of the K'thibh the conjunction ן, an error which is here corrected in the K'ri.]

Ver. 15.—רַע in רְעַ יֵרוֹעַ is probably not Infin. abs. Kal. (which should be רֹעַ), but a substantive, here used adverbially and attached to the reflexive Future Niphal יֵרוֹעַ to strengthen the idea. [Fuerst, while giving רַע as an intransitive Infin. also, also suggests that it *may be* a noun, giving it however the place and power of a masc. and not a neuter, and making it the subject, "*der Schlechthandelnde*,"—"he that manages ill."]

Ver. 25.—יֹרֵא is either to be taken as the Imperf. Hophal of ארי=ירה, or by change of pointing to be read יָרֵא and this is then to be regarded as another form of יָרְוָה (Hitzig; comp. Ziegler and Elster).

EXEGETICAL.

1. Vers. 1–11. Eleven proverbs on the value of a just demeanor towards one's neighbor, and on the curse of unrighteousness.—With vers. 1 comp. xx. 10, 23, and also Meidani's collection of Arabic proverbs, III., 538, where the first member at least appears, and that too expressly as a proverb of Solomon.—**A true weight**, lit., "a full stone;" comp. Deut. xxv. 13, where אֶבֶן in like manner signifies the weight of a balance.—Ver. 2. **Pride cometh, then cometh shame;**—lit., "there hath come pride, and there will come shame," *i. e.*, on the proud; comp. xvi. 18; xviii. 12.—**But with the humble is wisdom**.—That wisdom, namely, which confers honor (iii. 16; viii. 18). "The humble," derived from צנע, which in Chaldee signifies "to conceal," denote strictly those who hide themselves, or renounce self (ταπεινοί, ταπεινόφρονες).—Ver. 3. **The** (faithlessness of the false) **perverseness of the ungodly destroyeth them**.—"**Destroyeth**,"—from the root שׁדד which means "violently to fall upon and kill," and not merely to "desolate" (comp. Jer. v. 6). כֶּלֶף should in accordance with the Arabic be explained either by "falseness, perverseness" (as ordinarily), or with Hitzig "trespass, transgression."—Ver. 4. **In the day of wrath**, *viz.*, the Divine wrath and judgment; comp. Zeph. i. 18; Ezek. vii. 19; Job xxi. 30. With reference to the general thought comp. chap. x. 2.—Vers. 5 and 6 are exactly parallel not only each to the other, but also to ver. 3. Comp. also iii. 6; x. 3.—**And by their lusts are the wicked taken**.—Literally, "and by the lusts ('cravings' as in x. 13) of the wicked (false) are they (the wicked) taken;" the construction is the same therefore as in Gen. ix. 6; Ps. xxxii. 6; comp. also ver. 3.—Ver. 7.—A further development of the idea in the second clause of x. 28.—**The unjust expectation**.—Lit., "the expectation of depravities, of wickedness" (אוֹנִים plur. of אָוֶן). Most interpreters regard the noun here as an abstract for a concrete: "the expectation of the ungodly, the wicked" [so De W., E. V., H., N., M. W.]. Ewald interprets it in accordance with ver. ix. 4 by "sorrows" (continuance of sorrow); others in accordance with Is. xl. 26, render it by "might." In support of our interpretation see Hitzig on this passage. [Fuerst suggests that the form may be participial from the verb אין with the signification "the troubled, the sorrowing," and Böttcher, § 811, 3, deriving it as a participial form from אָנָה, reaches the same meaning; this is also Stuart's view, while Kamph. agrees with our author—A.] The antithesis in idea between the first and second clauses which is lacking in this verse, the LXX attempts to supply by reading in the first clause "when the righteous man dieth, hope doth not perish" (τελευτήσαντος ἀνδρὸς δικαίου οὐκ ὄλλυται ἐλπίς); they thus put the hope of the righteous reaching beyond death in contrast with the hopeless end of the life of the ungodly. This thought the original text certainly does not express; but immortality and a future retribution are yet presumptively suggested in the passage, as Muntinghe, Umbreit, Lutz (*Bibl. Dogmatik*, p. 100, *etc.*) and others have correctly assumed. Comp. the "Doctrinal" notes.

Ver. 8. **The righteous is delivered from trouble**, *etc*.—This proposition presented so conclusively "cannot be the result of experimental observation, but only the fresh, vigorous expression of *faith* in God's justice, such as believes where it does not see" (Elster).—Ver. 9. **The flatterer** (hypocrite) **with his mouth destroyeth his neighbor**.—For the verbal explanation of חָנֵף which, according to the old Rabbinical tradition, and according to the Vulgate, denotes a hypocrite (Vulg., *simulator*), comp. Hitzig on this passage. He moreover needlessly alters this first clause in harmony with the LXX (in the mouth of the hypocrite is a snare for his neighbor), and gives to the second member also a totally different form; "and in the misfortune of the righteous do they rejoice."—**By the knowledge of the righteous are they delivered**;—they, *i. e.*, his neighbors; the sing. "his neighbor," which is altogether general, admits of being thus continued by a verb in the plural. The meaning of the verse as a whole is "By the protective power of that knowledge which serves righteousness, they are delivered who were endangered by the artifices of that shrewdness which is the instrument of wickedness" (Elster).

Ver. 10. **In the prosperity of the upright**—בְּטוּב, an infinitive construction; literally, "when it goes well to the righteous," as in the second clause בַּאֲבֹד, "in the perishing," when they perish. Comp. xxix. 2.—Hitzig strikes out this verse mainly to secure again within vers. 4-11 a group of seven proverbs, as before in x. 29—xi. 3, but without being able to allege any ground whatever of suspicion that is really valid.—Ver. 11 gives the reason why the population of a city rejoices at the prosperity of the righteous and exults at the downfall of the wicked.—**By the blessing of the righteous is the city exalted,**—*i. e.*, by the beneficent and salutary words and acts (not by the benevolent wishes only) of the righteous (literally, "the straight, true, straightforward") is the city raised to a flourishing condition and growth, *exaltabitur civitas* (Vulg.). Not so well ELSTER: "is the city made secure"—as if the idea here related to the throwing up walls of defence.

2. Vers. 12-15. Four proverbs against talkativeness, a slanderous disposition, foolish counsel and thoughtless suretyship.—**He that speaketh contemptuously of his neighbor.**—This is the rendering here required to correspond with the antithesis in the second clause ; comp. xiv. 21; xiii. 13. [The E. V. and HOLDEN invert this relation of subject and predicate, while DE W., K., N. S., and M. agree with our author in following the order of the original—A.]—Ver. 13. **He that goeth about as a slanderer betrayeth secrets.**—With this expression, "to go tattling, to go for slander," comp. Lev. xix. 16; Jer. ix. 3. With the expression גֹּלֶה סוֹד, *revelavit arcanum*, "to reveal a secret," comp. xx. 19: xxv. 9; Am. iii. 7. That not this "babbler of secrets" is subject of the clause (HITZIG), but "he that goeth slandering," the parallel second clause makes evident, where with the "slanderer" is contrasted the faithful and reliable, and with the babbler the man who "concealeth the matter, *i. e.*, the secret committed to him." Comp. Ecclesiasticus xxvii. 16.

Ver. 14. **Where there is no direction.**—For this term comp. i. 5.—**In the multitude of counsellors there is safety.**—This thought recurring again in xv. 22; xxiv. 6, is naturally founded on the assumption that the counsellors are good and intelligent persons, and by no means conflicts with the conditional truth of the modern proverb, "Too many cooks spoil the broth ;" or this, "He who asks long errs long," *etc.*

Ver. 15. **He shall fare ill that is surety for a stranger.**—"Ill, ill does it go with him,—ill, very ill will he fare,—ill at ease will he be," *etc.* Instead of "who is surety," *etc.*, the original has literally "if one is surety," *etc.*—With the second clause comp. remarks above on chap. vi. 1 sq. Instead of תֹּקְעִים (partic.) we ought probably to read here תֹּקְעִים (subst.) (HITZIG), or to take the plural participle in the sense of the abstract "striking hands" (instead of "those striking hands)." Thus, *e. g.*, UMBREIT. Not so well the majority of commentators (EWALD, BERTHEAU, ELSTER, among others), who read "he that hateth sureties," *i. e.*, who will not belong to their number, who avoids fellowship with such as lightly strike hands as sureties, who therefore does not follow their example.

3. Vers. 16-23. Eight proverbs of miscellaneous import, mostly treating of the blessing that attends righteousness and the deserved judgment of impiety.—**A gracious woman retaineth honor and strong men retain riches.**—So reads the Hebrew text, according to which there is a comparison made here; as mighty men (lit., "tyrants, terrible men," comp. βιασταί, Matth. xi. 12) retain their wealth and will not allow it to be torn from them, with the same energy and decision does a "gracious woman" (comp. v. 19) watch over her honor as an inalienable possession. Comp. the similar sentiment, chap. xxix. 23 (where we have the same, "holdeth fast honor"); and as to the force of comparative sentences formed thus simply with the copulative conjunction ו, comp. xxv. 25; xxvi. 9; Job v. 7; xii. 11 ; xiv. 18, 19, *etc.*—The LXX, whom ZIEGLER, EWALD, HITZIG follow, read חֲרוּצִים (*i. e.*, diligent men, comp. x. 4), and besides insert two clauses between the first and second of this verse, so that the whole proverb has this expanded form :

"A gracious woman obtaineth honor;
   but a throne of disgrace is she that hateth virtue.
The idle will be destitute of means,
   but the diligent will obtain wealth."

For the authenticity of this fuller form may be urged especially the vigorous expression "throne of disgrace" (θρόνος ἀτιμίας), which is hardly the product of later invention, but rather agrees antithetically with the expression which is several times found, "a seat or throne of honor" (כִּסֵּא כָבוֹד, 1 Sam. ii. 8; Is. xxii. 23; Jer. xvii. 12. [While RUEETSCHI (as cited above, p. 138) seems to admit the antiquity of the form reproduced in the version of the LXX, he thus defends and amplifies the sense of the shorter form found in the Masoretic text, "A woman is powerful by her grace as the mighty are by their strength. In grace there lies as great force as in the imposing nature of the mighty ; nay, the power of the strength of the latter gains only more property, while the woman gains honor and esteem, which are of more worth."]

Ver. 17. **The benevolent man doeth good to himself.**—Lit., "the man of love," who by the goodness which he manifests towards others, benefits his own soul. The second clause in its contrast with this: "And his own flesh doth the cruel trouble," does not aim to characterize any thing like the unnatural self-torture of gloomy ascetics, but to express the simple thought that on account of the penalty with which God requites cruel and hard-hearted conduct, such conduct is properly a raging against one's self. Thus the LXX had correctly expressed the idea, and among modern interpreters HITZIG, ELSTER, *etc.*, while the great body (UMBREIT, EWALD, BERTHEAU among them), comparing Ecclesiast. xiv. 5, find the meaning of the verse to be directed against niggardliness, or ascetic self-torture: He who deals harshly and unkindly with himself will treat others also no better."

Ver. 18. **The wicked gaineth delusive gains,**—*i. e.* such as result in no good to himself, such as escape from under his hands. Comp. x. 2, and with reference to פְּעֻלָּה, gain, acquisition, x. 16.—**But he that soweth righteousness,**

a sure reward.—The "sure reward" (שָׂכָר אֱמֶת) perhaps in its sound in intentional accord with שֶׁקֶר in the first member) is also governed by the verb "gaineth" or "worketh out" (עָשָׂה); comp. Jer. xvii. 11, etc. For this figure of "sowing righteousness," *i. e.* the several right acts, which like a spiritual seed-corn are to yield as their harvest the rewards of God's grace, comp. James iii. 18; 1 Cor. ix. 11; 2 Cor. ix. 6; also Job iv. 8; Gal. vi. 8, etc.—**Whoso holdeth fast integrity (cometh) to life.**—כֵּן before צְדָקָה (righteousness) if genuine, (the LXX and Syriac versions read instead בֵּן, "son"), can be only an adjective or participle derived from the verb כּוּן " to be firm," having the meaning " firm" (comp. Gen. xlii. 11, 19); it therefore denotes "the steadfast in righteousness," *i. e.* as the antithetic phrase in the 2d member shows, "he who holds fast to righteousness, who firmly abides in it." Thus ZIEGLER, EWALD, UMBREIT, ELSTER, etc. Others, like COCCEIUS, SCHULTENS, MICHAELIS, DÖDERLEIN, take the word as a substantive—steadfastness (?); still others regard it as a particle in the ordinary meaning "thus" (by which construction however the verse would lose its independent character, and become a mere appendage to the preceding proverb); and finally, HITZIG conjecturally substitutes בְּנֵס and translates "As a standard is righteousness to life."

Vers. 20, 21. Two new maxims concerning the contrasted lot of the righteous and the wicked, serving to confirm vers. 18 and 19. With ver. 20 comp. ii. 21; xvii. 20.—**Assuredly,** literally, " hand to hand," a formula of strong asseveration, derived from the custom of becoming surety by clasping hands (ver. 15), and therefore substantially equivalent to "I pledge it, I guarantee it." Comp. the German formula which challenges to an honest self-scrutiny, *"die Hand auf's Herz!"* (the hand on the heart!); and for the sentiment of the 1st clause compare xvi. 5. [FUERST and K regard the formula as one of asseveration: GESEN., DE W. and NOYES interpret, by the analogy of some similar expressions in cognate languages, as referring to time, "through all generations;" H., M., S. and W. retain the rendering of the E. V., "though hand join in hand." The exceeding brevity of the Hebrew formula stimulates inquiry and conjecture without clearly establishing either interpretation.—A.]—**But the seed of the righteous escapeth,** literally, "delivers itself" (נִמְלָט), a Niphal participle with reflexive meaning), that is, in the day of the divine wrath, comp. vers. 4, 23. The "seed of the righteous" is not the posterity of the righteous (*soboles justorum,* SCHALLER, ROSENMUELLER, BERTHEAU) but is equivalent to the multitude, the generation of the righteous, Comp. Isa. lxv. 23, "the seed of the blessed of Jehovah."

Ver. 22. **A gold ring in a swine's snout; a fair woman that hath lost discretion.**—This last phrase (סָרַת טָעַם) literally denotes "one who has turned aside in respect to taste," *i. e.* one who lacks all moral sensibility, all higher appreciation of beauty and sense of propriety, in a word, a chaste and pure heart,—an unchaste woman. Only with this conception does the figure of the swine agree, and not with that given by ROSENMUELLER, BERTHEAU, EWALD, ELSTER, " without judgment," *i. e.* stupid, weak. Compare furthermore the Arabic proverb here cited by HITZIG (from SCHEID'S *Selecta quædam ex sententiis, etc.,* 47): *"Mulier sine verecundia est ut cibus sine sale.* [a woman without modesty is like food without salt]. For the "gold ring" (ring for the nose, נֶזֶם, not circlet for the hair, LUTHER) comp. Gen. xxiv. 47; Isa. iii. 21, and also in general what is cited by UMBREIT, in connection with this passage, on the habits of the Eastern women in respect to this kind of ornament.

Ver. 23. **The desire of the righteous is good only,**—*i. e.* nothing but prosperity and blessing, because God rewards and prospers them in everything. Comp. x. 28, and with the 2d clause where " wrath" denotes again God's wrath, comp. ver. 4 above.

4. Vers. 24–26. Three proverbs against avarice, hard-heartedness and usury.—**Many a one scattereth and it increaseth still.**—Comp. Ps. cxii. 9 (2 Cor. ix. 9), where the same verb is used of the generous distribution of benefactions, of scattering (σκορπίζειν) in the good sense (different from that of Luke xv. 13). For it is to this only true form of prodigality, this " sowing of righteousness" that the expression applies, as the two following verses plainly show.—**And many save only to poverty,** literally, "and a withholder of wealth only to want;" (thus BERTHEAU correctly renders, following SCHULTENS, etc.). With the participial clause (וְחוֹשֵׂךְ כִּי־יֹשֶׁר) the affirmative of the preceding clause (יֵשׁ, there is, there appears) still continues in force. HITZIG's attempted emendation is needless, according to which we ought to read שֵׁי וְחוֹשְׂכִים in correspondence with the language of the LXX, *εἰσὶ δὲ καὶ οἱ συνάγοντες.* Others, like SCHELLING, UMBREIT, EWALD, ELSTER (comp. also LUTHER), translate "who withholdeth more than is right;" but thus to give a comparative force to כִּי after חֹשֵׂךְ has no sufficient grammatical support, and instead of כִּי־יֹשֶׁר we should, according to xvii. 26, rather expect עַל־יֹשֶׁר. The signification "wealth," *opulentia* for יֹשֶׁר is abundantly confirmed by the corresponding Arabic word.

Ver. 25. **A liberal soul is well fed.** lit., " a soul of blessing is made fat," comp. xiii. 4; xxviii. 25; Ps. xxii. 29; Isa. x. 16; xvii. 4, etc. —**And he that watereth others is likewise watered,** lit., "he that sprinkleth others is also sprinkled" (comp. Vulgate, *"inebriat . . . . inebriabitur").* The meaning of the expression is unquestionably this, that God will recompense with a corresponding refreshing the man who refreshes and restores others. Comp. Jer. xxxi. 14, and with reference to the general sentiment Eccles. xi. 1; Ecclesiast. xi. 11, etc.

Ver. 26. **Whoso withholdeth corn, him the people curse.**—The withholding of grain is a peculiarly injurious form of the " withholding of property" mentioned in ver. 24. לְאֹם, people, multitude, as in xxiv. 24. With the 2d clause comp. x. 6.

5. Vers. 27–31. Five additional proverbs relating to the contrast between the righteous and the wicked and their several conditions.— **Seeketh favor**, that is, God's favor, *gratiam Dei*; comp. Ps. v. 12; Isa. xlix. 8. With the sentiment of ver. 27 compare in general x. 24; Am. v. 14 sq.

Ver. 28. **He that trusteth in his riches shall fall**.—Comp. x. 2; Ps. xlix. 6; Ecclesiast. v. 8.—**But as a green leaf shall the righteous flourish**. Comp. Ps. xcii. 12; Isa. lxvi. 14. "As a leaf," *i. e.* like a fresh, green leaf on a tree, in contrast with the withered, falling leaf, to which the fool should rather be compared who trusts in his riches. JAEGER and HITZIG (following the LXX) read וִיחַיֶּה "and he who raiseth up," that is, raiseth up the righteous man, proves himself their helper in time of need. On account of the appropriate antithesis to the 1st clause this reading is perhaps preferable.

Ver. 29. **He that troubleth his own house**, lit., "saddeneth" (as in ver. 17), *i. e.* the avaricious man, who is striving after unjust gains, straitens his own household, deprives them of their merited earnings, oppresses and distresses them, *etc.*; comp. chap. xv. 27 : 1 Kings xviii. 17 (where Elijah is described by Ahab as the man that "troubleth" Israel, *i. e.* allows them to suffer, brings them into calamity).—**Shall inherit wind**, *i. e.* with all his avaricious, hard-hearted acting and striving will still gain nothing. Comp. Isa. xxvi. 18; Hos. viii. 7.—**The fool becometh servant to the wise in heart**, that is, this same foolish niggard and miser by his very course is so far reduced that he must as a slave serve some man of understanding (a master not avaricious but truly just and compassionate). Comp. ver. 24.

Ver. 30. **The fruit of the righteous**, *i. e.* that which the righteous man says and does, the result of his moral integrity, and not in an altogether specific sense, his reward, as HITZIG maintains (in accordance with Jer. xxxii. 19). —**Is a tree of life** (comp. note on iii. 18), a growth from which there springs forth life for many, a fountain of blessing and of life for many. UMBREIT, ELSTER and others unnecessarily repeat "fruit" (פְּרִי) before the "tree of life" (עֵץ חַיִּים): "is a fruit of the tree of life."—**And the wise man winneth souls**, by the irresistible power of his spirit he gains many souls for the service of God and for the cause of truth. [The E. V. which has the support of H., S., and M., here again inverts the order of subject and predicate, conforming to the order of the original. The parallelism seems to favor our author's rendering which is also that of DE W. and N. Both conceptions are full of meaning and practical value.—A.] HITZIG here again alters in accordance with the LXX, substituting חָכָם for חָכָם; "but violence taketh life" (?!). ZIEGLER, DÖDERLEIN, DATHE, EWALD transpose the clauses of vers. 29 and 30 into this order: 29, 1st; 30. 1st; 29, 2d; 30, 2d. For arguments against this violent transposition of clauses see UMBREIT, BERTHEAU and HITZIG on this passage.

Ver. 31. **Behold the righteous shall be recompensed on earth**. That the "shall be recompensed" denotes specifically requital *by punishment*, and therefore the retribution of the sins of the righteous, cannot be positively maintained on account of the comprehensiveness of the idea of recompense (שָׁלֵם). Yet a comparison with the 2d clause unquestionably makes this specific meaning very natural; the whole then appears as an *argumentatio a majori ad minus*, and LUTHER's rendering, "Thus the righteous must suffer on earth," substantially hits the true meaning. On the other hand the Alexandrian version introduces a foreign idea when it renders, "If the righteous be scarcely saved" (Εἰ ὁ μὲν δίκαιος μόλις σώζεται,—see also the New Testament's citation, 1 Pet. iv. 18); for the verb שׁלם never signifies "to be delivered."

DOCTRINAL AND ETHICAL.

That it is chiefly that righteousness which is to be manifested in intercourse with one's neighbor that is commended in the proverbs of our chapter, and against the opposite of which they all warn, needs no detailed proof. For the first eleven verses relate solely to this antithesis, and in the second and larger section of the chapter also there are added to the proverbs which refer to the duties of justice for the most part only commendations of merciful, and censures of cruel, hard-hearted conduct (vers. 17, 18, 24–26, 29, 30). Those proverbs which have reference to the lack of intelligent counsellors (14), to inconsiderate suretyship (15), and to feminine grace and purity (16, 22), take their place among the precepts which enjoin righteousness in the widest sense (in so far as wisdom in rulers is an absolutely indispensable condition of prosperity in civil, and a wise economy and womanly honor in domestic society). The separation of these interspersed proverbs, it is true, renders it impossible to demonstrate within the section before us (vers. 12–31), any grouping as undertaken according to a definite principle of classification.

To that which is comparatively new in the dogmatical or ethical line, as presented in our chapter, there belongs above all else the suggestion of a *hope of immortality* in ver. 7. With the death of the ungodly all is over for him; from the future life he has nothing more to hope; he has had his good here below in advance; his reward has been paid him long beforehand; there awaits him henceforth nothing more than a cheerless, hopeless condition of unending pain, "a fearful awaiting of judgment and fiery indignation that shall consume the rebellious" (Heb. x. 27; comp. Luke xvi. 25: Matt. vi. 2, 16; vii. 23; xv. 12, *etc.*). This is the series of thoughts which is inevitably suggested by the proposition "with the death of the wicked hope perishes;" the bright reverse of this here quite as distinctly as in the similar representations of the Psalms, especially in the 49th Psalm, which is so preeminently important for the doctrine of the Old Testament concerning immortality and future retribution, depicts the certainty that the righteous will attain to an eternally blessed life,—a certainty whose foundation is in God (comp. Ps. xlix. 14, 15, and in connection with this HOFMANN, *Schriftbew.*, II. 2, p. 467). ELSTER denies that the sentiment of the verse points indirectly to a life after death, because "according to the doctrine of Proverbs the hope of the righteous is already fulfilled in the earthly life" (comp. also BRUCH, *Weisheitslehre, etc.*, p. 117). But the doctrine of retribution set forth in our book is (see below, remarks on xiv. 32) as far from being an exclusively earthly one, limited to the present life, as that of the Psalms or the Book of Job (comp. DELITZSCH on Job xix. 26 sq.: and also KÖNIG, *Die Unsterblichkeitslehre des Buches Hiob*, 1855). And as respects our chapter in particular, the two-fold allusion to the divine wrath (vers. 4, 23), and the assurance which is expressed altogether without qualification, that "the wicked will not go unpunished" (ver. 21; comp. notes above on this passage), point with sufficient clearness to this conclusion, that to the religious consciousness of the author of our Proverbs a retribution beyond the grave was an established fact. The closing verse of the chapter, "Behold, the righteous is recompensed on earth; how much more the ungodly and the sinner!" is by no means opposed to this view. For the main stress here falls not upon the "on earth," but upon "the righteous" (comp. the exegetical explanation of the passage); and it is not the certainty of a visitation of sin occurring *within the earthly life*, but the certainty of such a visitation in general upon the wrong committed on the earth (by the righteous as well as the wicked), that forms the proper substance and object of the expression.

Besides these, characteristic utterances of our chapter that are of special dogmatical and ethical significance are, the announcements concerning the blessing which goes forth from wise and upright citizens upon their fellow-citizens (vers. 10, 11, 14, comp. especially the exegetical comments on the last passage); concerning the serious injury which the hard-hearted and cruel does above all to himself, especially when he leaves his own house and his nearest connections to suffer from his avarice (vers. 17, 29, comp. 1 Tim. v. 8); concerning the blessing of beneficence, and the injurious and perverse nature of avarice in general and of avaricious usury in particular (vers. 24-26); and finally concerning the life-giving and soul-refreshing power which the conduct of a just and truly wise man has, like a magnet endowed with peculiar attractive power and working at a distance (ver. 30, comp. Matt. xii. 30, the "gathering with the Lord").

HOMILETIC AND PRACTICAL.

Homily on the entire chapter. Not justice only, which gives and leaves to every one his own, but love, which from spontaneous impulse resigns its own to others, and even for God's sake and in reliance on Him scatters it without concern,—this is the conduct of the truly wise. For "love worketh no ill to his neighbor: therefore love is the fulfilling of the law" (Rom. xiii. 10).—Comp. STÖCKER: Justice, as Solomon here commends it, relates 1) to private life (vers. 1-9); 2) to civil life (vers. 10-15); 3) to domestic life (vers. 16-31); it is therefore *justitia privata, publica, œconomica.*—STARKE:—The advantage which the pious have from their piety, and the injury which the wicked experience from their wickedness: 1) from righteousness and unrighteousness in business in general; 2) from good and evil conduct with respect to the honorable fame of one's neighbor (vers. 12, 13); 3) from good and evil government (vers. 14, 15); 4) from seeking or contemning true wisdom (vers. 16-23); 5) from beneficence or uncharitableness (vers. 24-31).

Vers. 1-11. MELANCTHON (on ver. 1): Weight and balance are judicial institutions of the Lord, and every weight is His work. But marriage compacts also, political confederacies, civil compacts, judgments, penalties, *etc.*, are ordinances of Divine wisdom and justice, and are effectively superintended by God.—(on ver. 2): Usually in prosperity men become remiss both in the fear of God, and also in prayer. If in this way God's fear is at length wholly stifled, men in their carnal security allow themselves all manner of encroachments on the rights of their neighbor. Experience has, however, taught even the heathen that certain penalties do by Divine ordinance infallibly overtake such pride and arrogance when these pass beyond the bounds of one's calling, and they have therefore designated this law of the Divine administration of the world according to which pride is the sure precursor of a speedy fall by the expression ἀδράστεια, "inevitability." Comp. 1 Pet. v. 5 sq. [ARNOT: God claims to be in merchandize, and to have His word circling through all its secret channels.—BRIDGES: Commerce is a providential appointment for our social intercourse and mutual helpfulness. It is grounded with men upon human faith, as with God upon Divine faith.—JERMYN: Such a *perfect stone* is a perfect jewel, and a precious stone in the sight of God.—Ver. 2. TRAPP: The humble man, were it not that the fragrant smell of his many virtues betrays him to the world, would choose to live and die in his self-contenting secrecy.]—J. LANGE (on vers. 1-3): Pride and malignity are, so to speak, the first nurses of injustice in business, Ecclesiast. x. 15, 16.—[Ver. 6. TRAPP: Godliness hath many troubles, and as many helps against trouble.—Ver. 8. BRIDGES: The same providence often marks Divine faithfulness and retributive justice.]—GEIER (on vers. 7, 8): The righteous man is in the end surely free from his cross; if it does not come about as he wishes, then assuredly it does as is most useful for him; if not before his temporal death then in and by means of this.—(On vers. 10, 11). The growth and prosperity of a civil community is to be ascribed not so much to its political regulations as rather to the prayers of its pious citizens, who therefore deserve above others to be protected, honored and promoted.—J. LANGE (on vers. 10, 11). Pious and devout rulers of a city or a land are a great blessing, for which we should diligently pray, lest God should peradventure chastise us with tyrannical, selfish, ungodly masters.

Vers. 12-15. GEIER (on vers. 12, 13): Taciturnity is never too highly praised, nor is it ever thoroughly acquired. Disgraceful and injurious as loquacity is, equally admirable is true reserve in speech.—(On ver. 14): The welfare of a land does indeed by all means depend on wise and faithful counsellors; yet to God, the supreme source of all prosperity, must the highest honor ever be rendered.—RUEDEL (on ver. 14—in ROHR'S *Predigermagazin*): Means by which we all may work beneficially from our domestic upon the public life (by the fidelity of our action, by purity of morals, love of peace, and a genuine religious sensibility).—VON GERLACH (on ver. 14): In the affairs of a city, a state, a society, we should look far more after the spiritual than after the external means and appliances.—WOULFARTH (on vers. 9-15): The blessing which the pious confers even here, and the curse that goes forth from the sinner.

Vers. 16-23. ZELTNER (on ver. 16): Zealous as tyrants are to acquire and keep their wealth, so diligent should the pious man be in attaining and preserving his true honor, which is the fear of God and virtue.—[ARNOT (on ver. 17): In every act that mercy prompts there are two parties, who obtain a benefit. Both get good, but the giver gets the larger share.—J. EDWARDS (on ver. 19): Solomon cannot mean *temporal* death, for he speaks of it as a punishment of the wicked, wherein the righteous shall certainly be distinguished from them.]—GEIER (on ver. 17): The gifts which have been received from God one may enjoy with a good conscience, only it must be done with a thankful heart in the fear of God, and in connection with it the poor may not be forgotten.—(On ver 18): The hope of the ungodly is deceptive. For the object of their labor they do not attain, because death suddenly overtakes them (Luke xii. 19). Their accumulated wealth does not reach the heir of the third generation, they leave behind them an evil name, and the worm of conscience continually preys upon them.—(On ver. 22): External physical beauty without inner beauty of soul is like a whitewashed sepulchre, that within is full of dead men's bones, Matth. xxiii. 27.—[FLAVEL (on ver. 20): God takes great pleasure in uprightness, and will own and honor integrity amidst all the dangers which befall it.]—VON GERLACH (on ver. 22): Personal beauty is like the mere ornaments of an animal, attached to it only externally, and often standing in sharp contrast with itself; it is that within which makes the man a man.—*Berleburg Bible* (on ver. 23): The righteous desire nothing but what is good, and are by God really made partakers of these things which they desire. The ungodly, on the contrary, instead of what they hoped for, are made partakers of God's wrath.

Vers. 24-26. CRAMER: Almsgiving does not impoverish, as many men from lack of love suppose.—HASIUS: Though God may not requite our beneficence in every instance by increasing the abundance of our possessions, yet He does in this that it contributes to our true welfare.—VON GERLACH: God as invisible regulator of human fortunes stands behind visible causes; He bestows His blessing upon the insignificant and increases it, His curse upon the abundant, and it wastes away. Thus every where it is the deeper causes that determine advance in wealth or impoverishment. The blessing which we diffuse among others turns to our account; he who waters the dry land of others thereby brings advantage to his own.—[T. ADAMS (on ver. 24): The communication of this riches doth not impoverish the proprietary. The more he spends of his stock, the more he hath. But he that will hoard the treasure of his charity shall grow poor, empty and bankrupt.—ARNOT (on ver. 25): To be a vessel conveying refreshment from the fountain-head of grace to a fainting soul in the wilderness is the surest way of keeping your own spirit fresh, and your experience ever new.—TRAPP: Bounty is the most compendious way to plenty, neither is getting but giving the best thrift.—CHALMERS: God in return not only enriches and ministers food to such as have willingly parted with their carnal things, but increases the fruits of their righteousness.]

Vers. 27-31. STARKE (on ver. 27): The opportunity to do good one should not let slip from his hands, Gal. vi. 10. If thou art always deferring from one time to another, it is easy that nothing should come of it —(On ver. 28): If thou wilt be and continue truly prosperous, then seek eagerly the righteousness of Jesus Christ, and not the perishable riches and pleasures of this world.—(On ver. 30): To win gold and possessions is far from being so great wisdom as to win souls and deliver them from the way of destruction.—[TRAPP (on ver. 28): Riches were never true to any that trusted to them.—Lord BACON (on ver. 29): In domestical separations and breaches men do promise to themselves quieting of their mind and contentment; but still they are deceived of their expectation, and it turneth to wind.—J. EDWARDS (on ver. 31): The persecutions of God's people, as they are from the disposing hand of God, are chastisements for sin.—Bp. JOS. HALL (on ver. 31): Behold even the most just and holy man upon earth shall be sure of his measure of affliction here in the world; how much more shall the unconscionable and ungodly man be sure to smart for his wickedness, either here or hereafter.]—MELANCHTHON (on ver. 31): If even the righteous in this life suffer correction and affliction, which nevertheless tend to improvement, how much more surely will they who defiantly and fiercely persist in their sinful course be punished, if not in this life, then in the life to come (Luke xxiii. 31; 1 Pet. iv. 18).—VON GERLACH (on ver. 30): From the righteous there go forth life and blessing, as from a tree of life, wherefore he also gains ascendency over the souls of many, just as the tree of life was the centre of Paradise, and from it went forth the prosperity of the whole.

β) With reference to domestic, civil and public avocations.

Chap. XII.

1 He that loveth correction loveth knowledge;
 but whosoever hateth rebuke is brutish.
2 The good man obtaineth favor from Jehovah;
 but the man of wicked devices doth he condemn.
3 A man shall not be established by wickedness;
 but the root of the righteous shall not be moved.
4 A good wife is the crown of her husband,
 but one that causeth shame is as rottenness in his bones.
5 The thoughts of the righteous are justice;
 the counsels of the wicked are deceit.
6 The words of the wicked are a lying in wait for blood,
 but the mouth of the upright delivereth them.
7 The wicked are overturned and are no more;
 but the house of the righteous shall stand.
8 According to his wisdom shall a man be praised;
 but he that is of a perverse heart shall be despised.
9 Better is the lowly that serveth himself,
 than he that boasteth and lacketh bread.
10 The righteous careth for the life of his beast;
 but the sympathy of the wicked is cruelty.
11 He that tilleth his land shall be satisfied with bread:
 but he that followeth after vanity is void of understanding.
12 The wicked desireth the spoil of evil doers,
 but the root of the righteous is made sure.
13 In the transgression of the lips is a dangerous snare,
 but the righteous escapeth from trouble.
14 From the fruit of a man's mouth shall he be satisfied with good;
 and the work of one's hands shall return to him.
15 The way of a fool is right in his own eyes,
 but he that hearkeneth to counsel is wise.
16 The vexation of the fool is at once known;
 but he that hideth offence is wise.
17 He that uttereth truth proclaimeth right,
 but the lying tongue deceit.
18 There is that talketh idly like the piercings of a sword:
 but the tongue of the wise is health.
19 The lip of truth shall be established forever;
 but the lying tongue only for a moment.
20 Deceit is in the heart of those who devise evil,
 but to those who give wholesome counsel is joy.
21 There shall no evil befall the righteous;
 but the wicked are full of calamity.
22 Lying lips are an abomination to Jehovah;
 but they that deal truly are his delight.
23 A prudent man hideth knowledge:
 but the heart of fools proclaimeth foolishness.
24 The hand of the diligent shall rule:
 but the slothful shall be obliged to serve.
25 If heaviness be in the heart of man it boweth it down;
 a good word maketh it glad.

26 The righteous guideth his friend aright;
   but the way of the wicked leadeth him astray.
27 The idle catcheth not his prey,
   but a precious treasure to a man is diligence.
28 In the path of righteousness is life:
   but a devious way (leadeth) to death.

GRAMMATICAL AND CRITICAL.

Ver. 11.—רֲחֻמַי. [This plural is cited by BÖTTCHER, § 699, among the examples of that, ideally extended and abstract, which vividly and agreeably impresses the spirit, and therefore is fitly represented by a plural; comp. 'אֲשֶׁר, etc.]

Ver. 17.—פִיחַ אֱמוּנָה (comp. פִיחַ כֹּזְבִים, chap. vi. 19) is to be regarded as a relative clause. [BÖTTCHER, however, regards פִיחַ here and in vi. 19; xiv. 25, xix. 5, 9; Ps. xii. 6; xxvii. 12, as a Hiphil participle of peculiar form, found only in a few instances in connection with roots containing a labial that would closely follow the כ which is the ordinary prefix of the Hiphil participle. The omission of this כ gives a form approaching the Kal. BÖTTCHER objects to EWALD's description of this as an intransitive Kal participle (§ 169, a), that this verb is not intransitive, etc. See § 994, 9 and 4).—A.]

Ver. 28.—An additional objection to the ordinary interpretation (see exegetical notes below) is the absence of Mappiq in the ה of נְתִיבָה, which must nevertheless be regarded as a third pers. suffix referring to צְדָקָה, "the way of its path."

EXEGETICAL.

1. Vers. 1-3. Three proverbs on the contrast between good and evil in general.—**Whosoever hateth correction is brutish.**—בָּעַר, brutus, stupid as a beast; a peculiarly strong expression. Comp. chaps. xxx. 2; Ps. xlix. 10; lxxiii. 22; xcii. 6. HITZIG prefers to read בֹּעֵר, which alteration, however, appears from the passages just cited to be unnecessary.—Ver. 2. **The good man obtaineth favor from Jehovah.** For the use of this verb "obtain" (lit. "to draw out") comp. iii. 13; viii. 35.—**But the man of wicked devices doth he condemn.**—i. e., Jehovah. Others regard the verb as intransitive, e. g., the Vulgate, "impie agit," and now HITZIG, who finds expressed here the idea of "incurring penalty." But for this signification of this Hiphil there is wanting the necessary illustration and support; and as evidence that the וְאִישׁ מְזִמּוֹת may be regarded as an accusative without the sign אֵת comp., e. g., x. 11; Ps. lvi. 8; Job xxii. 29, etc.—With ver. 3 compare x. 25, and with the second clause in particular ver. 12 below.

2. Vers. 4-11. Eight proverbs on the blessings and banes of domestic life, and on the cause of both.—Ver. 4. **A good wife is her husband's crown.** Literally, a woman of power, i. e., of moral power and probity, such as manifests itself in her domestic activity; comp. xxxi. 10; Ruth iii. 11. The "crown" or the garland (עֲטָרָה) is here regarded evidently as an emblem of honor and renown, comp. the "crown of rejoicing" (στέφανος καυχήσεως), 1 Thess. ii. 19; also Prov. xxxi. 23, 28.—**But like a rottenness in his bones is she that causeth shame.**—Literally a worm-eating, i. e., a ruin inwardly undermining and slowly destroying; comp. xiv. 30; Job iii. 16.—Ver. 5. **The thoughts of the righteous are just; the counsels of the wicked are deceit,**—i. e., the very thoughts of the pious, much more then their words and deeds, aim at simple justice and righteousness; the shrewd counsels, however, by which the wicked seek to direct others (תַּחְבֻּלוֹת, comp. xi. 14), are in themselves deceitful and unreal, and therefore lead solely to evil.—Ver. 6. **The words of the wicked are a lying in wait for blood,**—i. e., they mean malice, they are the expression of a bloodthirsty and murderous disposition; comp. i. 11 sq.; xi. 9.—Altogether needlessly HITZIG alters the phrase אֱרָב־דָּם to אֹרֵב בָּם, "are a snare for them."—**The mouth of the righteous, however, delivereth them,**—that is, the righteous (comp. xi. 6), or it may be also the innocent who are threatened by the lying in wait of the wicked for blood (comp. xi. 9). [So WORDSW. and MUENSCHER].—Ver. 7. **The wicked are overturned and are no more.**—The infin. abs. הָפוֹךְ here stands emphatically for the finite verb, and furthermore, for this is certainly the simplest assumption, in an active or intransitive sense [comp. however in general on this idiom BÖTTCHER, § 990, a.—A.]; "the wicked turn about, then are they no more" [comp. the proverbial expression "in the turning of a hand"]. To regard it as a passive (EWALD, ELSTER, HITZIG) [K., M., S.] is unnecessary; this gives a stronger meaning than the poet probably designed, i. e., "the wicked are overthrown" (or even "turned upside down," HITZIG). The subsequent clause "and are no more" would not harmonize with so strong a meaning in the antecedent clause, especially if, as HITZIG supposes, the verb really designs to remind us of the overthrow of Sodom and Gomorrah (Gen. xix. 21). With the second clause comp. x. 25; Matth. vii. 25.

Ver. 8. **According to his wisdom.**—לְפִי [literally "in the face or presence of"], "in proportion to," "according to the measure of," as in Judges i. 8 and frequently elsewhere.—**But he that is of a perverse heart shall be despised.**—lit., "the crooked in heart," i. e., the perverse man, who does not see things as they are, and therefore acts perversely and injudiciously (HITZIG).

Ver. 9. **Better is the lowly that serveth himself.**—With this use of "lowly, insignificant," comp. 1 Sam. xviii. 23. The phrase

וְעֹבֵד לוֹ the Targum, ABEN EZRA, BERTHEAU, ELSTER [DE W., N., S.], regard as expressing this idea, "and he has at the same time a servant." But the parallelism demands the meaning early given in the LXX, Vulgate and Syr. versions [and now preferred by K., H., M., W.], "*ministrans sibi ipsi,*" serving himself, which is here evidently put in contrast with the foolish, impoverished pride of birth mentioned in the second clause,—whether we retain the Masoretic reading, or, with ZIEGLER, EWALD and HITZIG, read וְעֹבֵד לוֹ (participial).—**And lacketh bread.**—Comp. 2 Sam. iii. 29. With the general sentiment compare the passage which undoubtedly grew out of this, Ecclesiast. x. 30.—Ver. 10. **The righteous careth for the life of his beast,**—*i. e.*, he knows how his beast feels, he concerns himself, he cares for his domestic animals, does not allow them to hunger. [ARNOT: When the pulse of kindness beats strong in the heart, the warm stream goes sheer through the body of the human family, and retains force enough to expatiate among the living creatures that lie beyond]. Comp. Ex. xxiii. 9, "Ye know the heart of the stranger," from which parallel passage it appears that ZIEGLER, ELSTER, *etc.*, are in the wrong in translating נֶפֶשׁ here by "hunger." For examples of this use of the verb יָדַע, "to know," in the sense of "to concern one's self, to care for something," comp. also xxvii. 23; Gen. xxxix. 6; Ps. i. 6, *etc.*—**But the compassion of the wicked is cruelty,**—lit., "is cruel."—With the whole proverb comp. Ecclesiast. vii. 23.—Ver. 11. **But he that followeth after vanity.**—רֵיקִים is probably not the designation of "vain persons," as in Judg. ix. 4; 2 Sam. vi. 20; comp. 2 Kings iv. 3 (UMBREIT, BERTHEAU, *etc.*), but is to be regarded as neuter, *i. e.*, as an abstract, and therefore as meaning vain things, vanities, and, as the contrast with the first clause shows, specially "idleness, inaction, laziness." Comp. the LXX, who have here rendered the expression by μάταια, but in the passage almost literally identical, chap. xxviii. 19, by σχολήν; in like manner SYMMACHUS (ἀπραγίαν), Vulgate (*otium*), *etc.*

3. Vers. 12–22. Eleven additional proverbs with regard to virtues and faults in civil relations, especially sins of the tongue and their opposites.—**The wicked desireth the spoil of evil doers,**—*i. e.*, one wicked man seeks to deprive another of his gains, one of them is evermore seeking the injury and ruin of another, so that no peace prevails among them (Is. xlviii. 22; lvii. 21); they are rather "by the conflict of their selfish strivings ever consuming one another." Thus, and doubtless correctly, UMBREIT and ELSTER [to whose view K. gives a qualified assent], while BERTHEAU, following the Targum, translates מְצוֹד by "net," and to illustrate the meaning thus obtained, compares chap. viii. 35 [this is also the rendering of the E. V., which is followed by W., M., H.; S. renders "desireth an evil net," *i. e.*, destruction, being so intent upon his evil deeds as to disregard the consequences; N. renders in seeming agreement with our author "the prey of evil doers," the genitive being however possessive and not objective, *i. e.*, such prey as evil doers take]; EWALD however and HITZIG regard the passage as altogether corrupt, on account of the widely divergent text of the ancient versions (LXX, Vulg., Syr.), and therefore propose emendations (EWALD, "the desire of the wicked is an evil net;" HITZIG, "the refuge of the wicked is crumbling clay"). It is certainly noteworthy that the LXX and Vulgate offer a double rendering of the verse, first one that widely departs, and then one less seriously differing from the form of the Masoretic text.—With the second clause comp. ver. 3, second clause. For the verb יִתֵּן it is probably not needful to supply as subject the word "Jehovah," which has been omitted (UMBREIT, BERTHEAU, ELSTER [WORDSW. (?)], *etc.*) [nor with LUTHER, DE W., E. V., N. and M. to supply an object,—giveth or yieldeth (fruit)]; but, as in the instance in x. 24, to change the punctuation to the passive יֻתַּן, or again, to write יִתֵּן (derived from יָתַן, *firmus fuit*, comp. the proper name אֵיתָן) with the Targum, REISKE, HITZIG [STUART], *etc.*—Ver. 13. **In the transgression of the lips is a dangerous snare;** *i. e.*, he who seeks to ruin others by evil speaking is himself overthrown in the same way. BERTHEAU proposes to construe so as to give the meaning "is a snare of or for the wicked," which, however, is contrary to the analogy of Eccles. ix. 12.—After this verse also the LXX introduces a peculiar addition consisting of two clauses, which, however, is probably nothing more than an old gloss on the following verse; comp. HITZIG on this passage.

Ver. 14. **From the fruit of a man's mouth is he satisfied with good.**—Lit., "from the fruit of the mouth of the man doth he satisfy himself with good;" *i. e.*, it is the good fruit which one brings forth in wise, intelligent, benevolent discourse, that results in blessing to him. Comp. xiii. 2; xviii. 20. In the second clause to good words good works are added, and as "returning upon him" (comp. Ps. vii. 16); they are therefore represented as being in a sense the personified bearers of reward and blessing. Compare the similar thought, referring however to future retributions, and therefore somewhat differently expressed, Rev. xiv. 13, "their works do follow them."—Vers. 15 and 16 belong together, as both refer to the fool and his opposite.—**The way of a fool is right in his own eyes,**—*i. e.*, according to his own judgment (comp. iii. 7), which presents to him his own mode of action in a light favorable enough, although others may ever so often, and in a way ever so convincing, point out its perverseness. The exact opposite of this is found in the conduct of the wise man, the willing listener to wise counsels. Comp. xiv. 12; xvi. 25; xxi. 2.—**The vexation of the fool is at once known.**—lit., "is known even on the same day," *i. e.*, at once, after a short time (Vulgate, *statim*). In contrast with this passionate breaking out of the offended fool, the wise man exercises a prudent self-control in a seemly disregard of the insult put upon him, as Saul once did, 1 Sam. x. 27.—Ver. 17. **He that uttereth truth proclaimeth right,** *i. e.*, always gives utterance to that which is strictly just; so especially in judicial examinations as witness. This "truth" (אֱמוּנָה) is subjective truth, fidelity to one's own convictions (πίστις, LXX), the opposite to the lies which characterize the false witness; comp. xiv. 5, 25.

Ver. 18. **There is that talketh idly, as though it were thrusts of a sword,** lit., "like piercings of a sword," or "like knife thrusts" (HITZIG); *i. e.*, he breaks out with speeches so inconsiderate and inappropriate, that the persons present feel themselves injured as if by sharp thrusts. This rude and inconsiderate babbling of the fool is here fitly described by the verb בָּטָה, which is equivalent to בָּטָא, used in Lev. v. 4; Numb. xxx. 7; Ps. cvi. 33 (of speaking hastily, rashly, unadvisedly). — **But the tongue of the wise is health.** — "Medicine, healing" (comp. iv. 22), forms here an exceedingly appropriate antithesis to the inwardly wounding effect of the inconsiderate babbling mentioned before.

Vers. 19. **But the lying tongue only for a moment.** — Literally, "till I wink again, till I complete a wink of the eye;" comp. Jer. xlix. 19 and l. 44. This is therefore a detailed poetical circumlocution for the idea of a little while, an instant (Is. liv. 7); the verb here employed (הַרְגִּיעַ) is a denominative derived from רֶגַע a wink.— **Deceit is in the heart of those who devise evil.** — "Deceit, malignity" (comp. ver. 17, second clause) might here be made antithetic to "joy," because the necessary effect of deceit is sorrow and trouble. Therefore this noun מִרְמָה is not to be transformed to כְּרֵרָה bitterness (HOUBIGANT), nor to be interpreted by "self-deception," or by "joy in evil" (*Schadenfreude*) with UMBREIT.—**But to those who give wholesome counsel is joy.** — The common rendering (as also that of UMBREIT, ELSTER, *etc.*), is "who counsel peace;" comp. the old reading of the LXX, οἱ βουλόμενοι εἰρήνην, and the εἰρηνοποιοί of Matth. v. 9. But שָׁלוֹם is here to be taken in the general sense of "welfare, that which is salutary," as, for example, in Ps. xxxiv. 14; xxxvii. 37. The special signification "peace" would not correspond with the "evil" of the first clause, which is nowhere equivalent to strife, division (not in Judges ix. 23, as UMBREIT thinks). The "joy" of the well-meaning counsellor is furthermore probably to be conceived of as one to be found in the heart, the inward cheerfulness and happy contentment of a good conscience (as HITZIG rightly maintains against BERTHEAU and others).

Ver. 21. **No evil befalleth the righteous.** —For this verb (Pual of אָנָה) comp. Ps. xci. 10; Ex. xxi. 13. אָוֶן here signifies not "sin," but "evil, misfortune, calamity," like the parallel term in the second clause, or the רָעָה in the 91st Psalm cited above.—With respect to the sentiment, which naturally should be regarded as a relative truth, not as unconditionally illustrated in every experience, comp. chap. x. 3; xi. 23; xii. 2, 3, *etc.*—With ver. 22 compare xi. 20.

It is unnecessary to alter the plural עֵינַי into the singular עֵשֶׂה (with the LXX, many MSS., HITZIG, *etc.*).

9

4. Vers. 23–28. Six proverbs which relate to the contrast between the wise and the foolish, the diligent and the slothful.—With reference to the first clause of ver. 23 compare x. 14, 17; with the second clause, xiii. 16; xv. 2.—Ver. 24. **The hand of the diligent will rule; but the slothful will be obliged to serve.**—With the first clause compare x. 4; with the second, xi. 29.—רְמִיָּה, "slothful," is doubtless an adjective belonging to the noun יָד (hand), and not an abstract substantive "sloth," standing here for the concrete, "the sluggard," as J. D. MICHAELIS, DÖDERLEIN, BERTHEAU and ELSTER suggest.— "Will be obliged to serve," literally, "will be for tribute, for service," *i. e.*, will be forced to labor as one owing tribute.—Ver. 25. **If trouble be in the heart of man it boweth it down.**—The suffix attached to the verb seems like that connected with the parallel verb, which, moreover, rhymes with this, to refer to the noun "heart," and this as a synonym with נֶפֶשׁ "soul," has here the force of a feminine. [BÖTTCHER, § 877, e, cites this among the examples of the use of the fem. singular as a neuter with reference to objects named before not conceived of as neuter. See also GREEN, § 197, b—A.] In this connection it is indeed remarkable that דְּאָגָה (trouble), also contrary to its natural gender, appears here construed as a masculine. Hence the varying views of many recent expositors, *e. g.*, that of UMBREIT and ELSTER: "if trouble be in a man's heart, let him repress it (the sorrow);" or that of HITZIG, who refers the suffixes of both these verbs to the noun "hand" of the verse preceding, and accordingly renders (at the same time in a peculiar way reproducing the rhyme):

"Is sorrow in the man's heart, he bends it (*i. e.*, the hand, down).
But if gladness, he extends it."

[HITZIG's rhyme is made with the verbs *senket* and *schwenket*, which are rather violent equivalents to the Hebrew terms, but are perhaps fairly matched by *bends* and *extends*, or *abases* and *raises*.—A.] In favor of the rendering which we prefer are the old versions, and among recent expositors ROSENMUELLER, DATHE, DÖDERLEIN, EWALD, BERTHEAU.

Ver. 26. **The righteous guideth his friend aright.**—The verb יָתֵר, Hiphil of תּוּר (which is equivalent to תּוּר), means "to set right, to guide to the right way, ὁδηγεῖν;" רֵעַ is then equivalent to רֵעַ, friend, companion, as in Gen. xxvi. 26; Judges xiv. 20; xv. 6. [So GESEN., RÖD., FUERST, EWALD, BERTHEAU, K., S., M. and W.]—Others, especially LUTHER, M. GEIER, *etc.*, following the Chaldee version, regard יָתֵר as an adjective followed by the object of comparison: "better than his friend is (or fares) the righteous man." [So the E. V., which is followed by NOYES]. Others still, like DATHE, J. D. MICHAELIS, ZIEGLER and HITZIG (the latter changing the verb to יָתֵר), read כְּרִעֹה, "his pasture," and so reach the meaning "the righteous looketh after his pasture," *i. e.*, his path in life. It seems, however, altogether needless to depart from the above explanation, which is grammatically admissible, and gives a meaning which agrees well with that of the second clause—**But the way of the wicked leadeth them astray;** them, *i. e.*, the wicked. The construction is the same as in chap. xi. 6, and probably also xii. 6.

Ver. 27. **The slothful catcheth not his prey.**—"The slothful," properly here again an adjective, "idle" hand, expresses the idea of sloth, and then, as an abstract for the concrete, stands for "the sluggard, the slothful." חָרַךְ then, an ἅπαξ λεγόμενον in the Old Testament, is explained by the Rabbins, following the Aramean (Dan. iii. 27), by "to singe, to roast;" therefore BERTHEAU, *e. g.*, still translates "the slothful roasteth not his prey," and then supplies the idea, "because he is too lazy to catch it." [M. adopts this explanation, and S. doubtfully.] Others, more simply, and in conformity with the old versions, render "the idle man catcheth not his game" [so K., H., and N.], for which signification of hunting, catching, seizing, HITZIG cites lexical analogies from the Arabic. [FUERST, criticising this interpretation, and defending the other, urges 1) that not to catch game is no sure sign of laziness, and 2) "his prey" must be already in hand—A.]—**But a precious treasure to a man is diligence.**—To reach this meaning it is necessary either to take חָרוּץ exceptionally in the abstract sense of diligence, or with C. B. MICHAELIS and HITZIG to read as an infinitive חָרוּץ, "to bestir one's self, to show one's self diligent." — Others, like KÖHLER, UMBREIT, ELSTER, *etc.*, resort to a partial transposition of the words, yielding the meaning "but precious treasure belongeth to the diligent man"—an alteration which is favored in advance by the Syriac version, and to some extent also by the LXX.

Ver. 28. **But a devious way** (leadeth) **to death.**—This is doubtless the interpretation to be given with HITZIG to this clause; for in Judges v. 6; Is. lviii. 12, נְתִיבָה in fact signifies (in contrast with אֹרַח) a crooked winding by-path, and the modification of אֶל to אַל seems the more justifiable in proportion as the combination on which the ordinary rendering rests is otherwise unknown (אַל־מָוֶת as equivalent to לֹא־מָוֶת); "and the way of its path is not-death" (which is to be understood as "immortality," EWALD, UMBREIT, ELSTER [K., E. V., N., S., M.], *etc.*). Furthermore, the form of expression (דֶּרֶךְ before נְתִיבָה) indicates plainly that to the second of the terms employed not its ordinary sense, but a quite peculiar signification, a quasi adjective import is to be given. [HODGSON and HOLDEN express a decided preference for this view].—With the general sentiment of the verse compare x. 2; xi. 19.

DOCTRINAL AND ETHICAL.

The contrasts between diligence and indolence, wisdom and folly, which present themselves as the strongest characteristics of the second and fourth of the groups of verses found in this chapter, lead us to refer the proverbs of these groups mainly to *private* or *domestic* life,—while the predominating reference of the third main group (vers. 12-22) to sins of the tongue or lips, leads us to regard *social* or *civil* life as the special department here chiefly contemplated. Still this classification is after all only a general one, and proverbs of a more general moral tendency and bearing, like those contained in the introductory group (vers. 1-3) are interspersed through each of the three large groups (*e. g.* in vers. 5, 6, 12, 21, 26, 28); these therefore show the impossibility of carrying through a division of the contents of the chapter according to definite and clearly distinct categories.

Moral truths to which an emphatic prominence is given are found in the very first verse, on which UMBREIT pertinently remarks, "The thought seems weak, and to a spirit practised in reflection hardly worth recording, yet on its truth rests the possibility of a spiritual progress in the human race, its development to a higher humanity; one might even say, the very conditions of history lie in that proverb." Again we find them in ver. 10, a proverb which sets forth that tender care for animals as man's fellow-creatures, which impresses itself on so many other passages of the Old Testament, *e. g.* Ex. xx. 11; xxii. 29, 30; Lev. xxii. 27; Deut. xxii. 6 sq.; xxv. 4; Ps. xxxvi. 6; civ. 27; cxlv. 15 sq.; cxlvii. 9; Job xxxviii. 39 sq.; xxxix. 5 sq.; Jonah iv. 11, *etc.**

We find like important truths in ver. 13, as also in general in all the proverbs that relate to the right use of the lips and tongue (compare besides vers. 14, 16-19, 22, 25); so also in the commendation of a willingness to receive good counsel, ver. 15, with which we may appropriately compare THEOGNIS, *Gnom.*, V., 221-225 (see the passage in UMBREIT, p. 158):—and again in the admonition to a wise self-command and presence of mind under experience of injury, ver. 16, with which should be compared admonitions of the New Testament against persistent anger and heat of passion, such as Rom. xii. 19; Eph. iv. 26, 31; James i. 19, 20, *etc.*—It has already been made evident that the concluding verse of the chapter (ver. 28, 2d clause) unlike chapter xi. 7, probably contains no hint of a hope of immortality.

HOMILETIC AND PRACTICAL.

Homily on the entire chapter. On the true wisdom of the children of God, as it ought to appear 1) in the *home*, under the forms of good discipline, diligence and contentment; 2) in the *state* or in the intercourse of citizens, under the forms of truthfulness, justice, and unfeigned benevolence (ver. 12-22); 3) in the *Church* or in the religious life, as a progressive knowledge of God, a diligent devotion to prayer and striving after eternal life (vers. 23-28).—Comp. STÖCKER: —On true discipline: 1) its general utility (vers. 1-8); 2) the blessing on those who receive discipline, and the curse on those who hate and despise it (vers. 9-16); 3) comprehensive repetition of what has been taught concerning the salutariness of discipline (vers. 17-28).—STARKE: —On the injurious nature of ungodliness and

---

* Comp. ZÖCKLER, *Theologia Naturalis, Entwurf einer systematischen Naturphilosophie*, *etc.*, 1, pp. 535 sq.

the utility of piety; 1) in general (vers. 1–3); 2) in particular, *a*) in the marriage relation (ver. 4); *b*) in common life (vers. 5–8); *c*) in the care of cattle and in agriculture (9–11); *d*) in the use of the tongue (12-23 ; *e*) in attention to one's calling (24-28).—*Calwer Handbuch:*—The heart, the action and the speech of the fool and the wise man,—or, of the life that is to be found in the way of righteousness, and the ruin that is to be found in the way of ungodliness.

Vers. 1-3. GEIER:—No one is so perfect that he might not sometimes fail, and consequently need a chastisement not only on the part of God, but also on the part of men.—(On ver. 3): He who by faith and love is rooted in God (Eph. iii. 17) will not possibly ever be rooted up by anything; Ps. lxxiii. 25 ; John x. 28.—STARKE:—It is better to be with true sympathy chastised by a just man, than to be deceitfully praised.— *Berleburg Bible:*—He who suffers himself to be guided comes constantly nearer to wisdom, *i. e.* to Christ, and for such a one His fellowship with all its blessedness stands open.—VON GERLACH (on ver. 1):—All that raises man above the brute is secured to him by training, by the wholesome discipline of his parents and teachers.—(On ver. 3): The ungodly has no ground in which he is rooted, no stability in assaults from without, while the righteous man is rooted in the eternal nature of the Creator Himself. Hence the righteous man is a tree by a river's side, a house on a rock,—the ungodly, however, is a fleeting storm-cloud, a tree in a dry land, a house built on the sand, and even chaff that the wind driveth away, Ps. i. 3 sq.; Isa. xliv. 4, *etc.* —[ARNOT (on ver. 1):—The fool casts away the precious because it is unpalatable, and the wise man accepts the unpalatable because it is precious. Nature hates reproof; let grace take the bitter potion and thrust it down nature's throat, for the sake of its healing power.—A. FULLER (on ver. 1):—He, and he only, that loves the means loves the end. The means of knowledge are "instruction" in what is right, and "reproof" for what is wrong. He who is an enemy to either of these means is an enemy to the end. —BRIDGES (on ver. 3):—Firm and unshaken is the condition of *the righteous.* Their leaves may wither in the blast. Their branches may tremble in the fury of the tempest. But *their root*—the true principle of life—*shall not be moved*].

Vers. 4-11. GEIER (on ver. 4):—By vicious conduct a woman destroys her husband as it were with subtle poison, but even then harms herself the most.—ZELTNER (on ver. 4):—He who will enter into the marriage relation should begin with God, with hearty prayer, sound reflection, and devout purposes, lest he be compelled afterward bitterly to bewail his folly, Tob. viii. 4 sq.—(On ver. 9): An honorable life in narrow circumstances is much better and more peaceful, and besides not subject to so many temptations, as when one lives in ever so high a position in the view of the world. To make a great figure and to aim at being great is the ruin of many a man, Tob. iv. 14 ; Ecclesiast. iii. 19, 30.— *Würtemberg Bible* (on ver. 10):—The brute has no one that can do him good but man ; therefore treat it kindly, with reason and moderation —[TRAPP (on ver. 5)]:—If good thoughts look into a wicked heart, they stay not there, as those that like not their lodging.—(On ver. 7): There is a council in heaven will dash the mould of all contrary counsels upon earth.— (On ver. 11): Sin brought in sweat (Gen. iii. 19), and now not to sweat increaseth sin.—LORD BACON (on ver. 10) :—The tender mercies of the wicked are when base and guilty men are spared that should be stricken with the sword of justice. Pity of this sort is more cruel than cruelty itself. For cruelty is exercised upon individuals, but this pity, by granting impunity, arms and sends forth against innocent men the whole army of evil-doers.—CHALMERS (on ver. 10):— The lesson is not the circulation of benevolence within the limits of one species. It is the transmission of it from one species to another. The first is but the charity of a world. The second is the charity of a universe].

Vers. 12-22. MELANCHTHON:—In everything are we exhorted to good, and to striving after truth, in the knowledge of God, in science and arts, in all honorable occupations and compacts ; and because truthfulness belongs to the most glorious and eminent virtues, therefore the vice opposed to it is condemned in strong language, and pronounced (ver. 22) an offence and abomination in the sight of God.—OSIANDER :—We use the gift of speech rightly when we employ it to God's glory and to our neighbor's benefit.— ZELTNER:—As one has here used his tongue, whether for good or evil, he will hereafter be recompensed. Truth is a daughter of righteousness ; apply thyself diligently to this, and thou hast the true witness in thyself that thou art of the truth and a child of God (1 John iii. 18, 19). Fidelity and veracity have indeed in the world, whose watchword is only hatred, a poor reward; but so much the more precious are they in the sight of God (Ps. xv. 1, 2).—[ARNOT (on ver. 13): When a man is not true, the great labor of his life must be to make himself appear true; but if a man be true, he need not concern himself about appearances.—TRAPP (on ver. 20) :—Such counsellors shall have peace for peace: peace of conscience for peace of country].—On ver. 20, TISCHER (in ZIMMERMAN's "*Sonntagsfeier,*" 1865, No. 41):—Every one can become acquainted with himself from his social intercourse.—[SOUTH (on ver. 22):—A lie is a thing absolutely and intrinsically evil: it is an act of injustice, and a violation of our neighbor's right. The vileness of its nature is equalled by the malignity of its effects; it first brought sin into the world, and is since the cause of all those miseries and calamities that disturb it; it tends utterly to dissolve and overthrow society, which is the greatest temporal blessing and support of mankind ; it has a strange and peculiar efficacy, above all other sins, to indispose the heart to religion. It is as dreadful in its punishments as it has been pernicious in its effects].

Vers. 23-28. HASIUS:—The ordinary modes of acquisition are always the safest and best. Him who loves crooked ways and devices we never find prospering; but those who walk in ways of innocence and justice, cannot become unsuccessful.—OSIANDER :—Follow thy calling in the fear of God and with diligence, and thy possessions will be with God's blessing richly multiplied.—STARKE:—He who squanders time, shuns toil and buries his pound in a napkin, is unworthy to dwell on earth (Luke xix. 20, 24).—WOHLFARTH (on ver. 25):—*The friendly word.* Where we can help by actual deeds, such real help is by all means better than mere consolation in words. If however the means for such aid are wanting to us, if the evil is of such a sort that no human help whatever is possible, then it is a double duty to cheer the depressed with friendly words; yes, consolation is then often in itself help because it leads to God, the true helper in all need!—[TRAPP (on ver. 27):—Jabal and Jubal, diligence and complacence, good husbandry and well contenting sufficiency, dwell usually together.—CHALMERS (on ver. 28):—The deeds of the hand have a reflex influence on the state of the heart. There is life in spiritual-mindedness; and it serves to aliment this life to walk in the way of obedience].

γ) With reference to the use of temporal good, and of the word of God as the highest good.

CHAP. XIII.

1 A wise son hearkeneth to his father's correction,
  but a scorner to no rebuke.
2 By the fruit of one's mouth doth he enjoy good,
  but the delight of the ungodly is violence.
3 He that guardeth his mouth keepeth his life,
  he that openeth wide his lips shall be destroyed.
4 The sluggard desireth, but without the satisfying of his desire,
  but the desire of the diligent is abundantly satisfied.
5 Deceit the righteous hateth,
  but the ungodly acteth basely and shamefully.
6 Righteousness protecteth an upright walk,
  but wickedness plungeth into sin.
7 One maketh himself rich and hath nothing,
  another professeth to be poor yet hath great riches.
8 A ransom for a man's life are his riches,
  but the poor heedeth no threatening.
9 The light of the righteous rejoiceth,
  but the lamp of the wicked goeth out.
10 By pride cometh only contention,
  but wisdom is with those who receive counsel.
11 Gain through fraud vanisheth away,
  but he that gathereth by labor increaseth it (his gain).
12 Hope deferred maketh the heart sick,
  but desire accomplished is a tree of life.
13 Whosoever despiseth the word is bound to it,
  he that feareth the commandment is rewarded.
14 The instruction of the wise man is a fountain of life
  to escape the snares of death.
15 Kindly wisdom ensureth favor,
  the way of the ungodly is desolate.
16 The prudent man doeth all things with understanding,
  but a fool spreadeth abroad folly.
17 A bad messenger falleth into trouble,
  but a faithful messenger is health.
18 Poverty and shame (to him) that refuseth correction;
  he that regardeth reproof is honored.
19 Quickened desire is sweet to the soul,
  and it is abomination to fools to depart from evil.
20 Walk with wise men and become wise!
  but whoso delighteth in fools becometh base.

21 Evil pursueth sinners,
   but to the righteous God repayeth good.
22 A good man leaveth an inheritance to his children's children,
   and the wealth of the sinner is laid up for the just.
23 The poor man's new land (yieldeth) much food,
   but many a one is destroyed by iniquity.
24 He that spareth his rod hateth his son,
   but whoso loveth him seeketh correction.
25 The upright eateth to the satisfying of his hunger,
   but the belly of the wicked shall want.

GRAMMATICAL AND CRITICAL.

Ver. 2. [The literal rendering is "*the soul of the wicked* (shall feed upon) *violence.*" Substantially this rendering is given by the E. V., by H., N., S. and M. ZÖCKLER [see exeg. notes] regards this verse as conveying the two ideas that violence is the wicked man's delight, and that it is his recompense. He feeds on it while he lives, and dies by it. Conceiving the former to be the more prominent idea here he gives to נֶפֶשׁ a secondary and figurative meaning,—the *longing*, the *delight*. We think that he has lost rather than gained by this refining.—A.]

Ver. 4. According to the Masoretic punctuation the clause would be literally rendered "His soul—the sluggard's—longeth [strongly desireth], and there is nothing," ["His appetite." Z.] The suffix in נַפְשׁוֹ would then stand pleonastically before the appended genitive עָצֵל [as *e. g.* Num. xxiv. 3; Deut. xxxii. 43]; וָאַיִן would however be introduced as a parenthesis between the predicate and the subject, and would express substantially the idea "without satisfaction, without finding anything." It appears simpler and less forced, however, to change the punctuation as HITZIG does, thus: כְּתַאֲוָה וְאַיִן נַפְשׁוֹ עָצֵל, in which case נֶפֶשׁ receives the meaning by metonymy "object of desire" (comp. Ps. xxxv. 25; Isa. lviii. 19), and the meaning of the whole clause is as in our version.

Ver. 5. [בָּאִישׁ, which Z. regards as equivalent to בַּעֲבִישׁ, BÖTT. (see § 1147, C. b.) regards as substituted for it by a mere interchange of weak and kindred consonants. The verbs are nearly related, בָּאַשׁ being used of that which is offensive to the sense of smell, בּוּשׁ of that which changes color, by turning pale or otherwise. The one describes misconduct as offensive, the other as shameful.—A.]

Ver. 9. The verb יְעַג seems to form a designed accord with יִשְׂכַּח; comp. xii. 25.

Ver. 11. [The different renderings grow partly out of different conceptions of the meaning of the noun הֶבֶל and partly from different syntactical constructions. הֶבֶל, originally "breath," then "nothingness" or "vanity," is by most interpreters taken in some metaphorical sense. The rendering of the E. V., followed by H., is ambiguous, "by or through vanity." M. and ST. render "without effort;" FUERST agrees with Z. in giving it no ethical meaning,—that which is morally nothing, nothing right, nothing good. It so describes fraud and iniquity. GESEN., NOYES, etc., retain the primitive meaning, and treat the כְּ as comparative. See Exeg. Notes.—A.]

Ver. 15. [The rendering of שֶׂכֶל־טוֹב in the E. V., is again ambiguous: "good understanding." H., N., S., M. agree substantially with Z., interpreting the phrase as descriptive of prudence or discretion joined with kindness. Others, *e. g.* FUERST, give it, with less probability, the passive meaning of "consideration" or "reputation."—A.]

Ver. 16. Instead of בְּכָל we should read כֹּל, in accordance with the correct rendering of the Vulg.: *Astutus omnia agit cum consilio.* [The English commentators without exception, so far as we know, follow the E. V. and the LXX. translate according to the pointing of the Mas. text: πᾶς πανοῦργος; "every wise man," *etc.* Z.'s rendering is certainly more forcible, and justifies the vowel change.—A.]

Ver. 19. [The weight of authority has been decidedly against the author's conception of the poetic נִהְיָה. GESEN. and FUERST are against him, as well as the commentators cited. KAMPH. may be added to those who agree with Z. in rendering this Niph. participle "become" as meaning "come into being," "developed," while the other conception is that it describes what has been "completed, accomplished." Comp. ver. 12, b, "desire that hath come," which is generally understood to be satisfaction. We cannot think that the proverb relates to the pleasure of desiring, but to that of being satisfied. The 2d clause is by H. regarded as an inference, "therefore," *etc.*; E. V., N., S., M. regard it as an antithesis—notwithstanding their certain disappointment fools cling to evil. K. shapes the antithesis differently; "a new desire is pleasant to the soul, but if it be evil fools abhor to renounce it." Z.'s view appears in the notes.—A.]

Ver. 20. [For the imper. use of the inf. abs. see GREEN § 268, 2 and grammars generally. יָרוּעַ Niph. Imperf., more distinct than יֵרַע which might be a neuter Kal. BÖTT. § 1147, A.—A.]

EXEGETICAL.

1. With chap. xiii HITZIG would have a new section commence, extending to chap. xv. 32, and consisting of three subdivisions of symmetrical structure. The first of these subdivisions would be chap. xiii., consisting of four groups of six verses each; the second, chap. xiv., five groups of seven verses each; the third, chap. xv., four groups of eight verses each—altogether 91 verses, precisely the same number as the preceding Section (chaps. x.-xii.) contained.— How arbitrary these assumptions are appears partly from the difficulties, often utterly insuperable, which meet the attempts to point out real divisions at the beginning and end of the several alleged groups of verses. It appears further from the fact that here again it is necessary to stamp as spurious one verse at least (xiii. 23), a violent critical expedient to secure the symmetrical relation of groups that is demanded. Comp. above, Exeget. notes on chap. x., No. 1.

With respect to the groups of verses that do develop themselves with satisfactory distinctness, and in general with reference to the order and progress of thought in the chapter before us, see the Doctrinal and Ethical notes.

2. Vers. 1-3. Three introductory proverbs, general in their import.—**A wise son hearkeneth to his father's correction.**—In this first clause we must supply "hearkeneth" from the second as predicate. The conception of others, e. g. J. D. MICHAELIS, BERTHEAU, etc.: A wise son is his father's correction, i. e. the object of his correction,—is less natural on account of its harshness. Parallel to the milder expression "instruction, correction" (מוּסָר) in clause a, we have in b the stronger term "rebuke" (גְּעָרָה, as in xvii. 10).—No rebuke, no threatening, no earnest enforcement of law makes any impression on the "scorner" (i. 22; ix. 7), the heedless reviler of religion, who has long ago thrown aside all childlike piety, and reverence for the holy. With ver. 2, clause a, comp. xii. 14; with b comp. x. 6.—**The delight of the ungodly is violence**, i. e. the eager desire (נֶפֶשׁ) of maliciously disposed sinners is for violence (חָמָס), which they wish to exercise upon others, and which therefore in turn recompenses them. "Violence," therefore, stands here with a twofold meaning [active and passive] as in chap. x. 6. [See Critical Notes].—**Shall be destroyed.**—מִחִתָּה, ruina, "destruction," just as in x. 14.—["Take heed that thy tongue cut not thy throat;" an Arabic proverb quoted by TRAPP from SCALIGER, Arab. Prov. i. 75.—A.]

3. Vers. 4-12. Nine proverbs relating mainly to the worth and right use of wealth.—**The sluggard desireth, but without the satisfying of his desire.**—[See Critical Notes].—**But the desire of the diligent is abundantly satisfied**, literally, "is made fat," comp. xi. 25.—Ver. 5. **Deceit the righteous hateth.**—דְּבַר־שֶׁקֶר appears to be not "word of falsehood," deceitful language (UMBREIT, BERTHEAU), but a designation of everything falling under the category of the deceitful (דָּבָר being therefore equivalent to πρᾶγμα); comp. Ps. xli. 9; Isa. xliv. 4; it means therefore lies and frauds, deceit.—**But the ungodly acteth basely and shamefully.** [See Critical Notes]. יַבְאִישׁ, lit., "maketh offensive, stinking," stands here as equivalent to יֵבֹשׁ, "acteth basely, or causeth shame;" comp. chap. xix. 26. The Hiphil form יַחְפִּיר, which is found also in the parallel passage, here has an active meaning, "acteth shamefully," while in Isa. liv. 4 it stands as passive: cometh to shame, or is put to shame. [So the E. V., H., N, and M., while S., K., etc., give the causative rendering—A.].

Ver. 6. **Righteousness protecteth an upright walk**, lit., "innocence of way," an abstract for the concrete, and therefore equivalent to "such as walk uprightly" (comp. x. 29). **But wickedness plungeth into sin.**—Wickedness (רִשְׁעָה), literally, "perverse, malicious disposition" describes that evil state of the heart which necessarily leads to sinful action (חַטָּאת). The verb, which is here used in its natural meaning, "overturn, plunge into something," has the end of its action, sin, connected with it without a preposition (comp. xix. 13). The old versions, and among modern expositors BERTHEAU, [FUERST, H., N., M., S.], take the object as an abstract for the concrete, and therefore translate "wickedness overthroweth sinners," by which rendering a more exact parallelism between a and b, it is true, is secured.

Ver. 7. **One maketh himself rich, and hath nothing at all.**—Comp. xii. 9, a maxim, which, like the one before us, is aimed at foolish pride of birth and empty love of display on the part of men without means. The "boasting one's self" there corresponds with the "representing one's self rich" here. Comp. also the similar proverb of the Arabs, in MEIDANI, III. 429. [The second clause is differently understood; W. interprets it as referring to the "being rich in good works, and sacrificing all worldly things for God and His truth." So HOLDEN; while TRAPP, BRIDGES, N., S. and M. regard the clause as referring to the deceitful concealment of riches. The parallelism requires this view.—A.]

Ver. 8. **A ransom for a man's life are his riches**, i. e. the rich man can and under certain circumstances, as e. g. before a court, or when taken captive by robbers or in war, must employ his wealth for his ransom.—**But the poor heedeth no threatening**, i. e. no warning or threatening however sharp ("rebuke" as in ver. 1) will be able to force anything from him who has nothing; the poor is deaf to every threat that aims at the diminution of his possessions, for "where there is nothing, there the Emperor has lost his rights." The spirit of this maxim, in itself morally indifferent, seems like that of the similar proverb, chap. x. 15, to be directed to the encouragement of industry, and of some earthly acquisitions though they be but moderate. ELSTER is certainly in the wrong, in holding that the proverb depicts, not without a shade of irony, "the advantages as well of great wealth as of great poverty." Against various other conceptions of the verse, especially of clause b, comp. BERTHEAU in loco. [HOLDEN construes interrogatively: "Doth not the poor," etc., understanding it of the helplessness of the poor; N. and M. understand it of the safety of the poor in his poverty; W. of his light-hearted independence; S. of the viciously or heedlessly poor, whom nothing can arouse to virtuous industry.—A.]

Ver. 9. **The light of the righteous burneth joyously.**—The verb is here intransitive: "is joyous, i. e. burns brightly, with vigorous blaze." HITZIG rightly directs attention to the fact that the same root (שׂמח) in Arabic signifies to "laugh, or sport."—**But the lamp of the wicked goeth out.** The "lamp" of the wicked (נֵר) does not seem to be emphatically contrasted as a dim night lamp with the bright light of the righteous, but is probably a simple synonym of אוֹר determined by the parallelism; comp. Job xviii. 5, 6; xxi. 17; xxii. 28; xxix. 3.

Ver. 10. **By pride cometh only contention.**—"Only" (רַק) although in the Hebrew put first in the clause, belongs nevertheless to the subject (בְּזָדוֹן), and not to the "by pride" בְּזָדוֹן [as in E. V., and STUART]; as though the meaning were, only by pride (or, only in excitement, ebullition of passion, UMBREIT) does one begin strife. Comp. rather as an example of this pretixing of "only" (רַק), Ps. xxxii. 6 [where HUPFELD and others do not admit this explanation "only to him," etc.]; and for similar hyperbata with גַּם and אַף comp. Prov. xix. 2; xx. 11; Isa. xxxiv. 14. [N. and M. agree with our author. H. takes רַק as a noun, "ignorance" with pride, etc. But if it be objected to the simple and obvious rendering of the words in their Hebrew order, that pride is not the only or chief cause of contention, it may no less be objected that contention is not the only or chief result of pride. Why may not the proverb be interpreted as comparing two dispositions, the proud, self-sufficient spirit, of clause a, and the modest inclination to consult and consider others, of clause b? Only by the former of these two is contention produced.—A.]—**But wisdom is with those who receive counsel.**—Comp. xii. 15, b. Instead of נוֹעָצִים, "the well advised, those who hearken to counsel," HITZIG proposes to read עֲנָוִים, the "modest." An unnecessary change to correspond with xi. 2.

Ver. 11. **Gain through fraud vanisheth away.**—[See Critical Notes]. The הוֹן מֵהֶבֶל is used to describe "gain coming from nothingness, from the unreal," i. e. secured in an unsubstantial, inconsiderate, fraudulent way (EWALD, LUTHER, etc.). Or (with ZIEGLER, DÖDERLEIN, ELSTER, HITZIG) let the pointing be מְהֻבָּל (Pual part.); i. e. a hastily, fraudulently acquired wealth, substantia festinata, Vulg.—To regard כְּהֶבֶל as a comparative, "sooner than a breath" (UMBREIT, NOYES and others), has this against it,—that a "vanishing away," a "diminution" cannot be well predicated of a הֶבֶל, a nothing, a mere phantom, but may be naturally of a possession gained in an unsubstantial or unworthy manner.—**But he that gathereth by labor increaseth it.**—עַל־יָד is either "handful after handful" (EWALD, BERTHEAU, ELSTER, etc.), or, "according to his ability," pro portione s. mensura sua (HITZIG). In both cases it describes the gradual and progressive accumulation of wealth, resulting from diligence and exertion, and so is in significant contrast with the impatient dishonesty of the preceding clause.

Ver. 12. **Hope deferred maketh the heart sick;** comp. x. 28. The predicate is not a substantive, "sickness of heart" (UMBREIT), but a Hiph. partic.—For the figure of the "tree of life" in clause b comp. xi. 30. ["Desire that hath come," (Kal part.) is by common consent of lexicographers and commentators desire accomplished. This should be remembered in the exposition of ver. 19 a.—A.]

4. Vers. 13-17. Five proverbs relating to the value of the divine word as the highest good, and exhorting to obedience to it.—**Whosoever despiseth the word is in bonds to it,** i. e. the word or the law of God (comp. for this absolute use of the term "word" דָּבָר) e. g. xvi. 20). The word of divine revelation is here, as it were, personified as a real superhuman power, whose service one cannot escape, and in default of this he comes in bondage to it, i. e. loses his liberty. [The verb according to this rendering describes mortgages, bonds and other such legal obligations; "wird verpfändet," Z.—A.] Thus SCHULTENS, EWALD, ELSTER correctly render, while many others, e. g. UMBREIT, BERTHEAU, [K., E. V., N., S., M.] explain "for him is destruction provided, he shall be destroyed." HITZIG. however, altogether arbitrarily takes the "word" of clause a in the sense of "command," and the "command" (כְּצָוָה) of clause b in the sense of "prohibition," and accordingly translates "whosoever despiseth the command is seized by it, and whoso avoideth (heedeth) the prohibition is rewarded" (?). For the phrase "he is requited, to him is requital," comp. xi. 31.

Ver. 14. **The instruction of the wise man is a fountain of life.**—Comp. x. 11, where the "mouth of the righteous," and xiv. 27. where the fear of God is described by this figure. In the latter passage the 2d clause of our verse appears again. "Snares of death" an established formula for the description of mortal perils; comp. Ps. xviii. 5; Prov. xxi. 6, and also the Latin laquei mortis, HOR. Od. III. 24, 8.

Ver. 15. **Kindly wisdom produceth favor.**—Comp. iii. 4, where however the שֵׂכֶל־טוֹב expresses a somewhat different idea, viz., passively, "good reputation." [See Critical Notes].—**The way of the ungodly is desolate.**—אֵיתָן, perennis, elsewhere descriptive of a brook or river that flows inexhaustibly, seems here to denote either a "standing bog" (J. D. MICHAELIS, UMBREIT), or, which is perhaps more natural, it belongs as an adjective to the noun "way" (דֶּרֶךְ), and characterizes the way of transgressors as "ever trodden," i. e. altogether hard, solid, and therefore desolate and unfruitful (BERTHEAU, EWALD, ELSTER, etc.). [As compared with the more common conception of the hard way as rough, stony (FUERST, H., S., M., W.) this has the advantage of following more naturally from the radical idea of continuance and permanence.—A.] HITZIG prefers to read אֵיתָן, makes hateful, produces hatred (?). [This is NOYES' explanation].

Ver. 16. [See Critical Notes]. For the meaning "the wise man doeth all things with understanding," comp. xii. 23; xv. 2.—Ver. 17. **A bad messenger falleth into trouble.**—A "bad messenger" (lit., "wicked") is not, as might be thought, one who is indolent, tardy, as in x. 26 (so BERTHEAU), but one who is faithless, not true to his master, betraying him. He "falls into trouble" as a punishment for his faithlessness. ARNOLDI and HITZIG unnecessarily substitute the Hiphil for the Kal, and render "throws into trouble." The antithesis between a and b is at any rate not an exact one.—**But a messenger of fidelity, a faithful messenger.**—Comp. xiv. 5; xx. 6, and for this participial form of the epithet, xxv. 13.—For this use of "health," healing medicine, comp. xii. 18.

5. Vers. 18-25. Eight additional admonitory proverbs, pointing to the blessedness of obedience to the divine word.—**Poverty and shame (to him) that refuseth correction.**—The participial clause is to be taken as conditional, "if one refuses correction" (comp. Job xli. 18). The connection with the main clause is "not grammatically complete, because intelligible of itself," comp. Prov. xxvii. 7 (Hitzig). For the meaning of the verb comp. i. 25; iv. 15; viii. 33.—With clause *b* comp. xv. 5, 32.

Ver. 19. **Quickened desire is sweet to the soul.**—[See Critical Notes.] "Desire that has come to be " (Niph. part.) cannot be designed to describe "appeased desire" (Vulg., LUTHER, BERTHEAU, EWALD, ELSTER [FUERST, H., N., S., M., *etc.*], but, as the import of clause *b* and a comparison of 12, *b* suggest, a desire that is just originated, has just attained its development, now first vividly experienced but not yet satisfied (UMBREIT, HITZIG). Now that this desire is in many instances directed toward evil, and that this evil desire is especially hard to appease,—this is the truth to which clause *b* gives expression (comp. James i. 14, 15). The second clause is not then antithetically related to the first, but it makes strongly prominent a single side of the general truth already uttered. [To what is said in the Critical Notes RUEETSCHI's comment may be added (*Stud. u. Krit.*, 1868, p. 139). He renders clause *a* like the Vulg., E. V., *etc.*, regarding it as the statement of a general psychological fact, while *b* supplies a particular case, illustrative and not contrasted. His practical use of the sentiment of the proverb is embodied in the appeal "Therefore see to it that thy desire be a good one in whose accomplishment thou mayest rightly rejoice!" He pronounces HITZIG's and Z.'s rendering of נִהְיָה as untenable lexically, and false to fact.—A.]

Ver. 20. **Walk with wise men and become wise.**—So according to the K'thibh: an infin. abs. [used as an imperative] followed by an imperative instead of a consecutive clause,—which is to be preferred to the K'ri [which is followed by LXX, Vulg., E. V., H., N., S. and M.]. The latter makes the language less spirited and needlessly assimilates it in form to the 2d clause.—**But whosoever delighteth in fools becometh base.**—In the Hebrew there is a play upon words: he who tendeth fools (רֹעֶה) showeth himself base יֵרוֹעַ. [This might be thus imitated in English: he who attendeth fools tendeth to folly]. For this use of the verb רָעָה, to follow or attach one's self to some one, *sectari aliquem*, to cultivate intercourse with one, comp. xxviii. 7; xxix. 3; Jer. xvii. 16. From this is derived רֵעַ "friend, comrade."

Ver. 21. **To the righteous God repayeth good.**—As subject of the verb we should supply in this instance not the indefinite subject, " one," *man*, but rather Jehovah (unlike the instances in x. 24; xii. 12). HITZIG needlessly substitutes יְקַדֵּם as an emendation, "meeteth," suggested by the καταλήψεται of the LXX. For the meaning comp. x. 25; xi. 3, 5, *etc.*

Ver. 22. **A good man leaveth an inheritance to his children's children.** For this absolute use of the Hiph., "causeth to inherit, transmitteth his estate," comp. Deut. xxxii. 8. For the sentiment comp. Job xxvii. 17; Eccles. ii. 26.

Ver. 23. **The poor man's new land (yieldeth) much food.** The noun נִיר according to Hos. x. 12; Jer. iv. 3, describes "newly broken, newly ploughed land," *i. e.* a field newly cleared, and therefore cultivated with much effort (Vulg. correctly *novalia*: LUTHER less exactly "furrows" (*Furchen*). If such a field nevertheless yields its poor possessor "much food," he must be a devout and upright poor man, and so possess the main condition of genuine prosperity, which is wanting to the man mentioned in clause *b*, who is evidently a man of means, a rich man, who in consequence of his iniquity (lit., " by notjustice") is destroyed.—HITZIG on the ground of the phraseology, which is certainly somewhat hard and obscure, pronounces the verse corrupt, and therefore reads נָגִיד instead of נִיר, and so gets for clause *a* the meaning "A great man who consumes the income of capital" (!). Furthermore he pronounces the whole verse spurious, and thinks it originally formed a marginal comment on xi. 24 (!!) but then by the mistake of some copyist was introduced into the text just at this point. [RUEETSCHI (as above quoted) interprets clause *a* in like manner of the righteous poor man's newly cleared land, which, although wrought with difficulty, abundantly rewards the labor. The יֵשׁ of clause *b* he regards not as a verb "there is," but as a substantive (comp. viii. 21), with the meaning "substance, wealth." This is destroyed where there has been unrighteousness.—A.]

Ver. 24. **He that spareth his rod hateth his son.** See iii. 12; xxiii. 13, 14; xxix. 15; Ecclesiast. xxx. 1.—**But whosoever loveth him seeketh it, correction.** The suffix of the last verb here, as in ver. 22, refers to the object immediately following, and this noun is here used actively in the sense of "chastisement, discipline which one employs with another." Others take the suffix as the indirect object, equivalent to לוֹ, "for him;" he seeketh for him (the son) correction. This, however, is not grammatically admissible. HITZIG maintains that the verb is here to be taken after the analogy of the Arabic in the sense of "tame, subdue," and that the noun is a second accusative object (?),—and that we should therefore translate "he restraineth him by correction." So also HOFMANN, *Schriftbew.* II. 2, 377 (follows him up with correction). With ver. 26 comp. Ps. xxxiv. 10 (11), Prov. x. 3, *etc.*

DOCTRINAL, ETHICAL, HOMILETIC, AND PRACTICAL.

The idea which appears in the very first verse, of salutary discipline, or of education by the word of God and sound doctrine, also reappears afterward several times in a significant way (vers. 13, 14, 18, 24; comp. vers. 6, 10, 20, 21); it therefore to a certain extent controls the whole development of thought throughout this Section, so far as we may speak of anything of the kind. We have also here again as in chap. iv. (see above, p. 74,) a chapter on the true religious training of children. Only it is here specifically training to the wise use of earthly blessings (so in particular the group vers. 4-12), and to the knowledge of God's word as the chief blessing (so especially in the 2d half, vers. 13-25); this is urged by most of the proverbs that are here grouped. Hence the frequent allusions to the blessing of constant diligence, and patient labor in one's earthly calling in reliance upon God (vers. 4, 11, 23, 25); also to the great value of earthly possessions gathered under God's gracious help, as important instrumentalities for the fulfilment of the spiritual duties also involved in one's calling (vers. 8, 11, 12, 18, 22); further to the hateful and harmful nature of pride and vanity (vers. 7 a, 10, 16, 18); to the evil consequences of unfaithfulness, since it necessarily "smites its own lord" (vers. 2, 5, 15, 17); to the importance of good company, and of a decided abhorrence of that evil companionship which corrupts the morals (vers. 1, 6, 20; comp. 1 Cor. xv. 33), etc.

Therefore, in the *homiletic* treatment of the *chapter as a whole*, we have as a subject "The true Christian education of children." 1) Its basis: God's word (vers. 1, 13, 14); 2) its means: love, and strictness in inculcating God's word (vers. 1, 18, 24); 3) its aim: guidance of the youth to the promotion of his temporal and eternal welfare (vers. 2 sq., 16 sq.) Or, on the right use of God's word as the basis, the means, and the end in all human culture. Or, on the word of God as the most precious of all possessions (comp. Matt. vi. 33; xiii. 44-46; 1 Pet. i. 23-25).—STÖCKER:—The wise man's discipline (*Disciplina sapientis*). 1) Wherein it consists (1-10); 2) What qualities the well-trained wise man possesses, viz. chiefly, *a*) Moderation and prudence in the use of earthly good; *b*) Humility and modesty; 3) What is the blessing of a wise training.

Vers. 1-3. STARKE:—No one is born pious; every one brings sin with him into the world; therefore from the tenderest childhood upward diligence should be employed with youth that they may grow up "in the nurture and admonition of the Lord" (Eph. vi. 2). There are spirits that from merest infancy onward have their jests at everything that belongs to virtue and piety (Gen. xxi. 9); to improve such always costs much work and prayer.—(On vers. 2, 3): If words spoken heedlessly before a human tribunal are often so dangerous that they can bring one into the greatest misfortune, how can evil words be indifferent in the view of God the Supreme Judge (Matt. xii. 36)?—WOHLFARTH:—On what does the happy result of education depend? 1) On the side of parents, on the strictest conscientiousness in the fulfilment of their duties as educators (ver. 1); 2) On the side of children, on their thankful reception of this training (vers. 2-9).

Vers. 4-12. STARKE (on ver. 5):—The natural man shuns lying and deceit on account of the outward shame and reproach; the pious abhors them with all his heart for God's sake.—(On ver. 7): A man's condition may not be with certainty inferred from the outward appearance: "all is not gold that glitters" (Eccles. viii. 4; 1 Sam. xvi. 7). The spiritually poor who feels his inward poverty stands in the right relation, in which he can become truly rich in the grace of God.—(On ver. 8): The poor man may have many advantages over the rich, in case he knows how to use his poverty aright.—(On ver. 11): That many men of means become poor is caused by the fact that they do not wisely apply what is theirs, but waste it on all manner of useless things.—(On ver. 12): If thou hast made some promise to thy neighbor, defer not long the fulfilment of the promise. He who gives promptly gives double.—[BRIDGES (on ver. 5): —It is not that a righteous man never lies. Nor is it a proof of a righteous man that he avoids lying. But true religion brings in the new taste—conformity to the mind of God.—TRAPP (on ver. 9):—A saint's joy is as the light of the sun, fed by heavenly influence, and never extinct, but diffused through all parts of the world.—(On ver. 11): Ill-gotten goods fly away without taking leave of the owner.—(On ver. 12): We are short-breathed, short-spirited. But as God seldom comes at our time, so He never fails at His own; and then He is most sweet because most seasonable.—ARNOT (on ver. 12):—If the world be made the portion of an immortal spirit, to want it is one sickness, to have it is another. To desire and to possess a perishable portion are only two different kinds of misery to men].—J. LANGE (on ver. 12):—Children of God must often hope long under the cross for their deliverance. Yet when this comes at length, it is so refreshing and joyful, that they begin as it were to live anew.—ZELTNER (on ver. 12):—Set thy hope not on the vain, uncertain and transient, but on the imperishable and eternal, on God and His word, 1 Cor. iv. 18; 1 Tim. vi. 17.

Vers. 13-17. *Tübingen Bible* (on ver. 13):—It is very great wisdom gladly to receive correction when one has erred; but it is folly to be angry when one is warned against everlasting destruction.—GEIER:—Faithful discharge of the duties that devolve on us secures a good conscience and reward from God and men.—[TRAPP (on ver. 15):—Natural conscience cannot but do homage to the image of God stamped upon the natures and works of the godly.—ARNOT:—It is far-seeing mercy that makes the way of transgressors hard; its hardness warns the traveller to turn that he may live].—STARKE (on ver. 16): —If thine act and project are to prosper, begin with prudence and good counsel, and so continue till thou hast done.—WOHLFARTH:—Wisdom as the fountain of true life. Its correction like its counsel is health and blessing; its yoke is soft and light, because it urges us to act and to walk simply according to our destination.—VON GERLACH (on vers. 13 sq.):—A despiser of God's word involves himself in its penalties, he falls sooner or later under its chastisement: while on the contrary his reward never fails the righteous.—(On ver. 17): While the wicked messenger prepares misfortune for himself as well as for his master, the faithful makes good even his lord's mistakes.

Vers. 18-25. *Berleburg Bible* (on ver. 18):—Where one finds a spirit that can tolerate no correction, is always excusing and defending itself, or throwing the blame on others, from such a one there is no good to be hoped.—(On ver. 20): It is very profitable to cultivate friendship and familiar intercourse with spiritually-minded men, because one is in general wont easily to take to one's self the spirit of those with whom one associates.—ZELTNER (on ver. 20):—If thou shunnest an infected house, how much more shouldst thou shun the company of the ungodly, that thou mayest not be touched by the poison of their sins and vices.—[ARNOT:—The issue to be decided is not what herd you shall graze with a few years before your spirit return to the dust; but what moral element you shall move in during the few and evil days of life, till your spirit return to God who gave it].—STARKE (on ver. 21):—Sin evermore draws after it God's wrath and judgments as the shadow always closely follows the body.—[T. ADAMS (on ver. 22):—The usurer lightly begets blind children that cannot see to keep what their father left them. But when the father is gone to hell for gathering, the son often follows for scattering. But God is just].—MELANCHTHON (on ver. 23):—It is better to possess small means, but use them well, and enjoy them with pious and contented mind, than to heap up great treasures, that pass not away without offences of many kinds.—OSIANDER (on ver. 23).—God gives to a pious man who is poor nevertheless nourishment enough if he only labor diligently in his calling and forsake not prayer.—J. LANGE (on ver. 24):—A good father follows his children unweariedly with prayer, correction and counsel, that he may not be forced afterwards bitterly to deplore omitting correction at the right time.—VON GERLACH (on ver. 24):—A loving father strives to correct his child early; he does not wait till urgent need forces him to it.—[JOHN HOWE:—Fond parents think it love (that spares the rod); but divine wisdom calls it hatred.—BRIDGES:—The discipline of our children must commence with self-discipline. Nature teaches us to love them much. But we want a controlling principle to teach us to love them wisely. The indulgence of our children has its root in self-indulgence].

β) With reference to the relation between the wise and the foolish, the rich and the poor, masters and servants.

CHAP. XIV.

1 Woman's wisdom buildeth her house,
   but folly teareth it down with its own hands.
2 He that walketh uprightly feareth Jehovah,
   but he that is perverse in his ways despiseth him.
3 In the mouth of the foolish is a rod for his pride,
   but the lips of the wise preserve them.
4 Where there are no oxen the crib is clean,
   but much increase is by the strength of the ox.
5 A faithful witness cannot lie,
   but a false witness uttereth lies.
6 The scorner hath sought wisdom, and findeth it not,
   but to the man of understanding is knowledge easy.
7 Go from the presence of the foolish man ;
   thou hast not found (with him) lips of knowledge.
8 The wisdom of the prudent is to understand his way,
   the folly of fools is a deception.
9 The sacrifice maketh sport of fools,
   but to the righteous there is favor.
10 The heart knoweth its own bitterness,
   and let no stranger intermeddle with its joy.
11 The house of the wicked is overthrown,
   but the tent of the upright shall flourish.
12 There is a way that seemeth right to man,
   but the end thereof is the ways of death.
13 Even in laughter the heart will be (perchance) sad,
   and the end of joy is sorrow.
14 He that is of a perverse heart shall be satisfied with his own ways,
   but a good man (shall be satisfied) from him (E. V. " from himself").

15 The simple believeth every word,
   the wise giveth heed to his way.
16 The wise feareth and departeth from evil,
   but the fool is presuming and confident.
17 He that is quick to anger worketh folly,
   and the man of wicked devices is hated.
18 The simple have secured folly,
   but the wise shall embrace knowledge.
19 The wicked bow before the good,
   and sinners at the doors of the righteous.
20 The poor is hated even by his neighbor,
   but they that love the rich are many.
21 Whosoever despiseth his friend is a sinner,
   but he that hath mercy on the poor—blessings on him!
22 Do not they go astray that devise evil?
   and are not mercy and faithfulness with them that devise good?
23 In all labor there is profit,
   but mere talk (leadeth) only to want.
24 The crown of the wise is their riches,
   the folly of fools (is evermore) folly.
25 A true witness delivereth souls,
   but he that uttereth lies is a cheat.
26 In the fear of Jehovah is strong security,
   and to His children He will be a refuge.
27 The fear of Jehovah is a fountain of life,
   to escape the snares of death.
28 In the multitude of the people is the king's honor,
   but from want of people (cometh) the downfall of the prince.
29 He that is slow to wrath is great in understanding,
   but he that is hasty of spirit exalteth folly.
30 The life of the body is a quiet spirit,
   but passion the rottenness of the bones.
31 He that oppresseth the poor hath reproached his Maker,
   whosoever honoreth him hath had mercy on the poor.
32 By his wickedness is the wicked driven forth,
   but the righteous hath hope (even) in his death.
33 In the heart of a man of understanding doth wisdom rest,
   but in the midst of fools it maketh itself known.
34 Righteousness exalteth a nation,
   but sin is a reproach to any people.
35 The king's favor is towards a wise servant,
   but his wrath against him that is base.

GRAMMATICAL AND CRITICAL.

Ver. 1.—Read חָכְמוֹת, as in i. 20; ix. 1, and not חַכְמוֹת (fem. plur. constr.), as though "the wise ones among women" (comp. Jud. v. 29) were to be here designated (so the LXX, Vulg., LUTHER). [So substantially the E. V., NOTES, etc., distributing the plural on account of the singular of the verb. FUERST regards חָכְמוֹת as merely another form of the abstract noun. BÖTT. does not admit the possibility of this, but explains the form in the text as an indef. or distributive plural, holding, nevertheless, that the antithesis with אִוֶּלֶת requires here the usual abstract. §§ 700, c and n. 4, and 702, c, e.—A.]

Ver. 2.—The ו in וּבְלוֹז is one of the few examples in the early Hebrew of the Hholem plen. in emphatic verbal forms beginning or ending a clause. See BÖTT., § 167.—A.]

Ver. 3.—The form הִשָּׁמְרוּם should probably be changed to תִּשְׁמְרֵם, since the assumption of the lengthening of the vowel (vocal Sheva) in the syllable preceding the accent seems hardly justified by analogies like Ex. xviii. 26; Ruth ii. 8. Comp. HITZIG on this passage. [BÖTT. defends the form doubtfully, and regards it as probably an illustration of the speech of the common people. The fem. form of the verb is indicated only by the prefix, and not by its ordinary termination. See §§ 367, b, 1043, 4 and n. 3, and 1047, e. See GREEN, § 105, d.—A.]

Ver. 5.—[כָּזָב, one of BÖTTCHER's examples of the "Fiens licitum," what may or can be; § 950, c, β; will not=can not.—A.]

Ver. 6.—[בִּקֵּשׁ, a "relative" perfect, like חָרַד and חוֹנֵן in ver. 31; "hath been seeking .... and it is not," "hath already virtually reproached his Maker," "hath already shown mercy."—BÖTT., § 950, 1.—A.]

נָקֵל is undoubtedly a neuter participle,=נְקַלָּה, a trifle, a small, easy matter.

Ver. 7.—[Three points come under consideration: 1) the meaning of לְ נֶגֶד, 2) the force of the perfect tense יָדַעְתָּ, and 3) the meaning of the connective וְ. On the first, in addition to the arguments of Z. in the exegetical notes, RUETSCHI urges (as before cited, p. 140) that with verbs of motion the only natural rendering is "from before," the לְ being justified by Deut. xxviii. 66 as well as the passage in Judges. In regard to the second the simple perfect is easier than a predictive perfect; thou hast not=thou surely wilt not. Z. omits the connective וְ in his version; "and" might be equivalent to "in case, or where thou hast not," etc. RUETSCHI somewhat more unnaturally renders "otherwise;" he obtains the very forcible meaning "otherwise thou hast not known lips of knowledge"—hast not learned their nature, and art now making this evident. DE WETTE agrees with ROSENMUELLER in rendering clause b as a relative clause—"and from him in whom thou hast not," etc.—A.]

Ver. 10.—[יֶעְרָב — for ־ in final syllable under the influence of the guttural, GREEN, §119, 1; BÖTT., §§ 378, 1, 1055. In כָּרַת, derived from כָּרַר, we have one of the few instances of a doubled ר. See GREEN, § 60, 4, a, BÖTTCHER, §392, 2, c.—A.]

Ver. 12.—[דֶּרֶךְ is used in the first clause as masc., in the second as fem. In the historical books, Jerem. and Proverbs, this confusion is common. See BÖTT., §§ 657, 2; 877, γ, e.—A.]

Ver. 13.—The suffix in וְאַחֲרִיתָהּ refers to the following שִׂמְחָה, as in the passages cited above in connection with xiii. 4. To divide וְאַחֲרִית שִׂמְחָה (J. D. MICHAELIS, HITZIG) is an alteration altogether unnecessary in the case before us, where the expression "joy" in clause b is nothing but a repetition of that of "laughter" in clause a.

Ver. 14.—To change to וּבְמִגְלָלָיו (L. CAPELLUS, JAEGER, etc.), or to עֲלָיו (ELSTER, comp. EWALD) is plainly needless in view of the simple and obvious interpretation of מֵעָלָיו given in the notes.

[BÖTT. proposes with great confidence to amend clause b by substituting for אִישׁ the verb יָמִישׁ; §§ 460, 2, a, and 1143, 6; "good will depart from him."—A.]

Ver. 15.—[Observe the emphatic change of accent and vocalization in פֶּתִי.]

Ver. 17.—In view of the explanation which may be given of the text, attempted emendations appear needless and inappropriate, such, e. g., as EWALD's, who proposes instead of יִשְׂנֵא to read יְשַׁנֶּה ("he quiets his anger," "keeps his equanimity"); or that of HITZIG, who to secure the same meaning reads יְשַׁאן, etc. [RUETSCHI emphatically defends the received text.]

Ver. 18.—[Observe the change of tense; וְ נָחֲלוּ, "Perfectum repentinum," used of that which is easily and quickly done; יַכְתִּירוּ "Fiens licitum," are disposed or incline I to wait, etc. BÖTT., §§ 950, B; 940, 2; 943, c, a.—A.]

Ver. 25.—[פֵחַ, as in vi. 19; xii. 17; xix. 5, 9, an irregular participial form.]

Ver. 28.—[רוֹזֵן is a collateral form of רוֹן, as עָשׁוֹק of עֹשֶׁק. The expression here stands as a parallel to מֶלֶךְ, as the plural רוֹזְנִים often stands side by side with מְלָכִים.

Ver. 30.—[בְּשָׂרִים, plural, probably, on account of the following עֲצָמוֹת. BÖTT. however (§ 695, 5) explains it as an example of the "pluralis extensivus" used also of the entire, the complete, the large,—"the life of the whole body."—A.]

EXEGETICAL.

1. Vers. 1–7. On wisdom and folly in general.—**Woman's wisdom buildeth her house.** [See critical notes]. It is plain that in contrast with this wisdom of the godly we are to understand by "folly" in clause b especially woman's folly.—With ver. 2, a, compare x. 9; with b, ii. 15; iii. 32.—Ver. 3. **In the fool's mouth is a rod for his pride.**—lit., "a rod of pride." [Is this genitive subjective or objective? a rod which his pride uses, for himself, or others, or both, as it has been variously understood,—or a rod by which his pride is itself chastised? The antithesis commends the latter, which is the view of BERTHEAU, KAMPH., etc., as well as Z. According to S., "pride" is the subject and not a limiting genitive—A.] HITZIG unnecessarily proposes to understand גַּאֲוָה in the sense of גַּו "back," a meaning which even in Job xli. 7 hardly belongs to the word [although given by AQUILA, JEROME, etc.] (Comp. DELITZSCH on the passage.)—**But the lips of the wise preserve them**—For the construction comp. xi. 6; xii. 6, etc.; for the meaning, x. 13, 14.—Ver. 4. **Where there are no oxen the crib remaineth empty.**—אֵבוּס, "crib," not "stall" (UMBREIT); בַּר, in itself meaning "pure, clean," is here "empty;" so sometimes קַן. The drift of the proverb is not quite the same as in x. 15; xiii. 8 (a commendation of moderate wealth as a means of doing good and as a preservative from spiritual want). Rather is this the probable meaning: "He who will develop his wealth to a gratifying abundance must employ the appropriate means; for "nothing costs nothing, but brings nothing in" (ELSTER, HITZIG).—With ver. 5 comp. xii. 17; with b in particular vi. 19.—Ver. 6. **The scorner hath sought wisdom, and findeth it not,**—lit., "and it is not," comp. xiii. 7. The bearing of this proverb is plainly directed against that superficial, trivial, seeming culture of the scoffers at religion, (who, in the perverted sense of the word, are "the enlightened"), which lacks all genuine earnestness, and for that very reason all really deep knowledge and discernment—**But to the man of understanding is knowledge given.**—See critical notes.

Ver. 7. **Go from the presence of the foolish man.**—So LUTHER had already correctly rendered; also DE WETTE, BERTHEAU, ELSTER; for לְנֶגֶד [from the front, from before] does not describe motion directly toward or at one (EWALD, comp. UMBREIT), but remoteness from him, as Is. i. 16; Am. ix. 3; and for the connection with לְ which, it is true, is unusual, comp. Judges xx. 34. [See critical notes].—HITZIG, following the LXX and Syr. vers., writes the first word of the verse כֹּל instead of לְךָ, and in clause *b* reads בְּלִי־דַעַת instead of בַּל יָדְעָה, from which the meaning is obtained "The foolish man hath every thing before him, but lips of knowledge are a receptacle of understanding" (LXX: ὅπλα δὲ αἰσθήσεως). But the idea of the second clause experiences in this way no possible improvement, but only an injury (observe the tautological character of the expressions "lips of knowledge" and "receptacle or vessel of knowledge"), and for this reason we should retain the meaning given above for the first clause also.—In clause *b* the verb is a proper perfect, "thou hast not known or recognized lips of knowledge," this is, if thou soughtest any such thing in him. [W. is wrong in rendering "over against," and "wilt not know."—A.]

2. Vers. 8–19. Further delineation of the wise and the foolish, especially with reference to their contrasted lot in life.—**The wisdom of the wise is to understand his way,**—lit., "observe his way." For this use of the verb with the accusative, in the sense of to "observe or consider something," comp. chap. vii. 7; Ps. v. 2. For the sentiment of the verse comp. xiii. 16, and ver. 15 below.—**The folly of fools is deception.**—"Deceit" here in the sense of self-deception, imposition on self, blindness, which is at last followed by a fearful self-sobering, a coming to a consciousness of the real state of the case (comp. Ps. vii. 15; Job xv. 35).

Ver. 9. **The sacrifice maketh sport of fools,**—*i. e.*, the expiatory sacrifice which ungodly fools offer to God is utterly useless, fails of its object, inasmuch as it does not gain the favor of God, which is, on the contrary, to be found only among the upright (lit., "between upright men," *i. e.*, in the fellowship of the upright or honorable, comp. Luke ii. 14). Thus BERTHEAU, EWALD, ELSTER [STUART and WORDSWORTH], *etc.*, while the majority, disregarding the singular member in the verb, translate "Fools make a mock at sin" [E. V., M., N., H.] ("make sport with sin," UMBREIT, comp. LUTHER). [HODGSON, rightly conceiving the grammatical relation, but making both subject and object concrete, renders "sinners mock at fools"]. HITZIG here again proposes violent emendations, and obtains the meaning "The tents (?) of the foolish are overthrown (??) in punishment; the house (?) of the upright is well pleasing."

Ver. 10. **The heart knoweth its own bitterness,**—lit., "a heart knoweth the trouble of its soul," *i. e.*, what one lacks one always knows best one's self; therefore the interference of strangers will always be somewhat disturbing. If this be so, then it follows that it is also not advisable "to meddle with one's joy," and this is the point that is urged in clause *b*. A precept applicable unconditionally to all cases is of course not designed here. The author of our proverbs will hardly be put in antagonism to what the Apostle enjoins in Rom. xii. 15. It is rather a hard and intrusive manifestation of sympathy in the joy and sorrow of one's neighbor, that is to be forbidden.—With 11, *a*, comp. xii. 7; Job xviii. 15; with *b*, Is. xxvii. 6.—With ver. 12, *a*, comp. xii. 15; xvi. 2.—**But the end thereof are ways of death,**—*i. e.*, the way of vice, which at the beginning appears straight (the way is not directly described as the way of vice, yet is plainly enough indicated as such), at length merges itself wholly in paths that lead down to mortal ruin; comp. ver. 4; vii. 27.—The same verse appears again below in xvi. 25. Ver. 13. **Even in laughter the heart will be** (perchance) **sad.**—The Imperf. of the verb here expresses a possible case, something that may easily and often occur. The contrasted condition is suggested by Eccles. vii. 4: "Though the face be sad, the heart may yet be glad." [Notwithstanding HOLDEN'S observation, that "though sorrow may be occasioned *by* laughter, it does not exist *in* it," it is a deeper truth, that in circumstances producing a superficial joyousness, there is often an underlying profounder sorrow.—A.]—**And the end of joy is sorrow** [not by a mere emotional reaction, but] in such a case as this; the heart, which under all apparent laughter is still sad, feels and already anticipates the evil that will soon have wholly transformed the gladness into grief.

Ver. 14. **He that is of a perverse heart shall be satisfied with his own ways,** *i. e.*, he who has departed from God (lit., "he that is turned aside in heart," comp. Ps. xliv. 19) is surfeited with his own ways, partakes of the ruinous results of his sinful action; comp. xii. 14; xiii. 2; xxviii. 19.—**But a good man (shall be satisfied) from him,** *i. e.*, the good man solaces himself in the contemplation of the wicked and his fate (chap. xxix. 16; Job xxii. 19; Ps. xxxvii. 34; lviii. 11); or, it may be, the upright man enters into the possession of the good which the other loses (comp. xi. 8, 29; xiii. 22). מֵעָלָיו, strictly "from with him," expresses here this idea.—"from that which belongs to him as its foundation" (HITZIG), and therefore "from his experience, from the sorrowful occurrences of life in which he is deservedly involved." [E. V., H., N., M. render reflexively "from himself," and make the experiences parallel; each shall be satisfied "with his own ways," or "from himself." The third pers. suffix has this reflexive meaning after בְּעַל distinctly in 1 Sam. xvii. 22, 39; Jonah iii. 6. The suffix in clause *a* is reflexive, "his own ways," and we must regard the same construction as the simplest and most natural in *b*—A.]

Ver. 15. **The simple believeth every word,** —ELSTER: "every thing." But as objects of belief, it is, in the first instance and most directly, words alone that come under consideration, and reference is made here precisely to the unreliableness of *words* as used by men, as in chap. vi. 1 sq.; x. 19; Eccles. v. 1 sq.; Ps. cxvi. 11, *etc.*—With clause *b* compare above ver. 8 *a*.—Ver. 16. With clause *a* compare xvi. 6, 17.—**The fool is presuming and confident.** —Comp. xxi. 24; xxviii. 16. The latter of these descriptive terms unquestionably describes a false security, and carnal arrogance, which is the opposite of the fear of God. The former epithet means "self-exalting, bearing one's self insolently," or it may be (like the Kal conj. of the same verb in chap. xxii. 3) "boldly rushing on, overriding" (HITZIG, comp. LUTHER, "rushes wildly through").

Ver. 17. **He that is quick to anger worketh folly.** — Strictly, "he who foams up quickly, who flies into a passion," contrasted with the man who is "slow to anger," ver. 29. [אַפַּיִם, the nostrils, then the breathing, which by its quietness or its excitement, marks the state of the temper]. — **And the man of wicked devices is hated.** — Literally, "the man of shrewd reflections, well contrived counsels" (comp. remarks on i. 4, and also chap. xii. 2; xxiv. 8; Ps. xxxvii. 7), who is not here set as a contrast, but as a counterpart to the passionate man; the crafty and subtle man, who, in spite of all his show of mildness, is still as thoroughly hated as the irascible and passionate man. The relation of the two clauses is accordingly not antithetic, but that of a logical parallel. With one manifestation of an evil disposition another is immediately associated, with a suggestion of the results which are in accordance with it; comp. chap. x. 10, 18.

Ver. 18. **But the wise shall embrace knowledge.** — יַכְתִּרוּ (comp. Ps. cxlii. 8), literally, "surround, enclose," cannot here mean "they crown themselves, or are crowned" [the verb is not reflexive" (UMBREIT, comp. LUTHER [DE W., E. V., H., N., S., M., W.]), but, as the parallel verb in clause *a* indicates, must convey simply the meaning of "laying hold upon," *i. e.*, gathering, accumulating [so FUERST, BERTHEAU, KAMPH., etc.].

Ver. 19. **And the wicked at the doors of the righteous.**—*i. e.*, they bow there (the verb is to be repeated from the first clause). The figure lying at the basis of this representation is that of the ambassadors of a conquered people, who, kneeling at the doors of their conqueror's palace, await his command. For the general sentiment comp. xiii. 9, 22; also Psalm xxxvii. 25, etc.

3. Vers. 20-27. On riches and poverty in their causal connection with wisdom and folly.—**The poor is hated even by his neighbor.**—Comp. xix. 4; Ecclesiast. vi. 7 sq.; xii. 8 sq. Numerous parallels from classic authors (*e. g.*, THEOGNIS, V. 621, 697; OVID, *Trist.*, I., 9, 5, 6), and also from Rabbinical and Arabic authors, may be found in UMBREIT's Commentary *in loco*. "is hated," *i. e.*, "is repelled as disagreeable, is obnoxious" (comp. Deut. xx. 15; Mal. i. 3). How this may come to pass, how former friendship between two persons may be transformed into its opposite on account of the impoverishment of one of them, is impressively illustrated by our Lord's parable of the neighbor whom a friend asks for three loaves (comp. Luke xi, 5-8.) —Ver. 21. **Whosoever despiseth his friend is a sinner**, *i. e.*, he who neglects a friend that has fallen into destitution (comp. ver. 20 *a*), who does not render him assistance, sins just as surely as his act is praiseworthy who is compassionate to the poor or wretched (read עֲנָיִים with the K'thibh). With the benediction in clause *b* compare xvii. 20.

Ver. 22. **Do they not err that devise evil?** —The figurative expression "carve evil" (comp. iii. 29; vi. 14) has as its counterpart in the second clause the kindred figure "carve out good," *i. e.*, contrive or devise good (*bona machinari*). Instead of יִתְעוּ "they err, or go astray" (comp. Job xv. 31) HITZIG reads יָרֵעוּ (from רעע): "Ought it not to go ill with them that devise evil?" But the language of the text characterizes with sufficient strength and clearness the unsettled and disastrous condition of those who have departed from God's ways.—**And are not mercy and truth with those that devise good?**—The interrogative particle affects the second clause as well as the first (so UMBREIT, and doubtless correctly, in opposition to most modern interpreters [*e. g.*, E. V., DE W., BERTHEAU, H., M., S., K., while NOYES agrees with our author]). The construction is like that in xiii. 18.— "Mercy and truth" are probably God's manifestations of Himself toward them, as in Gen. xxxii. 11; Ps. lxi. 7, and not human attributes, as above in chap. iii. 3 (see note *in loco*), or as in xvi. 6; xx. 28. [So TRAPP and others, while M. and S. make them human,—M. making these the *experience*, and S. the *action* of those who devise good.—A.]

Ver. 23. **In all labor there is profit, but idle talk (leadeth) only to want.**—(Comp. xi. 24; xxi. 5); in the latter passage "profit" and "want" are contrasted precisely as here.—"Idle talk;" in the Hebrew literally, "word of the lips;" comp. Isa. xxxvi. 5; Job xi. 2; xv. 3. The sentiment of the entire verse is moreover plain: "One should beware of idle talk more than of the hardest toil" (BERTHEAU). Comp. Matt. xii. 36.

Ver. 24. **The crown of the wise is their riches**, *i. e.* the well-earned possessions of the wise become his honor, are a real adornment to him, for which he is with good reason praised. "The folly of fools, on the other hand, is and continues folly," though he may ever so much parade and swell with it, though he may in particular studiously employ any riches he may chance to possess in splendidly decorating himself, and giving himself a magnificent appearance by all manner of outward trifles and finery (comp. BERTHEAU, UMBREIT, ELSTER on this passage). [TRAPP: "Why, was it not foolishness before they were rich? Yes, but now it is become egregious foolishness"].—HITZIG has here again needlessly felt constrained to amend. He reads in clause *a* "their prudence," עָרְמָם, and in clause *b*, as the subject, "ostentation," אִוֶּלֶת instead of אִוֶּלֶת; so he obtains the meaning, "The crown of the wise is their prudence (?); the pomp of fools is—drunken (??)."

Ver. 25. **A true witness delivereth souls**, *i. e.* from the death involved in some false charge brought against them before the court, and which therefore threatens them in case a truthful witness does not clear them and bring their innocence to light.—**But he that uttereth lies** (comp. ver. 5; vi. 19) **is a cheat.**—Compare xii. 17, where, however, "deceit" מִרְמָה is object of the preceding verb "showeth forth," and not predicate. Here the abstract "deception" stands emphatically for the concrete, "a deceitful man, one without substance or reliableness;" comp. above ver. 8, *b*. [ROEETSCHI (as above,

p. 142) would simplify the construction by retaining כָּצֵל as the common predicate of both clauses, and would give to the second object the meaning "wrongful or unrighteous possession," citing as a parallel Jer. v. 27. We cannot commend the suggestion.—A.] HITZIG instead of "deceit" (מִרְמָה) reads כִּרְמָה "be destroyeth" (*i. e.* souls), in order to obtain as exact an antithesis as possible to the "delivereth" in the first clause.

Ver. 26. **In the fear of Jehovah is strong security**, or, the fear of Jehovah is strong security, is a sure reliance; for the preposition may properly stand before the subject as the בְּ *essentiæ*, as in Isa. xxvi. 4; lvii. 6 (so HITZIG).— **And to His children He will be a refuge.**— "To His children," *i. e.* doubtless to His worshippers, those faithful to Him, who for that very reason are His favorites and objects of His care (comp. Deut. xiv. 1). This reference of the suffix to Jehovah Himself is unquestionably more natural than to refer it to the pious, an idea which must first be very artificially extracted from the "fear of Jehovah" (contrary to the view of UMBREIT, EWALD, BERTHEAU, ELSTER, [H., N., M., S.]). HITZIG reads לְבֹנָי "to its builders," *i. e.* to them who seek to build up that strong fortress, that "security" of the fear of Jehovah (?). With ver. 27 comp. xiii. 14. [RUEETSCHI (as above, p. 142) supports the idea rejected by ZÖCKLER, that the divine protection extends to the children and the children's children of such as honor God. Although not without grammatical warrant for the construction, and conveying beautifully a precious scriptural truth, we must regard the rendering as here somewhat forced.—A.]

4. Vers. 28-35. Continued parallels between the wise and the foolish, the rich and the poor— with the addition of the closely related comparison of masters and servants. —**From want of people** (cometh) **the downfall of the prince.** "People" (לְאֹם) as in xi. 26. Whether in the choice of the word rendered "prince" there is a hidden allusion to the ordinary meaning. "consumption" (HITZIG, comp. UMBREIT) must remain in doubt. For this use of מְחִתָּה, downfall, ruin, comp. x 14; xiii. 3.

Ver. 29. **He that is slow to anger is great in understanding.**— Literally, he that is long or slow in anger, βραδὺς εἰς ὀργήν, James i. 19; therefore, the forbearing, the patient. "Great, *i. e.* rich in understanding" (comp. "great in acts," 2 Sam. xxiii. 20); comp. the Latin *multus prudentia*.—**But he that is hasty in spirit** (quick-tempered) **exalteth folly**, *i. e.* makes much of it, carries it to excess. Thus HITZIG, and doubtless correctly, while the majority take the verb in the sense of "to exalt before the view of men," *manifestare, declarare*, for which idea however the parallel passages xii. 23; xiii. 16 are by no means conclusive [H., S., M., W. all take this view].

Ver. 30. **The life of the body is a quiet spirit.**— Lit., "life of the members (see Critical Notes) is a heart of quietness" (בָּשָׂר not meaning here "health," but composure, a tranquil condition, as in xv. 4; Eccles. x. 4).—**But passion the rottenness of the bones.**—Comp. xii. 4, and for this use of קִנְאָה, "passionate zeal," violent excitement in general (not specifically envy or jealousy) Job v. 2.—Ver. 31. With clause *a* compare xvii. 5, with *b*, xix. 17 *a*, and above ver. 21.

Ver. 32. **By his wickedness is the wicked driven forth**, driven forth, *i. e.* from life; he is by a violent death swept away from this earthly life (comp. Ps. xxxvi. 12; lxii. 3).—**But the righteous hath hope** (even) **in his death.** He "is confident," viz. in Jehovah; comp. Ps. xvii. 7, where the same absolute use of the participle "trusting" occurs (the "trustful" in general, believers). As in chap. xi. 7, and if possible even more distinctly than in that passage, we have expressed here a hope in the continuance of the individual life after death, and a just retribution in the future world. HITZIG, to avoid this admission, reads in accordance with the LXX (ἐν τῇ ἑαυτοῦ ὁσιότητι) בְּתֻמּוֹ, in his uprightness, "but in his innocence doth the righteous trust." But may not this divergent reading of the LXX owe its origin to the endeavor to gain an antithesis as exact as possible to the "in his wickedness" of the first clause? [RUEETSCHI (as last cited) preserves the recognition of a hope of immortality and also the poetical parallelism, by giving to the word "evil," רָעָה, a physical rather than an ethical meaning: "in his misfortune (or adversity) the wicked is overthrown, but the righteous has confidence even in his death." For the wicked all hope is gone. This seems to us a happy reconciliation of the grammatical and spiritual demands of the two parts of the verse.—A.]

Ver. 33. **In the heart of a man of understanding doth wisdom rest**, *i. e.* quietly, silently; comp. x. 14; xii. 16, 23, and for this use of the verb 1 Sam. xxv. 9.—**But in the midst of fools it maketh itself known**, *i. e.* not "fools draw out the wisdom of the wise," which is naturally quiet, in opposition to them and their folly (HITZIG), but, fools carry their wisdom, which is, however, in fact, only folly, always upon their tongues, and seek most assiduously to make it known (comp. xii. 23; xiii. 16; xv. 2). The expression is pointed and ironical, and yet not for that reason unintelligible, especially after expressions like those in vers. 8, 16, 24, *etc*. It is therefore unnecessary with the Chaldee version to supply the noun "folly" again with the verb.

Ver. 34. **Righteousness exalteth a nation.** Righteousness, צְדָקָה, is here used with a very comprehensive import, of religious and moral rectitude in every relation and direction, and is therefore not to be restricted, as it is by many recent commentators (UMBREIT, HITZIG, etc.), to the idea of virtue. Just as little is the idea of "exalting" to be identified with the idea of "honoring" (as ELSTER, HITZIG, etc., would have it); it is rather a general elevation and advancement of the condition of the people that is to be indicated by the term; comp. above, ver. 29.—**But sin is a reproach to the people.** —For the Aramaic term הֶסֶד, "shame," comp.

xxviii. 22 (also xxv. 10), and Job vi. 14. And yet in this national reproach and disgrace there is to be included the corresponding injury and misery of other kinds, so that in this view there is a certain justification for the Vulgate's rendering. "*miseros facit*" (which however rests upon the different reading יחסר; comp. the LXX and the Syr. vers.), and for LUTHER's "*Verderderben*," destruction.

Ver. 35. With clause *a* comp. xvi. 12.—**But his wrath will find out the base**,—lit., "his wrath will the base be;" comp., *e. g.*, xi. 1, where "his abomination" means the object of his abhorrence. To supply the preposition "to," ל, from clause *a*, is therefore needless (in opposition to the view of UMBREIT, BERTHEAU).

DOCTRINAL AND ETHICAL.

The representation of the entire chapter is plainly shaped by the contrast between the wise and the foolish, and it is only toward the end (vers. 20 sq.) that the kindred contrast between the rich and the poor, and at the very last (vers. 27 sq.) that between rulers and servants, is added.—Ethical truths to which a significant prominence is given, are contained especially in the following proverbs:

Ver. 1. The building of the house by the wisdom of woman. "Only the characteristic wisdom of *woman* (not that of the man) is able to build itself a house,' *i. e.*, to make possible a household in the true sense of the word; for the woman alone has the capacity circumspectly to look through the multitude of individual household wants, and carefully to satisfy them; and also because the various activities of the members of the family can be combined in a harmonious unity only by the influence, partly regulative and partly fostering, of a feminine character, gently but steadily efficient. But where there is wanting to the mistress of the house this wisdom attainable only by her and appropriate to her, then that is irrecoverably lost which first binds in a moral fellowship those connected by relationship of blood—that which makes the house from a mere place of abode to become the spiritual nursery of individuals organically associated." (ELSTER).

Ver. 6. The impossibility of uniting a frivolous disposition and jests at religion with true wisdom and understanding. "It is not by a one-sided action of the thinking power, but only by undivided consecration of the whole nature to God, which therefore involves above all other things a right relation of the spiritual nature to Him, that true knowledge in Divine things can be attained. The wise man, however, who has found the true beginning of wisdom, in bowing his inmost will before the Divine, not as something to be mastered by the understanding, but as something to be simply sought as a grace by the renunciation of the very self,—he can easily on this ground which God's own power makes productive, attain a rich development of the understanding." (ELSTER).

Ver. 10. The disturbing influence of an uninvited interference in the sorrow and the joy of one's neighbor. "Every one has his own circle of sorrows and joys, which his neighbor must leave to him as a quiet sanctuary for himself. For in the liveliest sympathy of which one may ever be conscious, it will still often be altogether impossible to enter into the peculiarity of others' sensibility with such a participation as is really beneficent. Therefore a Turkish proverb (in VON HAMMER, *Morgenl. Kleebl.*, p. 68) also says 'Eat thine own grief and trouble not thyself for another's'" (UMBREIT).—Comp. above, our exegetical notes on this passage.

Ver. 12. The self-deception of many men in regard to their courses, imagined to be healthful, but in reality leading to eternal ruin. Comp. MELANCHTHON: "The admonition relates to the mistiness and weakness of man's judgment, and his many and great errors in counsel, for it is manifest that men often err in judging and in their deliberations. Now they are deceived either by their own imaginations, or by the example of others, or by habit, *etc.*, and being deceived, they rush on all the more fascinated by the devil, as is written of Judas in John xiii. 27."

Ver. 14. The fool ever accumulating nothing but folly, and the wise man gaining in knowledge. Like ver. 24 this proverb is especially instructive with respect to the deep inner connection that exists on the one hand between foolish notions, and a poor, unattractive, powerless earthly position, destitute of all influence,—and on the other hand between true wisdom and large ability in the department both of the material and the spiritual. VON GERLACH pointedly says, "There is a certain power of attraction, according as a man is wise or foolish; the possessions also which the one or the other attains, are in accordance with his disposition."

Ver. 28. A sentiment directed against feeble princes who nevertheless array themselves with disproportionate splendor; and this, as also ver. 34, is designed to call attention to the principle, that it is not external and seeming advantages, but simply and solely the inward competence and moral excellence, whether of the head or of the members of a commonwealth, that are the conditions of its temporal welfare.

Ver. 31. Compassion to the poor is true service of God; comp. James i. 27. Since God has created both rich and poor (1 Sam. ii. 7), since He designs that they shall exist side by side and intermixed (Prov. xxii. 2), since the poor and lowly man is in like manner a being created in His image (James iii. 9), therefore he who deals heartlessly and violently with the poor insults that Being Himself who is the Maker and Ruler of all. The compassionate, on the contrary, discerns and honors His disposition toward His creatures, and the love which he manifests toward them, even the humblest and most unworthy, is in fact manifested toward God Himself; comp. Matth. xxv. 40.—Ver. 32. The confidence which the righteous man possesses even in his death. Compare the exegetical explanation of the passage.

HOMILETIC AND PRACTICAL.

Homily on the entire chapter: The wisdom and folly of men considered in their respective foundations, natures and results; and 1) within the sphere of *domestic* life (vers. 1-7); 2) within that of *civil* life (vers. 8-25); 3) within that of *political* or national life (vers. 26-35).—STÖCKER: Of human wisdom as the fruit of a right culture,—and 1) of the wisdom of *domestic* life (*prudentia œconomica*, vers. 1-25); 2) of the wisdom of public life (*prudentia politica*, vers. 26-35). STARKE: The results of piety and ungodliness 1) in the household, and in social life generally (1-25); 2) in the relations of rulers in particular (26-35).

Vers. 1-7. *Berleburg Bible:*—That wise women build their house, is to be understood not so much of the edifice consisting of wood, stone, plaster, as rather of the family and the household economy, which a wise woman always strives to keep in good condition and to improve. Ps. cxxvii. 1.—*Tübingen Bible* (on vers. 3): He who is wise keepeth his mouth and still more his heart, that he may not in connection with outward consideration and high dignities fall into pride.—(On ver. 4): He that doth not work also shall not eat; the poverty of many springs from this, that they lack industry and diligence.— STARKE (on ver. 6): He who in seeking wisdom has for his end pride and ambition, will never attain true wisdom, unless he changes his views. —(On ver. 7): Evil one always learns more quickly and easily than good; therefore avoid evil company.—[A. FULLER (on ver. 6): If our inquiries be influenced by a spirit of pride and self-sufficiency, we shall stumble at every thing we meet with; but he who knows his own weakness and conducts his inquiries with humility, shall find knowledge easy of attainment.— ARNOT: Those who reject the Bible want the first qualification of a philosopher, a humble and teachable spirit. The problem for man is not to reject all masters, but to accept the rightful One. Submission absolute to the living God, as revealed in the Mediator, is at once the best liberty that could be, and the only liberty that is.—TRAPP (on ver. 6): He that would have heavenly knowledge must first quit his heart of corrupt affections and high conceits.]

Vers. 8-17. *Tübingen Bible* (on ver. 8):— Steady watchfulness and attention to one's self is a great wisdom.—(On ver. 9): To make sport of sin is the height of wickedness.—STARKE (on ver. 10): He who knoweth the heart alone knoweth the needs of thy heart, which no other besides doth know. He can likewise give thee joy where no other can create it for thee.—(On ver. 16): Reverence and love to God must be with us the strongest motive to avoid sin.—(On ver. 17): Between the hasty trespasses of passionate natures, and the deliberate wickedness of malicious men, there is always a great distinction to be made.—VON GERLACH (on ver. 10): How hard it is to console and soothe others, Job's answers to the discourses of his friends are a signal illustration.—(On ver. 12): In connection with the deceptive, seductive show made by impiety, it is important to give more careful heed to one's way in life.—(On ver. 17): A man who quickly falls into a passion does indeed commit a folly, but yet is far preferable to the coldly and selfishly calculating villain. One may well be indignant at the first—the last makes himself odious.—[LORD BACON (*Advancement of Learning,*

Book VIII.), on vers. 8 and 15: He who applies himself to the true wisdom takes heed of his own ways, foreseeing dangers, preparing remedies, employing the assistance of the good, guarding himself against the wicked, cautious in entering upon a work, not unprepared for a retreat, watchful to seize opportunities, strenuous to remove impediments, and attending to many other things which concern the government of his own actions and proceedings. But the other kind of wisdom is entirely made up of deceits and cunning tricks, laying all its hope in the circumventing of others, and moulding them to its pleasure; which kind the proverb denounces as being not only dishonest, but also foolish, *etc.*—T. ADAMS (on ver. 9): Mocking is the medium or connection that brings together the fool and sin: thus he makes himself merry; they meet in mockery. Through many degrees men climb to that height of impiety. This is an extreme progress, and almost the journey's end of wickedness.—ARNOT (on ver. 10): The solitude of a human being in either extremity of the experiences of the human heart is sublime and solemnizing. Whether you are glad or grieved, you must be alone.—(On ver. 12): The result accords not with the false opinion, but with the absolute truth of the case. There is a way which is right, whatever it may seem to the world, and the end thereof is life. God's way of coming to us in mercy is also our way of coming to Him in peace.—(On ver. 15): Trust is a lovely thing; but it cannot stand unless it get truth to lean upon.—JOHN HOWE (on ver. 14): The good man is not the first fountain of happiness to himself, but a subordinate one a good man is, and so is satisfied from himself—a fountain fed from a higher fountain—by derivation from Him who is all in all, and more intimate to us than we ourselves. But the wicked man is the prime and first fountain of all misery to himself.—FLAVEL: The upright is satisfied from himself, that is, from his own conscience, which, though it be not the original spring, yet is the conduit at which he drinks peace, joy and encouragement.—R. SOUTH (on ver. 18): 30th of Posthumous Sermons].

Ver. 18-25. ZELTNER (on ver. 19): Bear patiently the pride of the ungodly; it lasts not long.—STARKE (on vers. 20, 21): The many promises that God will graciously reward kindness to the poor must make the Christian joyous and willing in labors of love.—(On ver. 22): Virtue and piety reward those who cherish them, but vices and sins cause nothing but pain and trouble.—GEIER (on ver. 23): Prating and boastful men are like an empty vessel; if one strike it, it does indeed give forth a sound, but for all that nothing goes in.—(On ver. 25): Be intent upon truth in thy words, gestures, acts, and in thy whole walk.

Vers. 26-35. STARKE (on ver. 28): It is the duty of the lords of the land to see to it that their land be well cultivated, and in particular that "mercy and truth dwell in the land, righteousness and peace kiss each other" (Ps. lxxxv. 11).—(On ver. 29): Impatience opposes the will of God, and is therefore the greatest folly.—(On ver. 30): Passion and wrath shorten the life, and care makes old before one's time.—(On ver. 31): Despise no man, be he ever so humble, for thou knowest not but in that act thou art despising a true child of God.—(On ver. 32): There is surely a future life to be hoped for after death; otherwise how could the righteous be so comforted in their death?—(On ver. 34): Sin is the cause of all misery under the sun.—(On ver. 35): If the fidelity of his subjects is pleasing to a king, how much more will God take pleasure if one serves Him faithfully and with the whole heart, through the strength of Jesus Christ!—[ARNOT (on ver. 25): The safety provided for God's children is confidence in Himself, the strong tower into which the righteous run.—(On ver. 31): The necessary dependence of human duty upon Divine faith.— S. DAVIES (on ver. 32): 1) Every righteous man has a substantial reason to hope, whether he clearly see it or not; 2) Good men in common do in fact enjoy a comfortable hope; 3) The hope which the righteous hath shall be accomplished. —SAURIN (on ver. 34): As there is nothing in religion to counteract the design of a wise system of civil polity, so there is nothing in a wise system of civil government to counteract the design of the Christian religion. The exaltation of the nation is the end of civil polity. Righteousness is the end of religion, or rather is religion itself. —EMMONS (on ver. 34): It is the nature of sin 1) to lessen and diminish a people; 2) to sink and depress the spirit of a people; 3) to destroy the wealth of a people; 4) to deprive them of the blessings of freedom; 5) to provoke the displeasure of God and draw down His judgments.]

e) With reference to various other relations and callings in life, especially within the sphere of the religious life.

CHAP. XV.

1   A soft answer turneth away wrath,
    but a bitter word stirreth up anger.
2   The tongue of the wise maketh knowledge attractive,
    but the mouth of fools poureth forth folly.
3   The eyes of Jehovah are in every place,
    beholding the wicked and the good.
4   A mild tongue is a tree of life,
    but transgression therewith is a wound in the spirit.
5   The fool despiseth his father's correction,
    but he that regardeth reproof is wise.
6   In the house of the righteous is a great treasure,
    but in the gain of the wicked is trouble.
7   The lips of the wise spread knowledge,
    but the heart of fools (doeth) not so.
8   The sacrifice of the wicked is abomination to Jehovah,
    but the prayer of the upright is his delight.
9   An abomination to Jehovah is the way of the wicked,
    but he loveth him that searcheth after righteousness.
10 There is sharp correction for him that forsaketh the way;
    he that hateth reproof must die.
11 Hell and the world of the dead are before Jehovah,
    how much more the hearts of the sons of men?
12 The scorner liketh not that one reprove him;
    to wise men will he not go.
13 A joyous heart maketh a cheerful countenance,
    but in sorrow of the heart the spirit is stricken.
14 An understanding heart seeketh after knowledge,
    but the face of fools feedeth on folly.
15 All the days of the afflicted are evil,
    but he that is of a joyful heart—a perpetual feast.
16 Better is little with the fear of Jehovah
    than great treasure and trouble with it.

17 Better is a dish of herbs, when love is there,
than a fatted ox and hatred with it.
18 A passionate man stirreth up strife,
but he that is slow to anger allayeth contention.
19 The way of the slothful is as a hedge of thorns,
but the path of the righteous is a highway.
20 A wise son maketh a glad father,
but a foolish man despiseth his mother.
21 Folly is joy to him that lacketh wisdom.
but the man of understanding goeth straight forward.
22 Failure of plans (cometh) where there is no counsel,
but by a multitude of counsellors they come to pass.
23 A man hath joy through the answer of his mouth,
and a word in due season, how good is it!
24 An upward path of life is the way of the wise
to depart from hell beneath.
25 The house of the proud will Jehovah destroy,
and he will establish the border of the widow.
26 An abomination to Jehovah are evil devices,
but pure (in his sight) are gracious words.
27 He troubleth his own house that seeketh unjust gain,
but he that hateth gifts shall live.
28 The heart of the righteous studieth to answer,
the mouth of the wicked poureth forth evil.
29 Jehovah is far from the wicked,
but the prayer of the righteous he heareth.
30 A friendly look rejoiceth the heart,
good tidings make the bones fat.
31 The ear that heareth the reproof of life
will abide among the wise.
32 He that refuseth correction despiseth himself,
but he that heedeth reproof getteth understanding.
33 The fear of Jehovah is a training to wisdom,
and before honor is humility.

GRAMMATICAL AND CRITICAL.

Ver. 1.—[דְּבַר־עֶצֶב undoubtedly means wrathful words, bitter words; GES. reaches this through a subjective meaning of עָצַב, labor, pain to the wrathful spirit; FUERST takes the objective, cutting words, that cause pain to their victim; the latter retains most of the radical meaning of the verb.—A.]

Ver. 2.—[הֵיטִיב, lit., maketh knowledge good; but the radical idea of the Heb. טוֹב is that which is good to the sense, especially sight; therefore bright, brilliant,—and afterward, that which is agreeable to other senses, hearing, taste, etc. The etymological meaning here best suits the sense "make knowledge appear attractive."—A.]

Ver. 5.—[BÖTT. (§ 1055, 111.), commenting on the three passages where the defective form יָרֻם occurs, proposes as the probable reading יְיָרֻם.—A.]

Ver. 6.—[נֶעְכָּרֶת (from עָכַר, chap. xi. 29) is a neuter partic. used substantively in the sense of ruin, destruction; comp. in Is. x. 25 נֶחֱרָצָה, and also מְחִתָּה in ver. 16 below.

[Ver. 7.—Masc. verb with the fem. שִׂפְתֵי, as in ver. 2; x. 21, 32.]

Ver. 9.—[BÖTT. (§ 412, 3) suggests rhythmical reasons for the peculiar and solitary form אֹהֵב, usually אָהֵב. Comp. GREEN, § 112, 5, c.—A.]

Ver. 15.—The construction is elliptical; טוֹב־לֵב is logically a genitive limiting the יְמֵי of clause a, and מִשְׁתֶּה is a predicate to it: "the days of him who is cheerful in heart are a feast," etc. Comp. HITZIG on the passage.

Ver. 21.—The Infin. לֶכֶת without לְ made dependent on the verb יְיַשֶּׁר (EWALD, Lehrb., § 285, a.)

Ver. 22.—The Infin. abs. הָפֵר is here naturally prefixed, instead of the finite verb, as e. g., in xii. 7. [Active used instead of passive, with an indefinite subject, in Hiphil and Piel as well as Kal. infinitives. See BÖTTCHER, § 990, 1, a.—A.]

Ver. 25.—Instead of וְיַצֵּב we must with HITZIG, etc., and in accordance with the anc. versions read וְיַצֵּב; for the optative rendering "and let him establish," etc. (BERTHEAU) does not agree with the parallelism. [BÖTT. regards it as a Jussive, expressing that necessity which is seen to be involved in the moral order of the world (§ 964, 7).—A.]

EXEGETICAL.

1. Vers. 1-7. Against sins of the tongue of various kinds.—**A soft answer turneth away wrath**,—lit., "bringeth or turneth back passion," comp. Is. ix. 11, 16, 20. The opposite of this "turning back" or "beating down" the violence of wrath is the "stirring it up," causing wrath to flash up or blaze out. Comp. Eccles. x. 4; Ps. xviii. 8, 9.—With the use of the epithet "soft, gentle" (רַךְ), comp. xxv. 15.—"A bitter word" (see critical notes) is more exactly "a word of pain," i. e., a smarting, offensive, violent word such as the passionate or embittered man speaks.

Ver. 2. **The tongue of the wise maketh knowledge attractive**, lit., "maketh knowledge good" (see critical notes); i. e., presents knowledge in apt, well arranged and winning ways (comp. xxx. 29; Is. xxiii. 16). In contrast with this "the fool's mouth poureth forth folly," i. e., in its repulsively confused and noisy utterances, brings to view not wisdom and true discernment, but only folly. "Poureth forth," a decidedly stronger expression than "proclaimeth," chap. xii. 23.

Ver. 3. Comp. 2 Chron. xvi. 9; Ecclesiast. xv. 19; xvii. 16; xxiii. 28; also Ps. cxxxix. 1 sq.; Matt. x. 30; Heb. iv. 13.

Ver. 4. **Gentleness of the tongue is a tree of life.**—With this use of the noun rendered "gentleness" (not "health") comp. xiv. 30, and for the expression "tree of life," xi. 30.—**But transgression therewith is a wound in the spirit.**—The noun כֶּלֶף probably does not here mean "perverseness" (BERTHEAU; E. V., etc.), but apparently "trespass, transgression," which seems to be its meaning also in chap. xi. 3 (comp. HITZIG). Transgression with the tongue is, however, probably not here falsehood (LUTHER, and the older commentators; comp. EWALD, "falling with the tongue"), but its misuse in the exciting of strife and contention, and so "irritation, excitement" (UMBREIT, ELSTER). "A wound in the spirit," i. e., disturbance and destruction by restless passion of the regulated and normal state of the spirit; comp. Is. lxv. 14.— HITZIG conjectures a corruption of the text, and therefore translates the second clause in partial accordance with the LXX, Syriac and Chaldee versions, "and whoso eateth its fruit (the tree of life), stretcheth himself comfortably (!?).— [RUEETSCHI (as before cited, p. 143) carries the idea of gentleness through the two clauses as the central idea; "it is precisely with this gentle speech which otherwise does so much good, that the wicked is wont to deceive, and then one is by this more sorely and deeply stricken and distressed than before."—A.]

Ver. 5. Comp. i. 7; xiii. 1.—**But he that regardeth reproof is wise** (reproof on the part of his father, or in general from his parents). For this verb, "is wise, prudent, dealeth prudently," comp. xix. 25; 1 Sam. xxiii. 22.

—Ver. 6. **In the house of the righteous is a great treasure**,—lit., "house of the righteous," probably an accusative of place. The treasure stored up in such a house is the righteousness that prevails in it, a source and pledge of abiding prosperity. [HOLDEN and some others make the earthly treasure too prominent, as though the direct teaching of the verse were that "temporal prosperity attends the righteous." We find in the verse rather an import that holds equally good in the absence of outward abundance.—A.] The direct opposite of this is the "trouble" that is found in the gains of the wicked.—Ver. 7. With clause *a* compare x. 31. [A rendering of יְזָרוּ is urged by RUEETSCHI, that is more in keeping with its general import, and particularly its meaning in chap. xx. 8, 26, *viz.*: to "sift," or "winnow;" the lips of the wise *sift* knowledge, separating the chaff, preserving the pure grain. —A.]—**But the heart of fools (doeth) not so**, *i. e.*, with him it is quite otherwise than with the heart of the wise man which spreads abroad wisdom and knowledge; a suggestion, brief indeed but very expressive, of the mighty difference between the influences that go forth from the wise man and the fool. HITZIG, to avoid this interpretation of לֹא־כֵן, which, as he thinks, is "intolerably flat," explains the expression in accordance with Is. xvi. 6, by "that which is not so as it is asserted to be," and therefore by "error or falsehood;" he therefore takes this as an accusative object to the verb "spread abroad," which is to be supplied from clause *a*. The LXX and Syr. adopt still another way, according to which כֵּן is an adjective with the meaning "sure, right,"—"the fool's heart is not sure," not certain of its matters, and therefore incompetent to teach others (so also BERTHEAU). This last explanation is doubtless possible, and yet the first seems at all events the simplest and most obvious. [This is also the rendering of the E. V., *etc.*; S., N., M., W. agree substantially with the last view, but differ in the grammatical connection of the word "sound, right," S. and M. making it a predicative epithet, N. and W. making it the object, "what is not sound," "folly."—A.]

2. Vers. 8-15. Of God's abhorrence of the wicked heart of the ungodly.—With ver. 8 comp. xxi. 27; xxviii. 9; also ver. 29 below. "Sacrifice" and "prayer" are not here contrasted as the higher and the lower [so BURGON, quoted by WORDSWORTH]; but "sacrifice" is a gift to God, "prayer" is desiring from Him. Comp. Is. i. 11, 15, and besides passages like Hos. vi. 6; Mic. vi. 6-8; Jer. vii. 21; Ps. xl. 6 (7); li. 17 (18), *etc*.—Ver. 9 stands in the relation, as it were, of an explanation of or a reason for ver. 8; comp. xi. 20; xii. 22.—**But he loveth him that searcheth after righteousness.**— "Searcheth after" ["pursueth," as it were, Piel part.], stronger than "followeth," chap. xxi. 21; comp. xi. 19; also Deut. xvi. 20; Ps. xxxiv. 14 (15).

Ver. 10. (There is) **sharp correction for him that forsaketh the way**, lit., "is to the one forsaking the path," *i. e.*, the man that turns aside from the right way (comp. ii. 13).—**He that hateth reproof must die**,—lit., "will die." Comp. Rom. viii. 13. This "death" is the very "sharp correction" mentioned in the first clause, just as he who hates correction is identical with the man who forsakes the way. Comp. x. 17.—Ver. 11. **Hell** (Sheol) **and the world of the dead are before Jehovah,**—*i. e.*, are not concealed from Him, lie open and uncovered before His view, comp. Ps. cxxxix. 8; Job xxvi. 6. In the latter passage אֲבַדּוֹן, lit. "place of destruction, abyss of the pit" stands, as it does here, as a synonym of Sheol; so likewise in Prov. xxvii. 20.—**How much more** (אַף כִּי as in xi. 37) **the hearts of the sons of men**; comp. Jer. xvii. 10; Heb. iv. 13.—Observe furthermore how this proverb also stands related to the next preceding, giving its reason, as in vers. 8 and 9.

Ver. 12. **To wise men doth he not go**; among them he will find deliverance from his folly—by stern reproof, it is true, and censure and reprimand; comp. xiii. 1, 20. HITZIG unnecessarily proposes to read, with the LXX, "with" instead of "to," "with wise men he doth not associate."

Ver. 13. **A joyous heart maketh the countenance cheerful.**—The verb "maketh good" (ver. 2), "maketh pleasant" is here equivalent to "brighteneth."—**But in sorrow of the heart is the spirit stricken.**—Others, UMBREIT, HITZIG, *etc.*, render "is the breath oppressed, made laborious." It is true that in this way there is produced a better parallelism with the "cheerful countenance" in clause *a*. But in chap. xvii. 22 also (comp. Isa. lxvi. 2) a "broken spirit" is described by this phrase, and not a labored breathing; and instances in which, instead of the outward effect, the inward cause which underlies it is named in the second clause, are by no means unknown elsewhere; comp. x. 20; xii. 22, *etc.*

Ver. 14. With clause *a* compare xiv. 33.— **The face of fools feedeth on folly.**—The K'ri and the ancient versions read פִּי (mouth) instead of פְּנֵי (face) for which reason many moderns adopt the same reading, *e. g.*, BERTHOLD [DE W., BERTHEAU, E V, S., N., M., H., who plead not only the authority of the Versions, but the singular number in the verb, and the greater naturalness of the expression]. But as in Ps. xxvii. 8, a "seeking" is predicated of the face [according to the rendering of HITZIG, in which he stands almost alone, "seek him, my face,"— while the vast majority of interpreters make God's face the object sought], so here there might very fitly be ascribed to the face a "feeding on something," a *pasci*, especially as this verb is here employed only in a figurative way, to denote dealing with a matter (comp. xiii. 20). [FUERST (Lex., *sub verbo*) takes the verb in quite a different sense; he makes a second radical meaning to be "to unite with," and then "to delight in." He also recognizes distinctly the use of this plural noun with verbs in the singular. See also NORDHEIMER, *Heb. Gram.* § 759, 3, *a.*—A.].

Ver. 15. **All the days of the afflicted are evil.**—עָנִי is here not the outwardly distressed, the poor, but the inwardly burdened and afflicted, as the parallel in clause *b* shows.— **But he that is of a joyful heart** (hath) **a perpetual feast,**—or, a perpetual feast are his days. The meaning of the verse is a tolerably exact parallel to ver. 13. [To this view of the ver. RUEETSCHI (as above, p. 144) objects that the very general *usus loquendi* refers עָנִי to outward circumstances, and when inward conditions are described by this term it is never in the way of depreciation, other terms being used to describe distress. He renders "all the days of a poor man are (indeed) evil (in regard to his outward circumstances); but whosoever is of a joyful heart has (nevertheless) a continual feast."—A.].

3. Vers. 16-23. Of various other virtues and vices.—With 16, *a*, comp. chap. xvi. 8.—**Than great treasure and trouble with it.**—Trouble, θόρυβος, here probably not the anxiety which apprehends losing the treasure again (BERTHEAU), but the care which accumulated the wealth, and constantly seeks to increase it, Ps. xxxix. 6 (7), (HITZIG). [RUEETSCHI observing the more general use of the noun, understands it to refer to the confusion and disorder in human society attendant upon riches without the fear of God.—A.].

Ver. 17. **Better is a dish of herbs, when love is there,**—literally, "a portion of green," *i. e.*, vegetables (Jer. xl. 5; lii. 24; 2 Kings xxv. 30). Vegetables represent simple fare in general (comp. Dan. i. 2), while meat, as always and every where in the East, is holiday fare, especially the flesh of fatted oxen (Luke xv. 23, 30).—Observe, furthermore, how the verse before us exhibits on the one hand a meaning exactly parallel to the preceding, while on the other hand it presents a climax to its ideas (fear of God—love to one's neighbor; trouble— hate).—As a substantial parallel compare the proverb in MEIDANI II. 422: "Want with love is better than hatred with riches."—With ver. 18 comp. above, ver. 1, as also xxvi, 21; xxviii. 25; xxix. 22; Ecclesiast. xxviii. 11-13.

Ver. 19. **The way of the slothful is as a hedge of thorns,** *i. e.*, because he is always encountering obstacles and hinderances, does not come away having accomplished his life's work, but must find his foot every where entangled and kept back. [The special aptness of this figure in Palestine is amply illustrated in HACKETT's *Scripture Illustrations,* THOMSON's *The Land and the Book, etc.*—A]. It is otherwise with the "upright," *i. e.*, the man who unmoved and unremitting goes about the performance of his duty, and continues with vigorous efficiency in the work of his calling. His way is, according to clause *b*, "built up," *i. e.*, lit raised by throwing up a ridge (Isa. lvii. 14; lxii. 10; Jer. xviii. 15, *etc.*), a way which leads easily and surely to its end.—HITZIG without any necessity reads עָרִיץ for עָצֵל, to obtain as he thinks a more appropriate antithesis to the word "upright," (יְשָׁרִים). But that the slothful may be very fitly contrasted with the upright or righteous, appears abundantly from proverbs like x. 26; xxviii. 19; vi. 10, *etc.*

Ver. 20. With clause *a* compare the literally identical first half of x. 1.—**But a foolish man,** lit. "a fool of a man;" comp. xxi. 20, and the similarly constructed expression "a wild ass of a man," Gen. xvi. 12. BERTHEAU wrongly renders "the most foolish of men."

Ver. 21. **Folly** (here unreasonable conduct, senseless action) **is joy to him that lacketh wisdom.** Comp. x. 23.—**Goeth straight forward**, lit. "maketh straight to go." Going straight forward is naturally acting rightly in moral and religious matters.

Ver. 22. (There is) **Failure of plans where there is no counsel.** Literally, "a breaking of plans" is, comes to pass, "where no counsel is." For the meaning comp. xi. 14, especially also with respect to clause b.—**They come to pass,** i. e., the plans. The singular of the verb is used in the Heb. distributively, as in chap. iii. 18 (see notes there).

Ver. 23. **A man hath joy through the answer of his mouth, and a word in due season, how good is it!** That the second clause cannot be antithetic to the first (HITZIG), but stands as its explanation or its climax is evident; for the "word in its time" is just the "answer" of clause a, exciting joy because apt and exactly meeting the inquiry.—Comp. furthermore parallels like x. 20, 31, 32, etc.

4. Vers. 24-33. Of several other virtues especially of the religious life.—**An upward path of life is the way of the wise;** lit. "a path of life upward is to the wise," i. e., the man of understanding walks in a way which as a way of life leads ever upward, to ever higher degrees of moral purity, elevation and power, but also in the same ratio to an ever-increasing prosperity. A reference to heaven as the final limit of this upward movement of the life of the righteous is so far forth indirectly included, as the antithesis to the "upward;" the "hell beneath" (hell downwards, hell to which one tends downward), suggests a hopeless abode in the dark kingdom of the dead, as the final destination of the sinner's course of life. Therefore we have here again the idea of future existence and retribution (comp. xi. 7 ; xiv. 32)—a meaning which BERTHEAU and HITZIG seek in vain to take from the proverb. Comp. ELSTER on this passage.

Ver. 25. **The house of the proud will Jehovah destroy.** For the verb comp. ii. 22. By "house" is here meant not the mere dwelling, but also the family of the proud, just as in xiv. 11; compare also xiv. 1.—**And establisheth the border of the widow,** i. e., the innocent widow who is in danger of being wronged by the proud through encroachment upon her borders. Comp. moreover with this expression Deut. xxxii. 8.

Ver. 26. Compare xi. 20.—**But pure (in His sight) are gracious words,** here probably specifically words sweetly consoling, words of love and compassion toward troubled souls, comp. xvi. 24. Such words are in Jehovah's judgment pure or precious, i. e., with a pure and genuine ring; comp. Ps. xix. 8, 9 (9, 10).—HITZIG proposes instead of טְהוֹרִים to read טֹפְלִים [adhere, cleave] from which comes the meaning strengthening the antithesis of the parallel: "and pleasant words cleave fast (?)."

Ver. 27. **He troubleth his own house that seeketh unjust gain.** For the last expression "spoileth spoil," i. e., goes after unlawful gains, seeks plunder, comp. i. 19; for the former phrase "disturb or trouble the house," xi. 29. The sentence as a whole seems to be aimed especially at unjust judges, who are willing to be bribed by gifts, in contrast with the judge that "hates gifts," and so is incorruptible and unchangeably upright; comp. xxviii. 16.

Ver. 28. **The heart of the righteous studieth to answer,** i. e., reflects upon its answers with all care, that it may utter nothing evil or perverse, while the wicked thoughtlessly "pours forth" his evil and perverse thoughts (pours forth, comp. ver. 2); compare Matth. xii. 35.—With ver. 29 comp. ver. 8.

Ver. 30. **A friendly look rejoiceth the heart.** Lit. "lustre of the eyes:" it denotes, like the "light of the countenance" in chap. xvi. 15, the cheerful beaming of the eye of the friendly, which exerts on one's neighbor also an influence refreshing to the heart, especially at the time when, as clause b indicates, it communicates a "good message," "joyful tidings" (comp. xxv. 25). For this "rich nourishing of the bones" (lit., making fat), comp. xi. 28; xiii. 4; also xvi. 24.—In this conception of the verse which is the simplest and on all sides well guaranteed, according to which clause b only defines more exactly the import of clause a, there is no need either of giving an objective cast to the idea of "brightness to the eye," as though it meant "friendly recognition" (LUTHER, DE WETTE, BERTHEAU), or of changing מַרְאֵה to מְאוֹר (HITZIG).

Ver. 31. **The ear that heareth the reproof of life,** i. e., reproof which has true life for its end, which points out the way to it, and for that very reason already in advance has life in itself and imparts it.—**Will abide among the wise,** i. e., will itself become wise (xiii. 20), and therefore permanently belongs to the circle of the wise. For this verb to "abide" (לִין), lit. to pass the night, i. e., to tarry long at some place, comp. Ps. xxv. 13; xlix. 12 (13); Job xix. 4. The ear here stands by synecdoche for the hearer, as in Job xxix. 11; Ex. x. 26; 1 Kings xix. 18.

Ver. 32. **He that refuseth correction despiseth himself,** lit. "undervalues, lightly values his soul," in so far as he does not ensure life, in so far as, without knowing and willing it, he loves death more than life (comp. viii. 36).—**But he that heedeth reproof getteth understanding;** comp. iv. 5, 7; xvi. 1. The man who "getteth understanding" is, however, according to xix. 8 the very man who does not hate his own soul but loves it.

Ver. 33. With clause a compare i. 7; ix. 10.—**And before honor is humility.** Humility here plainly appears as the necessary correlate to the fear of God, and as a chief manifestation of wisdom, which is elsewhere named as that which confers honor, e. g., iii. 16; viii. 18. Compare xviii. 12, b, where the second clause of the verse before us occurs again —The entire verse, by virtue of its somewhat general character, is equally well adapted to close a long series of proverbs, and to open a new section. It is therefore unnecessary, as HITZIG does, to transfer it to the following chapter, and to regard it as a sort of superscription to the second half of that division of the Book of Proverbs in which we now are (chap. xvi.-xxii.).

DOCTRINAL AND ETHICAL.

Among the proverbs of the chapter before us, which hardly admit of a grouping according to any well-established, clearly conspicuous principle of classification (comp. the four divisions which are distinguished in the "Exegetical Notes:" vers. 1-7; 8-15; 16-23; 24-33), several stand out as of no slight theological and soteriological importance,—especially the beautiful reference to the omniscience of God, the holy and righteous Ruler, in ver. 3 and ver. 11,—and the twice repeated emphasizing of the religious worthlessness of outward shows of reverence for God, without true devotion and consecration in the heart, vers. 8 and 29. The last mentioned truth is among the favorite ideas of the enlightened prophetic teachers and men of God in the Old Testament; (compare the parallel passages cited above in connection with vers. 8). It lets the clear light of that evangelical saving grace, which was already operative under the economy of the law, but which only in Christ rose as a full-orbed sun, shine with quite peculiar brightness on the dark ground of Old Testament life. In this connection there is, it is true, the distinction to be made (noticed above under ver. 8) between "sacrifice" and "prayer;" that the former term describes a gift brought to God, the latter a desire directed to Him. Yet this is by no means an essential difference; for both, sacrifice and prayer, which indeed falls likewise under the category of offering in the broadest sense (Ps. cxix. 105; Heb. xiii. 15), come under consideration here only as general tokens of reverence for God; and the value of both is clearly defined by this test, whether the state of heart in those who bring them is or is not well pleasing to God (comp. Isa. xxix. 13; Matt. xv. 7 sq.); in other words, whether the offering brought is a purely outward act, or the fruit of a sincere self-consecration of the entire personality in spirit and in truth, a "reasonable service" in the sense of Rom. xii. 1.

Closely related to the scope of these proverbs is what was said above, on ver. 17, of the worthlessness of outward shows of beneficence, especially free hospitality without inward love (comp. 1 Cor. xiii. 2).—Furthermore a specially serious consideration is due to the warnings against low greed and avarice, as leading, nevertheless, to the destruction of one's own home: ver. 6 and 27; to the repeated allusions to the necessity that one readily submit himself to reproof and correction for his faults: vers. 5, 10, 12, 31, 32; to the beautiful commendation of humility as the first step to true honor: ver. 33; and finally to the reiterated reference to the righteous judgment of God, which reaches its completion only in the life to come: ver. 25 (see notes on this passage).

HOMILETIC AND PRACTICAL.

Homily on the entire chapter: Right sensibility or a pure heart the only true service of God (1 Sam. xv. 22), demonstrated 1) in good and perverse conduct with the mouth and tongue (ver. 1-7); 2) in proper worship or the religious life (ver. 8-15); 3) in the intercourse of man with his neighbors (vers. 16-33).—Or again; Love (to God and men) as the germ and the true norm of all religious rectitude (Hos. vi. 6; Matt. ix. 13; xii. 7).—Comp. STÖCKER: How true prudence (wisdom) must guard man against sins 1) of the tongue (1-9); 2) of the heart and the hands (10-22); 3) against other sins of various kinds (23-33).—In a similar way WOHLFARTH: The effect of prudence; a means of guarding one's self against sins of various kinds.

Ver. 1-7. STARKE (on vers. 1, 2); when genuine piety exists there will not be wanting other manifestations of friendliness and gentleness. Even where there is occasion for earnestness in the punishment of transgressions, a friendly spirit must still be combined with it. Earnestness without friendship profits as little as friendliness without earnestness — GEIER (on ver. 3): If God knows all things then He knows also His children's need, and is intent on their help and deliverance.—(On ver. 5): If even to the most capable and powerful spirits there is still need of good discipline and instruction, how much more to the indolent and drowsy!—(On ver. 6): In connection with temporal blessings be intent upon righteousness in their attainment, contentment in their possession, prudence and system in their employment, submission in their loss!—[ARNOT (on ver. 1): Truth alone may be hated, and love alone despised; man will flee from the one and trample on the other; but when truth puts on love, and love leans on truth, in that hallowed partnership lies the maximum of moral power within the reach of man in the present world.—TRAPP (on ver. 6): Every righteous man is a rich man, whether he hath more or less of the things of this life. For *first*, he hath plenty of that which is precious. *Secondly,* propriety: what he hath is his own].

Vers. 8-10. CRAMER (on ver. 8): It is not works that make the man good, but when the man is justified, then his works are also good; God in His grace makes well-pleasing to Himself the works that come of faith, even though great imperfections still mingle with them.—STARKE (on ver. 11): The doctrine of God's omniscience is already in the Old Testament revealed frequently enough, and so clearly that no one can excuse himself on the ground of ignorance concerning it.—(On ver. 12): He is wise who gladly associates with those from whom he can learn something, though it be disagreeable to the flesh to do so.—ZELTNER (on vers. 13 sq.): He is the most prosperous man who possesses the treasure of a good conscience and seeks to preserve it; be can always be joyful in God (Acts xxiv. 16).—WOHLFARTH (vers. 13-17): *The joyous heart.* What can all the good things of this earth profit us when our inner nature is in trouble and our countenance sad? How rich are we, even with little earthly possession, if we only possess the one good of a conscience at peace, and a heart joyful in God!—VON GERLACH (on ver. 19): The sluggard lets his paths grow over, i. e., his means of acquisition go to waste, and his resources decay.—[CHARNOCK (on ver. 11): God knows the whole state of the dead—things that seem to be out of all being; He knows the thoughts of the devils and damned creatures, whom He hath cast out of His care forever into the arms of His justice; much more is He acquainted with the thoughts of living men, etc.]

Vers. 20-33. HASIUS (on vers. 22, 23): Many eyes see more than one, and many souls think more than one; therefore never esteem thyself so wise that thou shouldst not seek others' counsel. . . . A good thought on which one falls at the right time is not to be valued with much gold.—WOHLFARTH (on vers. 22-26): Important as it is in general that one testify the truth, as important is the way in which this is done.—VON GERLACH (on ver. 24): The very direction of the way which the wise enters saves him from extreme disasters; it leads toward God, toward the kingdom of eternal light, welfare and life.— (On ver. 33): Honor one can attain in the way of truth only by giving honor to the Lord alone, i. e., by profound humility (1 Peter v. 6).—J. LANGE: True humility consists not in all manner of outward gestures, but in the fact that one in perfect self-denial agree with the will of God, Luke i. 38.—[W. BATES (on ver. 33): Humility preserves the true and noble freedom of the mind of man, secures his dear liberty and peaceful dominion of himself. This is the effect of excellent wisdom].

2. *Admonition to a walk in the fear of God and obedience.*

CHAP. XVI. 1.—XXII. 16.

a) Admonition to trust in God as the wise Ruler and Governor of the world.

CHAP. XVI.

1   Man's are the counsels of the heart,
    but the answer of the tongue is Jehovah's.
2   All the ways of a man are pure in his own eyes,
    but Jehovah weigheth the spirits.
3   Commit thy works to Jehovah,
    so will thy plans be established.
4   Jehovah hath made every thing for its end,
    even the wicked for the day of evil.
5   An abomination to Jehovah is every one who is proud in heart,
    assuredly he will not go unpunished.
6   By mercy and truth is iniquity atoned,
    and through the fear of Jehovah one departeth from evil.
7   If Jehovah hath pleasure in the ways of a man,
    he maketh even his enemies to be at peace with him.
8   Better is a little with righteousness,
    than great revenues without right.
9   Man's heart deviseth his way,
    but Jehovah directeth his steps.
10 Decision belongeth to the lips of the king,
    in judgment his mouth speaketh not wickedly.
11 The scale and just balances belong to Jehovah,
    His work are all the weights of the bag.
12 It is an abomination to kings to commit wickedness,
    for by righteousness is the throne established.
13 A delight to kings are righteous lips,
    and he that speaketh uprightly is loved.
14 The wrath of a king (is as) messengers of death,
    but a wise man appeaseth it.
15 In the light of the king's countenance is life,
    and his favor is as a cloud of the latter rain.
16 To gain wisdom—how much better is it than gold!
    and to attain understanding to be preferred to silver!

17 The path of the upright departeth from evil;
   he preserveth his soul that giveth heed to his way.
18 Before destruction cometh pride,
   and before a fall a haughty spirit.
19 Better is it to be humble with the lowly,
   than to divide spoil with the proud.
20 He that giveth heed to the word findeth good,
   and he who trusteth Jehovah, blessed is he!
21 The wise in heart shall be called prudent,
   and grace on the lips increaseth learning.
22 Understanding is a fountain of life to him that hath it,
   but the correction of fools is folly.
23 The heart of the wise maketh his mouth wise,
   and increaseth learning upon his lips.
24 As honey of the comb are pleasant words,
   sweet to the soul and health to the bones.
25 There is a way that seemeth right to man,
   but its end are ways of death.
26 The spirit of the laborer laboreth for him,
   for his mouth urgeth him on.
27 A worthless man searcheth after evil,
   and on his lips is as it were scorching fire.
28 A perverse man sendeth abroad strife,
   and a backbiter separateth friends.
29 A violent man enticeth his neighbor,
   and leadeth him in a way that is not good.
30 Shutting his eyes to devise mischief,
   biting his lips, he bringeth evil to pass.
31 A crown of glory is the hoary head;
   in the way of righteousness it shall be found.
32 He that is slow to anger is better than the mighty,
   and he that ruleth his spirit than he that taketh a city.
33 The lot is cast into the lap,
   but from Jehovah is all its decision.

GRAMMATICAL AND CRITICAL.

Ver. 1.—In בַּיהוָה the כְּ stands as simply synonymous with the לְ *auctoris* of the first clause.

Ver. 3.—[A masc. verb agreeing with the fem. subject מַחְשְׁבֹתֶיךָ, which is less unnatural where the verb precedes; see Bött., § 936, a.—A.]

Ver. 4.—[לַמַּעֲנֵהוּ distinguished by the article and the daghesh as the noun מַעֲנֶה with preposition and suffix, and not the comp. preposition לְמַעַן with a suffix. See Green, *Heb. Gram.*, § 246, 2, a.—A.]

Ver. 7.—יַשְׁלִם, Hiph. Imperf. written *defective*. Bött. suggests the proper reading as יַשְׁלִם "absimilated" from the following ן. See § 1013.—A.]

Ver. 13.—[Ordinarily feminine forms of adjectives are employed in Hebrew to supply the lack of neuter and abstract forms. Occasionally as in יְשָׁרִים masc. forms are used in elevated style. See Bött., § 707, 2.—A.]

Ver. 16.—[Both the masc. and fem. forms of the Infin. constr. are here used, קְנֹה and קְנוֹת, but with a masc. predicate, the Niph. part. נִבְחָר, which has here the meaning of the Latin part. in *dus*. Bött., §§ 930, 3, β, and 997, 2, c.—A.] For examples of the form קְנֹה comp. xxi. 3; xxxi. 4.

Ver. 19.—שָׁפָל in שְׁפַל־רוּחַ is here probably not to be regarded as the adjective, as in xxix. 23; Is. lvii. 15 (so Bertheau, Elster, and others regard it), but an Infinitive, which is therefore equivalent to *humiliari* (Vulgate, comp. Ewald, Umbreit, Hitzig, *etc.*) For in the second clause an Infin. is the corresponding term: חַלֵּק שָׁלָל, "to divide spoil;" comp. with this Is. liii. 12. [Fuerst, however (*Lex.*, *sub verbo*), pronounces decidedly in favor of the adjective construction. Bött. regards it as an Infin., § 987, b, a.—A.]

Ver. 20.—הַשְׂכִּיל appears in Neh. viii. 13 construed with אֶל instead of עַל: compare, however, for this interchange of אֶל and עַל chaps. xxix. 5; Jer. vi. 10, 19, *etc.*

Ver. 27.—שְׂפָתָיוֹ is one of the few instances in which in the Masoretic punctuation a dual or plural form is disregarded in the vocalization of the suffix. Cases of the opposite kind are not rare. Bött., § 886, c. The LXX conform to the K'thibh.—A.]

Ver. 28.—נִרְגָּן (ψίθυρος, Ecclesiast. v. 14), is cognate with נָרַד, a verb which in the Arabic means *susurro*, to whisper.

Ver. 30.—עָצָה, related to עָצַם, *clausit*, is found only here in the Old Testament. [It is a gesture accompanying and expressive of crafty scheming; FUERST, s. v.]

Ver. 33.—For the impersonal use of the passive יוּטַל with the accusative, comp. Gen. iv. 18; xvii. 6; Jos. vii. 15; Ps. lxxii. 15, *etc.*

EXEGETICAL.

1. Vers. 1–3. Of God as the wise disposer and controller of all things in general.—**Man's are the counsels of the heart, but the answer of the tongue is Jehovah's.**—The "answer of the tongue" might indeed of itself signify the answer corresponding to the tongue, *i. e.*, the supplicating tongue, and so denote "the granting of man's request" (ELSTER, comp. UMBREIT, BERTHEAU, *etc.*) But since the *heart* with its hidden plans and counsels (lit., "arrangements:" מַעַרְכֵי, equivalent to the more common fem. מַעַרָכוֹת) is here plainly contrasted with the tongue as the instrument in the disclosure of such plans (comp. x. 8; xiv. 20, and numerous exx.), therefore the "answer of the tongue" must here be "the movement and utterance of the tongue," and Jehovah comes into the account as the giver of right words, from which health and life go forth, as the dispenser of the wholesome "word in due season" (chap. xv. 23); comp. Matth. x. 19, 20; also Rom. viii. 26; 2 Cor. iii. 5. LUTHER therefore renders correctly "But from the Lord cometh what the tongue shall speak;" in general HITZIG is also right, except that he would unnecessarily read "to" Jehovah לְ instead of לְ‍, and so thinks too exclusively of Jehovah merely as the judge of the utterances of man's tongue. The idea "Man proposes, God disposes" (*der Mensch denkt, Gott lenkt*), forms moreover quite as naturally the proper subject of discourse in the verse before us, as below in vers. 9 and 33. [Our English version sacrifices entirely the antithetic nature and force of the verse.—A.]

Ver. 2. **All the ways of a man are pure in his own eyes**, *i. e.*, according to his own judgment, comp. xii. 15. Lit., "something clean;" comp. EWALD, *Lehrb.*, § 307, c. — **But Jehovah weigheth the spirits**, *i. e.*, he tries them, not literally ponderable, with reference to their moral weight; he wishes to test their moral competence. The "ways" and the "spirits" here stand contrasted as the outward action and the inward disposition; comp. 1 Sam. xvi. 7. In the parallel passage, chap. xxi. 2, "hearts" (לִבּוֹת) occurs instead of "spirits" (רוּחוֹת) (compare also xxi. 12) and "right" (יָשָׁר) instead of "clean" (זַךְ).

Ver. 3. **Commit thy works to Jehovah.** —For this phrase to "roll something on some one," *i. e.*, to commit and entrust it wholly to him, comp. Ps. xxii. 8 (9), also xxxvii. 5 (where עַל is used instead of אֶל, "upon" instead of "to").—**So will thy plans be established.** —*i. e.*, thy thoughts and purposes, those according to which thou proposest to shape thy "works," will then have a sure basis and result. Comp. xix. 21; Ps. xc. 17.

2. Vers. 4-9. God's wise and righteous administration in respect to the rewarding of good and the punishment of evil.—**Jehovah hath made everything for its end.**—The noun מַעֲנֶה here signifies, not "answer," as in ver. 1, or in xv. 1, 23; but in general that which corresponds with the thing, the *end* of the thing. The suffix refers back to the "all, all things." The Vulgate renders "*propter semet ipsum*," but this would have לְמַעֲנוֹ. [See critical notes. BERTHEAU, KAMPH., DE W., N., S., M., *etc.*, agree with our author in the interpretation which is grammatically most defensible, and doctrinally least open to exception. An absolute Divine purpose and control in the creation and administration of the world is clearly announced, and also the strength of the bond that joins sin and misery.—A.]—**Even the wicked for the day of evil**, *i. e.*, to experience the day of evil, and then to receive His well merited punishment. It is not specifically the day of final judgment that is directly intended (as though the doctrine here were that of a predestination of the ungodly to eternal damnation, as many of the older Reformed interpreters held), but any day of calamity whatsoever, which God has fixed for the ungodly, whether it may overtake him in this or in the future life. Comp. the "day of destruction," Job xxi. 30; the "day of visitation," Is. x. 3. [HOLDEN'S rendering "even the wicked He daily sustains," is suggested by his strong aversion to the doctrine of reprobation, but is not justified by the use of the Hebrew phrase, or by the slightest requirement or allowance in the parallelism. Liberal interpreters like NOYES find not the slightest reason for following him. —A.]

Ver. 5. With clause *a* compare xv. 9, 25, 26; with *b*, xi. 21.—In regard to the two verses interpolated by the LXX (and Vulgate) after ver. 5, see HITZIG on this passage.

Ver. 6. **By mercy and truth is iniquity atoned.**—"Mercy and truth" here unquestionably, as in chap. iii. 3 (where see notes), describes a relation of man to his neighbor, and not to God, as BERTHEAU maintains (see in reply to his view especially HOFFMANN'S *Schriftbew.*, I., 518 sq.). [Nor is it God's mercy and truth, as HOLDEN suggests]. Loving and faithful conduct towards one's neighbor is, however, plainly not in and of itself named as the ground of the expiation of sin, but only so far forth as it is a sign and necessary expression of a really penitent and believing disposition of heart, and so is a correlative to the fear of God, which is made prominent in the second clause; just as in the expression of Jesus with reference to the sinning woman; Luke vii. 47; or as in Isa. lviii. 7; Dan iv. 24, *etc.*—**One departeth from evil,** lit., "there is remaining far from evil," *i. e.*, this is the result: so ver. 17.—"Evil" is here according to the parallelism *moral evil* (not misfortune, calamity, in conformity with vers. 4, 27, as HITZIG holds). This is however mentioned here with an included reference to its necessary evil results and penalties; therefore, if one chooses, it is evil and calamity together; comp. vers. 17.—With vers. 7 compare xxv. 21, 22, where as means to the conciliation of enemies there is mentioned the personal loving disposition of the man involved, who here appears as an object of the divine complacency.—With vers. 8 comp. xv. 16; with clause *b* in particular, xiii. 23.—Ver. 9. **Man's heart deviseth his way.** The Piel of the verb here denotes a laborious consideration, a reflecting on this side and that.— **But Jehovah directeth his steps.** He determines them, gives them their direction, guides them (comp. notes on ver. 1, *b*). UMBREIT, BERTHEAU, EWALD, ELSTER, [NOYES, STUART,] "he makes them sure." But then another conjugation (Pilel, יָכִין) would probably have been necessary, as in Ps. xxxvii. 23. For the Hiphil comp. moreover Jer. x. 23.

3. Vers. 10-15. Of kings as intermediate agents or instruments in God's wise administration of the world.—A divine **decision belongeth to the lips of the king.** קֶסֶם, oracular decision or prediction, here used in a good sense of a divine utterance (*effatum divinum*; comp. in the Vulg., *divinatio*). As representative of Jehovah, the supreme ruler and judge, a king, and especially the theocratic king of Israel, speaks words of divine validity and dignity (comp. Ps. lxxxii. 6; John x. 34), which give an absolutely certain decision, particularly in contested judicial questions. Therefore that continues true which the second clause asserts: **In judgment his mouth doth not speak wickedly.** "He deceives not, sins not" is not possibly, a *wish* ("his mouth should not err in judgment," UMBREIT, BERTHEAU), but "the passage rather lays down the principle: *the King can do no wrong*, in a narrower assertion of it, and with this difference, that it is here no political fiction, but a believing conviction. Righteousness at least in the final resort was under the theocratic monarchy of the Old Testament so absolute a demand of the idea, that one could not conceive it to be unrealized" (HITZIG). [We have here the theory of the king's relations and obligations, and a clear statement of the presumptions of which he should, according to the divine order, have the benefit. These must be clearly overthrown by him, before the people are entitled to set them aside. Comp. Rom. xiii. 1, 2. Had this proverb been penned near the end, instead of near the beginning of the Jewish theocracy, it would have been difficult to avoid the suggestion that the ideal and the actual are often strangely, sharply at variance.—A.].

Ver. 11. **The scale and just balances belong to Jehovah.** The proposition expresses the idea of an ownership in Jehovah as the first cause; for like agriculture (Ecclesiast. vii. 15) God instituted weights and measures, as an indispensable ordinance and instrument in just business intercourse.—**His works are all the weights of the bag.** His weights the oriental merchant (in Persia, *e. g.*, even at the present day) is wont to carry in a bag; comp. Deut. xxv. 13; Mic. vi. 11. Stones were in preference employed as weights because they do not wear away so easily, as iron, *e. g.*, which from rusting easily changes its weight. Comp. UMBREIT on this passage. BERTHEAU is quite too artificial. "His work is all of it stones of the bag, " *i. e.*, is as sharply and accurately defined "as the smallest and finest weights (?)."—Vers. 12, 13. Two verses closely connected, expressing a single truth, which is brought out first negatively and then positively.—It is an abomination to kings to commit iniquity; *i. e.*, injustice practised or at least attempted by their subjects is an abomination to them, representing, as they do, God and divine justice. Comp. ver. 10, and with clause *b* also especially xxv. 5.—**And he that speaketh uprightly is loved.** For this use of the plur. masc. of יָשָׁר, upright, which is therefore "upright things, uprightness," comp. Dan. xi. 17; also Job iv. 25.—The verb אָהֵב is either to be taken with an indefinite subject, "him one loveth," *i. e.*, he is loved (UMBREIT, ELSTER, *etc.*), or distributively, "him he loveth," *i. e.*, whoever is king for the time being.

Vers. 14, 15. Verses in like manner closely connected, and essentially expressing but one thought.—**The wrath of the king** (is as) **messengers of death.** This plural in the predicate of the sentence hints that when the king is enraged manifold means and instruments stand at his command for the immediate destruction of the object of his wrath. Remember the despotism and the capricious arbitrariness of Oriental sovereigns, and compare xix. 12; xx. 2; Eccles. viii. 3, 4.—**In the light of the King's countenance is life.** The "friendly countenance," lit. "light of the countenance," as in Ps. iv. 6 (7), is contrasted with the "wrath" ver. 14, *a.* as also are "life" and "death."—**As a cloud of the latter rain.** The harvest rain or latter rain (Vulg., *imber serotinus*) is a rain falling shortly before the harvest, in March or April, whose timely and abundant occurrence is indispensable to the success of Eastern harvests, especially so in Palestine; comp. xi. 14; Jer. iii. 3; v. 24; and particularly Job xxix. 23, 24, which latter passage is here a general parallel. [See THOMSON's *Land and Book*, I. 130, II. 66].

Vers. 16-26. Of God's righteous administration in respect to the wise and the foolish.—**To gain wisdom — how much better is it than gold,** *i. e.*, than the acquisition of gold; compare, for an example of this abbreviated comparison (*comparatio decurtata*) Job xxviii 8; Ps. iv. 7 (8), *etc.* For the general sentiment of the ver. compare iii. 14; viii. 10, 11, 19.

Ver. 17. **The path** (the raised, well-graded road מְסִלָּה) **of the upright departeth from evil,** lit "is abiding far (to abide far) from evil," as in ver. 6; comp. also x. 17; xi. 5, 20.—Hitzig expands the verse by four clauses which he introduces from the LXX, and in such an order that the second clause of the Masoretic text is separated from the first by three of the inserted clauses, and a sixth is appended as a final clause.

Yet he fails to give satisfactory proof that this expanded form was the original, three verses being now represented by one.

Ver. 18. Comp. xv. 25, 33.—The word here rendered "fall" (כִּשָׁלוֹן, tottering, downfall) is used only in this passage in the Old Testament.—With respect to the sentiment of the ver. compare also the Arabic proverb, "The nose is in the heavens, the seat in the mire" (*Nosus est, nates in fimo*), and the expression of HORACE "... *feriuntque summos fulgura montes*" (Odes, II. 10: 11, 12).

[. . . . . And ever, where
The mountain's summit points in air,
Do bolted lightnings flash."
—THEO. MARTIN'S Translation.]

Ver. 19. **Better is it to live humbly with the lowly.** עֲנָוִים (with which reading of the K'thibh the LXX agrees, while the K'ri reads עֲנִיִּים) describes those who are bowed down by troubles, the sufferers, the lowly; comp. Zech. ix. 9.

Ver. 20. **He that giveth heed to the word findeth good**, *i. e.*, naturally, to the word of God, the word *par excellence*; comp. xiii. 13.—With the expression "findeth good, or prosperity," comp. xvii. 20; xix. 8. "Blessed is he!" (אַשְׁרָיו) comp. xiv. 21.

Ver. 21. **The wise in heart shall be called prudent**, understanding, knowing, a possessor of בִּינָה, discernment. Comp. xiv. 33. —**And grace on the lips** (lit. "of lips") **increaseth learning**, *i. e.*, secures for learning an easy access in ever widening circles, comp. 23, *b*. The "grace" or literally the "sweetness" of the lips is here represented as a necessary attendant and helper of wisdom, as in chap. xv. 2.

Vers. 22. **A fountain of life is understanding to him that hath it**, lit. "is the wisdom of its possessor." The thought is here in the first instance unquestionably of the blessing which comes directly to the possessor from his wisdom, and not of its life-dispensing, life-promoting influence on others, as BERTHEAU thinks. For this figure of a "fountain of life" compare x. 11; xiii. 14; xiv. 27.—**But the correction of fools is folly**. The subject, according to the antithetic parallelism, is "folly," as "wisdom" is in clause *a*. The meaning can be no other than this; the folly of fools is for them a source of all possible disadvantages and adversities; the lack of reason is its own punishment (comp. HITZIG on this passage). [So N. and W., while H., M., and S. give to מוּסַר its active meaning, "the instruction of fools," *i. e.*, that which they give, "is folly."—A.].

Ver. 23. Comp. remarks on ver. 21.—**And increaseth learning upon his lips**. "Upon his lips," so far forth as the word that comes from the heart rests on the lips, comp. ver. 27; Ps. xvi. 4; and also the expression "on the tongue," Ps. xv. 3 [where the original expresses more than mere instrumentality (*with* the tongue); "who beareth not slander *on* his tongue" (HUPFELD, on the passage), *etc.*—A.].

Ver. 24. **As honey of the comb are pleasant words**, lit. "words of loveliness," as in xv. 26.—For a like reference to the "honey-comb" see Ps. xix. 10 (11).—**Sweet to the soul**. The adj. מָתוֹק, for which we might expect the plural is to be regarded as a neuter used substantively; something sweet, sweetness; comp. Ezek. iii. 3, and also ver. 2 above.

Ver. 25. Literally identical with xiv. 12:—stricken out by HITZIG from the passage before us, because it is superfluous in the group (vers. 22-30) assumed to consist of eight only (?).—

Vers. 26. **The spirit of the laborer laboreth for him**, *i. e.*, supports him in his labor, impels him to greater perseverance and exertion to gain his daily bread. [ZÖCKLER renders "the hunger," *etc.* So KAMPHAUSEN. This seems to us unnecessary. נֶפֶשׁ is often the animal soul or spirit as distinguished from the higher intellectual, moral and religious nature. It is this spirit that feels the pressure of life's necessities, and impels to effort for their relief; comp. x. 3, *etc.*—A.].—**For his mouth urgeth him on**, *i. e.*, as it longs for food. This verb (construed with עַל and the accus. of the person) denotes, according to Arabic analogies "to heap a load or burden on one" (comp. אָכַף, a weight, burden, Job xxxiii. 7) [E. V. "be heavy upon thee"]; and here specifically, to bind one, to drive and force him to do something" (Vulg., *compulit*).—With the general sentiment compare Eccles. vi. 7.

5. Vers. 27-33. A new delineation of God's justice in punishing the wicked and rewarding the pious. Vers. 27-30 form here one connected description of the ungodly, nefarious conduct of the evil men on whom God's judgment falls. Vers. 31, 32 contrast with these wicked men the upright and the gentle in spirit as the only happy men; ver. 33 is a general conclusion pointing us back to the beginning of the chapter.

Ver. 27. **A worthless man** ("man of Belial") **searcheth after evil**, literally "diggeth evil, shovels out evil for himself," *i. e.*, from the pit which he prepares for others, to destroy them (comp. xxvi. 27; Jer. xviii. 20 sq.). For this expression "man of Belial" compare vi. 12.—**On his lips is as it were scorching fire** (comp. ver. 23). The words of the worthless man are here on account of their desolating effects, compared to a blazing or scorching fire (comp. Ezek. xxi. 3; Prov. xxvi. 23; Job xxxi. 12; James iii. 5 sq.).

Vers. 28. With clause *a* compare vi. 14, 19.—**And a backbiter separateth friends**, lit. "divideth off the friend." The singular is not here used collectively, but in a certain sense distributively; "divideth a friend from his fellow." So in xvii. 9; comp. xix. 4.—For the use of נִרְגָּן, "backbiter" comp. xviii. 8; xxvi. 20, 22.

Ver. 29. With clause *a* compare iii. 31; i. 10 sq. With *b* compare Ps. xxxvi. 4 (5); Isa. lxv. 2.—[RUEETSCHI (as above cited, p. 145) thinks these verses (27-29) more expressive in each the first words are regarded as the predicates, prefixed for emphasis and stronger contrast; "a worthless man is he, *etc.*;" "a perverse, contentious man is he, *etc.*," "a backbiter is he, *etc.*;" "a man of violence is he, *etc.*;" although he may excuse his conduct as mere sport. —A.].

Ver. 30 describes more precisely, by two participial clauses which belong to the "man of violence" in ver. 29, the way in which this wicked man executes the ruin which he devises.— **Shutting his eyes to devise mischief**, lit. "to meditate craftiness;" comp. ii. 12, vi. 14.— **Biting his lips**. With this description, "pressing in, pressing together his lips," comp. vi. 13; x. 10, where this verb is used of the corresponding action with the eyes.

Ver. 31. With clause *a* comp. iv. 19; xx. 29, with *b*, iv. 10 sq., iii. 2.

Ver. 32. With *a* compare xiv. 29.—**And he that ruleth his spirit than he that taketh a city**. רוּחַ here not merely the spirit or the soul, but the *temper*, the passionate movement and excitement of the spirit. Comp. *Pirke Aboth* cap. iv. 1, where the question, Who is after all the true hero? is answered by a reference to the proverb of Solomon now before us. The Lord, moreover, in Matth. v. 5, promises to the meek that they shall inherit the earth.

Ver. 33. **The lot is cast into the lap**. HITZIG: "In the bosom the lot is shaken," a rendering which does indeed conform more closely to the import of חֵיק, "the bosom of the clothing," but to us who are not Orientals gives a meaning easily misunderstood. For we are wont to call the doubled or folded front of the dress the "lap."—**But from Jehovah is** (cometh) **all its decision**, the final judicial sense as it were, ("judgment," comp. Numb. xxvii. 21) in which the result of the lot is reached. Comp. xviii. 18, where, however, the discourse is specifically limited to the settling of judicial disputes by lot, while here attention is evidently directed to lots in general (and therefore to cases like Josh. vii. 19; 1 Sam. xiv. 37 sq., Numb. xvi. 8; Ps. xxii. 18 (19), *etc.*)

DOCTRINAL AND ETHICAL.

A course of thought running with any unity through the entire chapter it is here again impossible to detect. Only small groups of connected proverbs stand forth here and there from the general level; *e. g.*, vers. 1-3, vers. 10-15, vers. 27-30 (comp. especially the remarks on vers. 27 sq.). HITZIG's endeavor to develop here and in the two following chapters (*i. e.*, in general terms throughout the section xv. 33— xix. 2), symmetrically constructed groups of eight verses each, is quite as unsuccessful as his similar assumptions in respect to the construction of the general division, chap. x.—xxii. 16, on definite numerical principles (comp. above, remarks on x. 1 sq.; and on xiii. 1).

A decided pre-eminence belongs in the chapter, as it is now defined, to the idea that *God controls the action of man altogether according to His own wise judgment and good pleasure*. That "man proposes but God disposes,"—this truth which summons to humble confidence in God, and a child-like and unconditional surrender to the fatherly guidance of the Lord's hand, stands at the head of the section as a whole (ver. 1), with a special emphasizing of the divine influence exerted over the manner and the results of human speech. It recurs again in vers. 10-15 before the connected delineation of the authority of human kings, as counterparts and representatives of the great King of heaven; and here there is special reference not to the speech but to the action of men (ver. 9). Finally it forms the conclusion of the chapter, and that in the form of a reference to the supreme control which God holds in His hand over the lot as any where employed by men (ver. 33). It is the doctrine of the divine government of the world (the *gubernatio*, with its four prominent forms or methods, *permissio*, *impeditio*, *directio* and *determinatio*); or again the doctrine of the divine co-operation with the free self-determined acts of men (the *concursus* as it exists *tam ad bonas quam ad malas actiones hominum* [with reference both to the good and to the evil actions of men]), that is asserted in these propositions and developed in various directions. Especially does the intermediate place which human kings and judges assume as representatives of the divine justice, and in a certain sense prophets of the divine will (ver. 10), also as typically gods on earth (ver. 13-15; comp. Ps. lxxxii. 6), in their relation to the destiny of individual men, stand out in a significant prominence; it thus affords instructive premonition of the exhortations of the New Testament to obedience to the magistrates who stand in God's place,—such as are found in Matth. xxii. 21; Rom. xiii. 1 sq.; 1 Pet. ii. 17, *etc.* Compare what MELANCHTHON observes on ver. 10 sq.; "These words affirm that the whole political order, magistrates, laws, distinctions in authority, contracts, judgments, penalties are works ordained by the wisdom of God within the human race. Therefore since we know that political order is God's work, let us love it, and seek to maintain it by our duty, and in modesty obey it for God's sake, and let us render thanks to God the preserver, and let us know that the madness of devils and of men who disturb the political order is displeasing to God, *etc.*"

Other ethical truths to which a significant prominence is given are contained particularly in Ver. 6. A reference to the fear of God, and penitent and believing consecration to God as the only way to the development of genuine fruits of love and of righteousness (see notes on this passage).

Ver. 20. Combined view of the two chief requisites to a really devout life; 1) obedience to the word of God, and 2) inspiring confidence in God.

Vers. 21 and 23 (comp. also ver. 24). The stress laid on the great value of an eloquent mouth, as an appropriate organ for a wise heart exercising itself in the service of the Lord.

Ver. 32. Reference to gentleness of spirit and the ruling of one's own passions, as the best and surest means to the attainment of real power and greatness—an expressive Biblical testimony against all uncharitable advancement of self in the way of strife, and against the combative spirit of brawlers and duellists.

[ANDREW FULLER: The doctrine of verse 7 stands in apparent contradiction with 2 Tim. iii. 12. The truth seems to be that neither of the passages is to be taken *universally*. The peace possessed by those who please God does not extend so far as to exempt them from having enemies, and though all godly men must in some form or other be persecuted, yet none are persecuted at all times. The passage from Timothy may therefore refer to the native enmity which true godliness is certain to excite, and the proverb to the Divine control over it.]

HOMILETIC AND PRACTICAL.

Homily on the chapter as a whole; Of God's wise and righteous government of the world, as it is exhibited 1) in the life of men in general (1-9); 2) in the action and administration of earthly rulers (10-15); 3) in the endeavors and results of human wisdom (16-26); 4) in the righteous retribution which awaits both, the good and the evil (27-33).—STÖCKER: On God's gracious care for men. 1) *Proof* that such a paternally upholding and governing providence of God over men exists, *a*) in general (vers. 1-9); *b*) through the government of the world in particular (10-15). 2) The duties of the pious in recognition of this paternal providence and government of God (vers. 16-33).—WOHLFARTH:—On the providence and government of God, and man's duty. Man proposes, God disposes,—usually otherwise than we devise and desire, but always more gloriously and better than we could do. Hence humility, prudence and trust in God are the chief duties of man in return.

Vers. 1-3. MELANCHTHON:—It is well to consider that our resolves are a different thing from their success. That we may form successful and salutary resolutions we need God's aid in two forms; in examining the different possible ways, and then in conforming our course to them. We must therefore at all times be of this firm purpose, to let our whole life be ruled by God's word, and for all things to invoke God's help.—GEIER (on ver. 1): Teachers, preachers and rulers especially must call earnestly on God for the careful government and sanctification of their tongue, in order that in the fulfilment whether of their public or their private duties the right word may always stand at their command, and nothing unseemly or injurious may escape them. —(On ver. 3): The duties of our calling we must indeed fulfil with fidelity and diligence, but yet in all patience await from the Lord blessing and success.—*Berleb. Bible:* If one is not able without God to utter a word that one has already conceived, how much less will one be able to bring any thing to pass without God's aid. And how much more will this be true within the sphere of the spiritual life, since man is wholly "insufficient of himself to think any thing as of himself" (2 Cor. iii. 5), but must receive all from the Lord, *etc.*—[ARNOT (on ver. 2): The human heart is beyond conception cunning in making that appear right which is felt pleasant. The real motive power that keeps the wheels of life going round is this: men like the things that they do, and do the things that they like.]

Vers. 4-9. *Würt. Bible* (on ver. 4): God's providence extends over good and wicked men (Matth. v. 45); through His ordaining it comes to pass that the ungodly are punished in their time and as they deserve.—VON GERLACH (on ver. 4): The wicked man also fulfils God's design, when the day of calamity comes upon him; all without exception must serve Him.—[CHARNOCK (on ver. 4): If sin ends in any good, it is only from that Infinite transcendency of skill that can bring good out of evil, as well as light out of darkness.—WATERLAND (on ver. 4): God bridles the wicked by laws and government and by the incessant labors of good men; and yet more immediately by His secret power over their hearts and wills, and over all their faculties; as well as over all occurrences and all second causes through the whole universe; and if He still affords them compass enough to range in, yet notwithstanding He rules over them with so strong and steady a hand, that they cannot move a step but by His leave, nor do a single act but what shall be turned to good effect.—BEVERIDGE (on ver. 4): God in His revelations hath told us nothing of the second causes which He hath established under Himself for the production of ordinary effects, that we may not perplex ourselves about them, but always look up to Him as the first cause, as working without them or by them as He sees good. But He hath told us plainly of the final cause or end of all things, that we may keep our eyes always fixed on that, and accordingly strive all we can to promote it.—Bp. HALL (on ver. 6): It is not an outward sacrifice that God regards in His remission of the punishment of our sin; but when He finds mercy to the poor, and uprightness of heart towards Himself and men, then He is graciously pleased to forbear His judgments; inasmuch as these graces, being wrought in us by His Spirit, cannot but proceed from a true faith whereby our sins are purged. —BONAR (on ver. 6): Forgiveness, ascertained forgiveness, conscious forgiveness, this is the beginning of all true fear. This expels a world of evil from the human heart and keeps it from re-entrance. It works itself out in such things as these—obedience, fellowship, love, zeal].—STARKE (on ver. 6): Not of merit but of grace are the sins of the penitent forgiven for Christ's sake. One of the chief fruits of justification is, however, the exhibition of fidelity and truth towards one's neighbors (Eph. ii. 8, 9; iv. 25).—(On ver. 7): Think not that thou wilt thyself subdue and overcome thine enemies, but only seek to have God for thy friend; He can of all thy foes make thee friends.—[BATES (on ver. 7): Many sins are committed for the fear of the anger of men, and presumption of the mercy of God; but it is often found that a religious constancy gains more friends than carnal obsequiousness.—TRAPP (on ver. 7): When God is displeased, all His creatures are up in arms to fetch in His rebels, and to do execution. At peace with Him, at peace with the creature too, that gladly takes His part, and is at His beck and check].—ZELTNER (on ver. 9): Be presumptuous in none of thy schemes, but thinking of thine own weakness put as the foundation of every undertaking "if the Lord will" (James iv. 15).— [ARNOT (on ver. 9): The desires of human hearts and the efforts of human hands go into the processes of providence and constitute the material on which the Almighty works.]

Vers. 10-15. MELANCHTHON; comp. Doctrinal and Ethical notes.—STARKE (on ver. 10): For the right conduct of the office of ruler and judge it is not enough to understand well secular laws and rights; Divine wisdom is also absolutely essential.—(On ver. 12): Kings are not only not to do evil, or to let it be done by others with impunity; they are to hate and abhor it with all energy.—Von Gerlach (on ver. 11): Weight and measure as the invisible and spiritual means by which material possessions are estimated and determined for men according to their value, are holy to the Lord, a copy of His law in the outer world; taken up by Himself into His sanctuary, and therefore, as His work, to be regarded holy also by men.—(On ver. 14): Seasonable words of a wise man can easily avert the wrath of kings, destructive as that is. Therefore let each one mould himself into such a wise man, or find for himself such a one.

Vers. 16-26. [Chalmers (on ver. 17): The reflex influence of the outward walk and way on the inner man.—Arnot (on ver. 17): Doctrine, although both true and Divine, is for us only a shadow, if it be not embodied in holiness.—Waterland (on ver. 18): Shame and contempt the end of pride, *a*) by natural tendency; *b*) because of God's detestation and resolution to punish it.—Muffet (on ver. 19): It is a pleasant thing to be enriched with other men's goods: it is a gainful thing to have part of the prey: it is a glorious thing to divide the spoil. It is better to be injured than to do injury; it is better to be patient than to be insolent; it is better with the afflicted people of God to be bruised in heart and low of port, than to enjoy the pleasures or treasures of sin or of this world for a season.—Trapp (on ver. 20): He that, in the use of lawful means resteth upon God for direction and success, though he fail of his design, yet he knows whom he hath trusted, and God will "know his soul in adversity"].—Geier (on ver. 20): In doubtful cases to hold fast to God's word and believingly hope in His help, ensures always a good issue.—Starke (on vers. 21, 22): Eloquence combined with wisdom is to be regarded as an excellent gift of God, and produces so much the more edification and profit.—Lange (on ver. 21): One must first learn to think rightly before he can speak well.—Von Gerlach (on ver. 26): Since that which causes us labor and trouble becomes a means of our subsistence, it in turn helps us overcome labor and trouble, for this very thing, by virtue of God's wise, regulating providence, becomes for us a spur to industry.—[Lawson (on ver. 26): Self-love is a damning sin where it reigns as the chief principle of action; but the want of self-love where it is required is no less criminal.]

Vers. 27-33. Starke (on vers. 27 sq.): The lack of genuine love for one's neighbor is the source of all deception, persecution and slander of the innocent.—Hypocrites can indeed by an assumed mien of holiness deceive men, but before the eyes of God all this is clear and open, to their shame.—(On ver. 32): The greatest heroes and conquerors of the world are often just the most miserable slaves of their lusts.—E. Lösch (on ver. 31—see *Sonntagsfeier*, 1841, No. 27): Age, its burdens, its dignities; means to the attainment of a happy old age.—Saurin (Sermon on ver. 32): On true heroism—what it is, 1) to be ruler of one's spirit; 2) to gain cities and lands.—Von Gerlach (on ver. 33): Chance there is not, and man can never give more than the outward occasion for the decision, which lies wholly in the hand of the Lord.—[Trapp (on ver. 30): Wicked men are great students. . . . Their wits will better serve them to find out a hundred shifts or carnal arguments than to yield to one saving truth, though never so much cleared up to them.—Muffet (on ver. 31): Commendable old age leaneth upon two staves—the one the remembrance of a life well led, the other the hope of eternal life.—See Emmons' Sermon on ver. 31.—J. Edwards (on ver. 32): The strength of the good soldier of Jesus Christ appears in nothing more than in steadfastly maintaining the holy, calm meekness, sweetness and benevolence of his mind, amidst all the storms, injuries, strange behaviour, and surprising acts and events, of this evil and unreasonable world.—Lawson (on ver. 32): The meek obtain the noblest victories and enjoy the happiest kind of authority.—South (on ver. 33): Sermon on "All contingencies under the direction of God's providence."]

β) Admonition to contentment and a peaceable disposition.

Chap. XVII.

1 Better a dry morsel and quietness therewith
 than a house full of slain beasts with strife.
2 A wise servant shall have rule over a degenerate son,
 and shall have part of the inheritance among the brethren.
3 The fining pot is for silver, and the furnace for gold,
 but he that trieth hearts is Jehovah.
4 Wickedness giveth heed to lying lips,
 deceit giveth ear to a vile tongue.

5 He that mocketh the poor hath reproached his Maker,
  he that rejoiceth over a calamity shall not be unpunished.
6 The crown of the old is children's children,
  the glory of children is their parents.
7 High speech doth not become the fool,
  how much less do lying lips the noble!
8 As a precious stone is a gift in the eyes of him that receiveth it,
  whithersoever it turneth it maketh prosperous.
9 He that covereth trangression seeketh after love;
  but he that repeateth a matter estrangeth friends.
10 A reproof sinketh deeper into a wise man
   than to chastise a fool an hundred times.
11 The rebellious seeketh only evil,
   and a cruel messenger shall be sent after him.
12 Meet a bear robbed of her whelps,
   and not a fool in his folly.
13 He that returneth evil for good,
   from his house evil shall not depart.
14 As a breaking forth of waters is the beginning of strife;
   before the strife poureth forth, cease!
15 He that acquitteth the wicked and he that condemneth the just,
   an abomination to Jehovah are they both.
16 Why this price in the hand of a fool?
   (It is) to get wisdom, and he hath no heart to it.
17 At all times the friend loveth,
   but the brother is born of adversity.
18 A man void of understanding is he who striketh hands,
   who becometh surety in the presence of his friend.
19 He loveth sin that loveth strife,
   and he that buildeth high his doors seeketh destruction.
20 He that is of a false heart findeth no good,
   he that goeth astray with his tongue falleth into evil.
21 He that begetteth a fool doeth it to his sorrow,
   and the father of a fool hath no joy.
22 A joyous heart promoteth health,
   but a broken spirit drieth the bones.
23 A gift from the bosom a wicked man will receive
   to pervert the ways of justice.
24 Before the face of the wise is wisdom,
   but the fool's eyes are in the ends of the earth.
25 A grief to his father is a foolish son,
   and a trouble to her that bare him.
26 Also to punish the righteous is not good,
   to smite the noble contrary to right.
27 He that spareth his words hath knowledge,
   and he that is quiet in temper is a man of understanding.
28 Even a fool who keepeth silence will be counted wise,
   and he that shutteth his lips is wise.

GRAMMATICAL AND CRITICAL.

Ver. 4.—כְּרִי is probably not a Hiph. part.: "a wicked man," but an abstract substantive, as the parallel term שֶׁקֶר indicates (EWALD, HITZIG); and מֵזִין stands, according to the parallel מַקְשִׁיב for מַאֲזִין. [BÖTT. insists upon regarding the form as a Hiph. part. masc., distinguished by the vocalization from כָּרִי "friend" (see §§ 112f, A; 76f, c); FUERST gives to the full form כְּרִיעַ, which never occurs, but is assumed as the singular of מְרֵעִים, the active signification "malefiens," evil doer, but maintains that כְּרִי, which occurs only here except with a pausal modification, has naturally the neuter abstract meaning. See also GREEN, § 140, 5.—A.]

Ver. 10.—From the infin. הַבּוֹת there is easily supplied as an object מַכָּה.—תֵּחַת is the Imprf. of the verb נָחַת, to descend, to penetrate (comp. Is. xxx. 30): the form without abbreviation would, according to Ps. xxxviii. 3, have

הִנֵּה been. [So Bütt. who also defends the position of the accent on the ground of emphasis (§ 497, 3), and criticises, both on the ground of specific form and general construction, Fuerst's assigning it as an apoc. Imperf. to חָרָה.—A.]

Ver 11.—That רָע is the subject of the clause, and not possibly כָּרִי, as the Syr., Chald., Umbreit, Ewald, etc., maintain, appears from the position of אַךְ before the latter word, and also from the unquestionable reference of the בּוֹ in the 2d clause to רָע as a masculine substantive. [Ruetschi (as above, p. 146) replies that אַךְ may as well throw its emphasis on an entire proposition as on a single word (see Nordheimer, § 1072, 4) and that בּוֹ refers to כְּרִי the subject of the proposition, which is an abstract in the sense of a concrete. Versions and interpreters are very equally divided; with our author emphasizing כְּרִי as object, "only rebellion, nothing but rebellion," are the E. V., V. Ess, Bertheau, K., S.; with Ruetschi are De W., M., N., and substantially H. and W. We render with the latter in opposition to Zöckler's view.—A.].

Ver. 13. The K'thibh לֹא־תַכְשִׁיט is to be retained, since the Hiphil הִכְשִׁיט has in Ps. lv. 12 also the intransitive meaning "depart."

Vers. 19. Aben Ezra, Geier, Schultens, etc., take the expression "to make high the door, or gate," as meaning "to open wide the mouth, to utter a vehement outcry" (פֶּה being taken as equivalent to פֶּה, as ostium is to os; comp. Ps. cxli. 3; Eccles. xii. 4). But the idea would then be very obscurely expressed, and instead of כִּנְבִיָה we should expect כַּנְדִיל.

Vers. 22. גֵּהָה is not equivalent to גֵּוָה or גְּוִיָה, "body," (Chald., Syr., Bertheau, etc.) but is to be derived from the radical גָהָה, Hos. v. 13,—and therefore means "healing, recovery" (Hitzig, "the closing up of a wound"?) [Fuerst prefers the rendering of the Targ., Syr., etc.; Gesen. that adopted by the author.—A.].

Ver. 27. The rendering which we give conforms to the K'thibh, קַר רוּחַ, to substitute for which with the K'ri (which is followed by the Vulg., Luther, etc.) יְקַר רוּחַ, "of a noble spirit," seems here less appropriate. [The LXX follow the K'thibh.]

EXEGETICAL.

1. Vers. 1-9. Admonitions to contentment and a wise moderation in earthly possessions, and in the use of the tongue.—**Better a dry morsel and quietness therewith.** "A dry piece of bread," without wine, without even vinegar (Ruth ii. 14) or water with it (1 Sam. xxv. 11). The thing contrasted with it is זִבְחֵי, not "sacrificial banquets" (Umbreit, Elster, [Fuerst]), but animals slaughtered for sacrifice, as constituting the chief element in a rich, sumptuous meal; comp. chap. ix. 2; Gen. xliii. 16. For the general meaning compare xv. 16, 17; xvi. 8.

Ver. 2. **A wise servant** (comp. xiv. 35) **shall have rule over a degenerate son**, lit., "a bad, unprofitable son," who becomes impoverished and even a slave, because he has squandered his means, etc.—**Among the brethren shall he divide the inheritance**, i. e. among brethren who are sons of the testator, while he himself who inherits with them, is not a son but only a servant. Comp. Abraham's apprehension in regard to his servant Eliezer, Gen. xv. 3 sq. With this expression "in the midst of the brethren" compare a similar one in Hos. xiii. 15.—Ver. 3. With clause a compare xxvii. 21 a (which is literally identical): with b compare xv. 11; xvi. 2; xxi. 2; xxiv. 12.

Ver. 4. **Wickedness giveth heed to lying lips.** See critical notes. The meaning is plainly this: "A wicked heart, inwardly corrupt, gladly attends to lying talk; and deceit "—so clause b asserts in addition—i. e. a heart full of inward insincerity and hypocrisy, a hypocritical man given to lying (abstract for concrete), "hearkens to a perverse tongue," i. e. finds pleasure in wicked discourse, which supplies words to its own base thoughts, and develops them into definite evil propositions and designs.

Ver. 5. With a compare xiv. 31.—**He that rejoiceth over a calamity shall not be unpunished** (comp. xi. 21; xvi. 5). "Sudden misfortune," according to clause a probably sudden poverty. Comp. Job xxxi. 29, a similar utterance regarding the penal desert of an uncharitable delight in calamity.

Ver. 6. With clause a comp. Ps. cxxvii. 5.—**The glory of children is their fathers.** As the pride and honor of the gray-headed is the family circle that surrounds them, or the advancing series of their children, grandchildren, etc., so "on their part children, so long as they are not also parents, can only reach backward; and with the genealogy, the farther back it reaches, the honor of the family increases" (Hitzig).

Ver. 7. **High speech doth not become the fool.** "A lip of excess, of prominence" plainly denotes an assuming, imperious style of speech,—not the "elevated, or soaring," as Ewald, Elster, Umbreit claim; for the parallel "lip of deceit" in clause b indicates its sinful character. **How much less do lying lips the noble?** "The noble," the spirit of lofty dispositions (comp. ver. 26),—to whom deceitfulness, and crafty, sly artifices of speech are less becoming than to any other man,—stands contrasted with the "fool" just as in Isa. xxxii. 5 sq.

Ver. 8. **As a precious stone is a gift in the eyes of him that receiveth it.** Lit., "a stone of loveliness," a costly stone, *gemma gratissima* (Vulg.); comp. i. 9.—The "master" of the gift is here evidently not its giver (Elster, comp. Luther, and many of the older expositors), but he that receives it, he who is won by it; and the "gift" is here to be taken not in the bad sense, of bribery (as below in ver. 23), but rather of lawful presents; comp. xviii. 16.—**Whithersoever it turneth it maketh prosperous**; i. e. to whomsoever it may come it will have a good result and secure for its giver supporters and friends. The expression conforms to the idea of the "precious stone" in clause a (although it is not the jewel, but the gift that is subject of the verb "turneth"). For a really beautiful and well-cut stone sparkles, whichever way one may turn it, and from whichever side one may view it; just so is it with the good result of a well-directed generosity, by which the hearts of all are necessarily won. A truth which naturally is to be taken quite in a relative and conditional sense.

Ver. 9. **He that covereth transgression seeketh after love**, *i. e.* not "seeks to gain the love of others" but "seeks to exercise love, a truly charitable spirit" (so HITZIG with undoubted correctness, in opposition to BERTHEAU). [BRIDGES and M. also take this view, which commends itself both as the deepest and the most disinterested representation.—A.]. For the "covering transgression" comp. x. 12, and the remarks on the passage.—**But he that repeateth a matter separateth friends** (see xvi. 28). "Repeateth a matter" (שֹׁנֶה בְדָבָר) is not "to return with remarks" or "with a word" [*i. e.* to repeat] (EWALD, BERTHEAU, ELSTER, FUERST, *etc.*), but "to come back with a matter," [GESEN.] *i. e.* to be continually reverting to something, repeatedly to bring it up and show it forth, instead of letting it alone and covering it with the mantle of charity. This expression is different both from the Latin, "*ad alios deferre, denuntiare*" (WINER) and also from the Greek δευτεροῦν λόγον. Comp. furthermore Ecclesinst. xix. 6-10.

2. Vers. 10-20. Admonitions to a peaceable spirit; warnings against a contentious and uncharitable disposition.—**A reproof sinketh deeper into a wise man than a hundred stripes into a fool**, (comp. Deut. xxv. 3); lit., "than to smite the fool with a hundred." With the meaning of the verse compare SALLUST'S *Jugurtha*, c. 11: *altius in pectus descendit*, and the common phrase "to make a deeper impression."

Ver. 11. Clause *a*, see critical notes for the reasons for our departure from ZÖCKLER'S rendering.—**And a cruel messenger shall be sent after him**, *i. e.* by God, against whom we are to regard the "rebellion" mentioned in clause *a* as directed. So the LXX and Vulg. rendered in their day, and among recent interpreters BERTHEAU, *e. g.*; for to think of a mere human messenger, as in xvi. 14, is forbidden by the analogy of passages like Ps. xxxv. 5, 6; lxxviii. 49; HITZIG'S rendering, however, "and a cruel angel (a wild demon of passion, as it were), is let loose within him," is altogether artificial, and rests upon modern conceptions that are quite foreign to the Old Testament; besides we ought probably to have found בְּקִרְבּוֹ "in the midst of him," instead of בּוֹ.

Ver. 12. **Meet a bear robbed of her whelps**. The Infin. abs. here stands for the Imper. or Jussive; comp. Gen. xvii. 10; Deut. i. 16; Jer. ii. 2, *etc.* For the use of the epicene דֹּב for the she-bear comp. Hos. xiii. 8; 2 Sam. xvii. 8.—The "fool in his folly" is naturally a fool who is peculiarly malignant, one who is in a very paroxysm of folly, and whose raving is more dangerous than the madness of a wild beast. Comp. SCHILLER: "*Gefährlich ists den Leu zu wecken,*" *etc.* ['Tis perilous to wake the lion].

Ver. 13. With clause *a* compare 1 Sam. xxv. 21; with *b*, 2 Sam. iii. 29.—"Evil" here in the sense of misfortune, the penalty for acts of injustice done the good.

Ver. 14. **As a breaking forth of waters is the beginning of strife** [ZÖCKLER: "he letteth forth waters," *etc.* Z. also conceives of the latter part of the clause as meaning literally "who (lets loose) the beginning of strife;" in his view the participle is to be repeated before the word רֵאשִׁית "beginning." The use of the verb פָּטַר in the sense of "send forth, bring out" is confirmed by the Targum on Ex. xxi. 20. The participle cannot, however, in Z.'s view, be taken here in a neuter sense, as EWALD maintains (so UMBREIT). FUERST maintains the view of E. and U. and cites analogous forms of verbal nouns. We adopt it as justified by verbal analogies and simplifying the construction.—A.] LUTHER expresses the substantial idea thus: "He who begins strife is like him that tears away the dam from the waters."—**Before the strife poureth forth, cease!** The meaning of the verb הִתְגַּלַּע which is best attested is here, as in xviii. 1; xx. 3, "to roll forth." Here, as in verse 8, the figurative conception employed in clause *a* influences the selection of the verb in *b*. The strife is conceived of as a flood which after its release rolls on irresistibly. UMBREIT, ELSTER, *etc.*, following the Chald. and Arabic, explain "before the strife becomes warm;" HITZIG (and EWALD also) "before the strife shows its teeth." As though an altogether new figure could be so suddenly introduced here, whether it be that of a fire blazing up, or that of a lion showing his teeth! [As the word occurs but three times, and the cognate roots in the Hebrew and its sister languages are not decisive, the moral argument may well turn the scale; and this certainly favors the view in which Z. has the concurrence of FUERST, BERTHEAU, STUART, *etc.*—A.]

Ver. 15. Comp. xxiv. 24; Isa. v. 23.—**An abomination to Jehovah are they both**; lit., "an abhorrence of Jehovah are also they two;" comp. 2 Sam. xix. 31, where גַּם, also, expresses as it does here the associating of a second with the one.

Ver. 16. **Why this price in the hand of a fool**, *etc.* [While there is no essential disagreement among expositors in regard to the general meaning of the verse, they are divided as to the punctuation and the mutual relation of the clauses. The Hebrew points are not decisive. Z. agrees with the Vulg., E. V., H., S., *etc.* in making the sentence one complex interrogative sentence. DE DIEU, SCHULTENS, VAN ESS, DE WETTE, NOYES, *etc.*, make two interrogative clauses, followed by one affirmation. We have chosen the more equal division of the LXX.—A.] The getting or buying of wisdom is by no means a thing absolutely impossible, as appears from chap. iv. 5, where express admonition is given to do this. But for earthly gold, for a price, it is not for sale, and especially not for the fool, who has no understanding. For the last clause, "and heart, understanding, is not, does not exist," compare the substantially equivalent expression in Ps. xxxii. 9; also Jer. v. 21, *etc.*

Ver. 17. Compare xviii. 24; also Ecclesiast. xii. 7.—**But the brother is born of adversity**. The ideas "friend" and "brother" are related the one as the climax of the other. The "friend," the companion with whom one preserves a friendly intercourse cherishes a constant good-will toward his comrade; but it is only necessity that develops him further into a "brother," as it gives the opportunity to attest his loving disposition by offerings of love, such as in truth only one brother makes for another. Comp. ENNIUS, in CIC. Lǣl. c. 17: *Amicus certus in re incerta cernitur*; and also the Arabic proverb (Sent. 53 in ERPENIUS *Gramm.*): "The friend one finds out not till one needs him."— יִוָּלֵד "he is born," as a new being, into the new conditions of the actual, brotherly relation. לְצָרָה must here mean "of adversity" (HITZIG, K.), not "in adversity" (UMBREIT, N.), or "for adversity" (EWALD, BERTHEAU, ELSTER, DE W., S., M., *etc*.). [The grammatical justification of Z.'s view is found mainly in the fact that לְ is ordinarily used when in a passive construction the efficient cause is to be expressed: see GESEN. *Lehrgeb.* § 221, ROD. GESEN. *Heb. Gram.* § 140, 2. Of course it may also denote the final cause. —A.]—For ver. 18 compare vi. 1-5; xi. 15.

Ver. 19. With clause *a* compare James i. 20; with *b*, Prov. xvi. 18.—**Who buildeth high his doors**; *i. e.* seeks to transform his simple residence into a proud and splendid edifice, but by that very process only hastens its "destruction" (lit., "shattering, downfall," comp. the similar term in x. 14, *etc.*). [SHARPE'S *Texts of Bible explained, etc.*: "Private houses were sometimes built ostentatiously with a lofty gateway which would naturally breed jealousy in the neighbors, and invite the visits of the tax-gatherer; and in a time when law was weak and property very unsafe, might easily lead to the ruin of its owner."—A.] The sentiment is therefore directed against pride as the chief source of a quarrelsome spirit, and the most common cause of ruinous contention.

Ver. 20. With clause *a* compare xi. 20; xvi. 20.—**He that wandereth with his tongue**, *i. e.* speaks now this way, now that; therefore has a deceitful tongue, "a wayward tongue," x. 31 (comp. viii. 13).—**Falleth into evil**; see xiii. 17. Observe the climax existing in the negative expression "no good" in *a*, and this "evil."

3. Vers. 21-28. Proverbs of various content, directed especially against want of sense, and loquacity.—**He that begetteth a fool doeth it to his own sorrow**. Comp. x. 1; xviii. 13; and the converse of the thought here presented, chap. xxiii. 24; also xv. 20.

Ver. 22. **A joyous heart promoteth health**. See critical note. For the sentiment comp. xv. 13; with clause *b* in particular, iii. 8.

Ver. 23. **A gift from the bosom a wicked man will receive**. "From the bosom," *i. e.* secretly and stealthily; comp. xxi. 14. The term "gift" is here used naturally of unlawful bribery.—With clause *b* compare xviii. 5; Am. ii. 7.

Ver. 24. **Before the face of the wise is wisdom**. "Before the face," here it would seem "very near" and therefore "close before the face" (BERTHEAU, ELSTER, *etc*.): or again with ZIEGLER, HITZIG, *etc*., the explanation may be in accordance with Deut. xvi. 16, "Wisdom floats before the man of understanding, he has it in his eye" (comp. xv. 14).—**But the eyes of the fool** (range) **to the end of the earth**, *i. e.* "his mind is not on the subject, but roams in undefined, shadowy distance" (HITZIG): he thinks of many and various things, on every possible thing,—only not of the very thing that is needful and important; comp. iv. 25.—Ver. 25. Comp. ver. 21 and x. 1.

Ver. 26. **Also to punish the righteous is not good, to smite the noble contrary to right**. The also (גַּם) plainly gives prominence to the verb that immediately follows, and this verb should be allowed to retain its ordinary signification, "to punish with a fine, to impose a pecuniary fine" (comp. xxii. 3). The fine as a comparatively light penalty, which may easily at one time or another fall with a certain justice even on a "just" man (*e. g.* when he from inadvertence has in some way injured the property of another), stands contrasted with the much severer punishment with stripes; and as these two verbal ideas are related, so are also the predicates "not good" (comp. ver. 20), and "contrary to right" (above desert, beyond all proportion to the just and reasonable), in the relation of a climax. On the other hand the "righteous" and the "noble" (as in ver. 7) are essentially persons of the same class. The proverb, which evidently contains an admonition to mild and reasonable treatment of upright men, or a warning against the inhuman enforcement of penal laws upon active and meritorious citizens, has been in many ways misunderstood and falsely applied; and this is true of most of the recent expositors with the exception of UMBREIT, who alone interprets with entire correctness. (BERTHEAU and ELSTER are also essentially right, except that they do not take the עַל־יֹשֶׁר "contrary to right" as the predicate, but are disposed to connect it by way of more exact definition with the phrase "to smite the noble"). [The LXX, Vulg., followed by the E. V., W., M., H., N., render "for their equity." S. and K. agree with Z., both in the meaning and the predicative construction.—A.]

Ver. 27. With *a* comp. x. 19.—**And he that is of a quiet temper**. Comp. the opposite of the "coolness of spirit" here intended (*i. e.* cautious, moderate, quietly considerate deportment); Ps. xxxix. 3 (4).—Ver. 28. Comp. Job xiii. 5; Prov. x. 19, *etc*.

DOCTRINAL AND ETHICAL.

The introductory verse with its commendation of contentment and a peaceable spirit at the same time, or of contentment as the source and basis of a peaceable disposition and conduct, may be regarded as a prefatory announcement of the main subject of the chapter. Contentment is furthermore commended (at least indirectly) in vers. 2, 5, 8, 16, 19, 22-24; a peaceable and forbearing disposition in vers. 4, 9-15, 17, 19, 23,

26.—The summons which comes out in the opening verses, 1-9, to combine with contentment the appropriate restraint and regulation of the tongue,—*or to be abstemious not merely with the mouth but with the tongue* (by truthfulness and gentleness in speech, and by a taciturn disposition, ver 28),—recurs again in the last two verses. It may therefore to a certain extent be regarded as in general the fundamental idea of the entire section. In the asceticism of the early Church and of the monasticism of the middle ages, this idea that there must be an inward organic coexistence of bodily and spiritual fasting, or that one should bring the tongue under a serious and strict discipline, as *the organ not merely of taste, but also of speech,* found as is well known only too prolific practical appreciation. For, appealing to the supposed model of Christ's forty days of fasting in the wilderness, men added to the injunctions of fasting unnaturally strict prescriptions of silence in many forms (see my "Critical History of Asceticism," pp. 297 sq.). Apart from these extravagances and exaggerations, the organic connection, and living reciprocity of influence between the activity of the tongue as an organ of taste and an organ of speech, such as exists in every man, is a matter deserving distinct recognition; and sins of the tongue in both directions must be with all earnestness shunned, and together subdued and destroyed (comp. James iii. 22).

Other ethical sentiments of special value and compass are found in ver. 4: the heavy guilt not only of the tempter, but also of the tempted, who, on account of his inward corruption and vileness, gives a ready hearing to the evil solicitations of the former; comp. James i. 14 sq.—

Ver. 6. The blessing of a consecrated domestic life, as it shows itself in both the parents and their posterity, in their mutual relations and demeanor. The opposite of this appears in vers. 21, 25.

Ver. 16. The pricelessness of true wisdom, and the worthlessness of earthly possessions and treasures in the hand of a fool.

Ver. 17. The great worth of a true friend in time of need.

Ver. 26. The necessity of a mild, considerate bearing on the part of persons in judicial and magisterial station, toward deserving citizens of the state, in cases where they have perchance gone astray or come short of duty. Comp the exegetical remarks on this passage.

[LAWSON, ver. 4: "Wicked men have a great treasure of evil in their hearts, and yet have not enough to satisfy their own corrupt dispositions.

Ver. 15. Justifying the wicked has an appearance of mercy in it, but there is cruelty to millions in unreasonable acts of mercy to individuals.—Ministers are guilty of the sin of condemning the righteous when they preach doctrines unscripturally rigid, making those things to be sinful which are not condemned in the word of God, or carrying the marks necessary to discover grace to a pitch too high to suit the generality of true Christians, or applying to particular persons those terrors that do not justly belong to them. Such was the fault of Job's friends."]

HOMILETIC AND PRACTICAL.

Homily on the entire chapter: A peaceable spirit and contentment as the sum of all wisdom; its opposite (contentiousness and foolish aspiring after things that are high, see especially ver. 19) as the source of all failure in things temporal as well as spiritual.—STÖCKER: Of true temperance in controlling all unseasonable debate and strife; 1) the causes of these last (vers. 4-13); 2) the most important means of averting them (14-19); 3) the serious injuries and disadvantages which grow out of them (20-28).

Vers. 1-8. HASIUS (on ver. 2): To attain to power and influence in this world more depends on understanding and prudence than on birth and outward advantages.—LANGE (on ver. 3): All human investigations and theories concerning the interior world of thought in man are inconclusive and deceptive. The searching of the heart of man is one of the kingly prerogatives of God.—[TRAPP (on ver. 3): God tries us that He may make us know what is in us, what dross, what pure metal; and all may see that we are such as, for a need, can "glorify Him in the very fires" (Is. xxiv. 15)—BRIDGES (on ver. 4): The listening ears share the responsibility of the naughty tongue.]—ZELTNEN (on ver. 4): According as the heart and disposition of a man are moulded, he delights either in good or in evil discourse.—WOHLFARTH (on ver. 7): Force not thyself above, degrade not thyself below thy condition.—VON GERLACH (on ver. 7): The outward and the inward must always be in harmony, else a distorted and repulsive display results. As the fool cannot fitly speak of high things, so senseless must a falsehood appear to the noble.—LANGE (on ver. 8): Though one may effect much with an unjust judge by presents, how much better will it be if thou bringest thine heart to the Lord thy God as a gift and offering!

Vers. 9-15. [Lord BACON (on ver. 9): There are two ways of making peace and reconciling differences; the one begins with amnesty, the other with a recital of injuries, combined with apologies and excuses. Now I remember that it was the opinion of a very wise man and a great politician, that "he who negotiates a peace, without recapitulating the grounds of difference, rather deludes the minds of the parties by representing the sweetness of concord, than reconciles them by equitable adjustment." But Solomon, a wiser man than he, is of a contrary opinion, approving of amnesty and forbidding recapitulation of the past. For in it are these disadvantages: it is as the chafing of a sore; it creates the risk of a new quarrel (for the parties will never agree as to the proportions of injuries on either side); and, lastly, it brings it to a matter of apologies; whereas either party would rather be thought to have forgiven an injury than to have accepted an excuse.]—MELANCHTHON (on vers. 9-12): As the monitor must show sincerity and love of truth, and guard against a slanderous love of censure, so in him who is admonished, there is becoming a readiness to be instructed, and both must keep themselves free from φιλονεικία, from an ambitious quarrelsomeness.—CRAMER (on ver. 10): To him who is of a noble sort words of rebuke are more grievous than blows, and he yields to the discipline of mere words.—STARKE (on ver. 13): If God sharply punishes ingratitude, from this it is also evident how dear to Him, on the other hand, thankfulness must be.—(On ver 14): From a little spark a great fire may arise (James iii. 5): but he who buries in the ashes the kindling contention may thereby avert a great disaster.—[TRAPP (on ver. 10): The fool is beaten, but not bent to goodness; amerced but not amended.— (On ver. 13) : To render good for evil is Divine, good for good is human, evil for evil is brutish, evil for good is devilish.—BRIDGES (on ver. 15): If God *justifies the wicked*, it is on account of righteousness. If he *condemn the just*, it is on the imputation of unrighteousness. Nowhere throughout the universe do the moral perfections of the Governor of the world shine so gloriously as at the Cross of Calvary.]

Ver. 16-22. ZELTNER (on ver. 17): The most reliable and faithful friend, on whom one may depend most confidently in the very time of need, is the Lord Jesus. Strive for His friendship above all things, and thou hast treasure enough!—[ARNOT (on ver. 17): In the Scriptures we learn where the fountain of true friendship lies, what is its nature. why its flow is impeded now, and when it shall be all over like the waves of the sea. Our best friendship is due to our best friend. He deserves it and desires it. The heart of the man Christ Jesus yearns for the reciprocated love of saved men, and grieves when it is not given.].—STARKE (on ver. 19): He who first leaves room for one sin falls afterward into many others.—Contention and pride are almost always sisters, and of a most destructive sort.— VON GERLACH (on ver. 22): The heart, the fountain of life, works to bless the whole of man's condition when it is really sound, *i. e.*, when the grace of Jesus Christ has healed and renewed it.—[TRAPP (on ver. 22): When faith hath once healed the conscience, and grace hath hushed the affection, and composed all within, so that there is a Sabbath of spirit, and a blessed tranquility lodged in the soul; then the body also is vigorous and vigetous, for most part in very good plight and healthful constitution, which makes man's life very comfortable.—BRIDGES (on ver. 22): Liveliness needs a guard lest it should degenerate into levity; a grave temperament lest it should sink into morbid depression. Christian principle on both sides is the principle of enlarged happiness and steady consistency.]

Ver. 23-28. STARKE (on ver. 24): The more one gapes after vanity, the more foolish does the heart become.—(On ver. 25): A wise father has indeed now and then a foolish son; if he has not himself perchance deserved this, by neglect in education, let him bear his cross with patience. —(On ver. 26): He sins doubly who declares evil good, and besides visits the goodness of a righteous man with penalties.—*Berleburg Bible* (on vers. 27, 28): It is better to say nothing than foolish things.—VON GERLACH (on ver. 28): By silence a fool abates something of his senselessness, and since he gets the opportunity to collect himself and to reflect, a beginning of wisdom is developed in him.

γ) Admonition to affability, fidelity in friendship, and the other virtues of social life.

CHAP. XVIII.

1 He that separateth himself seeketh his own pleasure;
against all counsel doth he rush on.
2 A fool hath no delight in understanding,
but that his heart may reveal itself.
3 When wickedness cometh then cometh contempt,
and with shameful deeds reproach.
4 Deep waters are the words of man's mouth;
the fountain of wisdom is a flowing brook.
5 To have regard to the wicked is not good,
(nor) to oppress the righteous in judgment.
6 The lips of the fool engage in strife,
and his mouth calleth for stripes.
7 The mouth of the fool is his destruction,
and his lips are a snare to his soul.
8 The words of a slanderer are words of sport,
but they go down into the innermost parts of the body.
9 He also who is slothful in his work
is brother to the destroyer.

10 A strong tower is the name of Jehovah;
   the righteous runneth to it and is safe.
11 The possessions of the rich are his strong city,
   and as a high wall in his own conceit.
12 Before destruction the heart of man is haughty,
   and before honor is humility.
13 He that answereth before he hath heard,
   it is folly and shame to him.
14 The spirit of a man will sustain his infirmity,
   but a wounded spirit—who can bear?
15 An understanding heart gaineth knowledge,
   and the ear of the wise seeketh knowledge.
16 A man's gift maketh room for him,
   and bringeth him before the great.
17 He that is first is righteous in his controversy;
   then cometh his neighbor and searcheth him out.
18 The lot causeth contentions to cease,
   and decideth between the mighty.
19 A brother resisteth more than a strong city,
   and (such) contentions are as the bars of a palace.
20 With the fruit of a man's mouth shall his body be satisfied;
   with the revenue of his lips shall he be filled.
21 Death and life are in the power of the tongue;
   he that loveth it shall eat its fruit.
22 Whoso findeth a wife findeth a good thing,
   and shall obtain favor of Jehovah.
23 The poor shall use entreaties,
   and the rich will answer roughly.
24 A man of (many) friends will prove himself base,
   but there is a friend that sticketh closer than a brother.

GRAMMATICAL AND CRITICAL.

Ver. 1.—It would perhaps be admissible with Hitzig (following the LXX and Vulg.) to exchange לְתַאֲוָה for the rarer לְתֹאֲנָה (Judg. xiv. 4), from which we should obtain the meaning "He that separateth himself seeketh after an occasion (of strife);" Vulg.: *Occasiones quærit, qui vult recedere ab amico.* For the use of בִּקֵּשׁ with בְּ see also Job x. 6. [The E. V. in the text understands the בְּ as indicating the condition, and so supplying the motive of the seeker; the reading of the margin is "according to his desire." H., N., S., M., etc., agree with our author in connecting it with the object desired. The views of commentators, which are very diverse, may be found in considerable number in MUENSCHER, *in loco*.—A.]

Ver. 3.—Instead of רָשָׁע we shall be obliged, with J. D. MICHAELIS, HITZIG, UMBREIT, etc., to point רֶשַׁע as the parallel קָלוֹן (i. e., "infamy, infamous conduct," *turpitudo*) indicates.

Ver. 6.—[A masc. verb again with the fem. noun שְׂפָתֵי, as in ver. 2; x. 21, 32; xv. 7.—A.]

Ver. 10.—Without any necessity Hitzig proposes to read יָרוּם instead of יְרוּן, and to translate "by it (the name of Jehovah) riseth up high." [RUEETSCHI (as above, p. 147) concurs in rejecting both Hitzig's emendation and his conception of the proposition. He justifies by examples like 1 Kings x. 26; 1 Sam xxv. 26; Joshua xxiii. 7, etc., the use of בְּ after verbs of motion,—and suggests that the concluding participle marks the quick and sure result of the preceding act.—A.]

Ver. 17.—The K'ri' יָבֹא; the K'thibh is perhaps more appropriately יָבֹא.

Ver. 19.—The LXX and Vulg. appear to have read נוֹשָׁע (βοηθούμενος, *adjuvatur*) instead of נִפְשָׁע; Hitzig proposes to read by emendation פֶּשַׁע אָהוּב, "to shut out sin is better than a strong tower," etc.

Ver. 24.—לְהִתְרוֹעֵעַ, which is probably to be derived from the root רֹעַ, רֵעַ, and to be regarded as the reflexive of the Intensive form (comp. the Niphal form יָרוֹעַ, chap. xi. 15), must have the copula הָיָה supplied to give a full verbal sense (comp. chap. xix. 8); it therefore means "is to prove himself base, serves for this, to show himself base (i. e., here specifically an unworthy comrade, a bad friend)." The alliteration which is doubtless intentional between רֵעִים and הִתְרוֹעֵעַ led even the early translators (Syr., Chald., Vulg., and also THEODOT.) to derive the latter word from רָעָה, *associare*, and accordingly to explain it by "to make one's self a friend, to cultivate friendly intercourse" (comp. Ps. lxv. 4). So recently Hitzig: "There are companions for sociability,"—for he also reads שֵׁי (or אַשׁ, Mic. vi. 10) for יֵשׁ, appealing to the Syr. and Chald., who appear to have read the text in the same way. [BÖTT. supports this emendation or restoration (§ 458, 2,) and proposes without asserting the derivation of the verb from רָעָה, as a denominative (§ 1126, 2)]. But אִישׁ is proved to be original by the Vulg., THEODORET, etc.; and between clauses *a* and *b* there appears to be a proper antithesis and not merely a climax. This strictly antith-tic relation is also interfered with by the method of explanation adopted by those who, like UMBREIT, ELSTER, etc., render the verb by "ruin themselves, make themselves trouble;" (EWALD's conception resembles this, except as it has a still more artificial double import "must be a friend to trouble"); the result follows no less from the derivation from רוע, *jubilare* (so the Vers. Venet.: ἀνὴρ φίλων ὥστε ἀλαλάζειν, and of recent interpreters HENSLER: "He that hath friends may exult").

[Of the English commentatores HOLDEN renders "is ready to be ruined;" NOYES, "brings upon himself ruin;" STUART, "will show himself as base;" MUENSCHER, "will be ruined;" WORDSWORTH, "*for his own destruction*,"—his fate is not to be helped by his many friends, but to be ruined by them." Of the Germans not cited by Z., DE WETTE, "*hat viel Umgang zu seinem Untergang*;" BERTHEAU, "*ist um sich als schlechten zu erweisen*;" KAMP., "*so wird einem ubel mitgespielt*;" FUERST, "*muss sich als schlecht erweisen.*"—A.]

EXEGETICAL.

1. Ver. 1-9. Against unsociableness, love of controversy, and other ways in which an uncharitable and foolish disposition manifests itself — **He that separateth himself seeketh after his desire**, *i. e.* he who in an unsocial and misanthropic spirit separates himself from intercourse with others, will as a general rule hold in his eye only the satisfaction of his own pleasure and his own selfish interest.— **Against all counsel** (wisdom) **doth he rush on**, *i. e.* against all wise and prudent counsel (comp. iii. 21) he sets himself, and will hear nothing of it. In respect to the verb, comp. remarks on xvii. 14. HITZIG in this passage as in that holds to the signification which he there assumes, and therefore translates, "Against all that is fortunate (?) he gnashes his teeth."

Ver. 2. Compare similar censures of the loquacity of fools, and their delight in their own discourse, as they prefer above all besides to hear themselves speak, and gladly display everywhere their imagined wisdom,—in passages like xii. 23; xiii. 16; xv. 2, *etc.*

Ver. 3. **When wickedness cometh then cometh contempt**. For the sentiment comp. xi. 2.

Ver. 4. **Deep waters are the words of man's mouth**. "Deep," *i. e.* hard to fathom and exhaust (xx. 5; Eccles. vii. 24). This is true, naturally, only of the words of discreet and wise men, who, according to the parallel in clause *b*, are evidently alone intended here. Only they indeed can be called a "flowing brook," *i. e.* a brook never drying up, one always pouring forth an abundant supply of refreshing water; compare a similar phrase in Am. v. 24. Others regard the meaning of the second clause as contrasted with the first, as they either define "deep waters" in a bad sense, of dark, obscure, enigmatical words (DÖDERLEIN, ZIEGLER), or, in spite of the parallel in xx. 5, read כֵּי בְעִמְקִים instead of מַיִם עֲמֻקִּים, and understand "waters of excavation," and think of the contrast between cistern waters which readily fail, and a genuine spring of water, Jer. ii. 13 (so HITZIG).

Ver. 5. **To have regard to the wicked is not good**. The last phrase used as in xvii. 26. The first, lit., "to lift up, to show respect to the face of some one" (LXX: θαυμάσαι πρόσωπον), as in Lev. xix. 15; Deut. x. 17, *etc.* [Z. renders still more specifically "to take part, to take sides," *etc.*].—With clause *b* comp. xvii. 23; Isa. x. 2; Am. ii. 7, *etc.*; with the sentiment as a whole, xvii. 15.

Vers. 6 and 7 are in close connection; for the former comp. xix. 29; for the latter, xiii. 3. To the idea, which occurs in the parallel passage also, of "destruction, or ruin," there is here added by way of exemplification the figure of a "snare," as employed by huntsmen; comp. xii. 13; xiii. 14; xiv. 27

Ver. 8. **The words of a slanderer are as words of sport.** The slanderer, or backbiter, as in xvi. 28. The predicative epithet כְּמִתְלַהֲמִים is here, as also in xxvi. 22, where the whole verse is literally repeated, very variously interpreted. It is most obvious to go back to a root להם assumed to be cognate with להה, "to play, to sport" (comp. remarks on xxvi. 10), and accordingly to find contrasted the design of the inconsiderate words of the backbiter, intended, as it were, sportively, and their deeply penetrating and sorely wounding power (see clause *b*). So C. B. MICHAELIS, BERTHEAU, ELSTER, *etc*. Others explain differently; *e. g.* SCHULTENS, UMBREIT (following the Arabic), as "dainty morsels" [so GESEN., DE W., M., W.]; EWALD, "as if whispering;" HITZIG, "like soft airs;" [FUERST, "like murmured, mysterious, oracular words;" while the rendering given in the E. V., as also by some commentators, supposes a transposition of the radical consonants (for הלם); BERTHEAU and STUART agree substantially with our author. The whole matter is conjectural, the word occurring in the Hebrew Scriptures but twice, and no sure analogy existing for our guidance.—A.]—**Into the innermost parts of the body**, lit., "into the chambers," *etc.*; comp. xx. 27, 30; xxvi. 22.

Ver. 9. **He also who is slothful in his work is brother of the destroyer**, lit., "of the master of destruction,"—for the participle form מַשְׁחִית is here impersonal as in Ezek. v. 16: "the master of destruction" means "the destroyer" (xxviii. 24) and here the squanderer, who wastes his possessions, the *dissipans sua opera* (Vulg.), and not the highway robber or the captain of banditti as HOFMANN, *Schriftbew.* II., 2, 377, maintains.

2. Vers. 10-16. Seven proverbs of miscellaneous import, referring especially to confidence in God, and humility as the only true wisdom.—**A strong tower is Jehovah's name**; *i. e.* the revealed essence of God, His revelation of Himself in the history of salvation, with its blessed results, shows itself to those who confide in it, who in a childlike spirit submit themselves to its guidance, as a stronghold securely protecting them (so Ps. lxi. 3 (4).) [KUEETSCH: "The name always designates Himself, as man knows Him, as he receives Him to his knowledge and faith, and bears Him in his heart. It is precisely what man knows of God that is for him a strong tower. When man stumbles or falters it is precisely because he has not run to this refuge, has, as it were, not reminded himself where his strong

tower is"].—**The righteous runneth to it and is safe**, lit., "and is lifted up," *i. e.* gains a high and at the same time sheltered station, where the shafts of his enemies can do him no harm. Comp. another form of the same verb in xxix. 25.

Ver. 11. With clause *a* comp. x. 15.—**And as a high wall in his own conceit**. בְּמַשְׂכִּיתוֹ (comp. Ps. lxxiii. 7) the old Vers. Venet. renders quite correctly by ἐν φαντασίᾳ αὐτοῦ, while the Vulg., the Chald., *etc.*, read בְּמִשְׁבַּתּוֹ, "in his enclosure," an expression which would be superfluous with the "high wall." [FUERST, starting from this idea of figured or carved work, furniture, *etc*, understands the allusion to be to a "hall of state." Neither the simple meaning nor the complicated construction seems admissible; "and as behind a high wall is he in his hall of state."—A.]

Ver. 12. With *a* compare xvi. 18; with *b*, xv. 33.
Ver. 13. Compare Ecclesiast. xi. 8.
Ver. 14. **The spirit of a man will sustain his infirmity**, lit., "supports his sickness." The spirit that does this is naturally a strong, courageous spirit (comp. Num. xxvii. 18), the opposite of a "smitten" spirit, which rather needs, according to the second clause, that one sustain it. Furthermore the רוּחַ in clause *a* is used as a masculine, because it here appears engaged in the performance of manly action; in clause *b*, on the contrary, as a feminine, because it is represented as powerless and suffering.

Ver. 15. Comp. xiv. 33; xv. 14.—**The ear of the wise seeketh knowledge**. The ear here comes into consideration as an organ working in the service of the heart; for it is properly only the heart that pursues the acquisition of wisdom, and which actually acquires it,—not indeed without the co-operative service of the senses (especially hearing, as the symbol and organ of obedience, Ps. xl. 7).

Ver. 16. **A man's gift maketh room for him** [and nowhere more than in the East; see *e. g.* THOMSON's *Land and Book*, II., 28, 369]. כְּתָן here and in xix. 6 undoubtedly equivalent to שֹׁחַד in chap. xvii. 8, and therefore used of lawful presents, and proofs of generosity, whose beneficent results are here emphasized, as also there, without any incidental censure or irony (as many of the old expositors, and also UMBREIT hold). Altogether too far-fetched is HITZIG's idea that the "gift" is here "spiritual endowments or abilities," and is therefore substantially like the χάρισμα of the N. T.

3. Vers. 17-21. Against love of contention and misuse of the tongue.—**He that is first is righteous in his controversy**; *i. e.* one thinks that he is altogether and only right in a disputed matter,—then suddenly comes the other and searches him out, *i. e.* forces him to a new examination of the matter at issue, and so brings the truth to light, *viz.* that the first was after all not right. Comp. the same verb in xxviii. 11; also Job xxix. 16, where however the investigator is the judge, and not one of the two contending parties.

Ver. 18. Comp. xvi. 33.—**And decideth between the mighty**, *i. e.* it keeps from hostile collision those who in reliance on their physical strength are especially inclined to quarrel. Comp. Heb. vi. 16, where a like salutary influence is claimed for the judicial oath as here for the lot.

Ver. 19. **A brother (estranged) resisteth more than a strong city**. The participle נִפְשָׁע, which, according to the accents, is predicate of the clause, is to be taken in the sense of "setting one's self in opposition, resisting." Now a brother who resisteth or deficth more than a strong city is necessarily an alienated or litigious brother. Furthermore the whole connection of the verse points to this closer limitation of the idea of "brother," and especially the second clause, which aims to represent the difficulty of subduing the passion once set free, under the figure of the bars of a fortress, hard to thrust back or to burst.

Ver. 20. Comp. xii. 14; xiii. 2.
Ver. 21. **Death and life are in the power of the tongue**. Comp. James iii. 5 sq.; and also the Egyptian proverb: γλῶσσα τύχη, γλῶσσα δαίμων (PLUTARCH, Is. p. 378).—**He that loveth it shall eat of its fruit**; *i. e.* he that suitably employs himself with it, employs much diligence in using it in discourse, whether it be with good or bad intent, as εὐλογῶν or κακολογῶν, blessing or cursing, (James iii. 9; comp. 1 Cor. xii. 3), will experience in himself the effects of its use or its abuse. Against the one-sided application of this "loving the tongue" to loquacity (HITZIG), is to be adduced the double nature of the expression in the first clause, as well as the analogy of the preceding verse.—The LXX (οἱ κρατοῦντες αὐτῆς) seem to have read אֹחֲזֶיהָ (those laying hold upon it) instead of אֹהֲבֶיהָ, but this reading can hardly have been the original; comp. rather viii. 17, where the verb "to love" expresses essentially the same idea as here, that of a cherishing and cultivating or careful developing.

4. Vers. 22-24. Of conjugal, neighborly and friendly affection.—**Whoso findeth a wife findeth a good thing**. It is naturally a good wife that is meant, a partner and head of the household such as she should be, a wife who really stands by her husband's side as a "help-meet for him" (Gen. ii. 18, 20). The epithet "good," which the LXX, Vulg., *etc.*, express, is therefore superfluous (comp. also xix. 14; xxxi. 10), and is probably quite as little an element in the original as that which in the same version is appended to our verse: "He that putteth away a good wife putteth away happiness, and he that keepeth an adulteress is foolish and ungodly." With clause *b* compare furthermore iii. 13; xii 2; Ecclesiast. xxvi. 3. [ARNOT's view is more defensible: The text which intimates that a prudent wife is from the Lord tells a truth, but it is one of the most obvious of truths: the text which intimates that a wife is a favor from the Lord, without expressly stipulating for her personal character, goes higher up in the history of providence, and deeper into the wisdom of God. So substantially MUFFET, LAWSON and others].

Ver. 23. **The poor useth entreaties, but the rich answereth roughly**, lit., "opposeth hard things" (contrasted with the supplications of clause a). Comp. the similar proverbs directed against the hardness of heart of the rich: chap. xiv. 21; xvii. 5.

Ver. 24. **A man of many friends will prove himself base.** The "man of friends," of many friends, the "friend of all the world," will show himself a bad friend,—he with whom is contrasted in clause b the instance which is indeed rare and isolated, of a true friendly love, which endures in every extremity (xvii. 17), and even surpasses the devotion of one who is a brother by nature. See Critical notes for an exhibition of the many meanings found in the verse, etc.

DOCTRINAL AND ETHICAL, HOMILETIC AND PRACTICAL.

That the chapter before us treats mainly of the virtues of social life, of sociability, affability, love of friends, compassion, etc., appears not merely from its initial and concluding sentences, the first of which is directed against misanthropic selfishness, the latter against thoughtless and inconstant universal friendship, or seeming friendship, but also from the various rebukes which it contains of a contentious, quarrelsome and partizan disposition, e. g. vers. 5, 6, 8, 17-21. But in addition, most of the propositions that seem to be more remote, may be brought under this general category of love to neighbors as the living basis and sum of all social virtues; so especially the testimonies against wild, foolish talking (vers. 2, 7, 13, comp. 4 and 15); that against bold impiety, proud dispositions and hardness of heart against the poor (vers. 3, 12, 23); that against slothfulness in the duties of one's calling, foolish confidence in earthly riches, and want of true moral courage and confidence in God (vers. 9-11; comp. 14). Nay, even the commendation of a large liberality as a means of gaining for one's self favor and influence in human society (ver. 16), and likewise the praise of an excellent mistress of a family, are quite closely connected with this main subject of the chapter, which admonishes to love toward one's fellow-men; they only show the many-sided completeness with which this theme is here treated.

[CHALMERS:—Verse 2 is a notabile. Let me restrain the vanity or the excessive appetite for sympathy which inclines me to lay myself bare before my fellow-men.—LAWSON (on ver. 13):—"Ministers of the word of God are instructed by this rule, not to be rash with their mouths to utter anything as the word of God in the pulpit, but to consider well what they are to say in the name of the Lord; and to use due deliberation and inquiry before they give their judgment in cases of conscience, lest they should make sins and duties which God never made, etc."].

Therefore as a *homily on the chapter as a whole:*—Of love (true love for the sake of God and Christ) as the "bond of perfectness," which must enfold all men, and unite them in one fellowship of the children of God.—Or again: On the difference between true and false friendship (with special reference to ver. 24.)—STÖCKER:—Against division (alienation, contention) between friends. Its main causes are: 1) Within the sphere of the Church impiety (vers. 1-4); 2) Within the sphere of civil life, pride and injustice (vers. 5-10); 3) In domestic life, want of love (vers. 19-24).—*Calwer Handbuch:*—Testimony against the faults which chiefly harm human society.

Vers. 1-9. GEIER (on ver. 1):—Love of separation (*singularitatis studium*) is the source of most contentions in Church and State.—(On ver. 4):—Eloquence is a noble thing, especially when its source is a heart hallowed by the Holy Ghost. —*Berleburg Bible:*—When the soul has once attained steadfastness in God, then words go forth from the mouth like deep waters, to instruct others and to help them; for it is a spring of water, inasmuch as the soul is in the Fountain. —STARKE (on ver. 6):—Calumniators do not merely often start contentions; they themselves seldom escape unsmitten.—VON GERLACH (on ver. 9):—Slothfulness leads to the same end as extravagance.

Vers. 10-16. VON GERLACH (on ver. 10):—The name of Jehovah (He that is) reveals to us His eternally immutable essence; in this there is given to mutable man living here in time the firmest ground of confidence, by which he may hold himself upright in trouble.—STARKE (on ver. 11):—Money and property can, it is true, accomplish much in outward matters; but in the hour of temptation and in the day of judgment it is all merely a broken reed.—[BRIDGES (on vers. 10, 11):—Every man is as his trust. A trust in God communicates a divine and lofty spirit. We feel that we are surrounded with God, and dwelling on high with Him. A vain trust brings a vain and proud heart—the immediate forerunner of ruin.—BATES (on ver. 10, 11):—Covetousness deposes God, and places the world, the idol of men's heads and hearts, on His throne; it deprives Him of His regalia, His royal prerogatives, etc. The rich man will trust God no further than according to visible supplies and means].—ZELTNER (on ver. 14):—Wouldst thou have a sound body; then see to it that thou hast a joyful heart and a good courage, a heart which is assured of the grace of God and well content with His fatherly ordaining.—[T. ADAMS (on ver. 14):—The pain of the body is but the body of pain; the very soul of sorrow is the sorrow of the soul.—FLAVEL:—No poniards are so mortal as the wounds of conscience.—WATERLAND:—On the misery of a dejected mind].

Vers. 17-21. [LORD BACON (on ver. 17):—In every cause the first information, if it have dwelt for a little in the judge's mind, takes deep root, and colors and takes possession of it; insomuch that it will hardly be washed out, unless either some clear falsehood be detected, or some deceit in the statement thereof.—ARNOT:—Self-love is the twist in the heart within, and self-interest is the side to which the variation from righteousness steadily tends in fallen and distorted nature.]—STARKE (on ver. 17):—He that hath a just cause is well pleased when it is thoroughly examined; for his innocence comes out the more clearly to view.—ZELTNER (on ver. 19):—The sweeter the wine the sharper the vinegar; accordingly the greater the love implanted by nature, the more bitter the hate where this love is violated.—[TRAPP (on ver. 19):—No war breaks out sooner or lasts longer, than that among divines, or as that about the sacrament: a sacrament of love, a communion, and yet the occasion, by accident, of much dissension].—*Tübingen Bible* (on ver. 20, 21):—Speak and be silent at the right time and in the divine order, and thou shalt be wise and blessed.

Ver. 22. LUTHER (marginal note on ver. 22): The married who is truly Christian knows that, even though sometimes things are badly matched, still his marriage relation is well pleasing to God, as His creation and ordinance; and what he therein does or endures, passes as done or suffered for God.—STÖCKER: Praise of an excellent wife (*probæ conjugis commendatio*): 1) how such a one may be found; 2) what blessing her husband has in her.—ZELTNER: The great mystery of Christ and His church (Eph. v. 32) must ever be to married Christians the type and model of their relation.—VON GERLACH: The great blessing of a pious wife can only be found, not won or gained by one's own merit.

Vers. 23, 24. STARKE (on ver. 23): If poor men must often enough knock in vain at the doors and hearts of the rich of this world, this should be to them only an impulse, to plead and to call the more on God who surely hears them. (On vers. 24): Pour out your heart before the Lord in every extremity; He is a friend whose friendship never dies out.—VON GERLACH (on ver. 24): The number of one's friends is not the thing.—they are often false, unfaithful, and forsake us in misfortune. Let none despair for that reason; there are friends who are more closely and intimately joined to us than even brothers.—[ARNOT: The brother and the friend are, through the goodness of God, with more or less of imperfection, often found among our fellows; but they are complete only in Him who is the fellow of the Almighty.]

δ) Admonition to humility, mildness, and gentleness.

CHAP. XIX.

1 Better is the poor that walketh in his integrity
 than he that is perverse in speech and is a fool.
2 Where the soul hath no knowledge there likewise is no good,
 and he that is of a hasty foot goeth astray.
3 The foolishness of man ruineth his way,
 yet against Jehovah is his heart angry.
4 Wealth maketh many friends,
 but the poor is parted from his friend.
5 A false witness shall not go unpunished,
 and he that speaketh lies shall not escape.
6 Many court the favor of the noble,
 and every one is friend to him that giveth.
7 All the brethren of the poor hate him,
 how much more doth his acquaintance withdraw;—
 he seeketh words (of friendship) and there are none.
8 He that getteth understanding loveth his soul,
 he that keepeth wisdom shall find good.
9 A false witness shall not go unpunished,
 he that speaketh lies shall perish.
10 Luxury becometh not the fool,
 much less that a servant rule over princes.
11 The discretion of a man delayeth his anger,
 and it is his glory to pass over a transgression.
12 The king's wrath is as the roaring of a lion,
 but as dew upon the grass is his favor.
13 A foolish son is trouble upon trouble to his father,
 and the contentions of a wife are a continual dropping.
14 House and riches are an inheritance from fathers,
 but from Jehovah cometh a prudent wife.

CHAP. XIX. 1–29.

15 Slothfulness sinketh into inaction,
   and an idle soul shall hunger.
16 He that keepeth the commandment keepeth his soul,
   he that despiseth his ways shall die.
17 He lendeth to the Lord, that hath pity on the poor,
   and his bounty will He requite for him.
18 Correct thy son while there is still hope,
   but to slay him thou shalt not seek.
19 A man of great wrath suffereth punishment,
   for if thou wardest it off thou must do it again.
20 Hearken to counsel and receive instruction,
   that thou mayest be wise afterward.
21 There are many devices in a man's heart,
   but Jehovah's counsel, that shall stand.
22 A man's delight (glory) is his beneficence,
   and better is a poor man than a liar.
23 The fear of Jehovah tendeth to life;
   one abideth satisfied, and cannot be visited of evil.
24 The slothful thrusteth his hand in the dish,
   and will not even raise it to his mouth again.
25 Smite the scorner and the simple will be wise,
   reprove the prudent and he will understand wisdom.
26 He that doeth violence to his father, and chaseth away his mother,
   is a son that bringeth shame and causeth disgrace.
27 Cease, my son, to hear instruction
   to depart from the words of wisdom.
28 A worthless witness scoffeth at judgment,
   and the mouth of the wicked devoureth mischief.
29 Judgments are prepared for scorners,
   and stripes for the back of fools.

GRAMMATICAL AND CRITICAL.

Ver. 15. Altogether unnecessarily Hitzig proposes to read הָכִיל instead of הָבִיל and הֲרָדִים instead of הָרְדְכָה, and translates "slothfulness gives tasteless herbs to eat." [K. calls this a "remarkable alteration of the text;" and Rueetschi pronounces it "nothing but a shrewd fancy of Hitzig's"].

Ver. 16. Instead of the K'thibh יוּמָת, "shall be put to death," (the familiar expression of the Mosaic law for the infliction of the death penalty), the K'ri reads more mildly יָמוּת, which is probably original in chap. xv. 10, but not here.—Instead of בּוֹזֶה Hitzig reads in accordance with Jer. iii. 13 בּוֹזֵר: "He that scattereth his ways," but by this process reaches a meaning undoubtedly much too artificial, which furthermore is not sufficiently justified by an appeal to xi. 24; Job xxxi. 7. [While Green makes the primary meaning of בּוּז "to tread under foot," Fuerst makes it "to scatter, divide, waste," and interprets the "dividing one's ways" as a want of conformity to the one established worship. This is in his view the antithesis to "keeping the commandment." The only other passage in which he finds this literal meaning of the verb is Ps. lxxiii. 20, where De Wette (see Comm. in loco) admits that this would be a simpler completion of the verse, but thinks himself obliged to take the verb, as has usually been done, in the sense of "despise." Fuerst's rendering and antithesis seem preferable.—A.].

Ver. 19. Instead of the K'thibh גְרָל (which would probably require to be explained by "hard" or "frequent," as Schultens and Ewald explain it from the Arabic), we must give the preference to the K'ri, which also has the support of the early translators [Fuerst takes the same view]. Hitzig's emendation, גֹּמֵל instead of גְרָל (he that dealeth in anger) is therefore superfluous.

Ver. 23. רָע "Calamity, evil" is attached to the passive verb יָפָּקֵד as an accusative of more exact limitation.—Hitzig reads instead of יָפָּקֵד פָּחַד, so that the resulting meaning is: "one stretches himself (?) rests, fears no sorrow" (?).

Ver. 25. הוֹכִיחַ in clause b is either to be regarded as an unusual Imperative form (= הוֹכֵחַ), [so B., M., S.], or, which is probably preferable, as a finite verb with an indefinite pronoun to be supplied as its subject (τις, quisquam, Einer, one); so Mercer, Hitzig. [Fuerst calls it an Inf. constr., and Dörr. would without hesitation read תּוֹכִיחַ (§ 1051, d).—A.].

Ver. 27. Hitzig alters לִשְׁמֹן to לִשְׁמֹעַ which according to Arabic analogies is to be interpreted "to be rebellious, to reject."

EXEGETICAL.

1. Ver. 1-7. Admon. ions to meekness and tenderness as they are to be manifested especially toward the poor.—**Better is a poor man that walketh in his integrity than he that is perverse in speech and is a fool.** The "crooked in lips" (comp. the crooked or perverse in heart, xi. 20; xvii. 20) is here doubtless the proud man who haughtily and scornfully misuses his lips; for to refer the expression to strange and false utterances is less natural on account of the antithesis to "the poor" in clause *a*. The ideas contrasted are on the one hand that of the "poor" and therefore humble, and "perverse of lips," and on the other hand the predicates to these conceptions, "walking in innocence," and the "fool" (*i. e.*, foolish and ungodly at the same time, the direct opposite of humble innocence). There is therefore no need of substituting some such word as עָשִׁיר (rich, mighty) for כְּסִיל (the fool), as the Syr., Vulg. and HITZIG do, nor yet of conceiving of the fool as the "rich fool," as most of the later interpreters judge. Chap. xxviii. 6, where, with a perfect identity in the first clauses, the "rich" is afterward mentioned instead of the "fool," cannot decide the meaning of this latter expression, because the second member differs in other respects also from that of the proverb before us, "his ways" being mentioned instead of "his lips."

Ver. 2. **Where the soul hath no knowledge there likewise is no good.** גַּם, also, stands separated by *Hyperbaton* from the word to which it immediately relates, as in chap. xx. 11 (see remarks above on xiii. 10); the "not-knowing" of the soul, is by the parallel "of hasty foot," in clause *b*, more exactly defined as a want of reflection and consideration; the soul finally, is here essentially the *desiring* soul, or if one chooses, the "desire," the very longing after enjoyment and possession (comp. xiii. 2; xvi. 26). So likewise "he that hasteth with his feet" is undoubtedly to be conceived of as one striving fiercely and passionately for wealth; comp. the "hasting to be rich," chap. xxvii. 20, and also 1 Tim. vi. 9, 10.

Ver. 3. **The foolishness of man ruineth his way.** The verb סָלַף is not "to make rugged or uneven" (UMBREIT, ELSTER) but *præcipitare*, "to hurl headlong, throw prostrate, bring suddenly down," which is its ordinary meaning; comp. xiii. 6; xxi. 12. The verb in clause *b* is to rage, to murmur, *i. e.*, here to accuse Jehovah as the author of the calamity; comp. Ex. xvi. 8; Lam. iii. 39; Ecclesiast. xv. 11 sq.

Ver. 4. Comp. xiv. 20; also, below, vers. 6 sq. —**But the poor is parted from his friend**, that is, because the latter wishes to have no further acquaintance with him, separates his way wholly from him; comp. ver. 7, *b*.

Ver. 5. **A false witness shall not go unpunished**; comp. xvii. 5, and for the expression "uttereth or breatheth out lies" in clause *b*, comp. chap. vi. 19; xiv. 5. The entire proverb occurs again in ver. 9, literally repeated as far as the "shall not escape" at the conclusion, for which in the second instance there appears "shall perish." HITZIG it is true proposes also the exchange for the phrase "he that speaketh lies" in 9, *b*, "he that breatheth out evil;" but the LXX can hardly be regarded as sufficiently reliable witnesses for the originality of this divergent reading.

Ver. 6. **Many court the favor of the noble**, lit. "stroke the face," *i. e.*, flatter him (Job xi. 19) who is noble and at the same time liberal, him who is of noble rank (not precisely "a prince" in the specific sense, ELSTER) and at the same time of noble disposition, comp. xvii. 7, 26. If accordingly the "noble" expresses something morally valuable and excellent, the "gift" in clause *b* cannot express anything morally reprehensible, but must rather be employed in the same good sense as in xviii. 16. "The man of a gift" will therefore be the generous, he who gives cheerfully, and the "aggregate" or "mass" of friends (כָּל־הָרֵעַ) whom he secures by his gifts, will be lawfully gained friends and not bribed or hired creatures. The right conception is expressed as early as the translation of the Vulg., while the LXX, Chald and Syr., embodying the common assumption which finds in the verse a censure of unlawful gifts for bribery, go so far as to read כָּל־הָרַע "every wicked man" (πᾶς ὁ κακὸς, *etc.*).

Ver. 7. Comp. ver. 4, *b*.—**How much more do his acquaintance withdraw from him.** רֵעַ (comp. remarks on chap. xii. 26) we shall be obliged to take here as an abstract with a collective sense ("his friendship" = his friends), for only in this way is the plural of the verb to be explained (for which HITZIG arbitrarily proposes to write יִרְחַק).—**He seeketh words** (of friendship)—**and there are none.** In some such way as this we must explain the third clause, with which this verse seems remarkably enriched (comp. UMBREIT and ELSTER, on the passage); the K'thibh is to be adhered to, [so BÖTT. II., p. 60, n. 4) which evidently gives a better meaning than the K'ri, לוֹ הֵן in interpreting which so as to conform to the context expositors have vainly labored in many ways (*e. g.* EWALD: "he that seeketh words, to him they belong;" in like manner BERTHEAU).—The LXX instead of this third clause, which does indeed stand in an exceptional form, like the fragmentary remnant of a longer proverb, have two whole verses; the second of these: ὁ πολλὰ κακοποιῶν τελεσιουργεῖ κακίαν, ὃς δὲ ἐρεθίζει λόγους, οὐ σωθήσεται ["he that does much harm perfects mischief; and he that uses provoking words shall not escape:" BRENTON's Transl. of the LXX], seems at least to come tolerably near to the original sense of the passage. HITZIG through several emendations obtains from this the sense "He that is after gossip hatcheth mischief, hunting after words which are nothing."

Others, as BERTHEAU, *e. g.*, infer from the οὐ σωθήσεται of the LXX, that the original text instead of לֹא הֵמָּה (they are not) exhibited לֹא יִמָּלֵט (shall not escape), but they supply no definite proof that this is original. At any rate we must conclude that our present text is defective, inasmuch as verses of three members in the main division of the Book of Proverbs which is now before us occur nowhere else. (This is otherwise, it is true, in Division I.; see remarks above on chap. vii. 22, 23, and also in the supplement of Hezekiah's men: Comp. Introd., § 14).

2. Vers. 8–17. Further admonitions to mildness, patience, pity, and other prominent manifestations of true wisdom.—**He that getteth understanding** (comp. xv. 32) **loveth his soul**; comp. the opposite, viii. 36; xxix. 24.

For the construction of the predicate לִמְצֹא טוֹב in clause b compare notes on xviii. 24; for the expression of chap. xvi. 20, etc.

Ver. 9. Comp. notes on ver. 5.

Ver. 10. **Luxury becometh not the fool.** Comp. xvii. 7; xxvi. 1; and for clause b, xxx. 22: Eccles. x. 7; Ecclesinast. xi. 5.—Inasmuch as luxury naturally and originally belongs only to princes and the like exalted personages, clause b stands as the climax of a. That "servants rule over princes" will, it is true, not readily occur among common slaves in their relation to their masters; it may however the more easily happen at the courts of oriental despots, who frequently enough exalt their favorites of humble rank above all the nobles of the realm.

Ver. 11. **The discretion of a man delayeth his anger,** makes him patient, lit. "lengthens, prolongs his anger," [in the sense of defers rather than extends it; his patience is what is "lengthened out" and not his passion]; comp. Isa. xlviii. 9, as well as chap. xiv. 17, above, in regard to impatience as the token of a fool.—**And his glory is to pass over transgression,** lit., "to go away over transgression," comp. Mic. vii. 18.

Ver. 12. **Roaring like that of a lion is the wrath of a king;** comp. xxvi. 2; also xvi. 14; xxviii. 15. With the figure of the sweetly refreshing dew in clause b compare xvi. 15; Ps. lxxii. 6.

Ver. 13. **A foolish son is stroke upon stroke to his father.** The plural "troubles, calamities," expresses the repetition, the succession of many calamities; UMBREIT and HITZIG therefore will translate "ruin upon ruin;" comp. also ZIEGLER "a sea of evils."—**And the brawling of a wife is a continual dropping;** for this latter phrase see also xxvii. 15; a pertinent figure, reminding of the distilling of the dew in 12, b, although contrasted with it in its impression. The scolding words of the bad wife are as it were the single drops of the steady rain, as her perpetual temper pours itself out.

Ver. 14. Comp. xviii. 22, and the German and English proverb according to which "marriages are made in heaven" ["a proverb which," says Archbishop TRENCH, "it would have been quite impossible for all antiquity to have produced, or even remotely to have approached"].—Ver. 15. **Slothfulness sinketh into torpor;** lit, "causeth deep sleep to fall" (comp. Gen. ii. 21), brings upon man stupor and lethargy; comp. vi. 9, 10.—With clause b compare x. 4; xii. 23.—Ver. 16. With clause a comp. xvi. 17: Eccles. viii.

5.—**He that taketh no heed to his ways shall die.**—See critical notes.—Ver. 17.—With clause a compare xiv. 31; with b, xii. 14; with the general sentiment (which appears also in the Arabic collection of MEIDANI), Eccles. xi. 1; Matth. xxv. 40; Luke vi. 30-35.

3. Vers. 18–21. Admonition to gentleness in parents and children, with respect to the work of education.—**Correct thy son while there is still hope,**—that is, that he may reform and come to the true life. This last phrase "while there is hope" appears also in Job xi. 18: Jer. xxxi. 16 sq.—With b compare xxiii. 13. [RUEETSCHI calls attention to the deep import of this second clause, ordinarily misunderstood. It is not a caution against excess of severity, but against the cruel kindness that kills by withholding seasonable correction. He suggests as further parallels xiii. 24; iii. 12; xxii. 15; Ecclesinast. xxx. 1.—A.]

Ver. 19. **A man of great wrath suffereth punishment.**—One "great of wrath" is one who has great wrath (Dan. xi. 44; 2 Kings xxii. 13); comp. Jer. xxxii. 19: "One great in counsel."—**For if thou wardest it off thou must do it again.**—For this use of חָצַל, lit., "deliver,"—with reference to the ruinous action of angry and contentious men specifically to "avert or ward off" (HITZIG), comp. 2 Sam. xiv. 6. [But this very passage favors more the common rendering; for the object is personal, which requires the meaning "take away, i. e., deliver," while the rendering preferred by Z. and HITZIG demands for the object the עֹנֶשׁ, punishment, of clause a. DE W., B., N., S., M., W. agree with this view, while K. supports the general idea of Z.—A.] The last phrase can express only the idea that such an interposition must be frequently repeated, and therefore that in spite of all efforts to the contrary the wrathful man must still at last fall into calamity and punishment. The entire verse accordingly gives a reason for the dissuasion in ver. 18 against too violent passion in the correction of disobedient children [but see the supplementary note in regard to the true meaning of clause b]; yet this is not done in any such way that the "thou must do it again" would refer to frequent corrections, and so to the sure prospect of real reformation, as many of the older expositors maintain.

Ver. 20. Comp. xii. 15. **Afterward**—lit., in thy future, comp. Job iii. 7; xlii. 12.—Ver. 21 gives the constant direction toward God which the wise conduct of the well trained son must take during his later life. Comp. xvi. 1, 9.

4. Vers. 22-29. Miscellaneous admonitions, relating especially to humanity, truthfulness, the fear of God, etc.—**A man's delight is his beneficence.**—חֶסֶד (comp. note on iii. 3) is here to be taken in the sense of the active manifestation of love, or charitableness, for it is not the loving disposition, but only its exhibition in liberal benefactions and offerings prompted by love to others, that can be the object of man's longing, desire or delight: [FUERST renders "Zier," ornament, honor.] Comp. Acts xx. 35: "It is more blessed to give than to receive." With this conception of clause a the preference

expressed in *b* best corresponds,—that of the poor and lowly to the "man of lies," *i. e.*, the rich man who promises aid, and might give it, but as a selfish, hard-hearted man, still fails to render it.—The LXX and Vulg. deviate somewhat in the first clause from the literal rendering of the original. From their readings, which moreover differ somewhat the one from the other, HITZIG has by combination reached what he represents as the original meaning: "From the revenue (?) of a man comes his kind gift."

Ver. 23. With *a* compare xiv. 27.—**One abideth satisfied and cannot be visited of evil**,—because Jehovah does not suffer such as fear Him to hunger (x. 3), but in every way protects, promotes and blesses them (x. 29; xiv. 26; xviii. 10, *etc.*). The subject of the verbs in clause *b* is strictly the possessor of the fear of God, the devout man.

Ver. 24. **The slothful thrusteth his hand in the dish**, *etc*—An allusion to the well-known method of eating among Oriental nations, which needs no knife and fork. A similar figure to characterize the slothful is found in chap. xii. 27. Compare also the proverb in chap. xxvi. 15, which in the first half corresponds literally with the one before us.

Ver. 25. **Smite the scorner and the simple will be wise.**—Since the scorner, according to chap. xiii. 1 (see notes on this passage), "heareth not rebuke," but is absolutely irreclaimable, the simple who "becometh wise" in view of the punishment with which the other is visited, will be such a one as is not yet quite a scorner, but is in danger of becoming so, and therefore must be deterred by fear of the penalty. In contrast with this "simple" one who walks in the right way only by constraint (comp. remarks on i. 4), the "man of understanding," he who is really prudent, learns at once on mere and simple reproof, because he has in general finer powers to discriminate between good and evil (Heb. v. 14), and has moreover a reliable tendency to good.

Ver. 26. **He that doeth violence to his father.**—The verb שָׁדַד signifies "to assail violently, roughly, to misuse," as in xxiv. 15; Ps. xvii. 9.—הִבְרִיחַ is then "to cause to flee, thrust or chase away."—With *b* compare xiii. 5; with בֵּן מֵבִישׁ in particular x. 5.

Ver. 27. **Cease, my son, to hear instruction to depart from the words of wisdom.**— Two conceptions are possible: 1) The "instruction" is that of wisdom itself, and therefore a good, wholesome discipline that leads to life; then the meaning of the verse can be only ironical, presenting under the appearance of a dissuasion from discipline in wisdom a very urgent counsel to hear and receive it (so EWALD, BERTHEAU, ELSTER). [To call this "ironical" seems to us a misnomer. "Cease to hear instruction only to despise it." What can be more direct or literally pertinent? Cease to hear "for the departing," *i. e.*, to the end, with the sole result of departure.—A.] 2) The "instruction" is evil and perverted, described in clause *b* as one that causes departure from the words of wisdom. Then the admonition is one seriously intended (thus most of the old expositors, and UMBREIT [W., H., N., S., *etc.*]). We must choose for ourselves between the two interpretations, although the connection in which the proverb stands with the preceding verse seems to speak decidedly for the former of the two.

Ver. 28. **A worthless witness scoffeth at judgment**—*i. e.*, by the lies which he utters.— **And the mouth of the wicked devoureth mischief**,—*i. e.*, mischief is the object of his passionate desire; it is a real enjoyment to him to produce calamity; he swallows it eagerly as if it were a sweet fruit (Job xx. 12; Is. xxviii. 4); he "drinketh it in like water" (Job xv. 16). Thus apprehended the expression "to devour mischief or wrong" has nothing at all offensive in it, and we do not need either with the Chaldee (comp. GEIER, *etc.*) to get rid of it by exchanging the idea of "devouring" for that of "uttering," or in any other way; nor with HITZIG (following the LXX) to read instead of "mischief" (אָוֶן) "justice" (דִּין), and to translate accordingly "and the mouth of the wicked devoureth justice."

Ver. 29. **Judgments are prepared for scorners and stripes for the back of fools.** —The "scorners" are quite the same as the "fools," as the first clause of ver. 25 shows; and the "stripes" (the term the same as in xviii. 6) are a special form of "judicial penalties or judgments." The verse as a whole, with which chap. xiv. 3; xxvi. 3 should be compared, stands in the relation of an explanation to the preceding, especially to the idea that the wicked eagerly devours calamity. [Their eagerness is not forgotten by a just God, and fitting judgments await them.—A.]

DOCTRINAL, ETHICAL, HOMILETIC AND PRACTICAL.

In the considerably rich and varied contents of the chapter, that which stands forth most conspicuously as the leading conception and central idea is the idea of the gentleness and mildness to be manifested in intercourse with one's neighbors. Gentleness and an humble devotion, ready even for suffering, man ought to exhibit first of all toward God, against whom it is not proper to complain even in calamity (ver. 3), who is in all things to be trusted (vers. 14, 17), according to whose wise counsels it is needful always to shape the life (ver. 21), and in whose fear one should ever walk (ver. 23). Not less is a gentle demeanor a duty for the married in their mutual intercourse (ver. 13, 14); for parents in the training of their children (vers. 18, 19, 25); for children toward their parents (vers. 20, 26); for the rich in dispensing benefactions among the poor (vers. 1, 4, 7, 22); for rulers and kings toward their subjects (ver. 12; comp. vers. 6, 10); for men in general in their intercourse with their neighbors (ver. 11; comp. vers. 19, 27, 28). By far the larger number of the proverbs in the chapter are therefore arranged with reference to this leading and underlying conception of gentleness; the whole presents itself as a thorough unfolding of the praises and commendations of meekness in the New Testament, which are well known; *e. g.*, Matth. v. 5; James i. 20, 21.—Only some single proverbs are less aptly classified in this connection, such as the warning against hasty, inconsiderate, rash action (ver. 2); that against untruthfulness (vers. 9, 28); against slothfulness (vers. 15, 24); against folly and a mocking contempt of the holy (vers. 8, 16, 29). And yet these interspersed sentences of a somewhat incongruous stamp do not by any means essentially disturb the connection of the whole which is maintained and ruled by the fundamental idea of gentleness.

Therefore we may very suitably, in the *homiletical treatment of the chapter as a whole*, take this as the general subject: The praise of meekness, as it is to be exhibited, 1) in respect to God, by the quiet reception of His word (James i. 21), and bringing forth fruit with patience (Luke viii. 15); 2) in relation to one's neighbors, by humility, obedience, love, compassion, *etc.*— Comp. STÖCKER: Against contempt of poor neighbors: 1) Dissuasion from this peculiarly evil fruit of wrath and uncharitableness (vers. 1-15); 2) enumeration of some of the chief means to be used against wrath in general (*remedia, s. retinacula iræ*, vers. 16-29).—WOHLFARTH: On contempt of the poor, and the moderation of anger.

Vers. 1-7. GEIER (on ver. 1): To the pious poor it may impart a strong consolation, that notwithstanding their poverty they are better esteemed in the sight of God than a thousand ungodly and foolish rich men.—*Berleburg Bible* (on ver. 1): He who has nothing that is his own, who accounts himself the poorest of all men, who sees nothing good in himself, and yet with all this stands in the uprightness of his heart and in all simplicity, is far more pleasing to God than the souls that are rich in endowments and in learning, and yet despise and deride the simple.— STARKE (on ver. 4): Art thou forsaken by thy friends, by father and mother, by all men, be of good comfort! if it be only on account of goodness, God will never forsake thee.—(On vers. 6, 7): We often trust in men more than in God, but find very often that this hope in men is abortive, and is brought to shame.—[ROBERT HALL (on ver. 2): Sermon on the advantages of knowledge to the lower classes.—T. ADAMS (on ver. 4): Solomon says not the rich man, but riches; it is the money, not the man, they hunt.]

Vers. 8-17. [MUFFET (on ver. 8): Every one hath a heart, but every one possesseth not his heart. He possesseth his heart that, furnishing it with knowledge of the truth, holdeth his heart firm and fast therein, not suffering his courage to fail, nor losing that good possession which he hath gotten.]—CHALMERS (on ver. 10): With all the preference here expressed for virtuous poverty—the smallness of rank and the violence done by the upstart rule of the lower over the higher, are not overlooked.]—MELANCTHON (on ver. 10): The ungoverned and uneducated are in prosperous conditions only the more insolent and base, as, *e. g.*, Rehoboam, when he became king, Alexander the Great after his great victories, *etc.* —*Tübingen Bible* (on ver. 11): It is great wisdom to bear injustice with patience, and to overcome and even to gain over one's persecutors with benefits, 1 Pet ii. 19; Matth. v. 44 sq.—(On vers. 13, 14): God's wise providence manifests itself very specially in the bestowal of good and pious partners in marriage.—VON GERLACH (on ver. 17): The poor the Lord regards as specially His own, and therefore adjusts those debts of theirs which they cannot pay.—*Berleb. Bible:* With that which the righteous man dispenses in benefactions to the poor, he is serving God in his counsels with respect to men.—[Lord BACON (on ver. 11): As for the first wrong, it does but offend the law; but the revenge of that wrong putteth the law out of office. Certainly, in taking revenge a man is but even with his enemy, but in passing it over he is superior.—TRAPP (on ver. 11): The manlier any man is, the milder and readier to pass by an offence. When any provoke us we say, We will be even with him. There is a way whereby we may be not even with him, but above him, and that is, forgive him.— ARNOT: The only legitimate anger is a holy emotion directed against an unholy thing. Sin, and not our neighbor, must be its object; zeal for righteousness, and not our own pride, must be its distinguishing character.—MUFFET (on ver. 17): The Lord will not only pay for the poor man, but requite him that gave alms with usury, returning great gifts for small. Give, then, thy house, and receive heaven; give transitory goods, and receive a durable substance; give a cup of cold water and receive God's Kingdom —W. BATES: As there are numerous examples of God's blasting the covetous, so it is as visible He prospers the merciful, sometimes by a secret blessing dispensed by an invisible hand, and sometimes in succeeding their diligent endeavors in their callings.]

Ver. 18-21. *Tübingen Bible:* Cruelty to children is no discipline. Wisdom is needful, that one in the matter of strictness may do neither too much nor too little to them.—ZELTNER: Too sharp makes a notched edge, and too great strictness harms more than it helps, not only in the discipline of children, but in all stations and relations.—STARKE (on ver. 21): God is the best counsellor. Who ever enters upon His cause with Him must prosper in it.—[J. FOSTER: The great collective whole of the "devices" of all hearts constitutes the grand complex scheme of the human race for their happiness. Respecting the object of every device God has His design. There is in the world a want of coalescence between the designs of man and God; an estranged spirit of design on the part of man. God's design is fixed and paramount, and "shall stand "]

Vers. 22-29. MELANCTHON (on ver. 25): Not all, it is true, are improved by the warning example of the correction which comes upon the wicked, but some, that is, those who are rational and not insane, those who hearken to admonition and follow it.—STARKE (on ver. 25): The final aim of all penalty should be the improvement as well as him who is punished as of others who may there see themselves mirrored.—(On ver. 26): He who would not experience shame and sorrow of heart from his children, let him accustom them seasonably to obedience, to the fear of God and reverence.—J. LANGE: God's word is the right rule and measure of our life. Whosoever departs from this, his instruction is deceitful and ruinous.—HASIUS (on ver. 29): Every sin, whether great or small, has by God's ordinance its definite penalty. Happy he who recognizes this, and knows how to shun these punishments.

[Bp. HALL (on ver. 22): That which should be the chief desire of a man is his beneficence and kindness to others; and if a rich man promise much and perform nothing, a poor man that is unable either to undertake or perform is better than he.—ARNOT: A poor man is better than a liar; a standard has been set up in the market place to measure the pretences of men withal, and those who will not employ it must take the consequences.—CHALMERS (on ver. 23): Religion may begin with fear, but will end in the sweets and satisfactions of a spontaneous and living principle of righteousness.—Bp. SHERLOCK (on ver. 27); Since the fears and apprehensions of guilt are such strong motives to infidelity, the innocence of the heart is absolutely necessary to the freedom of the mind. We must answer for the vanity of our reasonings as well as the vanity of our actions, and if we take pains to invent vain reasoning to oppose to the plain evidence that God has afforded us of His being and power, and to undermine the proofs and authority on which religion stands, we may be sure we shall not go unpunished.]

ε) Admonition to avoid drunkenness, sloth, a contentious spirit, etc.

CHAP. XX.

1 Wine is a mocker, strong drink boisterous,
whosoever is led astray thereby is not wise.
2 As the roaring of a lion is the dread of the king;
he that provoketh him sinneth against his own soul.
3 It is an honor to a man to dwell far from strife,
but every fool breaketh forth.
4 The sluggard plougheth not because of the cold;
he seeketh in harvest and hath nothing.
5 Counsel in the heart of a man is as deep waters,
but a wise man draweth it out.
6 Many proclaim each his own grace;
but a faithful man who can find?
7 He who in his innocence walketh uprightly,
blessed are his children after him!
8 A king sitting on his throne,
searcheth out all evil with his eyes.
9 Who can say, I have made my heart clean,
I am pure from my sin?
10 Divers weights and divers measures,
an abomination to Jehovah are they both.
11 Even a child maketh himself known in his deeds,
whether his work be pure, and whether it be right.
12 The ear that heareth, and the eye that seeth—
Jehovah hath created them both.
13 Love not sleep, lest thou come to poverty;
open thine eyes, and be satisfied with thy bread.
14 "It is bad, it is bad!" saith the buyer,
but when he is gone his way then he boasteth.
15 There is gold, and a multitude of pearls;
but a precious vase are lips of knowledge.
16 Take his garment that is surety for a stranger,
and for strangers make him a bondsman.
17 Bread of deceit is sweet to a man,
but afterward his mouth is filled with gravel.
18 Plans are established by counsel,
and with good advice make war.

19 He that goeth about as a talebearer revealeth secrets ;
    with him that openeth wide his lips have nothing to do.
20 He that curseth father and mother,
    his light goeth out in utter darkness.
21 An inheritance that is hastily gained in the beginning,
    its end will not be blessed.
22 Say not: Let me avenge the evil!
    wait on Jehovah ; he will help thee.
23 An abomination to Jehovah are diverse weights,
    and a deceitful balance is not good.
24 Man's steps are of Jehovah ;
    man—how shall he understand his way?
25 It is a snare to a man that he hath vowed hastily,
    and after vows to inquire.
26 A wise king sifteth the wicked,
    and bringeth the (threshing) wheel over them.
27 The spirit of man is a candle of Jehovah,
    searching all the chambers of the body.
28 Grace and truth preserve the king,
    and he upholdeth his throne by mercy.
29 The glory of young men is their strength,
    and the honor of old men is the grey head.
30 Wounding stripes are a correction of evil,
    and strokes in the inner chambers of the body.

GRAMMATICAL AND CRITICAL.

Ver. 2. [כְּתִיַּבְּרוּ] is either to be pointed with Hitzig כְּתִיַּבְּרוֹ (partic. with suffix from a denominative verb of Aramaic form תִיַּבֵּר, "to throw into a passion, to excite wrath" [יַעְבְּרָה], or, which is probably simpler, with EWALD, BERTHEAU, [FUERST, etc., to conceive of it as a flithp. participle, whose ordinary meaning, " to become excited against any one," (comp. xxvi 17) here passes over into the transitive idea, "to excite some one against one's self, to call some one forth against one's self. Altogether too artificial, and in conflict with the old versions (LXX: ὁ παροξύνων αὐτόν; Vulg.: qui provocat eum) is UMBREIT'S explanation: "he that arouseth himself (riseth up) against him (the king)." [E. V., H., S., M., etc , agree with our author; DE W. and NOYES, with UMBREIT].

Ver. 3. שֶׁבֶת is according to the Masoretic punctuation the Infinitive of יָשַׁב [as in Isa. xxx. 7] and not, as most of the recent Interpreters [among them UMBREIT, EWALD, HITZIG, [FUERST. M . etc]], regard it, a substantive from the root שָׁבַה, for which derivation certainly no other support could be adduced than Ex. xxi. 19.

Ver. 4. The K'ri וְשָׁאַל is doubtless preferable to the K'thibh יִשְׁאַל (Ps. cix. 10), for "to beg in harvest" would give a meaning too intense. [So H., S., etc.]—HITZIG changes חָרֶף into כְּתָרֶף, which, according to Arabic analogies, should mean "a fruit basket;" he then reads יִשְׁאַל "he demands, desires," and obtains the meaning:

"A paneler [?] the sluggard doth not provide [?],
trieth to borrow [?] in harvest, and nothing cometh of it [?]."

Ver. 9. [טָהַרְתִּי, cited by BÖTT. § 948, c, as one of the examples of the "stative" perfect, used to describe spiritual states. אֹמַר, one of his examples of the "Fiens licitum," the Imperf. used to express what can be: " who can say;" § 950, 3. —A.].

Ver. 10. [לְקַח] standing emphatically at the beginning of a verse, one of the few instances of the full Imperative form; BÖTT. § 1101. 2—A.].

Ver. 18. EWALD proposes instead of עֲשֵׂה to read the Infin. עָשֹׂה, as in chap. xxi. 3; but the Imperative seems more appropriate, and gives to the expression greater vivacity.

Ver. 22. [וְיֹשַׁע לָךְ], one of the few examples of double accent, the penultimate accent marking the rhythm, that on the ultima sustaining its vowel; BÖTT. § 482. e. f.—The Jussive form with ו consec. is used to assert a sure result; BÖTT. " a firmativ consecutiv."—A.].

Ver. 25. יָלַע, essentially identical with לָעָה, signifies, according to the Arabic, "to speak inconsiderately, to promise thoughtlessly;" קֹדֶשׁ is here not a substantive, but an Infinitive continuing the finite verb. According to this simple explanation, which is lexically well justified, EWALD'S conception of יָלַע as a substantive, which should be pointed יֶלַע, and translated, " hasty vow," may be dismissed as superfluous ; and also the derivation preferred by JEROME, LUTHER and both rs of the older expositors, from the root לוּעַ " to swallow" [Vulgate: devorare sanctos; LUTHER : " das Heilige lästern "]. [GESEN. and FUERST are authorities for the view adopted by our author, while BÖTT., with great positiveness (§ 964, 5 and n. 7] pronounces the form a Jussive form with a "permissive" meaning, from יָלוּעַ or יֶלַע ; "let him only, i. e if he only hurry or hasten too much."—A.].

Ver. 29. בַּחוּרִים, young men, juvenes, as distinguished from בְּחֻרִים, youth, juventas ; comp. BÖTT., § 408, β —A].

12

EXEGETICAL.

1. Vers. 1-5. Various precepts of prudence and integrity, (especially directed against drunkenness, a contentious spirit and indolence).—**Wine is a mocker.** The spirit of wine, and in like manner that of "mead" or "strong drink" (שֵׁכָר, σίκερα, Luke i. 15),* a frequent accompaniment or substitute of wine (comp. Lev. x. 9; Num. vi. 3; Judg. xiii. 4 sq.; Isa. v. 11; xxviii. 7, etc.), appears here "personified, or represented as in a sense an evil demon, which excites to frivolous wantonness, to wild and boisterous action, and by the confusion of the senses into which it plunges man, robs him of all clear self-possession" (ELSTER).—**Whosoever is led astray thereby is not wise.** With this phrase "to stagger, or reel because of or under something" comp. v. 19. For the general meaning, Isa. xxviii. 7.

Ver. 2. With clause a compare xix. 12 (which is literally identical with the clause before us, except that this has אֵימָה, "dread" [terrible word, an utterance that spreads terror] instead of זַעַף).—**He that provoketh him sinneth against his own soul.** For the first phrase see Critical Notes.—"Sinneth against his own soul" (נַפְשׁוֹ, an accusative of respect); comp. kindred although not identical expressions in viii. 36; vi. 32.

Ver. 3. **It is an honor to a man to dwell far from strife.** See Critical Notes. To "dwell far from strife" is an apt expression to describe the quiet, peaceable demeanor of the wise man, in contrast with the passionate activity of the contentious multitude. For the meaning and use of the verb of clause b, יִתְגַּלָּע, comp. xvii. 14; xviii. 1; with the meaning of the whole expression comp. xix. 11.

Ver. 4. **The sluggard plougheth not because of the cold**, that is, because the season in which his field should be cared for is too disagreeably rough and cold for him. [For illustration see THOMSON's *Land and Book*, I., 207]. In consequence of this indolent procedure "he seeketh in harvest"—"for fruits of his field"—"and there is nothing." See Critical Notes. [RUEETSCHI, *ubi supra*, p. 149, retaining the general meaning, objects that the term here used is not the one that of itself describes the cold and stormy harvest time; he therefore retains the temporal meaning of the preposition, and renders, "from the time of the (fruit) harvest onward," *etc.*, this being the proper time for the ploughing and sowing, a time which none can suffer to pass by.—A.]

Ver. 5. **Counsel in the heart of man is as deep waters**, *etc.; i. e.* the purpose that one has formed may be difficult to fathom (see the same figure, chap. xviii. 4); a wise man nevertheless draws him out, elicits from him his secret, and brings it to light. דָּלָה means to "draw" water with a bucket (דְּלִי, Isa. xl. 15), to bring it up laboriously from a deep place (Ex. ii. 16, 19)—a metaphor suggested by the figure in clause a, and evidently very expressive.

2. Vers. 6-11. On the general sinfulness of men.—**Many proclaim each his own grace** (or love). The verb which is originally to "call" is here to "proclaim, to boast of," *prædicare*. אִישׁ, "each individual" of the "many a man," the mass or majority of men.—**But a faithful man who can find?** For the phrase "a man of fidelity," comp. xiii. 17; xiv. 5; for the general meaning, Ps. cxvi. 11; Rom. iii. 4.

Ver. 7. **He who in his innocence walketh upright.** Thus, taking צַדִּיק attributively, as an adjective subordinated to the participle, the LXX, Vulg., Syr., had already treated the construction, and later EWALD and HITZIG [and KAMPH.]; while recent expositors generally render, "is a righteous man" [H. and N.], or in other instances treat the "righteous" as the subject (UMBREIT, ELSTER, *etc.*), [S. and M., E. V., and DE W.].—With this benediction upon the descendants of the righteous in clause b comp. xiv. 26; with the אַחֲרָיו, "after him," *i. e.* after his death, Gen. xxiv. 67; Job xxi. 21.

Ver. 8. **A king . . . . searcheth out all evil with his eyes.** The natural reference is to the king as he corresponds with his ideal, that he be the representative on earth of God, the supreme Judge. Comp. xvi. 10; also Isa. xi. 4, where similar attributes to these are ascribed to the Messiah, as the ideal typically perfect king. With this use of the verb "to sift or winnow," to separate, comp. ver. 26.

Ver. 9. **Who can say: I have made my heart clean, I am pure from my sin?** The question naturally conveys a decided negative by implication: "No one can say," *etc.*; comp. ver. 6 b, and ver. 24 b. It is not a permanent purity, a "having kept one's self pure" (from birth onward) that is the subject of the emphatic denial in this proverb (in opposition to BERTHEAU's view), but a having attained to moral perfection, the having really conquered all the sins that were in existence before, that is denied. We should therefore bring into comparison not passages like Job xiv. 4; xv. 14; Ps. li. 5 (7), but such as 1 Kings viii. 46; Eccles. vii. 20; 1 John i. 8; James iii. 2, *etc.* With this expression, "I have made my heart clean," comp. Ps. lxxiii. 13.

Ver. 10 draws attention to deception in business intercourse as a peculiar and prominent form of that universal sinfulness which has just been spoken of as having no exceptions. Comp. chap. xi. 1, and ver. 23 below. With the language in clause b compare xvii. 15 b.

Vers. 11. **Even a child maketh himself known in his deeds.** With regard to the גַּם, "even," which does not belong to the word next following, but to the נַעַר, "child" (as GEIER, UMBREIT, ELSTER, HITZIG rightly interpret), comp. remarks on xix. 2.—"His deeds" EWALD and UMBREIT are inclined to render by "plays, sports," in disregard of the uniform meaning of the word, and in opposition to the only correct construction of the "even." מַעֲלָלִים is rather the works, the actions, the individual results or

---

* For a full and valuable discussion of the meaning of these and kindred terms, see an article by Dr. LAURIE in the *Bibliotheca Sacra*, January, 1869.—A.

the child's self-determination, from which it may even now be with confidence inferred of what sort "his work" is, *i. e.* the entire inner tendency of his life, his character (if one prefers the notion), the nature of his spirit (HITZIG).— That this thought also stands related to the fact of universal sinfulness needs no fuller demonstration. Comp. the familiar German proverb, "*Was ein Dörnchen werden will spitzt sich bei Zeiten*" [what means to become a thorn is early sharpening].

3 Vers. 12-19. Admonitions to confidence in God, to industry, prudence and integrity.—**The ear that heareth, and the eye that seeth—Jehovah hath created them both.** An allusion, plainly, not to the adaptation, the divine purpose and direction in the functions of hearing and seeing (HITZIG), but to God's omniscience as a powerful motive to the fear of God and confidence in Him; comp. xv. 3, and especially Ps. xciv. 9.

Ver. 13. With *a* compare vi. 9, 10.—**Open thine eyes, and thou shalt be satisfied with bread.** The imperative clause, "be satisfied with bread," has here the meaning of a consecutive clause, as in iii. 4. [This illustrates what BÖTT., § 957, 6, calls the "desponsive" use of the Imperative, conveying sure promises]. With this language compare xii. 11. To "open the eyes" is naturally the opposite of sleep and drowsiness, and therefore the description of wakeful, vigorous, active conduct.

Ver. 14. "**It is bad, it is bad!**" **saith the buyer, but when he is gone his way** (וְאָזֵל לוֹ), for which we should perhaps with HITZIG read אָזַל לוֹ, corresponds with the German, "*und trollt er sich*" [when he takes himself off], when he has gone his way) **then he boasteth,** *i. e.* of the good bargain that he has made. The verse therefore censures the well-known craft, the deceitful misrepresentation, with which business men seek to buy their wares as cheap as possible, below their real value if they can. In opposition to the true meaning of קָנָה, as well as inconsistently with the idea of boasting in the second clause, SCHULTENS and ELSTER (and LUTHER likewise) render: "It is bad, it is bad! saith the owner (?) of his possession: but when it is gone(?) then he boasteth of it (?)."

Ver. 15. **There is indeed gold and a multitude of pearls,** *etc.* As these precious things are compared in chap. iii. 14, 15; viii. 11, with intelligent, wise dispositions and discourse, so are they here compared with wise lips, that is, with the organ of wise discourse. In this connection we should doubtless notice the difference between "gold and pearls" as valuable native material, not yet wrought into articles of ornament, and on the other hand, the lips as an artistic "vase" or other "vessel" (that has come forth from the hand of the divine artificer, and is adorned and embellished by man's wise use of it).

Ver. 16. Comp. vi. 1-5; xi. 15; xvii. 18. Instead of the warnings that are there found against foolish suretyship, we have here in a livelier style a demand to give over at once, without hesitation as bondsman any such inconsiderate surety.—**And for strangers make him a surety.** Instead of the K'ri "for a strange woman," *i. e.*, an adulteress, we should unquestionably retain here the K'thibh, "for strangers, unknown people;" while in the corresponding passage, chap. xxvii. 13, נָכְרִיָּה "the strange woman" is undoubtedly the correct reading.

Ver. 17. **Bread of deceit is sweet to a man,** *i. e.*, enjoyments and possessions secured by means of deceit; comp. xxiii. 3; ix. 17.—For this use of "sand, gravel," (an appropriate emblem to describe a thing not to be enjoyed) comp. Lam. iii. 16.

Ver. 18. **Plans are established by counsel.** עֵצָה here equivalent to סוֹד, counsel which one takes with another,—comp. xv. 22.— **And with good advice make war.** The "advice" or management (comp. i. 5) is plainly contemplated as the result of the counsel that has been taken; comp. xxiv. 6.

Ver. 19. With clause *a* compare xi. 13; with *b*, xiii. 3.

4. Vers. 20-23. Against hatred of parents, legacy-hunting, revenge, deceit.—**He that curseth father and mother,** and so in the boldest way transgresses the fifth commandment of the law, (Ex. xx. 12, comp. Ex. xxi. 17; Lev. xx. 9).—**His light goeth out in utter darkness.** The same figure is used also in xiii. 9, here as there serving to illustrate the hopeless destruction of life and prosperity.—In regard to אִישׁוֹן the "pupil of the eye, blackness, midnight"— for which the K'ri unnecessarily demands the Aramaic אֱשׁוּן—comp. notes on vii. 9.

Ver. 21. **An inheritance that hath been hastily gained in the beginning.** In favor of the K'ri כְּבֹהֶלֶת, "hurried, hastened" (comp. ESTHER, viii. 14, and also remarks above on chap. xiii. 11), we have the testimony of the ancient versions, the parallel in xxviii. 20, 22, and besides the position of this verse after verse 20. For it is precisely the wayward son, who despises and curses his parents, that will be very readily disposed to seize upon his inheritance before the time against their will (comp. Luke xv. 12), and possibly even to drive his parents violently out of their possession (comp. xix. 26). That no blessing can rest upon such possessions, that as they were unrighteously acquired at first so they must in the end be wasted and come to nought, is a truth which clause *b* in a simple way brings to view. The K'thibh מְבֹהֶלֶת would either signify "cursed," in accordance with Zech. xi. 8 (so ELSTER, *e. g.*, regards it), or in accordance with the Arabic, "acquired by avarice" (so UMBREIT). [H., N., W., S., M., BERTHEAU, KAMPH, *etc*, agree in supporting the exposition adopted by our author].

Ver. 22. **Say not: let me avenge the evil;** *i. e*, do not desire to requite evil with evil, do not avenge thyself for offences that have been done thee; comp. xxiv. 29; Deut. xxxii. 35; Rom. xii. 17; 1 Pet. iii. 9.—The second member of clause *b* is evidently a consecutive clause, as the Jussive frequently is after the Imperative;

comp. Isa. viii. 10; 2 Kings v. 10. The Vulgate correctly renders "*et liberabit te,*" while the LXX, ROSENMUELLER, EWALD, *etc.*, treat the words as a final clause; "that he may keep thee."

Ver. 23. Comp. ver. 10. **A deceitful balance is not good**; (Z., "is shameful," lit. is "not good, is no good," as in xvii. 26; xviii. 5); a *litotes*, expressing the idea of that which is *very* base.

5. Ver. 24-30. Miscellaneous admonitions to the fear of God and integrity.—**From Jehovah are man's steps**; comp. xvi. 9; Ps. xxxvii. 23. The "steps" are naturally "not acts in their subjective ethical aspect, but these acts according to their result, their several issues in a parallel series of experiences,—and therefore those events depending on the action of man which make up its external counterpart" (HITZIG).—In regard to the emphatic negative import of the question in clause *b*, compare remarks on ver. 9.

Ver. 25. Before the קֹדֶשׁ יָלַע [he hath vowed hastily] there should be supplied the conjunction אִם, "if;" therefore render literally "it is a snare to a man, vows he hastily," *i. e.*, if he in a hasty manner promises to devote a thing to God as sacred (as κορβᾶν, Mark vii. 11). See Critical notes.—Furthermore hasty consecrations, and in like manner, according to clause *b* the hasty assumption of vows, are here called a "snare" (קְרֵשׁ, comp. remarks on xviii. 7), because he who makes the rash vow afterward easily repents of it, and falls under the temptation sinfully to break or to recall his vow (comp. Numb. xxx. 3; Eccles. v. 3).

Ver. 26. **A wise king sifteth the wicked.** To "sift" or "winnow" expresses here, just as it does in ver. 8, a discriminating separation of the chaff from the grain; comp. for this familiar and pertinent figure Ps. i. 4; Isa. xvii. 13; Am. ix. 9.—**And bringeth the wheel over them**, *i. e.*, the wheel of the threshing cart (Isa. xxviii. 27 sq.), which however is contemplated here not so much as an instrument of harvesting, as rather in the light of a means and emblem of the severe punishment of captive enemies (in accordance with 2 Sam. xii. 31; 1 Chron. xx. 3; Am. i. 3). There is therefore no offence to be taken in view of the fact that in the operation of threshing the crushing with the wheel preceded the winnowing or sifting, while here it is not mentioned until after it (in reply to BERTHEAU).

Ver. 27. **The spirit of man is a candle of Jehovah;** lit., "man's *breath*," for this is the first meaning of the Hebrew term נְשָׁמָה (Gen. ii. 7); yet it is not the *soul* which pervades and animates all the members of the body (as HITZIG renders), according to the view of many of the elder expositors, as also STARKE, VON GERLACH, *etc.*, but the *spirit*, as the higher manifestation of soul-life, or if any one prefers, the *reason*, *self-consciousness* (UMBREIT, ELSTER) that is intended by the expression. For all analogies are wanting, at least within the range of the Bible, for a comparison of the *soul* with a light (the Arabic maxim in KAZWINI *Cosmog.* I. 355, in which the soul, *Nephesch*, is designated the light of the body, plainly has no bearing on our present object). On the contrary the inner light or eye, (τὸ φῶς τὸ ἐν σοί) of which the Lord speaks in Matth. vi. 22, 23, is unquestionably an organ or factor of the higher spiritual soul, more precisely designated as the νοῦς or the reason. In support of the idea that נְשָׁמָה in the passage before us signifies essentially this and nothing else, there may be adduced the identity of נִשְׁמַת חַיִּים with רוּחַ חַיִּים as indicated by a comparison of Gen. vi. 17 with Gen. ii. 7. The expression "candle of Jehovah" moreover seems to point rather to the *spirit* as that factor in human personality which proceeds immediately from God, than to the *soul* which inheres in the physical life, and does not rise essentially above it.*—[WORDSW. and some other English expositors understand the allusion to be specifically to the conscience; the majority are content with the more comprehensive term *spirit*, including intellectual and moral factors.—A.].—**Searching all the chambers of the body**, *i. e.*, looking through its whole interior,—which clearly suggests the *ruling* relation of this "searcher" to the body, the sphere of its activity, and so is very pertinent with respect to the spirit, but not to the soul. In regard to the "chambers of the body" comp. ver. 36, and xviii. 8.

Ver. 28. **Grace and truth preserve the king.** "Mercy and truth," or "love and truth," not quite in the sense of ili. 3; the attributes of a king are intended by the terms, which should rather be rendered "grace and truth." With this idea of "preserving," comp. Ps. xxv. 21; with that of "upholding" in clause *b*, Isa. ix. 6.

Ver. 29. Comp. xvi. 31; xvii. 6.

Ver. 30. **Wounding stripes are a correction of evil and strokes** (that reach) **to the chambers of the body;** *i. e.*, stripes or blows that cause wounds, such as one administers to his son under severe discipline (comp. xix. 18), have this beneficial effect, that they intend a salutary infliction or correction "on the evil" in this son, as a scouring of the rust which has gathered on a metal cleanses and brightens the metal. And not merely does such an external chastening as this accomplish the sharp correction of the son; it penetrates deep into the inmost parts of the body (comp. remarks on ver. 27), *i. e.*, to the innermost foundations of his personal life and consciousness, and so exerts a reforming influence on him. Thus EWALD and ELSTER correctly render, and substantially UMBREIT also (comp. LUTHER's version, which expresses the true meaning at least in general), while BERTHEAU regards תַּמְרוּק, "remedial application," as the subject, and (after the analogy of Esther ii. 3, 9, 12) understands it to refer to "the application of ointments and perfumes for beautifying" (!?); HITZIG, however, naturally emends again, and by changing הַמְרִיק to תָּמֹר יָקֵב obtains the meaning: "Wounding stripes drop (?) into the cup of the wicked (?) and strokes into the chambers of the body."—[Our English version is defective from its obscurity: *The blueness of a wound cleanseth away evil.*

---

* VON RUDLOFF, *Lehre vom Menschen*, 2d Ed., p. 48, also takes a correct view of the passage.

Recent expositors are clearer in their renderings, and differ but slightly in their choice of terms. Stuart; *Wounding stripes* (II.; *the bruises of a wound*) *are the remedy for the base* (II.; *are a cleanser in a wicked man*); N. and M.; *The scars* (*stripes*) *of a wound are a cleansing from evil;* Wordsw, paraphrasing somewhat more: *The stripes of a wound are the* (only) *wiping away of* (certain cases of) *evil.*]

DOCTRINAL AND ETHICAL.

It is evidently impossible to derive the many maxims of the chapter from a single primary and fundamental thought. The warning against drunkenness or the passion of the intemperate, which introduces the diversified series, has in the further progress of the discourse no successor whatsoever of similar form, and could be retained as the theme or the germinal thought for the whole only by the most artificial operations, such as Stöcker, *e. g.*, and others of former times undertook (comp. the introductory paragraph to the Homiletic hints). Much more readily might a *contentious and revengeful spirit* be regarded as the chief object of the admonitory representations and suggestions of this section (see vers. 2, 3, 6, 14, 19, 22). But a space at least equally large is given to the dissuasions from *indolence and deceit* (vers. 4, 10, 13, 14, 17, 23), and again to the commendations, somewhat more general in their form, of *wise and upright conduct* (vers. 7, 9, 11, 15, 18, 24—26, 29). Only a single group of proverbs in this chap. stands out from the mass of diverse and isolated maxims and aphorisms, as contemplating one object with considerable compactness and unity of view. This is the division which relates to the *general sinfulness* of men (vers. 6-11). And this in fact presents also the richest and most important doctrinal material which the chapter anywhere contains. Starting with the fact, alas! too palpable, that really faithful men, *i. e.*, men who are on all sides reliable, free from all falsehood and untruth, are to be found nowhere on the earth (ver 6; chap. John vii. 46, and the passages cited above in notes to ver 6), the representation brings into the foreground the ideal of moral innocence, uprightness, and the practical prosperity which belongs to it, as this ought actually to be realized by humanity (ver. 7). It then at once suggests the crying contrast which exists between the real moral condition of humanity and the ethical aim of its perfect state, pointing to the manifold and numberless forms of evil in conflict with which, in judicial exposures and punishments of which, earthly kings even now are engaged (ver. 8). It next gives an outright expression to the universal need of purification and improvement (ver. 9), and then brings forward a special and conspicuous example of the deceitful acts and endeavors of all men, so odious to God (ver. 10). It concludes at length with a hint of that corruption in the devices and impulses of the human heart which appears even in the earliest periods of youth (ver. 11; Gen. viii. 21). The most important of these utterances, which are perhaps intentionally arranged as they are with reference to the very line of thought that has been indicated, is at all events the testimony given in ver. 9 to the impossibility of ever attaining in this present human life to a complete moral purity and perfection. We have here a proverb which, in addition to the universality, guiltiness and penal desert of the original corruption of human nature, attests very distinctly also its *permanent* character, *i. e.*, its continued obstinate and ineradicable inherence in the soul and body of man, its "*tenacitas, sive pertinax inhæsio.*" by virtue of which a certain spark of evil (or tinder for evil), a concealed germ and root of sinful lust (*fomes peccati s. concupiscentia*) remains in all men, even the most sanctified and morally elevated, until their very death. This proverb is also especially noteworthy, because "in contrast with the style of conception which is elsewhere predominant in the proverbs, according to which the imperfection of all human piety is but slightly emphasized, and he who is relatively pious is allowed to pass as righteous, it gives expression to the unsatisfying nature of all moral endeavors, as never conducting to the full extirpation of the sense of guilt, and a perfect feeling of peace with God; *it accordingly suggests the need of a higher revelation, in which the sense of guilt, and of an ever imperfect fulfilment of duty shall finally be wholly overcome*" (Elster).

Memorable doctrinal and ethical truths are furthermore contained, particularly in ver. 1, with its significant personification of the demon of mockery, and wild, boisterous recklessness, which as it were lurks concealed in wine and other intoxicating drinks;—in vers. 12 and 24, with their allusion to the mightily pervading influence of God, the Omniscient, over all the acts and fates of men;—in ver. 22, with its dissuasion from avenging one's self and the spirit of retaliation, so suggestive of the New Testament command of love to enemies;—in ver. 25, with its warning against the hasty assumption of religious vows;—in ver. 27, with its beautiful illustration of the all-embracing authority, and the moulding influence which man's spirit, as his inward divine light, must exercise over his entire physical and spiritual life (and in the normal self-determination does actually exercise);—and finally, in ver. 28, with its admirable exaltation of the loving, faithful, upright disposition of kings as the firmest prop to their thrones. Compare above, the Exegetical explanations of all these passages.

[Lawson (on ver. 7): The integrity of the just man is not like the pretended integrity of the moralist, for it includes piety, justice, sobriety, and a conscientious regard to every precept of God, without excluding those that appear to vain men to be of small importance, or those that most directly oppose the prevailing disposition of the mind.—Chalmers (on ver. 27): In order to salvation, the Spirit must deal with the subjective mind, and illuminate the ruling faculty there, as well as set the objective word before us, which is of His own inspiration. A more vivid conscience will give us a livelier sense of God's law; a more discerning consciousness, reaching to all the thoughts and tendencies of the inner man, will give us a more convincing view of our sad and manifold deficiencies from that law.]

HOMILETIC AND PRACTICAL.

Homily on the chapter as a whole: The general sinfulness and need of salvation on the part of all men, demonstrated 1) from the magnitude and variety of the vices that prevail in humanity; 2) from the rareness of a sincere striving after virtue; 3) from the absolute impossibility of finding complete purity and holiness except in Christ.—STÖCKER (less in harmony with the proper and chief contents of the chapter; comp. what has been said above): Of intemperance in drinking, and its evil consequences: 1) Delineation of the *ἀπωρία vini*; 2) Reference to the *incommoda* (the inconveniences), and 3) to the *remedia ebrietatis* (the remedies of drunkenness).—In like manner WOHLFARTH, *Calwer Handb.,* etc.; against the intemperance and the wildness of the scoffer.

Vers. 1–5. STARKE (on ver. 1): He who is inclined to physical drunkenness will not be vigorous spiritually; Eph. v. 18 (comp. VON GERLACH: A wild, unconscious excitement is far from a holy wisdom).—GEIER (on ver. 2): The wrath of an earthly king is intolerable; how much more the infinite eternal wrath of the King of all kings against persistent sinners at the judgment!—[LAWSON (on ver. 3): A fool is so self-conceited that he can bear no contradiction; so impertinent that he will have a hand in every other man's business; so proud that he cannot bear to be found in the wrong; and so stubborn that he will have the last word, although his lips should prove his destruction].—ZELTNER (on ver. 4); On observing times (Rom. xii. 11; Eph. v. 18) everything depends in physical as well as spiritual things.—J. LANGE (on ver. 5); For the testing, searching, and discriminating between spirits, there should be a man who is furnished with the spirit of Christ.

Vers. 6–11. ZELTNER (on ver. 6): It is far better to show one's self in fact pious, benevolent, true and upright, than merely to be so regarded and proclaimed.—[TRAPP (on ver. 7): Personal goodness is profitable to posterity: yet not of merit, but of free grace, and for the promise' sake].—STARKE (on ver. 8): When Christ, the Lord and King of the whole world, shall at length sit in judgment, then will all evil be driven away by His all holy eyes, brought to an end and punished.—(On verse 9): The justified have and keep sins within them even to their death; but they do not let these rule in them, Rom. vi. 11. He betrays his spiritual pride and his entanglement in gross error, who imagines, and, it may be, also maintains, that he has within himself no more sins, 1 John i. 8, 9.—(On ver. 11): He that has charge of the training of children, benefits not them only, but the whole of human society, when he incites flexible, well-disposed spirits to good, and seeks to draw away the vile from evil with care and strictness.

Ver. 12–19. MELANCHTHON (on ver. 12): To the successful conduct of a state two things are always needful: 1) good counsels of the rulers, and 2) willing obedience of the subjects. Both Solomon declares to be gifts of God, when he describes Him as the Creator both of the hearing ear and of the seeing eye.—GEIER (on ver. 12): It is God from whom we possess all good as well in temporal as in spiritual things (James i. 16): as He has given us eyes and ears, so will He also give us a new heart (Ezek. xi. 19).—ZELTNER (on ver. 14): Acknowledge with thanks God's present bounties, as long as thou hast them, and employ them aright, that God may not suddenly take them from thee, and thou then for the first time become aware what thou hast lost.—EGARD (on ver. 17): It is the way of sin and fleshly lust that it at first seems attractive to man, but afterward, when conscience wakes, causes great disquiet and anguish.—[Lord BACON (on ver. 18); The greatest trust between man and man is the trust of giving counsel... Things will have their first or second agitation; if they be not tossed upon the waves of counsel, they will be tossed upon the waves of fortune, and be full of inconstancy, doing and undoing, like the reeling of a drunken man.]—*Tübingen Bible* (on ver. 18): To wage war is allowed, for there are righteous wars; but they must be conducted with reason and reflection (compare General YONK's prayer and motto at the beginning of every battle: "The beginning, middle, end, O Lord, direct for the best!").—J. LANGE (on ver. 19): Rather hear him much who reveals to thee what harms thee, than him who flatters thee.—VON GERLACH (same verse): In all inconsiderate talking about others there is always some delight in evil or slander running along through it; just as also all tattling and idle gossip of this kind always has something exceedingly dangerous in it.

Ver. 20–23. MELANCHTHON (on ver. 21): It is of moment always to wait for God's ordinary call, to distinguish the necessary from the unnecessary, and to attempt nothing outside of our lawful calling.—LANGE (same verse): That for which one strives with inconsiderate craving in unlawful ways turns not into blessing, but to a curse.—ZELTNER (on ver. 22): To withstand passion, to wait in patience for the Lord's help, and to plead for the welfare of the evil doer is the best revenge on an enemy.—*Berleburg Bible* (same verse): Revenge always springs from pride; thou wouldst willingly be like God, and be thine own helper, avenger and judge; this pride then kindles thine anger within thee, so that thou for heat and violence canst not wait until God disposes of the matter for thee.—[LAWSON: By indulging your revengeful spirit, you do yourself a greater hurt than your greatest enemy can do you, for you gratify his ill nature when you suffer it to make a deep impression on your spirit, without which it could do you little or no hurt; but by committing your cause to God, you turn his ill-will to your great advantage, making it an occasion for the exercise of the noblest graces, which are attended with the sweetest fruits, and with the rich blessing of God.]

Ver. 24–30. GEIER (on ver. 24): No one can rightly begin and walk in the way to the kingdom of heaven, who would enter without Christ; John xiv. 6; xv. 5.—[CHALMERS (on ver. 24): Man can no more comprehend the whole meaning of his own history, than he can comprehend the whole mind of that God who is the Sovereign Lord and Ordainer of all things.]—*Berleburg Bible* (on ver. 25): In vows it is important to reflect with the utmost circumspection, before one forms a definite purpose. But what one has once vowed, against it he should seek no pretext of any kind to annul it.—STARKE (on ver. 25): The outward service of God without real devotion becomes a snare to many, by which they deceive their souls and plunge into ruin.—(On ver. 27): Know the nobility of the human soul, this candle of the Lord! Beware therefore of all conceit of wisdom and contempt of others about thee. Give rather to the illumination of Divine grace its influence on all the powers of thy soul, that when thine understanding is sufficiently enlightened thy will also may be reformed.—[STODDARD: The Spirit does not work by giving a testimony, but by assisting natural conscience to do its work. Natural conscience is the instrument in the hand of God to accuse, condemn, terrify, and to urge to duty.]—A. SCHRÖDER (on ver. 28—in the *Sonntagsfeier*, 1840): How the relation of the king to his people and of the people to their king can be a blessed one solely through the purity and sincerity of both).—RUST (same verse—same source, issue for 1834); Of the exalted blessing which a living Christianity ensures to all the relations of the State.—LANGE (on ver. 29): Art thou still a youth in Christian relatious; prove thy strength by conquest over thyself; art thou become grey and experienced in them, prove thy wisdom by love and a blameless life; 1 John ii. 13, 14.—(On ver. 30): There is much evil about and within us from which we must be cleansed and purified; God uses to this end the inward and outward trials of this life.—Comp. LUTHER's marginal comment on ver. 30: "*Mali non verbis sed verberibus emendantur;* pain is as needful as eating and drinking."

ζ) Admonition to integrity, patience, and obedient submission to God's gracious guidance.

CHAP. XXI.

1 Like streams of water is the heart of a king in Jehovah's hand;
  he turneth it whithersoever he will.
2 Every way of man is right in his own eyes,
  but Jehovah trieth hearts.
3 To do justice and judgment
  is more acceptable to Jehovah than sacrifice.
4 Haughty eyes and a proud heart—
  the light of the wicked is (nought but) sin.
5 The counsels of the diligent (tend) only to abundance;
  but every one who is over hasty (cometh) only to want.
6 The getting of treasures by a lying tongue
  is a fleeting breath of them that seek death.
7 The violence of the wicked sweepeth them away,
  because they refuse to do justice.
8 Crooked is the way of the guilty man,
  but the pure, his work is right (or. straight).
9 It is better to dwell in a corner of the house top,
  than with a contentious woman in a thronged house.
10 The soul of the wicked desireth evil;
   his neighbor findeth no mercy with him.
11 When the scorner is punished the simple is made wise,
   and when the wise is prospered, he will gain knowledge.
12 The Righteous (God) marketh the house of the wicked;
   He hurleth the wicked into destruction.
13 He that stoppeth his ear to the cry of the poor,
   he also shall call and not be answered.
14 A gift in secret allayeth anger,
   and a present in the bosom strong wrath.
15 It is a joy to the just to do justice,
   but destruction to them that work iniquity.
16 A man who wandereth from the way of understanding,
   shall dwell in the assembly of the dead.

17 He becometh a poor man who loveth pleasure;
     he that loveth wine and oil shall not be rich.
18 The wicked becometh a ransom for the righteous,
     and the faithless for the upright.
19 It is better to dwell in a desert land,
     than to live with a contentious and fretful woman.
20 Precious treasure and oil are in the dwelling of the wise,
     but a foolish man consumeth them.
21 He that followeth after righteousness and mercy
     shall find life, righteousness, and honor.
22 A wise man scaleth the city of the mighty,
     and casteth down the strength of its confidence.
23 He that keepeth his mouth and his tongue,
     guardeth his soul from troubles.
24 A proud (and) arrogant (man)—scorner is his name;
     he acteth in insolence of pride (overflowing of haughtiness).
25 The desire of the slothful killeth him,
     for his hands refuse to labor.
26 He desireth intensely all the day long;
     but the righteous giveth and spareth not.
27 The sacrifice of the wicked is an abomination;
     how much more when it is brought for evil!
28 A false witness shall perish,
     the man that heareth shall speak evermore.
29 The wicked putteth on a bold face,
     but he that is upright establisheth his way.
30 No wisdom, no understanding,
     no counsel (is there) against Jehovah.
31 The horse is made ready for the day of battle,
     but from Jehovah is the victory.

GRAMMATICAL AND CRITICAL.

Ver. 3.—The Infinitive form עָשֹׂה like קְנֹה in chap. xvi. 16.

Ver. 4.—Hitzig writes נֵב (=נִיב), sprout or shoot) instead of נֵר and translates the second clause: "The fruit of the wicked (i. e., pride) bringeth to destruction"—an emendation plainly not less unfortunate than the corresponding one, נִּב for נִיר, which he proposed in chap. xiii. 23. Compare notes on this passage. [The shortening of the long vowel in נִיר is undoubtedly facilitated by the initial ר of the following word.]

Ver. 6.—הֶבֶל cannot be stat. constr., for it would be separated from its genitive by the adjective נִדָּף.—EWALD, BERTHEAU, etc., read with the LXX and Vulg.: מוֹקְשֵׁי instead of מְבַקְשֵׁי and render "snares of death" instead of "seekers of death." Hitzig, in addition, proposes נֶרֶד instead of נִדָּף, as well as in clause a פֹּעֵל instead of פֹּעַל, so that he reaches the meaning (which corresponds pretty closely with the LXX and Vulg.): "He that getteth treasures by a lying tongue runneth after vanity into snares of death."

Ver. 7.—בְּאָנ is one of BÖTTCHER'S "relative" perfects; they have before this destruction, be it earlier or later, refused, etc.—See §950, 1.—A.]

Ver. 8.—הֲפַכְפַּךְ "winding, crooked" (as נְרֵפָה is elsewhere used, comp. xvii. 20) is not stat. constr. (BERTHEAU, "one crooked in his way"), but a predicate for emphasis prefixed to its subject דֶּרֶךְ, as the parallelism shows.—זָךְ at the beginning of clause b seems to be purposely chosen to correspond with דֶּרֶךְ at the end of clause a. Comp. זָךְ in chap. xx. 11. [This זָךְ is one of the very few words in Hebrew in which an initial ו remains, not being weakened into י. It seems to be an ancient judicial term, and etymologically corresponds with the familiar Arabic word Vizier; comp. also Charge d' Affaires. See BÖTT., FÜRST, etc.—A.]

Ver. 9.—(טוֹב לְשֶׁבֶת, a masculine predicative adjective notwithstanding the fem. form of the Infinitive. BÖTT. § 1840, 3, β.—A.]

Ver. 10.—[BÖTT. strongly maintains the existence of a Passive of the Kal. conj., and cites יֻחַן as one of the examples. See §906, e. As is well known, it has usually been called a Hophal form; no Hiphil forms are in use, and this is in meaning an exact passive counterpart to the Kal.—A.]

Ver. 14.—Instead of יְכַבֶּה (from יָעַז, a verb occurring only here, which must mean "to bend or beat down"), HITZIG proposes to read, with SYMMACHUS, the Vulg. and Targ. יְכַבֶּה "extinguishes."

Ver. 22.—The ה in כְּבָטְחָה without Mappiq, on account of the distinctive accent; comp. Jer. vi. 6; Is. xxiii. 17, 18; xlv. 6, etc.—יַעֲלֶה one of BÖTTCHER's "*empirical Perfects*;" it has been a matter of experience; see § 950, 3.—A.]

Ver. 28.—HITZIG, partially following the LXX (changing לָנֶצַח to לָנֶצַח, and שֹׁמֵעַ to שֹׂמֵחַ), amends thus: The man that rejoiceth to deliver (??) shall speak.

EXEGETICAL.

1. Ver. 1–3. *Of God's all directing providence and government.*—**Like streams of water is the heart of a king in Jehovah's hand.**—The *tertium comp.* is, according to the second member of the parallelism, the capability in the "streams of water" of being directed and guided at pleasure,—the allusion being to the canals and ditches constructed for the irrigation and fertilizing of meadows, gardens and fields. [See HACKETT's *Illustrations of Scripture*, and similar works; also HORACE, *Od.* III., 1, 5–8.—A.] Since for the accomplishment of their object there must always be a number of them, the plural "streams" is used, although only one king's heart is spoken of. Whether in the second line the pleasant, refreshing influence of the rivulets, dispensing blessing and increase, comes into account as a point in the comparison is uncertain (comp. Is. xxxii. 2); this, however, is not improbable, inasmuch as the heart of a king may in fact become in an eminent degree a fountain of blessing for many thousands, and according to God's design ought to be so. See also the comparison of royal favor with a "cloud of the harvest rain," in chap. xvi. 15, and in the opposite direction comp. xx. 2, 8, 26.

Ver. 2. Almost precisely like xvi. 2; comp. also xiv. 12; xvi. 25. [FUERST, unlike most others, renders the verb of the second clause "determineth," *i. e.*, determines the direction,—instead of "weighing, trying," or the old English term of our E. V., "pondereth."—A.]

Ver. 3. **To do justice and judgment is more acceptable to Jehovah than sacrifice.** Comp. xv. 8; Ps. l. 7 sq.; 1 Sam. xv. 22; Mich. vi. 6–8.—For this combination of righteousness and justice comp. besides, *e. g.*, 2 Sam. viii. 15; Jeremiah ix. 23. For the נִבְחָר "more acceptable," lit., "chosen," *i. e.*, desired, well-pleasing, valuable, comp. xxii. 1; and also vii. 10, 19. ["This maxim of the Proverbs was a bold saying then.—It is a bold saying still; but it well unites the wisdom of Solomon with that of his father David in the 51st Psalm, and with the inspiration of the later prophets." STANLEY, *Jewish Church*, II., 257].

2. Vers. 4–9. *Against pride, avarice, deceit, violence, and vicious dispositions in general.*—**Haughty eyes and a proud heart**; lit. "to be lofty of eyes and to be swollen of heart," for רוּם and רְחַב are infinitives. "Swelling of heart" is however here and in Ps. ci. 5, where it stands again in connection with "loftiness of eyes," a proud, arrogant disposition chastened by no care; comp. also Isa. lx. 5; Ps. cxix. 32.—**The light of the wicked is only sin.** נֵר רְשָׁעִים, which is plainly an appositive to "haughty eyes and a proud heart," may be translated either by "the fallow, or newly ploughed land of the wicked" (comp. נִיר, chap. xiii. 23), and refer to "the very first fruits of a man's activity (so EWALD, ELSTER, *etc.*), or, which is surely preferable, it may be taken as meaning the same as נֵר (comp. 1 Kings xi. 36, where instead of נִיר we find נֵר in the sense of "light"), and in accordance with chap. xx. 37, it may be regarded as a figurative representation of the entire spirit of the wicked, *i. e.* their proud disposition, flaring and flaming like a bright light. Thus the LXX (λαμπτήρ), Vulg., SCHULTENS, DATHE, BERTHEAU—except that the latter interpret the "light" less pertinently of the brilliant prosperity of the wicked. In like manner LUTHER also, GEIER, DÖDERLEIN, ZIEGLER, UMBREIT, who, however, find in the last term not an appositive to the two preceding expressions, but a third subject co-ordinate with them. [To those who adopt "light" as their rendering, may be added, although with some diversity in the grammatical relation and the interpretation of the term, K., DE W., H., S., M., N., and the E. V. in its marginal reading. The old English expositors generally follow the text of the E. V., "ploughing," which is also preferred and defended by WORDSW., as suggesting an "evil execution" of the "proud aspirations and covetous ambition" of the wicked "in a deliberate action."—A.].—The predicate of clause *b* is with no more propriety here than in chap. x. 16 to be explained by "ruin" (disaster, destruction),—which is contrary to the view of UMBREIT, HITZIG, *etc.*,—but retains the meaning which is predominant in the Old Testament; for to trace back all proud conduct and action to *sin* is plainly the proper drift and import of the proverb before us; comp. ver. 24, below.

Ver. 5. **The counsels of the diligent** (tend) **only to abundance; but every one who is overhasty** (cometh) **only to want.** "Abundance" and "want" stand contrasted here as in xiv. 23. The "hasty," however, in contrast with the "diligent," the man who labors in substantial and continuous methods (comp. xii. 27), must be he who in the pursuit of gain is in excessive haste, the impatient, restless fortune-hunter, who besides is not above base and deceitful modes of acquiring, and for that very reason for a punishment is plunged into destitution and penury; comp. xix. 2; also xx. 21; xxviii. 20; and with respect to the general sentiment still further xii. 11; xiii. 11.—This explanation, which is as simple as it is congruous with the context, makes HITZIG's conjecture superfluous (instead of אָץ, אֹגֵר, "the collector," *i. e.* the niggard); comp. xi. 24. [RUEETSCHI, *ubi supra*, p. 152, defending the common rendering, expands somewhat the implied contrast between the *plans* according to which the diligent toils, and the *impatient haste* which cannot wait to plan.—A.].

Ver. 6. **The getting of treasures by a lying tongue is a fleeting breath of them that seek death.** The second member is literally rendered according to the text: "is fleeting breath, those seeking death,"—the latter phrase not to be regarded as a limiting genitive (see Critical Notes), but the two a *hendiadys;* the idea "fleeting breath of those seeking death" being resolved into the two co-ordinate ideas, "fleeting breath" and "seekers of death." [WORDSW.: "*vanity driven like chaff;*"—"the *work* of the wicked and covetous man is *chaff* and his harvest is *death.*" KAMPH., while favoring a simple emendation (that of EWALD, *etc.;* see Critical Notes), would refer the "seekers," if the text is to be retained, to the *treasures:* "treasures unlawfully gained are not only themselves without substance, but also bring on destruction for their deceitful possessor." H.: "a vanity agitated by them that seek death;" N.: "scattered breath of them," *etc.;* S.: "a fleeting breath are they who seek death;" M.: "(like) a fleeting vapor to those who seek death." The phrase plainly requires somewhat violent grammatical constructions, or an emendation. Our author's *hendiadys* making the plural participle an *apparent* appositive of the singular noun is not the most forced.—A.] With reference to the phrase "seekers of death," comp. viii. 36; xvii. 19; with respect to the expression "a fleeting vanity," Job xiv. 2; xiii. 25; and PINDAR's well-known phrase, σκιᾶς ὄναρ ἄνθρωπος. It is hardly possible that we have here any suggestion of the mirage (Isa. xxxv. 7), the "tremulous mist of the desert, vanishing again in quick deception,"—for the noun הֶבֶל nowhere else occurs with this signification (this in opposition to ARNOLDI, and to some extent UMBREIT also).

Ver. 7. **The violence of the wicked sweepeth them away.** The "violence" is not designed here to describe the destruction intended for the wicked (comp. Job v. 22; Isa. xvi. 6), but is used in the active sense, of the rapacious or murderous violence practised by them (comp. xxiv. 2. So the Vulg., LUTHER, UMBREIT, HITZIG.) The latter, to illustrate the idea, appropriately suggests the case in which an incendiary is consumed in the fire which he sets. But examples like i. 18, 19; vii. 23; serve also for illustration. With clause *b* compare (above) ver. 3, *a*.

Ver. 8. **Crooked is the way of the guilty man.** "Burdened, laden" signifies, as the corresponding word in Arabic does, "the guilt-laden," and so the vicious man, the malefactor, in contrast with the "pure or clean."

3. Vers. 9-18. Various warnings against foolish, hard-hearted, uncharitable, unrighteous conduct.—**It is better to dwell in a corner of the housetop,** and so on the one hand, solitary and forsaken (comp. Ps. cii. 7 (8)), and on the other, exposed to all winds and weathers, in an exceedingly inconvenient, uncomfortable position. [See HACKETT's *Illustrations of Scripture,* and similar works].—**Than with a contentious woman in a thronged house:** lit., "than a woman of contentions (comp. xix. 13; xxvii. 15) and a house of companionship" (οἶκος κοινός, LXX),—an example of *hendiadys*, therefore like ver. 6.—On account of the correspondence of the idea with ver. 19, which certainly is remarkably close, HITZIG proposes to remove the "contentious woman" entirely from the text, for (freely following the LXX) he reads מִשְׂאֵת instead of בָאֵשׁ, and so from clause *b* gets the meaning: "than that strife arises and the house is common."

Ver. 10. For the expression in *a* comp. xiii. 4.—**His neighbor findeth no mercy with him,** lit., "his neighbor is not compassionately treated by his eyes," *i. e.,* on account of his violent wickedness and selfishness even his friend experiences no sympathy from him.

Ver. 11. With *a* comp. xix. 25.—**And when the wise is prospered, he will gain knowledge,** *i. e.* the simple, who must be the subject again in clause *b,* inasmuch as it can hardly be said of the wise that it is his prosperity that first helps him to knowledge. Usually, "and if one instruct the wise," as if the verb הַשְׂכִּיל were here transitive in the sense of "warning, instructing," and thus stood for הוֹכִיחַ, xix. 25. But the wise man needs no longer such instruction as may for the first time give him understanding; and this verb is found, *e. g.* also in Prov. xvii. 8 (comp. Isa. lii. 13), used in the sense of "possessing or finding prosperity." The whole proverb therefore demands that "the simple" be deterred by the punishment of the fool, as well as made intelligent and stimulated to good by the prosperity of the wise.

Ver. 12. **The Righteous marketh the house of the wicked.** That by this righteous one God is meant, the supreme judge and rewarder, appears beyond all controversy from clause *b,* as well as from the parallel passage xxii. 12 (comp. also Job xxxiv. 17). ROSENMUELLER, EWALD, BERTHEAU, ELSTER take the correct view, while HITZIG here again endeavors to emend (substituting בֵּיתוֹ for בֵּית, and making רָע, "wickedness," the subject of clause *b*); UMBREIT, however, harshly and ungrammatically makes the "righteous" in *a* a righteous man, and then in *b* supplies God as the subject of the predicative participle. [So the E. V., which is followed by WORDSW.; NOYES makes the righteous man the subject of both clauses,—while DE W., K., H., S. and M. more correctly refer both to God.—A.]

Ver. 13. Comp. Matt. xviii. 23-35, a parable which fitly illustrates the meaning of this sentence, pronounced against hard-heartedness; see also Matt. xxv. 41 sq.; Luke xi. 13.

Ver. 14. Comp. xvii. 8; xviii. 16; xix. 6. As in these passages so in the one before us it is not prohibited presents or bribes that are spoken of, but lawful manifestations of liberality, though bestowed in all quietness (in secret), *i. e.* without attracting needless attention.—**A present in the bosom,** is the same as the "gift from the bosom" in chap. xvii. 23, a present brought concealed in the bosom (not a "present *into* the bosom," as ROSENM., BERTHEAU, *etc.*, would have it).

Ver. 15. **It is a joy to the just to do justice, but (it is) destruction only to them that work iniquity.** "Confusion, terror" (comp. x. 29) is all right action to evil doers, since they distinctly feel "that its consequences must condemn and punish their own course and conduct" (ELSTER); for they practise their ungodly folly with pleasure and delight (x. 23; xv. 21); they have a real satisfaction in their works of darkness (comp. Rom. i. 32; John iii. 19). [The E. V., followed by H., N., S., M. makes "destruction" the subject of clause b, and not a second predicate, as DE W., K., etc., do, like our author. The latter construction best brings out the antithesis between a "joy" and a "terror." The same course of conduct is thus differently viewed by and related to the contrasted classes. —A.]

Ver. 16. With a compare ii. 15; iv. 14 sq.; with b, ii. 18; ix. 18.

Ver. 17. **He becometh a poor man who loveth pleasure** (lit. "a man of want"). "Joy" is here specifically intoxicating delights, such as are to be found in luxurious banquets, where "wine and perfume," these familiar symbols of social festivity (Ps. civ. 15; Prov. xxvii. 9; comp. Amos vi. 6), play their part. The Vulgate, therefore, if not with verbal accuracy renders by "qui diligit epulas."

Ver. 18. **The wicked becometh a ransom for the righteous**, i. e. so far forth as the divine wrath turns from him who is comparatively righteous to fall upon the head of the evil doer; comp. xi. 8. Thus according to Isa. xliii. 3 the heathen nations atone for the comparatively purer and more upright Israel (comp. HITZIG on this passage).

1. Vers. 19-25. Admonitions of an import similar to that of the preceding series, directed especially against uncharitableness, folly and sloth.—With ver. 19 comp. ver. 9 above.—**With a contentious, fretful woman**, lit., "with a woman of contentions and of worry;" the genitives are naturally genitivi effectus.

Ver. 20. **Precious treasure and oil are in the dwelling of the wise, but a foolish man consumeth them**, i. e. wastes whatever he possesses of valuable treasures and spices. "A fool of a man," as in xv. 20. To "swallow up," i. e. to waste, destroy and ruin, as in Eccles. x. 12; Lam. ii. 2-8; Job x. 8, etc.—HITZIG in clause a changes וְשֶׁלִי to שָׂכִי and reads פֶּה instead of נָוֶה, and thus obtains the meaning, "Precious treasure is in a wise mouth, but a fool of a man swallows it down (?)."

Ver. 21. **He that followeth after righteousness and mercy shall find life, righteousness and honor**. The second "righteousness," although wanting in the LXX, is not for that reason to be regarded an error (in opposition to ZIEGLER, ELSTER). It denotes the judicial righteousness of the man who, on account of his striving after righteousness, is sanctified and blessed by God (just as in chap. viii. 18; Job xxxiii. 26).—while in clause a the righteousness intended is a moral quality of the wise man who keeps the law. The relation is the same in the N. T. between δικαιοσύνη as a present possession of the believer (e. g. Rom. iii. 28; Gal. iii. 21), and δικαιοσύνη as an object of Christian hope; Gal. v. 5.—With this use of the terms "life" and "honor" comp. iii. 16.

Ver. 22. **A wise man scaleth a city of the mighty**; i. e. even a fortress well defended by numerous and strong warriors does not long withstand the sagacious counsel of the wise; comp. xxiv. 5, and also Eccles. ix. 15,—where, in a reversed relation, one wise man successfully defends the city against a whole army.—For the expression, "the bulwark of its confidence," in clause b, comp. xiv. 26.

Ver. 23. Comp. xiii. 3; xix. 6.

Ver. 24. **A proud and arrogant (man)— scorner is his name**; i. e. not, "he might reasonably be called scoffer," but, "the universal moral judgment of men really calls him so, looks upon him as a scoffer, as an 'infidel' (DELITZSCH; comp. Introd., § 3, N. 2), a man to whom there is nothing holy." For יָהִיר, superbiens, "arrogant, conceited," comp. Hab. ii. 5.

Vers. 25 and 26 form a continuous representation of the slothful, in contrast with the righteous and therefore diligent man, who, however, on account of his diligence is also beneficent.— **The desire of the slothful killeth him**, i. e. his desire for food and drink, his hunger, for the quieting of which he is nevertheless unable to employ the proper means—labor in behalf of his physical sustenance. Comp. xiii. 4; also xix. 24. [STUART understands "his desire of slothful repose;" which is less easily reconciled with clause a of ver. 26. His desires are not so intense and consuming for repose, passivity rather than activity characterizing whatever is voluntary about him; his involuntary appetites, for which he neglects to provide, destroy him.—A.] —**He desireth intensely all the day long**; lit., "Every day he wisheth a wish," i. e. he carries constantly the same intense longing for possession and enjoyment, but stops with this indolent wishing and dreaming, without passing over into energetic action. It is otherwise with the upright, who by his honorable industry is put in circumstances to distribute rich gifts among others also; comp. xi. 24 a.

5. Vers. 27-31. Of God's righteous judgment on the wicked and disobedient.—**The sacrifice of the wicked is an abomination** (comp. xv. 8), **how much more when it is offered for evil**. בְּזִמָּה might mean "with transgression, with evil intent" (not "with deceit," as BERTHEAU holds), comp. Ps. xxvi. 10; cxix. 150. But it seems to be more appropriately taken here as a statement of the motive of the abhorred sacrifice, and therefore to be "for transgression," for some iniquity wrought with evil intent, which is to be expiated by a sacrifice,—and by a sacrifice only, and not by true contrition and repentance (comp. HITZIG on this passage). Mal. i. 13 is therefore not so true a parallel as Ecclesiast. xxxiv. 21-25.

Ver. 28. With a comp. xix. 5, 9.—**The man that heareth shall speak evermore**; i. e. the modest and teachable, who, instead of talking on heedlessly at random, gives thoughtful attention to all profitable teaching, and ponders quietly all that he has heard, that he may be able to give reliable testimony (comp. Solomon's "hearing heart," I Kings iii. 9)—such a one will be constantly called forth anew to testify, and so become one "speaking evermore," a testis sive orator perpetuus, a witness to the truth universally esteemed and much desired, in contrast with the heedless, gossiping, lying witness (comp. xviii

13). For this interpretation the parallel in xii. 19 is decisive, from which appears especially the inadmissibility of rendering לְנֶגֶד *secundum veritatem*, according to truth (so *e. g.* UMBREIT: "he who hears the truth"). [KREETSCHI (as above, p. 152) brings out the antithetic force of the verse thus: "To hold to the truth is just what the lying witness fails to do; therefore must he cease to speak; his way perishes, Ps. i. 6. But the man that hearkens, *etc.*, to the truth shall evermore speak 'as a witness and otherwise, living happily shall always be able to speak, and shall be gladly heard' (EWALD), and so by no means perish."—A.]

Ver. 29. **The wicked putteth on a bold face**, lit., "the man of wickedness maketh boldness with his face." The predicate as in vii. 13, denotes the immovable fixedness of features behind which the shameless villain seeks to hide his criminal intentions and crafty dispositions. Whether we are here to think specifically of a false witness implicated in some criminal conspiracy (from the suggestion of 28, *a*), must remain doubtful from the indefiniteness of the expression (in opposition to BERTHEAU, HITZIG). **But he that is upright establisheth his way**. Instead of יָכִין the K'ri, with which the LXX agree, proposes יָבִין, and some modern interpreters prefer this reading, *e. g.* HITZIG: "considereth his way." But just as it may be said of God (chap. xvi. 9) so it might be said of a pious man, that he makes his way or his steps *firm*, *i. e.* sure and fixed (comp. Jotham's example, 2 Chron. xxvii. 6); and the antithesis between *a* and *b* becomes decidedly stronger with the reading of the K'thibh. [The E. V., which is followed by B., N. and M. adopts a weakened and ambiguous rendering, "directeth,"—"considereth" being in the margin. S. and WORDSW. decidedly prefer the stronger rendering "establisheth," W. bringing out the contrast between the wicked man's *hardening* his face, and the good man's *hardening* his way. As KREETSCHI urges, both the verbs and their objects contribute to the completeness of the antithesis. "The wicked man looks only to the outside, the forms, the appearance and show, the transient result; but the good man aims at the real, the actually good; he therefore establishes his ways, his mode of life and action, his whole course."—A.].

Ver. 30. **No wisdom, no understanding, no counsel is there against Jehovah.** לְנֶגֶד is by no means merely "before God," *i. e.* according to God's judgment, as UMBREIT, *etc.*, say, but "over against, in opposition to." The meaning is that a human wisdom which would assert itself in opposition to the divine, is not wisdom, but sheer folly (comp. 1 Cor. iii. 19), that in comparison with the divine wisdom that of man is altogether nought (comp. Isa. xxix. 14).

Ver. 31 continues the thought of the preceding verse. As human wisdom, so likewise is human strength and reliance on human aid and might nothing; comp. Ps. xx. 7 (8); xxxiii. 17.—**The horse is made ready for the day of battle.** The participle expresses the permanence of the matter; therefore, lit. "stands prepared, is prepared" (HITZIG).—With *b* compare also David's language to Goliath, 1 Sam. xvii. 47: "The battle is Jehovah's;" *i. e.*, on Him depends the decision of the war, its favorable issue, its victorious result.

DOCTRINAL, ETHICAL, HOMILETIC AND PRACTICAL.

According to the introduction and conclusion of the chapter, its contents refer mainly to the all-directing providence of God, the ruler of the world, just as in chap. xvi.,—which furthermore in regard to several of the ethical precepts, or rules of virtue connected with these considerations about providence, stands in quite close relations to the admonitory substance of the section before us; comp. *e. g.* xvi. 5 with xxi. 4, 24; xvi. 10, 12 with xxi. 1; xvi. 11 with xxi. 6; xvi. 6 with xxi. 21; xvi. 17, 20 with xxi. 23; xvi. 32 with xxi. 22; xvi. 26 with xxi. 25, 26. Among the virtues the practice of which is commended as a chief means of putting one's self in the right relations to the administrative and judicial government of God over the world, *righteousness* or *obedience* to God's word, which is better than sacrifice (vers. 3, 27; comp. vers. 8, 12, 15, 18, 21, 28, 29), is the most conspicuous. Side by side with this stands patience in the sense of the New Testament (comp. ὑπομονή, Luke viii. 15; James i 4), *i. e.*, steadfast endurance in labor and in suffering, such as the service of the Lord brings with it (vers. 5, 17, 25, 26). There are more isolated warnings against deception (vers. 6, 28), hard-heartedness (vers. 10, 13), luxurious extravagance (ver. 17, 20), scoffing (vers. 11, 24). Since however these without difficulty group themselves about the central idea of obedience to the divine command, this obedience may itself be considered in a general way as the controlling idea in the substance of the section, and accordingly some such theme as "the man who hearkens" (ver. 28; comp. 1 Kings iii. 9), or again "obedience more acceptable to God than sacrifice" (ver. 3; comp. 1 Sam. xv. 22), may be prefixed as a theme or motto to all the rest.

For a *homily* then *on the chapter as a whole*: God as ruler and judge over all the world, and man's duty of obedience to Him, consisting in walking in righteousness, patience, love, and truth. Or more briefly: Obedience to God's word as the sum of all human duties and virtues. Comp. STÖCKER: Of God's gracious and righteous government, as it shows itself in the good and the evil.—The *Berleburg Bible* puts it very well: God is to rule, not self-will.

Vers. 1-3. CRAMER (on vers. 1, 2): God not only knows the thoughts of men, but also has their hearts in His hands, and turns and moulds them as the potter the clay. In matters of faith therefore we are not to proceed according to the fancy of our own hearts, but according to God's command.—GEIER: Pray God earnestly that He may not leave thine heart intent on any evil, but that he may draw it to Himself to walk steadfastly according to his word.—WOHLFARTH: Not merely the plans of the lowly, but also the counsels and undertakings of the mighty depend on God, who as chief ruler of His world with wisdom that never deceives and power that never fails shapes all according to His design.—STARKE (on ver. 3): All outward ceremonies of worship avail nothing, if there is lacking the true inward service of God, worshipping God in spirit and in truth (John iv. 24).—[LAWSON: Sacrifices had no goodness in their own nature; and when men rested on them they were abominable to God. Judgment and justice are a part of the image of God in man, and have an everlasting excellency in their nature].

Vers. 4-8. CRAMER (on ver. 5): A measure is good in all things; therefore hasten deliberately. —GEIER: He is cruel against himself who heaps up riches unrighteously: he is gathering up his own ruin at the same time.—*Calwer Handb.* (on vers. 5-7): Industry and activity, not excess of haste, leads to good success; furthermore, not falsehood, or deceit, or robbing others.—VON GERLACH (on 7, 8): The desolation which the ungodly bring upon others at length sweeps them away; for no one, who persistently refuses to do right can stand, since right is precisely the stability, the order of things.—[TRAPP (on ver. 6): Many a wretched worldling spins a fair thread to strangle himself both temporally and eternally].

Vers. 9-18. [CHALMERS (on ver. 10): The claims of friendship are overborne by the strength of that evil desire on the part of the wicked, which is bent on the objects of their own selfishness]—STANKE (on ver. 10): We should not so often act contrary to the law of love to our neighbors, if we reflected always what we should desire in our neighbor's place (Matth. vii. 12).— (On ver. 13): An uncompassionate spirit toward the poor is punished by God with want of pity in return, according to the justice of an exact requital.—HASIUS (on ver. 14): Even with trifles, with slight manifestations of love, one may frequently avert much evil, and soothe spirits.— GEIER (on ver. 15): Joy and peace of conscience follow a joyful obedience to God's command; a scornful contempt and disobedience of it is followed by constant disquiet and fear.—[LAWSON (on ver. 15): Many do judgment without taking pleasure in it; their consciences will not suffer them to do otherwise, but their hearts are on the side of sin; or they will do many good things with pleasure, because their constitutional and beloved sins are not affected by them; but there are other things at which they stop short, *etc.*— TRAPP (on ver. 16): He that deviateth from the truth according to godliness cannot possibly wander so far as to miss of hell].—CRAMER (on ver. 17): He who will consume more than his plough can yield must utterly perish (Ecclesiast. xix. 32).—(On ver. 18): God often turns the leaf over so that the evil that was designed for the pious comes upon the ungodly.—VON GERLACH (on ver. 18): Every man deserves punishment here since none is guiltless. Since however the righteous acknowledges his guilt and walks in humility before the Lord, He remits his penalty, and before his eyes punishes the ungodly in full measure, that by the sight he may be made wise.

Vers. 19-26. HASIUS (on ver. 20): Where true wisdom is lacking in the administration of temporal things, there even with a regal or princely income destitution and want may enter.—GEIER (on ver. 22): Let every Christian and especially every Christian teacher exert himself by virtue of heavenly wisdom to tear down the fortresses and bulwarks of the kingdom of hell.—CRAMER (on ver. 22): Let no one trust in walls, castles or fortresses. What human hands have constructed human hands can pull down again.— (On ver. 23): God as the Creator of our human nature has set a double wall before the tongue, —the teeth and the lips,—to show that we should keep and guard the tongue with all carefulness. —[BP. HALL: He that looketh carefully to his tongue takes a safe course for preserving his life, which is oft in danger by much and wild talking].—GEIER (on ver. 24): Vices hang together like a chain; from pride springs contempt, from contempt wrath, from wrath mockery and many insults.—ZELTNER (on ver. 25, 26): Lazy thieves of time are not worth their bread: he that worketh not, neither shall he eat, 2 Thess. iii. 10.— [MUFFET: Wishers and woulders are neither good householders nor yet long livers].

Vers. 27-31. ZELTNER (on vers. 28, 29): To receive kind suggestions with thankfulness, and to reform, is no shame but an honor in the sight of God and men.—[TRAPP (on ver. 30): Human wisdom while it strives for masteries is overmastered].—MELANCHTHON (on ver. 30, 31): It is a wholesome rule for the whole of life, to fulfil the duties of one's calling, and in connection with this trustfully to invoke God's aid and succor. If we do this our works under God's aid in blessing us succeed well. Unrighteous labors, those undertaken without any call from above, as well as without trust in and prayer to God, on the contrary undoubtedly fail, be they entered upon with ever so much shrewdness and cunning.—SAURIN (sermon on ver. 30): On the futility of the means which human passions oppose to God,—viz. 1) earthly exaltation; 2) political prudence; 3) sensuality; 4) stoical endurance. —*Berleburg Bible* (on vers. 30, 31): No beginning, devising, striving of ours can possibly oppose that which God purposes with us. Is it not then the best thing to commit ourselves wholly to His guidance, without giving ourselves much labor in vain? We indeed prepare all in accordance with our idea and understanding; but God gives success wholly according to His will. In everything then let the charge be left to Him!

η) Admonition to secure and keep a good name.

Chap. XXII. 1–16.

1 A (good) name is to be chosen rather than great riches;
  better than silver and gold is good will.
2 The rich and the poor meet together;
  Jehovah is the maker of them all.
3 The prudent seeth the evil and hideth himself,
  but the simple pass on and must suffer.
4 The end of humility (and) of the fear of God
  is riches, honor and life.
5 Thorns, snares are in the way of the wayward;
  he that guardeth his soul let him keep far from them.
6 Train up a child in the way he should go;
  even when he is old he doth not depart from it.
7 The rich ruleth over the poor,
  and the borrower becometh servant to the lender.
8 He that soweth iniquity shall reap calamity,
  and the staff of his haughtiness shall vanish away.
9 He that hath a bountiful eye shall be blessed,
  for he giveth of his bread to the poor.
10 Chase away the scorner and contention goeth out,
   and strife and reproach cease.
11 He that loveth with a pure heart,
   whose lips are gracious, the King is his friend.
12 The eyes of Jehovah preserve knowledge,
   but the words of the false doth He overthrow.
13 The slothful saith: (There is) a lion without,
   I shall be slain in the streets.
14 A deep pit is the mouth of the strange woman;
   he that is accursed by Jehovah falleth into it.
15 Foolishness is bound in the heart of the child;
   the rod of correction driveth it far from him.
16 One oppresseth the poor only to make him rich;
   one giveth to the rich (and it tendeth) only to want.

GRAMMATICAL AND CRITICAL.

Ver. 1. [The Niphal part. נִבְחָר here as in xvi. 16 is to be rendered like the Latin pass. periphr.—*ndus est*, "is to be chosen, ought to be chosen;" comp. BÖTT, § 937. 2. *c*.—A.].

Ver. 2. [See Exeg. notes for the reason why כֻּלָּם is preferred to שְׁנֵיהֶם. The lit. rendering is "their totality, the whole of them." For minute explanations of the use of כָּל and the ordinary form of its suffixes see *e. g.*, BÖTT, § 876. *c*, § 883, *d*.—A.].

Ver. 3. [See Exeg. notes for reasons why the K'thibh is to be preferred to the K'ri. The vocalization is of course that of the K'ri נִבְהָל and not that of an Imperf. Kal. The time implied in the verb רָאָה is of course a "relative perfect;" he hath first seen, and then *will* hide himself.—A.].

Ver. 5. יָקֵשׁ is in the Vulg. correctly regarded as a genitive with דֶּרֶךְ; so most of the modern interpreters regard it.

Vers. 7, 8. [The full forms יִמְשׁוֹל and קוֹצֵר (K'thibh) are preserved by the emphasis thrown on the ultimate syllables. According to BÖTT, § 1005, 5, *c*, while these forms are the prevalent forms in the dialects of Ephraim and Simeon they are found in the period of Judah only under the influence of special emphasis or a following pause.—A.].

Ver. 11. [In the reading of the K'ri the Uholem is exceptionally shortened to Kamets-Hhatuph before Makkeph. The K'thibh has the *st st. constr.* in its ordinary form. See GREEN, § 215, 1, *c*.—A.].

Vers. 12, 13. [The perf. נָצְרוּ in ver. 12 is classed by BÖTT, with the "empirical" perfects; this is a fact of experience, it has been found true; the אָכְבֵד of ver. 13 is classed with the "effective" perfects: he has virtually said, it is in effect as though he had said, *etc.*—A.].

Ver. 15. [The pass. part. קְשׁוּרָה illustrates the principle that in Hebrew, whatever be the time to which this participle relates it describes a state and not a process,—something that is, and not something that is coming to be; Gerou. *ist verknupft* not "*wird v.*" See Bött. § 997, 2, *e*.—A.].

[It can hardly be accidental that in this group of proverbs so many of the important words begin with עָ; thus עֹשֶׁר (ver. 1), עָשִׁיר and עֹשֶׂה (ver. 2), עָרוּם (ver. 3), עֵקֶב and עֲנָוָה (ver. 4) עִקֵּשׁ (ver. 5), *etc*.—A.].

EXEGETICAL.

1. On account of the brevity of this section beginning with chap. xxii. 1, but plainly ending with ver. 16, as well as on account of the supposed construction of the section with some reference to the number *five* (which is said to have had a modifying influence also on chap. xxi.), HITZIG conjectures that its latter and larger half has been lost, and thinks that the portion which has disappeared may be recognized in the section xxviii. 17—xxix. 27. All this rests on the basis of assumptions as subjective and arbitrary as the general principles of this critic which relate to the supposed numerical structure of the oldest and main division of the whole collection of proverbs. See remarks below, on chap. xxv. 1, and also on xxviii. 1 (Doctrinal and Ethical).

2. Vers. 1-5. On a good name as dependent not on riches and treasures, but on prudence, humility and right sensibilities.—**A** (good) **name is more precious than great riches.** The absolute term "name" here denotes, like ὄνομα in the parallel passage, Ecclesiast. xli. 12, a *good* name (ὄνομα καλόν, LXX); so likewise in Eccles. vii. 1; Job xxx. 8.—**Better than silver and gold is goodwill.** The "good" (טוֹב) does not belong as an adjective [attributive] to the noun "favor" (as the Rabbins render, and UMBREIT also: "*Schöne Gunst*" [E. V., M., S., DE W., *etc*]), but is a predicate (comp. viii. 19), parallel with "more precious, or choice," but put at the end of its clause for the sake of a more emphatic stress upon the objects compared with it, gold and silver. [So E. V. in the margin, WORDSW. (?), H., N., K., *etc*.].

Ver. 2. **The rich and the poor meet together;** *i. e.*, they are found side by side (comp. xxix. 13; Isa. xxxiv. 14), as classes both of which are alike created by Jehovah, and therefore have each its own peculiar object and calling to fulfil in God's creation. Comp. xiv. 31; xvii. 5; Job xxxi. 15.—Since both "rich" and "poor" are collective ideas, it is said that God has created "all of them" (כֻּלָּם, and not "both of them, or the two," שְׁנֵיהֶם, as in xx. 12). [The verb "strike against, or encounter each other," of course does not here imply such an antagonism as too often exists in disordered human society, but simply the ordinary encounter or intermixture of social life. The word of God no where endorses the jealousies and collisions that result from sin.—A.]

Ver. 3. **The prudent seeth the evil and hideth himself.**—The K'thibh (וַיִּבָּחֵר, an Imperf. Niph.) is to be preferred to the K'ri (וְנִכְבָּה), because the hiding one's self is a consequence of seeing the coming calamity, and this consequence is expressed by the Imperf. with ו *consec* ; comp. 1 Sam. xix. 5. The K'ri originates from xxvii. 12, where the verse, with this exception, literally recurs.

But the simple pass on and must suffer ("are punished," E. V. and most of the English commentators). In the last verb we have a perfect preceded by a simple copula, because the heedless pressing on of the simple into calamity, and their "expiating" it, or suffering injury, are conceived of as cotemporaneous ; compare 2 Sam. vii. 9; Ezek. xxv. 12, *etc*.—The plural "the simple ones" over against the one "prudent man" of clause *a*, seems to be chosen not without an intentional reference to the disproportion that actually exists numerically in life between the two classes of men.

Ver. 4. **The end of humility** (and) **of the fear of God is riches and honor and life.**—The copula is wanting before "the fear of God," because this "fear" is in its idea so closely connected with "humility" that it can be appended as in a sense an appositive to it. Thus BERTHEAU and ELSTER correctly render, following GEIER, ROSENMUELLER, SCHELLING, *etc.* More commonly (and as early as the LXX and Vulg.) the "fear of Jehovah" is regarded as the first effect or consequence of humility, like riches, honor and life; this, however, gives no specifically appropriate idea. This is also true of HITZIG'S emendation (רָאָה for יִרְאַת), the "beholding Jehovah;" for "riches, honor and life" could hardly be the elements into which the "beholding Jehovah" should be resolved ; this idea is rather in the Old Testament also (*e. g.*, Ps. xi. 7; xvii. 15) always one that belongs not to the present, but only to the future life —With *b* compare moreover iii. 16; viii. 18.—[Our author's idea is also that of DE W. and K., the E. V., H., N., S., M., WORDSW., *etc*. The grammatical objection urged by HITZIG, UMBREIT and RUEETSCHI is the harshness of the *asyndeton* ; they agree in making the latter part of clause *a* the predicate, a more natural construction unquestionably, if the resulting meaning is admissible. UMBREIT interprets the humility of which "the fear of God" is the reward, as humility in human relations—a rendering hardly consistent with the Hebrew *usus loquendi*. RUEETSCHI takes the words in their ordinary sense, and the structure which is most obvious, and explains : "The genuine religious wisdom which is equivalent to 'the fear of Jehovah' (more precisely, of which the fear of the Lord is the beginning), is the highest reward of humility; it is to him who attains it all (riches, honor, life), all that man desires and strives for beside, his greatest riches, his highest honor, his true life." In this view clause *b* is an analysis of the predicate of *a*.—A.]

Ver 5. **Thorns, snares are in the way of the false.**—Here again we have an *asyndeton*, consisting in the associating of the two ideas which are in their import essentially equivalent, of "thorns" (comp. Job v. 5) and "snares, nets" (chap. vii. 23 ; Ps. lxix. 22; Job xviii. 9, *etc*.). HITZIG proposes instead of the latter explanation to read כְּפֻחִים: "Thorns are poured out, are spread on the way of the false (?)." [Those who agree with Z. in the general structure of clause *b*, in his selection of the subject and predicate, very generally, at least our English expositors, make the verb affirmative rather than hortative. RUEETSCHI (as above, p. 155), on the ground of the very general idiom of the book of Proverbs, and in regard to this phrase in particular, שֹׁמֵר נַפְשׁוֹ, considers the clause as inverted: "he who keepeth far from the thorns and snares that strow the way of the false, destroying him, notwithstanding all his cunning, saveth his life."—A.]—With *b* compare xvi. 17.

3. Vers. 6-12. Of good discipline, frugality, uprightness, love and fidelity as further important means for the preservation of a good name.— **Train up a child** (early) **in the way he should go** —The verb which, according to Arabic analogies, is equivalent to *imbuit, initiavit* (comp. SCHULTENS on this passage), denotes here the first instruction that is given to a boy, his early education and the formation of his habits. Compare the expression of HORACE (Ep. I., 2, 69): *Quo semel est imbuta recens, servabit odorem Testa diu;* and also the modern proverbs *Jung gewohnt, alt gethan* [Young accustomed is done old]: or "*Was Hänschen nicht lernt, lernt Hans nimmermehr*" ["What little Johnnie does not learn, John learns never." So our English proverb—"Just as the twig is bent the tree's inclined."]

עַל־פִּי דַרְכּוֹ can have no other meaning than "according to the standard of his way" (Gen. xliii. 7; Lev. xxvii. 8, *etc*.), *i. e*., according to the way that is determined for him, according to the calling and the manner of life for which he is intended. With this interpretation, which is as simple as it is pertinent, HITZIG's emendation may be dismissed as superfluous: עַל־פִּי רְבוּ, "according to his tenderness, since he is still tender." [Notwithstanding the "simplicity" of the interpretation "in accordance with his way, or his going," three different meanings have been found in it. It may be, *a*) "his way" in the sense of his own natural and characteristic style and manner,—and then his training will have reference to that to which he is naturally fitted; or *b*), the way in life which he is intended by parents or guardians to pursue; or *c*) the way in which he ought to go. The last is moral and relates to the general Divine intention concerning man's earthly course; the second is human and economical; the first is individual and to some extent even physical. Yet although the third presents the highest standard and has been generally adopted and used where little account is made of the original, it has the least support from the Hebrew idiom. So DE W., B., K., S., H. (?), and others.—A.]

Ver. 7 **The rich ruleth over poor men.**—Observe here again the significant interchange between singular and plural like that above in ver. 3, corresponding with the actual conditions of human society. The same relation of dependence comes in play however in like manner between borrowers and lenders; indebtedness always destroys freedom, even though no sale into slavery of him who was unable to pay should ever take place.

Ver. 8. **He that soweth iniquity shall reap calamity.**—Comp. Job iv. 8, and the converse sentiment, Prov. xi. 18.—**And the staff of his haughtiness vanisheth away;**—*i. e*., the staff with which in the ebullitions of his anger (Isa. xiv. 6) he smote others comes to nought, as though dried up and rotten. Compare for the verb "to come to nought, to come to an end," Gen. xxi. 15; 1 Kings xvii. 16; Isa. x. 25. According to the last mentioned passage, UMBREIT, EWALD [DE W.] and ELSTER explain: "and the staff of his punishment is already prepared."

But the verb כלה in that instance acquires the meaning "to be ready, to be already prepared," solely through the context,—and the noun (עֶבְרָה) means not "punishment," but always simply anger, passionate excitement. And to employ "staff of his anger" to describe "the rod of the Divine anger aroused against him" would surely be an unusually condensed and harsh expression.—HITZIG reads וְשֵׁבֶט עֶבְרָתוֹ "and be that renounces (?) his service perishes," a meaning clearly quite insipid and little appropriate as the result of a very artificial and violent emendation, for which the text of the LXX neither in ver. 8 *b*, nor in the spurious verse which this version exhibits appended to our verse, offers any adequate support whatsoever.—[FUERST distinguished two radical meanings in the verb אן, from one of which the derived noun has the meaning "nothingness, vanity," here adopted by E. V., and B.; the other gives the meaning "calamity," and in this sense the word is here understood more forcibly and appropriately, by DE W., K., H., N., M., S.—RUEETSCHI vigorously supports our author's interpretation of clause *b*.—A.]

Ver 9. **He that hath a bountiful eye shall be blessed.**—He who is "good in the eye" is the exact opposite of the man "evil in the eye" (chap. xxiii. 6); it is he therefore who looks around not wickedly but in kindness and friendliness. Such a one will besides always be charitable in disposition and action, and therefore as he dispenses blessing he will also receive blessing. The conjunction (כִּי) as the beginning of the second clause should doubtless be regarded rather as a causal, than, with HITZIG, as a conditional particle; it is therefore not "*if* he gives" (that he does this is in fact already implied in his being described as having "a bountiful eye"), but "**since**," or "**for he gives,**" *etc*.

Ver. 10. **Chase away the scorner and contention goeth out.**—That scoffing is a chief source of contention and strife was already expressed in chap. xxi. 24. Contention "goeth out," *viz*., with the scoffer, when he leaves the assembly in which he has given forth his scoffing utterances (the LXX rightly supply ἐκ συνεδρίου). —**And strife and reproach cease,**—for the evil example of the scoffer had excited the whole assembly to mutual abuse and recrimination (קָלוֹן has here this active meaning).

Ver. 11. **He that loveth with a pure heart, whose lips are gracious, the king is his friend.**—Thus, without doubt correctly, UMBREIT, ELSTER, HITZIG; for the passages xiii. 4. 24; xiv. 13 present no sufficient analogy for EWALD's interpretation of the last clause, "he is the king's friend;" and BERTHEAU's conception of the phrase "grace of lips," as a second accusative object of the verb "loveth" ("he that loveth purity of heart, and grace on his lips, the king is his friend") has against it the decided inappropriateness of the expression "to love the grace of his lips" as conveying the idea of "cultivating a wise eloquence." Furthermore we have to compare chiefly xvi. 13; for it is really wise and good counsellors who are there as here designated the favorites of the king.—[Few verses in the Book of Proverbs whose reading is unquestioned have received more interpretations. In clause *a* "purity of heart" is made the object by almost every interpreter, instead of an adverbial adjunct as Z. makes it. The "grace of lips" in clause *b*, in addition to BERTHEAU's construction (see above), is made a part of the subject—"*to whom*, or *whose* is grace of lips," *e. g.*, by DE W., EWALD, K.; it is made the first part of the predicate "*to him*, or *his* is grace of lips," *e. g*, by the E. V. in the margin, by H., N., S., M., W.; while the text of the E. V. makes it adverbial. —A.]

Ver. 12. **The eyes of Jehovah preserve knowledge**,—*i. e.*, secure protection to him who possesses and evinces true discernment and knowledge (an example, therefore, of the *abstr. pro concreto*). With clause *b*, furthermore, the meaning seems to correspond better which HITZIG obtains, when he, perhaps in this instance emending wisely, writes רָעָה instead of רֶגַע: Jehovah's eyes observe wickedness.—For the verb in clause *b* comp. xiii. 6; xxi. 12. The "words" of the false here denote his proposals or plans, the faithlessness which he devises by himself and discusses with others. [HOLDEN thinks it necessary to render the "affairs of the transgressor." The necessity is obviated by the above explanation.]

4. Vers. 13-16. Of slothfulness, wantonness, folly and avarice, as further chief hinderances to the attainment of a good name.—**The slothful saith: (There is) a lion without,** *etc.*;—*i. e.*, he has recourse to the most senseless and ludicrous excuses, if in any way he may not be obliged to go out to labor; he therefore says, *e. g.*, a lion has stolen into the city, and may possibly destroy him in the midst of the tumult and crowd of the streets. Comp. xv. 19. [See critical notes for an explanation of the tense of the main verb.]

Ver. 14. **A deep pit is the mouth of the strange woman**,—*i. e.*, her seductive language: comp. ii 16; v. 3; vi. 24; vii. 5 sq.; and also xxiii. 27, where the harlot herself is described as a deep ditch.—**He that is accursed of Jehovah.**—The "cursed of Jehovah" the exact opposite of the man "blessed" (בָּרוּךְ) of Jehovah," therefore one visited by the curse of an angered God.

Ver. 15. **Foolishness is bound in the heart of the child,**—*e.*, it belongs to the disposition of all children, who are altogether and without exception νήπιοι,—infallibly so (comp. 1 Kings iii. 7), and must therefore necessarily be removed from them by the diligent employment of the "rod of correction" (comp. xiii. 24; xix. 18; xxiii. 13, 14). Comp. our proverb "*Jugend hat kein Tugend*" [Youth hath no virtue].— [KAMPH., from the absence of an adversative particle before clause *b*, judges it better to take the first clause as conditional: "If foolishness be bound," *etc.* Here is then the remedy for the supposed exigency. But this is surely needless, and vastly weakens the import of clause *a*, with its impressive declaration of an urgent and universal need.—A.]

Ver. 16. **One oppresseth the poor only to make him rich**;—*i. e.*, the oppression which one, perchance some rich landlord or tyrannical ruler, practises on a poor man, rouses his moral energy, and thus by means of his tireless industry and his productive labor in his vocation, brings it to pass, that he works himself out of needy circumstances into actual prosperity. On the other hand, according to clause *b*, all presents which one makes to an indolent rich man, prodigal, and therefore abandoned by the blessing of God, contribute nothing to stay the waste of his possessions that has once commenced. What one gives to him is drawn into the vortex of his prodigality and profligacy, and therefore is subservient, in spite of the contrary intention of the giver, only "to want," or to the diminution of his possessions (comp. xi. 24).—Thus most of the recent expositors correctly explain, especially EWALD, UMBREIT, ELSTER, HITZIG [DE W., K.], while BERTHEAU's conception of the passage: "He that oppresseth the poor to take for himself, giveth to a rich man (*viz.*, himself) only to want," approximates to the old incorrect rendering of the Vulgate, LUTHER, *etc.* See in reply HITZIG on this passage. [H., N., M., S. follow the E. V. in giving this reflexive meaning to the pronoun of clause *a*, while WORDSW. guardedly expresses a preference for the other view; God's providence overrules the rich man's rapacity, and turns obsequious liberality toward the rich against him whom it would benefit. For according to this view it is not the giver, as the E. V. suggests, but the receiver, that shall come to want. RUEETSCHI comes vigorously to the defence of the older explanation. The subject is then single: the rich man seeks to advance himself by oppression of the poor; he gives wrongfully to one that has, and God thwarts him. We prefer this elder exposition. —A.]

DOCTRINAL, ETHICAL, HOMILETIC AND PRACTICAL.

The doctrine of the great worth of a good name forms undoubtedly the main theme of the section before us; for all that follows the introductory proposition of ver. 1, which is expressly shaped with reference to this theme, may be easily and without any violence regarded as a statement of the most important means or conditions to the attainment and maintenance of a good name. These conditions are given in part negatively, as not consisting in riches (ver. 2, comp. ver. 16), nor in falseness of heart (ver. 5), nor in scoffing and love of abuse (ver. 10), nor in unrighteous dealing (ver. 8, comp. ver. 12), nor in sloth and licentiousness (vers. 13, 14). They are also given in part positively, as consisting in a genuine prudence (ver. 3), in humility and the fear of God (ver. 4), in a wise frugality and industry (vers. 7 and 16), in charity toward the poor (ver. 9), in purity of heart together with that grace of speech which rests upon it (ver. 11),—in a word, in all the excellent qualities as well as the inward and outward advantages to which a strict and wise training of children is able to aid the man who is naturally foolish and ignorant (vers. 6 and 15).

Homily on the entire section: On the great worth of a good name, and on the means to its attainment and preservation. Comp. STÖCKER: Of a good name: 1) How it is to be gained (vers. 1-4); 2) what chief hinderances threaten the possession of it (vers. 5-16).—In similar style, WOHLFARTH, *Calwer Handb.*, etc.

Ver. 1. MELANCHTHON: With reason dost thou say: I need a good conscience for God's sake, but a good name for my neighbor's sake. A good name is really a good thing well-pleasing to God, and must be esteemed and sought by us, because God would have the difference between good and evil brought to the day by the testimony of public opinion, so that accordingly those who do right may be promoted and preserved, the unjust, on the contrary, censured, punished and destroyed. From such public witness we are to become aware of the existence of a moral law, and should reflect, that a holy God and supreme avenger of all evil lives. We must therefore strive after a good name for two reasons: 1) because God would have us regard the judgments of upright men (Ecclesiast. vi. 1 sq.); 2) because He would also have us serve as a good example to others (1 Cor. x. 31 sq.; Phil. iv. 8).— STARKE: If a good name is better than riches, then it is our duty, in case of need, to defend our innocence (Am. vii. 11; John viii. 49), but no less to rescue the good name of others also (1 Sam. xx. 31 sq.).—[ARNOT: The atmosphere of a good name surrounding it imparts to real worth additional body and breadth.—MUFFET: a good name maketh a man's speeches and actions the more acceptable; it spreadeth his virtues unto his glory, and the stirring up of others; it remaineth after death; it doth good to the children of him who is well spoken of; and finally is a means of advancement.]

Vers. 2-5. MELANCHTHON (on ver. 2): Know that there is a Divine providence, and that not by chance but by God's ordinance some are rich, others poor. Therefore it is of moment that both walk before God according to their state and calling, that the poor therefore do not murmur against God, but humble himself under His hand, and take comfort in the promises of His word (Matth. v. 3),—that the rich, however, be not presumptuous, and do not set his trust on uncertain riches (1 Tim. vi. 17), *etc.—Tübingen Bible* (on the same verse):—If the rich were always humble and the poor patient, and both alike penitent, pious, loving and peaceable, then rich and poor might live happy and content together.—[R. HALL:—The rich and the poor meet together 1) in the participation of a common nature; 2) in the process of the same social economy; 3) in the house of God; 4) in the circumstances of their entrance into this world and in the circumstances of their exit out of it: 5) in the great crises of the future.—SAURIN:— That diversity of condition which God hath been pleased to establish among men is perfectly consistent with equality: the splendid condition of the rich includes nothing that favors their ideas of self-preference; there is nothing in the low condition of the poor which deprives them of their real dignity or debases their intelligence formed in the image of God, *etc.—See* BISHOP BUTLER'S Sermon before the Lord Mayor.—R. HOOKER (on ver. 3):—It is nature which teacheth a wise man in fear to hide himself, but grace and faith teach him where.—MUFFET:— Although God can save us only by His power, yet He will not without our own care and endeavor, nor without those means which He hath ordained to that intent and purpose].—HASIUS (on ver. 8): —The best hiding from danger and calamity is under the wings of the Almighty (Ps. xci. 1 sq.). —J. LANGE (on ver. 4):—He who would be exalted to glory, must first suffer himself to be well humbled.—(On ver. 5):—The ungodly finds in the path to hell nothing but thorns and snares, and yet he presses on in it! A sign of the greatness and fearfulness of the ruin of man's sin.

Vers. 6-13. [SOUTH (on ver. 6):—A sermon on the education of youth].—STARKE (on ver. 6):—The spirits of children are like plastic wax; according as good or evil is impressed upon them will their chief inclination be a good or evil one. —On ver. 8):—Upon unrighteousness and ungodliness there surely follows a terrible end. But who believes it? (Ps. lxxiii. 18, 19).—CRAMER (on ver. 10):—One sin ever develops itself from another. From mockery comes wrath, from wrath comes strife, from strife one comes to blows, and from blows comes reproach.—(On ver. 11): —A true heart and a pleasing speech are rarely found together, especially at the courts of this world's great ones, where there is only quite too much hypocrisy and unfaithfulness to be found, hiding behind smooth words.

Vers. 13-16. J. LANGE (on ver. 13):—He that loveth his own soul and therefore on account of comfort and tenderness will not go forth to carry on the Lord's work, will lose and eternally destroy his soul, John xii. 25.—(On ver. 15):— God's children must in their life have to experience sharp strokes of affliction in many forms, for, still as heretofore spiritually children, folly in many forms remains in their hearts, and the sin that yet dwells in them makes itself perceptible by frequent outbreaks.—GEIER (on ver. 15): —With more loving words and flattering speech can no child be happily trained; strict and wise correction must be added.—(On ver. 16):—Beware of all unrighteous means of becoming rich through others' injury. Better to have little with a good conscience than great treasure with injustice!—*Calwer Handb.* (on ver. 16):—He that enricheth himself on the poor, one richer than he will in turn impoverish him.—[EDWARDS (on ver. 15):—The rod of correction is proper to drive away no other foolishness than that which is of a moral nature. But how comes wickedness to be so firmly bound, and strongly fixed, in the hearts of children, if it be not there naturally?]

III. ADDITIONS MADE BEFORE HEZEKIAH'S TIME TO THE OLD NUCLEUS OF THE COLLECTION MADE BY SOLOMON.

Chap. XXII. 17—XXIV. 34.

First Supplement:—Various precepts concerning righteousness and practical wisdom.

Chap. XXII. 17.—XXIV. 22.

a) Introductory admonition to take to heart the words of the wise man.

Chap. XXII. 17-21.

17 Incline thine ear and hear words of the wise,
and apply thine heart to my knowledge!
18 For it is pleasant if thou keep them within thee;
let them abide together upon thy lips!
19 That thy trust may be in Jehovah,
I have taught thee this day, even thee!
20 Have not I written to thee excellent words,
with counsels and knowledge,
21 to make known to thee the certainty of the words of truth,
that thou mightest return words of truth to them that send thee?

b) Admonition to justice toward others, especially the poor.

Chap. XXII. 22-29.

22 Rob not the poor because he is poor,
and oppress not the wretched in the gate;
23 for Jehovah will conduct their cause,
and spoil the soul of those that spoil them.
24 Have no intercourse with an angry man,
and with a furious man thou shalt not go,
25 lest thou learn his ways
and prepare a snare for thy soul.
26 Be not among them that strike hands,
who become sureties for debts;
27 if thou hast nothing to pay
why shall he take thy bed from under thee?
28 Remove not the ancient landmark
which thy fathers have set.
29 Seest thou a man that is diligent in his business—
before kings shall he stand;
he shall not stand before mean men.

GRAMMATICAL AND CRITICAL.

Ver. 17. [Observe the interchange of the imperative הַט with the 2d pers. sing. of the Imperf. תָּשִׁית.—A.]

Ver. 18. [In יִכֹּנוּ we have illustrated, as in many other instances, the final disregard of the originally strict application of the suffixes to their own person and number: let *them* abide in *its* entireness, *etc.*—A.]

Ver. 20. [Bött. § 707, 2, explains the masc. adj. שָׁלִשִׁים of the K'ri as an example of masculines used in describing the pre-eminent and striking,—but on account of the הַיּוֹם of ver. 19 gives the preference to the K'thibh שִׁלְשׁוֹם. So Stuart and Muenscher.—A.]

Ver. 21. [לִשְׁלָחֶיךָ, one of the plural participles, not uncommon in our book, to be taken distributively, as applicable to each of all possible cases. Bött. § 702, e.—A.]

Vers. 22, 24, 26, 28. [Further examples of the Jussive with the negative adverb אַל, instead of a direct prohibition with the Imperative: comp. Latin, *ne facias*; Greek, μὴ γράφῃς (Kuehner, § 250, 5, Hadley, § 723, a); as though in prohibitions a sense of fitness or obligation were appealed to rather than an authority asserted.—A.]—(Ver. 24). בּוֹא אֶת here, in accordance with the later *usus loquendi*, is equivalent to אֶת הָלַךְ; comp. Ps. xxvi. 4.

Ver. 25. [The more compact form הָאֵלֶךְ for הָאֵלֵךְ under the influence of the preceding פֶּן; Bött. § 1059, d.—A.]

Ver. 27. [An example of what is called the *concrete* impersonal in Hebrew is found in יָקִים; why should *he*, any one do this? Bött. § 935, c.—A.]

Ver. 28. [יָתְבַּ; Böttcher's *Fiens licitum* or *debitum*, rendered by the German *darf*: it is his privilege or prerogative.—A.]

EXEGETICAL.

1. That a new division of the collection begins with ver. 17, coming from another hand than compiled the preceding main division, appears not merely from the expression "words of wise men," which reminds us of i. 6, but also from the characteristic style of the proverbs which are found from this point onward to the end of chap. xxiv. These no longer consist of verses of two clauses constructed according to the antithetic parallelism, but for the most part of longer sentences, which as a general rule comprise two verses, sometimes, however, three (*e. g.* xxiii. 1-3, 6-8), or even five (thus xxxii. 31-35; xxiv. 30-34). By the side of the isolated proverbs containing an antithesis of two members, such as are here and there interspersed (*e. g.* xxii. 28; xxiii. 9, 12, 19, 22; xxiv. 8 sq., 23 sq.), there are found in addition several verses constructed of three clauses (xxii. 29; xxiii. 5, 7, 31, 35; xxiv. 12, 31). There is prevalent everywhere the minutely hortatory or in turn admonitory style, rather than that which is descriptive and announces facts. The אַל which serves to introduce the utterance of warnings is found not less than *seventeen* times within the two and a half chapters before us, while in the twelve chapters of the preceding main division it occurred but *twice* (chap. xx. 13 and 22). Many linguistic peculiarities in the section appear, moreover, to indicate a later period; whether it be the earliest period after the exile, as Hitzig proposes, may indeed be the more doubtful and uncertain, since many peculiarities of the section, especially the expression, "words of the wise" (in xxii. 17), like the prevailing admonitory tone of the discourse, seem to favor the assumption of Delitzsch, that its author is identical with that of the introductory main division, chap. i.-ix. Comp. Introduction, § 12, p. 29.

2. Vers. 17-21. The introductory admonition to give heed to the words of the wise.

Ver. 18. **For it is pleasant if thou keep them within thee.** "Them," *viz.*, "the words of the wise," for only to these can the suffix relate, and not to "my knowledge;" so that accordingly this proposition in ver. 18 a, beginning with "for," serves to justify only the first half and not the whole of ver. 17. With 18 *b*: **let them abide together upon thy lips,** the admonitory discourse proceeds, and in the first instance attaches itself to the substance of 17 *b* (comp. v. 2). Against the common construction, which regards the verb יִכֹּנוּ as a continuation of the conditional clause, "if thou keep," etc., [so *e. g.* De W., N., S., M., Muffet, etc.], we adduce the absence of a second conditional particle, or at least a copula before the Imperf., which in its present position at the beginning of a clause clearly appears to be a Jussive. Comp. Hitzig on this passage.

Ver. 19. **That thy trust may be in Jehovah I have taught thee this day, even thee!** The perfect represents the work of teaching as already begun and now in progress, like the "I have given," chap. iv. 2.—אַף אַתָּה, *etiam te, inquam*, Germ. *ja dich!* yea, thee! even thee! The expression brings out strongly the idea that the present teaching is designed for the student of wisdom who is here addressed, for him and for no one else (Mercer, Geier, J. H. Michaelis, Ewald, De W., Bertheau, etc.). There is no occasion for Umbreit's interrogative conception of the words: "but thou?"; *i. e.* dost thou also attend to my teaching? and the same is true of Hitzig's attempted emendation, according to which we should read אַף אַתָּה, "this also, the very same."—The first member, moreover, gives not so much the substance as the object of the teaching, and that as consisting in the development of a firm trust in God, or in the increase and establishment of faith (comp. Luke xvii. 5).

Ver. 20. **Have I not written** (Z., "behold, I write) **to thee excellent words?** (The K'ri שָׁלִישִׁים from שָׁלִישׁ), which is equivalent to נָגִיד "a great man, a nobleman" (comp. Keil on 2 Sam. xxiii. 8), describes the words us of the highest, noblest worth, of pre-eminent value, as *verba eximia s. principalia* (comp. the similar term in viii. 6). So, and doubtless correctly, Ziegler, Ewald, Elster, etc. Comp. the early rendering, τρισμέγιστα, of the *Vers. Veneta*. [K. renders "expressive, or significant," *bedeutsam*]. Others interpret the K'ri differently, *e. g.* Hitzig: bequests, *Vermächtnisse* (in accordance with the Rabbinic שָׁל, *depositarius*;) the Vulg. and some of the older expositors, "three-fold, *i. e.* several times, in various ways" (so Luther): or even "in three forms," so that the reference will be to the Law, the Prophets, and the Hagiographa, as the three chief constituents of the divine word, or again, to the three books of Solomon, etc. The K'thibh is explained ordinarily, by supplying an omitted הֲמוֹל, in the sense of "before, formerly:" thus Umbreit, *e. g.*: "have I not formerly written to thee?" (In a similar way Bertheau). But the ellipsis of a "yesterday" before this עֹלְשׁוֹם would be without any linguistic analogy; and in a section which introduces subsequent admonitions a reminder of teachings formerly given seems little appropriate. For this reason the K'ri in the sense above given is unquestionably to be preferred [S. and M. prefer the adverbial rendering; the majority of the English commentators with the E. V. the substantive.—A.]—**With counsels and knowledge**, so far forth, *viz.*, as these are contained in the "princely words."

Ver. 21. **To make known to thee the certainty of the words of truth.** "Correctness, verity," as *e. g.* in the Targ. on Jer. xxii. 13, 15; Sam. Gen. xv. 6 (where it is made equivalent to צֶדֶק, "righteousness"). Comp. the Chaldee קְשׁוֹט in the Targ. on our passage.— **That thou mightest be able to return words of truth to them that send thee.** "Words, truth," a sort of apposition, describing the discourse to be conveyed as consisting of words which are "as it were themselves the truth" (UMBREIT, ELSTER). The expression is like the "words consolations, *i. e.* consoling words," in Zech. i. 13.—The "senders" (comp. x. 26) are here naturally the parents, who have sent their son to the teacher of wisdom, that he may bring back thence to them real culture of spirit and heart; or again, that "be may know how to bring home to them in all things true and not false or erroneous report" (HITZIG).—[HOLDEN unnecessarily makes the suffix of the participle represent an indirect object; "them that send unto thee." For the construction "words truth" see GREEN, § 253, 2.—A.]

3. Vers. 22-29. Admonition to justice toward others, especially the poor and distressed.—**Rob not the poor because he is poor**, דָּל is the depressed, the straitened, he who is deprived of help for judicial contests and other cases of want, and who therefore needs the protection of the more powerful and the more prosperous.— **And oppress not the poor in the gate**, *i. e.* in the place where courts are held; comp Job v. 4; xxxi. 21; Ps. cxxvii. 5.—[Comp. THOMSON'S *Land and Book*, I. 31; and other works illustrative of Oriental usages, *passim*.—A.]

Ver. 23. **For Jehovah will conduct their cause**. The emphatic announcement of the reason for the warning in the preceding ver.; comp. xxiii. 11. With respect to the just punishment threatened in clause *b*, comp. Matt. xviii. 32 sq.—[God is not merely a formidable because an all-just and almighty advocate, appearing before the unjust tribunal, in behalf of the wronged; He is not merely a judge sitting in a higher court of appeal; He is the executor of the universal laws of justice to which the judges as well as the arraigned of earth are alike amenable. When Jehovah "cheats or spoils" it is in vindication and not in violation of eternal justice and right. FUERST makes the "life" an adverbial modification, and not the object, so that it expresses the extent of his work, "even to the life."—A.]

Vers. 24, 25. Warning against intercourse with men of violent temper, like xxvi. 21; xxix. 22; comp. James i. 20.—**And with a furious man thou shalt not go**, lit., "go not along with him."—**And prepare a snare for thy soul**; *viz.*, the passion that would become a snare, a fatal net for thee (comp. xx. 25).—With the warning against suretyship in vers. 26, 27, comp. vi. 1-4; xi. 15; xvii. 18; xx. 16.

Ver. 28. Warning against the violent removal of boundaries; comp. the prohibitions of the Law; Deut. xix. 14; xxvii. 17; and also Job xxiv. 2; Hos. v. 10; and below, Prov. xxiii. 10, 11.

Ver. 29. **Seest thou a man diligent in business.** The verb, a Perf. Kal, is conditional; "if thou seest;" comp. vi. 22. כָּהִיר, apt, active, expert (LUTHER, *endlich*).—**Before kings shall he stand** (Z. "may he set himself"), *viz.* to serve them, to receive their commands, comp. 1 Sam. xvi. 21, 22.—**He shall not stand before mean men**. Lit., "men in the dark," *homines obscuri, ignobiles* (Vulg.). The antithesis to the "kings" is naturally an idea of a somewhat general and comprehensive kind, describing those who belong to the low multitude, the plebeians. To generalize the idea of "king" in like manner, as if it here expressed something like "noble, rich," is therefore unnecessary (in opposition to HITZIG on this passage). [LORD BACON says: Of all the qualities which kings especially look to and require in the choice of their servants, that of despatch and energy in the transactions of business is the most acceptable, *etc., etc.* There is no other virtue which does not present some shadow of offence to the minds of kings. Expedition in the execution of their commands is the only one which contains nothing that is not acceptable (*De Augmentis Scientiarum*, Lib. VIII.)].

DOCTRINAL, ETHICAL, HOMILETIC AND PRACTICAL.

There are only two main ideas with the presentation of which this section is concerned; these, however, are thoughts of no slight weight and significance. That true wisdom, which is indeed one with firm confidence in God, is to be secured and maintained above all things else, the introductory admonition (vers. 17-21) brings out with earnest emphasis. And that such wisdom as this should manifest itself in a demeanor toward one's fellow-men just and kind in all directions,—to impress this is the single aim and end of the hortatory and admonitory addresses that follow in vers. 22-29.—For not merely the warnings against the unrighteous plundering of one's neighbors (vers. 22, 23), against passion and a ruinous familiarity with the passionate, and against a wicked removal of boundaries, have this end in view,—but also the cautions against suretyship, which are apparently brought forward merely as prudential suggestions (vers. 26, 27), and against the wasting of executive talents and skill in the service of insignificant masters (ver. 29), fall under the same generalization, so far forth as both kinds of unwise conduct point to an intentional hiding of the talent received from the Lord, and to an inclination to the low and the common, which is as wilful as it is unprofitable and contemptible. He who through inconsiderate suretyship for unworthy men deprives himself of the means of a free and vigorous efficiency in life, puts his light under a bushel quite as really, and with no less guilt than he who fritters away his strength in a narrow and obscure sphere of labor, rather than by earnest striving for an influential station seeks to make the results of his activity the common property of many. Comp. Matth. v. 14-16; xxv. 24; John iii. 20, 21; vii. 4.

These two main truths,—the praise of wisdom as the source of all real confidence in God, and the subsequent admonition to righteousness in many particulars, meet in the idea of *Faith*, or obedient consecration to the invisible holy God, as the sum of all true wisdom (ver. 19). Put in form as the *leading thought* in a *homiletic discussion*, this fundamental idea would be expressed in some such way as this: On faith in God as the ground of all righteousness and the end of all wisdom;—or, Faith (confidence in God) as the basis and end of all wisdom.—STÖCKER (regarding the whole as a direct continuation of vers. 1-16): Admonition to seek after a good name.—STARKE: Admonition to obedience to the true wisdom (17-21), to right treatment of the poor (22, 23), to the avoidance of intercourse with bad men (24-27), and to a scrupulous regard for boundaries (28, 29).

Ver. 17-21. ZELTNER: All the world's pleasure is to be accounted nothing in comparison with the true, sweet pleasure which comes from the word of God. This they know who have tasted the sweetness of this word (Heb. vi. 5).—J. LANGE: Where the good will to obey is wanting, there all teaching and preaching are vain. This is the reason why so many hundred sermons are heard by the majority without profit.—He who is heartily and willingly obedient to Christ finds in this no burden; in Christ's obedience consists rather the highest joy.—R. FLOREY (on vers. 17-19; see *Hirtenstimmen an die Gemeinde im Hause des Herrn*, II., Leips., 1849): In the training of your children let your hope be directed to the Lord; for 1) the word of the Lord gives the right direction; 2) His service gives the right strength; 3) His grace gives the right power besides.—TH. HERGANG (*Reformationspredigt*) on vers. 17-19; (see *Sonntagsfeier*, 1861, p. 357): What a blessed duty is it to hold in honor the memory of such men as have deserved well in the true culture of their own and succeeding times! [A. FULLER (vers. 17, 18): If we study the Scriptures as *Christians*, the more familiar we are with them, the more we shall feel their importance; but if otherwise, our familiarity with the word will be like that of soldiers and doctors with death—it will wear away all sense of its importance from our minds.—TRAPP (ver. 19): Only a Divine word can beget a Divine faith.]

Vers. 22-29. STARKE (on vers. 22, 23): If the Lord efficiently sympathizes with those who are in outward poverty, still more does He do this for the spiritually poor, who are of broken heart and tremble at His word (Is. lxvi. 2).—[ARNOT (on vers. 22, 23): There is a causal connection and not merely a coincidence between the spread of God's word and the security of men's rights in a land. As worship rises to heaven, justice radiates on earth. If faith go foremost, charity will follow.—LAWSON (ver. 22): For magistrates to be guilty of the crime of oppression, is a perversion of an institution of God into an engine of abominable wickedness.—(On ver. 23): The unjust spoiler has the mercy of God against him as well as His justice.—TRAPP (on ver. 23). A poor man's livelihood is his life. God, therefore, who loves to pay oppressors home in their own coin, will have life for life.—LORD BACON (on ver. 24): It is of the first importance for the peace and security of life to have no dealings with passionate men, or such as easily engage in disputes and quarrels; for they will perpetually involve us in strife and faction, so that we shall be compelled either to break off our friendship, or disregard our own safety.—BRIDGES (on vers. 26, 27): In "devising liberal things" we must combine scrupulous regard to justice and truth. Else our charity will prove the scandal, instead of the glory, of our profession.]—MELANCHTHON (on ver. 28): The injunction (that boundaries are not to be removed) may by a simple allegory be expanded to this prohibition; that laws in general that are venerable from their age are not to be altered, except in case of the most pressing and obvious need.—VON GERLACH (On ver. 29): Peculiar facility and ability God will bring into an appropriate sphere of action.—[TRAPP: A diligent man shall not long sit in a low place. Or if he do all the days of his life, yet if his diligence proceed out of conscience, "he shall stand before the King" of kings when he dies.]

---

c) Warning against greediness, intemperance, impurity, *etc.*

CHAP. XXIII.

1 When thou sittest to eat with a ruler,
   consider well him who is before thee,—
2 and thou wilt put a knife to thy throat
   if thou art a gluttonous man.
3 Crave not his dainties,
   for it is deceitful food.

4 Labor not to be rich;
 cease from (this) thine own wisdom.
5 Wilt thou look eagerly after it—and it is no longer there?
 for assuredly it maketh itself wings,
 as an eagle that flieth toward the heavens.
6 Eat not the bread of him that hath an evil eye,
 and crave not his dainties.
7 For as he thinketh in his heart, so is he;
 "eat and drink" saith he to thee,
 but his heart is not with thee.
8 Thy morsel which thou hast eaten, wilt thou cast up,
 and wilt have lost thy pleasant words.
9 Speak not in the ears of a fool,
 for he would despise the wisdom of thy words.
10 Remove not old landmarks,
 and into the field of the fatherless enter thou not.
11 For their avenger is a mighty one;
 He will maintain their cause with thee.
12 Apply thine heart to instruction,
 and thine ears to words of knowledge.
13 Withhold not correction from the child;
 for if thou beatest him with the rod he shall not die.
14 Thou beatest him with the rod,
 and his soul thou deliverest from hell.
15 My son, if thine heart be made wise,
 my heart will rejoice, even mine;
16 And my reins will exalt,
 when thy lips speak right things.
17 Let not thine heart press on eagerly after sinners,
 but after the fear of Jehovah all the day;
18 for if the end come
 then thy hope shall not be destroyed.
19 Hear thou, my son, and be wise,
 and incline thine heart in a right way.
20 Be not among winebibbers,
 who devour much flesh.
21 For the drunkard and the glutton shall come to want,
 and the sleep of sloth clotheth in rags.
22 Hearken to thy father that hath begotten thee,
 and despise not thy mother when she is old.
23 Buy the truth and sell it not,
 wisdom, and discipline and understanding.
24 The father of a righteous man rejoiceth greatly;
 he that begetteth a wise man hath joy in him.
25 Let thy father and thy mother be glad,
 and her that bare thee exult.
26 My son, give me thine heart,
 and let thine eyes delight in my ways.
27 For a harlot is a deep ditch,
 and the strange woman a narrow pit.
28 Yea, she lieth in wait like a robber,
 and the false among men doth she multiply.
29 Who hath woe? who hath grief?
 who hath contentions,—who trouble,—who wounds without cause,
 who hath redness of eyes?
30 They that tarry long at the wine,
 who come to seek mixed wine.

31 Look not on the wine, when it is red,
   when it sparkleth in the cup,
   when it glideth smoothly!
32 At last it biteth like a serpent,
   and stingeth like an adder.
33 Thine eyes shall see strange things,
   and thine heart shall utter perverse things;
34 and thou shalt be as one that (is) in the midst of the sea,
   as one that lieth on the top of a mast.
35 "They have stricken me—I have not felt it—
   they have smitten me—I have not known it—
   when I awake I will seek it yet again."

GRAMMATICAL AND CRITICAL.

Ver. 1.—[We have in בִּין, as in גִיל, ver. 24, examples of the "spurious" ע״י verbs, or mixed ע״י and ע״ו. The present result is that we have here in ver. 1, and in the K'ri in ver. 24, forms apparently of the Inf. constr., where the idiom of the language requires an Inf. abs. See GREEN, § 158, 2, 3; BÖTT., §§ 988, 4, a; 1141; 1143, 1, 2, etc. The הָכִין is followed by a Perf. consec. to express the idea of the "*Fiens debitum*," what ought always to be, and so may confidently be expressed as a finished result. BÖTT., § 981, D. γ.—A.]

Ver. 4.—The punctuation לְהֶעָשִׁיר is unquestionably correct (see Exegetical notes); to alter it to לְהַעֲשִׁיר (LXX, Targ., HITZIG), as though the admonition were against laboring for the favor of *the rich man*, is unnecessary.

Ver. 5.—We render according to the K'ri יָעוּף, which is certainly to be preferred to the unmeaning K'thibh וְעִיף (for which many conjecture וְעוֹף, "as eagles and birds of the heavens"). [BÖTT., § 1132, 3, very confidently proposes יָעֹף, making the verb a Jussive.—A.]

Ver. 7.—[For the form אָכוּל comp. critical notes on xxii. 7, 8.—A.]

The verb (שָׁעַר) pointed and accented as here can be nothing but 3d pers. Perf. Kal, equivalent to the Chald. שָׁעַר, *cogitavit, meditatus est*; and this meaning of the expression gives a general sense so appropriate that we ought clearly to abide by it (with ABEN EZRA, UMBREIT, BERTHEAU, ELSTER, etc. [so the E. V., N., S., M., W., DE W., FUERST], although no support can be found for it any where in the Old Testament. The LXX rendered שֵׂעָר "hair" [so he eats and drinks, as if any one should swallow a hair]; the Chald., שֵׁעָר, "fool;" SCHULTENS, שָׂעַר, shuddering; EWALD and HITZIG, שָׂעַר divided ("as one who is divided in his soul") [HOLDEN and others, "as he is vile"]; but these are all unnecessary attempts at emendation.

Ver. 10.—[In שְׂדֵי BÖTT., § 821, Decl. 11, and n. 3, maintains that we have a *sing. constr.* from the original form שָׂדַי, and not a *plur. const.* collateral to שָׂדוֹת, as most of the grammars and lexicons hold. He compares עָרַי and עֲלַי.—A.]

Ver. 12.—[הָבָאָה, a poetical form, a lengthened Imper. pres. Comp. דִינָה in xxiv. 14.—A.]

Ver. 15.—[The supplementary אָנֹכִי conforms to the case of the preceding suffix of the same person, which is of course a genitive. BÖTT., § 855, 3.—A.]

Ver. 19.—אַשֵּׁר is here a real Piel with a factitive meaning, unlike its use in iv. 14.

Ver. 22.—[The demonstrative זֶה used, as it is occasionally in poetry and prophecy, not instead of a relative, but as the emphatic antecedent of an omitted relative. BÖTT., §§ 896, θ; 897, E.—A.]

Ver. 25.—[Instead of rendering the verbs as simple Imperf., to be rendered by the future, they may perhaps be made more expressive if made examples of the "consultative" use of the Jussive: "let thy father and thy mother," etc. The E. V. is "thy father and thy mother shall," etc.—A.]

Ver. 26.—[Instead of the K'thibh, הרצנה (=תִּרְצֶנָה), "let them delight in my words" (comp. xvi. 7), the K'ri, with all the old versions, calls unnecessarily for תִּצֹּרְנָה, "let them preserve or keep," etc.

Ver. 32.—[יִפְרֹשׂ BÖTT. would explain as shortened from יַפְרִישׁ and not from יַפְרִישׁ. See § 1013, ex.—A.]

Ver. 33.—[רָאוּ, a masc. form agreeing with a fem. subject, as the fem. תִּרְאֶינָה would have seemed perhaps to agree with עֵינוֹת. See BÖTT., § 936, A. a.—A.]

EXEGETICAL.

1. Vers. 1-8. Warnings against courting the favor of the powerful, against greed, and against intercourse with the envious. The first of these warnings, vers. 1-3, stands very plainly in immediate connection with the last verse of the preceding chapter. The counsel that one's powers be employed in the service of kings is followed by a warning against the dangers of a too confidential intercourse with powerful and honorable men, especially against the danger of being watched by them on occasion of their banquets, and possibly recognized as immoderate, as intemperate, as an epicure, etc. Comp. the Arabic proverb: He that eats the Sultan's soup burns his lips, though it be not till afterward (MEID., II., 741); or this other: With kings one seats himself at the table for the sake of honor, and not of surfeiting (*Thaâl Synt.*, p. 31); see HORACE also, *Ars poet.*, 434 sq., and Ecclesiast. ix. 13, 14: xxxi. 12-14.—**Consider well him who is before thee**, *viz.*, that he is not one of thine equals, but one much mightier and loftier (so LUTHER, UMBREIT, HITZIG [KAMPH., N., M.]

etc Others. Consider well *what* is before thee, *i. e.*, the food that is set before thee (LXX, Vulg., Ewald, Bertheau [E V., H, S, Wordsw.] *etc.* Both explanations are possible; the first seems more consistent with the connection.

Ver 2. **Thou wilt put a knife to thy throat** Lit, "and thou hast put '—for which reason Hitzig thinks it necessary to put this entire verse after verse 3, and to regard it as a continuation of the reference made in 3, *b*, to the danger of eating with great men But no ancient MS. or version exhibits any other order of the verses than the usual one, and besides this gives unquestionably a good logical progress in the thought It is grammatically unjustifiable to regard the verb as Imperative (LXX Vulg., Luther [E V, *etc.*]. "And put a knife to thy throat") [But Bött. justifies a rendering substantially the same (see Critical note) by saying "Although the legislator and teacher prescribes only for the future, yet the hearer and render (and their point of view must be taken) cannot regard the thing prescribed as merely future — Something that is in general terms enjoined he must, as soon as he becomes cognizant of it, not merely do in the future, but in case of need immediately, *etc.* This *Fiens debitum* remains then indeterminate in time" As between the two resulting ideas: "Thou hast virtually destroyed thyself if thou art a self-indulgent man," —and "Thou must at all hazards subdue thine appetite" we prefer the latter, with K, N., W, M, H, against S —A] **If thou art a gluttonous man**, lit. a master or owner of desire, not precisely one ruled by appetite (Umbreit), but a man cherishing and maintaining strong desires; comp "Master of dreams," Gen xxxvii 19.

Ver. 3 **Crave not his dainties** (comp 6, *b*, xxiv 1). for it is **deceitful food**, lit, "bread of lies" (comp. xx 17). *i e*. a deceptive meal, which in reality has another object than that which it seems to have.

Vers. 4, 5 **Labor not to be rich** Since what follows plainly emphasizes the fugitive and perishable nature of riches in itself, the sentiment as a whole doubtless aims to deter from striving after wealth, or from covetousness — **Cease from** (this) **thine own wisdom**, *viz* from that which has reference to the acquisition and preservation of riches — **Wilt thou look eagerly** (lit "let thine eyes fly") **after it.**—*a* we render in accordance with the K ri, which in spite of the fact that a Hiphil of this verb does not occur elsewhere. is to be preferred to the unintelligible K'thibh, and we do not need (with Hitzig) to substitute the rendering "if thou faintest, if thou art weary" (from עיף "to be feeble or powerless;" comp Jer iv 31, Judg. iv 21)— **And it is no longer thers**, has disappeared, is suddenly gone' Comp. the same expression, Job vii 9, also Gen v 24.— **For assuredly it maketh itself wings** precisely "it will make itself wings;" comp 2 Sam xv 1; 1 Kings i. 5, also the Latin phrase *alas sibi facere* (Sil Ital. 16, 351) and our proverbial expression ' to make one find his legs," or again " *Füsse kriegen und davon fliegen*" [to get feet and fly away] —**As an eagle that flieth towards the heavens** (see Critical notes).

Vers. 6-8. **Eat not the bread of him that hath an evil eye**, the jealous, the man of an evil eye is the opposite of the man with the "good eye," to him who is of a "kindly look," (comp. xxii. 9, Deut. xv 9; Matth vi. 23)

Ver. 7. **For as he thinketh in his heart so is he** See Critical notes

Ver. 8. **Thy morsel which thou hast eaten thou shalt cast up** and this under the constraint of the "evil eye" exciting vexation and disgust, under the feeling of bitterness which the envy and ill will of thine entertainer will excite in thee, and from the perception of the fruitlessness of thy friendly words which were intended to gain the false heart of this man

2 Vers. 9-11. **Warning against intercourse with fools, and against violence** — With ver 9 comp ix 8 —**And into the field of the fatherless press thou not**, lit "come not into them," *i e*, in the way of removing boundaries or other acts of violence. [Hackett (*Scripture Illustrations*) and other travellers in the East call attention to the simplicity of these landmarks, a single stone or small heap of stones,—and the ease with which an aggressor could encroach without detection —A].

Ver 11 *For their avenger* is a strong one, *i. e.*, Jehovah, who appears as the vindicator of outraged innocence (as גאל, Job xix 25, Jer 1. 34, *etc.*), when human deliverers and protectors are wanting to it. (For illustration of human "redeemers ' comp. Ruth iii 12). With *b* compare xxii. 23, also Ps lxviii. 6. Mal. iii. 5, *etc*.

3. Vers 12 18 **Admonition to the strict training of children, and to the striving after true wisdom and the fear of God**—**Apply thine heart to correction** For this phrase "to apply the heart to, incline the heart," comp. Ps. xc. 12, *b*; for the "words of knowledge," chap. i. 2.

Ver 12 can hardly be regarded as an introduction to all that follows as far as chap xxiv. 2 (in opposition to Bertheau); rather does the general exhortation contained in it, to the reception of a discipline of the understanding, prepare the way only for what immediately follows, —perhaps as far as ver 16, or 18

Ver 13 Comp iii 27, xix 18, xxii 15.

Ver 14 **And his soul thou deliverest from hell** *i e*. so far forth as correction leads to life. and is even itself life, comp iv 13; xv. 24; also vii. 27 sq, ix 18

Ver 15, 16 **My son if thine heart becometh wise** *i e*. if it as the result of wholesome discipline shall have become wise —**My heart will rejoice, even mine**—therefore not thine merely For the repetition of the suffix which expresses the genitive relation, by the *casus rectus*, compare. 1 Kings xxi. 19; 2 Sam xvii, 5, xix 1. and also chap xiii 19 above. The "reins" in 16, *a*, are plainly only an interchangeable expression for "heart ' (Ps. xvi. 7; xvii. 3), and the "right speaking of the lips" is the necessary effect or the outward sign of having become wise

Ver 17 **Let not thine heart press on eagerly after sinners, but after the fear of Jehovah all the day** Thus Schelling, Um-

BREIT, HITZIG, [K.] correctly render, while the greater number, following the LXX, Vulg., etc., restrict the effect of the verb קָנֵה to the first member, and for the second supply the Imper. of the substantive verb. For the general idea moreover comp iii 31; xxiv. i. 19. [HOLDEN gives a qualified endorsement to the interpretation which our author adopts; (N, M., S. follow the E V) in the line of the LXX rendering.— RUEETSCHI supports the view which makes the one expressed verb common to the two clauses, the shades of meaning varying as a person is the object in the former, a thing in the latter clause; in the former case the idea is very nearly that of "envy," in the latter "to be zealous for." A more delicate point discussed by It is the peculiarity of the compound connective כִּי אִם, in ver 17 and again in ver 18. In the former it is hardly more than the simple adversative "but" (see EWALD, Lehrb. 343, b); in the latter (see Z's. view below). it must be virtually a causal "for," or by conjectural emendation = אָז כִּי "for then," (as above, p. 157).—A.].

Ver. 18. **For if the end come.** So UMBREIT, BERTHEAU, ELSTER correctly render, for the connective is here not "rather" or "but rather" as in ver. 17, but כִּי is a causal (comp. xxiv. 20), and אִם supplies a condition, as in the similar passage xxiv. 14 The "end" is not specifically the hour of death (UMBREIT) but the terminus which is necessarily reached in all human relations (ELSTER), the hour of judicial decision, when God fulfils the hopes of the pious but visits the ungodly with righteous penalties. So far forth as this decisive end is ordinarily reached not till the future life, there is undoubtedly a hint of the hope of immortality and of a future retribution involved in this passage, as in xi. 7: xiv. 32

4. Vers. 19-25 Warning against intemperance and extravagance, and counsel to an obedient endeavor after truth.— **Hear thou, my son, and be wise** The pronoun is added to strengthen the appeal in the Imper. "hear" for the sake of the contrast with the disobedient in vers 20 sq.—**And incline thine heart in a right way,** lit "and let thine heart go straight forward in the way" (i. e., in the "way of understanding" chap. ix. 6). Comp. Job xxxi. 7.

Ver. 20. **Who devour much flesh.** This conception of the Hebrew phrase is the simplest and best supported by the authority of all the old translators. We are to think of gluttons who at their carousals with much wine consume also much flesh. Comp. vii. 14; ix 2; and for the association of וְזוֹלֵל "waster, consumer," with כָּבָא, "drunkard," comp. also Deut. xxi 20, as well as the expression of the New Testament, φάγος καὶ οἰνοπότης, Matth. xi. 19, which seems to be a free rendering of this fixed formula. It is arbitrary and contrary to the meaning of וְזוֹלֵל as established in the usage of the language, when EWALD and UMBREIT refer it to licentious voluptunries, who "dishonor or destroy their own body." Of the later commentators BERTHEAU, ELSTER, HITZIG have taken the right

view. [The author is perhaps too summary in his way of dismissing an interpretation, which has the support of Hebraists and expositors like GESEN., FUERST, DE W , N. : and yet we concur in his view, which is best supported by scriptural parallels, and is that favored by the LXX, Vulg., LUTHER, E. V., H., S , M , WORDSW., etc.—A.]

Ver 21 **And the sleep of sloth clotheth in rags** The noun נוּמָה "sleep," which occurs only here, according to the context describes the indolence and drowsiness into which the drunkard and glutton sinks in consequence of his excesses, and the necessary result of which is poverty.

Ver 22. **Hearken to thy father that hath begotten thee,**—and for that reason deserves obedience, as does the mother also, to whom, according to clause b, it is becoming to hearken in the time of her old age.

Ver 23 **Buy truth and sell it not.** The "buying" of the truth consists in the acquisition of it with labor, exertion and sacrifice (comp. iv 5, 7. xi. 16; Matt. xiii. 44, 46) The "selling" of it would consist in its gross disparagement, and its sacrifice for the sake of sensual enjoyment, or any unsubstantial seeming treasure ["Give up everything for truth," says Dr CHALMERS, "and let no bribery of any sort induce me to surrender it."]

Ver. 24. **The father of a righteous man rejoiceth greatly.** The K'ri is unquestionably to be preferred to the K'thibh, while in clause b we ought probably to give the preference rather to the K'thibh; we render therefore literally, "the begetter of a wise man—and he shall rejoice in himself."—With respect to the sentiment of this verse and the one following comp. x. 1; xv 20; xxvii. 11.

5. Vers. 26-28. Warning against licentiousness, introduced by a summons to a loving consecration to wisdom.—**My son, give me thine heart.** The speaker is evidently wisdom personified, who appears here as in chap. vii. 4, 5, in opposition to a treacherous harlot, and admonishes to a firm adherence to her "ways," i. e. to the principles and rules of life which are prescribed by wisdom.

Ver. 27. With a compare xxii. 14 a.—**And the strange woman a narrow pit**; therefore, those that have been ensnared by her artifices and brought to ruin, she releases again with as much difficulty as a narrow and deep well (possibly of a conical, or, the reverse, a funnel shape) permits one who has fallen into it to escape.

Ver 28. **Yea, like a robber doth she lie in wait.** חֶרֶף is used only here to describe a robber. Comp Jer. iii. 2, where a wanton harlot is compared to an "Arab of the desert" lurking about the roads —**And the false among men doth she multiply**; i. e. by her seductive arts she allures many to unfaithfulness, especially when it is married men among whom she practises her impurities. UMBREIT unnecessarily renders: she draweth to herself faithless ones (i. e. adulterers);—besides, the verb here used could hardly express this idea. But it is likewise inappropriate, with EWALD, BERTHEAU,

ELSTER, *etc.*, to understand by the "faithless" not so much adulterers, *etc.*, as rather robbers and murderers. No sufficient support from the language can be adduced for HITZIG's conception of בֹּגְדִים as equivalent to the abstract בֹּגְדָה "perfidy, faithlessness."

6. Vers. 29-35. Warning against the vice of intemperance, by means of a vivid picture of its ruinous results.—**Who hath woe? Who hath grief?** Lit., "to whom is ah? to whom alas?" The interjection אֲבוֹי, an expansion of אוֹי is found only here. Among the subsequent terms, the "trouble" is strictly anxious care, complaint; "wounds without cause" are wounds received in causeless or wholly unprofitable disputes, wounds and stripes such as come of the brawls of drunken men; finally the dark "redness of the eyes" is the revolting effect of excessive use of wine as it shows itself in the face, according to Gen. xlix. 12.

Ver. 30. **They that tarry long at the wine** (comp. Isa. v. 11), **who come to seek mixed wine.** There is hardly need of our supposing (in accordance with BERTHEAU's view) an actual entrance into a proper wine store or cellar (Song Sol. ii. 4),—but rather a concourse of several at the house of some one (comp. Job i. 4), to drink there strong spiced wine or mixed liquor (ix. 5).

Ver. 31. **When it sparkleth in the cup** (lit., "giveth out or showeth its eye"), **when it glideth smoothly** (lit., "goeth a straight or right way," *ingreditur blande* (Vulg.)). Comp. Song Sol. vii. 10. [The figurative use of the term "eye" in this vivid description has suggested two slightly different conceptions;—one, that of BÖTT., *etc.*, derived from the *brightness* of the eye; the other, that of FUERST, *etc.*, from its *roundness*, setting forth therefore the "bead, or pearl" of the wine. Two different interpretations have likewise been given to the latter part of the description; one of these is based upon the smooth flow in the glass of rich, oily old wine (so E. V., W., *etc.*); the other upon its smooth pleasant flow as it is swallowed, when "it goeth down aright" (so substantially LUTHER, DE W., K., Z., BERTHEAU, H., N., S., M.). The LXX gives a curiously divergent rendering: "For if thou shouldest set thine eyes on bowls and cups, thou shalt afterwards go more naked than a pestle."—A.]

Ver. 32. **At last it biteth like a serpent;** lit., "its end," *i. e.* its ruinous influence which finally becomes evident, its fearful after-pangs. **—And stingeth like an adder.** This Hiphil form, which occurs only here, can, in accordance with the Aramæan, have no other meaning than "to sprinkle, or spirt," for which in the case before us "poison" suggests itself as the natural object; (the serpent is the very poisonous species of viper mentioned also in Isa. xi. 8).

Ver. 33. **Thine eyes shall see strange things.** The "strange" (זָרוֹת) standing parallel with "perverse (things)," is evidently to be taken in a different sense from that required in xxii. 14; it therefore does not denote "strange women" (UMBREIT, BERTHEAU, ELSTER), but "strange, marvellous things," as the object of the drunken man's vision; thus, *e. g.*, the doubling of certain objects, their inversion, their tremulous or swaying motion, *etc.* (thus, correctly, ROSENM., EWALD, HITZIG).—With clause *b* compare xv. 28. [While the Book of Proverbs emphasizes the connection of drunkenness and licentiousness as kindred, and often contemporaneous or successive vices (see especially chap. vii.), still the rendering suggested by xxii. 14, and preferred by the E. V., DE W., N., M., H., S., *etc.*, is rendered less probable by the parallelism, which in Hebrew is not to be lightly disregarded.—A.]

Ver. 34. **And shalt be as one who** (is) **in the midst of the sea,**—*i. e.* probably not one who is out in the midst of the high sea (so UMBREIT, BERTHEAU, *etc.*), but one who is in the depths of the sea (Jonah ii. 4), and therefore one who is as unconscious, with the spirit as completely removed from all previous surroundings, as a drowned man lying upon the deep sea-bottom (HITZIG). [KAMPH., H., N., S., M. take the other view, which has this to commend it, that it refers to more common experiences, and experiences of living men, and harmonizes better with the second part of the description.—A.]—**As one that sleepeth on the top of a mast,**—a lively image of the condition of the drunken man, reeling, staggering hither and thither, rising and falling, as it were, and so exposed to imminent perils to his life. חִבֵּל "mast," (which is usually described by תֹּרֶן), a word occurring only here, and apparently related to the verb חָבַל, "to bind;" comp. Dan. iv. 20. [FUERST makes the primary meaning "to conduct, direct, guide," and therefore interprets the noun of the "steering apparatus, the rudder."—A.]

Ver. 35. **They have stricken me—I have not felt it,** *etc.* Evidently language of the intoxicated man, who first, in clauses *a* and *b*, tells how he feebly remembers having experienced, without really feeling, even blows and bodily abuse of other kinds, while he was in his intoxication,—and then in clause *c*, although still half-bewildered by the later influence of the wine, expresses his intense craving for more, and his fixed purpose to seek anew the prohibited enjoyment. The more characteristic this whole picture of the mode of thought and action of a confirmed inebriate, so much the more unnecessary is it, with HITZIG, to read in *a* and *b* "it hath stricken—it hath smitten me" (הִלְלֻנִי הִכָּנִי) and to make wine personified (as in ver. 32) the subject.—With *c* compare, moreover, the language of the sluggard craving sleep; chap. vi. 10.

DOCTRINAL AND ETHICAL.

There is hardly need of further demonstration to show, that it is several of the main forms of sensual self-indulgence of which our chapter treats in the way of warning and dissuasion. At first it is a very strong desire for the pleasures of great men's tables, as well as for the enjoyments and advantages which intercourse with envious men secures (vers. 1-3, 6-8), that forms the subject of the admonition. The remonstrance interposed between these two warnings, and relating to striving after riches, points to covetousness as the deep root not only of evils in general, but of this one in particular (vers. 4, 5: comp. 1 Tim. vi. 10).—[LAWSON:—Solomon often speaks of riches as a reward that wisdom frequently bestows on those who love her, but here he cautions us against supposing that wisdom encourages the love of riches]. There follows next a further warning against common, rude and uncultivated conversation (ver. 9).—[CHALMERS:—Let me know when to be silent as well as when to speak. There is a manifest contempt for what is said that should lay instant arrest upon me]. There is a like warning against the rough and greedy exercise of violence upon helpless orphans, and others who are weak and entitled to consideration (vers. 10, 11); against foolish doting, and a false carnal forbearance in the matter of the discipline of children (vers. 12-18);—[ARNOT:—The command is framed upon the supposition that parents often fail on the side of tenderness; the word is given to nerve them for a difficult duty. There is no ambiguity in the precept; both the need of correction and the tremendous issues that depend on it are expressed with thrilling precision of language];— next, against haughty contempt of the consideration due to parents, and disobedience to them (vers. 22-25); against intercourse with the gluttonous and profligate (vers. 19-21); against being ensnared by wanton women (vers. 26-28); against the vice of drunkenness (vers. 29-35). As a basis for the warning against these two chief forms of incontinence and fleshly indulgence we have at one time more prominence given to the nothingness and transientness of the possessions or enjoyments to be obtained by means of them (vers. 5, 21, 35), and at another to the heavy penalty in temporal and eternal death (vers. 11, 14, 18, 27 sq., 32). To the foolish sentiments and manner of life which lead down to such ruin, ver. 17, which is cast in a peculiarly comprehensive form, opposes the "fear of Jehovah," as the only means of deliverance and preservation. And as the glorious fruit and result of this we have extolled in ver. 18 a hope which outlasts the grave and death.—the same hope, therefore, of an eternally blessed life, which in some earlier passages of the Book of Proverbs had already come out significantly; comp. above, remarks on this passage, on p. 202.

HOMILETIC AND PRACTICAL.

Homily on the entire chapter:—The fear of God the only safeguard against the ruinous ascendency of fleshly lusts, especially avarice, extravagance, drunkenness and licentiousness.—Comp. STÖCKER: On intemperance in eating and drinking.—*Berleburg Bible:*—The art of living well, according to the rules of wisdom.

Vers. 1-3. LUTHER (marginal):—At court there is deceitful bread, for one is ever out-lying and out-flattering another that he may bring him down, and himself up. . . . It is bad eating cherries with lords.—MELANCHTHON:—To be seeking offices and positions of service with great men is allowable if we know ourselves to be in some measure fitted for it; yet one striving for these may never restrain the independent judgment of him who has the choice, or in general seek to attain its end by unjust means: otherwise it is a guilty ambition.—HASIUS:—He that cannot walk prudently in dangerous places does better to keep away from them.—GEIER:— At the table of the Lord's grace in the Holy Sacrament, one should appear with special reverence and humility; for there one has to do with the King of all kings.—STARKE:—Moderation and the careful testing of that which is and that which is not hurtful to the body must always be the rule of prudence, even though one have great stores on hand.—[ARNOT:—It is of the Lord that hunger is painful and food gives pleasure; between these two lines of defence the Creator has placed life with a view to its preservation. The due sustenance of the body is the Creator's end; the pleasantness of food the means of attaining it. When men prosecute and cultivate that pleasure as an end, they thwart the very purposes of Providence].

Vers. 4, 5. MELANCHTHON:—Diligence, industry, faithful striving to fulfil one's earthly calling this proverb does not forbid, but multiplicity of cares and a greedy eagerness under which man, from want of confidence in God, seeks with pain and self-imposed smart for the perishable goods of this world. From such wayward and unlawful striving it summons us back to the true sphere of our calling and to a prudent and diligent work therein with appeals for divine aid.— *Tübingen Bible:*—To toil for riches which are perishable and cannot satisfy the soul, is a sinful folly. In heaven should we be gathering treasures that endure forever, Matt. vi. 19 sq.— [T. ADAMS:—Solomon compares riches not to some tame house bird, or a hawk that may be fetched down with a line, or found again by her bells: but an eagle that violently cuts the air and is gone past recalling.—BP. HOPKINS:—It were a most strange folly to fall passionately in love with a bird upon his wing, *etc.* How much better were it, since riches will fly, for thyself to direct their flight towards heaven, by relieving the necessitous servants and members of Jesus Christ?]

Vers. 6-8. ZELTNER:—Learn to be pleased and content at little cost, and thou wilt be able easily to forget dainty morsels. Follow Paul: I have learned in whatsoever state I am therewith to be content (Phil. iv. 11).—WOHLFARTH:—Reflect how much ruin envy works, this annoyance at others' prosperity,—how it spares no means for the overthrow of the envied neighbor, how unhappy and discontented it also makes even its own slaves, to what grievous sins it forces them, *etc.* Consider this, and thou wilt not merely take to heart the prudential maxim: Beware of the envious,—but thou wilt seek to keep thyself also from this vice!

Vers. 9 sq. STARKE (on ver. 9):—To speak at the wrong time and in the wrong place brings always far more harm than profit.—(On vers. 10, 11):—Pious widows and orphans have, notwithstanding their forsaken and apparently helpless condition, the mightiest protection; Ecclesiast. xxxv. 16 sq.—(On ver. 12):—Not simply instruction, but also correction and punishment one must receive gladly if one would become wise.

Vers. 13-18. LUTHER (marginal comm. on ver. 13):—If thou scourgest thy son the executioner need not scourge him. There must be scourging once; if the father does not do it, then Master John does it; there is no help for it. No one has ever escaped it, for this is God's judgment.—J. LANGE:—Many parents deserve hell in their own children, because they have neglected to train them in holiness.—CRAMER (on ver. 15):—Next to the experience of God's grace there is no greater joy on earth than when one finds joy and honor in his children.—[II. MELVILL:—If a child do that which will make a parent happier he does that which will also make himself so. Heart-wisdom is the thing desired. No wisdom is thought worthy of the name that has not heaven for its origin and end, and the heart for its abode.—TRAPP (on ver. 17):—Men must wake with God, walk with Him, and lie down with Him, be in continual communion with Him, and conformity unto Him. This is to be in heaven aforehand.—BP. HOPKINS:—It is the property of grace and holiness, when there are no actual explicit thoughts of God, then to be habitually in the fear of God, possessing the heart and overawing it].—STARKE (on ver. 18): —The true good of the pious is still future; so much the less may they be enamored of the present seeming good of the ungodly.—REINHARD (*Gesam. Predd.*, Bd. II., 1804; Sermon on vers. 17, 18):—How much cause we have to hold true to the old unchangeable principles of a genuine fear of God.—SACKREUTER (Fast-day Sermon on vers. 17, 18,—see "*Sonntagsfeier*," 1839):—Of three excellent preservatives from sin, *viz.:* 1) the avoidance of evil example; 2) reverence for God; 3) frequent remembrance of the blessing of virtue.

Vers. 19 sq. [TRAPP (on ver. 19):—Let knowledge and affection be as twins, and run parallel; let them mutually transfuse life and vigor, the one into the other.—JOHN FOSTER:—On the self-discipline suitable to certain mental states]. —*Tübingen Bible* (on ver. 20, 21):—Gluttony and drunkenness are works of the flesh; they that do such things cannot inherit the kingdom of God, Gal. v. 19.—LANGE (on ver. 22):—In the eyes of wicked children nothing is wont to seem more worthy of contempt than the old mother; and yet he is accursed of the Lord who troubles his mother, Ecclesiast. iii. 18.—SAURIN (on ver. 23):—The investigation of truth involves the seven following duties: 1) be attentive; 2) do not be discouraged at labor; 3) suspend your judgment; 4) let prejudice yield to reason; 5) be teachable; 6) restrain your avidity of knowing; 7) in order to edify your mind subdue your heart.—[A. FULLER:—Solomon does not name the price of truth, because its value was beyond all price. Buy it at any rate! It cannot be too dear! And having got it make much of it! sell it not, no, not for any price!]—ZELTNER (on vers. 26 sq.):—The best and most welcome present that thou canst bring thy God is thy heart with all its desires and powers. Is it ruined? He alone can amend and cleanse it.—STARKE:— He who opens his heart to the prince of this world thereby shows himself the enemy of God and of eternal wisdom.—[BP. HOPKINS:—Whatever else we tender unto God if the heart be wanting, it is but the carcass of a duty].

Vers. 29-35. CRAMER:—All sins come in agreeably and taste well in the mouth; but afterward they are as bitter as gall, and fatal as the poison of vipers.—OSIANDER:—Wine is a noble gift of God; but its abuse is only the more ruinous, and therefore to be shunned like deadly poison.—STARKE:—That man only is really and in the spiritual sense drunken who does not discern the great peril of his soul, but under all correction becomes only the more confident and defiant (Jer. v. 3).—[TRAPP:—Such is the drunkard's lethargy; neither is he more insensible than sensual and irrecoverable.—LAWSON:—An inferior master in the art of moral painting gives us a just picture of drunkenness in these words, "Drunkenness is a distemper of the head, a subversion of the senses, a tempest of the tongue, a storm in the body—the shipwreck of virtue, the loss of time, a wilful madness, a pleasant devil, a sugared poison, a sweet sin, which he that has has not himself, and he that commits it, doth not only commit sin, but is himself altogether sin"].

---

d) Warning against intercourse with wicked and foolish men.

CHAP. XXIV. 1-22.

1 Be not envious of evil men,
    and desire not to be with them,
2 for their heart studieth violence,
    and their lips talk of mischief.—
3 By wisdom is the house builded,
    and by understanding is it established;
4 by knowledge shall the chambers be filled
    with all treasure that is precious and pleasant.

5 The wise man is full of strength,
    and the man of understanding increaseth strength;
6 for with wise counsel shalt thou make war,
    and victory is in abundance of counsellors.—
7 Wisdom is too high for the fool;
    he openeth not his mouth in the gate.
8 He that deviseth to do evil
    shall he called a mischievous person.
9 The device of folly is sin,
    and the scorner is an abomination to men.
10 If thou faint in the day of adversity
    thy strength is small.
11 Deliver them that are taken to death,
    and them that totter toward destruction, oh rescue them!
12 If thou sayest, Lo, we knew it not!
    He that weigheth hearts will He not mark it?
    He that watcheth over thy soul, will He not know it?
    and He requiteth man according to his work.
13 My son, eat honey because it is good,
    and honey comb which is sweet to thy taste;
14 so acquaint thyself with wisdom for thy soul;
    when thou hast found it and the end cometh
    thy hope also shall not be cut off.
15 Plot not as a wicked man against the dwelling of the righteous,
    assault not his dwelling-place;
16 for seven times doth the righteous fall and riseth again,
    but the wicked shall plunge into destruction.
17 When thine enemy falleth rejoice not,
    and if he stumbleth let not thine heart be glad;
18 lest Jehovah see it, and it be evil in His eyes,
    and He turn away His anger from him.—
19 Be not enraged at evil doers,
    envy not the wicked.
20 For no future shall there be to the evil;
    the light of the wicked shall be put out.
21 My son, fear thou Jehovah and the King,
    and go not with those who are given to change;
22 for suddenly shall their calamity rise,
    and the destruction of them both, who knoweth it?

GRAMMATICAL AND CRITICAL.

Ver. 6. לְךָ a *dativus commodi* ["for thyself, thy advantage or interest"]; comp. לָמוֹ, chap. xxiii. 20.

Ver. 7. רָאמוֹת, *scriptio plena*, as in 1 Chron. vi. 58; Zech. xiv. 10. [Comp. GREEN, § 156, 3, *etc.*].

Ver. 8. For the construction of קָרָא with לְ comp. xvi. 21.

Ver. 11. אִם stands here for לוּ, *utinam*, as in Ps. lxxxi. 9; cxxxix. 19; it is not to be regarded (as the LXX, Vulg., UMBREIT, *etc.*, take it) as a negative particle of adjuration, in the sense of μή, *ja nicht*, by no means. [See also FUERST, *sub* v. For the time implied in the Part. לְקֻחִים, comp. rem. on xxii. 15; such as have been taken and are now in that condition. For the full form תַּחְשׂוֹךְ comp. Crit. Notes on xxii. 7, 8.—A.].

Ver. 13. [נֹפֶת an apparent fem. construed here as masc. See BÖTT. § 648, *b*, and n. 1.—A.].

Ver. 14. דֵּעָה or as the best MSS. read, דְּעֵה is an Imper. from יָדַע instead of the usual form דֵּעָה. [Comp. BÖTT. §§ 396, 956, *c*, 960, *a*; and GREEN, §§ 97, 1, *b*, 148, 3.—A.].

Ver. 17. [For the form וּבְכָּשְׁלוֹ instead of the fuller Niphal form, see BÖTT. §§ 990, 1, *b*, 1036, 2; and GREEN, §§ 91, *b*, 231, 5, *a*.—A.].

EXEGETICAL.

1. Vers. 1, 2. Warning against intercourse with wicked men (lit. "men of evil," comp. xxviii. 5;) comp. ver. 19; xxiii. 17; with ver. 1, *a*, comp. also xxiii. 3, 6; with 2, *a*, comp. xv. 28.

2. Vers. 3-6. Praise of wisdom and its salutary results.—**By wisdom is the house builded** Comp. xiv. 1, where it is specifically the wisdom

of woman that is commended as builder of the house. For the expression in 3, *b*, comp. iii. 19; for ver. 4 comp. also iii. 10; viii. 21.

Ver. 5. **The wise man is full of strength**, lit., is "in strength," *i. e.*, furnished with strength, powerful; comp. the corresponding phrase in Ps. xxix. 4. The LXX, Syr., Chald., read מֵעֹז, *i. e.*, more than, better than strength; comp. xvi. 32. But the Masoretic reading plainly gives us a simpler and more pertinent meaning.— **And the man of understanding** (lit. "man of knowledge") **increaseth strength**, lit., "maketh power strong," (comp. ii. 14) he develops mighty strength (comp. the phrase in Job ix. 19), he makes it available as a quality of his own.

Ver. 6. **For with wise counsel must thou make war**, lit. "must thou carry on war for thyself," *i. e.*, must thou bring thy war to an end, carry it through. [So M., WORDSW., K., *etc.*]. Comp. xx. 18, and for clause *b*, xi. 14; xv. 22.

3. Vers. 7-10. Four separate proverbs, directed against folly, intrigue, scoffing and faint-heartedness.—**Wisdom is too high for the fool.** רָאמוֹת is strictly "heights" (*excelsa*, Vulg.), *i. e.*, unattainably distant things, objects which are altogether too high; comp. Ps. x. 5; Isa. xxx. 18. HITZIG conjectures a double meaning, so far forth as the word in the form before us could have meant at the same time also "corals, costly ornaments" (in accordance with Job xxviii. 18).—**He openeth not his mouth in the gate;** *i. e.*, in judicial consultations and transactions of his fellow-citizens (comp. xxii. 22) he can bring forward nothing. ["He were two fools if he should," says TRAPP, "for while he holds his tongue he is held wise"].

Ver. 8. **Shall be called** (him they call) a **mischievous person**—a master or lord of mischief (an expression equivalent to that in chap. xii. 2, "a man of wicked devices"). ["This is his property and ownership, mischief and wrong." WORDSW.]

Ver. 9. **The device** (meditation) **of folly is sin**;—*i. e.*, there also where folly (or the fool, *abstr. pro concr.*) acts with consideration, and goes to work with a reflective prudence (זִמָּה, a similar term to that in ver. 8), it still brings to pass nothing good, but always only evil. It is indeed even worse with the scoffer, who, according to clause *b*, is an abhorrence and abomination to all men, because he, with his evil plans and counsels, unites furthermore great shrewdness, subtle wit, refined speculation—in general the exact opposite of folly.

Ver. 10. **If thou hast shown thyself faint in the day of adversity** (anxiety, distress), **thy strength is small;**—*i. e.*, thou art a coward and weakling, whose courage is feeble, and whose moral power and capacity for resistance is, as it were, crippled. Less appropriately UMBREIT, ELSTER, *etc.* (following the Vulg., Targum, *etc.*) "then sinketh thy strength also" (*imminuetur fortitudo tua*). But HITZIG's emendation is also needless, רֻחְבָה, "thy courage," for כֹּחֲכָה, "thy strength,"—as is also his marvellous reproduction of the *paronomasia* (צָר—צָרָה) by: "*am Tage der Klemme—klamm ist dein Muth*" ["in the day of straits—straight is thy courage"]. BERTHEAU connects the verse closely with the two following: "Hast thou shown thyself faint in the day of trouble, was thy strength fearful, oh deliver," *etc.* (?). At all points EWALD has the right view, and in general LUTHER also: "He is not strong who is not firm in need." [The principle is familiar enough that courage and hopefulness are half of man's strength.—A.]

4. Vers. 11, 12. An admonition to a sympathizing and compassionate demeanor toward such as are in their innocency condemned to death, and are being borne to the place of execution. Comp. L. MOSHEIM: *Comm-ntatio ad loc.* Prov. xxiv. 11, 12; Helmstadt. 4to. [KAMPH. suggests an easy and natural transition to this exhortation from the preceding. That had reference to courage in time of one's own need, this to quick and sympathizing helpfulness in others' extremity. —A.]—**Deliver them that are taken to death** (the participle here used has the same meaning as the forms of the verb found in Isa. lvii. 13; Ps. xlix. 16). That this appeal is made specifically to a judge (UMBREIT), is, according to ver. 12 *a*, very improbable. He who is addressed seems rather to be one who is accidentally passing by in the vicinity of the place of execution, who is on the point of going on after the manner of the priest and the Levite in Luke x. 30 sq., with no sympathy, and without lifting a helping hand. That the author of the proverb, notwithstanding the singular which is immediately employed, still has in his eye a plurality, a whole host of such passers by, appears from the "Lo, we know it not," which in ver. 12, *a*, he supposes to be the answer to his appeal. HITZIG's assumption is arbitrary, that the hard-hearted judges are Persians, and those who are in their innocence condemned to death, Jews, or Syrians, Samaritans, or some other Persian subjects of the period next succeeding the exile, possibly of the time of Ezra (ix. 9). The same is true likewise of BERTHEAU's opinion that there is no reference whatever to a judicial execution, but to a bloody battle, during which one ought courageously to protect those assailed by the foe, and not timidly to leave them to the threatening destruction. [Hardly any two of our English expositors agree as to the structure of this sentence, although they are nearly or quite unanimous in explaining its general meaning. N. and M. agree with the E. V. in making the first verb an Infinitive (which is possible) depending on the final verb of the sentence: E. V.: "if thou forbear to deliver," *etc.*; N.: "to deliver, *etc.*, spare thyself not;" M.: "dost thou forbear to deliver," *etc.* H., S. and WORDSW. agree with our author in making it an Imper., although H. and W. make the last clause conditional, like 12, *a*. The explanation of Z., S., KAMPH., *etc.*, is probably to be preferred which makes the אִם a particle of wishing, and the verb transitive rather than reflexive or neuter.—A.].—**Lo! we knew it not!** —HITZIG, in agreement with the LXX, "Lo, we know him not!" But in verse 11 there is plainly enough mention made of a number who are dragged to death. [As KAMPH. suggests, the time when a plea of ignorance could fitly be put in, as well as the nature of the plea itself, tells

against this personal interpretation. And it is also to be observed how idle the plea of ignorance becomes when it is God rather than man to whom one's omissions are to be justified.—A.] **And he will requite man according to his work.**—The interrogative הֲלֹא of the second clause plainly has no further influence on this general sentence which concludes (comp. Ps. lxii. 13; Job xxxiv. 11; Rom. ii. 6).

5. Vers. 13, 14. Admonition to a diligent striving after wisdom.—**My son, eat thou honey because it is good,** *etc.*—A figurative injunction of a preparatory sort, serving as a basis for the admonition to strive after wisdom, contained in ver. 14. For this figure of honey and the honey-comb as the designation of something especially lovely and agreeable, comp. Ps. xix. 11.

Ver. 14. **So acquaint thyself with wisdom also for thy soul;**—lit., "know wisdom for thy soul, appropriate it to thyself, recognized as precious and exceedingly palatable!" [The E. V., following the Vulg., takes the peculiar form of the Imperf. for a peculiar form of the noun "knowledge," and supplies the substantive verb. H. and M. are in the same error.—A.]— **When thou hast found it, and the end cometh.**—This last clause is still part of the conditional protasis, corresponding to the common use of אִם יֵשׁ to introduce a conditional clause; comp. Gen. xxiii. 8; xxiv. 49; Judges vi. 36, *etc.* For making it a transition to the apodosis ("then cometh an end—then a future remaineth"—Hitzig, following the LXX, Vulg., Luther, *etc.* [so K.; E. V.: "then there shall be a reward;" so also H., N., M., W., while S. takes our author's view.—A.]), not a single supporting case can be cited, in which יֵשׁ introduces the apodosis, in the sense "then or so will be" (comp. Bertheau on this passage). For the general sentiment compare furthermore xxiii. 18.

6. Vers. 15–18. Warning against malicious violence and delight in mischief.—**Lie not in wait as a wicked man** (that is, with wicked and mischievous intent) **against the dwelling of the righteous;** assault not (verb as in xix. 26) **his resting place.**—Hitzig changes the verb in clause *a* to תַּקְרֵב and the noun to רֵעַ and thus obtains the meaning: "Bring not alarm near to the dwelling of the righteous," *etc.* (?).—

Ver. 16. **For seven times doth the righteous fall and riseth again;**—*i. e.*, many a misfortune overtakes him in life, yet he gives way before none, but always comes up again (Hitzig). Comp. Ps. lxxxvii. 24; Jer. viii. 4; and with reference to the symbolical number *seven*, particularly Job v. 19.—**But the wicked shall plunge into destruction**—lit., "stumble, are brought to a downfall by calamity;" comp. chap. iv. 19.

Vers. 17, 18 are closely connected with both the verses preceding, not merely by the recurrence of the ideas "fall" and "plunge" (stumble), but also by the substance of the thought; for delight in injury is the twin sister to a plotting intrigue and violence. **Lest Jehovah see it and it displease him**—lit., "and it be evil in his eyes."—**And He turn away His anger from him**—*i. e.*, from the enemy (מֵעָלָיו referring back to ver. 16, "thine enemy"), to turn it upon thee thyself instead of him.

7. Vers. 19–22. Warning against intercourse with wicked and seditious persons.—**Be not thou enraged at evil doers,**—*i. e.*, be not excited, envious (אַל־תִּתְחַר, "burn not," here equivalent to the "envy not" of ver. 1) with regard to the undeserved prosperity of ungodly men, which perhaps might only stimulate to the imitation of their wicked conduct; comp. Ps. xxxvii. 8; lxxiii. 2, 3; also Prov. i. 11 sq. [Fuerst and some others understand this of excitement, impatience *against* evil doers, which cannot wait for God's recompenses. This explanation, we think, is to be preferred here, although the other is clearly and frequently enough an injunction of the Scriptures.—A.]

Ver. 20. **For no future shall there be to the wicked.**—אַחֲרִית here in a different sense from that found in ver. 14 and in xxiii. 18. [The two ideas most frequently conveyed by this noun, which is literally an "after," something subsequent to the present, are a "future," and an "end or issue," *i. e.*, to present relations. It is this last idea that Z. finds in ver. 14 and xxiii. 18, the first in ver. 20. In the first two passages the "end" of the present suggests by implication and contrast a blessed future; this our verse denies to the wicked, not by implication, but by express assertion. It does not assert that he shall reach no end to his present relations, nor that he shall have no future whatever, but no future blessing. Some commentators are less exact in these discriminations, finding one general meaning in all the passages.—A.] With the general sentiment compare Job xx. 5; Ps. xxxvii. 2, 9, 38. With *b* in particular comp. chap. xiii. 9; xxi. 4.

Ver. 21. With *a* comp. Eccles. viii. 2 sq.; x. 20; 1 Pet. ii. 17.—**Go not with those who are given to change.**—שׁוֹנִים [cognate with שְׁנֵי, two], those "otherwise disposed, wishing otherwise," *i. e.*, opposing [the present order], seditious, revolutionary (Vulg., *detractores*). "Go not with them," lit., "mingle thyself not," as in xx. 19.

Ver. 22. **And the destruction of them both**—*viz.*, of those who rebel against God and of those who rebel against the king. Others (Umbreit, Bertheau, *etc.* [De W., N., S., M., Wordsw., the genitive being treated as a genitive of source, "the ruin *proceeding from* them both"]; "and the penalty, the retribution of them both," *i. e.*, the punishment that goes forth from both, God and the king; Hitzig (in accordance with the Targ. and Syr.), "and the end of their years" (comp. Job xxxvi. 11). Our interpretation, as the simplest, is supported by the Vulg., Luther, Ewald, Elster [Kamph.]—**Who knoweth it?**—*i. e.*, who knows the time of their ruin; who knows how soon it will be precipitated? Comp. xvi. 14.

[The LXX, *etc.*, introduce here several verses for which there is no authority in the present Hebrew texts. "A son that keeps the father's commandment shall escape destruction; for such a one has fully received it. Let no falsehood be spoken by the king from the tongue; yea, let no falsehood proceed from his tongue. The king's tongue is a sword, and not one of flesh; and whosoever shall be given up to it shall he destroyed; for if his wrath should be provoked, he destroys men with cords, and devours men's bones, and burns them up as a flame, so that they are not even fit to be eaten by the young eagles. My son, reverence my words, and receive them, and repent." Some of the editions also introduce at this point chap. xxx. 1–14.—A.]

DOCTRINAL, ETHICAL, HOMILETIC AND PRACTICAL.

To refer the ideas of this section, which are very various in their substance and their applications, to the one fundamental category of a "*Warning against intercourse with wicked and foolish men*," would not indeed answer in all respects and at all points; and yet the introductory and the concluding verses at least (vers. 1, 2, 19–22) do relate to this subject; and besides, the eulogiums upon wisdom which are interspersed (vers. 3–6, 7, 13, 14), and the counsels against malicious intrigue, mockery, trickery and delight in mis chief (vers. 8, 9, 15 sq., 17 sq.), may without any peculiar violence be brought under the same classification. There remains isolated, therefore, only the censuring criticism on an unmanly, faint-hearted bearing in hours of peril (ver. 10), and the warning against a heartless indifference to those who are innocently suffering (vers. 11, 12). The latter passage in particular deserves attentive consideration, and a careful estimate of its practical bearings, for it belongs among those prefigurations and precursors of the distinctively Christian ethics, which occur somewhat rarely in the stage of revelation reached in the law of the Old Testament, and, in general, in any specific form in the literature of wisdom which centres in the name of Solomon. For even in a higher degree than the warning contained in vers. 17, 18 of our chapter, against delight in injury, in one's attitude towards his enemies,—and, if one is so disposed to view it, even in a higher degree than the demand of love to one's enemies in chap. xxv. 21 sq.,—does this powerful enforcement of the duty of a courageous protection and deliverance of the innocent who are doomed to death, correspond with the culmination of ethical justice, and the perfect fulfilling of the law, which Christ exhibits for the members of the New Covenant, in the narrative of the good Samaritan (Luke x. 30 sq.), in His admonition to visit those in prison, and to the loving sacrifice of life itself in imitation of His own example, *etc.* (Matt. xxv. 36 sq.; John xii. 25; xv. 12-14). [Only a few of the exegetical and practical interpreters of our book have so well brought out this important point. LAWSON suggests it when he says: "The wise man represents this piece of charity as a duty which we owe to our neighbors without exception; and with him agrees our Lord in the parable of the good Samaritan. We are not the disciples of Solomon or of Christ if we show love to those only," *etc.* ARNOT puts the principle with more characteristic vigor: "Under God as Supreme ruler, and by His law, we owe every human being love; and if we fail to render it, we are cast into prison with other less reputable debtors. Nor will any thing be received in payment but the genuine coin of the kingdom; it must be love with a living soul in it and a substantial body on it."—A.]

In the *homiletic treatment of the whole passage* one might take just this demand that is contained in vers. 11, 12, of a compassionate love of one's neighbor, that will not shun even deadly perils, as the highest exemplification of wisdom, to the attainment and preservation of which all the counselling and dissuasory suggestions of the section summon us; the topic might then be announced: "Mercy the highest wisdom," or again: "The contrast between the wise man and the fool reaches its climax in the timid selfishness of the latter, and the former's self-sacrificing love for his neighbor."—Comp. STÖCKER: On patience and sociability. In what the virtue consists (ver. 1–12), and how one is to practise it (vers. 13 sq).—*Calwer Handb.:* Shun evil, choose wisdom.

Vers. 1 sq. *Tübingen Bible* (on vers. 1–2): It is one element in the prudence of the righteous to have no fellowship with the ungodly and to avoid their society.—LUTHER (marg. comment on vers. 3 sq.): When all is well ordered in a house it avails more than great labor; as, *e. g.*, when one gives, where, to whom, and as one ought, *etc.*—GEIER (on vers. 3 sq.): A household, if it is to be blessed, must not merely be wisely organized, but also prudently regulated and constructed.—Filling the chambers with temporal good is accounted great prosperity; but much more beautiful is it when the heart's chamber is filled with the treasures of heavenly wisdom and virtue.—(On vers. 5, 6): Strength of body without wisdom and prudence of heart, is like a giant who is robbed of the sight of his eyes.

Ver. 7–10. ZELTNER (on vers. 8, 9): As true piety has its degrees, so has ungodliness. But they are followed by righteous retribution and punishment.—STARKE (on ver. 10): Want and trouble is a genuine touchstone, with which one may determine how strong or how weak one is in faith and reliance on God.—VON GERLACH (same verse): In times of adversity the man whose strength stands fast in God has more power than usual. It is the fault of one's own indolence if this is not the case, though his strength be scanty and restricted.—[BP. HOPKINS: That thy patience may be perfect, it must be strong, as well as lasting. It must have nerves and sinews in it, to bear weighty burdens.]

Vers. 11, 12. MELANCHTHON: To unrighteous cruelty one should give no impulse; even private individuals ought, according to their strength and calling, to oppose tyrannical injustice without uproar or tumult.—GEIER: Man never lacks excuses; but many of them are by the Lord found to be too light, Luke xiv. 18 sq.—STARKE: To deliver men from bodily death is a great thing; but more glorious is it to aid a soul toward deliverance from spiritual and eternal death, James v. 20.

Vers. 13 sq. *Berleburg Bible* (on ver. 13): Charge it upon thyself that thou have such inward experience of wisdom, that thou shalt relish its sweetness like honey and the honey-comb.—STARKE (on ver. 16): To fall into sin and to fall into calamity are two different things. Beware of the former, and the Lord will not forsake thee in the latter.—CRAMER: Whosoever rejoices in others' adversity, his own calamity stands already outside the door.—[T. ADAMS: Let us beware that we do not slide; if slide, that we do not fall; if fall, that we fall forward, not backward. Be hold thy Saviour calling, thy Father blessing, the Spirit assisting, the angels comforting, the Word directing, the glory waiting, good men associating.—FLAVEL: Though repeated spiritual falling shows the foulness it does not always prove the falseness of the heart.—BRIDGES (on ver. 17):—What has grace done for us, if it has not overcome nature by a holier and happier principle? To rejoice in the fall of an enemy would he to fall deeper than himself; to fall not into trouble, but into sin.—TRAPP (on ver. 18):—Think thus with thyself, Either I am like my enemy, or else I am better or worse than he. If like him, why may I not look for the like misery? If better, who made me to differ? If worse, what reason have I then to insult?]

Vers. 19-22. STARKE (on vers. 19, 20):—He that would look on the prosperity of ungodly men without envy and offence need only make a comparison between the brief instant of their joy and the unending eternity of their pain and punishment.—ZOLLIKOFEN (Serm. on vers. 19, 20):—Nullifying the objection against the divine government of the world, which is made on account of the unequal distribution of external prosperity among men, and the earthly well-being of the ungodly (therefore a *Theodicy*).—[ARNOT:—Here it is not the first and direct, but the secondary and circuitous effect of bad example, that is prominently brought into view. Some who are in no danger of falling in love with their neighbor's sin, may be chafed by it into a hatred of their neighbor].—MELANCHTHON (on ver. 21):—God has given to men authority because He would have men hear and know His law, and thereby Himself, and also for this reason, because He would preserve human society from dissolution through endless disquiets and controversies. He has, however, ordained that we hearken to human governors for His sake, and that we must know that He punishes the rebellious.—[Bp. SHERLOCK:—The only lasting foundation of civil obedience is the fear of God; and the truest interest of princes is to maintain the honor of religion, by which they secure their own.—ARNOT:—Take away godliness, and your loyalty without being increased in amount, is seriously deteriorated in kind; take away loyalty, and you run great risk of spoiling the purity of the remanent godliness. In the Scriptures the feebler force is made fast to the stronger, and so carried through in trying times. Loyalty is most secure where it has godliness to lean upon].—GEIER (on ver. 22):—Certain as death in itself is, although we cannot know the time and manner of it, so surely does God's punishment follow ungodliness and rebellion, but its time and form remain uncertain.

Second Supplement:

CHAP. XXIV. 23-34.

a) Various admonitions to good conduct toward one's neighbors.

VERS. 23-29.

23 These also are from wise men.
   To be partial in judgment is not good.
24 He that saith to the wicked, "thou art righteous,"
   him the people curse, (and) nations execrate;
25 but to them that rebuke (iniquity) it is well,
   and upon them shall come a rich blessing.
26 He kisseth the lips
   who giveth a right answer.
27 Set in order thy work without,
   and make it ready for thyself in the field;
   afterward build thine house.
28 Be not witness against thy neighbor without cause;
   and wilt thou deceive with thy lips?
29 Say not: "As he hath done to me so will I do to him:
   I will requite the man according to his work."

b) Warning against indolence and its evil consequences.

VERS. 30–34.

30 By the field of a slothful man I passed along,
   and by the vineyard of a man void of understanding.
31 And, lo! it was all grown over with thorns,
   briars covered the face thereof,
   and its stone wall was broken down.
32 Then I looked and fixed my attention;
   I saw and took (to myself) instruction.
33 "A little sleep, a little slumber,
   a little folding of the hands to sleep;"—
34 then cometh thy poverty apace,
   and thy want as an armed man!

GRAMMATICAL AND CRITICAL.

Ver. 23. בַּל is equivalent to לֹא, as in xxii. 29; xxiii. 7, *etc.*

Ver. 27. [The Perf. with ו *consec.* בָּנִיתָ is used, as this tense so construed not unfrequently is, in the sense of an Imperative; and afterward thou hast built, *etc.*; predictions and injunctions sometimes taking this way of expressing an assurance that what should be will be. See BÖTT. §§ 977, 3; 981, 3; GREEN, § 265, *b*; EWALD, *Lehrb.* 332, *b.*—A.]

Ver. 28. [A Perf. with ו *consec.* to express what *ought* to be,—a suggestion rather than a precept.—BÖTTCHER'S *Fiens debitum*, § 981, B. γ.] וְהִפְתִּית. Because the interrogative particle occurs only in this instance immediately after the copula, EWALD proposes to change the form to וְהִפְתִּיתָ, "and thou wilt open wide," *i. e.* betray (comp. xx. 19), [so FUERST]; HITZIG, however, into וְהִפְרָהוּת, "and thou wilt whisper," *i. e.* speak with subdued voice (from a form הִפֶּת, to be explained in accordance with the Arabic); [so BÖTT., making it a Hiph. from פָּתַת and not a Piel from פָּתָה]. Both are alike arbitrary and unnecessary. [K., BERTHEAU, S. and M. take our author's view].

Ver. 31. [כָּרָב, a Pual with Kamets Ḥhatuph; see GREEN, § 9, *a*; הַחֲרֻלִּים, one of two examples in which ו in the ultima gives place in forming the plural to ־ with a doubled vowel. GREEN, 291, *c.*—A.]

EXEGETICAL.

1. Vers. 23–25. Warning against a partial administration of justice—**These also are from wise men.** According to the LXX, Vulg., MICHAELIS, UMBREIT, ELSTER, *etc.*, the לַחֲכָמִים should be understood "for the wise." [So the E. V., which is followed by HOLDEN]. In opposition to this we have not merely the usual meaning of the preposition in superscriptions, but over and above this we have the "also," which refers back to the next preceding collection of proverbs, whose originating with wise men was expressly emphasized, chap. xxii. 17.—**To be partial in judgment is not good:** strictly: to distinguish persons in judgment is not good. This short proverb, forming only a single clause, is plainly nothing but a preliminary observation or introduction to the two following verses, which treat more fully of partiality in dispensing justice. Compare, furthermore, the quite similar, and almost literally identical sentences, xviii. 5 and xxviii. 21.

Ver. 24. **He that saith to the wicked,** "**Thou art righteous.**" Comp. chap. xvii. 15; "He that justifieth the wicked." To the threatening intimation of God's displeasure there given, there corresponds here the threat of a condition in which one is hated and cursed on the part of the nations (comp. xi. 26; xxii. 14); for to turn justice into injustice by partiality in judgment impairs the well-being of entire nations and states.

Ver. 25. **But to them that rebuke** (iniquity) **it is well;** *i. e.* upright judges who punish evil-doers according to their desert (not merely with words but also with stringent disciplinary enactments), instead of the curse of men, obtain as a reward nothing but blessing and welfare from God.

2. Vers. 26–29. Four additional admonitions to righteous conduct toward one's neighbors.— **He kisseth the lips that giveth a right answer;** *i. e.* faithful and truthful answers, especially before a court of justice, affect one as favorably as the most agreeable caress, or a sweet kiss on the lips. The mention of the "lips" is to be explained simply by the remembrance of the *question* to which the upright and truthful answer corresponds. The author of the proverb passes wholly by the fact that hearing is the appropriate organ for the reception of the answer. Therefore HITZIG's conception of the first clause, which differs from the common one: "He commends (ingratiates) himself with the lips who," *etc.*, is plainly unnecessary. [BERTHEAU, KAMPH., DE W., N., *etc.*, agree in our author's construction and conception; while the E. V., MUFFET, H., S., M., *etc.*, understand the allusion to be to tributes of love and honor *paid to him* who answers rightly: "Every man (or, the people) shall kiss his lips." According to this view the people's curse (in ver. 24) is contrasted with their respectful and loving salutation; according to the other, which is grammatically simpler and probably to be preferred, the offence given by the partial or partisan judge is contrasted with the cheering, soothing power of him who answers rightly.—A.]

Ver. 27. **Set in order thy work without**; *i. e.* take care, by the profitable and diligent prosecution of your labors in the field, first of all for the needful and reliable support of your existence; then you may go on to the building up of your establishment. The "house" in clause *c*, is thus doubtless equivalent to "family, domestic establishment," as in Ruth iv. 11; comp. above, Prov. xiv. 1. The literal rendering given by Hitzig and others to this phrase, "build thy house," seems less appropriate, although Biblical parallels might be adduced for this also, *e. g.* the passage Luke xv. 28, which in its moral bearing is certainly kindred.

Ver. 28. **Be not witness against thy neighbor without cause.** "Without cause," *i. e.* without an actual reason, without necessity; comp. xxiii. 29; xxvi. 2; John xv. 25, *etc.* It is not so much a false witness that is meant, as one not called for, one who is incited to say injurious things by nothing beyond his own animosity.— **And wilt thou deceive with thy lips?** See Critical notes for various constructions of the verb. With regard to the expression "deceive with thy lips," comp. Ps. lxxviii. 36; "and they did flatter him with their mouth."

Ver. 29. **Say not, "As he hath done to me so will I do to him."** We can hardly find here (with Hitzig, who follows several of the earlier expositors) a special connection between this verse and the preceding, as though the man who had been wronged by the officious witness were herein introduced as speaking, and a warning were given him against allowing free course to his revenge. Comp. rather the similar thought in chap. xx. 22, which like this stands quite isolated.

3. Vers. 30-34. *The vineyard of the slothful:* a narrative in form closely resembling the parable. Comp. Isa. v. 1 sq., as well as the passages which correspond still more closely with the form of this narration, Joh v. 3 sq.; Ps. xxxvii. 35 sq. —**By the field of a slothful man I passed along.** The figure of the field is in the sequel entirely dropped, from a preference for the closely related one of the vineyard. The "man void of understanding" in clause *b*, is naturally another sluggard, one who is indolent from lack of understanding.

Ver. 31. **And lo! it was all grown over with thorns** [lit., "it came up all of it thorns"] (comp. the same word in Isa. xxxiv. 13, which is there also translated in the Vulg. by the term *urticæ*), **brambles covered the face thereof** (חֲרֻלִּים, lit., "what one may not touch, things not to be approached" [Fuerst, "stinging, burning things," nettles, *c. g.*], is an accusative subordinate to the verb in the Pual), **and its stone wall** (lit., "its wall of stones") **was broken down.** All these features are found also in the parable of the vineyard in Isaiah, which has been already cited, Isa. v. 5, 6; comp. likewise Ps. lxxx. 13, 14. [Travellers like Hackett (*Illustrations of Scripture*) call attention to the minute accuracy of the description as illustrated by the fact, that in the richer soils of Palestine it is thorny shrubs, of which twenty-two kinds are enumerated, that are specially quick to spring up and overspread a neglected field.—A.]

Ver. 32. **Then I looked.** Hitzig proposes to read וָאֶחֱזֶה instead of וָאֶחֱזֶה (comp. 2 Sam. iv. 10): "and I stopped" (from the intransitive verb הִתְיַצֵּב, *sistere*, to stand still). But the ordinary reading is abundantly confirmed by the parallel in clause *b*. [Kamph. calls attention to the introduction of the pronoun, as an element in the graphic fullness of the poet's description of his meditation.—A.]—**I saw and took** (to myself) **instruction**, lit., "a correction or reproof." What was contained in this admonition is expressed in what follows.

With vers. 33, 34 comp. the almost literally identical verses 10 and 11 of chap. vi., and the Exeg. notes there (p. 84), where the meaning of the divergent reading was also discussed.—**And thy want**: lit., "and thy wants," *i. e.* thy deficits, thy pecuniary embarrassments, on account of which now one thing and then another fails.

DOCTRINAL, ETHICAL, HOMILETIC AND PRACTICAL.

Righteous treatment of one's neighbor, and a prudent active industry in the discharge of duties to ourselves, are the two points to which the admonitory import of this section may be reduced, and in a way quite exhaustive. For as vers. 23-29, all of them with the sole exception of ver. 28 admonish to a strictly just and honorable bearing in intercourse with others, so not merely that 28th verse, but also the parabolic narrative in vers. 30-34, relates to the vice of sloth and an indolent carelessness in the performance of the domestic duties of one's calling. The general substance of this short section therefore bears a resemblance, at least partial, to that of the 6th chapter (which is indeed much richer in its fullness). In attempting to obtain from it a central idea for *homiletic* use, we should be obliged to proceed as we did in that instance (comp., above, p. 87). [With reference to ver. 29 in particular (comp. what is said above on vers. 11, 12), Dr. Chalmers says: It is pleasant to observe the outgoing of the earlier morality towards the later and more advanced—of that in the Old towards that in the New Testament.—A.] Therefore as a *homily on the whole:* Neither injustice nor faithlessness toward one's neighbor, nor want of fidelity in the fulfilment of one's own domestic duties, brings a blessing.—Or, Honorable conduct in relation to others is possible only on the basis of the industrious and conscientious performance of the duties of one's own calling.

Vers. 23-25. Starke: An unjust judge loads himself with sighs which God also hears; a righteous judge, on the contrary, will surely enjoy at the same time the blessing and the intercession of the pious.—Wohlfarth: The blessing of a wise severity in the State (in the administration of the laws).

Vers. 26-29. Geier (on ver. 26): If thou meanest to deal fairly with thine own soul, then rejoice heartily in good counsel given from the word of God; though it be disagreeable to the flesh, yet it is like a precious balsam (Ps. cxli. 5).—Stanke (on ver. 27): He who with all his carefulness in attention to his occupation yet forgets the one thing needful, builds his house on the sand, because in the midst of all outward prosperity he still suffers injury in his soul.—(On ver. 29): If thou wouldst be really like God as His child, then follow Him in compassion and leave the right of vengeance to Him alone: Lev. xix. 18; Rom. xii. 17 sq.

Vers. 30-34. STARKE: Indolence is extremely injurious to the Christian life. If one does not do good with earnestness and diligence, evil surely gains more and more the ascendency, and in all conditions, in Church and State and in domestic life, want and labor are multiplied as the result of neglect of official duty on the part of the servants and stewards instituted by God.—WOHLFARTH (on ver. 32): To become wise on the follies of others is in fact an excellent prudence.—[ARNOT: Even the sluggard's garden brought forth fruit—but not for the sluggard's benefit. The diligent man reaped and carried off the only harvest that it bore—a warning.—J. FOSTER; Lecture on Practical Views of Human Life. Let it never be forgotten in any part of the process that the efficacy of the instruction must be from the Supreme Teacher; without Him, the attraction and assimilation of the evil would, after all, be mightier than its warning and repelling force].

IV. LATER COLLECTION BY THE MEN OF HEZEKIAH.

True wisdom proclaimed as the chief good to kings and their subjects.

CHAPS. XXV.—XXIX.

SUPERSCRIPTION: CHAP. XXV. 1.

1 These also are proverbs of Solomon
which men of Hezekiah, the king of Judah, collected.

1. Admonition to the fear of God and righteousness, addressed to kings and subjects.

CHAP. XXV. 2-28

2 It is the glory of God to conceal a thing;
but the glory of kings to search out a matter.
3 The heavens for height, and the earth for depth,
and the heart of kings (are) unsearchable.
4 Take away the dross from silver,
and there cometh forth a vessel for the refiner;
5 take away the wicked from before the king,
and his throne shall be established in righteousness.
6 Display not thyself in the presence of the king,
and stand not in the place of the great;
7 for it is better that it be said to thee, ' Come up hither,"
than that they humble thee because of the king,
whom thine eyes have seen.
8 Go not forth hastily to strive,
lest (it be said to thee): " What wilt thou do in the end,
when thy neighbor hath put thee to shame?"
9 Debate thy cause with thy neighbor,
but disclose not the secret of another;
10 lest he that heareth it upbraid thee,
and thine infamy turn not away.
11 (Like) apples of gold in framework of silver
is a word fitly spoken.
12 (As) a gold ring and an ornament of fine gold
is a wise reprover to an ear that heareth.

13 As the coolness of snow on a harvest day
   is a faithful messenger to them that send him;
   he refresheth the soul of his master.
14 Clouds and wind and no rain—
   (so is) a man who boasteth of a false gift.
15 By forbearance is a prince persuaded,
   and a gentle tongue breaketh the bone.
16 Hast thou found honey—eat to thy satisfaction,
   lest thou be surfeited with it and vomit it.
17 Withhold thy foot from thy neighbor's house,
   lest he be weary of thee and hate thee.
18 A maul, and a sword, and a sharp arrow
   is the man that speaketh as a false witness against his neighbor.
19 (Like) a broken tooth and an unsteady foot
   is confidence in an unfaithful man in the day of need.
20 (As) he that layeth aside clothing in a cold day—(as) vinegar on nitre—
   is he that singeth songs with a heavy heart.
21 If thine enemy hunger, give him bread to eat,
   and if he thirst, give him water to drink:
22 for (so) dost thou heap burning coals on his head;
   and Jehovah will reward thee.
23 North wind produceth rain,
   so doth the slanderous tongue a troubled face.
24 It is better to dwell in a corner of the house top,
   than with a quarrelsome woman in a wide house.
25 As cold water to a thirsty soul,
   so is good news from a far country.
26 (Like) a troubled fountain and a ruined spring
   is the righteous man who wavereth before the wicked.
27 To eat much honey is not good,
   and to search out the difficult bringeth difficulty.
28 (As) a city broken through, without walls,
   is the man who hath no mastery over his own spirit.

GRAMMATICAL AND CRITICAL.

[In the section of the Book of Proverbs including chaps. xxv.—xxix. peculiar idioms are more numerous, peculiarities in radical forms and in inflections, some of them common to this section with some others in the Old Testament, others of an Aramaic type. These have usually been regarded (if explained at all) as resulting from the more miscellaneous character of this portion of the collection. BÖTT. finds here provincialisms characteristic of Ephraim, belonging more naturally to the section of the country most in contact with Syria. The correctness of this view needs to be established by close investigation. For the enumeration of particulars see BÖTTCHER'S *Ausführliches Lehrbuch*, §§ 29, 34, 35.—A.]

Ver. 4.—The Infin. abs. הָגֵה [old root הגה, see also GREEN, § 172, 2, for the peculiar form] is in both cases, in vers. 4 and 5, to be regarded as Imperative (so all the ancient versions, and also UMBREIT, EWALD, ELSTER), and not as in the first instance a substitute for the Indic. Imperf. (HITZIG, BERTHEAU), or as standing in both cases for the gerund (so STIER: is to be, should be taken away, etc.). [In ver. 4 this virtual Imper. is followed by a consec. Imperf., in ver. 5 by a consec. Jussive: "let his throne be established," etc. BÖTT., § 980, B, and n. 10—A.]

Ver. 7.—[אָמַר, an impersonal use of the Kal. Inf. constr., "good is the saying;" the rendering is often appropriately passive,—so here "that it be said to thee." Here and in ver. 27 the Infin. has a masc. predicate; in ver. 24 the fem. Infin. שֶׁבֶת takes the same. BÖTT., § 990, 1, a, and 3 β —A.]

Ver. 9.—[גַּל], a Piel Imperf. apocopate with lengthened vowel. See GREEN, § 174, 4; NORDH., § 451; BÖTT., § 1085, A, etc.—A.]

Ver. 11.—[דָּבָר, either a Kal Pass. Partic., written defectively,—or a Hoph. Partic. deprived of its initial מ, which is no uncommon loss; the form would then be דֻּבָּר; see BÖTT., § 994, 5, 6, 10.—אָפְנָיו, regarded by BÖTT. as well as by Z. and others as derived from אֹפֶן, wheel, the form is dual, the plural form with the same suffix being אוֹפַנָּיו; the meaning will then be "on its (pair of) wheels," readily, aptly. See BÖTT., §§ 678, 3, f.; 685, 42, and n. 4. FUERST gives the preference to another meaning supported from the Arabic and the Talm., "*nach seinen Arten*," according to its various uses and applications=fitly.—A.]

Ver. 16.—[הֲקָאֹתוֹ, a Perf. Hiph. with peculiarities in the vocalization and the suffix. BÖTT., §§ 1158, 2; 1166, 33.—A.]

Ver. 17.—הֹקַר, Imper. Hiph. from יָקַר (Is. xiii. 12; 1 Sam. iii. 1).

Vers. 19.—רֹעָה, Partic. fem. Kal from רָצַץ—רֹעַע. [Explained by OLSEN. as an Infin. fem. used substantively, but by FUERST, BÖTT., etc., as by our author,—a fem. part. passing into an adjective use.] Instead of מוּעֶדֶת, wavering, unsteadily, is either to be read מוֹעֶדֶת (Part. Kal from מָעַד), or the form is with R. KIMCHI, BERTHEAU, ELSTER, etc., to be regarded as a Puel part. with the omission of the performative כ (comp. 1s. liv. 11, etc.); comp. EWALD, Lehrb., 160 d. FUERST supports the latter explanation; GESEN., Lex. and Lehrgeb., BÖTT., GREEN (?) and others adopt the author's view. See esp. BÖTT., §§ 492, η and u. 2; 1063, C and n. 4.—A.]

Ver. 20.—מַעֲדֶה is usually taken as a Hiph. Part. from עָדָה, "he who taketh off clothing," etc. FUERST suggests the construing and rendering of it as a noun, with the meaning Pracht, splendor; BÖTT. strenuously maintains that it can be nothing else. Lehr., 11., p. 377, n. 1, and references there given.—A.].

EXEGETICAL.

1. Vers. 1. *The Superscription*—plainly belonging to the whole subsequent collection as far as the end of chap. xxix., and not merely to some such portion as xxv. 2—xxvii. 27, as HITZIG suggests; for there is in chap. xxviii. 1 no new superscription, and the assumption that in chap. xxviii. 17 sq. the central main division of the entire Book of Proverbs (xii.—xxii. 16) is continued, while xxviii. 1-16 is a fragment from a later hand, lacks all real support. Comp. remarks above on chap. xxii. 1.—**These also are proverbs of Solomon**—whether precisely in the strictest sense, or in the broader one of an authorship that is Solomon's only indirectly, on this point the expression gives us no definite knowledge. Proverbs of Solomon in the broader sense may very properly be included under the phrase.—**Which have been collected.**—In regard to the meaning of this verb see what is already said in the Introd., § 12 (pp. 26). The meaning "remove" (from the original place), "transfer, transplant, compile" is certainly lexically established, and is to be preferred without qualification to the explanations which differ from it; to "append" or "arrange" (*ordine disponere*), or to "preserve" (*durare facere, conservare*). Whether as the source from which the transfer or compilation of the following proverbs was made, we are to think simply of one book or of several books, so that the transfer would be the purely literary labor of excerpting, a transcribing, or collecting by copying (comp. the ἃς ἐξεγράψαντο of the LXX); or whether we have to consider as the source simply the oral transmission of ancient proverbs of wise men by the mouth of the people (HITZIG), must remain doubtful. It is perhaps most probable, that both the written and the oral tradition were alike sifted for the objects of the collection.—**By the men of Hezekiah.**—Possibly a learned commission created by this king for the purpose of this work of compilation, consisting of the most noted "wise men" of his time. Comp. Introd., § 3, and § 12, as cited above. [FUERST, in his *Kanon des Alten Testaments*, cites the Jewish tradition as holding a different view in several of these particulars. In regard to original authorship, the title is not interpreted as even claiming all for Solomon, though his is the chief and representative name; it is rather the aim and effect of the collection that is emphasized. Tradition, moreover, interprets the "these also" as showing that the preceding sections were likewise collected by the men of Hezekiah, the verb הֶעְתִּיקוּ in the superscription to this fourth collection meaning "continued." "The men of Hezekiah" furthermore are represented as not simply literati and poets of the king's court temporarily associated, and engaged in a specific work, but a "college" existing for similar purposes two hundred and eighty years, seven full generations. For details and references see FUERST'S *Kanon*, pp. 73-80.—A.]

2. Vers. 2-5. Of kings, their necessary attributes and duties.—**It is the glory of God to conceal a thing**—viz., so far forth as He, the "God that hideth Himself" (Is. xlv. 15), is incomprehensible in His being, and "unsearchable in His judgments" (Rom. xi. 33), so that accordingly all His action is a working out from the unknown, the hidden, a sudden revealing of hidden marvels (the "secret things" of Deut. xxix. 29). ["David says, 'The heavens *declare* the glory of God,' and Solomon adds, that God's glory is seen not only in what He reveals, but what He conceals—a profound observation, which is the best answer to many Scriptural objections to Divine Revelation, as has been shown by BP. BUTLER in his *Analogy*." WORDSW., *in loc*.].—On the contrary, it is **the glory of kings to search out a matter**, rightly to discern and to make clear debatable points in jurisprudence, and in general, on the ground of careful inquiry, investigation and consultation, to issue commands and to shape political ordinances. Comp. what GÖTHE once said (*Sämmtl. Werke*, Bd. XLV., p. 41) : "It is the business of the world-spirit to preserve mysteries before, yea, often after the deed; the poet's impulse is to disclose the my-tery;" and also LUTHER's marginal comment on our passage (see, below, the Homiletical notes).—דָּבָר is moreover in both instances to be rendered by "thing, matter," and not by "word" (Vulg., COCCEIUS, UMBREIT, *etc*); for in clause *b* in particular this latter meaning seems wholly inapposite.

Ver. 3. **The heavens for height, the earth for depth, and the heart of kings** (are) **unsearchable.**—חֵקֶר אֵין, "no searching out," is plainly the predicate of the subjects in clause *a* also, so that the entire verse forms but one proposition. And this is not a possible admonition to kings (not to suffer themselves to be searched out, but to preserve their secrets faithfully), as UMBREIT, VAN ESS, DE W., *etc*., think, but a simple didactic proposition, to bring out the fact, that while the heart of man is in general deep and difficult to fathom (Jer. xvii. 9; Ps. lxiv. 7), that of kings is peculiarly inaccessible and shut up within itself, much as may be depending on its decisions. [While, then, according to ver. 2, "it is a king's glory to get all the light he can" (STUART), it is his glory, and often an absolute condition of his prosperity and that of his kingdom, that he be able to keep his own counsel,—that of his heart there be "no searching out."—A.]

Vers. 4, 5. **Take away the dross from silver.**—The "dross," whose removal empowers the "refiner" or goldsmith to prepare a vase of noble metals, corresponds here, as in Jeremiah vi. 29, to the wicked or ungodly men who are to be purged out of a political commonwealth.—**Take away the wicked from before the king—**

i. e., before the court or by virtue of the king's judicial decision. The wicked is probably not to be designated as a "servant of the king" by the phrase "before the king" (contrary to the view of EWALD and BERTHEAU [KAMPH., DÖDERLEIN, II., *etc.*]).—With 5, *b*, comp. xvi. 12; xxix. 14.

3. Vers. 6, 7. Warning against arrogance in intercourse with kings and their nobles.—**Display not thyself in the presence of the king;**—lit., "bring not thy glory to view, make not thyself glorious" (STIER).—With the phrase "great men" in clause *b* comp. xviii. 6; 2 Sam. iii. 38; 2 Kings x. 6, *etc.*—With ver. 7 compare in general Luke xiv. 8-11, as well as the Arabic proverb (MEIDANI, p. 72), "Sit not in a place from which one may bid thee rise up."—**Than that they humble thee** (thy humbling) **before the king.**—Z. renders "because of a prince," and goes on to say: "Usually, ·before a prince, in his presence.' But then we should have expected rather the plural, 'before, in the presence of princes and nobles.' לִפְנֵי seems to require to be employed here rather in the sense of 'because of, in relation to' (comp. 2 Sam. iii. 31); and the following 'whom thine eyes have seen' seems to suggest the criminality, by no means ignorant, of the dishonor put on the dignity of the prince (thus HITZIG correctly explains)." [We cannot see the fitness of this departure from universal usage in regard to לִפְנֵי, which occurs hundreds of times in the O. T. with various modifications of the meaning "before," but has not in one conceded instance the meaning "on account of." It has been used twice just before with its ordinary meaning, and before the end of the chapter occurs again with the same meaning. There is room for difference of opinion as to the person *before whom* the humiliation is to be,—whether it be the king himself, or some prince or noble of his court, but there can be none as to the preposition required to express the idea. It is probably best to regard the king, who is chiefly affronted by such arrogance, as described here, not by his specific and official title, but as the *exalted* one who was to see and be seen, and before whom the humiliation is most crushing.—A.]

4. Vers. 8-10. Warning against contentiousness and loquacity.—**Go not forth hastily to strive;**—*i. e.*, do not begin controversies with undue haste (LUTHER: rush not forth soon to quarrel).—**Lest** (it be said to thee) "**What wilt thou do in the end,**" *etc.*—Lit., "at the end thereof, at its (the strife's) end," at the time, therefore, when the evil results of the contention have shown themselves. It is so natural to supply a verb of saying with the "lest" before "What wilt thou do?" that we may without hesitation have recourse to this expedient for filling out the form of expression, which certainly is perplexingly concise and elliptical (comp. UMBREIT, ELSTER, STIER [KAMPH., H., N., M.], *etc.*, and even a commentator as early as JARCHI, on this passage). At all events this solution is better than that devised by EWALD and BERTHEAU [DE W., S.], who take the "what" in the sense of "what evil, what terrible thing" ("lest disgracefully treated by thine opponent and excited to wrath, thou do some fearful thing!")

Ver. 9. **Debate thy cause** (strive thy strife) **with thy neighbor,** *etc.*—If the contest has become really inevitable, if it has come to process of law, then press thy cause with energy, but honorably, with the avoidance of all unworthy or low means,—and especially in such a way that thou do not by any possibility with a malicious wickedness betray secrets of thine opponent that may have been earlier entrusted to thee.

Ver. 10. **Lest he that heareth it upbraid thee.**—The "bearer" does not denote possibly the injured friend (LXX, SCHULTENS [WORDSW.], *etc.*)—which would be intolerably flat and tautological, but very indefinitely, any one who obtains knowledge of that dishonorable and treacherous conduct. The Piel חֵרֵף is used here only in the sense of "curse, despise;" comp. the corresponding noun "reproach" in chap. xiv. 34.— **And thine evil name turn not away,**—die not out again, depart not from thee. Comp. the use of שׁוּב of wrath that is allayed or quieted; Gen. xxvii. 44, 45, and frequently.

5. Vers. 11-15. Five symmetrically constructed and concise comparisons, in praise of wisdom in speech, of fidelity, liberality and gentleness.—Ver. 11. **Apples of gold in framework of silver.** מַשְׂכִּית which occurred in chap. xviii. 11, in the sense of "imagination, conceit," is unquestionably to be left with its usual meaning, "sculpture" (carved or embossed work); comp. Ezek. viii. 12; Lev. xxvi. 1; Num. xxxiii. 52. Under the term we are to understand some such thing as sculptured work for the decoration of ceilings, pillared galleries, *etc.*, which exhibits golden apples on a groundwork of silver. That in this case we must have expected the precise term for "pomegranates" (רִמּוֹנִים) is an arbitrary assertion of HITZIG's, in support of which we need neither emend with him, to read אֶשְׁכּוֹל־מַשְׁכֻּלֹת (from an alleged noun בְּמַשְׁכֻּלֹת palm bough) "or branches," nor with LUTHER give to the word in question the signification "baskets," which has no parallel to support it. [KAMPH., H., M., *etc.*, support this rendering of LUTHER's; DE W. and N. suppose the silver work to be inlaid or embossed on the golden apples; while BERTHEAU, GESEN., S., WORDSW., *etc.*, understand the description to be of golden fruit, represented either in solid or embroidered work on a ground-work of silver. FUERST seems to favor the application of the term to ornamented furniture or plate for the table; and this certainly has the advantage of natural probability in its favor—A.]—(Is) **a word fitly spoken** ["spoken in its time."—Z.] Comp. xv. 23, where however we have בְּעִתּוֹ instead of the unique expression found in our verse. That this peculiar form of speech, which appears to signify strictly "after the manner of its wheels, or on its wheels," is in reality equivalent to *justo tempore, in tempore suo,* is expressed as early as SYMMACHUS and the Vulg., as well as supported by the analogy of a similar Arabic expression, in which the radical word אוֹפַן is in like manner used to describe time revolving in its circuit, moving on in the form of a ring, or after the

manner of wheels. Comp. also the well known vision of Ezekiel; Ezek. i. 15 sq. [See Crit. Notes. BERTHEAU, H., favor the exposition above given; GESEN., S., M., WORDSW. favor the other and less figurative way of reaching the same idea.—A.]

Ver. 12. **A gold ring and an ornament of fine gold.** נֶזֶם, elsewhere a ring for the nose (xi. 22, etc.), is here, as clause b shows, rather an ear-ring or ear-drop (comp. Gen. xxxv. 4). חֲלִי is in general a pendant, a jewel, such as is usually worn on the neck or in the ears, (Song Sol. vii. 2; Hos. ii. 15); and is here naturally used in the latter sense, therefore possibly of the ornament of pearls which was hung below the ear-ring.—(So is) **a wise reprover to an ear that heareth.** "The reprover, or punisher," is a concrete, lively, illustrative expression instead of "rebuke or censure." The boldness of the expression still fails to justify HITZIG's attempted emendation, according to which חֵיךְ is to be read instead of מוֹכִיחַ, and this is to be taken in the sense of "conversation" ("rational conversation"—comp. the λόγος σοφός of the LXX). With the general sentiment comp. besides chap. xv. 31, 32.

Ver. 13. **As the coolness of snow on a harvest day**, i. e. probably, as a refreshing drink cooled by the snow of Lebanon amidst the heats of harvest labor. Comp. XENOPH. Memorab. II. 1, 30; PLIN. Hist. Nat., XIX. 4; and especially the passages cited by HITZIG from the "Gesta Dei per Francos" (Han. 1611), p. 1098: "The coldest snow is brought from Lebanon, to be mixed with wine, and make it cold as the very ice." [See HACKETT's Illustrations of Scripture, pp. 53–5, for illustrations of the usage, and statements in regard to the extent of the traffic. —A.] With clauses b and c comp. x. 26; xiii. 17; xxii. 21.

Ver. 14. **Clouds and wind and no rain—** (so is) **a man who boasteth of a false gift.** That is, a boaster who makes much talk of his liberality, and yet withal gives nothing (who "promises mountains of gold, but does not even give lead," (STIER), is like clouds of vapor borne aloft and driven about by the wind (נְשִׂיאִים lit. light rising vapors, which gather in clouds), which dispense no rain. With the same figure, with a similar application: Jude 12; 2 Pet. ii. 17; likewise in several Arabic proverbs, e. g. Exc. ex Sent. 43 (ed. SCHEID.): "A learned man without work, is as a cloud without rain."

Ver. 14. To the recommendation of liberality in the verses preceding there is very appropriately added an admonition to gentleness and mildness, especially in the use of the tongue. Comp. xv. 1.—**By forbearance is a judge persuaded**, lit., "talked over, misled," i. e., changed in his disposition, influenced, comp. Luke xviii. 4, 5. קָצִין here certainly means "judge," as in vi. 7, and not "King, prince," as some of the older expositors and LUTHER also, render it, and as UMBREIT is inclined to regard it. [Why not the "prince," acting in his judicial capacity, and in other relations also where the bearing and spirit of those about him will more or less consciously mould his action? He is the "decider" in more ways than one.—A.] **And a gentle tongue breaketh the bone**, i. e., subdues even the most obstinate resistance. Comp. the Latin: "Gutta cavat lapidem," etc., as well as the German, "Patience breaks iron."

6. Vers. 16-20. Warning against intemperance, obtrusiveness, slander, credulity and levity.—**Hast thou found honey—eat to thy satisfaction** (lit., "thy enough"). Comp. Samson and Jonathan as finders of honey (Judges xiv. 8 sq.; 1 Sam. xiv. 26), and also a warning against partaking of it to excess, ver. 27, and PINDAR, Nem. 7, 52: Κόρον ἔχει καὶ μέλι.

Ver. 17 first introduces the real application of this warning against eating honey in excess. **Withhold thy foot from thy friend's house.** "Make rare, keep back, seldom enter with it," etc. Comp. the σπάνιον εἴσαγε τὸν πόδα of the LXX.—Comp. besides the similar proverbs of the Arabs, which warn against obtrusiveness: "If thy comrade eats honey do not lick it all up," or "Visit seldom, and they love thee the more," etc. Also MARTIAL's sentiment: Nulli te facias nimis amicum.

Ver. 18. **A maul and a sword and a sharp arrow.** מֵפִיץ an instrument for crushing, a club shod with iron, a war-club (Nah. ii. 2; comp. the cognate terms in Jer. li. 20, and Ezek. ix. 2). For additional comparisons of false, malicious words with swords and arrows, comp. Ps. lii. 4; lvii. 5; lxiv. 4; cxx. 4, etc. See also the previous rebukes of false testimony; Prov. vi. 19; xii. 17; xix. 5, 9; xxi. 28.

Ver. 19. **A broken tooth and an unsteady foot (is) confidence in an unfaithful man,** etc. שֵׁן רֹעָה is to be explained either by a substantive construction, "tooth of breaking" (UMBREIT, STIER following ABEN EZRA), or by a participial construction, "a breaking tooth." The latter is to be preferred as the simpler (BERTHEAU, ELSTER, etc., [See Crit. Notes]); to change the punctuation so as to get the meaning, "a bad, worthless tooth," HITZIG, is at any rate unnecessary, since the meaning "decayed, rotten," is in general not questionable. "Trust in (lit., of) an unfaithful man" is here a foolish, credulous reliance on one who is false. For the figure comp. furthermore, especially Is. xxxvi. 6; 1 Kings xviii. 21.

Ver. 20. **He that layeth aside clothing in a cold day.** This is plainly a senseless proceeding, an entirely aimless and absurd movement. The same is true of the action suggested by the words following, "vinegar on nitre;" for the moistening of nitre (comp. Jer. ii. 22), i. e., doubtless carbonate of soda, or soda, with vinegar or acid destroys its substance, while to combine the same thing with oil, etc., produces a useful soap. Thus, and doubtless correctly, ROSENM, BERTHEAU, VON GERLACH, and substantially UMBREIT also (although he thinks rather of potash or saltpetre as the substance here designated). J. D. MICHAELIS (de nitro Hebræorum), J. F. VON MEYER, STIER, etc., think specially of the fermentation and the offensive odor which the nitre produces in contact with vinegar(?). SCHULTENS, EWALD and ELSTER understand נָתַר in accordance with the Arabic (and also in harmony with the ἕλκει of the LXX), of a *wound*, which is washed with smarting vinegar instead of soothing oil; against this view, however, we have of the other ancient versions except the LXX, especially the Vulg., SYMMACHUS, the Vers. Venet., *etc.* HITZIG finally emends here again according to his fancy, and obtains the meaning: "He that meeteth archers, with arrow on the string, is like him who singeth songs with a sad heart"(!)— [GESEN., FUERST and the lexicographers generally refer to descriptions of Egypt and its natural productions, in describing the material and its properties. H., N., M., WORDSW., *etc.*, take the same view, and multiply and vary the references. See THOMSON's *Land and Book*, II. 302, 303. WORDSW. expresses a decided preference for the rendering of clause *a*, which (see Crit. Notes) is preferred by FUERST, BÖTT., *etc.*, "display in dress" instead of comfort; "as he that tricks out a man in a gay dress in winter, he who busies himself about the fineness and brilliancy instead of the texture and warmth of the attire," *etc.* This certainly secures a better correspondence of incongruities.—A.] Moreover, the "singing songs with a heavy heart" (for these last words comp. the similar phrases in Gen. xl. 7; Neh. ii. 1, 2; Eccles. vii. 3), which is described by the two comparisons in clause *a*, as a senseless and perverse proceeding, is doubtless to be understood in the sense of Ps. cxxxvii. 1, 4, and not to be taken as possibly a disregard of the Apostolic injunction in Rom. xii. 15. For the heart is hardly that of another [E. V., DE W., H., N., S., M., WORDSW.: "*to* a heavy heart"], but most probably the speaker's own heart. The procedure against which the sentiment of the verse is directed seems therefore to be frivolity, and superficial, insincere conduct, and not a rude indifference and uncharitableness toward one's neighbor.

7. Vers. 21, 22. Admonition to the love of enemies.—**If thine enemy** (lit., "thine hater") **hunger, give him bread to eat,** *etc.* "Bread" and "water" are named here as the simplest and readiest refreshment. To name meat, wine, dainties and the like would have been quite too forced. In the citation in the N. T., in Rom. xii. 20, both objects are for brevity omitted and thereby the expression is made more like Matt. xxv. 35.—**For so thou dost heap burning coals on his head.** For this verb to heap, to pile up, comp. vi. 27. To "heap coals on the head of any one" cannot be the figurative representation of a burning shame which one develops in his opponent (GRAMBERG, UMBREIT), for shame glows in the cheek, and not above on the head. The figure is designed to describe rather the deep pangs of repentance which one produces within his enemy by rewarding his hatred with benefits, and in the production of which the revenge to be taken on him may consist, simply and solely. This correct view is first presented by AUGUSTINE, *De doctr. Christ.*, III. 16; and then especially by SCHULTENS, ROSENM., HITZIG, *etc.* These last at the same time adduce pertinent Arabic parallels, like MEIDANI, II. 721: "He who kindly treats such as envy him, scatters glowing coals in their face, *etc.* At all events, we must decidedly reject the interpretation of many of the Church Fathers, like CHRYSOSTOM,

THEODORET, THEOPHYLACT, *etc.*, who regarded the coals as the designation of extreme divine judgments (comp. Ps. xi. 6; cxl. 11) which one will bring upon his enemy by refusing to avenge himself. [In this last opinion our recent commentators, perhaps without exception, agree with the author. In regard to his first discrimination, if any have been inclined to limit the figure to the superficial blush or the transient emotion of shame, there would be a general agreement with him. If he means to discriminate sharply between shame and repentance, we must pronounce his distinctions too fine, as some will be inclined to regard his comment on the proper seat of the blush. A deep, true shame, may be the first step toward, the first element in repentance.—A.]

8. Vers. 23–28. Against slander, a contentious spirit, timidity, want of self-control, *etc.* **North wind produceth rain.** For the verb comp. Ps. xc. 2; for a description of the rainy wind of Palestine, which strictly blows, not from the North, but from the North-west and West, as רוּחַ צָפוֹן, comp. Am. viii. 12, where this "North" is contrasted with קָדְמָה "the East." Perhaps this term is equivalent to ζόφος as a designation of a dark, gloomy region, which we are by no means to seek directly north of Palestine (UMBREIT; comp. HITZIG). In no case is JEROME right (and ABEN EZRA), when in view of the predominantly dry, cold and rough character of the north of Palestine, he renders the verb by "*dissipat pluvias*, it scatters the clouds, and so ends the rain." [The author's view is that of DE W., KAMPH., BERTHEAU, MUFFET, H., N., S., M., WORDSW., GESEN., and the recent commentators and lexicographers almost without exception. Now and then JEROME's rendering, which is that of the E. V., is assumed to be right, and illustrated, as *e. g.* in THOMSON's *Land and Book* I. 131.—A.]—**So doth the slanderous tongue a troubled face** [lit., "a secret tongue"]; *i. e.*, artful calumny and slander (comp. Ps. ci. 5) produces gloomy, troubled faces, just as surely as the North-west wind darkens the heavens with rain-clouds. The *tertium compar.* in the figure is therefore the same as in Matt. xvi. 3; Luke xii. 54. Comp. besides the German proverb, "He makes a face like a three days' rain-storm." [Those who follow the E. V. in the rendering of the first clause, must with it invert subject and object in clause *b*, and change the epithet. "troubled," dark with sadness, for "angry," dark with passion; "so doth an angry countenance a backbiting tongue." TRAPP, *e. g.*, says: "The ready way to be rid of tale-bearers is to browbeat them; carry therefore in this case a severe rebuke in thy countenance, as God doth."—A.]

Ver. 24. Comp. the literally identical sentence, chap. xxi. 9.

Ver. 25. (**As**) **cold water to a thirsty soul is good news from a far country.** Naturally we must here think of those far removed from their home and kindred, who have long remained without tidings from them. Comp. xv. 30; Gen. xlv. 27; and for the figure, Jer. xviii. 14.

Ver. 26. **A troubled fountain and a ruined spring** (comp. for this figure Ezek. xxxii. 2; xxxiv. 18, 19) **is the righteous man who wavereth before the wicked.** The meaning of this is probably not the righteous man who *without fault of his* has been brought by evil doers into calamity, but he who through the fault of his timidity, his want of faithful courage and moral firmness, has been brought to waver and fall by the craft of the wicked. Compare STIER on this passage, who however understands the wavering perhaps too exclusively of being betrayed into sin, or some moral lapse. [LORD BACON (*De Augmentis, etc.*) gives the proverb a political application: "This proverb teaches that an unjust and scandalous judgment in any conspicuous and weighty cause is above all things to be avoided in the State," *etc.*; and in his Essay (LVI.) "of Judicature," he says: "One foul sentence doth more hurt than many foul examples; for these do but corrupt the stream, the other corrupteth the fountain."—A.]

Ver. 27. **To eat much honey is not good.** Since this maxim, like the similar one in verse 16, must convey a warning against the excessive enjoyment of a thing good in itself, we should look in the 2d clause for an analogous truth belonging to the spiritual realm. That clause is therefore not to be rendered: "And contempt of their honor is honor" (thus J. D. MICHAELIS, ARNOLDI, ZIEGLER, EWALD,—all of whom take חֵקֶר in the sense of "contempt" (comp. xxviii. 11); and HITZIG likewise, except that he [by a transfer of one consonant] reads כְּבוֹד כָּבוֹד, and "contempt of honor is more than honor"). But we must here reclaim for the noun כָּבֹד its original meaning "weight, burden," instead of כְּבֹדִים we must read כְּבֵדִים, "weighty things, difficulties," and then retaining the ordinary meaning of חֵקֶר we must render: "and searching out the difficult brings difficulty," *i. e.*, too strenuous occupation of mind with difficult things is injurious; pondering too difficult problems brings injury (comp. the common proverb, "To know everything makes headache"). So ELSTER alone [with NOYES among our expositors, and FUERST, substantially, of the lexicographers] correctly explains,—while UMBREIT and BERTHEAU [with whom S. and M. agree] take only the last כָּבוֹד in the sense of difficulty, and therefore explain "and searching out honor (or "their honor") brings difficulty;" in a similar way the Vulgate "*qui scrutator est majestatis opprimetur a gloria*" ["he who is a searcher after dignity will be crushed by glory." The E. V. renders "to search their own glory (is not) glory;" the assumed meaning of the noun demands a negative copula, such as has just been used in clause *a*; so GESEN.(?) KAMPH. enumerates the above and several other renderings, and pronounces all unsatisfactory. HOLDEN and WORDSW. retain the ordinary meaning of all the nouns, supply the usual copula, and render: "To search after their glory (their *true* glory) is glory." The sentiment is fine, but to attach it to clause *a* requires skill.]

Ver. 28. (As) **a city broken through without walls** (comp. 2 Chron. xxxii. 5; Nehem. ii. 13), **is the man who hath no mastery over his own spirit**, *i. e.*, the passionate man, who knows not how in anything to keep within bounds, who can put bit and bridle on none of his desires, and therefore is given up without resistance to all impressions from without, to all assaults upon his morality and freedom, *etc.* Let it be observed how nearly this proverb corresponds with the substance of the preceding.

DOCTRINAL AND ETHICAL.

In the noble admonition to the love of enemies, in vers. 21, 22, which bears witness for the New Testament principle of a perfect love even more definitely and in fuller measure, than the dissuasion contained in the preceding chapter against avenging one's self (xxiv. 29), we reach the culmination of those moral demands and precepts with which the wise compiler of the Proverbs comes in the present section before the kings and subjects of his people. Beside this, in the exceedingly rich and manifold variety of ethical material which this chapter exhibits, the admonitions that stand out significantly are especially those to humility and modesty (vers. 6, 7, 14), to a peaceable spirit (vers. 8, 24) to honor and considerate forbearance toward one's opponent in controversy (ver. 9, 10, 23), to the wise reception of merited reproof and correction (ver. 12), to gentleness (ver. 15), to fidelity and sincerity (vers. 13, 18-20), to moderation in all things, in enjoyments of a sensual as well as of a spiritual kind (vers. 16, 17, 27), to moral firmness in resisting the seductive influences of the wicked, and in subduing the passions (vers. 26, 28). In regard to doctrine it is especially the delineation contained in vers. 2-5, of the godlike dignity and authority of the King, that is to be accounted one of the pre-eminently instructive portions of the chapter. The earthly king is, it is true, in this unlike to God, the King of kings, that he can take his decisive steps only after careful consideration, examination, and conference with wise counsellors, and only thus issue his commands, so far forth as they are to result in the welfare of his subjects,—while with God, the being who is alike near and afar off, the all-wise and Almighty, counsel and act are always coincident. But in this again there can and should be an analogy existing between earthly rulers and the heavenly King, that their throne also is established by righteousness, that they likewise must watch with unfaltering strictness, by punishing the evil and rewarding the good, over the sacred ordinance of justice and the objective moral law (vers. 4, 5). And for this very reason there belongs to their action also something mysterious and absolutely irresistible; their heart too appears unsearchable, and wholly inaccessible to common men, like the heights of heaven and the depths of the earth (ver. 3); in a word, they in the political sphere stand in every point of view as God's representatives, as regents in God's stead and by the grace of God, and even, according to the bold expression of the poetical language of the Old Testament, as in a certain sense even "gods and children of the Most High" (Ps. lxxxii. 6; comp. John x. 34 sq.). From this then there results, on the one hand, to themselves the duty of strict justice, and the most conscientious conformity to God's holy will,—but on the other, for their subjects the duties of humble obedience (vers. 6, 7, 13) of earnest reverence for civil laws and ordinances, and peaceable deportment, (vers. 8-10, 18, 23, 24, *etc.*); in general therefore, the *fear of God* and *righteousness*, as the conditions of a true welfare of earth's nobles and nations, to be fulfilled on both parts, by princes as well as by the people.

HOMILETIC AND PRACTICAL.

Homily on the entire chapter: "Love the brethren; fear God; honor the King!" (2 Pet. ii. 17); three apostolical injunctions, which Hezekiah's wise men already preached to the Israel of their day.—Or, the fear of God, justice and love, as the three foundation pillars of a well-founded and well organized Christian commonwealth.—Comp. STÖCKER; Of true honor, such as wisdom confers: 1) in the state (ver. 2-15: *gloria politicorum*); 2) in the household (vers. 16-24: *gloria œconomicorum*); 3) in the church (vers. 25-28: *gloria ecclesiasticorum*).—*Berleburg Bible:* Divine political maxims.—WOHLFARTH: Honor and renown as wisdom's reward.

Vers. 2-5. LUTHER (marginal comment on ver. 2): In God's government we are not to be wise, and wish to know why, but believe everything. But in the secular kingdom a ruler should know, and ask why, and trust no man in anything!— STARKE: God's counsel concerning our blessedness is revealed to us clearly enough in His word; act accordingly, and in the presence of the mysteries of divine wisdom take thy reason captive under the obedience of faith.—[JEREMY TAYLOR: God's commandments were proclaimed to all the world; but God's counsels are to Himself and to His secret ones, when they are admitted within the veil.—BATES: God saveth us by the submission of faith and not by the penetration of reason. The light of faith is as much below the light of glory as it is above the light of nature.—R. Hall's Sermon on "the glory of God in concealing." 1) The Divine Being is accustomed to conceal much. 2) In this He acts in a manner worthy of Himself, and suited to display His glory.—LORD BACON (on ver. 3); Multitude of jealousies, and lack of some predominant desire, that should marshal and put in order all the rest, maketh any man's heart hard to find or sound].—GEIER (on ver. 3): Every one, even the greatest and mightiest, is to know that God knows his heart most perfectly and searches it through: Ps. cxxxix. 1, 2. —CRAMER (on vers. 4, 5): As well in matters of religion as in matters of justice (in the sphere of the church and in politics) the duty belongs to the ruler of removing all abuses and offences.

Vers. 6 sq. GEIER (on ver. 6): An excellent means against pride consists in looking to those who are better, more pious, more experienced, more learned than we are, rather than to estimate ourselves solely by those who are lower.— STARKE (on vers. 9, 10): If thou hast a reasonable complaint against thy neighbor, thou shouldst not mingle foreign matters with it, nor from revenge reveal secrets which weigh heavily against thy neighbor.—LANGE (on ver. 11); In religious discourses heart and mouth must agree: the orator must besides always examine what is best adapted to his congregation: 1 Pet. iv. 11.— [BP. HOPKINS: As the amiableness of all duties consists in the right timing and placing of them, so especially of this holy and spiritual discourse]. —HASIUS (on ver. 12): He who can hearken and gladly hearkens to rational reproofs, does his ears a far better service thereby, than if he adorned them with jewels of the finest gold, and with genuine pearls.

Vers. 13 sq. LUTHER (marginal comment on ver. 13): A true servant or subject is not to be paid for with gold.—STARKE (on ver. 13): A chief characteristic of able teachers of the divine word is that they as stewards over the mysteries of God (1 Cor. iv. 1, 2) seek to be found faithful.—(On ver. 14); Satan promises mountains of gold, but gives only smoke and empty vapor. Jesus keeps His word plenteously above all requests or understanding.—(On ver. 15): He who will everywhere put his head through the wall, will hardly succeed. But how beautiful and salutary is it to be gentle and full of love!— ZELTNER (on vers. 16, 17): Of all things, even the most charming and lovely one becomes at last weary. Therefore there is nothing better or more blessed than to strive for heaven and the eternal, where satiety is without weariness (John iv. 14), life without death (John vi. 50; Col. iii. 1, 2).

Vers. 19 sq. STARKE: Beside the confidence of believers in God every other hope is deceptive and unreliable as a brittle cake of ice or as a bending reed.—(On ver. 20): Even joyful music is not able to drive away cares and troubled thoughts, but an edifying song of the cross or of consolation may do it; Ps. cxix. 92; Col. iii. 16. —*Tübingen Bible* (on vers. 21, 22): True wisdom teaches us by gentleness to break down the haughtiness of enemies, and even to win them to one's self by benefits: Matth. v. 44 sq. But how excellent is it not merely to know these rules of wisdom, but also to practise them!—[TRAPP: Thus should a Christian punish his pursuers; no vengeance but this is heroical and fit for imitation.—ARNOT: This is peculiarly "the grace of the Lord Jesus." When He was lifted up on the cross He gave the keynote of the Christian life: "Father, forgive them." The Gospel must come in such power as to turn the inner life upside down ere any real progress can be made in this difficult department of social duty].

Vers. 23-28. GEIER (on ver. 23): Cultivate sincerity and honor, that thou mayest not speak evil things in his absence of one whom thou meetest to his face with all friendliness.— [BRIDGES: The backbiting tongue wounds four at one stroke—the backbiter himself, the object of his attack, the hearer, and the name of God].— ZELTNER (on ver. 25): When we hear from distant lands the glad news of the course of the gospel among the heathen, it must cause us hearty rejoicing, and urge us to thanksgiving to God (an application then of ver. 25 for a missionary festival sermon).—STARKE (on ver. 26): As a fountain made foul becomes in time pure and clear again, so likewise the stained innocence of a righteous man will in due time be revealed again in its purity; Ps. xxxvii. 6.—(On ver. 27): The laborious and diligent will never lack work, and the more vigorous and systematic he is in it, the more honor does it bring him.—*Calwer Handb.* (on ver. 27): Search not into things too hard.— STARKE (on ver. 28): A man who cannot govern himself cannot be usefully employed in conducting public affairs.—[BATES: Satan hath an easy entrance into such men, and brings along with him a train of evils].

---

2. Various Warnings, *viz.*:

a) Against dishonorable conduct,

(*especially folly, sloth and malice*).

CHAP. XXVI.

1 As snow in summer and rain in harvest,
   so honor befitteth not the fool.
2 As the sparrow flitting, as the swallow flying,
   so the curse undeserved: it cometh not.
3 A whip for the horse, a bridle for the ass,
   and a rod for the fool's back.
4 Answer not a fool according to his folly,
   lest thou be like him.
5 Answer a fool according to his folly,
   lest he become wise in his own eyes.
6 He cutteth off the feet, he drinketh damage,
   who sendeth a message by a fool.
7 Take away the legs of the lame,
   and the proverb in the mouth of a fool.
8 As a bag of jewels on a heap of stones,
   so is he that giveth honor to a fool.
9 As a thorny staff that riseth up in the hand of a drunkard,
   so is a proverb in the mouth of a fool.
10 An archer that woundeth everything,
   and he that hireth a fool, and hireth vagrants (are alike).
11 As a dog that returneth to his vomit,
   so the fool (ever) repeateth his folly.
12 Seest thou a man wise in his own eyes,
   there is more hope of a fool than of him.—
13 The slothful saith: There is a lion in the way,
   a lion in the midst of the streets.
14 The door turneth on its hinges,
   and the slothful on his bed.
15 The slothful thrusteth his hand in the dish;
   he is too sluggish to bring it to his mouth again.
16 The sluggard is wiser in his own eyes,
   than seven (men) who give wise judgment.
17 He layeth hold on the ears of a dog
   who passing by is excited by strife that is not his.
18 As a madman who casteth fiery darts,
   arrows and death,
19 so is the man that deceiveth his neighbor,
   and saith: Am I not in sport?
20 Where the wood faileth the fire goeth out,
   and where there is no talebearer the strife ceaseth.

21 Coal to burning coals and wood to fire;
   so is a contentious man to kindle strife.
22 The words of the talebearer are as sportive (words),
   but they go down to the innermost part of the breast.
23 Silver dross spread over a potsherd,—
   (so are) glowing lips and a wicked heart.
24 With his lips the hater dissembleth,
   and within him he layeth up deceit.
25 When he speaketh fair believe him not;
   for seven abominations are in his heart.
26 Hatred is covered by deceit,
   (yet) his wickedness shall be exposed in the assembly.
27 He that diggeth a pit falleth into it,
   and he that rolleth a stone, upon himself shall it return.
28 The lying tongue hateth those that are wounded by it,
   and a flattering mouth will cause offence.

GRAMMATICAL AND CRITICAL.

Ver. 3. [The form נֵז (comp. x. 13; xix. 29) is ordinarily explained as derived from נָוָה the more common נֶז (Lex.), נֶז as from נוּג; Böтт. (§ 498, 17) suggests that the form נֵז is used, as in numerous similar cases the forms with weaker, flatter vowels are employed, to convey in their very sound the idea of the weak, the suffering, the miserable; נֵז then, in every instance except perhaps one, is used to describe a back that is beaten or threatened.—לַחֲמוֹר a form with the article, as is indicated not by the vocalization alone, but by the parallel לָכוּב; Böтт. I., p. 403, n. 1.—A.].

Ver. 6. [בִּקְצֵה a Piel part., therefore active in its meaning, and not to be rendered by a passive, nor need it be exchanged for the Pual (pass.) part. as Ewald proposes. The emendations of בִּקְצֵה רַגְלַיִם in clause a which have been proposed by recent expositors are unnecessary; e. g., Ewald's reading בִּקְצֵה רוֹ "is deprived of his feet, etc." Hitzig would read בִּקְצֵה רוֹ immediately connecting the following words; "from the end of the feet he swallows injury (?!) who sends messages by a fool."—A.].

Ver. 7. דָּלְיוּ is taken most simply as Imper. Piel from דָּלָה, to "lift out, draw out" (Ps. xxx. 2). [So Fuerst; Green, § 141, 1; Nordh. § 452. Böтт. § 1123, 4, and § 300 b, makes it from דָּלַל. This resolution of ל and substitution of י for the second ל Böтт. regards as a probable sign and characteristic of the Ephraimite dialect which he is inclined to find in this section of the Book of Proverbs. Gesen., Thes., was at first disposed to take it from דָּלַל, but in the supplement brought out by Rödiger appears to have changed his view, taking it as a fuller form of דָּלִי. The rendering of Böтт., etc., would be "the legs of the lame hang useless."—A.].

Ver. 14. [הַסּוֹב, illustrates Böттcher's Fiens solitum, "is wont to turn," and in ver. 20 תִּכְבֶּה and יִשְׁתֹּק his Fiens debitum; "must go out, must cease." See Lehrb. § 950, b, and c, ε.—A.].

Ver. 18. כְּהִתְלַהְלֵהַּ from לָהַהּ or perhaps from a root תָּלָה still preserved in the Arabic.

Ver. 26. [וְהִבָּכֶה; the ת of the Hithp. prefix is elsewhere not assimilated.—A.].

Ver. 28. [לְשׁוֹן as here used Böтт. regards as one of the traces of an Ephraimite dialect, the noun with this meaning being otherwise feminine.—דָּכָיו Gesen. derives from דָּךְ in the active sense the form being plural with suff. and the construction acc. as object. Fuerst makes it a peculiar derivative (without suffix) from דָּכָה in the sense of "bowed down, humble, pious." Böтт. pointing דְּכָיו as the K'thibh, makes it from דְּכִי with the suffix of the singular. See Exegetical notes for the various interpretations.—A.].

EXEGETICAL.

1. Vers. 1–3. Three proverbs against folly, symmetrical in their structure (in each case bringing two related ideas into comparison).—**As snow in summer and rain in harvest.** According to Jerome, Comm. in Am. iv. 7, rain in harvest time is in Palestine a thing not heard of, and even impossible. Comp. 1 Sam. xii. 17 sq., where a sudden thunderstorm at this season appears as a miracle from God, and also the confirmatory statements of modern observers, like Robinson, Pal. II. 307: "In ordinary years no rain at all falls from the end of the spring-showers till October or November, and the sky is almost always clear," etc.—Comp. furthermore the remarks above on chap. xxv. 13, as well as, for clause b, chap. xix. 10; and also ver. 8 below.—Ver. 2.—**As the sparrow flitting, as the swallow flying:** lit. "as the sparrow for fleeing or wandering, as the swallow flying," viz. is fitted. Comp. the similar construction in chap. xxv. 3, and also the similar comparison in xxvii. 8. [The Inf. with ל may be rendered by the abl. as readily as by the dative of the gerund or verbal noun; by or in respect to flying, etc.]—**So the curse** (that is) **undeserved: it cometh not.** "A curse that is in vain, that has been uttered without just

ground, that is unmerited," like that, *e. g.*, in 2 Sam. xvi. 5 sq., or that in 1 Kings ii. 8. For the "in vain" comp. xxiv. 28 and the remarks on the passage.—Instead of לֹא תָבֹא K'ri calls for לוֹ

תָבֹא: "to him, to the fool who utters it, will it return," it will find its fulfilment in his own case (thus the Vulg. and JARCHI). But the verbal expression agrees poorly enough with this rendering, and moreover the two comparisons in *a* plainly favor rather the idea expressed by the K'thibh. [Such a curse is then fugitive, transient as a bird; it does not come to stay. The E. V. suggests the idea very blindly. TRAPP explains: "As these may fly where they will, and nobody cares or is the worse; so here." He would carry the comparison farther: as birds after their aimless flight return to their nest, "so the causeless curse returns to the authors. Cursing men are cursed men." A.]—Ver. 3. Comp. x. 13; xix. 29; Ecclesiast. xxx. 25-27.—The assertion of J. D MICHAELIS that the ideas "whip" and "bridle" in clause *a* are not rightly distributed between the horse and the ass, is refuted by Nah. iii. 2; Ezek. xxxix. 9, where express mention is made of riding whips in connection with horses, as well as by Ps. xxxii. 9, where with horses mules are also mentioned as bridled animals. [GESEN. *Thes*., *s. v.*, abundantly illustrates the nobler nature of the Eastern ass, and the higher estimate put upon it. See also HOUGHTON'S article in SMITH'S *Dictionary of the Bible*, I. 182, Am. Ed. A.]

2. Vers. 4-12. Eight additional proverbs directed against the folly of fools (among them one consisting of two verses, vers. 4, 5).—**Answer not a fool according to his folly**, *i. e.*, speak not with him in accordance with his folly, conforming thyself to it, imitating it, and thereby becoming thyself a fool. On the other hand, ver. 5: **Answer a fool according to his folly**, *i. e.*, serve him in his senseless babbling with an appropriate, sharply decisive retort, use with the coarse block (blockhead) the heavy wedge that belongs to it. The proverb in ver. 5 does not then stand as a restriction on the meaning of ver. 4 (as EWALD holds), but yet adjusting it, and guarding against what might be misunderstood in the former language. [Says ANDREW FULLER: The terms in the first instance mean "in a foolish manner," as is manifest from the reason given. In the second instance they mean "in the manner which his folly requires." This is also plain from the reason given. A foolish speech is not a rule for our imitation; nevertheless our answer must be so framed by it as to meet and repel it. "This knot will be easily loosed," says MUFFET, "if it be observed that there are two sorts of answers, the one in folly, the other unto folly." A]

Ver. 6. **He cutteth off the feet, he drinketh damage, who sendeth a message by a fool.** Comp. the two figurative expressions in clause *a*, the first ("he cutteth off the feet," *i. e.*, his own feet, *amputat sibi pedes*—MICHAELIS, SCHELLING, BERTHEAU, ELSTER, STIER, [KAMPH. WORDSW.] *etc.*,) means: he deprives himself of the means of attaining the end, he puts himself into a helpless condition; [and the idea is better expressed in this way than if we adopt the ex-

planation of H., N., S., M.; he acts as though he cut off the feet of his messenger who chooses a fool for the errand. N. errs in completing a proposition in clause *a*: "he that has his feet cut off drinks damage." A.] The second phrase "he drinketh injury or wrong," according to Job xxi. 20; xxxiv. 7, is equivalent to "he suffers abuses, he experiences in the largest measure an injury self-devised." For similar use of the term "words" in the sense of commands, directions, a message, comp. Ex. iv. 28; 2 Sam. xv. 36. For the general meaning compare like complaints of bad and foolish messengers in x. 26; xxv. 13.

Ver. 7. **Take away the legs from the lame.** The verb דליו appears to be used here with the meaning, which it is true is not to be discovered elsewhere, of *tollere*, to take away. For the meaning of the comparison, according to *b*, seems to be this: Always take from the lame his legs, (*i. e.*, his lame legs), *for they are really useless to him*, just as the "proverb," (*i. e.*, the maxim of wisdom, the Maschal) in the mouth of the fool is useless, something that might without loss be never there; for the fool is and continues still a fool (ver. 9; xii. 16; xiv. 24, *etc.*). Thus UMBREIT, BERTHEAU, STIER [STUART, KAMPH.] correctly explain, while the rest take some one and some one or other way to explain the peculiarly obscure and difficult דליו. So LUTHER takes the phrase altogether arbitrarily in the sense of "to dance" ("as dancing to a cripple, so does it befit a fool to speak of wisdom"); in like manner JARCHI and LEVI BEN GERSON ("his legs are too long for the lame." דליו being taken as equivalent to נבה), and also GEIER, ROSENM, J. H. MICHAELIS, SCHELLING, *etc.*, who take דליו as a substantive equivalent to דליות in the sense of *elevatio*. [The E. V. renders "the legs of the lame are not equal"]. EWALD and ELSTER read דליו, "the legs of the lame are too loose" (ABEN EZRA had already given a similar rendering) [GESEN., "hang down," so DE W., N., WORDSW.; "are weak," H. M.]. HITZIG finally gives the Inf. abs. דלילו: "leaping of the legs on the part of a lame man—so is a proverb in the mouth of a fool," (the same meaning, therefore, substantially as in LUTHER'S conception.)

Ver. 8. **As a bag of jewels on a heap of stones, so is he that giveth honor to a fool.** If the noun כְּצרור which occurs only here expresses the idea "heap of stones," *acervus lapidum*, which is altogether probable from its derivation from רגם, to stone, to heap up stones, then the צרור אבן must be a parcel not of common, but of precious stones (comp. Ex. xxviii. 9; xxxv. 27, where אבן alone stands for *lapis pretiosior*), and this all the more since the 2d clause makes this rendering peculiarly natural. So R. LEVI BEN GERSON, then LUTHER, GEIER, SCHULTENS, GESENIUS, UMBREIT, STIER, ELSTER. [E. V. in margin, DE W., N., W.].—of whom LUTHER, GEIER, SCHULTENS, STIER [WORDSW.] think particularly of a heap of stones raised by the stoning of a malefactor, a *tumulus aggestus supra corpus lapidatum*, which is certainly more natural than with

JEROME, (Vulg., *acervus Mercurii*), several of the early Rabbis, JARCHI, V. E. LÖSCHER (in the "*Unschuldigen Nachrichten*," Vol. 13, p. 496), and OETINGER, to think of a Hermes, a heap of stones dedicated to Mercury (λόφος ἑρμαῖον, *statua mercurialis*). Others (BERTHEAU, EWALD [FUERST, KAMPH., E. V., in text, H., S., M.] etc.,) following the LXX and Chald., take מַרְגֵּמָה in the sense of "sling," and regard צְרוֹר as an infin.; "as the binding a stone fast to the sling";—but against this may be maintained the inappositeness of the figure as compared with the idea in clause *b*, and the fact that such a meaning cannot be proved to belong to the noun, and the circumstance that the sling is elsewhere always called קֶלַע.—HITZIG: "as a little stone on the beam of a balance," *etc.*,—for he says the noun כִּי means, according to the Arabic, "the beam of a balance," and אֶן יַ signifies a "bit or kernel of stone," a little stone serving to bind the balance (?).

Ver. 9. **A thorny staff that riseth up in the hand of a drunkard, (so is) a (wise) proverb in the mouth of a fool.** If in ver. 7 a Maschal, a maxim of wisdom, taken into the mouth of a fool was represented as something useless, destitute of all aim and effect, it here appears rather as something working absolute harm, wounding, injuring like thorns, and in particular like an instrument of correction heedlessly carried, striking in the wrong place, and so grossly misused. Comp. LUTHER's marginal note, which in the main point certainly interprets correctly: when a drunkard carries and brandishes in his hand a sweet briar, he scratches more with it than he allows the roses to be smelled; so a fool with the Scriptures or a judicial maxim oft causes more harm than profit."—HITZIG following the LXX, reads in clause *b* מָשָׁל instead of מָשָׁל, and furthermore takes the verb of clause *a* in the sense of "to shoot up," and therefore renders: Thorns shoot up by (under) the hand of the hireling (?) and tyranny by the mouth of fools." But we do not need to give to the verb here even as a secondary meaning the sense of growing up (as EWALD, UMBREIT, STIER, propose), as the simple original meaning of rising up; raising itself gives a meaning in every way satisfactory. [The rendering of the E. V., H., W., "as a thorn goeth up into the hand," etc., wounding unconsciously, is less forcible every way than that of the author, with whom DEW., K., BERTHEAU, N., S., ML, etc., agree. A.]

Ver. 10. **An archer that woundeth everything** (for this meaning comp. רָב, "an archer or dartsman," comp. Jer. l. 29; Job xvi. 43; for the verb in this sense, Is. li. 9), **and he that hireth a fool, and he that hireth vagrants** ("passers by," *i. e.*, therefore untried, unreliable persons, who soon run away again)—are alike; one of the three is as foolish as another. This interpretation, which is followed by SCHELLING, EWALD, BERTHEAU, STIER, [DEW., KAMPH., and virtually S. and M.], involves it is true a certain hardness, especially in the relation of the figure in *a* to the two ideas in *b*; it corresponds best, however, with the simple literal meaning of the passage. LUTHER, GEIER, SEB. SCHMID, [N.,

WORDSW.] render: "A master formeth all aright," *magister format omnia recte;* in a similar way ELSTER: "An able man formeth all himself" (in contrast with the fool, who seeks to hire others, and even incompetent persons of all sorts, stragglers and vagrants, etc., to transact his business). [The E. V., which is followed against his will by HOLDEN, interprets the "master" as God: "the great God," etc.]. UMBREIT and HITZIO [with another common meaning of רָב]: "*Much* produceth *all*," as though the meaning were similar to that in the ὅστις ἔχει δοθήσεται αὐτῷ, Matt. xiii. 11; xxv. 20. Others read רַב instead of רָב. *e. g.*, the Vulg., *judicium determinat causas*, and of recent expositors ZIEGLER, etc.

Ver. 11. **As a dog that returneth to his vomit** (comp. the New Testament citation of this passage in 2 Pet. ii. 22) **so the fool** (ever) **repeateth his folly;** lit., "so comes the fool for the second time again with his folly," comp. xvii. 9. Here is plainly meant not merely a constantly renewed return to foolish assertions in spite of all the rational grounds adduced against them, but a falling again into foolish courses of action after brief endeavors or beginnings at improvement (comp. Matt. xii. 46; John v. 14; Heb. vi. 4-8.)

Ver. 12. **Seest thou a man wise in his own eyes,** *i. e.*, who holds himself as wise, and by this very blind over-estimate of himself thoroughly and forever bars for himself the way to true wisdom (comp. xxx. 12), like the Pharisees mentioned in John ix. 41, who gave it out that they saw, but were in truth stone-blind.— With *b* compare chap. xxix. 20, where this 2d clause recurs literally.

3. Vers. 13-16. Four proverbs against sloth.— Ver. 13. Comp. the almost identical proverb in chap. xxii. 13.—**A lion is in the way.** שַׁחַל a synonym of אֲרִי designates the lion as a *roaring* animal, as *rugiens sive rugitor;* it does not contrast the male lion with the lioness (Vulg.), or again the young lion with the full grown, (LUTHER).

Ver. 14. Comp. vi. 10; xxiv. 33. With this figure of the door ever turning on its hinges but never moving from its place comp. the well-known words of SCHILLER—"*dreht sich träg und dumm wie des Färber's Gaul im Ring herum*" [turns lazy and stupid like the dyer's nag round in its circle.]

Ver. 15. Comp. the almost identical proverb, chap. xix. 24.

Ver. 16.—**The sluggard is wiser in his own eyes.** (comp. ver. 12) **than seven men who give a wise answer.** The number seven stands here not because it is the sacred number, but to express the idea of plurality in a concrete and popular way. Comp. ver. 25; also vi. 31; xxiv. 16; Jer. xv. 9; 1 Sam. ii. 5; Ecclesiast. xxxvii. 14.—With this use of טַעַם "taste" in the sense of "understanding, judgment," comp. 1 Sam. xxi. 14; xxiii. 33; Ps. cxix. 66; Job xii. 20; also remarks above on Prov. xi. 22, where is denoted in addition a quality of the moral life. "To give back understanding" is naturally equivalent to giving an intelligent, wise answer, as a sign of an intelligent disposition; comp. xvii. 18.

4. Vers. 17-19. Against delight in strife and wilful provocation.—**He layeth hold on the ears of a dog** (and so provokes the animal outright to barking and biting) **who passing by is excited by strife that is not his,** lit., "over a dispute not for him" (comp. Hab. ii. 6). For the use of this verb "to provoke or excite one's self," comp. the remark on xx. 2. This כְּתִעַבֵּר with the Part. עָבֵר forms an alliteration or polyptoton which (with STIER) may be substantially reproduced in German: *"wer vorübergehend sich übergehen (sich die Galle überlaufen) lässt,"* etc. There is no occasion for HITZIG's assumption, that instead of כְּתִעַבֵּר there stood originally in the text the כְּתִעָרֵב which is expressed by the Syriac and Vulg.; " he who *meddleth* in strife," etc. [The E. V. has taken this doubtless under the influence of those early versions.]

Vers. 18, 19. **As a madman who casteth fiery darts, arrows and death.** The כְּמִתְלַהְלֵהַּ which occurs only here, signifies, according to SYMMACHUS, the Vers. Venet., and ABEN EZRA, one beside himself or insane (ἐξεστώς, πειρώμενος). For the combination of the three ideas, fiery darts, arrows and death (*i. e.* deadly missiles), comp. the similar grouping in xxv. 18 *a*.—**So the man that deceiveth his neighbor.** רִמָּה is to "deceive, to deal craftily," not to "afflict" (UMBREIT), or "overthrow" (VAN ESS). —**And** (then) **saith: Am I not in sport?** The meaning of the simple "and saith" the Vulgate paraphrases correctly when it renders: *"et cum deprehensus fuerit, dicit,"* etc. ["Quipping and flouting," says MUFFET, "is counted the flower and grace of men's speech, and especially of table talk; but the hurt that cometh by this flower is as bitter as wormwood, and the disgrace which this grace casteth upon men is fouler than any dirt of the street."—A.]

5. Vers. 20-28. Nine proverbs against malice and deceit.—**Where the wood faileth the fire goeth out,** *etc.* Comp. the Arabic proverb expressing the same idea, aimed at slander (in SCHEID, *Selecta,* p. 18): " He who layeth no wool on the fire keeps it from burning." For this description of the "slanderer" comp. xvi. 28.

Ver. 21. The direct opposite to the contents of the preceding verse.—**Coals to burning coals;** lit., black coals to burning coals. For the "man of contentions" in clause *b* comp. xxi. 9; xxvii. 15.

With ver. 22 compare the literally identical proverb xviii 8.

Ver. 23. **Silver dross spread over a potsherd.** "Silver of dross" is impure silver not yet properly freed from the dross, and therefore partly spurious (Vulg., *argentum sordidum*), and not some such thing as a glazing with the glitter of silver made of plumbago (*Lithargyrus*), and so imitation of silver, as many think, and as LUTHER seems to have expressed in his *"Silberschaum."* חֶרֶשׂ, potsherd (Isa. xliv. 11), seems to be used intentionally instead of כְּלִי־חֶרֶשׂ "an earthen vessel," to strengthen the impression of the worthlessness of the object named.—

(So are) **burning lips,** *i. e.* fiery protestations of friendship, or it may be warm kisses (which BERTHEAU understands to be the specific meaning), which in connection with a genuinely good heart on the part of the giver are a sign of true love, but with a "wicked heart" are on the contrary repulsive demonstrations of hypocrisy, without any moral worth (comp. the kiss of Judas, Matt. xxvi. 48 so.). It is unnecessary to read with HITZIG חֲלָקִים, "smooth lips," instead of דֹּלְקִים, "burning" lips.

Vers. 24, 25. **With his lips the hater dissembleth.** For the verb which may not here, as in xx. 11, be translated "is recognized" (so LUTHER, following the Chald. and Vulg.), comp. the Hithp. of נָכַר, which elsewhere expresses the idea of "dissembling," *e. g.* Gen. xlii. 7; 1 Kings xiv. 5, 6.—**And within he prepareth deceit.** Comp. Jer. ix. 7, and with שִׁית מִרְמָה "to set, contrive, prepare deceit," compare the "setting or preparing snares," Ps. cxl. 6.—**For seven abominations are in his heart.** See remarks above, on ver. 16, and comp. the seven devils of Matt. xii. 45, which represent an intensified power in present moral deformity. That there is a specific reference to the six or seven abominations mentioned in chap. vi. 16-19, is an arbitrary conjecture of ABEN EZRA.

Ver. 26. **Hatred is covered by deceit.** כְּשָׁאוֹן from נָשָׁא, "to deceive," is doubtless correctly understood by the LXX, when they express the idea by δόλος (comp. also the *fraudulenter* of the Vulg.); here it designates specifically "hypocrisy, the deception of friendly language used to one's face" (UMBREIT). The suffix in רָעָתוֹ refers then by an obvious *constructio ad sensum* to him who conceals his hatred in this hypocritical way. The second clause gives assurance then of the certain occurrence of an exposure of this flatterer "in the assembly," *i. e.* before the congregation of his people assembled for judgment, who perhaps through some judicial process that ends unfortunately for him come to the knowledge of his villanies. HITZIG partially following the LXX (ὁ κρύπτων ἔχθραν συνίστησι δόλον), renders: He who concealeth hatred, devising mischief (?), his vileness is exposed in the assembly."

Ver. 27. **He that diggeth a pit falleth into it.** Comp. Eccles. x. 8; Ecclusiast. xxvii. 26; Ps. ix. 16, and with respect to the "falling back of the stone that has been (wickedly) rolled " in clause *b*, comp. Ps. vii. 17; Matt. xxi. 44.

Ver. 28. **The lying tongue hateth those that are wounded by it.** If the reading דַּכָּיו is correct this may be the rendering, and the "crushed" (plural of דַּךְ [E. V. the oppressed], Ps. ix. 10; x. 18; lxxiv. 21), *i. e.* the bruised (or oppressed or wounded—see UMBREIT and STIER on this passage) of the lying tongue, are then those whom this tongue has bruised or wounded, the victims of its wickedness—and not those possibly whom it proposes to wound or oppress (UMBREIT, DE W., VAN ESS), or again those who wound, *i. e.* punish, it (*conterentes sive castigantes ipsam*—LUTHER, GEIER, GESENIUS),

Inasmuch, however, as the proposition is by no means universally and in every case true, that the lying tongue, or that detraction hates its own victims, and since besides the second clause seems to demand another sense, it might be justifiable to read with EWALD and HITZIG אֶוֶן, accordingly "the lying tongue hates *its own master*," *i. e.* it hurls him into calamity, brings him to ruin—a meaning which also corresponds admirably with ver. 27. [See Critical notes for the three chief explanations of the form and derivation of the word. The passive rendering has this advantage, that it makes the fourth instance correspond with the other three in which the word is used; this presumption must be decidedly overthrown. This we do not think is done; so the E. V., H., N., S., M., W., KAMPH., *etc.*—A.] For the noun rendered "offence," in clause *b*, comp., moreover, the cognate verb in clause *a* of xiv. 32.

DOCTRINAL, ETHICAL, HOMILETIC AND PRACTICAL.

It is mainly three forms of dishonorably and morally contemptible conduct, against which the condemning language of the proverbs in this section is directed; foolishness or folly in the narrower sense (vers. 1-12;) sloth (vers. 13-16); and a wicked maliciousness (vers. 17-28), which displays itself at one time as a wilful contentiousness and disposition to annoy (17-19), and at another as an artful calumniation and hypocritical slandering (20-28). Original ethical truths, such as have not appeared in previous chapters, are expressed only to a limited extent in the proverbs which relate to these vices. The novelty is found more in the peculiarly pointed and figurative form which distinguishes in an extraordinary degree the maxims of this chapter above others. Yet there are now and then essentially new ideas; what is said in ver. 2 of the futility of curses that are groundless; in vers. 4, 5 of uttering the truth staunchly to fools without becoming foolish one's self; in vers. 7 and 9 of the senselessness and even harmfulness of proverbs of wisdom in the mouth of a fool; in vers. 12 of the incapability of improvement in conceited fools who deem themselves wise; and finally in vers. 27, 28 of the self-destroying reflex power of malicious counsels formed against one's neighbor.

Homily on the chapter as a *whole* —Of three kinds of vices which the truly wise man must avoid: 1) folly; 2) sloth; 3) wicked artifice.—STÖCKER: What kinds of people are worthy of no honor: 1) fools; 2) sluggards or idlers; 3) lovers of contention and brawling.—STARKE: A (warning) lesson on folly, sloth and deceitfulness.

Vers. 1-6, *Würtemberg Bible* (on ver. 1):—Honor is a reward of virtue and ability; wilt thou be honored, then first become virtuous and wise!—MELANCHTHON (on ver. 2): As a consolation against all calumnies and unjust detraction the assurance of the divine word serves us,—that false (groundless) curses, though they momentarily harm and wound, yet in the end appear in their nothingness, and are cast aside, in accordance with the saying: truth may indeed be repressed for a time, but not perish (Ps. xciv. 15; 2 Cor. iv. 9). ["Truth crushed to earth shall rise again; the eternal years of God are hers."—LAWSON: The curses of such men instead of being prejudicial, will be very useful to us, if we are wise enough to imitate the conduct of David, whose meekness was approved, his prayers kindled into a flame of desires, and his hopes invigorated by them].—GEIER (on ver. 3): One may not flatter his own unruly flesh and blood, but must seek to keep it properly in check.—STARKE (on vers. 4, 5): Great wisdom is needful to meet the different classes of our adversaries in an appropriate way.—(On ver. 6): Important concerns one should commit to skilful and able servants.

Vers. 7-12. LUTHER (Marginal comment on ver. 7): Fools ought not to be wise and yet will be always affecting wisdom.—[TRAPP: If thy tongue speak by the talent, but those hands scarce work by the ounce, thou shalt pass for a Pharisee (Matt. xxiii. 3). They spake like angels, lived like devils; had heaven commonly at their tongue ends, but the world continually at their finger ends].—STARKE (on vers. 7, 9): He who will teach others in divine wisdom, must first have mastered it himself (Ecclesiast. xviii. 19); then he will not only teach with profit, but also have honor from it.—(On ver. 9): He who misuses God's word does himself thereby the greatest injury.—(On ver. 8): Beware of all flattering of the ungodly; for one prepares himself thereby but a poor reward.—(On ver. 10): As is the master so is the servant. Bad masters like bad servants.—(On vers. 11): If all relapses in sickness are dangerous, so much more relapses into old sins.—(On ver. 12): Self-pleasing and self-relaxation is the prolific mother of many other follies.—WOHLFARTH (on ver. 12): Let no one esteem himself perfect, but let every one strive for humility and cherish it as his most sacred possession.—[LAWSON (on ver. 8): But does not God Himself often give honor to fools? Yes. He is the judge of nations who has a right to punish men by subjecting them to the power of fools. We are to regulate our conduct not by His secret but His revealed will.—ARNOT (on ver. 11): When the unrenewed heart and the pollutions of the world are, after a temporary separation, brought together again, the two in their unholy wedlock become "one flesh." Man's true need—God's sufficient cure is "Create in me a clean heart, and renew a right spirit within me."—J. EDWARDS (on ver. 12): Those who are wise in their own eyes are some of the least likely to get good of any in the world.—BRIDGES: The natural fool has only one hindernace—his own ignorance. The conceited fool has two—ignorance and self-delusion].

Vers. 13-16. LANGE: That the weeds of sin are ever getting the upper hand as well in hearts as in the Church, comes from this, that men do not enough watch and pray, but only lounge, are idle and sleepy: 1 Thess. v. 6.—*Berleburg Bible:* The sluggard remains year in year out sitting on the heap of his self-chosen convenient Christianity, reads, hears, prays, sings in the Church year after year, and makes no progress, never comes to an inner complete knowledge of truth;

just as the door always remains in one place, although it turns this way and that the whole year through, and swings on its hinges. This slothfulness is the mother of all the doctrines which encourage the old Adam, and in the matter of sanctification throw out the "cannot," where it is a "will not" that hides behind.—WOHLFARTH: The sluggard's wisdom. Rest is to him the sole end of life; only in indolence does he feel happy, *etc.*

Vers. 17-19. STARKE (on ver. 17): To mix one's self in strange matters from forwardness and with no call, has usually a bad issue.—OSIANDER (on vers. 18, 19): In the sight of God the wantonness and wickedness of the heart are not hid; moreover He does not let them go unpunished.—ZELTNER: Crafty friends are much more dangerous and injurious than open enemies.—LANGE: It testifies of no small wickedness when one alleges quite innocent intentions in injuring another, and yet with all is only watching an opportunity to give him a blow.

Vers. 20-28. HASIUS (on vers. 20 sq.): There would not be so much dispute and strife among men if there were not so many base spirits who nourish and promote it in every way.—STANKE: Slanders and contentions are to be regarded as a flame to which one should not supply wood, but rather water to quench them.—[TRAPP (on ver. 23): Counterfeit friends are nought on both sides].—VON GERLACH (on ver. 26): Though a deceitful man may succeed in cheating individuals, yet this is not possible before the whole Church (Acts v. 1-11).—(On ver. 27): A hypocritical tongue if it has injured any one follows him still further with lies to defend itself, and so it causes universal confusion.

---

b) Against vain self-praise and presumption.

CHAP. XXVII.

(*With an admonition to prudence and frugality in agriculture: vers. 23-27*).

1 Boast not thyself of to-morrow,
  for thou knowest not what a day will bring forth.
2 Let another praise thee and not thine own mouth,
  a stranger and not thine own lips.
3 Stone is heavy and sand weighty;
  the fool's wrath is heavier than them both.
4 Anger is cruel and wrath is outrageous;
  but who can stand before jealousy?
5 Better is open rebuke
  than secret love.
6 Faithful are the wounds of a friend,
  but the kisses of an enemy are deceitful.
7 The satisfied soul loatheth a honeycomb;
  to a hungry soul every bitter thing is sweet.
8 As a bird that wandereth from her nest
  so is a man that wandereth from his home.
9 Oil and perfume rejoice the heart,
  but the sweetness of a friend is better than one's own counsel.
10 Thine own friend and thy father's friend forsake not;
  and into thy brother's house enter not in the day of thy calamity;
  better is a neighbor that is near than a brother far off.
11 Be wise, my son, and make my heart glad,
  that I may know how to give an answer to him that reproacheth me.
12 The prudent man seeth the evil (and) hideth himself;
  the simple pass on and are punished.
13 Take his garment, for he hath become surety for a stranger,
  and on account of a strange woman put him under bonds!
14 He that blesseth his friend with a loud voice early in the morning,
  let it be reckoned a curse to him!

15 A continual dropping in a very rainy day
   and a contentious woman are alike.
16 He that will restrain her restraineth the wind,
   and his right hand graspeth after oil.
17 Iron sharpeneth iron;
   so doth a man sharpen the face of his friend.
18 Whosoever watcheth the fig-tree eateth its fruit,
   and he that hath regard to his master is honored.
19 As in water face (answereth) to face
   so the heart of man to man.
20 Hell and destruction are never full,
   and the eyes of man are not satisfied.
21 The fining pot is for silver and the furnace for gold,
   but man according to his glorying.
22 Though thou bruise a fool in a mortar
   among grain with a pestle,
   his folly will not depart from him.
23 Thou shalt know well the face of thy sheep;
   direct thy mind to thine herds;
24 for riches are not forever,
   and doth the crown endure forevermore?
25 The grass disappeareth, and the tender grass is seen,
   and the herbs of the mountains are gathered.
26 Lambs (are) for thy clothing
   and the price of thy field (is) goats;
27 and abundance of goat's milk for thy food, for the food of thine house,
   and subsistence for thy maidens.

GRAMMATICAL AND CRITICAL.

Ver. 4. אַכְזְרִיּוּת is used here only in the Old Testament.

Ver. 5. טוֹבָה is regarded by BÖTT. (§ 1133, 1 and n 3) as the 3d sing. fem. of the verb and not as the fem. of the adj.; the chief evidence being found in the participles following, which, according to Hebrew usage, more naturally follow a finite verb.—A.]

Ver. 9. [In רֵעֵהוּ we have one of the examples found in Hebrew in connection with words in wide and frequent use, in which the suffix loses all distinct and specific application; comp. in modern languages *Monsieur, Madonna, Mynherr*, etc.; therefore *one's* friend, a friend, and not *his* friend. BÖTT, § 876, c. עֵץ is regarded by GESEN., FUERST, DÖDERLEIN, DATHE, etc., as a fem. of עֵץ used collectively; the meaning in connection with נֶפֶשׁ is then, "more than fragrant wood." BÖTT. (§ 643, δ) pronounces all the examples cited in the lexicons for this use of the noun "more than doubtful;" and, as the exegetical notes show, nearly all commentators give to עֵץ its ordinary meaning.—A.]

Ver. 10. [רֵעֶה is one of three nouns whose full and original form appears only in the *stat. constr.*; the K'ri therefore points as though the *absol.* were used רֵעַ, while the K'thibh exhibits the form רֵעֶה. See GREEN, § 215, 1, e; BÖTT. §§ 721, 9; 794, Pect. IV.—A.]

Ver. 11. [וְאָשִׁיבָה an Intentional, or paragogic Imperf., connected to Imperatives by ו used as a final conjunction, "in order that;" BÖTT. § 965, B, c. And let me—that I may.—A.]

Ver. 14. הַשְׁכֵּם, an Infin. abs. used adverbially, as in Jer. xxv. 4; here on account of the pause written with ־ֵ instead of simple ־ַ.

Ver. 15. On the question whether נִשְׁתָּוָה is to be accented and explained as a 3d pers. Nithpaal, or whether, with KIMCHI, NORZI, and the most recent editors and expositors, we should point the form as Milel [with penultimate accent], and accordingly regard it as perhaps a voluntative Hithpael, with the ה_ of motion (therefore "let us compare"), consult BERTHEAU, STIER and HITZIG on the passage. [GESEN., Röd. (GESEN. *Thes.*, p. 1376, add. p. 114), FUERST, etc., make the form a Nithpaal; BÖTT. (§§ 474, 4, a and 1072, θ) agrees with HITZIG in making it a simple Niphal with a different transposition of consonants, and argues at length for this view. FUERST pronounces the form participial, in opposition to nearly all lexicographers and commentators who make it 21 sing. fem. GESEN. and some others, following Chaldee analogies, ren [lered], "are to be feared." RÖDIGER (*ubi supra*) and most others render, "are esteemed alike," or "are alike." Comp. also EWALD, *Lehrb.* § 132, d; GREEN, § 83, (2).—A.]

Ver. 16. קרא = קרה, according to an interchange which is common of א with ה. [In clause a we have a singular verb following a plural participle taken distributively as in xxii. 21; xxv. 13, *etc.*—A.]

Ver. 17. יָחַד is best regarded, as GEIER, BERTHEAU and STIER take it, as an Imperf. apoc. Hiphil from חרה = חדד "to sharpen." EWALD, ELSTER, *etc.*, needlessly take the first יָחַד in clause a as a Hophal: יֻחַד (comp. the Vulg. *exacuitur*) and would have only the second recognized as a Voluntative Hiphil (to be pointed יָחֵד or יָחֶד). [BÖTT. § 1124, β, insists that the Masoretic forms can be regarded as nothing but the ordinary adverb "together," and that the pointing must be changed to יַחַד, יָחַד, or יָחֵד, יָחֶד. GREEN, § 140, 1, makes it a simple Kal Imperf. FUERST regards it as a Niphhal

Imperf., no change of vocalization being required, although the more common form would be יֵחַד. RÜD. (Thes. GESEN, Ind. pp. 5, 88) regards the form as an apoc. Hiphil. for the more common יַחַד, used impersonally, "one sharpens, men sharpen."—A.]

Ver. 20. The parallel passage xv. 11 (see notes on this passage) shows that instead of אֲבַדֹּה (or again instead of אֲבֵדָה) we should read with the K'ri אֲבַדּוֹן, or that we should at least assume a transition of this latter form into the former, in the way of lexical decay (as in בְּגָדִי for בְּגָדוֹן). [BÖTT. (§§ 262, a; 293) notes this as a tendency in proper nouns, aided perhaps in the case before us by the following liquid.—A.]

Ver. 21. [בֹּעֵל, Instead of the more regular בֹּעֵל, mimetically sharpened in its vocalization at the end of its clause. See BÖTT., §§ 394, b; 409, 6.—A.]

Ver. 25. [עֲשְׂבוֹת with Dagesh dirimens or separative, indicating the vocal nature of the Sheva. See, e. g. GREEN § 24, b; 216, 2, a.—A.]

EXEGETICAL.

1. Vers. 1-6. Three pairs of proverbs, directed against self-praise, jealousy and flattery.

Vers. 1, 2. **Boast not thyself of to-morrow**, i. e., "do not throw out with proud assurance high-soaring schemes for the future" (ELSTER); do not boast of future undertakings as if they had already succeeded and were assured.—**For thou knowest not what a day will bring forth**; i. e., what a day, whether it be to-day or to-morrow, will bring in new occurrences, is absolutely unknown to thee. Comp. James iv. 13-15; also HORACE, Od., iv. 7, 17: Quis scit an adjiciunt hodiernæ crastina summæ Tempora Di superi?—

["Who knows if they who all our fates control
Will add a morrow to thy brief to-day?"
THEO. MARTIN'S TRANSLATION.]

and SENECA, Thyest. V. 619; Nemo tam divos habuit faventes Crastinum ut possit polliceri [No one has had the gods so favorable that he can promise himself a morrow].—With ver. 2 comp. the German Eigenlob stinkt, and Arabic proverbs like "Not as mother says, but as the neighbors say" (FUERST, Perlenschnüre, ii. 8), or "Let thy praise come from thy friend's and kinsman's mouth, not from thine own" (MEIDANI, p. 467.)

Vers. 3, 4.—**Stone is heavy and sand weighty**, lit., "weight of stone and heaviness of the sand." HITZIG fitly remarks with respect to the genitive combinations of this as well as the succeeding verse ("Cruelty of anger, etc.") "The genitive relation holding a figure before our eye instead of developing it in a proposition, possesses nevertheless the value of a combination of predicate and subject." [So K., W., etc., while S. and others make the relation directly that of subject and predicate].—**The fool's wrath**, i. e., probably not: the vexation and anger occasioned in others by the fool (COCCEIUS, SCHULTENS, BERTHEAU, [S.], etc.), but the annoyance and ill-humor experienced by himself, whether it may have originated in envy, or in a chafing against some correction that he has received, etc. Such ill-temper in the fool is a burden, heavier than stone and sand, and that too a burden for himself, but beyond this also for those who must besides suffer under it, whom he makes to feel in common and innocently his ill-will and temper.—**Anger is cruel and wrath is outrageous**, lit., "cruelty of anger and inundation of wrath." With regard to the genitives, compare remarks above on vs. 3, a. For the expression "overflowing of wrath" or "excess, outrageousness of wrath," comp. Is. xxx. 28, 30; Dan. ix. 27; xi. 22.—קִנְאָה in clause b, often "envy," is plainly "jealousy," as in vi. 34, 35, which passage is here to be compared in general.

Vers. 5, 6. **Better is open rebuke** (open, undisguised censure, honorably expressing its meaning) **than secret love**, i. e., than love which from false consideration dissembles, and does not name to one's neighbor his faults even where it should do so. Compare the ἀληθεύειν ἐν ἀγάπῃ, Eph. iv. 15, as well as the numerous parallels in classic authors (PLAUTUS, Trinummus, I. 2, 57; CICERO, Læl. 25; SENECA, Epist. 25); and MEIDANI, II. 64: "Love lasts long as the censure lasts," etc.—**Faithful** (lit. true, coming from a true disposition) **are the wounds of a friend, but deceitful are the kisses of an enemy.** נֶעְתָּרוֹת, from the root עָתַר, is if this be identical with עָשַׁר, largus fuit, as is generally assumed, equivalent to "plentiful" (comp. עָשִׁיר), in which case we must think of kisses "liberally bestowed but faithless," or it may be kisses "to be lightly esteemed" (so GESEN., UMBREIT, BERTHEAU, STIER [FUERST, S., W.]) And yet it corresponds better with the parallelism, as well as with the exegetical tradition (Vulg., fraudulenta), to derive from an Arabic root عثر to stumble (σφάλλειν, fallere, therefore falsus, false—so EWALD, ELSTER, etc.), or it may be from غدر = עדר in the sense of "to miss"—thus HITZIG,—both of which modes of explanation give the idea "deceptive, crafty, treacherous." With regard to the meaning compare, therefore, chap. xxvi. 23.

2. Vers. 7-14. Eight proverbs in praise of contentment, of friendship, prudence, etc.

Ver. 7. **A satisfied soul loatheth honey comb.** The verb literally means "tramples, treads under feet," comp. Dan. vii. 10; Judg. v. 21.—With clause b compare the German proverb "Hunger is the best cook;" and also Ecclesiast. iv. 2.

Ver. 8. **So is a man that roameth far from his dwelling-place.** As the preceding proverb is directed against a want of contentment in the department of food and drink, so is this against weariness of one's own home, against adventurous wandering impulses, and a restless roving without quiet domestic tastes. Comp. Ecclesiast. xxix. 28, 29; xxxvi. 28.

Ver. 9. With clause a compare Ps. civ. 15;

cxxxiii. 2.—**But the sweetness of a friend is better than one's own counsel.** The "sweetness" of the friend is according to xvi. 21 doubtless sweetness of the lips, the pleasing, agreeable discourse of the friend (lit. "of his friend;" the suffix stands indefinitely, with reference *i. e.* to every friend that a man really has; here with especial reference to the possessor of the נֶפֶשׁ). See also the critical notes. The מֵעֲצַת is best taken in the sense of comparison (with JARCHI, LEVI, COCCEIUS, UMBREIT, STIER): "better than counsel of the soul," *i. e.*, better than one's own counsel, better than that prudence which will help itself and relies purely on its own resources (comp. xxviii. 26). EWALD, ELSTER (in like manner also LUTHER, GEIER, DE WETTE [K., N.], *etc.*,) render: "The sweetness of the friend springeth from (faithful) counsel of soul," which is understood as describing the genuineness and the hearty honesty of the friend's disposition. BERTHEAU gives a similar idea, except that he supplies in *b* from *a* the predicate with its object: "The sweetness of a friend from sincere counsel maketh glad the heart" (?); [this is very nearly the conception of the E. V., H., S., M.]. HITZIG following the καταρρήγνυται δὲ ὑπὸ συμπτωμάτων ἡ ψυχή of the LXX, amends so as to read: "but the soul is rent with cares." [See critical notes for still other expositions of the phrase.]

Ver. 10. **Thine own friend and thy father's friend forsake not.** Whether one read with the K'ri רֵעֵ֨ךָ or with the K'thibh the *stat. constr.* of the emphatic form [or according to others the primitive form—see critical notes], in any event together with the friend of the person addressed "his father's friend" is also named, but as an identical person with the former, who, for that reason, has a value proportionally greater, and may so much the less be neglected, because he is as it were an heirloom of the family of long tried fidelity and goodness.—**And into thy brother's house enter not in the day of thy calamity.** HITZIG, who explains the three clauses of this verse as originally separate propositions, only "afterward forced together," fails to see a logical connection as well between *a* and *b* as between *b* and *c*. This is in fact in the highest degree arbitrary, for the common aim of the three members: to emphasize the great value of true friendship and its pre-eminence in comparison with a merely external relationship of blood, comes out to view as clearly as possible. The "near" neighbor is he who keeps himself near as one dispensing counsel and help to the distressed, just as the "far off" brother is he who, on account of his unloving disposition, keeps at a distance from the same. [Our commentators have in general agreed substantially with this conception of the scope of the verse.—A.].

Ver. 11. **Be wise, my son, and make my heart glad,** *etc.* Evidently an admonition of a fatherly teacher of wisdom addressed to his pupil (comp. i. 8 sq.; xxii. 21; xxiii. 15),—perhaps of the same one to whom the wise counsel of the preceding verse in regard to conduct toward friends likewise belonged.—**That I may know how to give an answer to him that reproacheth me** (literally, "and so will I then return a word to my reviler"), *i. e.*, in order that I, pointing to thy wise and exemplary conduct, may be able to stop the mouth of him who reviles me, the responsible teacher. Comp. Ps. cxix. 42; also cxxvii. 5; Ecclesiast. xxx. 2 sq.

Ver. 12. In almost literal accordance with xxii. 3.

Ver. 13. Almost exactly like xx. 16 (comp. notes on this passage.)

Ver. 14. **He that blesseth his friend with a loud voice early in the morning.** These words are directed against a friend who is flattering and profuse in compliment, but inwardly insincere; who, by his congratulations, hasty, and offered with boisterous ostentation, brings, instead of a real blessing to his friend, only a curse upon his house, at least in the general judgment of the people. For of them we must think in clause *b* as those who are to "reckon." For this last verb and its construction, "reckoning something to some one," comp. Gen. xv. 6. [This insincere and untimely praise may be accredited to its giver as no better than a curse in his intention, or more positively it may be regarded as veiling an evil intent, and so threatening an actual curse to him who is its object.—A.].

3. Vers. 15, 16. Two maxims concerning a contentious woman.—**A continual dropping in a very rainy day** (according to the Arabic כָּגְרִיר denotes "a rain poured as if out of buckets," and so "a pouring rain;" moreover the word occurs only here), **and a contentious woman are alike.** Like this, only more concise, is chap. xix. 13, *b*. [The peculiar force of this comparison to one who has been in the rainy season under the flat earthy roofs of Oriental houses, is commented on and illustrated, *e. g.*, in HACKETT'S *Scripture Illustrations*, p. 85, and THOMSON'S *Land and Book*, 1. 453. A.]—**He that will restrain her restraineth the wind** (צָפַן literally "to shut out, dam up, confine"), **and his right hand graspeth after oil,** *i. e.*, it grasps after something, encounters an object, seeks to retain something that is necessarily continually eluding it. [The idea of hiding her disagreeable and vexatious disposition from the view of others, which is expressed by the E. V., H., W., in both clauses, and by N. and M. in the second, is less appropriate and forcible than that given in the version of our author, K., S., *etc.*—A.].

4. Vers. 17-22. Six proverbs against haughtiness, selfishness, a greedy eye, self-praise and folly.—**Iron sharpeneth iron,** lit. iron to iron maketh sharp, or according to others, "iron is made sharp by iron,"—see critical notes]. **So doth a man sharpen the face of his friend.** Whether we render פְּנֵי by "face, look," or (as HITZIG maintains) by "edge, *acies ingenii*," the mental keenness," in either case the meaning is not: "One enrages, provokes the other" (STIER and in like manner BERTHEAU), but: One stimulates the other, polishes himself by mutual spiritual contact and friction with his fellow, contributes by such an interchange of one's own peculiarities with those of his fellow to the spiritual development of both (compare especially ELSTER and HITZIG on the passage). ["Conference hath incredible profit in all sciences," observes TRAPP. "A man by himself," says MUFFET, "is no man,

he is dull, he is very blunt; but if his fellow come and quicken him by his presence, speech, and example, he is so whetted on by this means that he is much more comfortable, skilful, and better than he was when he was alone." So most of our commentators, while STUART, and NOYES with a qualification, would find the idea of provocation, not as though anger were even indirectly commended, but " if men must enter into contest, let the antagonists be worthy of the strife" (S.): an exposition far weaker as well as more unnatural than the ordinary one.—A.].

Ver. 18. With the general proposition in a comp. xii. 11; xxviii. 19.—**And he that hath regard to his master is honored.** The honor which the master (*i. e.*, any master whatever, and not God especially, the master of all, as STIER holds) confers upon his faithful servant resembles the fruit which the fig tree yields to the proprietor or tenant who carefully cultivates it. "To regard one," *colere aliquem*, as in Ps. xxxi. 7; Hos. iv. 10.

Ver. 19. As (in) **water face** (answereth) **to face, so the heart of man to man.** פָּנִים, an accusative of place: "as in water," EWALD, § 221. The meaning will be like that of ver. 17, somewhat such as this: "As the mirror of the water reflects the likeness of one's own face, so one's heart is mirrored in that of his fellow, if one only has courage and penetration enough to look deeply into this " (EWALD; comp. STIER and BERTHEAU). There is contained in this at the same time an admonition to the wise testing and examination both of one's own heart and that of our fellow-men; or, the recommendation of a comprehensive knowledge of men, to be gained by thorough knowledge of one's self. The Vulgate already gives essentially the right idea: "*Quomodo in aquis resplendent vultus respicientium, sic corda hominum manifesta sunt prudentibus;*" while several other ancient expositors, whom ELSTER to some extent follows, find expressed in the passage a relation too exclusively ethical, *viz.*, that of arousing by love a reciprocal love, or that of the practical maxim, "*Si vis amari, ama*" [" Love if you would be loved "].—HITZIG thinks that clause *a* כַּמַּיִם must be the reading instead of כְּפָנִים: "What a mole on the face is to the face, that is man's heart to man," *viz.*, his disfiguring mole, his dark spot, his *partie honteuse* in the sense of Gen. viii. 21 (?). [Among our English expositors the mirror and the mirrored object have been somewhat variously understood; some retain while others dismiss the specific idea of reflection that is suggested by clause *a*. MUFFET and HOLDEN, *e. g.*, make a man's own heart the mirror in which he may truly know himself; WORDSW. makes the mirror the hearts of others on whom we act; while the great majority make the reflected object the oneness, especially the moral oneness of human nature, as discoverable from any heart into which we may look (so *e. g.*, BP. HALL, TRAPP, LAWSON, BRIDGES, S. and M.)—A.].

Ver. 20. **Hell and destruction are never** full [*i. e.*, not the world of the lost, but the world of the dead]. The meaning of clause *b* as indicated by this parallel in *a* cannot be doubtful. It relates to the really demoniacal insatiableness of human passion, especially the "lust of the eyes;" comp. 1 John ii. 16; James iii. 6; and in particular Prov. xxx. 16; Eccles. i. 8.

Ver. 21. With *a* compare the literally identical language in chap. xvii. 3 *a*.—**But man according to his glorying,** *i. e.*, one is judged according to the standard of that of which he makes his boast (the noun to be taken not in a subjective, but in an objective sense, of the object of one's glorying). If his boast is of praiseworthy things, then he is recognized as a strong, true man, *etc.* ; if he glories in trivial or even of evil things, he is abhorred; comp. above ver. 2. Thus EWALD, BERTHEAU, HITZIG, [K.], while the majority (the LXX, Vulg., LUTHER, *etc.*, also UMBREIT, STIER, ELSTER, *etc.*), translate the second clause: "so is man for the mouth of his praise," *i. e.*, for the mouth of the one that praises him [testing the nature and worth of the praise that is bestowed]—to which the figure in clause *a* can be made to correspond only by a considerably forced interpretation. [Here again among the English expositors who adopt this general idea, making the praise objective, there is diversity in carrying out the details. Is man the crucible or is he the object tested? N. and W. take the former view, according to which man tests or should test with careful discrimination the praise bestowed upon him; H., S. and M. take the other view, by which the praise is represented as testing him and disclosing his real character in the effects which it produces upon him.—A.].

Ver. 22. **Though thou bruise a fool in a mortar among grain** (" grains of wheat;" the word is used only here and in 2 Sam. xvii. 19), **with a pestle,** *etc.* The meaning of this proverb, which has at least its humorous side, is plain; lack of reason is to such a degree the very substance of the fool, is so intertwined in his inward and outward nature, that one might divide him into atoms without eradicating thereby this fundamental character of his. This idea is not so clearly connected with the preceding verse by its substance as by the similarity of the figures employed in the two (the crucible and the mortar); comp. HITZIG on the passage.

5. Vers. 23-27. Admonition to a prudent and frugal economy in connection with agricultural possessions.— **Thou shalt know well** (Z. "make thyself well acquainted with ") **the face of thy sheep.** "The look of the sheep" (comp. Gen. xxx. 40), *i. e.*, its condition and thrift.

Ver. 24. **For riches are not forever**—*viz.*, the supply of subsistence, on the abundant presence of which the good appearance of the flock depends above all things else.—**And doth the crown endure forevermore?** The question introduced by this interrogative (אִם) expresses the idea of a very strong negation, standing as a climax to the preceding: and even the crown, the royal diadem, has no perpetual existence. The נֵזֶר seems not to designate the metal of itself that composes the king's crown, but the kingly dignity and authority represented by it; the expression "from generation to generation " plainly indicates this. HITZIG's rendering is as trivial as it is contrary to the *usus loquendi:* that נֵזֶר means "grass, fodder" (because it sometimes signifies the hair of the head, and may therefore designate the herbage as a hairlike ornament to the earth!).

Ver. 25. **The grass disappeareth,** *etc.*; a reason for the admonition contained in the preceding verse, that one should be intent upon laying up ample supplies of nourishment for the flocks. The discourse passes over in vers. 25-27 to a richly diversified description of the beauty and abundance of rural nature, reminding us of Ps. lxv. 10-14, but in its present connection having this aim,—to show how God's creation liberally rewards the labor bestowed upon it by the active and industrious landlord. Neither this concluding picture, nor the entire passage from ver. 23 onward can be interpreted in some allegorical way (with various ancient expositors, SCHULTENS and STIER), and be applied to the conduct of the spiritual, pastoral office of the teacher of wisdom. As the utmost that is admissible this conception may have a place under certain conditions in the practical and homiletic treatment of the passage. [WORDSW. characteristically makes much of the secondary import of these verses.—A.].

Ver. 26. **And goats (as) price for the field;** *i. e.*, goats of such value that for each one a piece of arable land might be exchanged.

Ver. 27. **Abundance also of goat's milk . . . for subsistence for thy maidens.** חיים (with which we must repeat לְ from the preceding) "and life" is here equivalent to "substance, nourishment." Female servants, maidens, waiting women, were wanting in no large household among the Hebrews, not even in the royal palace and the temple; comp. 2 Sam. iv. 6; 1 Sam. ii. 22 sq. Here we must naturally think first of shepherdesses, milkmaids, *etc.*

DOCTRINAL AND ETHICAL, HOMILETIC AND PRACTICAL.

Modesty, contentment and prudence are the central ideas about which we may group the practical instructions of the section just expounded, if not in all their items at least in large measure. Especially may we throw under these categories what is said of the necessity of avoiding all vain self-praise, and of boasting in an inconsiderate extravagant way neither of our own prosperity nor of our neighbor's (vers. 1, 2, 14, 21); in like manner that which relates to the duty of moderation in ill temper and jealousy, in sensual enjoyments, in love of restless wandering and of sight-seeing (vers. 3, 4, 7, 8, 20); and not less, finally, the admonition which recurs in manifold transformations to a general prudence in life, as it should be exhibited in social and business intercourse with others, and in the diligent discharge of the domestic duties of one's calling (vers. 11, 13, 17-19, 23-27). If so inclined we might reckon among these commendations of an all-embracing practical wisdom even the warning against the contentiousness of a bad woman (ver. 15, 16), as well as the encomiums upon a genuine, unfeigned friendship, in vers. 5, 6, 9, 10; and in these especially, and above all in the command (ver. 10): to regard the love of a true friend more highly than the bonds of relationship of blood,—an injunction which reminds us of expressions in the New Testament, such as Matth. x. 37; xii. 48-50, we might see the very climax, and the main theme of the discourse of wisdom which constitutes this chapter. Over against this counsel, to give to the love of a true friend the preference above all vain passions and selfish interests, we have presented in a significant way the evidence which establishes the sad truth, that the fool is not disposed at any price to let go his selfish, vain, arrogant nature (ver. 22), in connection with which fact allusion is made to the natural corruption of human hearts in general and to the necessity for their being given up to the delivering and renewing influences of divine grace (comp. ver. 11).

Homily on the chapter as a whole: "Godliness with contentment is great gain" (1 Tim. vi. 6).—Or, boast neither of thy prosperity, nor of thy deeds, nor of any earthly and human advantages whatsoever, but only of the Lord (1 Cor. i. 31).—STÖCKER: Of conceit and vain presumption as a first and main hinderance to the progress of true wisdom (comp. besides comments on chapters xxviii. and xxix).—*Calwer Handbuch:* Of the means of attaining true honor.

Ver. 1-6. MELANCHTHON (on verse 1): That which is necessary and first demanded by our duty we must do before all else, conscientiously, and with appeals for divine help, lest in reliance upon our own strength or on foolish hopes we undertake needless and futile things.—STARKE: He walks the more cautiously who always considers that to-day may be the day of his death (James iv. 13 sq.; Ecclesiast. vii. 40).—Comp. the New Year's Sermon by RÖHR (*Sonntagsfeier,* 1844, No. 15): "The high and weighty import that each year of life has for us."—[J. EDWARDS: Not depending on another day, is a different thing from concluding that we shall not live another day. We ought not to behave ourselves in any respect as though we depended on another day.—ARNOT: This proverb contains only the negative side of the precept; but it is made hollow for the very purpose of holding the positive promise in its bosom. The Old Testament sweeps away the wide-spread indurated error; the New Testament then deposits its saving truth upon the spot.—A. FULLER (on verse 2): A vain man speaks well of himself; and Paul speaks well of himself. The *motive* in the one case is desire of applause; in the other justice to an injured character, and to the Gospel which suffered in his reproaches.—BP. HOPKINS: The tongue is of itself very apt to be lavish when it hath so sweet and pleasing a theme as a man's own praise].—*Tübingen Bible:* Self-praise is a sign of great pride, and must be in the highest degree offensive to the wise man when he has to hear it.—GEIER (on verses 3, 4): If even the pious man may easily transgress in his anger, how much more easily the ungodly!—LANGE (on vers. 5, 6): He who truly loves his neighbor is bound, when the occasion presents itself, to persuade, admonish and warn him; Ps. cxli. 5; Gal. vi. 1.—WOHLFARTH (on vers. 5, 6, 9, 10): Moral perfection the highest aim and blessing of true friendship.—VON GERLACH: A rebuke before the whole world is better than a love that proves itself by nothing, that only flatters in connection with a neighbor's faults.—[LORD

BACON: This proverb rebukes the mistaken kindness of friends who do not use the privilege of friendship freely and boldly to admonish their friends as well of their errors as their dangers.]

Ver. 8 sq. MELANCTHON (on ver. 8): Solomon here warns against our forsaking our lawful calling from weariness; Eph. iv. 1; 1 Cor. vii. 20.—LUTHER (marginal comment on ver. 8): Let no assault drive thee from thy calling; hold fast, and God will make thee prosper.—LANGE: By discontent with one's position and calling one only doubles his need, and sins grossly against God's holy providence.—[MUFFET: The wandering person is hated and despised by all; none honoreth his kindred, none regardeth his beauty, none careth for him, and none feareth to hurt him.—JOHN HOWE (on ver. 10): If it be an indecency, and uncomeliness, and a very unfit thing, that is, contrary to the precept of studying whatsoever is lovely, and thinking of those things, to forsake my friend and my father's friend, how much more horrid must it be to forsake my God and my father's God!]—STARKE (on vers. 9, 10): God is the best of all friends; strive with great care, that thou mayest obtain God's favor and friendship, and thou mayest never lose them.—VON GERLACH: Union of spirit with an old family friend from the father down is to be much preferred to mere relationship of blood.—[T. ADAMS (on ver. 12): The fool goes, he runs, he flies; as if God that rides upon the wings of the wind should not overtake him. Haste might be good if the way were good, and good speed added to it, but this is the shortest way out of the way. He need not run fast: the fool may come soon enough to that place from whence he must never return].

Ver. 14. sq. LUTHER (marginal comment on ver. 14): He who reproves much praises, and he who praises much censures; for they are not believed because they go too far.—*Tübingen Bible:* Too much praised is half censured. Trust not the flatterer who praises thee to excess.—[BP. HOPKINS: Let all thy reproofs be given as secretly and privately as thou canst; otherwise thou wilt seem not so much to aim at thy brother's reformation, as at his shame and confusion.—LORD BACON: Moderate praise used with opportunity, and not vulgar, is that which doeth the good.—ARNOT (on ver. 17): One half of the human faculties are framed for maintaining intercourse with men, and one half of the divine law is occupied with rules for regulating it].—MELANCTHON: Let us recognize our weakness, and see that the individual man is ignorant of much, errs and stumbles, and . . . . that God has furnished us men with the power of speech chiefly for this, that one may befriend another with counsel and instruction.—ZELTNER: The pious should arouse one another, and stimulate to all good works (Heb. x. 24), and that too in all circumstances.—GEIER (on ver. 18): Faithful labor and diligence find at length their rich reward—if not from men, at least from God; Heb. vi. 10.

Ver. 19 sq. LUTHER (marginal comment on ver. 19): As the outline in water trembles and is uncertain, so also are hearts. The lesson is: Trust not!—[BP. HOPKINS: In the world we see our own hearts unbowelled; and there we can learn what ourselves are at the cost of other men's sins].—LUTHER (on ver. 21): He who loves to hear himself praised is easily deceived: for he proves thereby that he is a reckless man who values his honor above all right.—STARKE (on ver. 21): If thou art praised, let it serve thee as a test, a humiliation, and a profit.—LANGE (on ver. 22): The urging and chastisement of the law makes no one pious, and does not change the heart. The power of the Gospel must change and renew the hard heart.—VON GERLACH: No outward cure helps at all where the inward part is obstinately corrupt.

Vers. 23-27. STARKE: Let every one labor diligently in his calling, let him indeed bring everything to counsel, and be thoroughly systematic in his actions.—GEIER: If it be important carefully to guard and to cherish silly sheep, oh, how much more Christ's sheep, the souls which He has redeemed with His precious blood! Acts xx. 28.—WOHLFARTH: The husbandman's prosperity (a sermon for a harvest thanksgiving).—VON GERLACH: To persevere is as needful as to acquire in every kind of possession.—[LAWSON: God's bounty is a great encouragement to our industry].

---

c) Against unscrupulous, unlawful dealing (especially of the rich with the poor).

CHAP. XXVIII.

1 The wicked flee when no man pursueth,
   but the righteous are bold as a lion.
2 In the rebellion of a land its princes become many,
   but through wise, prudent men one (the prince) continueth long.
3 A man who is poor and oppresseth the lowly
   is (like) a rain flooding and (bringing) no food.
4 They that forsake the law praise the wicked,
   but they that keep the law contend with them.

5 Evil men understand not judgment,
   but they that seek Jehovah understand all.
6 Better (is) a poor man that walketh in his uprightness,
   than he that walketh in crooked ways and is rich.
7 He that keepeth the law is a wise son,
   but the companion of profligates causeth his father shame.
8 He that increaseth his wealth by interest and usury
   gathereth it for one that pitieth the poor.
9 He that turneth away his ear from hearing the law,
   even his prayer is an abomination.
10 He that leadeth the righteous astray in an evil way,
   in his own pit shall he fall;
   but the upright shall inherit good.
11 The rich man thinketh himself wise,
   but a poor man that hath understanding searcheth him out.
12 When righteous men exult there is great glory,
   but when wicked men arise the people hide themselves.
13 He that hideth his sins shall not prosper,
   but he that confesseth and forsaketh them shall find mercy.
14 Happy is the man that feareth always;
   but he that hardeneth his heart shall fall into evil.
15 A roaring lion and a ravening bear
   is a wicked ruler over a poor people.
16 O prince, poor in understanding and abounding in oppressions;
   he that hateth unjust gain shall prolong his days!
17 A man laden with the blood of a soul
   fleeth to the pit; let them not detain him!
18 He that walketh uprightly shall be delivered;
   but he that walketh in crooked ways shall fall suddenly.
19 He that tilleth his land shall be satisfied with bread,
   but he that followeth vanity shall have poverty enough.
20 A faithful man aboundeth in blessings;
   but he that hasteth to be rich shall not go unpunished.
21 To have respect of persons is not good,
   and (yet) for a piece of bread (many) a man will transgress.
22 He that hath an evil eye hasteth after riches,
   and knoweth not that want shall come upon him.
23 He that reproveth a man shall afterward find favor
   more than he that flattereth with his tongue.
24 He that robbeth his father and his mother,
   and saith it is no wrong,
   he is companion to one that destroyeth.
25 He that is of a covetous heart stirreth up strife,
   but he that trusteth in Jehovah shall be richly rewarded.
26 He that trusteth in his own heart is a fool,
   but he that walketh in wisdom, shall be delivered.
27 He that giveth to the poor (suffereth) no want,
   but he that covereth his eyes hath abundance of curses.
28 When wicked men rise men hide themselves,
   but when they perish the righteous increase.

GRAMMATICAL AND CRITICAL.

Ver. 2. פֶּשַׁע might perhaps be more correctly read as an Infinitive: בִּפְשֹׁעַ—Comp. Hitzig on this passage. As the words of the original Hebrew now stand, we can supply a subject for יַאֲרִיךְ only the singular שַׂר ("the true prince"); in like manner the בְּ in בְּאָדָם must be taken in the sense of בִּהְיוֹת "when there is at hand;" the פֶּן however must be taken as an introduction to the concluding clause, like our "then" or "so." In all this there is indeed the difficulty remaining that the participles כְּבִין and יֹדֵעַ stand side by side without a copula—an anomaly that is hardly removed by referring to chap. xxii. 4 (Bertheau). And yet the construction thus brought out is, in spite of the manifold

CHAP. XXVIII. 1–28.

anomalies which it involves, after all better than, *e. g.* that of UMBREIT, who takes כֵּן as a substantive in the sense of "right" as dependent on יֹדֵעַ,—or then HITZIG's violent emendation (יָדֹעַ כָּרוֹז instead of יֹדֵעַ כֵּן יַאֲרִיךְ), the meaning resulting from which "but through a man of understanding contention ceases," does not agree very well with the context. [The E. V. takes כֵּן as a noun: "the state thereof," *etc.* So H. and M. (the stability"). N. without this specific rendering reaches the same result by finding for the verb "shall prolong its days, or endure" the subject "it" (the state) suggested in clause *a*. S. follows UMBREIT. BÖTT. (§ 935, β) regards the verb as furnishing an example of what he calls "concrete impersonals," having a general subject "one," a construction not uncommon where reference is made to public offices or functions. This reaches Z.s. result by a different path.—A.]

Ver. 17.—[The participle עָשֻׁק BÖTT. prefers an account of its peculiar vocalization to regard as a mutilated Pual part., deprived of its initial מ, and would therefore point עֻשָּׁק; so xxv. 11, *etc.* See § 991, 6, 10.—A.]

Ver. 18.—נֶעְקַשׁ דְּרָכַיִם is equivalent to עִקֵּשׁ דְּרָכַיִם in ver. 6.

Ver. 23.—אַחֲרַי a somewhat stronger form in its vowel elements than אַחֲרֵי, used here as אַחַר is elsewhere.

EXEGETICAL.

1. Vers. 1–5. Of the general contrast between the righteous and the ungodly (unscrupulous transgressors, men of violence).—**The wicked flee when no man pursueth.** "The wicked" (singular) is on the ground of its collective, or more exactly its distributive meaning, subject of a plural verb; compare similar constructions, κατὰ σύνεσιν: Job viii. 19; Isa. xvi. 4; and also below, ver. 4 of the present chapter; 1 Tim. ii. 15 (γυνή—ἐὰν μείνωσιν), *etc.* [See EWALD *Lehrb.* § 309, *a*, and other grammars].—**But the righteous are bold as a lion.** כְּכפִיר is to be explained as a relative clause and referred to the preceding "as a lion"—"which is confident, rests quietly" in the consciousness of its superior strength and the security which results from it, see the same figure in Gen. xlix. 9. [This seems to be needlessly artificial; according to a common Hebrew construction the verb may be a distributive singular after a plural, "the righteous." See *e. g.* GREEN, § 275, 6.—A.]

Ver. 2. **In the rebellion of a land its princes become many.** For this use of "transgression" in the sense of "rebellion, revolt," comp. the verb employed in this sense in 2 Kings i. 1; also Ex. xxiii. 21, *etc.* The allusion is plainly to the uprising of many petty chiefs or tyrants, or many pretenders to the throne, or usurpers opposing each other, in lands which, through revolt from the lawfully reigning house, have fallen a prey to political anarchy, as *e. g.* the Kingdom of Israel, especially in the period after Jeroboam II.,—to which the author of the proverb now under consideration might very well have had special reference. [On account of the form of clause *b* we prefer, with KAMPH., to understand the allusion to be to a rapid succession of half established kings, rather than to a number of competing claimants. THOMSON, *Land and Book*, 1., 498, cites an Arabic proverb: "May Allah multiply your sheikhs!" as embodying in its intense malediction a constant Oriental experience of fearful calamity. It is only incidentally illustrative of the proverb before us.—A.]—**But through wise, prudent men he** (the prince) **continueth long.** [See Critical notes.]

Ver 3. **A man who is poor and oppresseth the poor.** We are to think of some magistrate who is originally poor, an upstart, who seeks to enrich himself rapidly by oppression of his subjects. This man is in clause *b* very appropriately described as a "rain" that floods the sowed field or the fruitful district, and thus destroys the prosperous condition of the crops. [Here again, and more appropriately, THOMSON (*ubi supra*) illustrates, both from natural and political experiences common in the East, the impressiveness of this proverb to an Oriental mind.—A.]

Ver. 4. **They that forsake the law praise the wicked,** *i. e.* for his success; comp. Ps. xlix. 12, 19; lxxiii. 3, 10, 12.—**But they that keep the law** (xxix. 18) **contend with him;** lit., "with them;" comp. remarks above on ver. 1. For this verb, "to contend or dispute," comp. Jer. l. 24; Dan. xi. 10, *etc.*

Ver. 5. **Evil men** (lit., "men of evil," comp. remarks on vi. 23) **do not understand judgment;** their wickedness darkens their understanding likewise, which is especially the faculty for distinguishing between good and evil; comp. chap. xxix. 7. In contrast with them "they who seek God understand everything," *i. e.* everything that relates to the investigation and determination of right; comp. Eccles. viii. 5.

2. Vers. 6–12. Against wanton oppression of the poor by the rich.—With ver. 6 compare the quite similar proverb chap. xix. 1.—**Than he that walketh in crooked ways;** lit., "than one who is crooked in the two ways," or, "than one who is perverse in a double way" (the dual of the noun is used here as in ver. 18 [see GREEN, *Gram.* § 203, 3]), *i. e.* one who unskilfully and waywardly passes from one way to another, one who, with divided heart, stands midway between the right path and the bypath of immorality; comp. Ecclesiast. ii. 12; James i. 6.

Ver. 7. With clause *a* compare x. 1; xxix. 3. —**But the companion of profligates.** For the verb רָעָה, to cherish, to cultivate intercourse with some one, comp. xiii. 20. For the term "profligate or waster," comp. xxiii. 21.

Ver. 8. **He that increaseth his wealth by interest and usury.** The "interest" and "usury" are so distinguished according to Lev. xxv. 36, 37, that the former denotes the annual revenue of a sum of money loaned out, the latter an exaction in other things, especially in natural products. The former is then *fœnus pecuniarium*, the latter *fœnus naturale sive reale*. [Here again Orientals, ancient and modern, have a peculiarly deep and painful experience of the enormities of usury.—A.]—**He gathereth it for one that pitieth the poor,** *i. e.* for an heir who will at length show himself more liberal and compassionate toward the poor; comp. xiii. 22, and also Job xxvii. 16, 17. MERCERUS, EWALD, BERTHEAU,

ELSTER take the לְחוֹגֵן as an Infinitive of the intensive form: "*ad largiendum pauperibus*," for bestowal upon the poor, to show himself merciful to the poor. But such an involuntary giving is a harsh idea, difficult to realize; and the meaning, "to bestow, *largiri*," חנן has elsewhere only in the Kal conj., the participle of which corresponds best with the general context before us.

Ver. 9. Comp. xv. 8; and with clause *a* in particular Isa. xiii. 15.

Ver. 10. **He that leadeth the righteous astray in an evil way.** The "evil way" is unquestionably a way of sin and ungodliness, whether the ר׳ ע׳ be taken as a neuter substantive in the genitive (as in ver. 5; vi. 24), or, which is perhaps to be preferred here, as an adjective. With clause *b* compare xxvi. 27; with *c*, ii. 21. The "pit" in *b* is naturally the way of sin into which one betrays the upright, not as it is in itself, but in its ruinous issues to which he is finally brought. Comp. chap. xi. 6, 8.

Ver. 11. With *a* compare xxvi. 16.—**But a poor man that hath understanding searcheth him out;** *i. e.* he sees through him, and accordingly knows his weaknesses, and therefore outstrips him in the struggle for true prosperity in life.

Ver. 12. **When righteous men exult** (triumph). עָלַץ, lit., "to rejoice," here expresses the idea of the victory of the good cause over its opposers, in which victory "all the people" (according to xxix. 2) sympathize with great exultation. HITZIG's alteration is unnecessary (בַּעֲלֹץ into בַּחֲלֵץ, suggested by the διὰ βοηθείαν of the LXX): "when righteous men are delivered."—**But when wicked men rise,** come up, attain to power. Compare, with respect to this as well as the people's anxious "hiding themselves," ver. 28.

3. Vers. 13-18. Against the secret service of sin, hardening of the heart, tyranny, and thirst for blood.—With ver. 13 comp. Ps. xxxii. 1-5.

Ver. 14. **Happy is the man that feareth always,** *i. e.* he who lives in a holy dread of transgressing the will of God by sins of any kind whatsoever; comp. 2 Cor. v. 11; Phil. ii. 12, *etc.* The antithesis to this man "who feareth always" is the "confident," the carnally presumptuous, hardened in the service of sin; ver. 26 and also chap. xvi. 14.—With *b* comp. Ps. xcv. 8; Prov. xvii. 20.

Ver. 15. **A roaring lion and a ravening bear.** שׁוֹקֵק the ancient translators (LXX: διψῶν; Vulg. *esuriens, etc.*), already give with a substantial correctness, when they interpret it of the raging hunger or the blood-thirstiness of the bear; comp. Isa. xxix. 8; Ps. cvii 9. Not so well BERTHEAU and ELSTER (following KIMCHI, LEVI, COCCEIUS, *etc.*, [GESEN., FUERST, E. V., II., S., while LUTHER, DE W., K., N., M., RÜD., *etc.*, agree with our author]): "a roaming, ranging bear,"—for which rendering neither Joel ii. 9 nor Isa. xxiii. 4 can be adduced as decisive supports

Ver. 16. **O prince poor in understanding** (lit., in "discernments") **and abounding in oppression.** This conception of the first clause as an animated appeal to a tyrant (EWALD, BERTHEAU, ELSTER, *etc.*), seems to correspond better with the second clause than HITZIG's view, according to which clause *a* is a nominative absolute, not to be resumed by a suffix in *b*, or than STIER's still more forced translation: "A prince who lacks understanding—so much more does he practice oppression," *etc.* [LUTHER, E. V.. DE W., H., N., M. make the general relation of the clauses antithetic, each clause having its normal subject and predicate, although H., *e. g.*, admits the want of precision in the antithesis. K. agrees with HITZIG's abrupt sundering of the clauses; while S. makes the first a synecdochical clause, "as to a prince," *etc.* Our author's rendering if animated is certainly unusual.—A.]—**He that hateth unjust gain shall prolong his days.** For the generalizing plural שֹׂנְאֵי, which stands here quite as appropriately as *e. g.* iii. 18; xxvii. 16, the K'ri unnecessarily calls for the singular שֹׂנֵא. [So BÖTT., § 702, *c*].

Ver. 17. **A man laden with the blood of a soul.** For this participle, "burdened, loaded" (with the sense of guilt), comp. Isa. xxxviii. 14. [The E. V. loses the passive form and force of the expression; so LUTHER and H.; while DE W.. K., N., S., M, W. agree with Z.—A.]—**Fleeth to the pit,** is restless and a fugitive (like Cain, Gen. iv. 14), even to the terrible destruction toward which he is hastening by God's righteous decrees, and from which no human exertion is able to hold him back. Hence the warning exclamation at the end: "let no one detain him," *i. e.* let no one attempt the impossible, after all to recover him who is irrecoverably lost!

Ver. 18 forms an antithesis to the preceding verse, cast in a somewhat general form.—**He that walketh uprightly** (comp. Ps. xv. 2; Mic. ii. 7) **shall be delivered, but he that walketh in crooked ways shall fall suddenly.** Comp. "the perverse in a double way," in ver. 6. The "suddenly, at once," points to the fact that the one or the other of the two perverse ways which the ungodly alternately pursues, must bring him at last to ruin.

4. Vers. 19-28. Various warnings and cautions, directed mainly against avarice and violence.—With ver. 19 comp. xii. 11.— . . . . **is surfeited with poverty.** A stronger and more direct antithesis to *a* than the "is void of understanding" in xii. 11 *b*.

Ver. 20. **A faithful man aboundeth in blessings.** For the "man of fidelities," comp. the similar expression in chap xx. 6; also 2 Kings xii. 16; xxii. 7, *etc.*—**But he that hasteth to be rich,** naturally, in unfaithful, dishonorable ways. Comp. xx. 21; xxi. 5; and for the concluding phrase, iv. 29.

Ver. 21. With *a* compare the somewhat more complete expression, xxiv. 23.—**And (yet) even for a piece of bread** (many) **a man will transgress.** The morsel of bread (1 Sam. ii. 36) probably stands here not as an example of a peculiarly insignificant bribe, but as the concrete designation of a trifle, a very slight value or advantage of any sort. Comp. A. GELLIUS, *Noct. Att.* I., 15, where CATO says in proverbial phrase of the tribune Cælius, "*frusto* panis conduci potest, vel ut taceat, vel ut loquatur" [with a crust of bread he can be hired either to keep silence or to speak].

Ver. 22. **He that hath a covetous eye hasteth after riches,** lit., "with an evil eye," and therefore the envious; comp. xxiii. 6. For the idea of hastening after riches comp. xx. 21.—**And knoweth not that want shall come upon him.**—Instead of חָסֵר "want" (comp. Job xxx. 3 and a kindred term in Eccles. i. 15) the LXX read חֶסֶד (so likewise the *Edit. Bomberg.*, 1525, and the *Plantin.*, 1566). If this reading were original, then we must undoubtedly render in accordance with chap. xiv. 34; xxv. 10; by "shame, reproach." Yet the Masoretic reading also gives a good sense, as a comparison of vi. 11; xxiii. 5, and other passages that refer to the vanity and perishableness of riches teaches.

Ver. 23. **He that reproveth a man findeth afterward more favor,** *etc.*—"Later, afterward," in the general sense, and not possibly with ABEN EZRA, J. H. MICHAELIS, to be taken in the sense of "after me, *i. e.*, according to my precepts." With the flattering "smoothness of the tongue" in *b* compare xxix. 5; Ps. v. 10; cxl. 4; Rom. iii. 13.

Ver. 24. **He that robbeth his father and his mother.**—Comp. xix. 26; also Mal. i. 8; Mark vii. 11 sq.; and for the expression "companion of a destroyer" in clause *c*, chapter xviii. 9.

Ver. 25. **The covetous kindleth strife.**—רְחַב נֶפֶשׁ is certainly not the "proud" (Vulg., LUTHER, EWALD, BERTHEAU, ELSTER [GESEN., FUERST, DE W., E. V., N., S., M.], *etc.*), but the man of large cupidity (comp. Is. v. 14; Hab. ii. 5), the avaricious and insatiable, ἄπληστος (LXX, UMBREIT, STIER, HITZIG [K., H.]). By his covetous grasping and his overreaching others, he "kindles strife" (comp. xv. 18; xxix. 22), instead of living like the man who patiently trusts in the Lord's help in peaceful quietness and with the prosperous development of his possessions as they multiply under the Divine blessing. For the expression "shall be made fat," *i. e.*, shall be richly rewarded, compare xi. 25; xiii. 4.

Ver. 26. **He that trusteth in his own heart** —*i. e.*, not "he who relies on his own immediate feelings" (UMBREIT, ELSTER), but he who suffers himself to be guided solely by his own spirit (comp. Jer. xxx. 21), by his own inconsiderate, defiant impulse to act, and therefore follows exclusively his own counsel (xxvii. 9). Comp. HITZIG and STIER on the passage.

Ver. 27. **He that giveth to the poor** (suffereth) **no want.**—For the sentiment comp. xi. 24; for the elliptical construction (the omission of the pronoun "to him" with the "no want"), chap. xxvii. 7 *b*.—**He that covereth his eyes,** *i. e.*, turns them unsympathizingly away from such as need help, that he may not see their wretchedness; comp. Is. i. 15, as well as the similar expressions, Deut. xxxi. 17; 1 John iii. 17 (κλείειν τὰ σπλάγχνα).—**Hath abundance of curses**—of imprecations from the oppressed poor; the opposite, therefore, of ver. 20.

Ver. 28. Comp. 12 *b*.—**But when they perish the righteous increase;**—*i. e.*, the right-eous who were before oppressed and chased away come out to view again on all sides and form once more a numerous and strong party. Comp. xxix. 2; and also xi. 10, 21.

DOCTRINAL AND ETHICAL.

A peculiar "religious complexion" belongs not merely to the first half of the chapter, vers. 1–16 (as HITZIG asserts, who separates this portion from its older surroundings as a peculiar interpolation originating after the exile), but to the whole section, as is shown with reference to the second part, particularly by vers. 18, 20, 24, 25. That which gives to the chapter its specifically religious character is, the repeated admonitions to hear and keep the Divine law (vers. 4, 7, 9), to seek Jehovah (ver. 5), to trust in Him, (ver. 25, 26), to a walking in "faithfulness" (ver. 20), and in blamelessness or innocence (ver. 18), and therefore in a general consecration,—to fear of God's sacred anger (ver. 14); and also in no less degree the warnings against wanton and flattering suppression of the consciousness of sin (vers. 13, 24), against a hardening in the service of sin (ver. 14), and against the betrayal of others into sin (ver. 10). Undoubtedly it is the desire to exhibit as the "root of all evil" and as a main radical form of ungodliness and lawlessness in general, the vice which is most sharply censured and opposed, that of covetousness, or the mighty rapacity of the wicked,—and accordingly to warn against it in the most emphatic way,—that led the compiler to accumulate just in the passage before us so many thoughts with respect to the religious relation of men to God. For beside these admonitory and warning proverbs which refer directly to this relation, the substance of the chapter is made up almost exclusively of warnings against wicked violence on the part of rulers in their dealing with the lowly (ver. 1, 3, 12, 15, 16, 28), of rich with the poor (vers. 6, 8, 11, 24), and of the covetous and greedy of gain in their relation to the inoffensive and unsuspecting (vers. 19–22, 25, 26). A logically developed progress of thought, it is true, is wanting; the combination is mixed of many colors, in the style of the "strings of pearls" in the gnomic poetry of the East, in which it is rather external than internal contacts and analogies that determine the concatenation of the several proverbs or groups of proverbs.

HOMILETIC AND PRACTICAL.

Homily on the entire chapter. Of avarice as the foulest stain on the conscience, or as the mother of all vices (1 Tim. vi. 10)—Or, on walking in the fear of the Lord and a good conscience, and also on the chief dangers that threaten such a devout conscientious life.—Comp. STÖCKER: On the second hinderance to the attainment of true wisdom: an evil, terrified, timorous conscience; its source and characteristics, as well as the remedies for it (in a similar style, WOHL-FARTH).

Vers. 1 sq. LUTHER (marginal comment on ver. 1); One's own conscience is more than a thousand witnesses.—CRAMER: An evil conscience makes timid (Job xv. 21); but faith and a good conscience make the heart joyous, so that it is not terrified before death and the devil (Ps. xci. 7).—[ARNOT: No man pursueth; and yet a pursuer is on the track of the fugitive, otherwise he would not flee. When they escape from man, God is the pursuer of the guilty. By conscience chiefly God apprehends us—thereby chiefly we apprehend God].—LANGE (on ver. 2): When subjects are oppressed and vexed, they are not to rebel or curse the authorities, but seek the causes of such judgments in themselves, turn and bring forth fruits meet for repentance.—VON GERLACH (on ver. 5): To the understanding of the law there belongs a disposition to fear God, otherwise the clearest knowledge of the letter is of no avail; while men that fear God attain a sure comprehension of all.—[MUFFET: Albeit there is some light in the wicked man which is sufficient to make him inexcusable, yet he is always so blinded by natural ignorance and malice that both Christ and the law to him is a mystery.—BRIDGES: When knowledge stands in the stead of faith; when the man reasons instead of submitting to Divine teaching; knowledge abused becomes a positive hinderance to a correct understanding.]

Vers. 6–12. CRAMER (on ver. 6): As his riches do not help the rich man at all toward blessedness, so his poverty does not harm the poor in that direction.—(On ver. 8): God often rewards even here kindness shown to the poor, though it may show itself first to the children of the benefactors.— *Würtemberg Bible* (on ver. 9): He that would be heard by God in his prayer must first hear God in His word and subject himself to its direction.—[BP. HOPKINS: God stops His ears against their prayers who stop their ears against His law. And this is but equity with God.]—VON GERLACH: Even the best that man can do becomes a sin to him when he does it with a disposition of disobedience to the Divine word.—(On ver. 11): Trust in outward blessings easily brings with it false self-confidence, and it is very natural for the rich to wish to lay claim likewise to inward excellencies and advantages. The poor man standing by unconcerned and simple, nevertheless overlooks and searches him through, and by his very poverty has more of spiritual superiority.—STARKE (on ver. 12): A large proportion of subjects conform to the conduct of their superiors. Blessed is the land whose rulers govern piously and praiseworthily!—[TRAPP (on ver. 10): Heaven is kept for the upright, and they for heaven; how then should they miss of it?]

Ver. 13–19. MELANCHTHON (on ver. 13): As in all conversion repentance must be the first thing, *i. e.*, recognition of transgression and guilt, combined with a sore change of disposition,—so here confession of sin is demanded, and such a one as leads to sincere reformation of the feelings and conduct, like that of Paul, 1 Cor. xv. 9, 10. For necessarily in confession of sin every evil purpose must be given up, because with persistence in these penitence is no true penitence.—Comp. the Absolution-sermon on ver. 13 by WELCKER (*Sonntagsfeier*, 1839): Be not ashamed to confess, for he only who confesses will obtain mercy, and no competitor is crowned except he strive lawfully.—[LAWSON: To endeavor to shelter ourselves under coverings that are not of God's Spirit, is an additional provocation to the eyes of His glory.—TRAPP: Sin is a deformity that must be uncovered, or God will never cover it; see it we must to confession, or see it we shall to our confusion. No man was ever kept out of heaven for his confessed badness: many are for their supposed goodness.—ARNOT: Sin cast forth from the heart is harmless. It cannot then pollute the life; and it will not then remain an element of treasured wrath.—BATES (on ver. 14): Blessed is the man who considers that God's eyes are always upon him in order to judgment, and whose eyes are always upon God in order to acceptance.—J. HOWE: It is a very hopeful character upon you when you are really afraid lest a controversy should still depend, and not be taken up between God and you.—J. EDWARDS: A saint is apt to be sensible of his spiritual dangers, jealous of himself, full of fear when he cannot see his way plain before him, afraid to be left alone, and to be at a distance from God.]—STARKE: Searing and hardening the heart is a heavy judgment. If thou wouldst not fall into it, then hear betimes the grace that knocks at thy door.—(On ver. 18): There is only one way to eternal life; he that turns from that to the right or to the left, and would make himself sidepaths, will fall into ruin.—VON GERLACH (on ver. 19): As a reward for his vain striving the simple receives only vanity.—[LAWSON (on ver. 17): The murderer of his neighbor is his own murderer.]

Vers. 20 sq. [LORD BACON (on ver. 21): In a judge facility of disposition is more pernicious than bribery; for it is not every one that offers a bribe, but there is scarcely a case wherein something may not be found to bias the mind of the judge, if he be a respecter of persons.]—CRAMER (on vers. 20–22): Striving after riches has become to many a one a cause of many sins; and these are the very tares which (according to Luke viii. 14) choke the word of God.—*Tübingen Bible* (on ver. 23): Speak the truth always, even though thou see that it is bitter. The future will show that thou still farest better with this than do shameful flatterers.—(On ver. 24): To take any thing from parents the Spirit of God calls a theft, robbing the children of all prosperity and all blessing.—[FLAVEL (on ver. 28): There is no better way to secure our own interest in any man's heart, than to fasten it in his conscience by our faithfulness, and by being willing to hazard it for God's glory.—SOUTH (on ver. 26): Of all the fallacies and scurvy cheats put upon men by their trusting others, there are none so shameful, and indeed pernicious, as the baffles which men sustain by trusting themselves.]—GEIER (on ver. 26): In our own important affairs we should never rely upon ourselves alone, but ever hearken to others' counsel. Does not even a physician in his sickness employ the counsel of other physicians?—WOHLFARTH: Trust not in thine heart, but in the Lord.

d) Against stubbornness and insubordination.

Chap. XXIX.

1 He that being often reproved hardeneth his neck
  shall suddenly be destroyed and without remedy.
2 When the righteous increase the people rejoice,
  but when a wicked man ruleth the people mourn.
3 He that loveth wisdom maketh his father glad,
  but he that keepeth company with harlots spendeth his substance.
4 The king will establish the land by judgment,
  but a man (fond) of bribes destroyeth it.
5 A man who flattereth his neighbor
  spreadeth a net for his feet.
6 In the transgression of the wicked man is a snare,
  but the righteous will rejoice and be glad.
7 The righteous knoweth the cause of the poor;
  the wicked doth not discern knowledge.
8 Scoffers set on fire the city,
  but wise men turn back anger.
9 A wise man contendeth with the fool;
  but he rageth, and laugheth, and there is no rest.
10 Men of blood hate the upright,
  but the righteous seek his soul (to deliver it).
11 All his wrath doth the fool pour forth,
  but the wise quieteth it afterward.
12 A ruler that giveth heed to deceitful words,
  all his servants are wicked.
13 The poor man and the usurer meet together;
  Jehovah giveth light to the eyes of both.
14 A king who judgeth the poor faithfully,
  his throne shall be established for ever.
15 The rod and reproof impart wisdom;
  but a neglected son causeth his mother shame.
16 When the wicked are multiplied transgression increaseth;
  but the righteous shall see their fall.
17 Correct thy son, and he will give thee rest,
  and bring delight to thy soul.
18 When there is no revelation the people are ungoverned,
  but he that keepeth the law, blessed is he!
19 By words a servant will not be corrected;
  for he perceiveth them but doth not conform to them.
20 Seest thou a man hasty in his words;
  the fool hath more hope than he.
21 One bringeth up his servant tenderly from a child
  and afterward he shall be a son.
22 An angry man stirreth up strife,
  and a passionate man aboundeth in transgression.
23 A man's pride shall bring him low,
  but he that is of a lowly spirit retaineth honor.
24 He that is partner with a thief hateth his own soul;
  he heareth the curse and showeth it not.
25 Fear of man bringeth a snare,
  but he that trusteth Jehovah shall be preserved.

26 Many seek the favor of the ruler,
    but from Jehovah cometh man's judgment.
27 An abomination to the righteous is the unjust man,
    and an abomination to the wicked is he who is upright in his way.

GRAMMATICAL AND CRITICAL.

Ver. 5.—With בְּחֲלִיק we should, according to xxviii. 23, supply לָשׁוֹן; and עַל expresses here the dative relation as אֶל usually does; Comp. Ps. xxxvi. 3.

Ver. 6.—יָרוּן stands for יָרִין, illustrating a very common transition from ע״ע roots into the ע״י form; Ewald, § 138, a. [Green, § 140, 1; Bott. § 1147, A., etc.]

Ver. 10.—Between דִּכִּים and הֵם there seems to be an assonance intended.

Ver. 18.—[אֲשֻׁרֵיהוּ an instance of the attachment of the suffix of the singular to form *pluralia tantum*; comp. אֲשֻׁרָי in xiv 21; xvi. 20, the only other instances in which the noun occurs with the suffix of 3d pers. sing. Dött. suggests that this may be a trace of the dialect of Ephraim; § 886, δ and n. 1; § 888, 1.—A.]

Ver. 25.—חֶרְדַּת Bött. treats as a fem. Infin. (§ 990, 4, B and n.3), and notices the not uncommon sequence of a masculine predicate (990, 3, β.).—A.]

EXEGETICAL.

1. Vers. 1–7. Against various forms of obstinate unrighteousness, especially oppression, prodigality, flattery, etc.—**He that is often reproved, being stiffnecked.** A "man of corrections" or "reproofs" (for which Hitzig needlessly substitu s תּוֹכֵחוֹת "punishments" [which Gesen. would render "arguments," *i. e.*, a man who when censured defends himself]) is one who deserves many corrections, is continually bringing them upon himself (comp. the "man of sorrows," Is. liii. 8). Here he is described as such a man, who "maketh his neck hard," *i. e.*, the stiffnecked man who will everywhere defiantly carry through his own will (comp. Ex. xxxii. 9; xxxiii. 3; xxxix. 9; Deut. ix. 6; xxxi. 27, etc.; and also the "hardening of the heart" in chap. xxviii. 14). [The E. V. which is followed by nearly all our expositors, and which we have given in the general version of the chapter, makes the obstinacy not the original cause of the many corrections, that for which the offender is in the first instance reproved, but the disposition evinced by him under all reproofs whatsoever. The final difference is not great; sudden and utter destruction will follow and end unavailing reproofs.— A.]. With *b* compare the literally identical second clause of chap. vi. 15.

Ver. 2. **When the righteous increase.** According to chap. xxviii. 28 this is the same thing as "the wicked's perishing," Hitzig: "when righteous men attain to power,"—an unnecessary assimilation of the meaning of the verb to that in clause *b*. For the rest compare xxviii. 12.

Ver. 3. With *a* compare x. 1; with *b*, vi. 26; xxviii 7

Ver 4. **A king will establish the land by judgment,** (*i. e.*, by the maintenance of justice) For the verb comp. 1 Kings xv. 4. The "man of gifts (bribes)" is then naturally the unjust ruler who "perverts justice from love of gifts" (Bertheau). Rosenmueller and Hitzig explain the phrase as meaning "a man of taxes or assessments," in like manner Luther: "he who assesses the land excessively." This is possible, but not demonstrable with full certainty. The conception of the Vulgate is at any rate too general: *Vir avarus*, and also Stier's; "he who willingly receives presents." [K. agrees with Hitzig, etc.; H., N., S., M., take our author's view.]

Ver. 5 **A man who flattereth his neighbor;** see Critical notes.—**Spreadeth a net for his feet.** "He does this even when he is not intending it: the web of enticing errors before his neighbor's eyes, becomes, when he comes into contact with them, a net in which he is caught" (Hitzig). For the sentiment comp. xxvi 24, 25, 28.

Ver. 6. **In the transgression of the wicked man is a snare,** *i. e.*, for himself; comp. xviii. 7; xx. 25; xxii. 25. Hitzig proposes instead of the noun the corresponding verb (in the Niphal); "In the sin of the wicked he ensnareth himself." A change plainly as superfluous as that of Ewald, who, following the steps of some earlier expositors but clearly in violation of the order of words, combines the epithet "evil" with the "snare."—**But the righteous will rejoice and be glad,** *i. e.*, in his own happy escape from danger. For a like combination of רָנַן to exult, or shout for joy, and שָׂמַח to be glad, comp. Ps. xxxv. 27.

Ver. 7. **The righteous knoweth the cause of the poor,** *i. e.*, their judicial cause, their claims before a court. For this use of the verb "to know" comp. xii. 10; for the sentiment ver. 14; Job xxix. 12, 16.—**The wicked doth not discern knowledge** (others "know understanding"); *i. e.*, he listens to no reason, has no sensibility for right and equity (Hitzig). Comp. xxviii. 5. [This explanation, which is also Wordsworth's ("knowledge, which consists in piety and charity"), we prefer to the more external one given, *e. g.*, by H., S., M.; does not acquaint himself with the poor man's cause.—A.]

2. Vers. 8-11. Against scoffing, contentiousness, thirst for blood and passionateness.— **Mockers set on fire the city.** "Men of derision" is a more select expression for the common לֵצִים "scorners," one found likewise in Is. xxviii. 14 [intending and meaning more than would be ordinarily suggested by the rendering of the E. V ; "scornful men."—A.]. The "setting on fire" (lit. "blowing upon," comp. Ezek. xxi. 36) the city is a fitly chosen figurative expression for the excitement of the passion and the party spirit of the people of the city; קִרְיָה

stands here like πόλις in Matth. xii. 24 of the community of the city.—With *b* comp. xv. 1, 18; Eccles. x. 4. [The connection is not unknown in modern times of religious skepticism and rationalism, with political radicalism and a revolutionary spirit.—A.].

Ver. 9. **A wise man contendeth with a fool;—but he rageth and laugheth and there is no rest.** The first clause forms, somewhat like the *abl. absol.* in Latin, a clause by itself, the participle of which may be resolved into "if or when the wise contendeth, *etc.*" The subject of the verbs in *b* is the fool and not the wise man (EWALD, UMBREIT, ELSTER, STIER [DE W., MUFFET, N., *etc*, while BERTHEAU, K., H., S., *etc*., understand "the fool," the E. V., M. and others being ambiguous]), in which case the וְאֵין נָחַת (and there is no ceasing, no rest comes, comp. 1 Sam. xxv. 9) would form quite too short a conclusion; moreover the "raging" and the "laughing" appear to be much rather characteristic signs of the fool's conduct than of the wise man's; comp. ver. 11 and chap. xii. 16.

Ver. 10. **Men of blood hate the upright.** "Men of blood" as in Ps. v. 7; xxvi. 9; lv. 24; cxxxix. 19.—**But the righteous seek his soul,** *viz.*, to preserve and prosper it. That the "seeking the soul" here stands *bono sensu*, unlike its use in some other passages (*e. g.*, Ps. xl. 15; 1 Kings xix 10, *etc.*,) [on the other hand comp. דּוֹרֵשׁ לְנַפְשִׁי in Ps. cxlii. 5], appears from the contrast with clause *a*; HITZIG'S emendation is therefore unnecessary, substituting וִישָׁרִים for יְשָׁרִים, and thus obtaining as the meaning: "and seek to separate his soul, to isolate it" (!). [Of our expositors H. prefers the common rendering of the predicate, and makes "the upright" a nom. or acc. absolute.—A.]

Ver. 11. **All his wrath doth the fool pour forth.** "Spirit" is here plainly wrath, as in xvi. 32, and not "soul" (UMBREIT) or "mind " STIER, *etc.*; [so E V and some of our interpreters]).—**But the wise quieteth it afterward.** בְּאָחוֹר, which occurs only here, means "afterward, at length"; others explain this unusual expression by "back, *retrorsum;*" *e. g.*, DE W., STIER, HITZIG, GESEN., *etc.* : "Keepeth it back, restraining it, pressing it in as it were (?)."

3. Vers. 12-17. Admonitions to a just and mild mode of government, and also the strict discipline of children. With ver. 12 comp. Ecclesiast. x. 2, and also CIC. *De Leg.*, III. 13 and the Latin proverb; *Qualis rex talis grex*, "like king, like people."

Ver. 13. **The poor man and the usurer** (oppressor) **meet together.** The "man of exactions" should be interpreted with the LXX (δανειστής), Vulg (*creditor*), EWALD, HITZIG, FUERST, *etc.*, by "usurer," inasmuch as תְּכָכִים as a plural from תֹּךְ (τόκος) [?] is very probably equivalent in meaning to נֶשֶׁךְ "usury;" [RÖD., BÖTT., *etc.*, prefer the broader meaning "oppression"]. A "man of usury, money-lender" is furthermore only a more concrete expression for a "rich man," and this is the corresponding term in chap. xxii. 2.—**Jehovah giveth light to the eyes of both;** *i. e.*, according to the parallels cited, Jehovah has given to them both the light of their life ; from God comes to both the light of life and the joy of life ; comp. Ps. xiii. 4 ; Job xxxiii. 30 ; Eccles. xi. 7. ["Here is comfort to the poor in his sufferings; here is warning to the rich in his violence." WORDS.]

Ver. 14. **A king who judgeth the poor faithfully.** "In truth, or fidelity " is not here "conscientiously, with truth to his own convictions," but conformably to the state of the facts, "so that he permits true judgment (Zech. vii. 9) to reach the poor" (HITZIG). With the sentiment comp. xx. 28; xxv. 5.

Ver. 15. With *a* comp. xxiii. 13; xiii. 24; with *b*, x. 1 ; xvii. 21 ; xxviii. 7. The "neglected" is literally "he who is exempted from discipline, who is left to his own will."

Ver. 16. **When the wicked are multiplied transgression increaseth**, so far forth as the wicked who are found in the decided majority think that they may with impunity commit all manner of wickedness. With *b* comp. Ps. xxxvii. 34 where the joyful beholding of the destruction of the wicked is expressed by the same phrase.

Ver. 17. With *a* comp. xix. 18.—**And give delight to thy soul.** כְּעֲדָנִים not "delicacies, dainties" (BERTHEAU), but delights, joys in general, whose increasing variety is expressed by the plural (STIER).

4. Vers. 18-23. Against lawlessness, insubordination, a passionate temper, and pride.—**When there is no revelation the people are ungoverned.** חָזוֹן here denotes prophetic prediction, the revelation of God by His חֹזִים or רֹאִים, "seers" (1 Sam. ix. 9), [E. V. " when there is no vision"]; the chief function of these consisted in their watching over the vigorous fulfilling of the law, or in the enforcement of the demands of the law. By the phrase "in lack of vision " a time is described like that mentioned in 1 Sam. iii. 1, when "the word of the Lord was precious ;" or like those mentioned in Hos. iii. 4 ; Am. viii. 12; 2 Chron. xv. 3; Ps. lxxiv. 9, times distinguished by poverty in prophetic testimonies and activities. In such times the people must necessarily be "undisciplined and unbridled," (so Ex. xxxiv. 25 [where the E. V. incorrectly renders "naked"]).—**But he that keepeth the law blessed is he!** (comp. xiv 21; xvi. 20.) This benediction forms no strict antithesis to clause *a*. The connection of ideas seems to be this: But he who in such seasons of ascendant lawlessness nevertheless keeps God's law, *etc.*" (HITZIG).

Ver. 19. **By words a servant will not be corrected;** *i. e.*, mere words do not reform a servant, who rather needs a sharper correction.—**For he perceiveth them but doth not conform to them**; lit. "but there is not an answer," that is in action, by actual obedience, by ὑπακοή (2 Cor. x. 6, *etc.*). BERTHEAU is wrong: "For he will observe it—that there is no coming to blows—and there will be no answer;" no less is EWALD incorrect: "But he becomes intelligent (gains understanding) without an answer," and likewise VON HOFMANN, *Schriftbew.*, II. 2, 377: "if he has understanding no answer follows."

Ver. 20. Almost exactly like xxvi. 12. Comp. also Ecclesiast. ix. 18, where the προπετής ἐν λόγῳ αὐτοῦ corresponds precisely with the "hasty in his words" of our verse.

Ver. 21. **If one bringeth up his slave tenderly from a child afterward he will be a son.** The relation of the two clauses is like that in ver. 9, פנק "to fondle" is used here only in the O. T.; it is more common in Aramaic. מָנוֹן which according to the Rabbinic is cognate with בֵּן אֲבָלִים *suboles*, seems to be designed to distinguish "the son of the household," the free *filius familias* in contrast with the house-slave; comp. LUTHER's term "*Junker*" [a "squire"]. Others interpret the Παπαζλεγομ. differently, *e. g.* EWALD, following the Arabic: "he will be unthankful" [FUERST, "intractable"]: STIER "his end will be (evil) development;" VON HOFMANN, *ubi supra:* "there is at last a lamentation," etc. [HOLDEN: "shall be grieved"]. HITZIG reads כִּנּוּר which is to be interpreted, like Ps. xliv. 15 (14) "a shaking of the head," or even "a wringing of the hands!" To write כָּדוֹן would be more natural than this; "his end will be contention," as the Vulgate seems to have understood the expression, when it renders: *postea sentiet eum contumacem.*

Ver. 22. **An angry man stirreth up strife.** Almost precisely like xv. 18; comp. xxviii. 25.— **And a passionate man aboundeth in transgression;** for רַב in the sense of "great or rich in something," comp. xxviii. 20, 27. See chap. xxii. 24 for a phrase kindred to the "lord of passion," *i. e.*, the passionate man.

Ver. 23. With *a* compare xvi. 18; xxv. 7; with *b*, xvi. 19; xi. 16.

5. Ver. 24-27. Warning against the fear of man, disposition to please men, and complicity in transgressions.—**He that is partner with a thief hateth himself;** *i. e.*, inasmuch as he, as the concealer of a thief, brings upon himself the guilt and likewise the penalty of the full theft.—**He heareth the curse and showeth it not;** *i. e.*, he hears the curse which according to the law (Lev. v. 1 sq.) marks a theft as an offence deserving a heavy penalty, and yet does not reveal the perpetrators of the deed which is laden with such a curse, and thus brings the curse also upon himself. [The E. V. is altogether ambiguous and misleading.]

Ver. 25. **Fear of man bringeth a snare.** Fear of man (for which HITZIG conjectures חֶמְדַּת לְאָדָם, "desiring or delighting in man") is strictly "trembling before men;" comp. 1 Sam. xiv. 15. Such a fear of man "bringeth a snare," because it easily betrays into a participation in the sinful actions of men. With *b* comp. xviii. 10.

Ver. 26. **Many seek the face (favor) of the ruler;** they wait upon him, the potentate, in person, as a token of their homage, and in order to gain his favor. Comp xix. 6; 1 Kings x. 24.—**But from Jehovah cometh man's judgment;** *i. e.*, God, the Supreme Ruler, allots the destinies of men most justly and equitably; with Him one obtains the desired judgment more certainly than with any human ruler whatsoever. Comp. xvi. 33. HITZIG arbitrarily says: "judgment is here equivalent to rank, dignity."

Ver. 27. Comp. xi. 20; xxviii. 4; and for the expression "they that walk uprightly," or are "upright in the way," in clause *b*, see in particular Ps. xxxvii. 14, and also Prov. ii. 7.

DOCTRINAL AND ETHICAL.

When early expositors (STÖCKER, WOHLFARTH, *etc.*, comp. also STIER) represent the chapter before us as directed especially against stiff-necked obstinacy, or against wilful disobedience and persistent refusal of correction, this conception of its main subject not only corresponds with ver. 1, but also with the repeated occurrence of rebukes of lawless conduct and the bad training of children, such as the following series of proverbs exhibits (vers. 9, 12, 15, 17, 18, 19, 21). Besides the manifold warnings against violent temper and its evil consequences fall under the same category (vers. 8, 11, 22); in like manner the dissuasions against prodigality (ver. 3), oppression of the poor (vers. 2, 7, 13, 14), pride (ver. 23), flattery and bribery (vers. 4, 5, 12), injustice and deeds of wickedness in general (vers. 6, 10, 16, 27). As a peculiar form of insubordination, or persistent disregard of the divine law, there is brought out prominently toward the end of the chapter the *fear of man*, which has not before been expressly mentioned in the Book of Proverbs. And this is done in such a way as to distinguish three degrees of this fault; the concealing of a theft, as its rudest and lowest form (ver. 24); the "trembling before men," or pliability with respect to such conduct of wicked persons in general as is sinful and entices to sin (ver. 25); and the mere disposition to please men, or reliance on the protection and favor of powerful men, instead of on God alone (ver. 26).

A special adaptation to the theocratic political organization of the people of God under the Old Testament is given to the general direction which the chapter takes against wilfulness, insubordination and want of discipline, in ver. 18: When there is no revelation, the people become lawless; but he that keepeth the law, blessed is he! In this remarkable testimony to the need of prophecy as the living watch and ward of the law, there is evidently brought to view that thought which is doctrinally and in respect to the history of salvation the most significant in the section. This is a thought which could develop itself and find expression only after repeated periods had occurred in which prophecy was wholly or partially silent, and therefore only on the ground of sorrowful experiences that had accumulated in such seasons. The appearance of this thought, however, in the section before us by no means compels the assumption that this division of the book may not have originated till after Hezekiah, and this HITZIG also admits. Comp. above, the exegetical interpretation of the passage.

The great significance of prophecy for the moral life, both of the theocratic people of God and of Christian nations, has been well presented by ELSTER, in connection with this passage. "Where the continuity of these prophetic revelations (to which it belonged to maintain in life and to develop the fundamental revelation made in the law) was interrupted, this was the sign of a stagnation in the theocratic life, of an incapacity to understand the voice of God that ever continued to exist in Israel. Such a condition must therefore necessarily bring with it also a moral lawlessness in the people. For when the law was a vivid reality, it must necessarily develop prophetic manifestations, because there is in the law itself a struggling toward a higher perfection, so that the faithful keeping of the law stood in the most intimate reciprocity with the flourishing of prophecy.—Naturally the relation of this proverb to the life of Christian nations is thereby not excluded, for we must then contemplate the law as first revealed in its true import in the light of the gospel, and revelation as the continued working of the Spirit in the Church."

How far moreover in the life of Christian nations we can and must speak of an abiding co-operative work of prophecy (*i. e.*, naturally that of the New Testament), upon its successful development, religious and moral, Von Zezschwitz has shown with peculiar force and pertinence in his three discourses on "Domestic Missions, popular education and prophecy" (Frankfort on the Main, 1864); see in particular pp. 86 sq.

HOMILETIC AND PRACTICAL.

Homily on the chapter as a whole: The blessing of strict discipline on the basis of the word of God, or its necessity for the prosperity whether of individual persons and households, or of entire nations and States.—STÖCKER: Third hinderance to the attainment of true wisdom: obstinate disobedience or stubbornness; origin, characteristics and remedy of this evil.

Vers. 1-7. [TRAPP (on ver. 1): If men harden their hearts, God will harden His band.—J. HOWE: A fearful thing when the gospel itself shall not be my remedy!—CHALMERS: The hardening effect of continued resistance to the application of a moral force.—S. DAVIES: To follow the conduct of our own folly and refuse the advantage we might receive from the wisdom of others discovers an uncreaturely pride and self-sufficiency; and the career of such a pursuit, whatever be its object, will always end in disappointment and confusion.—HOOKER (on ver. 2): Religion unfeignedly loved perfecteth man's abilities unto all kind of virtuous services in the commonwealth.]—ZELTNER (on ver. 1): He that obstinately opposes the Holy Ghost and will not receive the wholesome corrections of God's word, his heart the evil spirit hardens; he thereby plunges himself into calamity.—(On ver. 3): Pious parents can experience no greater joy than when they see their children walk in true wisdom and the fear of God.—(On ver. 5): The caress of a flatterer is much more dangerous than the hatred of an enemy.—[SOUTH (on ver. 5): Three Sermons on Flattery.—BRIDGES (on ver. 6): There is always a snare in the ways of sin; always a song in the ways of God.]—LANGE (on ver. 7): Let judges and rulers take good heed lest they by their negligence in the cause of the humble be reckoned as among the ungodly.—VON GERLACH: By righteousness there is opened to man a view into all departments of life; especially may he transfer himself into the position and case of the oppressed; while to the wicked man, who looks on every thing superficially, such insight is denied, and he therefore easily comes to oppress the poor.

Vers. 8-11. HASIUS (on ver. 8): An unwashed mouth may easily stir up much evil; but it is a characteristic of wisdom to make the best of every thing.—STARKE: A true Christian is at the same time a good citizen in the commonwealth; for he seeks to produce and preserve peace.—[LORD BACON: Scorners weaken all the foundations of civil government; a thing the more to be attended to, because the mischief is wrought not openly, but by secret engines and intrigues.— LAWSON: The holy seed are the substance and strength of a land.—Lord BACON (on ver. 9): In this contest the chances are altogether unequal; seeing it is no victory to conquer, and a great disgrace to be conquered.]—LANGE: One should not suffer himself to be kept from the proclamation of the truth by the opposition of foolish people, 2 Tim. iv. 2: if one does not receive it, another does.—VON GERLACH (on ver. 11): Among the characteristics of folly there is always found a boisterous, ungovernable nature; to wisdom belongs self-command.

Ver. 12-17. MELANCHTHON (on ver. 12): The example of distinguished persons, such as rulers, teachers, *etc.*, avails and effects very much, and that in both directions, by promoting good as well as evil. Most rapidly, however, is the plague of base vices transmitted, especially in the circle of household companions, and in the daily retinue of these persons of high station.—[MUFFET: He that carrieth Satan in his ear is no less blameworthy than he which carrieth him in his tongue.] —CRAMER (on ver. 13): The Holy Scriptures are for poor and for rich; every one findeth his own chapter therein adapted to himself. But in order that the one as well as the other may see what is needful for them, both need enlightenment and divine help—STARKE (on ver. 14): Not so much by strength and might as rather by faithful, kind and righteous treatment of subjects is a government preserved and confirmed.—VON GERLACH (on vers. 15, 17): Mothers are wont to be most at fault in indulging their children, and must therefore bear away the chief shame of its fruits. —[CHALMERS: By joining with the reproof, the moral is sometimes the better enforced when there is added to it the physical appliance.]

Ver. 18. LUTHER: Without God's word man can do nothing but practise idolatry and his own will.—MELANCHTHON: As well princes as people must consider that pious governments, which God aids by His counsel and blessing, are more needful than all things beside: they must therefore beseech God for such a wholesome government, and not plunge themselves in sin and vice, lest God withdraw it from them as a judgment.— STÖCKER (special sermon for married people, based on ver. 18): On the indispensable necessity of the divine word to a blessed domestic relation: *a*) How Christian hearts should stand related to the word of God; *b*) What advantage and reward they have from its right use.—WOHLFARTH: Take religion from man and he sinks into the deepest barbarism.—[FLAVEL: The Spirit and the word of God usually come and go together.]

Vers. 19-27. ZELTNER (on vers. 19-21): As self-willed menials do when they are indulged, so likewise our own vile flesh and blood. If one leaves to this its own will even a little, it will quickly rule over the spirit, Gal. v. 17 sq.— [LORD BACON (on ver. 21): Princes and masters ought to keep a measure in conferring grace and favor on their servants. . . . Sudden promotion begets insolence; continual obtaining of desires begets impatience of refusal; and if there be nothing further to aspire to, there will be an absence of alacrity and industry.]—STARKE (on ver. 24): Both the bold sinner himself and he likewise who makes himself partaker in the sins of others, brings upon himself God's wrath and punishment.—(On ver. 25): It is a sinful fear of man when one from timidity acts to please others against his conscience.—A means against this fear of man is pre-eminently prayer for a joyous spirit (Ps. li. 12, 14), and faith and child-like reliance on God's protection. — [FLAVEL: Men vainly "hope to find mercy with God," but expect none from men; so the voice of conscience is drowned by the louder clamors and threats of adversaries.—ARNOT: It is not a transference of fear from man to God that makes a sinner safe; the kind of affection must be changed as well as its object. Safety lies not in terror, but in trust. Hope leads to holiness.]—VON GERLACH (on ver. 26): Justice and favor which princes can ensure are indifferent in the presence of God's decision. —(On ver. 27): It is no good sign for him who would be upright when he can be on friendly terms with the ungodly.

V. THE SUPPLEMENTS.

CHAPS. XXX. and XXXI.

First Supplement: The words of Agur.

CHAP. XXX.

a) INTRODUCTION: Of God's word as the source of all wisdom.

Vers. 1–6.

1 Words of Agur, the son of the princess of Massa.
The man's saying: "I have wearied myself about God,
wearied myself about God—then did I withdraw!
2 For I am a beast and not a man,
and the understanding of a man I have not;
3 neither have I acquired wisdom,
nor gained knowledge of the Holy.
4 Who hath ascended to the heavens and descended?
who hath grasped the wind in his fists?
who hath wrapped the waters in a garment?
who hath fixed all the ends of the earth?
what is his name and what is his son's name, if thou knowest?
5 Every word of God is pure;
a shield is He to them that trust in Him.
6 Add thou not to His words,
lest He rebuke thee and thou be made a liar."

b) Various expressive numerical proverbs, relating to the golden mean between rich and poor, to recklessness, an insatiable disposition, pride and arrogance, *etc.*

7 Two things have I entreated of thee,
refuse me not, before I die:
8 Deceit and lies keep far from me;
poverty and riches give me not;
cause me to eat the food allotted me;
9 lest I, being full, deny (God)
and say: Who is Jehovah?
and lest I, having become poor, steal
and take the name of my God in vain.—

10 Cause not the servant to slander his master,
   lest he curse thee and thou suffer (be destroyed).—
11 (There is) a generation that curseth their father,
   and doth not bless their mother;
12 (there is) a generation that are pure in their own eyes,
   and are not washed from their filthiness;
13 (there is) a generation, how haughty are their eyes,
   and their eyelids are lifted up;
14 (there is) a generation whose teeth are swords, and their jaw-teeth knives,
   to devour the poor from the earth, and the needy from among men!—
15 The leech hath two daughters: give, give!
   there are three (things) that are not to be satisfied;
   four say not: enough!
16 The world of the dead, the barren womb;
   the earth (which) is not satisfied with water,
   and the fire that saith not: enough!—
17 An eye that mocketh at its father,
   and despiseth obedience to its mother,
   the ravens of the valley shall pluck it out,
   and the young eagles shall eat it.—
18 Three things are too wonderful for me,
   and four I do not comprehend;
19 the way of the eagle in the heavens,
   the way of a serpent upon a rock,
   the way of a ship in the midst of the sea,
   and the way of a man with a maid.
20 Thus is the way of the adulterous woman:
   she eateth, and wipeth her mouth, and saith:
   I have done no iniquity!—
21 Under three things doth the earth tremble,
   and under four can it not stand:
22 under a servant when he ruleth,
   and a fool when he is satisfied with bread;
23 under a hated (rejected) woman when she is married,
   and a maid when she succeedeth her mistress.
24 Four are the little things of earth,
   and yet are they wise, quick of wit:
25 the ants, a people not strong,
   that prepare in summer their food;
26 conies, a people not mighty,
   that set their dwelling among rocks;
27 no king have the locusts,
   and yet they go forth organized all of them;
28 the lizard layeth hold with her hands,
   and dwelleth in kings' palaces.—
29 There are three that make stately their walk,
   and four that are comely in going:
30 the lion, mighty among beasts,
   and that turneth not before any:
31 the greyhound, slender in its loins, or the goat,
   and a king with whom there is no resistance (possible).—
32 If thou art foolish in exalting thyself,
   and if thou devisest evil—(put) thy hand on thy mouth!
33 For the pressing of milk giveth forth cheese,
   and pressing the nose giveth blood,
   and pressing wrath giveth strife.

GRAMMATICAL AND CRITICAL.

Ver. 6.—[In תּוֹכַף we have the single instance in which *daghesh lene* is omitted after a silent sheva. See GREEN, § 22 *b*; 66 (2), *a*; BÖTT., § 95.—A.]

Ver. 10.—[In אֵיתָן the suffix is of the form appropriate to the singular, as is not uncommon with *pluralia tantum*; BÖTT., § 886, 1, δ. In יְקַלְלֶךָ the verb has the sense of a subj. pres. in a negative or final clause; BÖTT., § 981, 2.—A.]

Vers. 15.—[The noun הוֹן, as a sort of independent accusative, becomes virtually an Interjection. BÖTTCHER, § 510, *b*, *d*.—A.]

Ver. 17.—[לִקְהַת for לִקֲהַת has a *daghesh dirimens* in the ק, the long Hhiriq being shortened; GREEN, § 14, *a*; 24, *b*; 57, 2, (3) *a*; BÖTT., § 309, *b*, 3; 458, 1, *d*.—A.]

Ver. 25.—[םכלים, a fem. noun construed as masculine; GREEN, § 200, *e*; BÖTT., § 715, ε.—A.]

Ver. 29.—[כי טבי, where it occurs the second time, drops the characteristic י as superfluous; BÖTT., § 171.—A.]

Ver. 31.—[For אִין BÖTT. would read רָאִן, the wild goat or antelope.]

EXEGETICAL.

1. *Preliminary Remark.* If our reading and explanation of the superscription in ver. 1 is correct (see what is said immediately below, under No. 2), the contents of this Supplement, like that of the one following (chap. xxxi. 1-9), can be accepted neither as from Solomon, nor from Hezekiah. For aside from the fact that it is quite as impossible that "Agur" as that "Lemuel" in chap. xxxi. 1 is some allegorical substitute for the name of Solomon, as many of the olden commentators claim (*e. g.*, STÖCKEL, J. LANGE, *etc.*, [so JEROME, RASHI, *etc.*, earlier, and WORDSW., *etc.*, more recently]), the name Massa clearly points to a land beyond the bounds of Palestine as the dwelling-place of the author or collector. The name must belong to the Massa mentioned in Gen. xxv. 14; 1 Chron. i. 30 with Duma, as the name of a district or tribe in northern Arabia,—which from the direction of Jerusalem (according to Is. xxi. 11) was beyond Seir, and therefore in any case south-easterly from Palestine, and which we shall be obliged to regard as an Ishmaelitish kingdom, or an Israelitish founded by members of the covenant people of the Old Testament who had wandered from home. DELITZSCH holds the former view (Article *Sprüche Salomo's* in HERZOG'S *Real-Encyclopädie*). His reasons are, that both sections, the "words of Agur" and the "words of Lemuel" contain numerous traces of an origin outside the Hebrew while yet Semitic (*e. g.*, the insatiable "Aluka" or blood-sucker, chap. xxx. 15; the Divine name אֱלוֹהַּ, chap. xxx. 15; the expressions יָקְהָה, xxx. 1, 17; הוֹן "enough," xxx. 15, 16; בַּר (בְּרִי), xxxi. 2; אֵין=אִן, xxxi. 4; עֲלֵי בְּנֵי, xxxi. 5, *etc.*); and because the reception into the canon of the prophecies of Balaam, and yet more that of the discourses of Job, a dweller in the land of Uz, which notoriously was never inhabited by Israelites, furnish proofs sufficiently weighty of the possibility of a transplanting into the soil of the sacred national literature of Israel, of the products of a religious literature originating beyond the bounds of Israel. The second of the views above mentioned HITZIG has endeavored to present as probable in his treatise on "the kingdom of Massa" (1844), already cited in § 12 of our Introduction, and likewise in pp. 310 sq. of his Commentary; and he has done it with arguments which we must deem more weighty than those adduced by DELITZSCH, and whose decisive weight is admitted by BERTHEAU also. These arguments for the Israelitish character of the land of Massa, and of its rulers Agur and Lemuel, whose wise maxims are before us in our two Supplements, are briefly the following. 1) Agur confesses expressly in chap. xxx. 9 his faith in Jehovah the God of Israel. 2) The introductory words in xxx. 1-6, as well as the utterances in vers. 7, 8, 14, 22, 32 of the same chapter, and in chap. xxxi. 8, 9, breathe forth that sense of justice and that humble subjection to the hand of God, which are peculiar to the theocratic reverer of the law who is of Israel, and such as appear in numerous other passages of our Book of Proverbs, of the Book of Psalms, the Prophets, *etc.* 3) The Massa of Gen. xxv. 14; 1 Chron. i. 30, is indeed in these passages numbered among the sons of Ishmael, and therefore characterized as a district inhabited mainly by Ishmaelites; but later Arabian and Jewish authors (especially BENJAMIN of Tudela in his accounts of the city of Telmâs see RITTER'S Arabia, II. 406) describe the region of Massa and the Duma which is its near neighbor, as occupied by numerous Jews,—and already among the prophecies of Isaiah from the time of Hezekiah there is found a prophecy which relates to Duma (Is. xxi. 11, 12), a "burden of Duma" which with great probability presents Hebrews as dwelling in this region. 4) The passage (1 Chron. iv. 38-43) expressly records a migration that occurred in the days of Hezekiah to Mount Seir, and so quite into the neighborhood of Massa and Duma,—a migration of Israelites of the tribe of Simeon who had settled in the region of the remnant of the Amalekites, and therefore in northern Arabia; and moreover from Micah i. 15; ii. 8-10; iv. xxviii. 12 there may be inferred as probable a considerable advanced movement of certain roving Israelites toward the South, as having occurred about that time. Therefore Agur and Lemuel might very probably be regarded as Arabian-Israelitish shepherd princes, or as kings (Emirs, Captains) of a colony of Israelites of the tribes of Simeon that had emigrated to northern Arabia,—and this Simeonite colony Massa, quite like Job's "land of Uz," should be conceived of as a district to a great extent if not chiefly occupied by kinsmen of the Old Testament people of God, who were believers in Jehovah. [BÖTT. in his *Lehrb.*, has

of course no occasion to enter into the details of this discussion. He does, however, § 29, 36, 37, refer to these chapters as probably largely of Simeonitish origin, and cites various words and constructions as plainly showing affinity with and the influence of the cognate Arabic and Aramaic dialects. STUART (*Comm.* pp. 401-407) enters very elaborately into the examination of the arguments for and against the generally received conception and construction, and decides strongly in favor of HITZIG's view, which our author adopts. Nearly every other English and American interpreter dismisses the subject with a few lines, quietly retaining the rendering of the E. V. possibly with slight modifications. KAMPH. rejects this part of HITZIG's theory while agreeing with it in many other points. BLEEK admits its possible correctness.—A.]

2. **The superscription to the discourses of Agur,** ver. 1, according to the Masoretic punctuation is literally rendered: "Words of Agur, the son of Jakeh, the divine utterance (prophetic utterance), the saying of the man to Ithiel, to Ithiel and Ucal." Inasmuch as of the four proper names which these words include, according to this conception of them, one at least, Ithiel, appears also in Neh. xi. 7 as an Israelitish name of a man, and since Agur is not to be at all suspected as a Hebrew personal name, whether we interpret the word (with HERDER and the majority) by "collector," and so regard it a collateral form of אָגַר (Prov. x. 5),—or whether with HITZIG, following the Arabic, we claim for it the signification "exile, the man living in a strange land," this interpretation of this difficult passage, which was already given in the Chaldee version, and partially in the Syriac, and has been retained by most moderns, seems to excite no suspicion, *if it be assumed* that we are to regard Ithiel and Ucal as sons or pupils of Agur, and are to conceive of the whole as the communication, not indeed of a dialogue of the teacher Agur with these pupils (so *e. g.*, DÖDERLEIN), but of a didactic address, or a "fatherly counsel" given to them. But this conception is lexically impossible. And 1) because neither "Jakeh" nor "Ucal" occurs elsewhere as a Hebrew proper name, nor can they even be satisfactorily explained as such (see HITZIG on this passage); [FUERST taking Jakeh as an irregular participial form interprets it symbolically "one holding to the assembly of the wise;"—GESEN more concisely "pious"]. 2) Because the remarkable doubling of לְאִיתִיאֵל can in no way be brought into harmony with the laws of the Hebrew modes of expression,—not even by the assumption of HERDER and UMBREIT that this is a solemn repetition produced "by the vehemence of parallelism." 3) Because, finally, הַמַּשָּׂא in the sense of "prophetic utterance, prophetic burden" would in connection with the following נְאֻם give a combination unknown in the whole prophetical literature of the Old Testament,—one to the justification of which neither Zech. ix. 1; xii. 1, nor any other passage whatsoever can be brought. [KAMPH. while admitting that only a greater or less degree of probability can at the best be reached, meets this difficulty by separating the two nouns whose combination is pronounced unexampled. The first he connects with Agur, while admitting the term is elsewhere used only in strict prophecy. The second he regards as describing the "utterance" of "the man," some friend or stranger, whose words are given in vers. 1-4, while Agur himself begins to speak in ver. 5. He fails to find any sufficient reason for taking כַּיָא as a proper rather than a common noun. STUART argues that in xxxi. 1 כַּשָּׂא must be a genitive limiting מֶלֶךְ, no other construction being grammatical; the noun must therefore be a proper noun, the name of the kingdom, and the noun must be presumed to be the same here.—A.]

The allegorizing interpretations are however likewise untenable, which have been attempted in various forms, taking the four proper names as either wholly or partially appellative. This was early done by the LXX and Vulg., the former of which appears to have regulated the text in a way wholly arbitrary, while the latter follows the text more closely, and renders Agur by *congregans*, Jakeh by *vomens*, Ithiel by *cum quo est Deus*, and Jucal by *confortatus*. Of modern expositors EWALD has taken at least the last half of the ver. in a similar way: Thus does the man speak to God-with-me, to God-with-me and I-am-strong. The אֻכָל according to this view stands for אוּכַל, and in combination with the appellative Ithiel composes a single name. Instead of נְאֻם however we should need to read נָאַם. Since the objections expressed above, especially those which relate to the name Jakeh, and the doubling of the name Ithiel are not removed, and still others are added to them, there is nothing left but to alter the reading of the verse thoroughly. Of the various emendations which are possible and have been in part already attempted, that of HITZIG commends itself most strongly, which we have made the basis of the version given above.

According to this we should in the first place read בֶּן־יִקְהָה כַשָּׂא "Son of her whom Massa obeys," or again בֶּן־יִקְהָה כ' (which is equivalent to בֶּן־יִקְהָה כ') "Son of her whose dominion is Massa," which in any case gives as the result "son of the ruler, the princess of Massa" (comp. No. 1)

Furthermore we must then read twice לָאִיתִי אֵל, "I have labored, have wearied myself upon, about, with God," *i. e.*, have sought with difficulty and effort to conceive and comprehend Him in His nature (comp. נִלְאָה in Is. xvi. 12; and also passages like Job xi. 7; Acts xvii. 27, *etc.*)

Finally the concluding word וָאֻכָל must either be pointed וָאֵכֶל, "and have become dull, am wearied," *i. e.*, in seeking after God (thus HITZIG); or, which seems to be lexically easier, וָאֵכֶל (from כלה, *evanuit*) "and have withdrawn, have become faint " (comp. Ps. lxix. 4; lxxxiv. 3; Job xix. 27, *etc.*), which latter reading is the one followed by BERTHEAU [KAMPH., S., *etc.*]. It is, indeed, true that even by these emendations the difficulties of the passage are not removed; and yet the meaning thus resulting for the second half of the verse agrees admirably with the further utterances of the Introduction, especially with vers. 3 and 4. Moreover the οὐ παύομαι of the LXX which corresponds with the ואכל at the end confirms on the whole the interpretation given to that obscure expression (and that of HITZIG as well as that of BERTHEAU, which besides are not essentially different). And as respects the expression, which is, it is true, somewhat harsh, בן יקהה לם, an indirect confirmation of this appears in the fact that the rare word קָהָה "obedience" (comp. Gen. xlix. 10) occurs again immediately below in ver. 17.

3. Vers. 2-6. Continuation and conclusion of the Introduction.—**For I am a beast and not a man**, *etc*. To the confession given at the outset, that he has wearied himself in vain in fathoming the divine nature, there is here appropriately added the admission of the author's ignorance, and his natural incapacity for higher spiritual knowledge. His vexation in view of the fact that his wisdom has come to shame in connection with God and things divine, finds vent for itself in strong expressions, which remind us of Ps. lxxiii. 22; comp. also remarks above on chap. xii. 1.—בַּעַר מֵאִישׁ is probably not "more stupid than any man" (as is commonly rendered, EWALD, BERTHEAU [E. V., DE W., H., N., S., M., W., K.] *etc.*), but "brutishly stupid, unlike (away from) a man," and so "a beast and not a man" (HITZIG). [We see no reason for preferring this to the common comparative rendering of מִן.—A.]

Ver. 3. **Nor gained knowledge of the Holy.** For this last clause comp. remarks on ix. 10.

Ver. 4. **Who hath ascended to the heavens and descended?** For the form of words here employed comp. Gen. xxviii. 12; also John iii. 13; Rom x. 6, 7. The ascending to heaven and descending thence, is like the "grasping the wind in the fists," the wrapping up the waters, *etc.*, an activity belonging exclusively to God, and characteristic of Him in His supermundane nature. That there is an activity of this sort, ruling the world and upholding the world, on the part of the invisible God, he knows; but who the invisible divine Ruler of all is, and how constituted, this has hitherto remained hidden from his view, and it is to this that his amazed inquiries relate, reminding us of Job xxvi. 14; Is. xl. 12, *etc*.— **Who gathereth the wind in his fists?**—so that he can at his pleasure restrain it and let it blow. בְּחָפְנָיו, lit. "in his two fists;" an expression employed probably because there are always two opposing currents of wind, of which now the one and again the other blows (comp. Eccles. i. 6.) [There seems to be no occasion for going beyond the fact that fists usually exist in pairs, to find in the remoter facts of nature an explanation for a very natural phrase.—A.]—**Who wrappeth the waters in a garment?** The water is the upper mass of waters, wrapped in the clouds of heaven as in a capacious garment, and so kept back from pouring down upon the earth. Comp. Job xxvi. 8; Ps. civ. 6; and above, notes on Prov. viii. 28.—**Who fixeth all the ends of the earth?** By this is probably intended the bounds of the continents against the sea (Jer. v. 22; Job xxxiii. 10, 11.)—**What is his name, and his son's name, if thou knowest?** In this question is contained the idea: No one knows God adequately, in His inmost nature; none is able to attain a genealogical knowledge of Him and His family, in such way as may be done among men; especially is the question, what is true of His son, veiled in inscrutable mystery. That God *has no son at all* is plainly not implied in this remarkable question, which is left unanswered (in reply to HITZIG); but only this, that no one knows the name of this son,—that his nature and his relation to the other manifestations of God's nature, *e. g.*, to His hypostatic wisdom (chap. viii. 22 sq.) is known to none. Agur therefore confesses here with sufficient distinctness the defectiveness of his knowledge of God the Son,—a fact which serves to confirm in the most welcome way our remarks on the passage viii. 22 sq. concerning the incompleteness, the embryonic imperfection of the doctrine of the Logos (or the Christology) of the proverbs in general. Both GEIER who identifies the "Son" of our passage without qualification with God's hypostatic wisdom, and J. D. MICHAELIS, who finds here ascribed to God with the clearness and precision of the New Testament an only Son, go too far and intermingle foreign ideas. [So STUART: "To think of the *Logos* here, under the name of בֵּן would be 'travelling very far out of the record.'" And yet we may well go as far as J. PYE SMITH (*Scripture Testimony, etc.*, I. 469) when he says: "The concluding clauses of this energetic passage are rationally and easily interpreted, if we admit that the ancient Jews had some obscure ideas of a plurality in the divine nature." The objections to as much of an inference as this are forced and feeble. It is *possible* that the meaning may be only this: We know neither himself nor his,—while in human relations the man and his genealogy are objects of eager inquiry and extensive knowledge. But the Messianic Psalms had already spoken of "the Son," mysteriously, perhaps, and yet enough to supply germs of knowledge as well as of faith. See HOLDEN, *etc*.—A.]—Strangely insipid and rationalizing is UMBREIT's view [held by NOYES, *etc.*], that by the Son is here intended the pupil of the philosopher who understands all the mysteries of the world and the world's government!— Furthermore the LXX instead of בְּנוֹ must have read בָּנָיו for they render ἢ τὸ ὄνομα τοῖς τέκνοις αὐτοῦ.

Vers. 5, 6. Instead of unprofitable puzzling about God and divine mysteries there is recommended the humble reception in faith of the only true divine revelation which affords light and peace, and needs no supplementing or perfecting on the part of man.—With 5 *a* comp. Ps. xix. 9; cxix. 140; with *a* and *b*, Ps. xviii. 31, where however יְהוָה takes the place of the divine name אֱלוֹהַּ which is characteristic of our passage. In regard to this comp. above, remarks under No. 1.—**Add thou nothing to His words.** A similar warning with respect to the law as a revelation of the divine will fully sufficient in itself and adequate occurs in Deut. iv. 2; xii. 32; comp. also Rev. xxii. 18.

4. Vers. 7-10. Prayer of the poet to Jehovah for preservation from all that is false, and from the two extremes of poverty and riches (vers. 7-9), together with a warning against the vice of slander. This last forms with ver. 17 the sole exception to that mode of constructing the proverbs which elsewhere in the section, vers. 7-33, is consistently carried through, viz., the numerical. Comp. on these peculiar numerical proverbs or *Middoth*, the Introd., § 14, and remarks on chap. vi. 16.—**Two things have I entreated of thee.** This double prayer is, as the 2d clause shows, a prayer not merely once offered, but the abiding utterance to God of the desire of the poet's heart, his importunate request from Him continued to his death.

Ver. 8. **Deceit and lies keep far from me.** "Deceit" (שָׁוְא) and "lying words" stand in the mutual relation of the devising of inward untruth and deceitful wickedness, and the false, lying utterance which springs forth from this as its necessary expression. No further justification is added for this first half of the prayer; the second, however, which relates to the golden mean between rich and poor, is more minutely explained and justified in ver. 8, c and ver. 9. [The idea "vanity" given in the E. V. and retained by H., M., W., *etc.*, is a secondary meaning of the noun whose primary meaning according to GESEN. is "evil," according to FUERST "insecurity, or slipperiness." It seems to be more than the unsubstantial, it is the positively deceitful that is here intended.—A.]—**Cause me to eat the food allotted me,** lit. "the food of my lot or portion." *i. e.,* the part or assignment that falls to me, so much as is intended and is needful for me, no more and no less. Comp. xxxi. 15; Gen. xlvii. 22; and also the ἄρτος ἐπιούσιος, the "daily bread" of the Lord's prayer, Matth. vi. 11, which is equivalent at least in a general way.

Ver. 9. **Lest I being full deny,** *etc.* Bold denial of the Holy One, and the mocking question "who is the Lord, or what can He do?" (comp. Ps. lxxiii. 11; Job xxi. 14) appears in other passages likewise as the indication of pride developed by surfeiting and luxurious enjoyment in life; see Deut. viii 12-15; xxxii. 15 sq.—**And lest I be poor and steal** (comp. vi. 30) **and take the name of my God in vain.** תפש "to lay hands upon or seize hold of something" here denotes the wicked profanation of the divine name which consists in mockery, cursing and contumely with respect to it. For such offences as these the bitter necessities of hunger and poverty may according to Isa. viii. 21 produce (comp. Prov. xix. 3), and not merely false swearing by the name of God in denying the guilt of theft, which alone is usually thought of here.

Ver. 10. **Cause not the servant to slander his master.** Usually rendered: "betray (or slander) not the servant to his master" (Vulg., LUTHER, UMBREIT [E. V., DE W., H., N., M.], *etc.*). But the Hiphil cannot have the same meaning as the Poel, Ps. ci. 5; it must mean "to cause one to slander, to excite one to calumny against another." The warning is not against slander in itself, but against incitement to slander, and more specifically betraying servants into tattling and accusations against their masters (thus correctly EWALD, BERTHEAU, HITZIG, ELSTER [KAMPH, S.], *etc.*).—**Lest he curse thee, and thou be destroyed.** The instigator to slander might easily hit upon the wrong person, a faithful, diligent servant, who instead of allowing himself to be misled, might rather curse the betrayer, and so bring merited calamity upon his head (comp. remarks on xxvi. 2).

5. Vers. 11-14. An utterance expressive of execration, vehement abhorrence, concerning a people or a generation characterized by four forms of ungodliness (not *quatuor genera detestabilia hominum,* as J. D. MICHAELIS and others hold). The דּוֹר which is four times repeated, may be taken either as a vocative, "Oh generation!" (EWALD, ELSTER), or as a nominative, which then expresses simply the existence of a generation of the kind described, and is used in a certain sense for יֵשׁ דּוֹר (LUTHER, E. V., *etc.* "There is a generation").—**A generation that curseth their father,** *etc.* Comp. chap. xx. 20; Ex. xxi. 17; and then with respect to ver. 12; Isa. iv. 4; with reference to ver. 13, Isa. x. 12; Ps. cxxxi. 2; Prov. vi. 17.—**And their eyelids are lifted up!** HITZIG finds in this exclamation, which appears at first to be only a rhetorically expanded parallel to "the loftiness of the eyes" in clause *a*, an allusion to the name עֲמָלֵק Amalek, which in the Arabic signifies "one looking with wide open eyes, a man with eyelids lifted up or painted." He therefore conjectures that the entire delineation of a reckless generation here before us refers to the people of the Amalekites, whose deadly national hatred toward the children of Israel (the "needy or poor," ver. 14 *b*) and whose warlike love of plunder are described in ver. 14 especially. With the assumption that Agur is the prince of a colony of Simeonites, Massa, founded in the Amalekite territory (see remarks above, No. 1), this hypothesis would admirably agree, on account of 1 Chron. iv. 53. And yet the conjecture is in itself too uncertain, and particularly too little established on the linguistic side.—With ver. 14 *a* comp Ps. lvii. 5; lviii. 7; with *b,* Jer. v. 17; xxx. 16; 1. 17; Isa. ix. 12, *etc.* [WORDSW. with his fondness for allegorizing finds in these "four evil generations" an undoubted reference to spiritual mysteries, *e. g.,* various offences within and against the church.—A.].

6. Vers. 15, 16. Of four kinds of insatiable things.—**The leech hath two daughters; Give, give!** The rare name Aluka (עֲלוּקָה) the old versions (the LXX, SYMM., the Venet., Vulg.) render by βδέλλη, *sanguisuga,* with which there should undoubtedly be taken into account the fact that *galuká* or *galoká* in the Indian is the name of the blood-sucker, and that essentially the same word (علوق) is in Arabic the designation of a ghostly demon (or according to Camus, possibly of a ravenous wolf). And this is the more confirmed by the fact that the

Targ. on Ps. xii. 9 speaks of "an Aluka going about in a circle, and sucking from men their blood," and by this is undoubtedly meant a vampyre-like spirit, a ghostly monster of the nature of the *ghouls* of the Arabs and Persians, or the Indian *dakini* (which congregate in graveyards, and live on the flesh and bones of the corpses). An Indian origin of the conception described by "Aluka" is indicated also by the occurrence of a proverb closely related to our own, with reference to the insatiableness of four things, in the *Hitopadesa* (ed. LASSEN, p. 66): "The fire is not sated with wood, nor the great sea with the streams; nor the god of death with all the living, nor the beautiful-eyed with men." The similarity of this Indian maxim to our passage is clearly much more significant, than that of the Arabic proverb in MEIDANI, III. 64, where only "death not to be satisfied with creatures, and fire not to be satisfied with wood" make up the objects compared. The assumption of a derivation both of the name Aluka, and of the entire proverb in its essential substance from the old Indian literature need the less excite any well-founded suspicion, since Agur's residence, Massa, doubtless lay quite near to the old highway of caravans leading from India and Persia to Petra and Teima, and on this Sabæan and other merchants will have brought, not only Indian articles of traffic, but Indian ideas and literary productions to the lands of South Western Asia (comp. HITZIG, p. 313). But the name Aluka and the proverb as a whole is conceived with substantial correctness by DÖDERLEIN and ZEIGLER, whom afterward GESEN., UMBREIT, HITZIG, BERTHEAU, DELITZSCH, and in general most of the recent interpreters have followed. [For illustration supplied by travellers in Palestine, see THOMSON's *Land and Book*, I. 368, and WOOD's *Bible Animals*, p. 646.—A.]

We must reject as untenable both JARCHI's interpretation of "Aluka" by Sheol, hell (so rendered in alleged accordance with the Arabic), and BOCHART's assertion, that the word signifies fate, μοῖρα, insatiable destiny. In this latter view there is only so much of truth, that "Aluka" does indeed appear generalized to a conception of quite a comprehensive sort, so far forth, plainly, as "personified insatiableness, craving in its highest intensity" (BERTHEAU) is denoted by it. Therefore, it appears also as a female spirit, and has two daughters ascribed to it. These two "daughters of the blood-sucker" are in the first instance designated by a double "give," in accordance with their character as craving, insatiable natures, and these are also expressly mentioned by name. For it is plainly these that are meant by the first two of the four insatiable things, which are named in vs. 16 *a* as "Sheol" and the "barren womb." Hell, or the kingdom of the dead, is also in Isaiah v. 14, as well as above in chap. xxvii. 20, personified as a spiritual power that with insatiable greediness gathers men to itself. The "closing of the "womb" (for עֹצֶר comp. Gen. xvi. 2; xx. 18), *i. e.*, the unfruitful womb of woman, in connection with which there is no conception and bearing of children, gives indications of itself, according to what is said in Gen. xxx. 1 sq. of Jacob's wives, likewise in an insatiable craving, in constant desire for sexual enjoyments. On this second example of insatiableness the most weight seems to be laid by the author of the proverb (comp. chap. xxvii. 20). He does not, however, externally distinguish it specially, and assigns it a prominent place in the series of his enumerations only by making it together with "hell" emphatically the daughter of the blood-sucker, while the "earth" as a third, and the "fire" as a fourth example he simply allows to follow in a subordinate place. The whole sentence evidently lacks the symmetrical, simply and clearly organized structure, which distinguishes the analogous Indian proverb above cited. Yet in this fact that just that which is the main thought, or the truth in the moral world among men which is to be illustrated by the associated similes from nature, the insatiableness of the craving of the barren woman, is pushed on to the second place, and so in a sense hidden (unlike the order in that Sanscrit proverb where the never satisfied "beautiful-eyed" are emphatically placed at the end), there is with the greatest probability involved a fully conscious intention of the author of the proverb, who wished by this artifice to give to his maxim the heightened charm of ingenuity, and to form, instead of a mere numerical proverb, a sharp enigmatical proverb (a חִידָה, comp. Introd., § 11, note 2). Of these numerical proverbs which are at the same time enigmas, our chapter contains several besides, especially vers. 18–20; vers. 24–28; and vers. 29–31. [As compared with the numerical proverbs that follow, the complexity and the more artificial character of the one before us at once arrests attention. They all have this in common, that whatever moral lesson they have to convey is less obvious, being hinted rather than stated, and in this view they may merit the name "enigmas." In the one now under consideration insatiable desire and the importance of its regulation seem to be the remote object. In the development, instead of the "three things" and "four things" which repeatedly appear afterward, we have the "leech," its two daughters, the three and the four. Some have regarded the two daughters as representing physical characteristics of the blood-sucker,—others as expressing by an Orientalism a doubly intense craving. Parallelism suggests making the first two of the four the two daughters apart from other considerations; other allusions of the Scriptures to the greediness of the world of the dead, justify the first, while the second alone belongs to human nature. We can see no other reason than this for making the second the most emphatic of the four as Z. is disposed to do.—Only the most unnatural theory of inspiration can take exception to the suggestion of a possible Indian origin for the substance and the external form of this proverb, its place and form here being secured by an appropriate and adequate influence of the Holy Spirit. The Book of Proverbs applies a very severe test to some theories of inspiration.—A.]

7. Ver. 17. The punishment of him who sins against his parents;—an ethical maxim introduced without any close connection into the series of the "Middoth" in our section, as ver. 10 is above. EWALD would have the insatiableness of the birds of prey, which are to execute the judgment on the

wicked man, regarded as the main idea of the proverb, connecting it with vers. 15, 16. This element, however, is plainly too far in the background, and the main thought is rather his desert of curse and penalty who daringly tramples under foot the fifth commandment; and from this there is a sort of connection with vers. 11–14.— **An eye . . . . the ravens of the valley** (lit., brook) (comp. I Kings xvii. 4–6) **shall pluck it out**, *etc.* [The נחל, the Arabic Wady, is sometimes the torrent, sometimes the valley through which it flows. See full illustrations and citations in STANLEY'S *Palestine*, p. 496.—A.]—The "raven" and the "eagle" (*i. e.*, vulture) are named here as birds that feed upon carrion; the "sons of the eagle," *i. e.*, the young eagles, are named because it is especially upon sons, wayward sons, it is true, that the penalty is to be inflicted. The punishment itself, however, consists in strangling and leaving the bodies unburied, so that they become food for the fowls of heaven; comp. 1 Sam. xvii. 44; 1 Kings xiv. 11; xvi. 4, *etc.*— [With reference to the raven consult WOOD's *Bible Animals*, p. 445; and to the eagle or griffin vulture, p. 346.—A.]

8. Vers. 18–20. Four incomprehensible things. —**The way of the eagle in the heavens,** *etc.*—Besides the ease with which the eagle, a large and heavy bird, soars high above in the air (comp. Job xxxix. 27), this circumstance is also surely an object of the poet's amazement, that it leaves behind no trace of its course; for the same thing is also true of the progress of the smoothly gliding serpent over the slippery rock, and also of that of the ship that swiftly ploughs the waves of the sea. Of the fourth of the ways here compared, the "way of the man with the maid" (or "in the maid"), *i. e.*, of the mysterious way in which the man in sexual intercourse has fruitful connection with the maid, this failure to leave any trace behind seems indeed to be less true. And yet the author in this connection doubtless thinks not of pregnancy and the woman's child-bearing as later results of sexual connection, but as ver. 20 shows, at first only of this, that the intercourse leaves behind it no traces immediately and directly apparent; man and wife, adulterer and adulteress, can the night following the accomplishment of the mysterious process be convicted of it by no one; the act is as little to be detected in them both as eating in him who after table has wiped his mouth (ver. 20, *b*, *c*). Moreover, the woman in ver. 19 is designated as עַלְמָה, *i. e.*, as *virgo pubescens*, as a young woman capable of sexual intercourse (comp. Gen. xxiv. 43; Is. vii. 14; Song Sol. vi. 8), undoubtedly for this reason, that she is to be put in contrast with the adulterous woman in ver. 20; in other words, the sexual intercourse between man and woman is to be described first in its pure and normal type (the first love of the bridegroom and the bride, comp. Gen. ii. 24; Eph. v. 31, 32; John iii. 29), and only afterwards in its degenerate form as adultery. Furthermore, the "Alma" of our passage has been in many ways interpreted also of the Virgin Mary, *e. g.*, by AMBROSE, LYRA, CORN. A LAPIDE, and FR GRISENIUS (in LÜSCHEN's "*Unsch. Nachrichten*," Vol. 13, p. 503) [and also by WORDSW. *in loco*].— DATHE has very unnecessarily been disposed to regard ver. 20 as a spurious addition by a later hand. It is not even necessary (with HITZIG) to regard the verse as a later addition coming from Agur himself, which he "had not originally had in view."

9. Vers. 21–23. Four intolerable things under which the earth trembles (not "the land," as LUTHER, UMBREIT, BERTHEAU, *etc.*, render, weakening the sense). With ver. 21 comp. Am. ii. 13; vii. 10.—**Under a servant when he becometh ruler.**—This is the first and most familiar example, by which the moral danger, and even the ruinous consequences of a sudden elevation of men from a depressed condition to an influential station and unwonted prosperity, are illustrated.—**And a fool when he is satisfied with bread.**—The "becoming surfeited" is usually attended by a becoming insolent (see ver. 9), especially in the case of a fool to whom not satiety but hunger is properly becoming (chap. xiii. 25; Job xxvii. 14).

Ver. 23. Under a **hated woman when she is married.** By the "hated woman" is meant, not one who is "odious," "worthy of hate" (ROSENM., [E. V., H., N., S., M.,]), nor again a woman already married and only neglected and disparaged by her husband (DATHE, UMBREIT,), but, as appears from the "when she is married," one who has remained waiting, the maiden (old maid) who at first could obtain no husband, but afterward when she has been married triumphs insolently, and deals harshly and contemptuously with her sisters or companions who are single (comp. Gen. xxix. 31, 33; Deut. xxi. 15-17.) The same will be the conduct, according to clause *b* of a maid "when she becomes heir to her mistress," *i. e.*, undoubtedly, when she supplants her mistress in the favor of her husband, and so becomes his all-powerful favorite.

10. Vers. 24–28. The four things that are small and yet wise (with respect to חֲכָמִים, made wise or quick of wit, comp. Ps. lviii. 6; lxiv. 7). Four species of small animals are thus described, which in spite of their comparatively diminutive size and strength of body, yet by virtue of their diligence (ver. 25), shrewdness (ver. 26), harmony (ver. 27), and flexibility (ver. 28) serve as instructive emblems for the domestic, social and political life of men.—With ver. 25 comp. vi. 7, 8.—For the "conies" (Z. "cliff-badgers") in ver 26, *i. e.*, the *hyrax Syriacus* which live in companies in Syria, Palestine and Arabia Petriea (not the marmot, the *mus sive dipus jaculus*, comp LINNÆUS, or the rabbit, as LUTHER renders the word, following the Chald. and the Rabbins), see Ps. civ. 18; Lev. xi. 5; Deut. xiv. 7. [See THOMSON's *Land and Book*, 1. 459, and also WOOD's *Bible Animals*, pp. 312-18; and for his illustration of the nature and habits of the ant of Palestine, pp. 616–22; for the locusts see pp. 596-604; and for the gecko, a species of lizard which he understands to be referred to in ver. 28 instead of the "spider," see pp. 643, 534 sq. A.].—For the "organized going forth" of the locusts. in ver. 27, comp. especially Joel ii. 2 sq., [and THOMSON, *Land and Book*, II. 109]. Finally the lizard in ver. 28 is as its name signifies the poisonous spotted lizard (*stellio*, Vulg.) in regard to which the thing here made prominent is

its sly entering into the interior of houses, and even into the palaces of the great. For this characteristic of the animal BOCHART brings forward various testimonies, *Hieroz.*, 1. iv. 7, p. 1090, Frankfort Ed. [GESENIUS, FUERST, etc., favor this rendering, and WOOD (*ubi supra*) describes and depicts the peculiar form of the feet by which the lizard, the Gecko, "layeth hold" even upon flat surfaces like the walls of apartments.—A.]

11. Ver. 29-31. The four creatures that have a stately movement; three animals, and the king in his all-ruling dignity and power. The whole description really turns upon the last.

Ver. 31. **The greyhound, slender in its loins.** This is the probable meaning of the difficult phrase זַרְזִיר מׇתְנַיִם (according to the Jewish interpreters, EWALD, BERTHEAU, [E. V., S., M.,] etc.). For זַרְזִיר is plainly derived from the root זָרַר "to compress," and therefore denotes a compact, slender animal; and the neighboring term seems to indicate the intention not to bring together exclusively examples of animal majesty of the high rank of the lion, but to give to the enumeration as a whole in a certain sense a ludicrous variety and an air of wit. The old versions (LXX, Vulg., Targ., etc.,) suggest the *cock*; with this meaning of the main noun the modifying term, however, does not at all agree, even though one were disposed to transform it into a Hithp. Part. מׇתְנַיִם. Others, like SCHULTENS, GESEN. (?), UMBREIT, ELSTER, HITZIG [DE W., K., MUFFET, N.] take the זַרְזִיר in the sense of "that which is girded about the loins, or panoplied," and therefore the *war-horse*,—a meaning however which is not surely demonstrable. [Starting with the same idea WORDSW. understands a "warrior," and WOOD an "athlete." FUERST's rendering is "stag"].—**And a king with whom no resistance** (occurs). In this way (with the Vulg., the Rabbins, GEIER, MICHAELIS, BERTHEAU, EWALD, [K., E. V., H., S., M.], etc.), we must interpret the words אַלְקוּם עִמּוֹ, although the אַל־כָּוָה of chap. xii. 28 is a very doubtful parallel for this way of regarding אַלְקוּם as a compound of אַל and קוּם. For the identification of this noun with the Arabic الْقَوْمُ "the people" (CASTELLIO, POCOCKE, UMBREIT, [DE W., N.], etc.), an argument might seem to lie in the fact that the meaning so reached, "the king at the head of his people," agrees almost literally with the δημηγορῶν ἐν ἔθνει of the LXX, and the similar version of the Syriac. But to bring in an Arabic word, especially one compounded with the article *al* is here quite too unnatural. HITZIG's emendation might better recommend itself, אֱלֹהִים instead of אַלְקוּם, and all the more because it gives a very pertinent sense: "A king with whom God is."

12. Vers. 32, 33. Warning against pride, haughtiness and love of strife, with an indication of three forms of evil resulting from these vices.—**If thou art foolish in exalting thyself** (comp. 1 Kings i. 5) **and if thou devisest evil.** To these two hypothetical antecedent clauses, which do not present an antithesis (the foolish and rational—as HITZIG explains), but two different forms of human error: foolish self-exaltation and wicked plotting, the sentence "the hand on the mouth," forms the conclusion, interjectional and imperative (comp. Job xx. 5).

Ver. 33 then justifies the warning by a significant intimation of three cases in which the foolish act of "pressing" (מִיץ) brings forth undesirable results,—strong cheese, flowing blood, sharp strife.—**And pressing** (forcing) **wrath produceth strife.** The last word supplies plainly the object of the whole discourse from ver. 32 onward. The dual אַפַּיִם stands doubtless intentionally (comp. Dan. xi. 20) to indicate that it is the wrath of two whose sharp pressing upon each other leads to the development of strife. [THOMSON, *Land and Book*, 1.398, describing the Oriental mode of churning by squeezing and wringing a leathern bag or bottle that contains the milk, makes more apparent and vivid the meaning of this comparison. The dual אַפַּיִם is employed probably because nostrils usually exist in pairs, and the transition is easy from the physical organ, through the heavy breathing of passion, to the metaphorical sense "wrath." Whether two or many are concerned in strife is not material.—A.]

DOCTRINAL AND ETHICAL.

As the confession of an Israelite, a believer in Jehovah in a strange land, one separated from his people of the ten tribes, who among Arabs and the sworn and mortal enemies of Israel, adheres firmly to the faith of his nation, this discourse of Agur is one of great doctrinal importance, and of no slight interest to the history of redemption. Its fundamental idea, which is put forward as a sort of programme, is contained in the six verses of the introduction, and comes out most clearly in ver. 5: Every word of God is pure; a shield is He to them that trust in Him. It is the truth, purity and saving power of the word of God alone, in contrast with the nullity and inadequacy of all human wisdom (vers. 2-5), that forms the starting point in the instructive discourse of this poet of wisdom, and to which all the manifold apothegms, numerical proverbs and enigmas which he combines in a varied series in vers. 7-33, sustain a closer or more remote relation.

While it appears at the first view that the flowers and fruits from the cornucopia of Agur's wisdom, original and in part so rarely fashioned, are heaped up wholly without order, yet they all agree in this, that they depict the glory and all-sufficiency of the word of God, dissuade from adding to it by any human supplements (see in particular ver. 7), and most urgently commend the fulfilling and following it by a pious life. There is hardly a single commandment of the Decalogue that is not directly or indirectly repeated and emphasized in these maxims. Observe the relation of the prayer for the hallowing of God's name (vers. 7-9), to the first and third commandments; the reference contained in ver. 11 and again in ver. 17 to the fifth commandment; the warnings against the transgression of the sixth commandment in ver. 14 as well as in vers. 32, 33; the reproving and warning aim of vers. 18-20, and 23, in their bearing upon the seventh; the allusion to the eighth in ver. 9, and to the ninth in ver. 10; and finally the reference, reminding us of the tenth, in vers. 15, 16, as bearing on the unsatiableness of evil desire (this "daughter of the blood-sucker" and sister of hell!). No one of these proverbs is wholly without an ethical value, not even the two numerical proverbs, vers. 24-28 and 29-31, which at the first view stand apart as incidental reflections on merely natural truths, but in reality hide under their ingenious physical drapery decided moral aims. For in vers. 24-28 four chief virtues of one's social and political avocation are specified through an allusion to a like number of examples from the animal world (comp. exeg. notes, No. 10), and vers. 29-31 run into a delineation of the high dignity and glory of a king by the grace of God (in contrast with the insufferable tyranny of base upstarts, vers. 21-23).

It is true that the point of view taken in the author's doctrinal and ethical knowledge nowhere rises above the level of the pure religion of the law. The law's doctrine of retribution he holds with inexorable strictness and severity, as is indicated particularly in the fearful threatening prediction in ver. 17 against children who are disobedient to their parents (γονεῦσιν ἀπειθεῖς, Rom. i. 30). Against those who do not belong to the people of God of the Old Testament he appears to cherish prevailingly dispositions of hate and abhorrence, as the utterance in vers. 11-14, which is probably directed against such non-Israelitish people, shows (see remarks above on this passage). With respect to knowledge in the department of theology and Christology his point of view seems in no respect more elevated than that of the author of chaps. i.-ix.; for in ver. 4 he confesses that he knows nothing of the name of the Son of God, and he nowhere makes reference to the existence and efficiency of the hypostatic wisdom of God, not even where this would have been natural enough (e. g. in vers. 4-6). He need not be charged in addition with the intermingling of impure and superstitious notions from polytheistic religions, for the Aluka with its two daughters, in ver. 15, is evidently mentioned by him only with a symbolical design, as a personification of insatiableness (an evil lust that nothing can quell), and is by no means represented as an actually existing spectre, or demoniacal nature.*

HOMILETIC AND PRACTICAL.

Homily on the entire chapter:—The all-sufficient power and the fullness of blessing in the divine word in contrast with the weakness of mere human wisdom: *a*) in general (vers. 1-6); *b*) with special reference to the glory and indispensable necessity of the Decalogue (vers. 7-33); comp. Doctrinal and Ethical notes.—Or again:

* The case appears to be otherwise with the spectre of the night לִילִית mentioned in Isa. xxxiv. 14; comp. DELITZSCH on this passage.

To God's word and law man is to add nothing (vers. 1-6), but he is also to take nothing away, not even one of its least commandments (vers. 7-33).— STÖCKER: All true wisdom comes from God alone (1-7), not from human nature, which is rather exceedingly corrupt (11-17), and whose understanding is greatly weakened (18-24).

Vers. 1-6. MELANCHTHON: Human wisdom is able to devise no means of preservation from the ignorance and spiritual weakness which naturally belong to us. But the Church in its divine revelation possesses a light which not only reveals to it the causes of its spiritual destitution, but also points out the means for its elevation and healing. Therefore this divinely revealed truth must be listened to by us, must be received in faith as well in its threatenings of punishment as in its consolatory contents, and be guarded from all corruption and perversion.—LUTHER (marginal comment on ver.2): Wise people know that their wisdom is nothing; fools know everything and cannot err.—GEIER (on vers. 2, 3): With the knowledge of himself and of the deep corruption that dwells in him the Christian must make the beginning in the contemplation of divine things.—[ARNOT: It is a precious practical rule to look toward heaven while we measure ourselves.—TRAPP: Godliness as it begins in right knowledge of ourselves, so it ends in a right knowledge of God.—EDWARDS: All true spiritual knowledge is of that nature that the more a person has of it the more is he sensible of his own ignorance].—STARKE (on vers. 4-6): Whoever is engaged in the investigation and exposition of God's word, let him take his reason captive to the obedience of faith, and not curiously scrutinize, that he may make divine mysteries comprehensible.—STÖCKER (on vers. 5, 6): On the glory of the divine word, especially its clearness, utility and perfectness.— *Berleburg Bible* (on ver. 6); How many counterfeiters there are who from their poor copper make additions to the royal gold currency of God's word, and thereby debase it!—[LAWSON: Our trust must be in the name of the Lord, as it is represented to us in the word of God: the seed and the ground of our faith in Him.—MUFFET: It is treason to corrupt or falsify the prince's coin; what high treason must it needs be then to counterfeit or corrupt the pure word of God!]

Vers. 7-17. Comp. P. GERHARD's poetical reproduction of vers. 7-9: "*Zweierlei bitt' ich von dir,*" etc. (*Gesamm. geistliche Lieder*, No. 41).— [TRAPP: God heaps mercies on His suppliants, and blames them for their modesty in asking.— ARNOT: Agur's requests are specific and precise; the temporal interests are absolutely subordinated to the spiritual prosperity of the suppliant; and a watch is set against the danger to a soul which lies in extremes either of position or of character.—BP. HOPKINS: There is a seeking of worldly advantages which is not to be branded with the black mark of self-seeking; *e. g.* when we seek them with a due subordination to the higher and more noble ends of piety and holiness, such as that we may escape those temptations which possibly the want of them might expose us unto.—FLAVEL: How much better were it for thee to endure the pains of hunger than those of a guilty conscience.—BATES: To receive no hurtful impressions by great changes of condition discovers a habit of excellent grace and virtue in the soul].—GEIER: Although poverty and riches of themselves can neither make us blessed nor damn us, yet both are wont incidentally and through the fault of men not rarely to bring after them consequences injurious to our spiritual welfare.—(On ver. 10): Keep thy tongue bridled, especially when it is disposed to rage against the needy and helpless; for though it is not right to curse thy neighbor, yet such curses when they have been uttered do not remain without effect, particularly if he who utters them is one who has been unjustly oppressed.—STARKE (on ver. 11-14): The natural corruption of men is great; yet it is possible that they be purged from it by the blood of Jesus Christ; 1 Cor. vi. 11; 1 John i. 7.—Unthankfulness (ver. 11), self-righteousness (ver. 12), pride (ver. 13), and unmercifulness (ver. 14) are usually associated as an unblessed quartette of sisters—WOHLFARTH (on vers. 15, 16): Many are the evil spirits that go about among men to spread misfortune and ruin, the cruel spectre of avarice is one of the most formidable enemies of our race. Like the vampyre which in the night attacks sleepers and sucks their blood, this demon rages in palaces and cottages, etc.—(On ver. 17): What Agur here says by way of warning of ravens and vultures, etc., has already gone a thousandfold into literal fulfilment in a horrible way on children who are wayward and in consequence of their disobedience to parents sunk in the deepest spiritual need; who were either driven to self-murder, or died on the scaffold.

Vers. 18-31. LUTHER (marginal, on ver. 19): Love (the mystery of love, Eph. v. 31, 32) is not to be thought out or expressed.—GEIER (on vers. 18-20): As it is with adulterers so it is with flatterers; they will never allow their vicious nature to be called by the right name.—(On vers. 21-23): It always causes manifold disquiet and misfortune, when they rule over others whom it would better befit to be subject to others.—(On vers. 24-28): Despise not things that at the first glance appear small and contemptible. Under a poor garment there is often a wise man hid; Dan. i. 18-20.—(On vers. 29-31): In matters belonging to one's office and public calling it is important to be courageous and firm, especially in times of need. It is not well then if one forsakes those over whom one is set; Ecclesiast. x. 31.—[LAWSON (on ver. 20): Do not imagine that the secrecy of sin is your security from punishment; it is the snare of your souls].

Vers. 32, 33. LUTHER (marginal, on ver. 32): Be not ashamed if thou hast chanced to err, and do not defend it. For to err is human, but to defend it is devilish.—LANGE: Strut not with lust of the eyes, fleshly lust and insolence. Thereby thou only provokest the wrath of God, that will come down too heavily for thee; Ecclesiast. v. 2 sq.—*Berleburg Bible:* He that would gladly shun strife must seek to avoid obstinacy and self-will. How many useless disputes in matters of religion might not in this way be escaped!—[EDWARDS: Silence attends humility.—MOFFET: He which falleth through pride should rise again to repentance].

Second Supplement:

The words of Lemuel, together with the poem in praise of the matron.

CHAP. XXXI.

a) Lemuel's maxims of wisdom for kings.

VERS. 1-9.

1 **Words of Lemuel the king of Massa**
  with which his mother instructed him:
2 Oh, my son! oh, thou son of my womb!
  oh thou son of my vows!
3 Give not thy strength to women,
  nor thy ways to destroy kings.
4 Not for kings, oh Lemuel,
  not for kings (is it becoming) to drink wine;
  nor for princes (wine) or strong drink;
5 lest he drink and forget the law,
  and pervert the judgment of all the sons of want.
6 Give strong drink to him that is perishing,
  and wine to him that is of a heavy heart.
7 Let him drink and forget his poverty,
  and let him remember his want no more!

8 Open thy mouth for the dumb,
  for the right of all orphan children.
9 Open thy mouth, judge righteously,
  and vindicate the poor and needy.

b) Alphabetical song in praise of the virtuous, wise and industrious woman.

VERS. 10–31.

10 A virtuous woman who can find?
   and yet her price is far above pearls.
11 The heart of her husband doth trust in her,
   and he shall not fail of gain.
12 She doeth him good and not evil
   all the days of her life.
13 She careth for wool and linen,
   and worketh with diligent hands.
14 She is like the ships of the merchant,
   from afar doth she bring her food.
15 She riseth up while it is yet night,
   and giveth food to her house
   and a portion to her maidens.
16 She considereth a field and buyeth it,
   a vineyard with the fruit of her hands.
17 She girdeth her loins with strength,
   and maketh her arms strong.
18 She perceiveth that her gain is good,
   her light goeth not out by night.
19 She putteth her hands to the distaff,
   and her fingers lay hold on the spindle.
20 She stretcheth forth her hand to the poor,
   and extendeth her arms to the needy.
21 She is not afraid of the snow for her household,
   for all her household is clothed in crimson.
22 Coverlets doth she prepare for herself;
   fine linen and purple is her clothing.
23 Her husband is known in the gates,
   when he sitteth with the elders of the land.
24 She maketh fine linen and selleth it,
   and girdles doth she give to the merchant.
25 Strength and honor are her clothing;
   she laugheth at the future.
26 She openeth her mouth with wisdom,
   and the law of kindness is on her tongue.
27 She looketh well to the ways of her household
   and the bread of idleness she will not eat.
28 Her sons rise up and praise her,
   her husband, he also boasteth of her:
29 Many daughters have done virtuously,
   but thou hast excelled them all!
30 Grace is deceitful, beauty is vanity,
   a woman that feareth the Lord; let her be praised!
31 Give to her of the fruit of her hands,
   and let her works praise her in the gates.

GRAMMATICAL AND CRITICAL.

Ver. 2.—[מַה, where it occurs the third time, is pointed בָּר, as is not uncommon in repetitions, to secure variety; see BÖTT., ₴ 499, c. The consonant succeeding is the same in the three cases.—A.]

Ver. 3.—Hitzig changes the לִכְחוֹת (Inf. Hiph. from כחה) to the fem. part. of לכח, "to leer or ogle," לְכֹחוֹת, "and give not thy way to them (the seductive courtesans) who leer after kings" (?). [Bött. prefers to make of it a Kal part. fem. plur. from כחה, and would point לְכֹחוֹת and render "the caressers of kings." This is certainly easier than the causative Infinitive with its abstractness. See Bött., § 1089, 2. כְּלָכִין, an Aramaic form immediately followed in ver. 4 by the regular plural twice repeated. Green, § 193, a; Bött., § 277, 3.—A.]

Ver. 4.—We render אִי "or" according to the K'thibh, which is recommended by like examples of a distributive location of this disjunctive particle (such as chap. xxx. 31 [where Bött. would read רָאוּ rather than allow the irregularity; Job xxii. 11). We do not need therefore to substitute for it אַי, "desire" (that is, "for strong drink," Gesen. and others), or to read with the K'ri אֵי, "where?" ("where is strong drink for princes?" comp. Gen. iv. 9). [Bött. regards it as a probable Simeonite synonym for הָאֲוָה, "desire," § 436, 3; 443, g. The two forms of the king's name, לְמוֹאֵל and לְמוּאֵל, a genitive in ver. 1 and a vocative in ver. 4, also deserve attention. The changing person of the verbs is no uncommon phenomenon. See Ewald, § 309, a.—A.]

Ver. 5.—כְּחֻקָּק, a Pual part. from חקק, signifies "that which is decided, the prescribed," and is therefore equivalent to חֹק, "law."

Ver. 6.—תְּנוּ the permissive use of the Imper.; Bött., § 959, 5.—A.]

Ver. 12.—גָּבַל is used with two accusatives as in 1 Sam. xxiv. 18.

Ver. 13.—[The fem. noun פִּשְׁתָּה seems to be used of the raw material, flax, while this plural form פֵּשֶׁת is used of the product, the materials for clothing.—A.]

Ver. 15.—טֶרֶף (comp. the verb הִטְרִיף in xxx. 8) is a strong expression for לֶחֶם, ver. 14 (comp. above in ver. 11, שָׁלָל, "spoil").

Ver. 16.—The K'thibh נָטַע, stat. constr. from נֶטַע, "planting," Is. v. 7, is undoubtedly to be preferred to the K'ri נָטְעָה, notwithstanding all the old versions prefer the latter (see Bertheau and Hitzig on the passage). [Bött. defends the Masoretic reading, and renders as a verb.]

Ver. 21.—[The short form of the part. לָבֻשׁ seems to be explained and justified by the close connection of words and the sequence of שׁ. Bött., § 934, 6.—A.]

Ver. 27.—Instead of the K'thibh הֵילִיכוֹת we must either with the K'ri read הֲלִיכוֹת, or regard the former as an Aramaic collateral form (וְהִלְכָה) for הֲלִיכוֹת.

Ver. 30.—יִרְאַת before יְהוָה is here the stat. constr. not of the abstract substantive יִרְאָה, but from the fem. part. יְרֵאָה, "the woman who feareth."

EXEGETICAL.

1. Ver. 1. *The superscription to Lemuel's discourse.*—**Words of Lemuel, king of Massa.**—That we must, in disregard of the Masoretic pointing, connect the "Massa" with the first clause, and regard it as a genitive governed by the כְּלָךְ, which has no article, was the right view taken as early as the Syriac version, when it interprets the כְּלָךְ מַשָּׂא by "king of utterance" (*regis prophetæ*). We might, however, here, as in chap. xxx. 1, to regard כְּשָׂא rather as the name of a country, and Lemuel, the king of the land, as perhaps a brother of Agur, and consider his mother as the same wise princess who was there designated as "ruler of Massa." To her therefore belong properly and originally the counsels and instructions for kings contained in vers. 1–9. And yet, since Lemuel first reduced them to writing, and so transmitted them to posterity, they may well be called also "words of Lemuel,"—a title which there is therefore no need of altering (with Hitzig) to "words to Lemuel." The name "Lemuel," or, as it is written in ver. 4 by the punctuators, "Lemoel," appears furthermore to be quite as properly a genuine Hebrew formation as "Agur" (see above, Exeg. notes on chap. xxx., No. 2). It is probably only a fuller form for that which occurs in Numb. iii. 24 as an Israelitish masculine name, לָאֵל, "to God, for God" (*Deo deditus*). That it is purely a symbolical appellative designation, a circumscribing of the name Solomon, and that accordingly by the "mother of Lemuel" no other than Bathsheba is intended, this opinion of many old expositors (and recently of Schelling, Rosenmüller [Words.], etc.) lacks all further corroboration. [The impossibility of regarding כְּלָךְ without an article as an appositive of לְמוּאֵל, even though מַשָּׂא be not a limiting genitive, but an appositive to דְּבָרַי, is not admitted by those who defend the prevailing interpretation of ver. 1. The construction is admitted to be exceptional, but claimed to be possible (see, *e. g.*, Green, § 247, a). Hitzig, Bertheau, Z. and others make this one chief reason for seeking a new rendering. Another is the peculiar use of מַשָּׂא out of prophecy, and as an appositive to the sufficient and more appropriate דְּבָרַי. Here as in xxx. 1 Kamph. retains the ordinary meaning of מַשָּׂא, while S., here as there, follows Hitzig.—A.] In regard to the peculiar linguistic character of the section vers. 1–9, which in many points agrees with Agur's discourse [and in which Böttcher again recognizes a Simeonitish cast], see above, p. 246.

2. Vers. 2–9. *The rules of wisdom from Lemuel's mother.*—**Oh my son! Oh thou son of my womb!** etc.—The thrice repeated מָה, usually "what"—which Luther appropriately rendered by "Ach!" is plainly "an impassioned exclamation expressing the inward emotion of the mother's heart at the thought that the son might possibly

fall into an evil way" (ELSTER); it is therefore substantially "What, my son, wilt thou do?" or "How, my son, wilt thou suffer thyself to be betrayed?" etc.—With "son of my vows" comp. 1 Sam. i. 11.

Ver. 3. **Give not thy strength to women** —i. e., do not sacrifice it to them, do not give thy manly strength and vigor a prey to them. It is naturally the ways of licentiousness that are intended, which ruin physically and morally kings and princes who give themselves up to them. See Critical notes.

Vers. 4. This warning against licentiousness is immediately followed by a dissuasion from drunkenness, which is naturally closely connected with the preceding.—**Also not for princes** (is wine) **or strong drink.**—See Critical notes. For לָמוֹ, "mead, strong drink," comp. notes on xx. 1.—[GESEN., BÖTT., DE W., H., N., S., M., etc., would render by "desire," if the K'thibh is followed, which they are disposed to do. The K'ri, pointing אֵי, suggests either the interrogative אֵי, "where," or an abbreviated form of the negative אֵין. FUERST renders אֵי as an interrogative here. —A.]

Ver. 5. **Lest he drink and forget the law** —i. e., the king, who is here in question. The construction ("drink and forget" instead of "drinking forget") is like that in chap. xxx. 9. **—And pervert the judgment of all the sons of want**—i. e., of all the poor and helpless. For the Piel שִׁנָּה, "in deterius mutare, to distort, wrest, destroy," comp. Job xiv. 20. For the sentiment comp. PLINY, Hist. Nat., XXIII. 25: In proverbium cessit sapientiam vino obumbrari. [It has become proverbial that wisdom is clouded by wine.]

Vers. 6, 7. The enjoyment of wine and strong drink is seasonable in its cheering influence upon the sorrowful, whom it is desirable to cause to forget their sorrow; comp. Ps. civ. 15; Matth. xxvii. 34.—**Give strong drink to him who is perishing**—the man who is on the point of perishing, who is just expiring, as Job xxix. 13; xxxi. 19: "the heavy in heart" are afflicted, anxious ones, as in Job iii. 20; 1 Sam. xxii. 2, etc. [That even these be made to drink to unconsciousness is not the recommendation, but that in their extremity, physical or mental, wine be given to fulfil its office in imparting elasticity, and increasing power of endurance, and taking the crushing weight from calamities that might otherwise be overwhelming. As there is a misuse pointed out before in drinking to the destruction of kingly competence and the thwarting of kingly duty, self-indulgence, sinful excitement and excess overmastering reason and conscience.—so it is a kingly grace to bear others' burdens by ministries of helpful kindness. As on the one hand there is nothing here to preclude the pressing of other pleas for abstinence, so on the other there is nothing to encourage the too early and willing resort to the plea of necessity, or to commend in any case drinking to utter oblivion.—A.]

Vers. 8, 9. Continuation of the exhortation, commenced in ver. 5, to a righteous and merciful administration.—**Open thy mouth for the dumb**—That is, help such to their right as are not able to maintain it for themselves; be to them a judge and at the same time an advocate (comp. Job xxix. 15, 16).—**For the right of all orphan children.**—"Sons of leaving, of abandonment or disadvantage" (not of "destruction," as EWALD and BERTHEAU would interpret here, with a reference to Ps. xc. 5; is. ii. 18), are clearly those left behind as helpless orphans; the word therefore conveys a more specific idea than the "sons of want" in ver. 5.

3. *The praise of the virtuous matron* (vers. 10–31) is an alphabetic moral poem (like Ps. ix., x., xxv., xxxiv., cxix.; Lam. i.—iv., etc.), "a golden A B C for women" according to DÖDERLEIN's pertinent designation, a highly poetic picture of the ideal of a Hebrew matron. Not the alphabetic structure indeed, which it has in common with not a few Psalms of high antiquity, partly such as come from David (comp. DELITZSCH, Psalms i. 69; II. 187), but very probably some traces that are contained in it of a later *usus loquendi*, especially the more frequent *scriptio plena*, even apart from the distinctive accents (comp. HITZIG, p. 334), and also in particular the position assigned it by the compiler, even after Hezekiah's supplement and Agur's and Lemuel's discourse, mark the poem as a literary work produced quite late after Solomon's time, and even as probably the latest constituent of the whole collection. Although separated from the "words of Lemuel" by no superscription of its own, it shows itself to be the work of a different person from the wise prince of Massa, and that probably a later poet, by its not sharing the linguistic idioms of that section, and by the whole of its characteristic bearing and structure. Besides, in its contents and general drift it does not stand in any particularly close and necessary connection with the maxims of wisdom from the mother of Lemuel. And that it has by no means steadily from the beginning held its place immediately after these, appears with great probability from the fact that the LXX attach it directly to xxix. 27, and give to the proverbs of Agur and Lemuel an earlier place (within the limits of the present 24th chapter). Comp. Introd., § 13, p. 30.

With the greatest arbitrariness. R. STIER (*Politik der Weisheit*, pp. 134 sq.) has felt constrained to interpret the matron of this poem allegorically, and to make the application to the Holy Spirit renewing men and educating them for the kingdom of God. The whole attitude of the section speaks against such an interpretation, most of all the praise bestowed in vers. 23 sq. upon the influence of the matron as advancing the standing of her husband in the political organization of the State, as well as what is said in ver. 30 of the fear of God as her most eminent virtue. Comp. VON HOFMANN, *Schriftbew.*, II., 2, 378. [According to WORDSW. we find here a prophetic representation *of the Church of Christ*, in her truth, purity and holiness, and as distinguished from all forms of error, corruption and defilement, which sully and mar the faith and worship which he has prescribed."—A.]

4. Vers. 10–22. The action and management of the virtuous woman *within her domestic sphere*. **A virtuous woman, who can find?** The "virtuous woman." as in xii. 4; chap. xi. 16. [The transition is easy, from physical strength to moral strength and probity. The word "vir-

tuous" is therefore to be taken in this high sense.—A.]. The interrogative exclamation "who will find?" express the idea of a wish, as מִי יִתֵּן does elsewhere; it is therefore equivalent to "would that every one might find so gracious a treasure!"—**And yet her price is far above pearls.** The "and" at the beginning of this clause is either the exegetical, "that is, that is to say," as in xxv. 13, *etc.* (thus HITZIG), or, which seems to be more natural, the adversative "and yet, however" (EWALD, ELSTER). For the figure comp. iii. 10; viii. 11. [THOMSON, *Land and Book*, II. 572 sq. illustrates the force and fitness of the successive points in this description in contrast with the ordinary ignorance, weakness and worthlessness of the women of the East.—A.]

Ver. 11. **And he shall not fail of gain.** שָׁלָל strictly "the spoil of war," is a strong expression to describe the rich profit to which the co-operation of the efficient wife helps her husband's activity in his occupation. According to HITZIG, "spoil, fortunate discovery," is to be taken here as in Ps. cxix. 162; Isa. ix. 2, figuratively, and to be interpreted of the joy which the wife prepares for her husband (?).

Ver. 12. **She doeth him good and not evil.** Comp. 1 Sam. xxiv. 12.

Ver. 13. **She careth for wool and linen;** lit., "she *seeketh* (busieth herself with) wool and linen," *i. e.*, she provides these as materials for the products of her feminine skill.—**And worketh with diligent hands;** lit., "and laboreth with her hands' pleasure" (UMBREIT, EWALD, ELSTER) [DE W., K., E. V., N., S., M.]. or inasmuch as חֵפֶץ might here signify "occupation" (as in Is. lviii. 3; Eccles. iii. 17): "and laboreth in the business of her hands" (HITZIG).

Ver. 14. **She is like the ships of the merchant,** so far forth as she selling her products to foreigners (ver. 24), brings in gain from remote regions (comp. *b*), and provides long in advance for all the necessities of her house.

Ver. 15. **And distributeth food to her house.** The "portion" of the next clause is not a possible synonym for the "food" of this, so that it should denote the definite allowance of food, the rations of the maidens (LUTHER, BERTHEAU [E. V., S., M.] *etc.*); what is described by it is the definite *pensum*, what each maid has to spin of wool, flax, *etc.*, and therefore the day's work of the maidens (EWALD, UMBREIT, HITZIG [DE W., K., H., N.] *etc.*).

Ver. 16. **She considereth a field and buyeth it,** that is, for the money earned by her diligent manual labor.—**A vineyard** (Z. "a vineyard-planting") **with the fruit of her hands.** A "planting of a vineyard" (*genit. apposit.*) is however the same as a planting of vines. See Critical Notes for another construction and rendering.

Ver. 17. Comp. ver. 25 *a*.

Ver. 18. **She perceiveth that her gain is good.** For this verb טָעַם "to taste," *i. e.*, to discern, to become aware, comp. Ps. xxxiv. 9. For the succeeding phrase, "excellent, charming is her gain," comp. iii. 14. What she now does in consequence of this perception of the pleasing nature of her gain, is shown in the 2d clause.

Ver. 19. **She putteth her hands to the distaff.** This is the usual rendering. But probably HITZIG'S rendering is more exact (following VATABL., MERCERUS, GESEN., *etc.*): "Her hands she throweth out with the whorl," for כִּישׁוֹר is not properly the "distaff," but the "whorl, or wheel," *verticulum*. "a ring or knob fastened upon the spindle below the middle, that it may fall upon its base, and may revolve rightly." [KAMPH. rejects this explanation, and gives an extract of some length from a "Book of Inventions, Trades and Industries," to justify his own, which is the old view. The word translated "fingers" is literally her "bent hands."—A.]

Ver. 20. **Her hand she stretcheth forth to the poor,** lit., "her hollow, or bent hand," in which she holds her gift.

Ver. 21. **She is not afraid of the snow for her household,** lit., "feareth not for her house from snow." The snow stands here for "winter's cold," and for this reason,—that the sharpest possible contrast is intended with the clothes of "crimson wool," woolen stuffs of crimson color with which her household go clothed in winter. The same alliterative antithesis of שָׁנִי and שָׁלֵג is found in Is. i. 18.—UMBREIT, EWALD, BERTHEAU, S., *etc.*, render שָׁנִים incorrectly by "purple garments" (see in objection to this BAEHR'S *Symbolik des Mosaischen Cultus*, I. 333 sq.), while the LXX, LUTHER, ROSENM., VAIHINGER, H., *etc.*, read שְׁנַיִם (*vestimenta duplicia*, "double clothing"), by which the strong contrast is sacrificed.

Ver. 22. **Coverlets doth she prepare for herself.** For the "coverlets" comp. vii. 16. An article of clothing can be intended no more here than there. In the costly articles of apparel which the woman wears, the contrasted colors, white and purple, recur again. The *byssus* (COPT. *schensch*) and the "purple" (reddish purple in contrast with the (violet) "bluish purple" (תְּכֵלֶת) are both foreign materials, the one an Egyptian, the other a Syro-phœnician production.—Comp. BAEHR, *ubi supra*; WINER in his *Realwörterb*. Articles *Baumwolle* and *Purpur*.

5. Vers. 23–31. The influence of the matron beyond the narrow sphere of the domestic life. —**Her husband is well known in the gates,** because the excellence of his wife not only makes him rich but important and famous. With this being "known in the gates," see also ver. 31 *b* (*i. e.*, well known in counsel), comp. HOMER'S: ἐναρίθμιος ἐνὶ βουλῇ, Iliad ii. 202.

Ver. 24. **She maketh fine linen,** *etc.* סָדִין=σινδών (comp. LXX here and in Judg. xiv. 12) fine linen and shirts made of it (comp. Mark xiv. 51; Is. iii. 23, and HITZIG on this passage). —**And girdles doth she give to the merchant,** lit. to "the Canaanite," the Phœnician merchant, who knows well how to prize her fine products, and to dispose of them.

Ver. 25. With *a* comp. ver. 17; Job xxiv. 14.—**She laugheth at the future.** In reliance on her ample stores, and still more her inward strength and skill, she laughs at the future as respects the evil that it may perchance bring. [E. V.: "She shall rejoice in time to come;" H., M., W.; while DE W., K., BERTHEAU, MUFFET, N., S., *etc.*, take our author's view. This "laughing at the future" is of course not to be understood as expressive of a presumptuous self-confidence, but only of a consciousness of having all appropriate and possible preparation and competence for the future.—A.]

Ver. 26. **Her mouth she openeth with wisdom.** HITZIG well says: "The mouth, which in 25 *a*, is smiling, is here a speaker."— The "law of kindness" in *b* is not "amiable, loving instruction, but that which is pleasing, gracious;" comp. Is. xl. 6; and especially Luke iv. 22 (λόγοι τῆς χάριτος).

Ver. 27. **She looketh well to the ways of her household**; lit. "she who looketh," *etc.*—for the partic. צוֹפִיָּה is probably to be connected, as HITZIG takes it, as grammatically an appositive to the subject of the preceding verse, so that according to this view, it is now the object of her pleasing instruction that is given. The "ways of the house" are naturally its organization and management, the *course* of the household economy (comp. LUTHER: "How it goes in her house").

Vers. 28, 29 describe the praise which the excellent housekeeper has bestowed upon her by her sons and her husband. The words of the latter are expressly quoted, but they are probably not to be extended through the last three verses (as UMBREIT, EWALD, ELSTER, *etc.*, would do), but to be restricted to ver. 29; for verse 30 immediately separates itself as a proposition altogether general, by which the poet comes in with his confirmation of the husband's praise. [So DE W., BERTHEAU, K., N., S., M.].—**Many daughters have done virtuously.** The husband says "daughters" and not "women," because as an elder he may put himself above his wife (comp. Heb. vii. 7). With the phrase "have done virtuously, or show themselves virtuous," lit. "make, produce, manifest virtue," comp. Num. xxiv. 18; Ruth iv. 11.

Ver. 30. **Grace is a deception, beauty a breath**; both are no real abiding attributes of man, and are, therefore, not to be praised. As an imperishable and therefore really praiseworthy possession, there is contrasted with them in *b* the disposition to fear God. Comp. Is. xl. 6; Ps. ciii. 15—18; 1 Pet. i. 24, 25. [Observe how our book just at its close dwells in a very different way, yet with a significant emphasis, upon that "fear of the Lord," which in i. 7 was pronounced "the beginning of wisdom."—A.]

Ver. 31. **Give her of the fruit of her hands**, *i. e*., of the praise which she has deserved by the labor of her hands.—**And let her work praise her in the gates** [not with Z., "let them praise her work in the gates," for the verb has its object in its suffix.—A.]. In the place where the population of the city gathers in largest numbers, in the assembly of the community at the gate (ver. 23), there must the praise of her excellent life and work resound.

DOCTRINAL, ETHICAL, HOMILETIC AND PRACTICAL.

The central idea to which we may trace back the two divisions of this concluding chapter, quite unequal, it is true, in their size, is this: *Of a pious administration, as the king should maintain it in the State, and the woman in her family*. For the fear of God quite as really constitutes the foundation of the virtues of chastity, sobriety, righteousness and compassion, to which Lemuel's mother counsels this son of her's (vers. 2–9), as it, according to ver. 30, forms the deepest basis and the glorious crown of the excellences for which the virtuous matron is praised (vers. 10 sq). It has already been brought out prominently in the exegetical comments, that the delineation which is shaped in praise of the latter, in turn falls into two divisions (which are only relatively different),—the first of which treats of the efficiency of the virtuous woman within the circle of her domestic relations, the second of her activity as extending itself beyond this sphere into wider regions.

Homily on the chapter as a whole:—Of the pious administration of the king in his State and the woman in her household: what both should shun and what they should strive for, with an exhibition of the blessed reward that awaits both. Or, more briefly: A mirror for rulers and a mirror for matrons, with the fear of God as the centre and focus of both.—STÖCKER: I. Instruction of Solomon the king by his mother. *a*) To be shunned: lust and drunkenness. *b*) To be practised: justice. II. Praise of a virtuous woman. 1) Her duties or general virtues; 2) her ornaments or special virtues (ver. 25–27); 3) her reward (vers. 28–31).

Vers. 1–9. *Tübingen Bible* (on ver. 1): How good is the report when parents, especially mothers, teach their children good morals. It is the greatest love that they can show them, but also their foremost duty!—GEIER (on ver. 2): If parents have dedicated their children from birth to the Lord, they must so much more carefully educate them from youth up, and so much more diligently pray for them.—(On ver. 3): Let every husband be content with the wife conferred upon him by God, let him live with her chastely and discreetly, and serve God heartily; that is a truly noble, kingly life.—STARKE (on vers. 6, 7): A draught of wine which is bestowed on a suffering member of Christ's body on his sick or dying bed is better appropriated than whole casks that are misemployed for indulgence. —VON GERLACH (on vers. 8, 9): The highest duty of kings is to befriend the helpless.

Vers. 10 sq. LUTHER: There is nothing dearer on earth than woman's love to him who can gain it. Comp. also P. GERHARD's poetical treatment of the passage, "*Voller Wunder, voller Kunst, etc.* (*Gesamm. geistl. Lieder*," No. 107).—MELANCHTHON: As virtues of the true matron there are named, above all the fear of God as the sum of all duties to God; then chastity, fidelity, love to her husband without any murmuring; diligence and energy in all domestic avocations; frugality, moderation and gentleness in the treatment of servants; care in the training of children, and beneficence to the poor.—ZELTNER (on vers. 11 sq.): God gives to pious married people their subsistence and their needed bit of bread, yea, He blesses them, yet not without prayer and work.—[ARNOT: Empty hours, empty hands, empty companions, empty words, empty hearts, draw in evil spirits, as a vacuum draws in air. To be occupied with good is the best defence against the inroads of evil].—GEIER (on ver. 23): A pious virtuous wife is her husband's ornament and honor (1 Cor. xi. 7). A vicious one, however, is a stain in every way (Ecclesiast. xxv. 22 sq.).—[ARNOT (on ver. 25): If honor be your clothing, the suit will last a lifetime; but if clothing be your honor, it will soon be worn threadbare].

Vers. 30, 31. LUTHER (marginal, on ver. 30): A woman can dwell with a man honorably and piously and be mistress of his house with a good conscience, but must to this end and with this fear God, trust and pray.—CRAMER: The fear of God is the most beautiful of all ornaments of woman's person; 1 Pet. iii. 4.—ZELTNER: If thou hast outward beauty see to it that thy heart and soul also be beautified before God in faith.—[TRAPP: The body of honor is virtue, the soul of it humility.—ARNOT: True devotion is chiefly in secret; but the bulk of a believer's life is laid out in common duties, and cannot be hid. Lift up your heart to God and lay out your talents for the world; lay out your talents for the world and lift up your heart to God].—STARKE (on ver. 31): Works of piety and love preserve among men a good remembrance, and are also rewarded by God of His grace in everlasting joy; Heb. vi. 10; Ps. lxi. 6. My God, let my works also graciously please Thee in Christ Jesus.

AMEN.

www.ingramcontent.com/pod-product-compliance
Lightning Source LLC
Chambersburg PA
CBHW032002230426
43672CB00010B/2236